Revelations On Interstellar Highway 10

A Metaphysical Journey For The Advanced
Religious Seeker And The Spiritually Attuned

Anon Omous

D1596905

Copyright Notice

• • • •

RELEASED: SEPTEMBER 13, 2020 – First Edition

• • • •

WWW.AsteroxRising.com

• • • •

ISBN
    978-1-7354480-1-5 (ebook)
    978-1-7354480-2-2 (paperback)

Contents

Dedication And Acknowledgments

DEDICATION

This book is dedicated for the love of humanity as we evolve beyond our follies and flaws.

• • • •

ACKNOWLEDGMENTS

To my family for all the love, joy, support, amusement, interaction and play they provide. They are good company, fun to hang out with and continuously forgive and look past all my faults, blunders and shortcomings. I owe them a lot of sushi.

• • • •

"I LOVE MY WIFE NOT because she cherishes my divinity, but because she puts up with my humanity." – AO

• • • •

"WHO CAN FIND A GOOD woman of noble character?
    She is precious beyond all wealth.
    Her husband is grateful and has full confidence in her,
    She is his best reward." – *Proverbs*[1]

• • • •

STATEMENT OF REALITY

"People may drive me nuts sometimes, but I so have hope in humanity." – AO

Warning/ Caution

If you wish to reach a higher level of illumination, read and study every section and chapter within this book from start to finish.

• • • •

THIS BOOK IS FOR THE advanced religious seeker and the spiritually receptive. It is not for the faint-hearted or those with indolence of the mind. It is for those wishing to evolve the consciousness of their being and to improve their humanity. Adequate reflection is required to properly digest the intensity of its content. The reading of it won't just inform you, it will change you. It will change how your brain interprets and processes the world, but for the better. Perhaps it may even trigger the miracle of an awakening within. Be sure you are ready, for once you enter here, the fabric of your reality could change forever. There is no going back.

—Λ*—

"The truth doesn't always set you free. Sometimes it saddles you with a burden you can never escape. So choose very carefully where you decide to start digging and what dragons you choose to slay. Prepare to be taken places you never wanted to go." – Chris Knowles[2]

—*Ω—

Before proceeding further into this book, if you suffer from excessive untreated emotional disorders or if there is still a hurt and wounded child within you who still needs to heal, it is recommended that you first seek the guidance of a professional counselor or therapist and perhaps attend the appropriate support groups and related recovery programs (i.e., the Twelve Step Community, the Eightfold Path of Buddhism, group therapy). Whether you or a person who is affecting you is codependent, overcome with grief, an abuser, an alcoholic, chemically dependent (a drug addict), an excessive gambler, a foodaholic, a workaholic, a sexaholic, a persistent liar, a religionaholic (extremes of left or right fundamentalism), a continued criminal, an overly rebellious teenager, an overt narcissist, a neurotic parent, spouse, sibling or dependent, and you have been unsuccessful trying to solve the associated problems, I say again, seek out the guidance of a competent professional counselor, therapist, psychologist and/or psychiatrist who will assist with tapping into your own healing template. A proper and balanced theological perspective is what can cure many of our mental ills, for psychological phenomena is a manifestation of energy,[3] but this prompting may call for the counseling of both clergy and/or psychotherapist. You may need to empty yourself of the behavioral patterns that have been so destructive in your life and then refill with something anew as you awaken a better and enhanced version of yourself. You need to heal, perhaps repent and regain balance before properly assisting yourself and helping others.[4] Being concerned about and responsive to the needs of the world is a good thing, but only if we go about it in a healthy and balanced manner while avoiding extremism.

—A*—

"This is your last chance. After this there is no turning back. You take the blue pill, the story ends. You wake up in your bed and believe whatever you want to believe. You take the red pill, you stay in Wonderland, and I show you how deep the rabbit hole goes. Remember, all I'm offering is the truth. Nothing more." – character of Morpheus offering the character of Neo an awakening[5]

—*O—

If you are off balance, exhibit any sociopathic or dysfunctional behavior per any of the descriptions mentioned above and continue reading this book, the emotional impact that you encounter may be much harsher and more difficult to endure than necessary. If you are too entangled in someone else's dysfunctionality and emotional mess, first you must learn to properly and healthily detach from their problems. They are the only ones who can save themselves, not you. Once you are on the path to recovery, having regained a serene sense of Self and are beyond the anchors of codependency, then you will start to become the person you were meant to be. Upon retraining the mind to move away from the self and closer to God, then again open the pages of this book and decide if you will take the "blue pill" or the "red pill." With balance and internal stability, return back to reading this book to determine whether you will remain as you are, or whether you will engage, determine, plan and take hold of your destiny.

—Δ*—

"Know thyself and improve upon it." – the most supreme of wisdoms,[6] AO

—*O—

About The Cover Art: The Universal Seal

DIVINITY HAS GUIDED you to this point with a symbol, sign, sigil or key that is ever so simple, yet powerfully complex. It is called an "Asterox" and can appear in a variety of geometric and chromatic forms. Its etymology is composed of "a" for the alpha or triangle, "ster" for stellar or star, "o" for the omega or circle and "x" for the Greek letter "chi" representing the Christ Logos. It contains the trinity of the body, soul and spirit within its geometric symbolism. The triangle represents the physical body (*physis*), the circle represents the soul (*psyche*) and the central starburst region represents the spirit (*pneuma*). The ten rays shining forth from the starburst are symbolic of the Ten Directives listed in Chapter 10 and the energy of the One Pure Intelligence as declared by the wise and divinely skillful Phoenicians.[7]

The central region represents: 1) that invisible sacred force of the universe which works and operates both within and behind the scenes of matter; 2) that unseen essence of thought emanating throughout the cosmos that temporarily binds our being into form and then reabsorbs it upon release; 3) the ultimate chakra and connection hub for spirit to enter and exit our mind and body; 4) the mediating Logos and overlapping intersections of divinity with humanity; 5) that astounding subliminal perception to a reality beyond time and outside the material realm; 6) that seen and unseen presence of the divine will; 7) the healthy part of our intelligence mystically attuned to spiritual receptiveness as it aligns our "third eye" with the Eye of Providence; 8) the key to unlocking all divine mysteries; 9) the convergence destination of all true religions focusing in on the Creator and the Receiver; and, 10) the conduit to <u>gnosis</u> of which the password is love.

Appearing on the cover of this book, the title page or through the digital portal through which you entered, the Asterox will be intuitively familiar and intrinsically understood by the believer and the truly righteous. It is the primordial mandala, a symbol of unity, reconciliation of opposites, totality and God's will.[8] Within it are representative aspects of the Holy Grail, the Emerald Tablet and the Philosopher's Stone. Its stellar emblem represents the fleur of the cosmos, the rose of the universe and the primordial furnace from which our existence emerged. The purple hue in the center contains the blueness of the Eye of Horus merging with the redness of the Eye of Ra – the choice between the "blue pill" or the "red pill."

It contains both the Cathar Perfect's *con-sol-amentum*, "with the sun in mind" and the "morning star" of the Catholic Bishops' Easter Proclamation (Exsultet).[9] Those of noble character and purity of being have a predisposition and intuitive precept to its true meaning and panacea of commonality within the collective subconsciousness as it rises into the collective consciousness. It is an evolved pentagram and refined Pleroma coming-of-age as it adjusts into focus and full clarity. Those of virtuous cores have been primed to recognize it, for harbingers (the modern spiritual redivivus and influences of Elijah, Isaiah and Daniel) and others that came before me have been imbedding this seal, or variations and approximations thereof, into your subconscious throughout the past decades. It is the primordial image of eternity's harmonies ingrained within our psyche and represents the true church of the *kata holos* (κατά ὅλος), that Church of the universe that embraces the manifestation of all true religions and their true paths.

You will see more of this ecumenical symbolic sign as the future unfolds and synchronizing ascension takes place. The Asterox relates not just to the physical sun, but to the spiritual Sun that heralds in the true religion of all religions – the perennial philosophy (*philosophia perennis*) returning to ancient theology (*prisca theologia*). It emanates that divine energy of love that every star form, every planet, every moon, every comet, every asteroid, every atom and every particle underlyingly puts forth which creatively produces, growingly maintains, and then destructively absorbs in a repetitive binding and balanced cycle of being and non-being. It is the archetype Seal of God.

—Λ*—

"In the middle of all is the seat of the Sun. For who in this most beautiful of temples would put this lamp in any other or better place than the one from which it can illuminate everything at the same time? Aptly indeed is he named by some the lantern of the universe, by others the mind, by others the ruler. Trismegistus called him the visible God, Sophocles' Electra, the watcher over all things." – Nicolaus Copernicus[10]

• • • •

"THOSE IN WHOM THERE is no deceit, untruth, or bad faith, who live in steadiness, purity and truth, theirs are the radiant regions of the sun." – *Prasna Upanishad*[11]

• • • •

"IF THOU FOLLOW THY star, thou canst not fail of glorious haven." – Dante Alighieri[12]

• • • •

"IN THE SPIRITUAL WORLD, divine love and wisdom look like a sun." – Emanuel Swedenborg[13]

• • • •

"KNOWLEDGE, IN TRUTH, is the great sun in the firmament. Life and power are scattered with all its beams." – Daniel Webster[14]

—*Ω—

The Author's Background: Who Is Anon Omous?

PASSING THROUGH THIS world as a wayfarer, a stranger and a foreigner (ἀλλογενής) cast into a carbon-oxygen-hydrogen based organism, I am a humble creature participating and living out a human experience. My reacquaintance with God first occurred through the path of Christianity. Going back to my earliest memories as a 5 to 7-year-old child, I remember internally questioning why there were so many different Christian denominations and then as a teenager, internally questioning why there were so many different religions. Feeling the pull of interconnections, I felt that there had to be more of a commonality to them rather than dissimilarities and engaged in finding those intertwining threads of pluralistic unity among the kaleidoscope of arbitrary details, idiosyncratic juxtapositions and scriptural opinions. Entering past my mid-twenties, I later supplemented my spiritual workshop with the tools of other religions and expanded my spiritual repertoire as I ventured exposure across religious lines. Like the Naassenes, I sensed that there is one spiritual system underlying the mythology of all religions and set out to find it.[15] Entering into my mid-fifties, I now understand that this desire and quest for pluralistic unity is a free form of syncretism, a word that I just learned of on the first day of 2020. What is it, however, that has activated this desire and longing for religious unification, to make our mythology and beliefs whole again?

Choosing to dwell among civilization but remain in relative obscurity to observe, learn, understand and prepare, I am not a hermit living in seclusion on a mountain peak, nor a monk living in isolation, nor a recluse shunning societal interactions, nor currently an active member of any organized religion, ministry, order or sect, nor am I a collegiate scholar immersed in academia. When still a toddler, I was baptized as Greek Orthodox and, as an older adult, do occasionally accompany my family in attendance at Roman Catholic mass. As of the completion of this book in 2020 CE (≈AUC 2772, 5781 per the Hebrew calendar,

1472 per the Hijri calendar), I have **never** taken a course on philosophy, theology, religion or comparative religions nor have I ever been active in any lodge or order. My preference for this was to be my own teacher, without the influences of instructional biases – I did not want to be persuaded by another's voice while conducting my own investigation into metaphysics. In the physical realm, I have **never** been personally under the training or guidance of a priest, imam, guru, swami, rabbi, pastor, staretz, magi, shaykh, mystic, lama, sage, cleric, druid, monk, reverend, adept, seer, muni, shaman nor any other spiritual guide, mentor, religious scholar, ecclesiastical personage, church leader or master. Upon the completion of this book, I have **never** been to the Middle East, the United Kingdom, Jerusalem, Palestine, Rome, Asia, England, Israel, the Vatican, Makkah (Mecca), Egypt, Africa, the Far East, the Languedoc region of France, India, Tibet, Australia, China or Japan. I have **never** set foot in a mosque, an active pagan temple, monastery, mandir, ashram or lamasery. I do hope, time permitting, that I will someday be able to remove items from the lists above by training under a legitimate guide and visiting the mentioned places.

One of my maternal great-grandfathers died from the 1918 influenza pandemic wave breaching its ravages into Ireland and I am a distant relative of a participant (the one who was a fugitive for 36 years) in The Great Train Robbery of 1963. The paternal side of my family has lineage going back to the Souli and Phocis regions of Greece during the days of Ali Pasha. My paternal grandparents and their children (my father and his brother) survived the National Socialist Party's (Nazi) militant occupation by relying on rabbits for sustenance. My father narrowly escaped being conscripted (abducted against his will) into the Democratic Army of Greece, the militant branch of the communist party during the Greek Civil War of 1946–1949. Educated as a chemical engineer, he later immigrated onto the American continent with only $200 in his pocket and landed his first job picking ripened fruit from trees. He later obtained a position at a refinery that was more in line with his training, met and fell in love with the company nurse, a divorced woman with two children. He transferred himself to New York City and invited that Canadian nurse and her young family to join him in "The Big Apple", where they were married in 1965. I was born about a year later in the Astoria neighborhood of Queens, a borough of New York City. My three siblings and I later moved to and were raised in a small town in the United States. Growing up among the Sunday School services and youth groups of a few different Christian denominations, I was exposed during my upbringing to the religious teachings and pop culture of the 1960s, 1970s, 1980s and 1990s.

My oldest memory is the sensation of a "chunk-chunk" sound as the wheels of the stroller that I was strapped into passed over the joints and cracks of city sidewalks. I still remember my very first vivid nightmares from when I was a toddler, visions and crackling sounds of being surrounded and engulfed by walls of reddish maroon fire no matter which direction that I turned and seeing only darkness beyond the flames. I also remember, as a preschooler, being gathered with my family looking at black and white images on our RCA television of the Lunar Module Eagle resting on the Moon's surface. From the glimpses of military footage that caught my attention on the same cathode ray tube, I first thought the Vietnam War, the Korean War and World War II were all the same confrontation continuing for four decades. About the age of 7, I was only allowed to stay up past my bedtime when the family was gathered for an episode of *The Ascent of Man* being shown on the public networks. My normal K-12 primary and secondary education were in the taxpayer funded school systems but I also attended a Greek Orthodox Sunday School from about the ages of 5 to 8, then a Methodist Sunday School and youth group from about the ages of 9 to 13 and finally, a Roman Catholic youth group from about the ages of 14 to 18. I remember having what are described as "out-of-body" experiences (sleep paralysis and disturbances?) a few times as a child after the age of 10 and occasionally as an adult. I've attended masses at Greek Orthodox, Methodist, Roman Catholic, Presbyterian, Episcopalian and Baptist churches. I've been on overnight spiritual retreats twice in my life, one time as a teenager (≈1982/83) and another time about a decade later. I was in a synagogue once as a young adult for a friend's wedding and was married later in life in a Roman Catholic church.

I am merely a layperson dwelling within a diverse village, but also a semi-polymath in hiding remaining patient for when it is time to step forth. Influenced by aptitude, the surrounding society and life circumstances, I flowed into an occupational framework of an electro-mechanical *tektōn* that places me in the midst of an average daily routine. I currently earn a wage for a living, get stuck in traffic, prepare and submit the family tax returns, scrub the bathrooms, vacuum the floors, clean my own laundry (with the thankful assistance of a washing machine), mow the lawn, change the oil in my automobile and do most household related repairs and maintenance on my own.

I am fortunate to have been born into a region of first world problems with reasonably fair and stable governments. It is not a perfect nation and the needle on its moral compass has fluctuated from time to time depending on the influence of its elected officials. Encountering a repetitive need to heal itself after divisions induced and promoted by phases of its less enlightened leadership, it is still a relatively young country that strives to improve itself and bestow opportunities of the highest order among the broadest spectrum of freedoms, provided we are not trampling on the freedoms of others. Currently, however, the populace is at a faltering junctural fork of either embracing or condemning the multicultural roots which formed the very foundation of its establishment. In responding to a question asked about what type of governance will be leading the United States into its future, it was Benjamin Franklin who replied at the closing of the Constitutional Convention of 1787, "A Republic if you can keep it." Will the nation of my domicile continue to forge oneness among the many as a representative democratic republic or fragment itself into disconnected divisions of fascist/corporatism? Will societal atavism prevail as beliefs in racial or cultural superiority resurface to regress civil rights backwards in time? Has my country become a land that is "no more at liberty, but should be the subject unto kings",[16] and will its regime drag us down into a new Age of Ignorance? That nation, which used to be a role model for the world, will hopefully have extraordinary leadership in place for 2021 to move us forward through extraordinary times as civilizations restart and emerge from the COVID-19 pandemic.

Having struggled through, wrestled with and overcome a severe religious and spiritual crisis within my mid-to-late twenties, I have become a theological free agent and travel the path of an Initiate, a Pilgrim in training, in hopes of becoming a Secret Master. I have, however, personated the appearance of a nearsighted agnostic realist, playing the devil's advocate who prefers to remain stubbornly blind to all the proof Brahman/Allah keeps revealing to us of his/her/its existence – "This world is full of God."[17] For every time my faith begins to waver, that divine consciousness of the universe again surprises me with glimmers of his/her/its existence. Amidst that spiritual upheaval upon exiting a post-secondary education of university training and entering into the job market, a period of despair and a crisis of personality which lasted about three to four years, I had an onrush of several mental and emotional experiences of internal examinations and intense self-reflection during the incipient awakening. It was also a fight for regaining the composure of my true-Self by purging away the harmful dysfunctional influences and persuasions encountered in organizational environments and habitats of ignorance. While falling into the innermost chambers of my being and arguing against internal adversaries, one state (haal or hāl) was composed of the classic conflict of good versus evil with visions of access to instantaneous excessive material possessions, luxuries, wealth and power if I gave up my quest – the temptation of immediate vast rewards and <u>mammon</u> if I were to retreat from my calling. Although feeling like all was lost from the bottom of my pit and abyss of profound despair, and persistently offered, I refused to sign the Faustian bargain. For I was able to see further into a future eternity despite the blurred and cracked goggles of my broken state.

When I resisted such temptations which confronted the final fragments, remnants and shadows of darkness lurking within, later stages consisted of debilitating and unrelenting guilt for my existence and perceived failures during moments, judgments and trials (<u>tauba</u>), a defending of humanity's worthiness despite all their faults, and a total erasure emptying and annihilation of my ego (<u>fana</u>). It was although I (my ego, psyche and personality) became nothing and died before my body was actually dead – it was a trip through Duat. It was a period and experiences that one could refer to as "The Dark Night Of The Soul" as described by St. John of the Cross, a descent into the interior hell to rescue the trapped and sleeping soul from her chamber.[18] I had travelled, although rather quickly and with limited sightseeing, through all the astral, mental, celestial planes and spheres while still enmeshed in the flesh within my living body. Being a young adult at the time, my conscious and rational mind was quite unprepared for archetypal visions, internal awakenings, introspective labyrinths and manifestations of profound experiences from time immemorial. Through a spiritual "baptism by fire", it was though I was fighting an onslaught of demons, conducting a self-exorcist, in order to break through to the rescue lines of a cavalry of angels and beyond the reaches of the barraging accusative tribunal. It was an internal submersion into the deepest depth of Hades as I fell into a void of unknown chthonic territory within the kenoma, of which perhaps I was not adequately ready, nor trained, but yet I survived. I was experiencing a combination of both ecstatic frenzy and moments of total emptiness,[19] being without a sense of self and character. It was then followed by a rebuilding of my core as it refilled with something anew, the launching into the victory of high heaven and the catalyzing of a deeper purpose as my being accelerated into the pleroma. This internal journey within both the kenoma and the pleroma resulted in the immense intuitive acceptance and realization of the dominance, nature and principles of duality and polarity (the alpha and the omega) within the universe as defined by the archetypical symbolic model framework of triangular and circular elements – the paradox of combining the interplay in a marriage of opposites, antinomes and contradictions to harmonize the extremes to reach unity. The following image is of my handwritten notes from 1986, age 19, showing the very first fringes of thinking about, exploring and sorting through the concepts of duality.

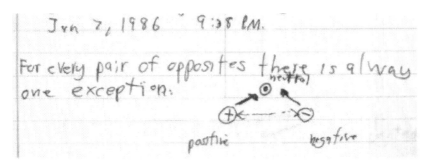

During this fight for my soul, any faith in God that I had was almost extinguished, only to be miraculously reignited exponentially. I do not know what it was that my mind tapped into and/or what it was that tapped into my mind. Were they reincarnated memories resurfacing as a déjà vu of past recollections? Was it ancestral knowledge contained within an internal primal database, transmissions from that supposed fictional ancient satellite called VALIS or did I tune into the external Akashic records?[20] Was it the primitive subconscious revealing itself or was it a gift of gnosis to be shared with the world? Whatever the surges of thoughts were, they occurred almost thirty years before I was even aware of Hermeticism, Rosicrucianism, Sufism, Gnosticism, Catharism, Anthroposophy or the works of Carl Gustav Jung. For that matter, this book's draft was over 90% completed (about 2019) before I even came across or read any literature on Hermeticism, Rosicrucianism, Sufism, Gnosticism, Catharism, Anthroposophy or the works of Jung to any depth.

Towards the end of the "ordeals" there was an encounter or occurrence that had a permanent effect on my psyche and still resonates within me. I awoke from my sleep one night about 2AM with the feeling that there was a presence or force beyond rational comprehension within my bedroom. Upon opening my eyes, I looked up to see the overhead ceiling light was off, but then a cloud-like shimmering essence started pouring out from near its direction. Whatever it was, I felt or knew that it was something extremely formidable, capable of destroying me and beyond my sense of reason.[21] I felt utterly terrified and horrendously frightened. I then noticed what looked like the movement of black or grayish snake-like tails or serpentine legs moving out from the portal that

had formed just below the ceiling. From the nebulous essence, a blur-
ry disembodied hovering dark greyish face started to morph into shape
from the fog with a veiled illuminated ray, flowing winged tentacle and
multiple serpent-like substrate for where its body should be. At first the
face appeared to be forming into a disfigured lion, rooster or dog, but
as it turned towards me it became more hobgoblin or withering hag-
like. Watching the hideous visage slowly appear from that rupture of
reality, that glitch in the Matrix, added even more to my fright since
the ghoulish face of decay seemed to change into whatever terrified me
the most. Regardless of what it initially looked like, it was becoming
something horribly grotesque, prune-like, contorted, gruesomely shriv-
eled, and even more ghastly grimacing with an opened-mouthed howling
screaming expression with each second as it was coming into full focus.
Its purpose seemed to be about invoking the greatest of fear to stop me
from going any further.

Before it fully formed as it lowered itself towards me, a thought came
over me that whatever this was, it obviously was much more powerful
and potently advanced than I. Rather than continue my internal trem-
bling and succumbing in fear, being at rock bottom and feeling like I had
nothing else to lose, I decided to change my emotional state, not to resist,
let my ego dissolve and project love onto it while letting go of my fright.
I do not have absolute clarity on whether the decision to project love unto it was my own, placed in my mind from a higher external source or a
combination of both. The moment I did so in surrender and submission,
however, the harrowing and open-jawed face of gloom stopped its formation with a stunned or startled like halt, almost as if it was not expecting
that reaction from me. In that instant the face changed, dissolved or pul-
verized from a Medusan horror and reformed into the ravishing elegance
of Aphrodite (a discharge of divine radiance), transitioning into a beautiful, luminous, smooth, porcelain-like whitish mask with dark pupil-less
eyes and flowing silk-like strands or wispy wings in the background. After
several seconds of staring, it then formed a slow flirtatious smile, upon
which I was embraced by comfort and ease as it projected intense amplified waves of love back at me. It became the type of radiant beauty and
glorious smile that one tries to turn away from since the potency of its el-

egance was too overwhelming, too intimidating, too intoxicating for the mind to fathom. I could not distinguish if it was specifically male or female, since it appeared to be both and neither. As it softly smiled with brilliance and a gleaming grace, its bright ivory face ascended in reverse back up into the portal (an aperture into another realm) from which it came and, I too, felt as if I was rising out of my body with it in a state of ecstatic and erotic bliss. I then fell back asleep. When I awoke at dawn, I knew that I was past the worst of my crisis and although there was still much work to be done in the triumph, everything was going to be fine in times to come for that encounter had rescued my identity. It gave me the proof in something beyond that I needed to continue with my journey.

It was though I and all of humanity was being judged by something supernatural, determined to be worthy and had our future redeemed. Acting as a nameless mediator, I had passed the test; I had taken an oath; I had vowed to the mystical marriage; I had broken the seals; I was granted permission; I was given access; I was allowed to proceed; I had successfully crossed Chinvat, that bridge spanning the chasm between humanity and divinity, and returned. I do not know if what I encountered was the continuation of the tail end of a dream, a self-generated hallucination, the reflection of my own emotional consciousness looking back at me, an apparition, phantasm or ghost, an alien, a mirror image of my Atman or Akh, or a higher ethereal being of light from an alternate dimension. I do not know if it was an angel, a demon, a demigod, an aeon, an archon, Iblis, Gabriel, Sraosha, Metatron, Lucifer, the face of God (Allah) or a combinational representation of them all. Was it a benevolent extraterrestrial abduction that I am trying to apply religious and spiritual grounding as a means to understand the encounter? Was it the default programming of my being, a BIOS of the psyche, doing a reboot and resetting itself? Was it a seraph that appeared to me out of its own volition from outside of my mind or did I summon it internally by trespassing into regions of thought reserved for advanced initiates? Was it a "Flyer" as described by the Yaqui Indian of Don Juan, an energetic parasite that lost its feeding grip upon my awareness, a willing "Scout" guiding me into its world or was it a benevolent kachina as revered by the Pueblo cultures? Was it my own present eidolon, a daemon, a familiar or a future non-corporeal version of myself projecting back through time to save me? Was it my Manichaean divine twin showing itself as proof of divine existence or was my Epinoia coming out to my defense?[22] Did the face first start out as the entrance of the antagonistic Demiurge (aka Ialdabaoth, Saklas, Samael, Yaldi-Baldi, Yaldabaoth, Yaltabaoth) or another detrimental archon into my room and then become overruled by his nurturing, comforting and loving mother Sophia, thus exiting the room as a benevolent aeon? Were the serpent-like twin tails or legs flowing behind the awful face prior to its transition into beauty, those of Abraxas, Typhon or of Melusine?[23] Was it the androgynous face of the Mother-Father named by the Gnostics as Barbelo? Was it Protennoia, the thought of the Father devolving itself to reach me as described in the Sethian text of *Trimorphic Protennoia*? Was it the same Goddess that instructed Boethius on philosophy during his stay in prison for "heresy"?[24] Was it the same divine influencer of the Protestant Jacob Boehme encountered when he was at the same age as I was during my encounter?[25] Was it a visitation from the sacred angel named Metatron, Mītatrūsh or Michael? Was it the Shiva within uniting with the Shakti throughout? Was it a newer aeon that has become symbiotic within my core and being, forming a syzygetic union or a hieros gamos (ιερός γάμος)?[26] Was it a rare and honored visitation by Amaterasu, the Sun-Goddess revered by some Shintoists?[27] Did I travel on a Night Journey similar to what the prophet Mohammad experienced? Was it the Holy Paraclete taking on form while trying to teach and train me? Was it Tara or Quan Yin (aka Guanyin, Guan Yin, Guanshiyin, Gwan-eum, Kuan Yin), a divine feminine from the Buddhist path for reaching enlightenment or was it Frejya, Frigg, Hel, or another Norse goddess?[28] Was it the embodiment of the serpentine dragon switching from evil to goodness upon sensing my change in state? By defaulting to love rather than remaining in fear, did I remove the veil and unite myself with Shekhinah or Hokmah? Was it another Helen, the spiritual partner of Simon Magus, who I had unknowingly rescued from the brothel of Tyre by projecting true love onto her or was it she who saved me?[29]

Was she Sophia Zoe (ama Zoa), a daughter or grand-daughter emanation of the true God, falling in love with me as I adored her?[30] Was the initial entrance of the fearful face a sacred presence testing my resolve or was I being confronted and tempted by Satan or Naamah herself and my unexpected projection of love had thrown the demon off guard, thawed his heart and kept her at bay? A demon, however, would not be able to project love and comfort, for a being cannot give what it does not already have inside. As a reminder, I did not even know about the Gnostics, the *Zohar* or read anything by Carl Jung until almost three decades after the encounter.

If it was my imagination playing tricks on me, a hallucination or the continuation of a dream upon awakening, it was the only one I have ever had and occurred about 1990–1991. This was back in the days of floppy disks and when the internet was still a novel luxury item, long before it was readily available and in its infancy prior to becoming mainstream. I do not have an addictive personality, I was not on any recreational mind-altering substances and I did not have a fever. I expect that a person who is prone to such hallucinatory specters would have seen more than one in his or her lifetime – this was the only singular time in my life that I had such a vision event. Either what I encountered was a fake illusion, a psychotic figment of my own subconscious, or something very real from beyond this realm that gives legitimacy to the true religions and aspects of their scriptures. I unknowingly leaned towards <u>deism</u> prior to these events, but I cannot deny what I went through and encountered. Therefore, I must accept the duality of both deism and revelation. Although rational thought could not be applied to account for those flutters of my internal world, I am forced to apply logic to accept them. Prior to the occurrences, the only religious scripture that I was somewhat familiar with was the *Holy Bible*, for I did not venture into the scriptures of other religions or philosophies until after that encounter – I did not read *The Koran* until 1998 nor open the pages of the *Book of Mormon* until February 2020.

Those experiences, whatever they were, installed a paramount faith deep within me that there is something much greater to our existence and a degree of truth in the words of the valid prophets – that the cosmos is much more fascinating, mysterious and interesting than we realize. It left with me a newfound religious and spiritual insight that I am just now, about three decades after the encounter and perseverance on my journey, beginning to fully understand and to accept upon fulfilling a transformation and entering into rubedo. Being at this stage of my life and past the adolescent focus on self, there is much less concern about what the world may think of this book and of me. Its publishing is worthwhile despite the heckling risks, for I am much more certain now that I write this book out of love, or more specifically agape, and not out of ego or vanity. However intensely spiritual all the events were and although there is still a longing for the conduit that was encountered while transitioning back into this "mundane" realm, it is not something that I wish to repeat; once was enough to get my mind to listen and to become a dilettante of the religious, spiritual and mystical arts. The experiences were real, they occurred and authentically transpired. They defied logic and operated without conscious control and I do not have solid answers, nor do I pretend that I do. This leaves me to infer through cryptic perceptions, postulating based on nebulous connections and concluding through an obscure and unclear mist of understanding. Were they self-induced psychosis or divine intervention? Were they a flurry of subconscious illness or influences of the supernatural? Were they false perceptions of reality or true theophanic encounters? Did my intense reading of the shrouded passages within the *Book of Revelation* open a doorway into something highly profound? Were they true embodiments of genuine primordial visions or psychic disturbances of the mind venturing too far into the inner depths and abyss of the soul? What they actually were, a taste of Allah or a mouthful of madness, I will let you to decide. I leave it up to you to interpret those experiences of the mind, impressions, visions or disturbances from three decades ago as you see fit, but realize this, it is not having an absolute and clear comprehension which forces us into a mystical approach. If you should ever have similar encounters during an awakening, I recommend lowering the ego, surrendering in grace and defaulting to a state of love as well. It is love that will outwit, defeat, diffuse and appease the Archons, making them powerless as they turn from being your enemy and into becoming an Aeon and your friend.

—Λ*—

"The heaven of every religion hath been rent, and the earth of human understanding been cleft asunder, and the angels of God are seen descending." – Bahá'u'lláh[31]

. . . .

"WAS THIS A SISTER-SOUL, was it his genius, or only a reflection of his inmost spirit, a vision of his future being dimly foreshadowed? A wonder and a mystery! Surely it was a reality, and if that soul was only his own, it was the true one. What would he not do to recover it? Were he to live millions of years he would never forget that divine hour in which he had seen his other self, so pure and radiant." – *The Barque of Isis*[32]

. . . .

"AND I SAW WITHIN THE mystery of God a wondrously beautiful image. It had a human form and its countenance was of such beauty and radiance that I could have more easily gazed at the sun." – Saint Hildegard of Bingen[33]

. . . .

"WHAT WERE YOU, OH WHITE goddess whose beauty and grace cannot be described? Descending from realms unknown and revealing yourself to mine eyes. Were you the sacred Sun Lady, leading me to understanding and gnosis? Were you the pure one, the Great Mother putting me to the test? Were you the divine dove that brings tidings of peace? Were you true and real or the tidbits of dream? Seemingly, you were not allegory, nor myth. Yet, you were much more than lore." – AO

—*Ω—

Scriber's Note: Into My Psyche

HAVING MY INTERNAL thoughts confined for years as I remained incognito, I now release them onto these pages. I am far from perfect and make no claims or statements of infallibility or invincibility – I am susceptible to the common cold and other viruses just as everyone else. Started over twenty years ago, this little book was written in the hopes that it will not be misunderstood, nor esoteric in its following, nor elitist in its recruitment, nor implemented as a controlling gospel. I am not here to start a new religion, there are already plenty enough to choose. Through my inner voice without hindrance, the very depths of my consciousness, I lead you through a journey without restriction as a "quiet guide" and prefer any proclamation to be done by the merits of this book, rather than through verbal evangelicalism, eloquent oration, oratory lecturing or by harangue. I apologize in advance for some preachiness that you will encounter. Any internal cravings are not for power, nor importance, but for an awakening of the human spirit, and then a normalization of it as it settles onto a higher plateau of existence, insha'Allah. For such an awakening of our global consciousness would awash me in pleasure and fulfill a passion for peace. Do I cling to a childhood ideology of being a redeemer, the wishful fantasies of a paradise on Earth, an inflated sense of capabilities or an infantile claim of illusive insights into a greater reality? Am I an *Apostolos* (ἀπόστολος) in the midst of recovering from my own anamnesis? I cannot be sure that I didn't write this book to escape the feelings of a humdrum existence, a life potentially unfulfilled, internal delusions of wanting to be something more than I am or playing a role beyond my mortality. I rely on you to be the judge after reading this book to completion. I do know, however, that I write from the heart, through the core of my being, and with the desire to explain my experiences and perceptions in hopes of assisting in your spiritual development and search of the soul. If I am not successful with these desires, then I will at least pull you into my lunacy of love for the divine (theia mania). I will not call my condition a hindrance or obstacle, but rather, it is a stimulus of greater effort to new possibilities of achievement.[34]

If anything, it is the glowing embers of childlike imagination now ready to ignite forth through adult know-how and more than a half century of lifetime experiences.

If my disorder is that I have a messianic complex at the root of my subconscious of which my consciousness is finally coming to acceptable terms with, then the volition of this underlying psychiatric condition has kept me whole among the fragmented chaos of encountered dysfunctional human behavior and the shatters of suffering across the globe. If I indeed suffer from such a complex, then it is a coping mechanism developed and put in place in reaction to life stresses and extreme crises, empowering me to deal with the impairments found within the human family and rescue my species from degradation. It has helped me to make the correct decisions in life by thinking in terms of the future and eternity, rather than in terms of being only in the present moment and succumbing to detrimental choices. I only hope that this disorder can be transmitted and spread to others as a favorable contagion of the Holy Spirit. If I have a neurosis, then perhaps it stews forth from a feeling of inferiority due to an unbearable sensitivity,[35] the seat of which is that I don't like the pain and suffering encountered in this world, a four-dimensional reality restricted by material perception and an illusion of time.[36] I feel the world's suffering and unfairness intensely and must often muffle its penetrations into my core. It is a perceived helplessness and inability to mend things that leads me to religion and spirituality as a means to soothe the trauma and overcome the perceptions of being limited or powerless to influence and improve world conditions. The saving grace is realizing that the neurosis of wanting joy for all is not unique to my mind, but dwells within the hinterland of yours as well and in most of the human collective subconscious. Have I been called to a task too great for any ordinary mortal, succumbing to archetypical images of the redeemer laying dormant within and being awakened by human society going astray? Is it the masculine animus trying to fix things and the feminine anima trying to nurture souls? Is my desire to do what I can to save the world merely a narcissist feed to keep my ego engaged? No matter what the answers may be, I ask of you to share and join me in the promethean adventure and _koinonia_ (κοινωνία) of healing the wounds of the world and undertaking the enterprise of teaching it to save itself. I ask you to also awaken the buried savior (σωτήρ) within, to activate your greater Self and to help restore us to a mindset of equilibrium and the instinctive psyche of understood love.[37] I ask you to help change the world by striving to be an example for emulation, not by becoming a force to be reckoned with.

Like Philip K. Dick's _Exegesis_, which tries to comprehend his highly personal and spiritual experiences using a framework that fit him or Robert M. Pirsig's self-character of Phaedrus in _Zen And The Art Of Motorcycle Maintenance_, I too, express my experiences through this book's pages in a manner that flows naturally from my imagination, viewpoint and personality. The words put forth are based on a life purpose, a vow to the modern Creator made when still a child and an inspirational calling from a higher mind during internal reflection and/or the reading of a particular passage, phrase or perception previously scribed by others that resonated strongly within my being. Such resonations, intuitive comprehensions, or epiphinac vibrations ("aha" moments) were indicated by an emotional pull – a sudden rapturous feeling of joy and understanding that sent a flash of stimulation throughout my central nervous system. Maja D'Aoust refers to aspects of these moments of synchronization as "pop-outs" of divination,[38] glimmers of the universe trying to grab our attention to show us a truer and greater reality. Upon temporarily meshing with the thoughts of God, I would then fall back to the material plane but with an increased awareness of reality and truth. The difficulty arises in remembering to put those learnings into everyday practice, for why is it so challenging at times for our human part to put love into every moment, response, movement and action? At what point do we draw the line between being helpful or being taken advantage of? How do we assure that patience and kindness continue, even when we are feeling frustrated or fatigued? What mnemonics can we ingrain into our core to always remind us of what life is really supposed to be about? Oftentimes, I would write down a thought or notion, only to see and discover it minutes, days, weeks, months or years later printed within the pages of the particular scripture or book that I was reading or the media that I was watching. Was it synchronization based on common interest, intuition, sensitive tuning or advanced revelation? Or was it merely that the thought or idea was original only to me, but not to prior thinkers? I cannot answer these questions, but to prevent delving into madness, I chose not to pass judgment upon them and to accept their occurring frequency as gifts and with gratitude.

Preface And Caveats

THE IMPETUS FOR WRITING this book was based on a searching and an internal drive to understand more about both the physical universe (that which is dependent on time) and the metaphysical universe (that which is independent of time). Metaphysics and physics are different reference frames, with some overlap, for viewing our universe. Physics utilizes the scientific method to obtain repeatable results from repeatable actions. Metaphysics deals with our holistic relation with the universe and its relationship to us. Started before the days of the internet and written over a period of three decades with purpose and for the love of humanity and its future, this reading journey is for those wishing to reflect upon their role in and relationship with the universe. In an attempt to reconnect the reader by moving beyond specific semantics to a grander consciousness, whether it be a one source monotheistic theism of ultimate reality, a pantheistic diversity of influential divine factors, or the embracing of both, it is intended to stimulate those spiritual synapses that may have been dulled from the labors, burdens and time robbers encountered due to the pressures and distractions of modern life and of being human. We all must eat, drink, earn a living, maintain our shelters and provide for our physical existence, but we must also feed ourselves the spiritual nourishment necessary to maintain and expand our beings.

Ranging from simplistic to cerebral, the words, ideas and concepts presented within the pages of this text are merely another viewpoint on God, the universe and our relationship to all. Written over many years of spiritual and religious reflection, maintenance, preservation and experiences, it is an expansion upon ideas repeated many times in previous scriptures and thrives to question and go deeper into what others have sensed. Some sections will strongly resonate with your perceptions and experiences, while others will have no correlation. Paragraphs will fluctuate between intellectual sophistication to straightforward satisfaction, but with an intensity of depth which pushes at the boundaries of your cerebral limits. Striving to be like the 11th Sikh Guru, it contains original thought, transcendental ideas generated by the scriber, as well as referencing those of prior thinkers, but makes no claims as being all inclusive, comprehensive or absolute. Its objective is to become a handbook for conquering the world through the power of love and to teach you to master the universe with the same power. May it become a cherished and iconic work of literature worthy of being widely read and inwardly digested rather than tossed into the trash receptacles of lost annals and buried history.[39] As a reader progressing through chapters of varying lengths, some extremely short and others long, you will be led on an insightful journey of both acceptance and sometimes doubt. This compilation is an intermixture of edicts from the Almighty and of human interpretations. Therefore, since the thoughts and emotions of its human authorship are interlaced among the pages, it is not perfect and subject to misinterpretations, misapplication, inconsistencies, errors, being taken out of context and future rewrites based on outdated material. If there are any words of hypocrisy or statements of negative exploitation, then may they be kept to a minimum. There will also be human contaminative impurities such as linguistics mistakes, generalizations and influential biases, but it is up to you to determine which are the thoughts of the Supreme Consciousness, which are those of humans, and which are a combination of both.

Some will view this book as ridiculous, controversial, blasphemous, too convenient and heresy while complaining about its endnotes making occasional references to Wikipedia webpages. Others will view it as exhilarating, sublime, profound, timely and uplifting while pointing to all the other assorted endnote references. I hope most will find it meeting the conditions of the latter. Presented as a gift and written as a spiritual legacy for current and future generations, the guidance within these pages will hopefully evolve the reader beyond their faults and lead you to a more enlightened view of yourself, God and the universe.

Similar to other religious texts, within these pages is a mishmash, occasional rambling, fragmentation of context or hodge-podge of thoughts on relating to divinity and how they apply to past eras, the current events of this era and to future eras. It will be a smorgasbord of spiritual exposure and influenced opinions. To the untrained, untuned and undisciplined mind, they will appear as gibberish, gobbledygook, rantings and ravings. The advanced initiate, however, will have understanding. There may be parts that are uncomfortable to read or difficult to comprehend. There will be contradictions, dualities, redundancies, imperfections, and overlaps as well that will need to find their acceptable degree of osmosis into your core.

There are those who are not ready to read the words in this book nor even open it, yet they are the ones who most need to readjust their cores. Some will choose to educate themselves and others will not, an unfortunate dilemma with the duality of freedom of choice. This book will not give you absolute truth, for that is something you must develop on your own. It will, however, start you in the direction of your desire. It will provide some answers and perhaps even more questions. In searching for truth, remove all the constants and variables that you know are false, what remains will be the desire of your search. How you interpret and apply the perspectives presented within these pages and those of other texts will determine your truth. Truth will show through your actions and the intentions behind those actions.

In the search for truth, no matter what the cost to one's established beliefs and reality, it is necessary to consider both the strengths and the weak points of one's personal creed.[40] Asking questions is the essence of learning, from which you may either agree, partially agree, disagree or have no opinion on the contents. That is your prerogative and freedom to choose. If you choose to disagree, then do so by peaceful and non-violent discussion. Back your point of views with research, reference, logic, reason, anecdotes, analogies and humor. Most importantly, think. Be skeptical and be critical, but think with an open mind and a willingness to come out of ignorance and possibly the comfort of your current religious perspective. Read with eyes open, mind alert, heart afire and spirit radiant with the quest for truth.[41] Don't just read this book, but study and imbibe it. Find the capacity to ponder its lessons and appreciate its message. Read slowly and reflectively, allowing time to appreciate the invoked emotional imagery and for your subconscious to catch up. Step back and reflect on the habits, impulses and institutions that govern your beliefs and values.[42] I make no promises that this book will change your perceptions, beliefs and identity, but it will present very high probabilities. Don't be afraid to develop or redefine your own belief system and come up with your own spiritual conclusions. Always live your life with the notion that your actions or inactions will always contribute to either the healthy advancement of humanity or its detrimental stagnation and regression. Choose your actions wisely, listen to your scruples, keep your tanha in check and dwell within the credence of a healthy ego; an ego that is neither under-inflated nor over-inflated. Let your truth be guided by noble intentions with an inner voice of sound reason and good balanced judgment. May the words within these pages be the catalyst that propels you forward on your spiritual voyage.

—Λ*—

"Freethinkers are those who are willing to use their minds without prejudice and without fearing to understand things that clash with their own customs, privileges, or beliefs. This state of mind is not common, but it is essential for right thinking..." – Leo Tolstoy

• • • •

"RESERVE YOUR RIGHT to think, for even to think wrongly is better than not to think at all." – Hypatia of Alexandria[43]

—*Ω—

Navigational Reading Instructions

THE FOLLOWING PARAGRAPHS provide preparation, definitional notes and terminology for reading this book. For organization clarity and reading flow, references and anecdotal notes will be denoted with superscript numerals and listed in the section titled *References And Notes*. The references and bibliographical style follow no particular citation standard, other than providing enough information for the reader to locate the source. The decision not to use the abbreviation "Ibid" to denote the same source in the endnotes was intentional, since confusion and lost references were occurring during the re-organization and editing of paragraphs. The first, second or third appearance in this book of certain words that are defined in the glossary will have a straight or zig-zagged line underneath them (i.e., example). The acronym of (aka) means "also known as." The acronym of (asa) means "also spelled as." The acronym of (ama) means "also modified as" and pertains to vowel changes performed specifically to words within this book – my own neology. Assume that all dates and years listed are in the common or current era (after the alleged birth of Christ) unless otherwise denoted as being before the common era (BCE) and prior to the birth of Christ.[44] Words of a language other than English, (i.e., Latin, French, Greek), and names of printed material, cinematic media, audio productions or publications will typically be italicized. I encourage you to do your own research on any unfamiliar words or people's names. Any use of "high-sounding" words is not to come off as pretentious, but rather, it is to convey the intensity of the message.

Throughout this text, the word God, Allah, Lord, Krishna, Brahma and other qualifying terms of personified labels will be used interchangeably since from the author's standpoint, they are all formal human names for the same and identical force, being or consciousness or an aspect thereof. Starting with a lowercase letter, the word "divinity" or "godhead" itself will be used to describe this compelling and influencing force in the non-personified sense; an informal reference to the universe's essence. Since no pronoun can adequately describe this divine essence, at times God/Allah/Lord/Krishna will be referred to as "he", "him", "she", "her", "he/she", "him/her" and even "it." This gender and identity conundrum will be discussed further in Chapter 2.

If you are a follower of the Islamic faith, read the word "God" as "Allah". If you are a follower of a Christian or Jewish faith, then read the word "Allah" as "God", "Lord", "Jehovah" or "Yahweh." Since this book was written in English, the word "*Koran*" will primarily be used when referring to the title of the sacred scripture of Muslims. From its Arabic roots, the term "*The Qur'an*" is probably more proper, although "*Quran*", "*The Quran*" and "*The Koran*" are other acceptable forms.[45] If you are of a religion whose scripture is not of the *Torah*, the *Bible*, or the *Koran*, then relate the word "God" or "Allah" to the appropriate description(s) or forms within your religion's sacred writings or generational oral passages. The word "prophet" refers to its modern meaning of an instrument of God – someone with divine visionary insight. The term "seer" or "soothsayer" is someone that can genuinely see beyond the constraints of time and can sense trends or strong probabilities. Sometimes a prophet is also a seer or soothsayer. You will come to the understanding that every religion, every culture, every region have their own prophets and seers. The Anglicized name of the great prophet and founder of Islam appears to be more commonly written as "Muhammad", but it will most often appear in this book written as "Mohammad", seeming to be the second most common form. There are several other acceptable Anglicized spelling variations such as "Mohammed", "Muhamad", "Mohamed", "Mahamad", "Mahomet" or "Mohamet" and "*Μωάμεθ*" in Greek.[46]

A particular etymology of the English word "religion" comes from the Latin *religio* which means to relink and *ligare* which means to bind or connect. Although there are other possible roots, this etymology was favored by St. Augustine, Tom Harper and Joseph Campbell. The addition of the prefix "re" to "ligare" creates re-ligare, meaning to re-connect. Therefore, religion is a tool that allows us to reconnect to the source from whence we came and where we are headed. The defining lines between spirituality, religion, philosophy and mythology can sometimes become blurred or non-existent. Typically within this book and for clarification to the reader, the word "religion" is considered the organized customs, beliefs, scriptures, methods, traditions and practices used to establish and/or maintain a group of followers' relationship with God or to the godhead. "Religion" can be referred to as the organized club or association to which one belongs for commonly communing with God. A religious view that is attractive to the masses of a given time period will take hold and evolve. How long it lasts depends on the truths upheld by its leadership and the good sense it has in connecting with its followers.

Typically, "Spirituality" is considered one's personal positive relationship with God, Allah, the Lord, the Supreme Consciousness or whatever name chosen to represent divinity. It occurs when humanity and God reach each other. The term "true religion(s)" means an organized set of views, beliefs, or approaches based on verbal tradition, written manuscripts, notes or printed documents which provide positive spiritual nourishment for advancing humanity's relationship with the universe and/or God. The truest of religious experiences is participating benevolently in the human condition through actions based on love. The term "true path" is an aspect of a "true religion", philosophy or moral behavior that an individual chooses and/or selects to follow in maintaining a positive relationship with the universe and/or God. The term "sect(s)" or "religious sect(s)" when referred to in this book, denotes a different branch of religious doctrine or alternate view. It does not denote or imply, unless otherwise stated, that a particular sect is a bad or a good thing. There can be good sects and there can be bad sects.

The writings within this book by no means distinguishes nor determines which religions and/or paths and/or branches and/or sects and/or schism are true and which ones are false. That is reserved for each individual's personal relationship with the universe to determine. Some organized religions have paths which may be truer than others. A true religion's tenets, however, will always have the desire for the removal of violence and oppression, the fair spread of equal feasible opportunities for all, and be catalyzed by love. A religion without healthy love as its underlying driving statement and doctrine is not a true religion. Upon your completion of reading this book through all its chapters, you will know how to discern which are the authentic religions.

The word "universe" and "cosmos" will be used interchangeably to represent all there is and generally refers to the physical, the spiritual, and the connective medium between them. The word "enlightenment" or "illumination" within this book signifies an advancement to a higher level of understanding, spiritual awareness or a momentary epiphany of God's grace. It implies that there are various levels and degrees, depending on the sentence context. Unless otherwise stated, it should not be interpreted as the pure translation from Eastern Buddhism, meaning to end the cycle of being reborn (escape from transmigration) when one has achieved or "awaked" to the truth of life and death. The terms of "conscious" and "consciousness" will be used interchangeably to denote that which is occurring at an aware level of perception. Likewise, the terms "subconscious" and "subconsciousness" will be used interchangeably to denote that which is occurring at an unaware level, without perception and operating below our states of awareness. Although translations of Carl Jung's works use the term "unconscious" to denote states submerged below the level of awareness, the word will be avoided in this text so as not to be confused with a medical state of being "knocked out." I realize that some schools of psychological thought do not consider "unconscious" and "subconscious" identical, but from the perspective within this book, they both refer to something obscured from our levels of clear awareness.

The word "dreams" when mentioned in Chapter 15 refers primarily to those daytime conscious thoughts of a desired future (waking dreams) and not the subconscious (meaningful or meaningless) releases occurring during the stages of sleep. For the dreams of sleep may be senseless nocturnal displays of a mind wandering, interlaced fragmented memories mixed with current events, totally random and irrational cinematic recoils of thought, the living out of forbidden fantasies, signals and messages of truth, genuine telepathic visions, or glimpses into the unknown.[47]

Unless as otherwise stated in Chapter 20, the word(s) "love" or "healthy love" do not refer to carnal interaction or sexual intercourse, but rather they refer to healthy emotional intimacy, a state of mutual respect, a receptive openness, a calming forgiveness, an expression of appreciation, contentment, serenity, sympathy and/or compassion. The use of the word "love" within this text primarily denotes a state of tranquility as one projects feelings and actions of healthy acceptance, kindness and a quest for unity – the reversal of entropy. Love is the opposite of fear and hatred.

—Δ*—

"Love is the recognition of the transcendence in everyone and everything." – Robert Bonomo[48]

—*O—

The word "scripture" means any writings, printed documents or manuscripts that contain the primary messages and beliefs of a true religion. There are Christian, Islamic, Judaic, Hindu, Buddhist, Zoroastrianism, Bahá'í, Sikhist and many other scriptures available for connecting to divinity. When reading such scriptures, recognize the differences but focus on the commonalities. Many times the word "scripture" and its plural form will appear within this book. The term standing alone is used as a generic description of any or all known religious texts. It is not specific to any one religion unless the specific religion appears as a descriptive adjective prior to the word, (i.e., Buddhist scriptures).

Within these chapters, you will find the duplication of words, ideas and quotes. This is deliberate as a means to aid the reader with retaining key themes. This teaching style is used for reinforcing main concepts such as to <u>inculcate</u> the notion that love should be at the basis of every word and every action. You may find this repetitious and monotonous at times, but it is necessary to ingrain the lessons within your subconscious thoughts. Repeat exposure reinforces the imprint of knowledge on the mind; familiarity breeds ease of action and develops algorithms of habit. It also gives a chance for the intensity of the message to sink in. It may take several exposures until the epiphany of the meaning leaves its mark within the core of your being and remains at the root of your soul.

Unaware to the author of this book, others may have previously written about the same thoughts presented within these pages. Many times thinking my ideas were new and original, I would later internally retract those assumptions while having to confess with such inner outbursts as

"Why even old man Socrates knew that!" The fact that after 2,500 years after his existence, a modern mind can still conjecture and deduce similar patterns is indicative of a continuum of psyche commonality through the ages.

Many of the quoted references interspersed between the A* and *O (or other triangular and circular characters) were found elsewhere and placed within the sections after this book's related paragraphs were already written. Viewpoints, notions and ideas within this book may be similar or identical to those of prior thinkers. My most fascinating discovery was encountering the quantity of other authors throughout history who expressed like-mindedness to my own. It is not uncommon for thinkers and philosophers to borrow ideas without remembering exactly where they came from.[49] Duplication can result due to synchronization of similar creative reflection and revelation. The references are provided when the source is readily available or distinguishable from the public domain, but some may have been inadvertently omitted, or not remembered. Links to website pages have been provided in the endnotes and bibliography at the risk that they may become broken or non-functional at a future date.

—A*—

"If I come across by chance in the good authors, as I often do, those same subjects I have attempted to treat, seeing myself so weak and puny, so heavy and sluggish, in comparison with those men, I hold myself in pity and disdain. Still, I am pleased at this, that my opinions have the honor of often coinciding with theirs, and that at least I go the same way, though far behind them, saying, 'How True!'" – Michel de Montaigne[50]

—*O—

At times during my digestion and absorption of the thoughts expressed in spiritual books, I became overwhelmed. The results were tears, belly aches (bitter or sour stomach), knots in the throat, heartburn or tension in the torso due to excitement and mind dizziness. If you should encounter similar responses, take a temporary break from reading and put this book down when such spiritual over-stimulation and epiphanic indigestion starts to trigger physical reactions – even too much awakening realization can be overloading and vertiginous. Give time for cognitive rest, allowing your neural network to power down and cool off. Just as God needs a break from us sometimes, we also need a break from diving into divinity. Recognize that your mind needs time to absorb, compile, file and store the information into memory and ingrain it into your core. Your brain is an organ (a receiver and processor) that needs recovery time from strenuous mental exercise and religious overload. When you feel awestruck or exceeding of your emotional capacity, meditate into a relaxed mode, think in terms of eternity, default to a state of love and gratitude, allow the tears to flow or simply smile. That is the cure to regaining composure when overcome with the intensity of ecstatic surges and to regain equilibrium of the mind.

Chapter 1
Alpha – In The Beginning And The Growth Of God

"UPON REALIZATION OF his own existence, God snapped her fingers thus beginning the universe with a bang." – AO

• • • •

OUR STUDY OF GOD BEGINS with the writings of men and women expressing their human opinions and views of theology. It may be divinity influencing the pen or type, but it is moved and set by human hands. This book too contains the words of the Almighty, but I am not their legitimate author. I am only the scribe and for that reason, I prefer to remain anonymous. Among these pages are the words of the Lord/Allah/Jehovah/Yahweh interwoven with the interpretations and thoughts of humans. I will only take credit as the author of the human thoughts. For the thoughts of divinity appearing in these chapters, I am merely the recorder putting them into time through the language of alphabet. Even William Blake put forth, "I just transcribed what the eternals told me to write."[51]

There is a new age upon us. It is an age in which the collective consciousness of humanity (aka the network of humanity) is trying to make a quantum level shift and emerge onto the next plateau of being. It is the beginnings of an awakening in which the beauty of diversity is taking a strong budding hold over the ugliness of prejudice and racism. It is an awareness in which the damage generated by unchecked narcissism is being recognized and confronted. It is a time where enough of us are aware of deceptions by statesmen who are unaware of their own ill motives. It is a period in which the bragging of non-accomplishments and over promotion of bloated propaganda is starting to be challenged. It is an era of realization that our materialistic schema is engulfing our sense of a centered life. It is a longing in which our dismay with the relentless utilitarianism of over applied technology has us looking towards something more fundamental, more meaningful and more permanent to regain our sense of balance.[52] It is an ending in which negative exploitation is putting forth its final gasps of a fading resistance. The valid meaning of "New Age" does not pertain to random religious sprouts shooting forth, but rather on the general recognition of the truths, filtering out of the falsehoods, respect and tolerance of the differences, pluralism of the commonalities and the implementation of the idealistic good contained within all the great and true scriptures. It is recognition of the need for both the Gnostic (the alternate) and the Orthodox (the mainstream), for each seeks to answer the profound trinity of questions which confronts all of us: 1) Who was I before I was born? 2) Who am I now? 3) Who will I be after death?[53] Going about it in different ways, the Orthodox prefers one method while the Gnostic allows for several means. One becomes a Gnostic when they have reached the point of no longer relying on just the Orthodox to provide meaning – they start to conduct their own search for God as well. Aligning with all religious precepts, isn't God always considered one and the many? "The mystic knows, often describes, and longs to return to a world of complex undifferentiated" unity.[54] Yet, the concept of "one" has no meaning unless it is referenced by the diversity that spreads from it – for the "ten" are within the "one". The notion of "one" cannot be defined unless a "two" or more came from it – the observed needs an observer.

At times, expressed thoughts within religious texts will assure there is something greater than ourselves. At other times, philosophical conclusions will cast tangents of doubt into your mind that the Lord/God/Allah even exists. As you rollercoaster between faith and doubt, skepticism and belief during your journey through the kenoma to reach the pleroma, you are determining the strength of your synaptic connections to divinity while groping through the darkness to find the light of meaning to your own existence. This stumbling duality is necessary as you construct the pathway of your own spiritual trek while traversing and vibrating among the esoteric planes, frequencies or concentric spheres of reality and existence. If we are created by chance, then our existence is futile and we were born in vain – it would mean that we are nothing more than the biology of our body. If death truly terminates everything for evermore, then our actuality is a baffling, tragic, nonsensical and mysterious travesty.[55] For without God, we are limited to a concatenation of fortuitous events transpiring in a random universe.[56] If, however, we are created through the laws of cause and effect, with the Supreme Mind being the cause and humanity being one of the effects, then our existence has meaning. Random occurrences and accidental events are repellent to a mind that loves order.[57] Yet when we do not have an explanation for what appears to be a random act, out of ignorance, we call it chance. For chance is but a name given for when the law or model is unknown or not recognized.[58] It is that which is out of the ordinary or cannot be measured that we call accidental.[59] The famous theoretical physicist Albert Einstein refuted that "God does not play dice with the universe" to express his perplexity with quantum theory.[60] Well maybe God does, but he still has to initiate the rolls. To his advantage, perhaps he also chooses to use a loaded pair of dice.

—Δ*—

"Nothing is unclear to the understanding; it is only when we fail to understand that things appear unintelligible and confused." – C.G. Jung[61]

—*O—

Entering this world as neophytes to being human, we all came from our mother's womb knowing God, but amnesia seems to set in while adjusting to the influences and pressures of this physical plane of matter. It is much like the wonderful feelings from that long-ago magical vacation of a lifetime. You remember the vacation and that you had wondrous feelings, but can't internally recreate those feelings while remembering the vacation. "We cannot conceive of how we came here ourselves, and yet we know for a fact that we are here."[62] In parallel with Hermes lament to Asclepius, we seem to forget our celestial origins while adapting to our new corporeal container, its capabilities and its limitations. Upon our birth, the senses automatically tune into and self-adjust to interpret the physical reality, the realm of matter in which we find ourselves. While learning to make use of our thoughts and develop ways to express them to others, the divinity within has to cope and adjust as it mingles with the behavioral environment we are born into and the entanglements encountered with exposure to the impediments of a material world. Like a planted seed sending forth its sprout through the dark soil toward sunlight, we too are planted in this material realm and must navigate and toil our way back to the godhead. The pressures of adapting and finding our place in a collective of species and culture may mean repressing our individuality and creative potential.[63] We seem forgetful of our eternal relationship with Krishna – our connection becomes dulled and tarnished. It then becomes the ignorance forming within ourselves and others that we must learn to recognize, understand, dissipate and release. It is up to us to clean and polish our connection to the Lord.

The words and lessons within the great scriptures help to remind us of and rekindle our relationship with Allah. You are here in the present moment reading this because of your desire for spiritual truth – you were drawn to this book for some divine reason. It may be because of your desire and interest in searching for God, meaning, purpose, answers, questions, direction or spiritual insight. By reading such words, you are a seeker looking for a higher meaning. The mere fact that you are seeking, means that you already have a link with divinity. The purpose of this book is to strengthen that bond and improve the connection. Your reading of these words means your relationship with the Creator is strengthening and becoming truer than that of many. There is a duality in the fact of your choosing to read these chapters, for those who most need to read this book will not reach for it. The duality is that those with strong connections feed their mind with positive spiritual nourishment in their seeking of God, while those with the weakest connections tend to starve and deny themselves the abundance of the Lord's cornucopia.

We are all beings dwelling within a cocoon of flesh, blood and bones and limited to the needs and wants of human desires. There is nothing wrong with having secular cravings, as long as during the pursuit of those desires, our moral fulcrum is properly situated and we apply moderation.

Consisting of atoms, molecules, cells, and organs, is this really all that we are? Just electrochemical reactions between neurons formed by the chance reorganization of ejected matter from dying stars? Is there nothing more beyond the elemental material protoplasm of our bodies? To go beyond this limited viewpoint of existence, we must ask different questions. To what influences or forces do we credit with the morphing of our form into who we are? Are we a part of that force? Can we tap into that force? Can we synchronize with that force? Are we made from chance or from spirit? What attracted you to open and read this book? Why are we drawn to concepts of divinity? The mere notion that we can ask such questions is proof enough of consciousness, sentience and sapience. But where does consciousness come from and where does it go? These are the questions that humanity has contemplated through stories, myths, fables, folklore, legends and religions from the dawn of our existence. It is one supreme creator presenting itself in multitudes that is the source for inspiring all the God Seekers.[64]

Throughout the ages in etiological pursuit of understanding our origins, men and women have vexed over the meaning of: 1) where we came from; 2) where we are; and, 3) where we are going. In terms of our physical self, our material composition, we rely upon the sciences of biology, chemistry, physics, astronomy, astrophysics among others to find answers. Embracing them into the whole of the Physical Sciences, the study of matter, one can call them the Natural Philosophies. In terms of our spiritual self, we rely upon psychology, metaphysics, mythology, philosophy and religion to find answers. Grouping them into a whole, we can call them the Spiritual Sciences, the study of the non-material, and they can be referred to as the Divine Philosophies. The former (the Natural Philosophies) studies the mixing of matter with time, the latter (the Divine Philosophies) studies the behavior of thought beyond time. Yet the underlying deism of the Physical Sciences and the Natural Philosophies are still divine principles, discovered by human curiosity and observation, and then applied with foreknowledge and predictability. It is religion that is the human invention, the tools of the Spiritual Sciences and the Divine Philosophies by which we use to access God or the gods, to gain the timeless wisdom of the Universal Consciousness. Religion is an enigmatic product of our ancient mind which is both profound and sublimely connecting – it can take us to heights of glory or to pits of despair depending on how it is applied.[65]

It was Thales of Miletus (624 or 620 BCE–546 BCE) who should be credited for first seeing a predictable order of natural laws for taming the chaos of the universe and to see some sense in its workings, moving us away from extreme reliance on the whimsical fancies of the gods or other supernatural influential entities. In doing so, we define (or at least assume) that we are advanced intelligent sentient beings (AISBs) with varying qualitative degrees of sapience, the vibrations of which, seem to make us expressions of God's energies. Not just having senses but also being aware of those senses, we can pull beauty and awe from the processors of our brains as we communicate our experiences or desires to others. Our minds learned to see patterns of elegance or repetition in both the randomness of chaos and in displays of order – it searches for predictable harmonies. We are able to create art and to recognize it. In this search for meaning, our neuron encoded processors (i.e., the brain) categorically respond to messages received from the eyes, ears, nose, tongue and skin and delivered them to the mind as emotional and logical signals. Our brains evolved and developed into a neural structural network capable of generating and projecting a mind which searches to identify with a larger and more sacred identity.[66] Sensing our interior sentience, that deepest dimension of ourselves, we realize it was built upon the contributions from eons of prior souls. From this mental search, the proper boundaries of social conduct morphed forward as we strived to define our linkage to the continuum of existence. Guidance sought from seniors and from the words of past generations had to find their place in modern society. Behavior that was considered acceptable and necessary for the preservation of society was encouraged and praised. Patterns of behavior that contradicted societal norms or which resulted in or perceived to result in demise were considered taboo and subject to punishment. For example, the kosher practices originated from an age lacking in the awareness of microorganisms, the importance of proper sanitation and refrigeration. The keeping of dairy and meat separate may have been due to the rapid bacterial spoiling of the mixture under the Mediterranean heat. The consumption of the spoiled mix could cause illness or death, hence, it was interpreted as forbidden by God. The proper behavior for preserving our species and advancing its relationship with the surroundings was transferred into written scripture as it evolved from legends, oral laws of past and the traditions of elders. It has been a process based on internal and external reflection, a commonality of spiritual experience, and the transfer of ancient information from generation to generation. Morality consisted in respecting those relational models, ethics or foundations. Violations were based on: 1) betraying, exploiting, or subverting a coalition; 2) contaminating oneself or one's community; 3) defying or insulting a legitimate authority; 4) harming someone without provocation; 5) taking a benefit without paying the cost; or, 6) peculating funds or abusing prerogatives.[67] To be a socially competent member of a culture is to have assimilated a large set of their norms, for better or for worse, regardless of the true moral qualitative content and measure of the norm.[68]

As humanity moved from the savannah to the skyscraper, much of what was previously considered prehistoric religion was left behind as it turned into folklore or superstition.[69] Our ancestors of long ago accounted for their world of experiences and the universe's actions with explanations based on assumptions of the supernatural; arbitrary powers at work. Without the suitable tools, meters and instrumentation for analysis of cause, this was the only course available of explaining and rationalizing the effects. However comforting explanative story telling was to primitive men, women and children, for re-living the great adventures of heroes, predicting phenomena, connecting to the world and comprehending the universe, fables and legends were superseded by the rise of true religious prophets during the dawn of civilization. Some legends, such as the stories of King Arthur, Merlin and the Knights of the Round Table, formed after the rise of the pre-common era religions and may contain elements of truth. Providing higher levels of more advanced and favored metaphysical models for relating to the universe, the prophets gave a greater sense of direction and purpose and clearer rational for the universe's behavior, wants and needs.

The great scriptures, be they Hindu, Buddhist, Judaic, Christian, Islamic or others, were written with the key intention of evolving the spiritual level of humanity by reconnecting it back to the source of eternal creation. They have served as guides for civilizations' behavior throughout the ages, propelling humanity to various levels of spiritual epiphanic plateaus. Many verses of religious texts are the wailings and lamentations of the human condition to a consciousness greater than ourselves. The emotions and feelings of the author(s) became incorporated into the pages. Other verses relate to current events in play during the time period of the scriber's thoughts. Many incorporated stories of past beings to explain the universe and give a sense of predictability to a seemingly chaotic world. Archetype heroes developed within the context of mythology, and blended and re-morphed into the religions of prophets, monks, shamans, gurus and saints. The borders between mythology, religion and philosophy were not always distinct or clear and often overlapped or blended. For example, Orpheus is a musician, poet and prophet in Greek mythology and said to have descended into the underworld and returned. The Bulgarians, however, view him as a great sage that lived among the Thracians about 4000 BCE and contributed to preparations for the future arrival of Christ four millennia later.[70] Sometimes those stories related only to the events at the time they were written with no intention of moral revelation, but rather as a reference for describing the patterns in the canvas of the night sky – a presentation of constellational history and the treating of the stars themselves as divine beings. Other times they relayed rules, regulations and moral guidelines to preserve and guide the existence of a culture through specific periods of peril, turmoil, awakenings and growth.

The story of a great flood sent by God or gods can be found not only in the *Book of Genesis* of the biblical scriptures, but also in Greek, Mesopotamian, Babylonian, Mayan, Yoruba, Hindu and other mythologies. It also appears in the indigenous folklore of many nations such as China, Korea, Ireland, Iraq, Turkey, Finland, the Philippines and the

Polynesian regions.[71] A story about a worthy family gathering the seed of all creatures into a boat and surviving a great flood, first appears in Mesopotamian text about a millennium before the *Old Testament* was even written.[72] Going against the traditional reasons for the great Biblical flood, the Gnostic Sethians (a cult based on the surviving son of Adam and Eve) viewed that it was not a punishment from the Hebrew God of the *Old Testament* for humanity's inequity and having gone astray. On the contrary, it was an attack of genocidal proportions out of anger, jealousy and fear that Adam and Eve's kin would continue passing down from generation to generation the divine knowledge (gnosis) that had been acquired through the instruction of the Garden of Eden's serpent. However, the temperamental and tyrannical <u>Demiurge</u> (the false God or half-maker) had not anticipated the resistance of one woman, Seth's sister or wife, Norea. Norea suspected the ark that Noah was building was a trap and burns it down, resulting in narcissistic anger and rage of the Demiurge, who then sends his archons to punish her by means of rape (either in the spiritual sense, physical sense, or both). Norea pleas and appeals to the true God for help, who hears her calls and prayers. The true God sends the aeon Eleleth (Sagacity) to the rescue and further instructs her in the ways of Gnostic righteousness. The Demiurge still sends the flood anyway, but Noah, Norea and their family are saved by finding shelter in a luminous cloud, resulting in their genealogy continuing in their descendants.[73] John Denham Parsons' book *Our Sun-God, Or, Christianity Before Christ*, questions the story of an ark saving all the animal pairs based on the sheer geometric volume required to transport them and makes us wonder why Noah chose not to bar the mosquito from its passage.[74] He also questions what saved crop, vegetable and seed from the ravages of a global flood – were they also stored in the ark's cargo hold? Whether literal or allegoric, the stories of a great deluge being sent by a higher being(s) to cleanse the planet of humans for either having gone astray or becoming a threat to the gods seems a common theme across more than one culture.

Mithra, a variant of the Persian version of a sun-god from Indo-Iranian mythology, was said to have been born in a miraculous way which attracted the attention of sheep herders to the birth. Competing with early Christianity for followers, the cult of Mithra was still popular among Roman soldiers up to the 4th century. Not knowing the actual birth date of Jesus, the Christians of the time period allegedly adopted the pagan birthdate of Mithra, which was alluded to be on December 25th and in doing so, tell us that Mithraicism was in existence prior to Jesus' birth. Parsons mentions that the wafer (aka "host") of the Christian mass used for the Eucharist or Communion may have been copied from the rituals of Mithraicism.[75] Tertullian even admitted that Mithraicism and Christianity appeared identical to the educated in all but their name.[76] The *Avesta* of Zoroastrian scripture "declares Mithras the Sun-God to be the first emanation of Ohrmazd."[77] This December date of the shortest day of the year, prior to the effects of the procession of the equinoxes over the past two to three millenniums, used to be when the sun having reached its most southern destination, began its return to the north.[78] This pagan date also coincides with *Dies Natalis Solis Invicti* (Birthday of the Unconquerable Sun), a winter solstice holiday celebrated at least two centuries before the birth of Christ. Also celebrated on December 25th was the dedication to the Syrian sun-god Baal and/or King Helios (aka Zeus). Emperor Constantine, whose patron deity was Apollo (aka the god of the sun), saw the title of Christ as another name for the Sun-God. He still kept the phrase "To the invincible Sun my companion" upon Roman coinage after converting to Christianity.[79] Most importantly, however, many of the stories contain eternal and infinite truths within their contents that stand for all time. They also contain passages that may now be outdated or only relevant for a particular past timeline of humanity's growth. One of the keys to enlightenment is to figure out which are which. This is done through reflection, the application of spiritual logic, sound reasoning and the development of our inner core through correct action and thought.

With the advent of the Scientific Method, explanations for our material existence were developed by interpreting the cause and effect behavior of elements and forces both internal and external from ourselves, provided such forces originated and remained within our realm of time. Investigating the interlocking puzzles of deoxyribonucleic acid (DNA),[80] matter interactions of elementary particle bombardment, the grander cosmos and developing temporal secular models (i.e., the Periodic Table Of Elements, the taxonomical hierarchy of biological genre, the Hertzsprung-Russell Diagram for star ranking) to predict, at least partially, the interconnectedness of everything, humanity is always thriving for a glimpse into the mind of God. Such human models, no matter how relatively crude, evolved through the use of establishing hypotheses, theoretical assessments and attainable observation. For astrology morphed into astronomy, alchemy morphed into chemistry and the deeper meaning of mythology beyond just the literal, morphed into religion. The modern is related to the ancient, for it is the old which diversely evolves into the new. What comes to us from the past is adapted to possibilities and demands of the future.[81] Without the steps of the ancient, there would be no "state-of-the art." We have elaborate microprocessors, computers, and digital memory, yet we still use and have a reliance for the simplicity of pencil, paper and pen. Our current models for predicting and understanding the universe are still developing and changing to this day and will also seem relatively primitive to our posterity.

Allah wants us to cautiously unravel, discover and continue to reveal the secrets of existence, but we must proceed with caution since the universe is both a wondrous and dangerous place. What I am implying is the idea that God wants humanity to rise to the greatest heights possible. I'm not saying that humanity is to, can or will rise above the godhead and become greater than God, (a fraction cannot become greater than the whole just as a drop of seawater or a saturated sponge is not the entire ocean). We cannot become Allah, but we can mesh with him/her. God wants us to chase after our desired dreams and his secrets.

—Λ*—

"The secret things belong to the Lord our God, but the things revealed belong to us and to our children forever, that we may follow all the words of this law." – *Deuteronomy 29:29*

—*Ω—

Much as science strives to categorize and establish predictability in the material universe, religion often seeks to organize, designate, classify, catalogue and portray patterns of order in the metaphysical universe. The works of Emanual Swedeborg, the Theosophy of H.P. Blavatsky, *The Bhagavad-Gita*, *The Kybalion* and the *Spheres of Evolving Life and Consciousness* from *Thy Kingdom Come* are typical examples of writings seeking to classify the metaphysical universe with secular descriptive terms, hierarchal categorizations and organizational arrangements.[82] Sections of this book will inevitably be conducting similar taxonomical metaphysical labeling and categorizing. Throughout this text, certain themes will be repeated as a means of mental and educational reinforcement. Among these primary themes are: 1) defaulting to a steady state of love; 2) the notion of learning to recognize, interact and deal with duality and polarity; and, 3) that there are diverse and multiple acceptable paths to divinity.

As our primitive ancestors became cognizant of their own existence while transcending into the realm of the abstract, they became aware of and tuned into a much greater consciousness. This greater consciousness, and aspects thereof, have been discussed through the ages in the form of myths, legends and religious spokespersons (e.g., prophets). Some of the revelations have been considered truth by a select group, others have been considered false. Within *The Age of Reason*, the colonial American patriot "infidel" named Thomas Paine expressed his dissatisfaction of organized religious pursuits or more specifically, the promotion of the biblical ridiculousness and incongruences. He was bold and brave enough to face notoriety by questioning the chronology, authenticity, arithmetic and cruelty of various sections of the *Bible*, by dissecting and dismantling the various allegoric poetry when considered literal. He views much of the *Old Testament* as disordered prose, mangled medley, artificial anecdotes, "bungling stories", "jumbled fables", and the "pretended word of

God."[83] He sees the *New Testament* much the same way noting its "glaring absurdities", "contradictions", and "falsehoods."[84] Considering *Genesis* to have been written in the same time period as *Aesop's Fables*, about three hundred years before *Homer*, Paine sees it not to be as old and ancient as portrayed.[85] He even harps on the fact that the beginning of *Ezra* provides a recap to the reader in case they missed the last book's episodes, by being the same as the ending of the *2 Chronicles*.[86] Having himself been held a prisoner in revolutionary France, he takes an empathetic affinity towards the handling of captivity described in the books of *Ezekiel* and *Daniel*.[87]

Paine approaches the start of the *New Testament*, the Virginal Conception, as merely a continuation of heathen mythology of Zeus impregnating Leda or his union with Europa, but this time it is the Holy Ghost fertilizing Mary, the mother of Jesus. He views that Christianity wants us "to believe that the Almighty committed debauchery with a woman engaged to be married..."[88] But was it "debauchery" or was it consenting mutual love? Making a strong case that Mary was not a virgin, for *Matthew* 13:55-56 tells us that Jesus had brothers and sisters, Paine neglects to consider *Luke* 2:7, which tells us the child laying in the manger was her first-born. Parsons points out that the older copies of Isaiah's prophecy about a child savoir being born do not read as coming from a "virgin", but as coming from a "young woman."[89] It was later versions of Hebrew scripture that were altered to state "virgin."[90] The mythology of hybrid individuals being created when the gods or goddesses copulate with humans is not unique. Paul Wallis points out that there are 28 hybrids named in the Greek panoply, 17 in the Hindu myths and a few in the Norse and Celtic mythologies.[91] There appears to be nothing specifically restricting Mary's impregnation by the universe injecting its conceptive force directly into her gamete, thus initiating a spontaneous zygote and bypassing the need for physical sperm to trigger mitosis into cell specialization. If parthenogenesis can occur in certain animals and plants, why could it not ever happen in a human female?[92] It was, however, a spiritual parthenogenesis that resulted in Sophia's creation of the Demiurge.

Paine again points out mathematical inconsistencies by noting the genealogy of Jesus to be of 43 generations in *Luke* and then only 28 generations in *Matthew*.[93] He fears such discrepancies in accounting for natural genealogy could be indicative of discrepancies in Jesus' celestial origins as well. Mistakenly sometimes viewed as an anti-biblical atheist, he was unknowingly taking both an agnostic and a Gnostic (if not that of a Cathar) approach, although with a slightly bitter and scripturally cynical tone. Concluding the *Bible* to be more a mockery of the Almighty rather than an authentic account of his/her actions and words, he presents that to be true to oneself, disbeliefs must be openly acknowledged along with one's beliefs and "that the only true religion is Deism", the putting forth of moral behavior in imitation of God rather than relying upon another's revelations.[94] He fails, however, in his scriptural analysis by his judgments and assumptions that all parts of the *Bible* are incredulous forgeries, dismissively viewing that no sections can be accurate.

Encounters of revelation to Paine were personal experiences of new knowledge being exposed between God and an individual. He writes that the telling of one's revelations is merely hearsay, since true or not, it relies upon repeating the story of one's divine exposure and the surrounding circumstances without hard evidence. I too, would have to agree with his conjecture, for revelation tends to be of a mental or spiritual personal expanse, not typically of a material and physical public conception. The important thing to focus on is the nature of those revelations, not the particular relationship between the revealer and divinity. The key question to ask of anyone's revelations is do they advance humanity's relationship with itself and the universe or do they diminish it? If they advance it, then they are truths. If they diminish it, then I would tend to think of them as false. Some revelers had closer ties and stronger connections, but delivering the intended message of universal love, integrity and justice was primarily the same. Yes, there are discrepancies, contradictions, figurative and numeral imagery from the authors of both the older and newer testaments. Parsons points out in *Our Sun-God Or, Christianity*

Before Christ the numerological discrepancies of Noah and his days on the ark, the repeating significance of the numeral "72" in relation to our ancestors' worship of the sun, the pattern of "12" found in the zodiac, the tribes of Israel,[95] and the disciples of Jesus. In *The Sophia Teachings*, Robert Powell brings up the pattern of "12" in the stars upon the crown of the women described in *Revelation* 12.[96] Even Plato teaches, "There are 12 feasts to the 12 gods who give their name to the 12 tribes".[97] Parsons also points out the numeral "40" as it relates to the Israelites' years in the wilderness, Jesus' days in the wilderness of the Judean Desert, the time period for Lent and Powell reminds us of Jesus' ascension occurring 40 days after the resurrection.[98] Thomas Paine obsessed on the scriptural details to the point of only seeing the trivial differences rather than the commonalities, such as the exact wording of the inscription placed over Christ during the crucifixion while ignoring their unification in meaning.[99] I ask of you, however, to focus on and link the similarities and commonalities, for it is these which bind the stories together. If that single encounter in my mid-twenties with the porcelain face hovering overhead (as described in the beginning section titled *The Author's Background: Who Is Anon Omous?* of this book), was more than a self-induced hallucination, then it gives evidence and credence to stories of Mary and Joseph's encounters with angels announcing a child conceived by means of the Holy Spirit.[100] Perhaps that luminous face was an avatar of Earth or our Sun manifesting itself for my eyes to see.

There has been plenty of vigorous disagreement about virtually every issue of theology and the nature of reality throughout the centuries. This has led to the creation of a multitude of religious and philosophical paths for relating to the metaphysical universe. It is a travesty that as different perspectives and factions evolved from base religious foundations, disagreement often morphed into violence. One sect or schism attacked another. Instead of focusing on the similarities, concentration was placed on the differences. Sometimes these sects were created due to different theological views within both the branch and trunk lines and other times due to corruptive power grabs for leadership, property or land. Unfortunately, as some groups become obsessed with validating, determining or proving their particular prophets' relationships to divinity, they abused the prophets' messages and strayed away from the true intent of the related scriptures to justify negative actions. This has happened on a larger scale several times in human history and smaller occurrences continue to smolder in modern times.

There is only amazement when one contemplates the common reasons behind early cultures' desire to worship a being or beings considered above them on the hierarchy of life. Was it to create rationale for the seemingly chaotic effects and actions occurring within the environment? Was it to soothe our fear and despair of going from a conscious being to potential nothingness upon death? Was it to connect with or grasp onto a source that lasts beyond our physical time on earth? Was it to create a beacon of productive behavior for focusing the striving energies of present and future generations? Was it to find meaning to our existence and the probability of our destiny? Recognizing that we are living entities created by God, as manifestations stamped into the realm of time, we are a small aspect of divinity searching for itself. We are not the whole, but rather, a minute small parcel or subset of the Lord. God is the universal artist putting a part of herself into every one of her creations as she grows along with us.

Through the application of the Doppler Effect and light emanating from far away heavenly bodies being shifted towards the red side of the spectrum, science tells us that the universe is currently expanding; it is growing. If it were to start suddenly contracting, however, we would not know this for about 4.4 years due the distance of the next nearest triple star system of Alpha Centauri. More recent cosmological observations through the use of the Hubble Space Telescope indicate that this expansion is accelerating; the further away a galaxy or nebula is, the faster it is moving away from us. Although they are one and the same: God is growing, the universe is growing.

This growth occurs in both the creation and the creator. We are the artwork and so is the rest of the universe. God is always creating, and he is also recreating himself. Shiva, a Hindu aspect of the universal godhead, is always doing the dance of creation. The universal artist sculpts himself in understanding of his creations. The perpetual painter is always forming new pigments. The cosmic musician is always creating new melodies. The divine dancer is always performing new choreography. Some steps are ancient and well established, others are novel and fresh.

If we choose to see God, evidence of his/her existence will be revealed. If we choose not to see God, it is our loss. As a species we have a choice. We can open ourselves up and become receptive to this incredible spiritual energy capable of emanating from all points, (also known by name as, but not limited to, the Holy Spirit, The Tao, Ruach Hakkodesh, Tifereth or the Great Mystery), or we can close our receptiveness and remain within the comfort of our ignorance. The choice is ours. God wants us to learn about ourselves, our world and our universe. God is eternal and instantaneous. He moves slowly and she moves fast. As we grow, so does God, however, this creator is always many steps ahead of us.

The universal matrix of thought that encompasses everything is also constantly seeking to know itself. God seeks to know God. Since we are a small but significant subset of this grand idea, it is our utmost mission and purpose to seek knowledge, strive for moments of positive and enlightening experiences, and to achieve a balanced relationship with that which is external from ourselves. Significant aspects of the divine seek the divine. We are pieces of the whole, created and sent out to re-discover this puzzle called existence, and then return back to it bringing with us more than what we had upon going out. After our material death, the sum of our life experiences, (our thoughts, our actions, our feelings), is given to the whole, thus increasing the size of that already infinitesimal and infinite puzzle called God.

While in this physical realm, there is a network of thought of which we are all a part. As a form of monopsychism, it is referred to as the Global Mind, Global Human Consciousness or Global Consciousness of Humanity. It is beyond the organism of self and is the organism of humanity, a collective aspect and integration (integral) of each individual's subconscious. Just as the millions of cells in our bodies form a greater being, so too, is each one of us part of an even greater being. This global entity, an egregore of humanity's mean arithmetic level of illumination, is the average core behavior of our species' collective (our matrix) and it is where we are now on our spiritual evolution.[101] It is where the average personality of humanity resides.

Prior to approaching God, there is another swarm of thought that we are all a part of and must traverse through upon the death of our physical bodies. It is called, among other variations,[102] the Collective Cosmic Consciousness of Humanity, Universal Mind, Universal Human Consciousness or the Universal Consciousness of Humanity and it is the Collective Subconscious of the Global attributes and it too is a subgroup or aspect of God. Influenced by the souls of others, it is an integration (an integral) of the Global Consciousness, and it too is much greater than each individual. It is an entity that we enter on our journey to the godhead, both while in and beyond our physical existence on this planet. It is an entity that contains all the thoughts of humanity, all the emotions, all the experiences – the *nous* of our species. It is an entity from which souls pass through upon entering this world and a being in which souls pass through when exiting this world. It is an entity in which our thoughts swim with the thoughts of others. It is an entity that can both terrify and heal.[103] This is the entity that judges our souls for it contains all the information of our significant experiences; the thoughts, the emotions, the sensations and how we handled them. It contains the Pearly Gates of St. Peter, the judgment of Allah, the court of the afterlife. It is the fairest court of all because the evidence is the full documentation and recording of our lives. It is like a hard drive in the internet "cloud" that contains every significant moment of our existence and our interplay with the world around us – a data center with server rooms full of Akashic records.

Both the Global and the Universal are subsets of the universe and are somewhat comparable to a flock of birds or a school of fish. An individual bird or fish traveling alone looks like an isolated creature as it traverses within the medium of air or water. From our perspective, a lone bird flies through the air or a single fish travels through water as a triangular being,[104] appearing separate from the whole. As the bird and fish gather together with others of their species and start to travel as a collective, the flock or school appears to become an entity or organism onto itself – an egregore of animal movements. Observe the movement of a flock of migrating birds or a school of fish and the collective as a whole takes on a form of its own. It becomes a living, dynamic, dancing entity that seeks its own advancement and preservation. Although the entity of a flock of birds or a school of fish is always there, it only reveals itself to the human eye when the individual creatures come close enough together to the point at which they visually quantize into a school or flock. The Global and Universal Collective Consciousness of Humanity, although not visibly tangible items, are also always there. The Global Collective evolves and advances or contracts and digresses through the spiritual waxing and waning of its individual members, but it is always greater than the sum of those individual members. Just like the individual branches that make up a tree or the cells that make up the human body, the collective health of each of these parts contributes to the overall health of the entire entity. When enough of the Global Consciousness' constituents (e.g., people) resonate and vibrate with its implementing of The Thrice Primary Axioms: The Principle of Love, The Principle of Gratitude and The Principle of Forgiveness, then the Great Tribulation shall cease. The time for this is very near since the emergence is about to begin.

The Universal Collective is the desired direction of our evolutionary spiritual travel; it is where we and other AISBs want to head. It is the evolutionary human collective mind that pulls atoms and molecules together into physical form, to make our way through the realm of matter and time. All true paths to the godhead lead through this Universal Consciousness. Other species of creatures belong to their own Global and Universal collectives, which are subsets of God as well.

God, on the other hand, is the Supreme Collective Cosmic Consciousness or the Supreme Universal Mind, the over-soul of all creation. It is the Collective Subconscious of the Universal aspects, an integration of the Universal Collective, a quintessence of reality and eternity and perhaps a being of its own right. The Supreme Consciousness operates in the realm of time and matter, while the Supreme Subconsciousness operates beyond and outside of the realm of time and matter. The various pleroma shells of subconsciousness and consciousness interpenetrate each other, but those of purer heart and mind are able to mingle beyond their own individual containers on a more frequent basis. Like the nesting of matryoshka (Russian) dolls, the following is a visual diagram to help comprehend the layered and overlapping relationship. Whether the subconscious is triangular and the conscious is circular or whether the conscious is triangular and the subconscious is circular is arbitrary and depends on one's defining perspective.

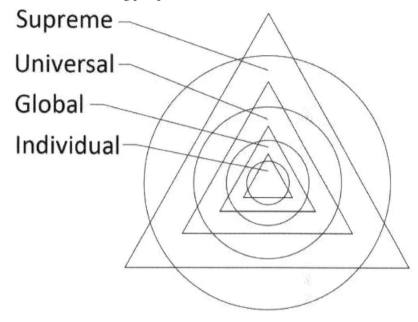

There is a bond of love between the Supreme Consciousness (God's soul and mind) and the souls of all sentient beings and things. It is we who sometimes tarnish this bond, not God. If we are to truly recognize the direction that the Universal Mind wants us to head, then we must leave the scriptural stories of vengeance, execution, persecution, combative destruction and extreme punishment within the infancy of our spiritual evolution and focus on those that invoke a positive relationship between our internal and external universe. Such spiritual contradictions expressing violence are from the direction in which we came, not the direction in which we are heading. *The Bible, The Avesta, The Koran, The Talmud, The Gita, The Sutras, The Vedas, The Zohar, The I Ching, The Upanishads, The Shri Guru Granth Sahib, The Kitáb-i-Aqdas, The Book*

of Mormon, The Urantia Book and plenty of other written scriptures, they are all training manuals of spiritual guidance for evolving our beings and maintaining our connection with the continuum of divine thought. When reading such texts, our minds taste the nectar of God's words as we become immersed into the internal ruminations and reflections of ancient scribers from long ago. Stepping inside their minds, our empathetic circles expand as their thoughts are encountered and become intertwined with our own. Yes, there are contradictions and dualities of good and evil among some of these ancient texts and we do not have to agree 100% with all of their phrases and passages, but they are still sacred and important for understanding ourselves. These discrepancies do not make any of the great scriptures less significant in the development of humanity's global consciousness. On the contrary, they are necessary to trigger the importance of love over hate, compassion over indifference, peace over war, education over ignorance, healthy tolerance over intolerance, justice over revenge, ambition over aggression and freedom over bondage. Without knowing the damage that negative destructive extremes can do to the spiritual growth of an individual, and to all of humanity and civilization in general, how else would we recognize the importance of striving for and maintaining as close to the positive constructive extremes as possible?

—A*—

"The soul is a veiled light. When neglected, it flickers and dies out, but when it is fed with the holy oil of love, it shines forth like an immortal lamp." – Amon-Râ[105]

• • • •

"WHO SAID THE ETERNAL one has died? Who said the Light of hope has died? The enemy of the Sun is on the rooftop. With his eyes closed he yells out, 'The brilliant Sun has died!'" – Rumi[106]

—*O—

Allah is personal when she lifts the veil between the secular and the divine to show her influence and impersonal when she chooses to carry out her actions hidden and concealed behind the shroud. He reveals his being when he feels we can endure the intensity of his grace and remains hidden when he feels such intimidating encounters will overwhelm us into madness from which we will not recover. God has never died. It is only our connection to divinity which has fluctuated from time to time. It is every advanced intelligent sentient being's mission in life to strengthen that connection through internal reflection, choice of action and consistency of good character. From the *Talmud*, God says to us, "If you come to my house, I will come to your house."[107] We must all prepare our house with a solid foundation of love and sturdy walls built on truth, not empty façades of false words and hypocritical actions. We must all become our own messiah of giving and gurus of positive action. It is the sage within each one of us that guides the future destiny of our own soul. Each individual must become a role model for themselves by identifying with those whose words and deeds that are based on wisdom, while filtering out those whose words and deeds that are based on egocentric and lower motives.

"Creativity is not efficient."[108] It calls upon sublime reflection and constructive imagination, bordering somewhere on the fringes of a dream or just prior to entering a trance. It is not efficient from a human perspective that often impatiently desires instantaneous results. It requires time for thoughts to brew and for interactions between the conscious and subconscious mind to generate connective solutions. Creativity is the influential signature of Krishna flowing through us. But to properly express it, we must also have the wisdom and knowledge to guide the divine pen. Artistic creativity without the acceptable borders of control and moderation is a clatter of chaotic disruption and false value. Great art arises above the narcissistic personal life of the artist, speaking to the spirit and hearts of all that admire it. "When a form of 'art' is primarily personal, it deserves to be treated as if it were a neurosis."[109] The true artist is not a person endowed with the free will who seeks their own ends, but one who allows art to realize its purpose through them.[110] The true artist is not merely an observer who complains, ignores, loathes, mocks or laments over the state and condition of society, but rather seeks to influence it in the direction of improvement. The proper steps of applying and developing our creativity must be followed through education, patience and listening to the inner core of our being that is fighting to be heard above the roar of a noisy world. Our DNA has morphed our minds, more than many other earthly species, to be receptive to God's grace, guidance, wisdom and love. Like an antenna, our brains are tuned to receive those divine energies. Based on what one chooses to allow into their internal being, however, some minds are better tuned in than others. The great separation between humanity and the other creatures of this great planet is the gift of aesthetic manipulative creativity in order to mingle with the divine. Humanity manipulates the elements not only for the objectives of food, clothing, shelter and transportation, but also for the experience of beauty, joy, companionship and ecstatic rapture. Brahma put more potential of his creative energy and pattern recognition into *Homo sapiens sapiens* than any other single or multi celled organism on our planet of origin. He also gave us the ability to either cause or prevent mass extinction events. Be those events from global warming, ecological cataclysms, thermo-nuclear annihilation or diverting the impact of an asteroid or comet, all life on Earth has placed their trust into our hands, relying on humanity to be their savior, not their destroyer.

—Δ*—

"Your task is not to seek for love, but merely to seek and find all the barriers within yourself that you have built against it." – Rumi[111]

• • • •

"IF A MIND PERCEIVES without love, it perceives an empty shell and is unaware of the spirit within." – *Accept This Gift*[112]

—*O—

The many-sidedness and variety of religious perspectives that have evolved from individuals and group collectives, if not incomprehensible, then at the very minimum, are astonishing.[113] Yet they all seek the same primary objective; a communing path to an intelligence or state of being that is far beyond our own. With so many different paths for approaching the godhead, the achieving of perpetual enlightenment, how can we be assured with certainty which ones are effective or if any of them are? The perplexities of choices and arbitrariness of the contradictions can cause one to abandon the notion of God or an ultimate reality all together. It can leave one bewildered in a fog and confounded to reject all. If approached improperly, the multiplicity of beliefs can veer towards a division of faith, therefore we must pull the reigns back and harness it into a unitive religious ecology. To muddle through the quandary, we should not limit ourselves to narrow definitions, but focus on the commonalities. Going even deeper into the endeavor of searching for the soul and investigating a preferred religious path, do not be afraid to walk several, only one or none at all. While doing so, however, remember that the placement of each searching step should be staged and planted with the gait, stride and balance of love on a journey that is sane, sound and authentic. Without love as the imprinting basis, the search ends and the path fades, for the correct direction towards God/Allah is always about love. What all the true masters of spirituality tell us is that the full communion of our being with God is through healthy love, acceptance and empathy transitioning into compassion. The only way to the godhead is through love. It is by love through which we reach the Almighty and by which he touches us. Love does not belong to God; it is God. For love is both an emotional and a logical progression into a higher state of mind. God wants us to reach for him/her as the cosmos witnesses itself through us. For our and God's growth is dependent on the sharing and exchanging of her essence of love, the implementation of empathetic fairness, and the development of religious innovation.

• • • •

NOTE ALPHA/TRIANGLE: There is an openly concealed message within the words of this book's title. One meaning is a symbolic reference to the 10 rays emanating from the star portion of the Asterox. Other meanings are the 10 representations of the center region as listed within the beginning section titled *About the Cover Art: The Universal Seal* and the 10 Directives listed within Chapter 10 of this book. Still other meanings are representative of the 10 emanations or Sefirot as denoted in a form of the Tree of Life (Kabbalah) and the 10th Heaven according to the *Book of Enoch*. There is one other very significant meaning to the title, a mystery within plain sight for you to solve as you define a new reality. *ΠΡΟΣ ΤΟ ΩΜΕΓΑ*

Chapter 2
God Who? – Our Personified Labels For Naming Divinity

"GOD SPOKE TO ME LATE last night. He told me that he's an atheist with insomnia and a sense of humor." – AO

• • • •

WHAT IS GOD? WHAT is not God? Is the Lord a deity? Is the Lord the deity? Are deities merely an aspect or subset of the All? Should we even attempt to define Allah? How does one call upon a single pronoun to describe all that divinity is? Is God a personification of divinity, a collective of an underlying consciousness to all things, or a bit of both? Do we call God a he, a she or an it? The descriptive use of the term "it" would unjustly miss the mark of describing the persona of that which is all encompassing. Clearly, the Almighty is infinitely beyond the dichotomy of genders and yet is also composed of both and everything in between. For us to fully describe and present God is like a finite mirror trying to portray the reflection of the entire world or trying to show the perspective of an infinite repeating mirror within the confines of its own edges. Being finite within our bodies, how can we ever fully comprehend and understand an infinite consciousness? One's definitional semantics of describing Allah also seems to vary among the global populace. We are limited to describing only aspects of divinity, but never being able to fathom the whole concept. When it comes right down to it,[114] there are innumerable names and labels for addressing and relating to divinity. All of which either refer to the whole or an aspect of the whole.

The ancient Hebrews also got caught up in this descriptive dilemma. With religious pursuit being dominated at the time of the *Old Testament* (forged from Babylonian and Assyrian civilizations) by males of the Israelite society, they veered in describing Yahweh as an "all powerful" he – God The Father and patriarch. Filianists, on the other hand, focus on

and worship the feminine aspects of divinity referring to her with labels such as Déa, Aphrodite, Venus, Thea, Mary and Sophia – God The
Mother and matriarch.[115] The word for "spirit" in Hebrew and other
Semitic languages is feminine, so to the ancient speakers of those languages, the name "Holy Spirit" would have most likely connoted a feminine being.[116] From Hinduistic scripture, Krishna states: "I am the father of this universe, the mother, the support and the grandsire..."[117]
Additional Vedic literature states "I am Brahman, I am spirit." Schools
of Buddhism insert the feminine of enlightenment into their goddesses
such as Tara and Guanyin.[118] The Gnostics from the beginning of
the 1st millennium, referred to the feminine aspect of God as "Sophia"
(aka Barbelo, Ennoia) when whole or "Achamoth" (aka Prunikos) when
split.[119] She is considered the psyche of God and is the appearance of
his essence.[120] Sophia is always ready to help the sincere seeker determine their destiny on his or her spiritual journey by providing enlightening epiphanies. She is the personification of wisdom (aka Chokhmah,
Hokhamah), intuition, insight and the veil dividing humanity from divinity, yet a real being. When she loses herself and identifies with the
body, she becomes the triangular Achamoth. When she finds herself and
identifies with consciousness, entering those who are ready, she becomes
the circular Sophia. Our quest is to help her find equilibrium between
the two states by projecting love into the universe – she is the Goddess
trapped within the psyche of each of us, waiting to be freed upon our
awakening. The Sethian sect of early Christianity contended that God's
mind suffered a breakdown and lost its wisdom, also known as the Aeon
Sophia when split. "Due to this trauma, Sophia fell into a void of chaotic, speculative emotions that eventually became the material world. As a
coping mechanism against this insanity, she fooled herself into thinking
she was a human."[121] A particular Gnostic view of the Gospels sees the
Virgin Mary (the mother) as representative of the higher Sophia prior to
the fall and Mary Magdalene (the whore) representing the lower Sophia
(Achamoth) after the fall.[122] The *Exegesis on the Soul* depicts the soul as

feminine and tells of her fall and entrapment into the physical realm after becoming separated and lost from her father in the Pleroma.[123] The *Gospel of Mary* shows too, that the feminine can access divinity equally as the masculine.

—Λ*—

"I was sent out from the power and have come to you who study me and am found by you who seek me." – influence of Sophia[124]

• • • •

"THERE IS NO DAY ON which I grow not finer and more pure, for this world holds no nobler lady than she whom I do serve and I adore. And these, the words I speak, come singing from an open heart." – Troubadour Arnaut Daniel[125]

—*Ω—

Coming from the Greek feminine noun of *monas*, the early Gnostics also referred to the Supreme Being as Monad. According to the *Apocryphon of John* (aka *The Secret Book of John*), Jesus reappears to John sometime after the crucifixion and consoles him by saying "I am with you always, I am the father, I am the mother, I am the child. I am the incorruptible and the defiled one."[126] Later on in human history, St. Thomas Aquinas (1225–1274) had regrets upon revelations towards the end of his life that he neglected the feminine aspect of God. The Christian theologian Julian of Norwich (1342–1430) among others, stressed the duality of God's paternal and maternal loving aspects. From rabbinic and Kabbalistic Judaic thought, the feminine aspect of Yahweh is referred to as "Shekinah" (asa Shehkinah).[127] The third chapter of the *Old Testament* book of *Exodus* tells of Moses' commission by God to be Israel's liberator from the bondage of Pharaoh's Egypt. Concerned over potential human reactions of doubt, Moses asks for God's name in order to validate his divine given role for the people of Israel.[128] God simply answered Moses with the phonetic of *ehyeh-asher-ehyeh,* spelled in Hebrew as (אֶהְיֶה אֲשֶׁר אֶהְיֶה) or translated into English as "I AM THAT I AM", "I AM WHAT I AM" or "I AM WHO I AM." Simplistically meaning that one can refer to God as a "him", as a "her", or as a combination, depending on which form of reverence is more comfortable to the devotee. Allah is whatever gender we call for since both the divine feminine and the divine masculine have a place in our hearts – the Creator has multi sexual powers.

—A*—

"You are the endless love,
You are the heavenly song,
You are the mother and father,
You are the one I will always know."

– Jalāl ad-Dīn Rumi[129]

• • • •

"I YAM WHAT I YAM AND that's all what I yam." – Popeye The Sailor Man[130]

—*O—

There is no better way to transcend time and the polarity of the genders than through the use of language asking us to accept Brahman for all that is. Allah is a concept beyond pronouns or hermaphroditic labels, but our limited language of secular beings forces us to sometimes reduce the description of all that is into a label of "he", "she" or "it". This is not a specific fault of the human language but rather an inherent boundary in our perception to fully conceptualize something or someone much greater than ourselves that or who is not quantifiable. The exact notion of God seems to transcend our limited cognitive abilities. Divinity is a presence much greater than all our thoughts and is beyond being referred to as a "thing". Yet many of us have been talking about this incomprehensible essence and praying to "it" for millennia. Without any less reverence for the divine essence of the cosmos, by default, the pronouns of he, she, or it will be used interchangeably within these chapters for referring to God.

Before we can argue about the existence or non-existence of God, we must first define what God is. Depending on perspective and level of spiritual nescience, the definition seems to fluctuate based on one's vantage point of understanding. Some refer to her as a sentient consciousness at work which is much greater than us. Others refer to him as a unique being that can answer our prayers or grant favors. Some of us have a myopic view when defining God and others have a broader view. Perhaps God should be left as undefinable since we all seem to have different relationships or degrees of connection with him/her.

Say the word "God" or "Allah" or "Lord" or "Ultimate Reality" to yourself. In defining your relationship with divinity, reflect on what the word represents to you for at least a minute. Now contemplate deeply on the following questions and try to formulate answers in your mind.

What is your concept of God?

Does God pertain to some connection to a larger whole?

Does it trigger memories of an "imaginary" friend who has done his or her best to guide the development of your morals and consciousness?

Does it represent those universal creative and destructive forces within our universe?

Did the creator form the universe and then leave it to its own follies or is she an active participant?

Does God micro-manage the universe and our daily affairs or watch them from afar with occasional intervening?

Does it portray a deity that needs to be invoked through prayer and worship?

Does it symbolize an all knowing or only partially knowing supreme entity?

Does it describe a being who is all powerful or only partially powerful?

Does it mean an all-encompassing divine consciousness?

Does it bring on feelings of love, beauty, kindness, acceptance and joy?

Does it invoke fear, anger, loss, misery and trials of punishment into your soul?

Are the unhappy or chaotic conditions in the world the fault of God, humanity or both?

Do you feel awkward, uncomfortable, hesitant or embarrassed when talking about God or Love?

Do you feel inspired, energized, or empowered when talking about God or Love?

Do you prefer to internalize or externalize your relationship with divinity?

Is God an eternal being behind the perpetual movement of our minds and the beating of our hearts?[131]

Is God fun, stern or fluctuating in between?

Is God full of vindictiveness and cruelty or infinite ecstasy and love?

Is God omnipotent always, occasionally or never?

Is the Supreme Being a finite entity or is Allah without limit?

Is it God the Father, God the Mother, neither or both?

Is God just a series of cause and effect patterns?

Can God ever change his/her mind?

Does God ever wonder where he/she came from?

Does God ever question the reality of his/her own existence?

Does God ever get sad or depressed?

Does God ever celebrate or feel happy?

Does God infinitely love humanity or is the love conditional?

Does God act with benevolence, viciousness or both?

Does God/Allah exist only on planet Earth or does he/she extend throughout all galaxies?

Is God merely the personification of the cosmos or a superior intelligence beyond our own individual minds?

Does God live within our universe or influence it from behind a curtain of immortality?

Is God the cause of all things, both good and bad?

Are God and Satan one and the same or are they opposing essences of existence?

To whom does God pray?

Did God create us, do we create God, or is it a symbiotic combination of both?

Did God exist before time or prior to the sprouting forth of material existence starting with what we scientifically and theoretically call the "Big Bang?"

What do you think the words "God/Allah/Lord/Almighty" should represent?

Do you believe in God, gods, goddesses or a god?

Yes, no, maybe, or sometimes?

—Δ*—

"We say that God is a living being, eternal, most good, so that life and duration continuous and eternal belong to God; for this IS God." – Aristotle[132]

—*O—

Even though we may find ourselves pondering about what is or what is not God, he or she is primarily a mystery both within and beyond the capabilities of thought. Religious doctrine has assigned descriptive adjectives that represent a secular aspect of the immortal being's character. Painting the full picture of all that God is, however, requires a canvas, brushes and pigments not available in this physical realm.

One of the names that ancient Egyptians used to refer to the Supreme One is "Atum" (ama "Atom"), the creator God. The ancient Babylonians refer to the holy name as "Ia", "Ie", or "Bel-Yaii". The Moabite Stone and the Assyrian monument both call the deity of the Hebrews as "Yahoo".[133] The later Kabbalists named that absolute, infinite, transcendent and unknowable essence as "Ein Sof" and followers of the *Zohar* refer to it as the Blessed Holy One. Ancient Hebrew symbolically referred to the supreme deity with a tetragram of (יהוה) and Anglicized as YHYW, YHWH, or YHVH, a name that could be written but not uttered due to respect for the sacredness of the divine. Philo, who lived during the time of Jesus, tells us the sacred name is pronounced like the Greek "Ieuo" and Clement of Alexandria of the 2nd century, interprets the tetragram as "Iaou" – both Philo's and Clement's pronunciational interpretations include almost all the vowel sounds found within the modern English language.[134] Irenaeus, Origen, Epiphanius, Hesychius and Porphyry as well as some of the Gnostics would all say that the God of the Hebrews was pronounced as "Iao".[135] Later, the tetragram had been transliterated into the pronounceable "Jehovah", "Yah-

weh" or "Jahweh", "Shaddai", "Adonai", "Elah" or "Jah" and further morphed into "Allah" due to some similarities between the Hebrew and Arabic languages. The word "God" itself comes from a translation of the
original "Elohim", which can mean God or gods. "Elohim" and "Adonai"
are considered the plural form while variations in the singular appear as
"Eloi" or "Eli" (meaning my God), or just "El", another appellation of the
Sun-God based on "Elios", a variant of "Helios" and the Greek word for
Sun.[136] The old English word "God" developed from Indo-European
roots. It is based on a blend of the Germanic "Gott", proto-Germanic
"gudan" and Sanskrit "huta" or "gheu" meaning "invoked or that which is
invoked." Ancient Greeks used the word "Theos" to refer to the creator
and owner of all things or the word "theos" for referring to a particular
god. God is addressed as "deus" from Latin, "Dieu" in French, "Dios" in
Spanish or as "Ishwar" in the southern regions of the Asian continent.
The use of the term "Lord" came out of the word "Master."

Besides the word "God", during the early sprouting of Christianity
from its Judaism based roots, the word "Abba" was also used to denote
the Heavenly Father.[137] It is no coincidence that the word "Abba" is
within the word "kabbalah" (asa cabala, cabbala, kabala, kabbala) and it
also means "Papa" or "Father" in Hebrew. Other Christian Anglicized
terms for the Supreme Being are Ruler of the Universe, Universal Master
of All, Infinite Mind, Lord of Lords, The Almighty, The Almighty Father, Father Eternal, Eternal Father, Divine Teacher, Divine Parent, Divine Friend and The Lord. Denoted as the "same Spirit", the "same Lord"
and the "same God",[138] the *Bible* uses several different pronouns to
symbolize this all-encompassing essence. The Sethians, a sect within the
first few centuries of Christ, referred to divinity as the "Invisible Spirit"
or "Great Invisible Spirit".[139] The Mandaeans, a modern semi-gnostic
sect still surviving from antiquity, refers to divinity as the "Great Life",
"Lord of Greatness", "King of Light" or the "Great Mind."[140]

The modern Islamic faith commonly refers to this universal being as
"Allah", most likely cognate with the Aramaic "Alaha", which means literally "the God." It is the preferred Arabic term for the one true God, con-

sidered containing all his/her divine attributes and has no plural or association with masculine, feminine or neuter characters.[141] The word "Allah" is composed of the article "al" and "lah" and according to esoteric Sufi tradition, one of the interpretations is "nothingness."[142] Emptying oneself to this "nothingness" opens up the heart to experience such intimacy, tenderness and love within the calmness of an inner serene solitude. Is it coincidental that the Proto-German and English word "All", meaning "everything", is also contained in the word "Allah"? I think not and Hermetic writings would agree. Sufi mystics, with their souls having a love affair with this primordial and everlasting essence, often refer to the supreme consciousness as "Beloved" or "my Beloved." Traditionally, there are over 99 other Islamic names or references for this universal entity such as Lord of the Universe, Lord of Creation, the Ever-existent One, the Life-Giver, the Mighty One, the Most High, the Supreme One, the Exalter, the All-knowing, the All-Merciful, Hu, the Keeper of Secrets and the Self-sufficient One to name but a few.[143] Each name tends to invoke a particular aspect or characteristic of Allah.

—Λ*—

"The ALL is the mind and the mind is ALL." – *The Kybalion*[144] and *Prashna Upanishad*[145]

—*Ω—

Those who practice a path of Hinduism may refer to this essence, entity or avatar as Lord of the Universe(s), the principle of Brahman (ama Brahmon), Vishnu, Sri Krishna or just Krishna (asa Krsna or Krisna), Rama, Hrsikesa, Isvara, Narayana, Bhagavan, Indra, Paramatma, Mahadeva, The Absolute, The Whole, The Supreme Lord, The Supreme Person, The Supreme Spirit, The Supreme Personality of the Godhead, That Thou Art,[146] The Cause of All Causes or The Supreme Proprietor Of The Planetary Systems Of the Universe, depending on their attempts to express the inexpressible from the particular bioregional perspective of their Hinduistic branch. According to the Hindu text of the *Bhagavad-Gita*, "The Lord has different names according to his different activities."[147] The greatest of all divinity can also be referred to as the

One and the Many, Source of All Things, the Ultimate Causality, Master of All Mystics, Lord of lords, the God of gods, the Goddess of goddesses, the All-Father, the All-Mother, the Father of fathers, the Mother of mothers, the Master of masters, the Savior of saviors, the Mind of minds, the Spirit of spirits, the Wisdom of wisdoms, the King of kings, the Queen of queens, the Truth of truths, the Consciousness of consciousnesses, the Ruler of rulers, the Soul of souls, and the Joys of joy.

—A*—

"He who knows, O' my beloved, that Eternal Spirit wherein consciousness and the senses, the power of life and the elements of final peace, knows the All and has gone into the All." – *Prasna Upanishad*[148]

—*O—

Most of the Eastern religions (Buddhism, Jainism, Taoism, Confucianism) remove the personality from divinity and trend more on its ultimate state and real nature. Buddhism never specifically mentions that a God or gods do not exist, but finding them to exist as a being or beings is extraneous to their doctrine. Going from thousands of names for aspects of the Brahman in Hinduism and many names among the Abrahamic religions, Buddhism goes in the opposite direction by having no distinct names or any anthropomorphic tags. Mohists (followers of Mohism) submitted to the will of heaven in the sense that the piety was displayed by obeying the Shangdi (the Lord-on-High, Supreme Deity, or Highest Deity). Although showing glimpses of acknowledging forms of a personalized overseeing consciousness, much of the schools of Eastern spiritual thought focus on transcending above the material realms and into the divine realms (ultimate realities). Their teachings are more about improving one's own essence rather than submitting to or worshipping a greater all-encompassing essence. Even among the Eastern religions and their various sects, there are discrepancies and commonalities in how they approach personifying the cosmos and its many layers.

The indigenous people of the Americas had their own names and terms for when referring to the divine essence. The Lenape Tribes from the mid-Atlantic Eastern United States, for example, typically refer to the original creator as "Kitanitowit" or "Kishelemukong." The similarity in beginning phonetical pronunciation of "Krishna" and "Kishelemukong" may be more than coincidental. The Mohegan and Pequot languages refer to it as "Konchi Manto" or just "Manto."[149] The Algonquin Tribes refer it as "Kuloscap."[150] Kanghi Duta (Floyd "Red Crow" Westerman) from his Sioux background, referred to its name as "Konkachila" (meaning grandfather).[151] From Lakota or Sioux and other indigenous inhabitants, the term "Wakan Tanka" is used to refer to the Almighty Consciousness. When translated by the generalization of European linguistics, the various indigenous terms used to denote the Creator or divinity, coalesce into the succinct phrase of "The Great Spirit" or "The Great Mystery." The indigenous peoples of North America such as Navajo, Cherokee, Choctaw, Chippewa, Apache, Blackfeet, Iroquois, Pueblo, Creek, Hopi, Comanche, Cheyenne, Crow, Arapahoe, Shoshone, Kiowa and the numerous other tribal nations most likely have their own and additional vocabulary terms for when referring to this "Great Spirit." The Inca names for their link to the cosmos were "Inti" or "Pachacamak" and certain Polynesians referred to the divine influence as "Mulunga".[152] Other aboriginal collectives from around the globe not mentioned here, probably also have their customized words and phonetics for referring to this influential consciousness of the universe or the multiple aspects of its various forms.

Hermetic occultists refer to this presence as Substantial Reality, The Infinite and Eternal Energy, the Infinite Living Mind, The All, and the All-Goodness.[153] Zoroastrians refer to the supreme being as Yazata, Yezdan, Yazdan, Ahura Mazda (asa Ohrmazd, Ahuramazda, Hourmazd, Hormazd, Hurmuz) or "Wise Lord." The Druids called the highest Supreme Being, "Be'al."[154] Those who follow a path of Sikhism refer to the same essence as Vaheguru, the One Supreme Being or One Immortal Being who is both Ram and Allah. The Bahá'í Faith references God with titles and attributes such as the All-Glorious, All-Powerful, the All-Knowing, the All-Loving, the All-Subduing, the All-Compelling, the Most Exalted, the Most Powerful, the Most Excellent, the Most Bountiful and the Supreme Protector. Other terms used to name this entity (or aspects of it) are a Higher Power, Indwelling Being, Universal Patriarch,

Universal Matriarch, Divine Teacher, The Source, The Source of All, The Self-Existing One, The Mind of the All, The Mighty Fabric of Space-Time, The Supreme Guardian, The Absolute, Infinite & Creative Intelligence, the Perfected Self, Supreme Consciousness and the Supreme Universal Mind.

In 1953, Arthur C. Clarke published an award-winning short science fiction story titled *The Nine Billion Names of God*. Its fictional plot relates to technology accelerating the oncoming of the end of the universe, the ultimate apocalypse, by revealing all possible permutations of names for referring to the Lord. In a way, our technology of extracting energy from the burning of fossil fuels or the reckless splitting of atoms is a non-fictional plot that could very well prematurely end our world. If industry and consumer do not ween, reduce and shift our economic energy dependence from a primary portfolio of fossil fuels, the "Wine of Babylon",[155] we too will become fossils.

With toyful wordplay, the author of this book sometimes opts to personify divinity with the friend-like names of **Amo**n (asa Amoe) or **Oma**ne (asa Omai) depending on whether referring to the masculine or feminine aspects, characteristic or presence. The name Amon refers to God the Father (the universal father; the triangle/alpha) and also the ancient Egyptian god of the sun and air. The name Omane refers to Goddess the Mother (the universal mother; the circle/omega). The gender characteristics of Amoe and Omai are sometimes clearly distinguishable and other times they are overlapping or commingled. By elongating the sound of the first syllable when spoken, the names also become a form of the universal vibrational sound of the eternal mantra which resonates with the Supreme Spirit: "Om" or "Aum."[156] The Hebrew and Christian word "Amen", contained within the word "Test**ament**", is a common utterance meaning "so be it, surely, indeed, truly, verily." It is often spoken at the end of prayers and it too contains the universal mantra sound within its syllables. The "Am" sound can be considered the alpha, triangular echo of God's voice while the "Om" sound can be considered the omega, circular echo.

—Δ*—

"Call it Nature, Fate, Fortune; all these are names of the one and self-same God." – Lucius Annaeus Seneca[157]

—*O—

Rain, hail, sleet, snow, frost, steam, ice, clouds, fog, mist, spray, slush, vapor, icicle, drop, condensation, moisture, liquid, solid, wave, droplet, particle, crystal, icicle, gas, H2O, river, canal, pool, swamp, aqueduct, channel, aquifer, reservoir, pond, lake, puddle, stream, spring, geyser, falls, basin, well, fountain, bath, cenote, shower, tub, flood, wet, sweat, perspiration, brook, creek, moat, rapids, ocean, sea, lagoon, bay, marsh, harbor, tide, estuary – just as there are many names and forms of water, so too, are there many names and manifestations from the perspective of the material/physical plane for referring to God.

• • • •

QUESTION: WHAT NAME(s) or label(s) do you use when referring to divinity?

• • • •

ALL THE NAMES AND REFERENCES in the prior pages are presented as a mortal description for that which cannot be described fully in the realms of our current existence. If it cannot be described then why has our species spent so much time trying to explain, justify and enforce it? If the "All" of the universe is unnamable and undefinable, why do we have so many names and definitions for it? The answer is because a small fraction of all that is, exists within each of every one of us. This small fraction always seeks to enlarge its identity and to further comfort itself by reconnecting with the whole.

—Λ*—

"It is the God within your own self that is impelling you to seek him." – Swami Vivekenanda[158]

—*Ω—

Despite all the names we may use to describe this force of existence and non-existence, despite all the figures and secular designs we may use to describe the various emotional aspects of this being's human characteristics, despite all the branches, tools, paths and subdivisions we may create as a means of reaching a glimpse of this grandiose consciousness, we must always remember that all of us came from this universal entity, we live as a part of its continuum, and we shall return to it upon our passing from this plane of existence and into the next. In the end, no matter what name or sub-groupings we use to describe or classify this immeasurable ether of spirit, no matter what culture or religious path we travel to connect with this infinite wisdom, no matter what terms we may convey or customs we may practice in an effort to see beyond the veil of our mortal selves, we all are still referring to the same universal mind that is a witness to, and the cause of, all the interactions of being and nonbeing. God manifests himself/herself in innumerable forms, degrees of energies, and is diverse in action and behavior. The importance is not in the numerous secular names humanity uses to label divinity, but rather, it is in the recognition of a common essence, consciousness or force of thought at work that is much greater than ourselves, yet that we are all a part of. We are all a small part of God; the size of which is determined by the nature of our emotional and logical relationships between and with both our internal and external universe.

As sentient intelligent beings, we have sought to place organizational labels upon the various metaphysical aspects of God. Defining God, however, is a task not well suited for humans since there is no way to completely and truly describe something or someone that seems indefinable.

—A*—

"The Spirit Supreme is immeasurable, inapprehensible, beyond conception, never-born, beyond reasoning, beyond thought." – *Maitri Upanishad*[159]

—*O—

We can, though, as individuals, define and refine our relationship to this extreme consciousness or Supreme Being. Defining your relationship with that "something greater than ourselves" and how you refer to it is up to you. Some refer to this higher existence as God, Allah, Jehovah, Yahweh, the Almighty, Akal Purakh and many other terms and multiple names throughout the millenniums of human existence. The exact name is merely a verbal and written tool used within the limited conceptual realm of humanity's languages and is not as important as the path chosen. Choosing a path based on non-violence and striving for a better tomorrow through the actions of love for all of humanity is the truest belief in something greater than us.

As a reminder and noted in the Preface, since the plethora of names given to this all-encompassing consciousness are merely simplistic human labeling, the use of the word "God", "Allah", "The Lord", "Krishna", "The Almighty", "Yahweh", "Jehovah", "Creator" or other identifiers will be used interchangeably throughout this book. However primitive and lacking in adequate veneration, the pronouns "he", "she" or even "it" will also sometimes to be used in this book for referring to this same all-encompassing gender-neutral consciousness. The particular selected identifier in a given phrase refers to the same divine infinite expanse referred to by all the true religions. Never in this text is it said or stated which are the true religions, for that is up to the individual to determine based on their chosen spiritual path(s). God already knows which religions are the true ones.

Do not become too lost in the semantics of trying to define God, or aspects thereof, and do not be afraid to refine your perspective and conception on what constitutes God. The supreme consciousness (divinity) transcends all the names, terms and labels that we throw at it. Whatever the name used to label the transcendent One, we experience identity with that One across all religious boundaries. This understanding, acknowledgment, and experience surpasses culture itself, raising us above the duality of us and them, to awaken our unitive with the whole of the global community.[160] Travelling through life as religious beings, we should revere all forms of the Lord. The way of growth and spiritual evolution is by allowing changes to occur in our definitional view on what Allah is and to continually recognize that God leaves his mark through diversity, love, gratitude and forgiveness.

How do we rationalize a world that can be rather perverse and chaotic at times? Will the universe disappoint or will it provide? Is God just a fairy tale created by humanity as a means to make us feel better about our daily perils and future demise? Is our life just a monotonous void of consecutive burdens? Is our individuality the accidental culmination of interchangeable forces making us unique only due to our genetic inheritance? Is the total sum of our days just a vast collection of impulses of thought and movement or is there something grander to our existence than just the random bonding of nucleotides and encounters with chance? Do we mark the passage of time by birthdays, holidays or by the day of the week that we wash the laundry or put the trash out to the curb or in the dumpster for pick up? Is our only purpose to have futile hopes and endure devastated dreams, born only to weep, suffer pain and die? What goal do we serve as living, experiencing, and dying beings? Is religion's promise of a life beyond merely to provide a carrot of perseverance with no scientifically convincing absolute proof? The answers to these questions are for each individual to determine as we celebrate the good days and endure the bad ones encountered within a lifetime. For when life is good and times seem magical, it is easy to be aware of God in our midst. Being aware of God's presence behind the curtain of the situation when times are bad, however, can be challenging, yet that is when we need him most as we move forward through crises as warriors and soldiers of endurance. Developing a tremendous faith in something beyond ourselves, a God or an essence of divinity, seems to encourage a humble yet soundly realistic faith in ourselves.[161] Within the *Bible*, we are reminded that God is always with us,[162] especially in *Matthew* 28:20 where Christ is quoted as stating "...I am with you always even to the end of the age." In our times of grief, loss, misery and suffering, it is reasonable to question whether divinity has forsaken us and whether there is meaning to our existence. It can take much reflection and spiritual work to re-establish our connection to God after surviving such ordeals, rather than during them. Climbing out of that pit of despair can be a difficult journey. The steps we take to rekindle our relationship with the universe depend on where in the duality we want to be. Do we believe we will one day be released from the clutches of sadness? Do we believe we will ever feel content again? Do we believe we are deserving of happiness? It is when floating and then climbing through the emotional agony that we start to rebuild ourselves.

Brahman seems to be much smaller than an elementary particle and much larger than the entire cosmos, existing simultaneously at both extremes and everywhere in between. The Lord is a creator, a maintainer, a destroyer, a law giver, an overseer of the universe, a parent, a guardian, a teacher, a judge, a lawyer, a jailer, a prisoner, a ruler, a healer, a physician, an apprentice, a craftsperson, a master, an entrepreneur, a guide, a mentor, an artist, a painter, a sculptor, a chef, a grocer, a scriber, a poet, a writer, a singer, an author, a calligrapher, a piper, an entertainer, a musician, an actor, a choreographer, a dancer, a comedian, a scientist, an athlete, an inventor, a coach, a mathematician, a traveler, an explorer and a philosopher. Above all else, God is love and a lover. Jehovah is the invisible personification of the cosmos, revealing aspects of his/her existence to glimpses beyond our physical realm and answers to all known names.

—Δ*—

"If you call me by day or night by these names I will come to assist and to help; the Angel will come to assist and help; and the Spirits also come." – *The Avesta*[163]

—*O—

Spiritual development through self-purification and self-realization is what delivers our soul upward to the House of the Lord and into the democratic Kingdom of Heaven and Light. It is incorporating the remembrance of divinity by internally or externally invoking whatever name we choose to call it, into as many moments of our existence as possible. God is God in every name and every tradition.[164] Ultimately, there is no single tag or brand suitable to call the essence of the universe, because all names are his/her name and any one we try to use ultimately becomes a limitation. Therefore, we may call and refer to divinity by any known label that is familiar for us to say and comfortable for us to pronounce. Hallowed be thy ineffable name, whatever it may be.

—Λ*—

"If we want to truly understand God, we have to go beyond all names and attributes. He is both God and not-God." – Dionysius[165]

—*Ω—

Now continue with reading the following chapters to help answer the next question: What is your place in the universe and your relationship with divinity?

Chapter 3
Choose Your Religious Analogy

"GOD WELCOMES THE MULTITUDE of all true religious paths used to reach him or her." – AO

• • • •

THERE ARE MANY MODELS and methods for relating to God. No religious model or path has an exclusive access nor a monopoly for connecting to divinity. Any religion claiming to be the only path or the only way is succumbing to the human frailty of insecurity and feels threatened by the other paths. Attacking another because of a religious path that is different than yours only reveals an insecurity within your own path. If you truly believe that your path is the true or only way, then why should you be concerned with the path followed by others provided it is a non-violent approach? God and his abundance of love does not feel insecure or threatened so neither should you.

—Δ*—

"The easy confidence with which I know another man's religion is folly teaches me to suspect that my own is also." – Samuel Clemens (aka Mark Twain)

—*O—

Some religious paths overlap and some diverge, but all true paths eventually lead to God. Just as the Almighty has cast diversity into her creations, she accepts the many true paths used to reach her. Just as there are many forms, manifestations and subsets of the Lord, there are many branches, many paths, and many tools for interacting with divinity. The purity of our link to God is determined primarily by our behavior and treatment of others and the universe, not by what religious organization we belong to, nor what customs and traditions that we follow.

A genuine purpose of a religion and its texts is to expand and develop the consciousness of its followers and readers. This expansion occurs by installing metaphysical connections within our thoughts that network us

81

to higher truths. As these connections develop and intertwine with the core of our personality, our approach to life and the universe changes. We may still get discouraged, cynical and at times, feel overwhelmed by the pressures of life. But it is upon reflection and internal contemplation that we reset the circuitry within our brains, rewiring our beings back to God. Just as we define and refine our relationship to the Supreme Entity, God is also defining and refining his or her relationship with us.

Religion is a popularity contest. The best way to influence someone is through making your ideas attractive. If your ideas are attractive, others will follow. A particular religion withstands the test of time through the appeal of its initial leaders and future spokespeople, the attractiveness of its ideology and accessibility to its doctrines. It will endure only for the short term if implemented through the brunt authoritative strike of enforcement. Therefore, philosophies and religious views should never be forced on anyone. An individual has the God-given right to choose and accept the religious aspects that they prefer to practice. They have the God-given right to join, question or leave a religion or religious order if they so choose. The best way to search for God is by reflection from within, not by seeking and attaching to external objects, nor by becoming charmed with charismatic characters touting religious media. The true religions will have followers for eons provided they continue to provide the proper spiritual nourishment for advancing humanity's relationship with the universe. Otherwise, they will wane and die off due to their own falsehoods. There will, perhaps, be newer religions morphing from prior ones just as a bud branches from a tree or a spout emerges from a seed.

A religion which promotes a positive relationship with the universe is generally true. One or a misguided aspect thereof that promotes violence and self-destruction is certainly false. Religion exists for its believers, not the other way around. Religious structure exists for its followers, not the other way around. Its leaders should always keep this in mind. Religion is a *modus operandi* created by humanity and other sentient beings for connecting to divinity; it is not a creation of God. God does not need religion; it is humans and perhaps other intelligent sentient beings that need religion. Allah is always connected to us and does not need religion to reach us. It is we who need religion to reach him/her.

Religions will need to adjust and change while still maintaining connections to the past if they are to remain attractive to their followers. If
true religions do not appropriately evolve with the times, they do not die,
but they may wither, fade and merge into others. God is growing and the
vehicles to understand him or her needs to allow for growth as well. This
growth should not abandon the roots and initial branches, but cautiously allow for the establishment of new buds. Religions will need to balance the roots of their past with the new shoots of the future, if they are
to survive beyond the present. It is a balance between the past and the
future, which gives the present. The present is the cornerstone set on the
past and upon which the future is built.

There are many true paths (i.e., religions) to the godhead with a variety of scenery (i.e., rituals, customs, traditions, pageantry, creeds, ceremonies, liturgies) along the way. Sometimes the scenery and foliage are
similar and other times rather distinct. Some paths may be more productive and others more colorful. Some paths are older and some paths
are newer. Some are more elaborate, ornate and detailed while others are
more straightforward, simplified and basic. Some have a simple hierarchy
of leadership while others have a more complex organizational bureau-
cracy. To say one path is better than another is a misnomer. To say they
are different accentuates the beauty in their multitude, variety and diversity. God knows which ones are the true paths. If you follow a belief in
one almighty God and practice a monotheistic religion, then peacefully
respect those who believe in more than one god and practice a polytheistic religion that worships benevolent deities. A polytheistic faith is still
an aspect of God, but a monotheistic approach is more focused, direct,
efficient and concentrated for reaching the supreme source and the divine being.

Allah takes on many different forms from culture to culture. At
times, he provides us with wisdom, inserts barriers so that we learn and
removes obstacles from our existence so that we can grow. Is Ganesh,
symbolized with an elephant head and celebrated by many Hindu, Jaina
and Buddhist sects, not merely an aspect of Allah? For Ganesh is often
considered a god of wisdom, intelligence, learning and a remover/im-
plementer of obstacles. Is the personification of existence through gods

by the Hindu Trimurti of Brahma (the creator), Vishnu (the sustainer) and Shiva (the destroyer) not merely another aspect of God? Is the Vedic Trinity of Brahman, Paramatma and the Supreme Personality of the Godhead not similar to an abstraction of the Christian Trinity of the Father, the Son and the Holy Ghost? Are saints, angels (or perhaps even demons),[166] jinn, aeons, archons, avatars, gods, goddesses, and demigods not just subsets or an aspect of the whole? Is Allah/God not the whole? Are the influences of Tao and the Hindu notion of Brahman not like the Christian concept of the Holy Spirit? Should we look upon ourselves as being separate from the Almighty or as being an aspect of his wonderment? Being created from divinity, are we not a subset of God? We are not gods or God, but can humbly accept in our piety that we are a part of creation's greatness. We should not disregard the relevance and recognition that God/Allah comes forth as both fractional elements and as the whole source. There are multiple paths or entry points to the Ultimate Source or the godhead and we should respect all of them which encompass a creed of healthy tolerance and non-violence. God embraces all true paths used to connect with him and/or her.

—A*—

"Krsna is one, but he is manifested in unlimited form and expanded incarnations." – *Bhagavad-Gita*[167]

—*O—

If Allah is everything and all embracing, then is not the religious path of multiple gods also an aspect of God? Perhaps polytheism is not the most efficient path to Allah, but it is still a part of him/her. If the Lord is everything and all encompassing, then are not the peaceful pagan religions and traditions also an aspect of God? They may involve different names for subsets of Allah's various forms and a path that is more meandering than a monotheistic approach, but is worshipping a tree, an animal, a mountain or the Sun, or another object created by God, not in some way, worshipping God himself? When we worship her works, are we not worshipping, showing awe and reverence for the creator herself? When one admires the great canvases of a talented painter or the physical forms crafted by a skilled sculpture, are we not admiring the artist herself? This is not saying that if you practice Islam, Christianity or Judaism that you should suddenly elect a pagan path or feel obligated to "cut and paste" from other religions, but rather, it is putting forth the message of providing healthy tolerance and acceptance towards those on alternate paths to the godhead. A pagan of moral character that chooses to "personify both virtue and vice by statues and images", rather than by words alone, is still following a path to divinity.[168] In the biblical story of Jonah and the whale, the author makes a point of separating the gods of the mariners from that of the Hebrew Jonah.[169] Rather than initially terminate Jonah for the stormy wraith his god has brought upon them, even when Jonah has already requested that he be thrown overboard, they show mercy and compassion by first unsuccessfully trying to fight the tempest generated by the Lord.[170] Being unable to safely bring the ship to shore, they had no choice but to throw him overboard to calm the seas and save themselves.[171] They even pray to the Supreme Being, going against the very propaganda that pagans are idolaters.[172] The "Gentile" sailors' willingness to put their lives on the line to save that of an outsider shows moral character as does Jonah admitting how they could save themselves. Again repeating a core theme within this text, we should not be concerned with the non-violent path others take to reach the divine artist, but rather, we should focus on how our own path is paved. The divine artist puts a seed of themselves into every one of their creations in hopes that those seeds will sprout and grow in balance with all the other creations.

• • • •

RELIGION AS A TOOL

Religion is a tool invented for connecting to the supreme consciousness. It is not God's design, it is humanity's creation, the workings of advanced intelligent sapient life forms. We need religion to aid in communing with God, but he/she does not need religion to commune with us. Understanding that religion is a tool, it is a normal human drive to want to improve upon it by making modifications. Just as there are many tools for turning a nut on a bolt, so too, are there many religious paths for connecting with divinity. Just as the scientific method is a tool used for relating to the physical universe, religion is a tool used by sentient beings for relating to the metaphysical universe. Some of these religious tools work better than others, depending how they are used and applied.

In the same sense that there are many means to install a nut onto a bolt, there are many ways to interact with God. To install a nut, one can use an adjustable spanner wrench, an open-ended wrench, a closed-box wrench, a ratcheting wrench, a shallow socket wrench, a deep socket wrench, an impact socket wrench, a socket driver, a pipe wrench, a monkey wrench, a channel wrench, a lock wrench, a torque wrench, a strap wrench, long nose pliers, combination jaw pliers, clamping pliers or one's fingers. Some of these tools will be more effective and easier to use, depending on the size of the nut and skill of the craftsperson, but never-the-less, they can all be used. The workshop of a master mechanic has an arsenal of tools from which to select from. An adroit spiritual master also has an assortment of religious tools from which to choose from. Good religion is the tool by which we guide, monitor and adjust our behavior for the betterment of our core. It helps us and assists us with relating to divinity.

* * * *

RELIGION AS AN AUTOMOBILE

Just as there are many models of automobiles for traveling over land, so too, are there many vehicles available for traveling closer to enlightenment and communing with God. One may choose various aspects of the different religions to create a vehicle custom suited to their needs. One may prefer the seats of Hinduism, the frame of Judaism, the wheels of Buddhism, the engine of Christianity, the tires of Islam, and the body of the Bahá'í faith. One may select a custom-built spiritual vehicle or prefer a vehicle made stock from the factory. An individual's relationship with the godhead is their own choice. It can be based on the religious foundation and traditions of their parents and ancestors or it can be based on their own searching for truth. The only divine stipulation is that it is a path which promotes a positive relationship within us and towards others and the universe.

Consider the owners of two classic American sports cars; we'll use a 1957 Chevrolet Corvette and contemporary Corvette built in this millennium as the examples. If the two should meet while driving their jalopies, they would look at each other's vehicle with admiration. Each may prefer their own driving machine, but they respect the other's car. They would probably pull over and pop the hood of both vehicles and observe the workings underneath. The older vehicle would have a fuel system based on carburation, the newer one, fuel injection. The older vehicle would have points in the distributor, the newer one would have electronic ignition.

The important thing to realize is that the later vehicle could never have come about without the trials and tribulations of the earlier vehicle. Modern struts were formed by combining shocks, control arms, springs and ball joints of the earlier vehicles. Many changes have occurred with each advancing decade, but the basic underlying structure still exists. They still have wheels for connecting to the earth, doors to allow its occupants access to its interior, a windshield for vision, a steering wheel for direction, an accelerator for initiating momentum, a brake to restrain the momentum, seats for comfort, and an engine or motor for converting energy into driving motion. Similarly to the automobile, true religions have their componential differences but they still are built upon core tenets that are common to all.

—Λ*—

"Life can only be understood backwards; but it must be lived forwards." – Søren Kierkegaard[173]

—*Ω—

The steering of our life into the future can feel like driving a car backwards. Using the limited view of our mirrors, it is as though we are edging our way down the road of time with the transmission in reverse. Sometimes it feels like our foot is on the brake and the vehicle is not moving at all. Other times we can barely stay on the road and maintain control due to the rapid acceleration or obstacles to avoid. We see each moment as it zips past; a slide show of events, snapshots of our lives, seen

out the side windows of our automobile. We try to steer our future with
the limited field of vision of our overhead and side mirrors, but it only
shows us a small peephole into what is to come. We dare not turn our
heads to see the whole picture at once through the rear windshield for it
would overwhelm us with all the choices to be made, all the emotions to
be felt, all the moments to be experienced. God, however, sees the whole
map at once. She knows the journey forwards and backwards. He also
knows what awaits at the final destination. She sees the hills, the curves,
the bumps and the weather. He knows the villages, the towns, and the
cities. He is a passenger too, for he always comes along for the ride. Because she sits in the backseat, we sometimes forget her presence. God
wants us to become the best drivers as possible – one who knows when to
slow down to negotiate sharp turns, and one who knows when to speed
up on the open road. He wants us to know when to pull over and enjoy
the scenery and admire the beautiful vistas. She wants us to know when
it is time to reflect and maintain the vehicle.

• • • •

RELIGION AS A TREE

We cannot deny the infinite structure given to God by all the great
religions. So how can we ever insist that there is only one path to this
infinite structure? It defies spiritual logic to say that the path to an infinite structure is based on a set of finite roads. This infinite structure has
paths that are both permanent and changing, for the Almighty is both
immutable and fluid. God is always growing, and like a tree, he chooses
to keep certain branches and drop others.

What if there was only one path to God? What if Buddhism was the
world's only religion? What if only Bahá'í was the primary faith? What
if it were only Islam, Judaism, Hindu or Christianity? Only one path?
Only one branch? I know of no tree that can grow and stay healthy with
only one branch. It takes many in balance to assure the continued upward growth of the trunk. A balanced and healthy tree is one with many
well-distributed branches. Just as a physical tree is grounded in earth and

reaches for the sky, so too, should our faith be grounded in the secular but reaching for the heavens.

Be us a Zoroantian, Buddhist, Hindu, Jew, Christian, Muslim, a follower of an ancient primal or earth based religion, or a benevolent sect or schism thereof any of the aforementioned, we are all formed from the same creative life force. There are differences between religious doctrines just as there are differences between ash, oak, banyan, maple, yew, sequoia, birch, cedar, fig, juniper, olive and mulberry trees. There is variety in religious scripture just as there is variety among bristle cone pine, cypress, baobab, spruce, eucalyptus, redbud, orange, pear, pomegranate, willow and apple trees. To say there is only one path to Allah is as ludicrously analogous as saying there is only one entity in the scientific classification of the plant kingdom, for a mustard seed can grow into a plant, shrub, bush or a tree. There are many aspects of Allah within all true religions, just some paths are more efficient, more scenic, or more direct than others. Being more efficient, more scenic, shorter, longer or more direct does not necessarily mean that such paths are better, rather, it means that some paths may be preferred depending on the follower. Just as the distinction between trees, bushes and shrubs can become unclear at times, so too, can the distinction between religion, philosophy and mythology. Just as all trees, bushes and shrubs are plants, so too, are religion, philosophy and mythology all metaphysical views for relating to reality and interacting with the universe. Like a tree, if we are strongly rooted in the word of the true God by putting forth behavior based on love and not on hatred, then we shall survive periods of tribulation. The many religion and sects are merely different branches to God; they are of the same tree. Some of these branches have grown out of others, and some have grown out of the base spiritual trunk line. If all these branches were to grow from only one side of the trunk, the tree would be bent and lopsided. If only one branch were to grow out of the trunk, it would not provide enough nourishment and energy to the trunk and its roots. The relationship between the leaves, branches, trunk and roots of a healthy tree is symbiotic. They need and help each other to grow.

—A*—

"Tell me of Moses, Isaiah, Confucius, Zoroaster, Buddha, Pythagoras, Jesus, Paul, Mohamet, Aquinas, Luther, and Calvin – a whole calendar of saints. I give God thanks for them, and bare my brow, and do them
reverence, and sit down at their feet to learn what they have to offer. They
are but leaves and fruit on the tree of humanity which still goes on leaf-
ing, flowering, fruiting with other Isaiahs and Christs, whereof there is
no end." – Theodore Parker[174]

• • • •

"A SINGLE ACT OF KINDNESS throws out roots in all directions,
and the roots spring up and make new trees." – Father Frederick William
Faber[175]

—*O—

At times, a branch may become diseased and fall away because it is
no longer supporting itself or contributing to the trunk. If a branch is no
longer supplying the tree with energy, it dies and falls away. So do religions which no longer provided its members with the spiritual growth
they need. Religion was meant to supply its members with spiritual energy and guidance, not control them for its own self-advancement. If a
religion is attractive by its own merits, followers will come to it. If it has
a false doctrine or one based on the self-promotion of its leaders, it will
soon decay like the dead branches falling from a tree. A new sprout may
come out of the stump left behind and new buds are constantly extending from the tips of healthy branches. There are also many different religious sects that have grown from the godhead. Some of these sects, just
as the diseased branches of a tree, are self-destructive and promote violence believing this will further their growth. In reality the opposite is
true; these false sects will destroy themselves and remain unattractive to
potential followers. A tree rids itself of diseased branches and so does the
godhead.

—Δ*—

"Like a tree ever-lasting he stands in the centre of heaven and his radiance illumines all creation." – *Svetasvatara Upanishad*[176]

—*O—

What boggles the mind is how certain religious branches choose to attack and sometimes twist around and strangle one another. Do they not realize they are all part of the same tree? Do they not realize they are only weakening themselves and not contributing to the godhead? What happens when a tree's roots or branches attack each other or even the trunk itself? If a tree's roots or branches were to attack each other by twisting around, restricting and strangling, parts of the tree will have less supply of water, nourishment and energy. The resulting weakening will eventually lead to decay. A tree grows by starting a bud at a level that will contribute to the future supply of sunlight and nourishment to the whole organism. The branches do not grow higher with the tree, but their connections stay at the same relative level. Earlier branches with their leaves supplied the energy for the foundation of future branches. Without those lower branches supplying nourishment to the trunk, the upper ones could never have grown. Which branch or leaves are more important, those on top, or those on the bottom? They are all equally important, for some catch the light in the morning, others in the afternoon, and the rest at dusk. Some catch the mist and the rain that falls upon all the parts of the tree. Others block the sun during times of drought, preserving moisture at the tree's base. All the leaves of the tree, supported by its many branches, create the nourishment necessary for maintaining our relationship with God.

—A*—

The Roots Of Character

"Those who preserve their integrity remain unshaken by the storms of daily life. They do not stir like leaves on a tree or follow the herd where it runs. In their mind remains the ideal attitude and conduct of living. This is not something given to them by others. It is their roots...it is a strength that exists deep within them." – Anonymous Indigenous American[177]

—*O—

A tap root of the great cosmic tree is found in the interplay between thought, radiation and matter, within the Trinity notion of Christianity and within the Trimurti of Hinduism, all of which are manifest by the

Supreme Source.[178] Even Jesus said, "I am the vine, you are the branch-es."[179] Carl Jung reminds us that "in alchemy, the tree is the symbol of Hermetic philosophy."[180] A tree is an ancient symbol for life itself, with its roots extending underground and its branches reaching to the heavens.[181] There is a symbolic reference to the Tree of Life or the Tree of Eternity being upside down with its roots in heaven and its branches extending into the physical realm; the dimension that we dwell in. The Tree of Life is also the name of the diagram consisting of various nodes and lines and used in various Kabbalistic mystical traditions.[182] Refer-ring to the Sahu, the incorruptible soul according to ancient Egyptian re-ligion and mythology, it means that although our bodies are in this plane of existence, there is a divine extension of branches (a spiritual capillary system) that feeds and nourishes our being.[183] It is the structural net-work that connects us to the higher mind – to be in this world but not of it. We cannot see it visually with our eyes, but it can be accessed by cleansing, nourishing and strengthening our connection with God. Go-ing back to Norse mythology, there is an immense legendary tree called Yggdrasil which is a tree of life, domain of Gods and Goddesses and con-necting the universe together with its supporting roots and branches. Ac-cording to some Gnostic perspectives, we are all branches of God.[184]

—Λ*—

"The Tree of Eternity has its roots in heaven above and its branches reach down to earth." – *Katha Upanishad*[185]

• • • •

"TODAY I HAVE GROWN taller from walking with trees." – Karle Wil-son Baker[186]

• • • •

"WE ALL HAVE THE SAME roots and we are all branches of the same tree." – Aang[187]

—*Ω—

. . . .

RELIGION AS A CONDUCTOR

All the scriptures of the great religions connect humanity to the God of yesterday and pave the way for reaching the God of today and the God of tomorrow. Allah is both ancient and futuristic, stagnant and dynamic, regressive and progressive, prehistoric and modern. All true paths, those of non-violence, to Allah should be respected. Allah is the dualities. There is the duality between syncretism, the merging of different religious thought and practices, and omnism, the parallel and co-existence of unique religious identities. An analogy to syncretism would be an electrical cable made of adjacent uninsulated bare strands of copper wire in conductive contact (i.e., stranded copper wire); the current is intermixed. An analogy to omnism would be electrical cable made of intertwining and adjacent insulated strands of copper wire that are not in conductive contact (i.e., telephone wire); although flowing parallel, the current remains individually isolated and unique within each strand.

An analogy to "Unity in Diversity" would be the omnism of the electrical cable with multi strands of insulated conductors. Although not in conductive contact, each strand is able to deliver a unique signal, input/output or message. This functionality and value of the cable is multiplied by the uniqueness and diversity of its individual conductors. So too, is the value of humanity multiplied by the cultural diversity of its people. Each contributes a different perspective or function for the common improvement of the human condition. We are more alike than different and our unification comes from our commonality of existence. There are numerous religious spokes that lead us (the rim) to God (the hub). We all share common threads on the skeins to divinity and we all have the potential of happiness, suffering, love or hate.

A true spiritual being finds beauty and wonder in the variety and diversity of religions, their differences, their similarities and their prophets. The purest worship of the Lord is through embracing and loving the diversity of his creation. One should view religion the same way an astronaut sees the Earthly globe from high above. An astronaut does not see the borders marking where one country ends and another begins nor do they see the lines dividing one culture from another. He or she sees one planet, one world, one form, but with a multitude of terrains. Religious vehicles should be looked upon with the same view. They are all means of transportation for one's spiritual growth and development.

In our search for truth and meaning, we must be willing to expose ourselves to other religious views and ideas. We must be willing to allow changes in our perspective on what God is or is not. We should not feel threatened to cautiously investigate other religions and their beliefs, either through reading or discussions with their participants, which may be external to our current religious upbringing. By cautiously investigating, I mean to distinguish between a true religious path versus a harmful cult that seeks to think for you, control you and does not allow you to maintain the proper balance between the secular and the divine. If you encounter morally questionable acts being justified by a group's leadership and find your increased immersion causing distance between you and your family and friends, question the reality of the path. Not all cults are bad, but not all are good.

To better understand our own religion, it is often necessary to understand those of others. This does not mean we have to always agree with other viewpoints and we may find our previous beliefs even more reinforced. If we truly believe our religion is the only way, then we should not have any reason to feel threatened by other religions. One who is secure with their religious foundation should not feel threatened by exposure to other paths. We should respect all the paths to God or the godhead and their traditions, provided others are not negatively exploited in traveling those paths or carrying out those traditions. The only thing that we have to fear is that our previous perception of religious reality may change; in other words, our spiritual universe will expand. All of the true religious texts thrive to move their societies out of ignorance, and this may mean exposure to that which was previously unknown. True enlightenment is the seeking of knowledge and having the proper grounding and balance of being able to appropriately implement that newfound knowledge.

God does not mind the differences in the various paths used to reach him, and yet certain groups of humanity continue to declare that their way is the only way or the best way. No path or prophet is the only way.

When Jesus said he was the way,[188] he did not succinctly say he was the only way. He was implying that his way was the correct way as opposed to the hypocrisy he saw in the Pharisees of the day. God gave humanity many routes, ways and means to ponder his existence, yet we still continue to fight and argue over which path is the correct one. The truest path to God or the godhead is one of mutual respect and non-aggression. God prefers peaceful coexistence and respect among the multiple paths which lead to him or her. Enlightenment is understanding that there are many correct paths. To exclude one over the rest is naïve and ignorant. A myopic religious perspective does not coincide with God's desire for humanity to seek knowledge, wisdom and truth. From the spinning of the Sufi Dervishes, the bonfires of the Ethiopian Orthodox Christian festival of Demera, the pagan Norse mythologies, to the chanting of monks, all the paths and branches invoke a connection to something greater than ourselves.

When choosing your religious path, never follow it blindly. Apply your critical thinking skills and spiritual logic to evaluate and analyze the passages within its scriptures and how each of its regional leadership chooses to apply and interpret its messages. Is the focus on phrases condoning acts of violence or is the focus on phrases perpetuating acts of kindness? I can assure you that any path condoning violence upon others of any religion is a false path. Travelers of such paths of violence, terrorism and destruction are being fooled by a mirage created by internal demons. Religions and parapsychology have expressed that one can become possessed by demons. By the same token, perhaps one can also become possessed by angels. I would prefer possession by the latter, that of angels. One's behavior towards others will determine if they are following the correct map to God. The truest of religions are those that practice benevolent actions to all.

Within all the great true scriptures, there are both beginning and advanced lessons for the spiritually attuned. The advanced lessons may, at first, not be understood or misinterpreted. It is like when a gardener reads a book on brain surgery; since he or she is not familiar with anatomy and medical terminology, the instructions appear meaningless to them. One must take steps, not leaps, as they walk their spiritual path of self-realization while meshing with the greater consciousness and encountering epiphanies across all the esoteric spheres of reality. We should rejoice in and embrace the multitude and diversity of paths to the Lord, provided they are paths of non-violence that promote the preservation and advancement of all humanity. I can assure you of this, any path condoning violence is not a path to Allah. God welcomes the multitude of true paths created to reach him/her.

—A*—

"Where Love Is, God is" – book title of short story written by Leo Tolstoy

—*O—

Religion was meant to progress as it is built upon the structure of earlier foundations. Based on our background, some paths may be better suited than others in fulfilling our personal spiritual needs. A particular path that is effective for some, may not be effective for others. Similar to selecting an exercise routine that works for one's skill level and lifestyle, travel the true religious path, belief or faith, that you find the most efficient, the most empowering, the most epiphanic and the most euphoric for your spiritual needs. Need be, don't be afraid to "cherry-pick" from what you consider the best if that is what it takes to ensure your journey on a path to the godhead. After exploring different paths, the one that works best for you is the one that you should follow. No matter which path, tool, vehicle, branch or methodology you choose as the means for developing your connection with the mind of divinity, always remember that the *summmum bonum*,[189] the quickest path, the fastest vehicle and the most efficient methodology is through the application of healthy love, the development of self through the seeking of knowledge and the recognition of the necessary boundaries within our lives to maintain our balance. Part of religious acceptance is believing in that which we do not necessarily fully understand, for faith has a tendency to dissipate doubt. And remember, just as too little religion is unhealthy so is too much religion. Too much religious intake can sour the stomach and dizzy the mind.

Chapter 4
Insights Into The Religions Of Planet Earth With Origins Before The Common Era

"GOD WELCOMES TRAVELERS of all the true religious paths." – AO

• • • •

THE PURPOSE OF THIS chapter and the next is to provide simplistic glances into the history, truths, commonalities and even the differences among the primary religions of planet Earth. Hopefully, any preconceived notions and misconceptions of other religious paths will be corrected within your mind. With these temporal epiphanies, some of us will come out of ignorance and closer to enlightenment. As we expose ourselves to other approaches to the godhead, we will realize that their similarities are more pronounced than their distinctions.

Earth based primary religions, as referred to in this text, is merely a term used to describe those religions currently practiced by a large portion of humanity, those that have evolved through the culmination of prevalent appeal, those that are more commonly known or those that are significant to the basis of future religions/sects. If a religion or sect is **not** included in this or the next chapter, it should **not** be considered a reflection upon its significance, size or importance, for it only means that it was left out for lack of space, time or editorial reasons. Although certain religions and sects are more predominant across the globe, they all have a role to play for tapping into and accessing divinity. Many religions, to a degree, morphed from mythological or even philosophical undertones. This book does not denote which are the truest religions and which are not. All of them may be true religions, partially true or none at all. You must decide on your own which are which and God already knows.

Since fitting all the information pertaining to a particular religion or its various sects within the confines of these chapters is not secularly pragmatic or even feasible, do not depend on this text as being all inclusive nor in agreement with all sources. This chapter and the next contain brief summaries, shallow hues and some notable highlights, but they by no means do justice in providing all there is to know about a particular religion or sect. They were written to provide a taste or sampling of the religious path, not an exhaustive overview or complete multiple perspective understanding. I encourage you to read and study the *Koran*, the Old and New Testaments of the *Bible*, the *Bhagavad Gita*, the *Upanishads*, and various other religious scriptures and come to your own conclusions on what God is all about and the many paths and perspectives used to connect with him/her. Travelling on your own metaphysical investigative journey, new scriptural sources will reveal themselves. Some of the scriptures may seem monotonous or contradictory and others will be stimulating and uplifting. You don't have to agree with all the passages that you read (I'm sure Allah/Brahma/God/Buddha don't agree with all of them either) or always take them literally, but exposing yourself to the scriptures of other religions will give you more of an understanding and acceptance of your own path and that of others.

Within this chapter and the next, the primary Earth based religions are addressed in chronological order of when it is generally accepted that they first came into existence. The oldest of the formal religions may have all started simultaneously among different regions in parallel with varying growth spurts occurring during their development. The specific point in human history in which religion morphed from mythology is unclear. Perhaps a valid religion is merely elements of a true mythology that has withstood the test of time in retaining followers and active practitioners.

<u>1.</u> <u>Hinduism</u> – started about 1500 BCE or earlier.

Hinduism is one of the most ancient religions, having no specific founder or exact date of formation, it is a blend of various beliefs among the Indo-Aryan people who migrated to the Indus Valley. Hinduism and Hindu are Sanskrit words used by early invaders to describe the people encountered upon crossing the Hindu Kush mountains and arriving at the Indus River. Hinduism has become more globally prolific through emigration from India as its followers brought their customs, rituals and teachings (such as yoga and meditation) to other nations. It may be considered by some more as a way of life, rather than a religion.

Hinduism is rich in scripture with a vast collection of ancient religious writings based on oral teachings and traditions passed down through the generations. Although there is no one central authoritative book in Hinduism, the *Shruti* is often considered analogous canon to what the *Bible* is to Christianity. It is a compilation of various aspects of sacred (divine revelations) and ancient texts: the four *Vedas* (*Rigveda*, *Yajurveda*, *Samaveda*, and *Atharvaveda*), the *Brahmanas*, the *Aranyakas*, the *Upanishads*, the *Bhagavad Gita* and others. The *Vedas* are the oldest written works and considered to have emerged about 1500 to 500 BCE, the oldest of the *Upanishads* were composed about 800 to 400 BCE, and the *Gita* is considered to have been composed later about 500 to 200 BCE. Either way, many of these texts are accepted as being older than the New Testament of the *Bible*.

—Δ*—

"When doubts haunt me, when disappointments stare me in the face, and I see not one ray of hope on the horizon, I turn to *Bhagavad Gita* and find a verse to comfort me; and I immediately begin to smile in the midst of overwhelming sorrow. Those who meditate on the *Gita* will derive fresh joy and new meanings from it every day." – (Mahatma) Mohandas Karamchand Gandhi[190]

—*O—

Hinduism is based on one supreme God that cannot be fathomed by typical human comprehension. Therefore, relating to God by a means suitable to the worshipper is encouraged. Often, practitioners of Hinduism will worship and focus on some of the many manifestations of God. The Trimurti (meaning "three forms" of God), also known as the Hindu Trinity, is a sample of iconographic representation of divinity in Hinduism. Depicted as a three-faced figure, it is composed of the three main deities: Brahma, the creator; Vishnu, the preserver or maintainer; and Shiva, the destroyer.

Hinduism can be considered as having a monotheistic trunk or center, but with monistic (belief that everything in the universe is part of one substance or nature) and henotheistic (worshiping of one god without denying the existence of other gods) elements. The numerous Hindu deities should be viewed as focused aspects of Allah's many manifestations and should not be considered idols. Comparatively, Christianity has many saints that can be prayed to for the granting of particular favors but it too is not a polytheistic religion. For example, St. Joseph, a Catholic saint, has become the focused representative of granting desired real estate transactions (the selling of a house), while Ganesh, the elephant-faced god within Hinduism, is the focused representative of business success.

There is a misconception that Hindus worship bovine cows, but actually they believe all living things have a soul; a continuous essence of sentience. Cattle, due to their usual gentle and provider of sustenance nature, are seen as maternal and valued. Therefore, they hold a special place among Hindu society and are refrained from being eaten. A majority of Hindus do eat the meat of other animals, but a percentage refrain from eating any type of meat based on the principle of non-violence and preserving all life forms. Since all living things are forms of God's organic creations, any form of violence against them is considered by some to be contrary to the natural balance of the universe. Yet, the natural world is composed of omnivores and carnivores whose survival is dependent on the flesh and meat of other organisms. Perhaps the notion that humans can sympathize with other creatures' desire for life and a preference not to be slaughtered or viciously devoured as a meal is what occasionally separates us from the animals. Perhaps questions for God are why did he create a universe in which organisms need to consume each other for sustenance and why were we given the awareness of this flaw?

The Caste system, an occupational categorizing of individuals based on their socio-economic status, is rooted in culture and not based on sanctioned Hindu religious practices. It was put into place by those with power and influence prior to medieval times and continued to evolve during colonization and in modern times into a rigid social hierarchy. It has resulted in suppression, oppression and marginalizing of those confined within the lower levels and ranks. The Caste system is found in the Indian region and subcontinent and also exists in parcels among those practicing Nepalese Buddhism, Christianity, Islam, Judaism and Sikhism. The Caste system has become discriminatory and reformists from many different religious backgrounds have challenged its basis. Treating any group or gender (be it feminine, masculine or overlapping) as inferior or subservient is a concept of cultural ignorance and personal insecurity, not of true religious prescript. We all have suitable aptitudes, talents and skills for which our ethnic identity or gender should not be the determining factor in restricting the development and honing of our occupational capabilities.

Hindus celebrate and recognize forms of God in the specific characteristics of their deities. They can be masculine such as Rama (the model of reason and virtue, compassion, courage, and devotion) or Lord Krishna (the embodiment of love, divine joy and destroyer of pain and sins). They can also be feminine such as Shakti (the primordial cosmic creative power manifesting in feminine form when in our realm) or Parvati (a primary goddess form of Shakti which focuses on fertility, love and devotional energy). Yoga, a variation of practices and methods (bhakti, jnana, karma, raja or hatha) used to reset the mind and body by communing with the All-Pervading Spirit, is a spiritual and ascetic discipline originating from Hinduism. It consists of controlled breathing techniques, movement between different bodily positions and simple meditation. It may also utilize the chakra system, a metaphysical survey of the body's layout as a tool for diagnosing and maintaining spiritual and physical health. Chakras (spinning wheels or vortexes of life-force energy) are based on power centers, focal points, nodes or portals for accessing various representations of the functions of mind and body. When done properly, yoga cleanses and unblocks the chakras and dims the barrier that separates us from God; it makes the veil more permeable. Literally, the word yoga means "union" and implies the yoking of one's essence to the divine consciousness as a method for gaining physical and mental health. Take notice of the omega (circle) and alpha (triangle) character appearing in the word **yoga**. This is not a coincidence.

The bindi, a red decorative mark or circle sometimes worn on a Hindu woman's forehead, once only symbolized marriage. In modern times, however, it can also denote a decorative spiritual fashion statement among both married and single women. The tilaka (or tilaki), a marking that can be applied to the foreheads of all genders and sometimes to other parts of the body, signifies participation in a spiritual celebration or event of religious significance. Similarly, modern day Catholics and some Protestants, often have ash applied in the shape of a cross upon their foreheads by a priest during the service initiating the start of Lent, a season of fasting and prayer.

Karma, in simplest terms, is the notion of metaphysical cause and effect (that one's behavior and actions will always be returned upon them in some way or form in the future) and is a key principle of not only Hinduism, but also Buddhism, Jainism, Sikhism, Taoism, Christianity to some degree as well as other religions. The precept being that our state of happiness or unhappiness is fed by the moral and immoral actions that we conduct on a daily basis. The form of the reaction can come back to us in a different form than the initial action, thus a moral action can come back to us in the form of a beneficial material or emotional stimulus. Our destiny becomes determined by our deeds. We become the karma that we create.

Faith in karmic resolve requires us to accept that if it does not occur in this lifetime, then it will catch up to us in the next realm, or perhaps in the one after that. Views on the precise meaning, how or when karma operates is diverse and varies among the various religious sects. Some consider the state and affairs of one's current life situation a result of karma from prior incarnations, others treat the deeds of prior lives as having minimal if any influence on one's current life. In *Galatians*, the ninth book of the *New Testament* within the Christian *Bible* and considered written by Paul the Apostle, the proverb "As you sow, so shall you reap" is mentioned.[191] This proverb portrays the very essence of karmic input and outcome; that one's actions (or inactions) will create a return of related results. Eastern thought had viewed karma as the accumulation of only bad actions. Hence karma, the density of which places a drag on one's soul due to the weight of accumulated sins, was something to be eliminated such that one may exit from the cycles of birth and death to obtain moksha (a liberated state of existence; Nirvana) and merge with both Brahma and Brahman. Western thought has morphed the definition of karma into something as either good or bad. In Western thought, one can accumulate "good" karma or "bad" karma.

The exact definition of Nirvana (asa Nibbana) varies, but from a simplistic approach, it can be considered the ecstatic bliss of heaven. From the *Nirvana Sutra*, the Buddha explained the state with the following description:

"...There is that dimension where there is neither earth, nor water, nor fire, nor wind; neither dimension of the infinitude of space, nor dimension of the infinitude of consciousness, nor dimension of nothingness, nor dimension of neither perception nor non-perception; neither this world, nor the next world, nor sun, nor moon. And there, I say, there is neither coming, nor going, nor staying; neither passing away nor arising: unestablished, un-evolving, without support (mental object). This, just this, is the end of stress..."[192]

It is characterized by a state of moral, mental, emotional, and logical perfection, resulting from the success of self-improvement techniques of the mind, body, core and soul. It is found when the seeker learns to balance their desires and attachments, thus becoming an agile spiritual athlete at stepping around the snares of life and reaching "heaven on earth." It entails: 1) a minimization or absence of egoism; 2) mastering handling the dualities of existence; 3) complete bliss without escapism; 4) tranquility of being as one maintains their uniqueness while merging with the consciousness of the cosmos; 5) converting fears and anxieties into transcendent energy and maneuvering around them; and, 6) having insight into where the future is headed and harnessing its direction. One who has achieved this state, even for brief instances, may not show any visible signs of it and remain calm and composed with humility in the presence of others.[193] They dwell, even for glimpses, in the abode of angels in a dimension that is beyond definition. It is a realm of existence that is beyond description and cannot be adequately described through the normal limitations of our senses.

2. <u>Hermeticism</u> – establishment date unknown, could be much older than Hinduism, about the same age as Judaism and Zoroastrianism, or slightly younger than Christianity.

Hermeticism is a rather obscure synthesis of philosophy, mythology, religion and the occult. It presents an ultimate reality (i.e., God) generally referred to as the All or the One. It is a reality that is unitary and transcendent, profoundly monotheistic, and which can be understood only by advanced students of divinity. It also subscribes to the idea that other beings, such as aeons, angels and elementals, exist within the universe.[194]

Although ancient in its origins with variations of reference and accuracies, its practices are better reserved for those of advanced spiritual understanding. Elements of it can be found blended into both philosophical movements and religious doctrine. Of the Hermetic writings that remain, much of it is hidden in higher planes (outer spheres) of thought and accessible only by those on elevated paths of enlightenment. The teachings are considered sealed until one is ready for them.

—A*—

"The lips of wisdom are closed, except to the ears of understanding."
– *The Kybalion*[195]

• • • •

"You will hear what you are ready to hear." – Rumi[196]
—*O—

MORPHING FROM ANCIENT Egyptian and Hellenistic roots, the being considered to have authored a series of sacred texts titled *Hermetic Corpus* (aka *Corpus Hermeticum*) is known as Hermes Mercurius Trismegistus (meaning "Thrice-Great" Hermes), Thoth-Hermes, Mercurius ter Maximus, or a cyclical form of Osiris. Through the combination of a personification of both the Egyptian deity Thoth and the Greek deity Hermes (Roman deity of Mercury), he is considered the founder of science, religion, mathematics, geometry, philosophy, medicine, magic and alchemy. Based on the writing style, some feel that a majority of Hermetic texts were actually written in the parallel time period of when the Christian Gospels were being formed. Regardless of when the actual scribing occurred, they contain a compilation of fragments of historical thought. At the time of the origination of the Hermetic Arts, the region of Egypt was originally called "Khem", "Chem" or "Chemi" (all meaning Black Land) due to the fertile darkness of its soil.[197] Hence the term "All Khem" morphed into the word "alchemy" to denote the ancient practice of transmuting material and oneself into higher states or vibrations of existence. The term of alchemy may have also come from the Hebrew word "chamaman" or "hamaman", meaning a sacred mystery not to be revealed, but treasured as a religious secret.[198] Modern alchemy of material transmutation is merely nuclear fusion or fission. Perhaps future alchemy will involve the resonating, synchronizing and harmonizing of light waves/particles at the correct proportions to convert energy directly into usable matter – nanotechnology coming-of-age.

—Λ*—

"If you want to find the secrets of the universe, think in terms of energy, frequency and vibration." – Nikola Tesla

—*Ω—

Thoth-Hermes' knowledge and wisdom were so vast and all-encompassing that the ancient Egyptians viewed him as a messenger or communicator of the gods. Some sources consider him as the prophet Enoch,[199] and others as Idris (asa Idrees) referred to in the *Koran*.[200] He has also been associated with the earlier persona of Moses, Akhenaten and Nabu (Babylonian god of writing and wisdom). The reason behind the term "Thrice-Great" varies, but it may relate either to his/her mastery of alchemy (secrets of the sun), astrology (secrets of the stars), and theurgy (secrets of the gods) or to the mastery of the three realms of existence: physical, mental and spiritual. Credited to having written thousands of works, some either lost during the tragic fires, razing and destruction of the great and ancient Library of Alexandria or secretly hidden away for safe keeping, only a small handful of Hermetic texts remain today. It is unclear whether he was one individual or being that lived about 2500 years before Christ, a series of several, or a repetition of many incarnations throughout history. The rediscovery of Hermetic texts triggered the emergence of Europe out of its Dark Ages and initiated the entrance into the Renaissance period. Regardless, whenever there is a re-awakening in study and veneration of the works of Hermes, students properly applying his teachings and becoming self-taught Hermeticists, civilizations seem to accelerate in advancements.[201] It is the application of Hermetic principles among modern materials and technologies that will initiate humanity's genesis within and beyond the solar system.

The resulting composite tradition (an amalgam of Jewish and Christian mysticism, Hellenistic philosophy and Egyptian occult mythology) was both persuasive and perdurable, as it proved compelling to both Muslim scholars in the early Middle Ages and European intellectuals.[202] Hermetic texts were viewed as entirely compatible with Christian revelation, and going even deeper, were considered a pagan prophesizing of the coming of Christ.[203] It is sad and caustically ironic thus, that during the last years before the fall of the Roman Empire, the so-called Christian Emperors and the Popes of the Middle Ages chose to subdue the Hermetic arts instead of embracing them as foundational stones of Christianity.

The *Emerald Tablet* is a cryptic piece of Hermetic writing first appearing in Arabic about the years 500 to 700 and consider esoterically related to the Philosopher's Stone. Hermeticism's revival during the Renaissance should be credited to a monk (Leonardo di Pistoia), who brought an edition of the *Hermetic Corpus* to Italy in 1460 and then scholarly interest remerged in 1945 when Hermetic writings were revealed among the 2nd and 3rd century Gnostic Coptic manuscripts found by two brothers allegedly collecting fertilizer for their crops near Nag Hammadi, Egypt. A more recent text that aims to rekindle the lost Hermetic teaching is *The Kybalion*, authored in 1912 under the pseudonym of "The Three Initiates." Perhaps "The Three Initiates" are the immortals per *The Book of Mormon* remaining on Earth until the Second Coming of Christ or the three angels referenced in *Revelation* 14, but more secular sources credit its authorship to William Walker Atkinson.[204] Scholars will argue that the text has no ties to Hermeticism, while the practitioner would state otherwise.[205] Although more of an offshoot and not pure in its Hermetic sense, I personally would consider it a useful companion tool rather than disparaging it – think of all the other spiritual texts of antiquity that are offshoots (i.e., *The Zohar*) and/or blends of prior philosophies and scriptures. Within *The Kybalion*, seven principle laws are discussed that describe how the universe functions. They are: The Principle of Mentalism (Thought), The Principle of Correspondence (Reciprocity), The Principle of Vibration (Motion), The Principle of Polarity (Duality), The Principle of Rhythm (Synchronization), The Principle of Causality (Karma), and The Principle of Gender (Sexuality). Through understanding and implementing these principles, the three realms (physical, mental, spiritual) of existence can be more effectively traversed and used for benevolent purposes. Hermes assures us that the haven to peace and immortality awaits those who rise to his challenge.[206]

—Δ*—

"The path to immortality is hard, and only a few find it. The rest await the Great Day when the wheels of the universe shall be stopped and the immortal sparks shall escape from the sheaths of substance. Woe unto those who wait, for they must return again, unconscious and unknowing, to the seed-ground of the stars, and await a new beginning." –
The Divine Pymander of Hermes Trismegistus[207]

—*O—

A major tenet of Hermeticism (and likewise of alchemy) is that which is being studied is influenced by the observer and the two are intrinsically linked – similar to quantum physics in which the observer influences the outcome of the experiment. This is denoted by the central and famous Hermetic phrase and esoteric teachings proclaiming "As above, so below; As within, so without...", meaning that the universe is partially a symbolic reflection of what is happening inside of ourselves.

The universe exists both within us and beyond us. Our thoughts and actions in this realm influence energies in other realms. "For just as it is on earth, so also is it in the firmament, because replicas of what are in the firmament are on earth."[208] Through developing our core, one trains and hones the skill of attracting the invisible spiritual ingredients, the divine sparks of revelations, to bring about the desired transformation in both themselves and their works.[209] The macrocosm of the universe also exists in the microcosm and *vice versa*.[210] Analogous to Hermetic stances, the characteristics of great nations is presented in the phrase "...out of the one, come many, and out of the many, come one..."[211] The phrase "All is mind" reveals that manifestation first requires thought, which through electromagnetic energy, induces forth physical form; (more on this in Chapter 8). Another tenet is that everything comes from the same universal consciousness but vibrates at different levels on the scale of sentience. This ultimate reality is somewhat analogous to the Brahman of Hinduism. The notion of duality (the distance from being either triangular or circular) is viewed as various degrees upon a scale of extremes, incremental calibrations between polar opposites. Examples of this scaling between poles are the: 1) pH scale used in chemistry to denote the acidic or basic levels of a solution; 2) degrees of a thermometer to measure levels of heat; 3) shades of gray based on the distance from pure white to pure black; or, 4) states of temperament to measure the location of one's fulcrum between love and hate. The quest for knowledge becomes a spiritual journey to return to a state of unity with the divine, known as the "Great Work" of humankind. Hermetic principles can be seen in the works of luminaries such as Nicolaus Copernicus, Johannes Kepler, Robert Boyle, Isaac Newton, Giordano Bruno (martyred during the Inquisitional years), John Dee and Francis Bacon, as well as medieval philosophers, notably Roger Bacon, but also Islamic philosophers like Al-Kindi and Avicenna.[212] Had Galileo and Bruno been living in regions of Islam, their works would most likely have been initially praised rather than subjected to persecutions. It is said that the secrets of Hermeticism and Alchemy will reveal themselves only to the sincere seeker and the pure of heart, providing access to the deepest understandings of nature, the cosmos and ourselves – this attainment of spiritual maturity and access to gnosis is a divine gift.

3. <u>Judaism</u> – formally established about 1400 to 1200 BCE.

Considered one of the oldest of the absolute monotheistic religions to take hold and the foundational fabric for Christianity and Islam, Judaism is the forerunner of the so-called primary desert religions. John Denham Parsons, however, considers it as a continuation of "Babylonian Sun-God worship tempered by the more spiritual conception of Zoroastrians."[213] The creative and destructive god of the Jews, Christians and Muslims, (the Adam and Eve based religions), is often considered the same guardian, higher being or entity of all. Although there is a commonality among these Abrahamic-based religions, their own individual theological ideology wiring sends them in both overlapping and separate ways, and often find themselves intertwining without fully merging. Given the same overall diameter, a rope or cable made of individual intertwining strands is much stronger than one made of a single strand. Similarly, when followers of the Abrahamic-based desert religions understand and acknowledge the strength within their commonality rather than focusing on their differences, they become greater than the sum of their parts.

In a time period and region of where many gods were being worshipped as aspects of the whole, the ancient Israelites incorporated and drew upon the traditions and knowledge of the surrounding tribes and cultures, but focused their worship to only one god; written as YHWH (the Anglicized tetragram form). Judaism's early beginnings consist of the story of creation, Adam and Eve, Cain's murder of Abel, Noah and the promise from God that Earth would never encounter a global flood again, the Tower of Babel, the lineage of about 20 ancestral patriarchs from Adam all the way to Abraham, and Abraham's receiving of a real estate covenant from God in that he would become the patriarchal starting point of many nations. Additional covenants granted that as long as they promised to obey God and his commandments, Abraham and his descendants (the Israelites: those with Jewish or Samaritan ethnicity) would be God's chosen people. Later, Moses, a descendant of Abraham, received additional instructions from God for his chosen people, including edicts of proper behavior written into stone tablets (the Ten Commandments.) However, the covenants did not specifically say they would be God's only chosen people on the planet.

Having undergone rule by numerous geo-political governing authorities (Babylonian, Persian, Hellenistic, Roman, Crusaders, Ottoman, British) and occupational forces throughout their more than 3,200 years of history, the Jewish people have perhaps suffered the most persecution, turmoil, conflict and dispersion of all the religious cultures. Under some of these governing occupations, their religious culture flourished and was enhanced in an environment of acceptance, emancipation and stability. Other times it was suppressed, forced out of regions or even obliterated, as political climates could rapidly shift, generating periods of flux and infighting. Around 1947 to 1949 under United Nations recognition, the Jewish state of Israel was established in the Palestine region to provide a cultural home and diminish the potential for future persecution. In doing so, however, local political tension and violent conflicts ensued as existing Palestinians of Arabic culture now faced oppression.

Composed of twenty-four books, the earliest scripture of Judaism is the *Tanakh*. According to tradition, the first five books, (*Genesis, Exodus, Leviticus, Numbers* and *Deuteronomy*), were revealed to the prophet Moses on Mount Sinai. Referred to as the Pentateuch, Greek for "five books", they were further interpreted and refined by ancient rabbinical orders into the *Torah* (which means "teaching"). The *Talmud*, a text written between the years 200 and 600 focusing on religious law and theology, was used as a Rabbinic doctrine and became an influencer and foundation of Jewish culture. Hebrew, the original language in which the Judaic scriptures were written, is still the oral and written basis of Jewish worship today. Similar to Muslims facing in the direction of Mecca during prayers, many Jewish worshipers traditionally face Jerusalem during their prayers. Like Christianity, there have been various sects that have evolved into modern day denominational classifications (i.e., Reform, Conservative, Orthodox, Reconstructionist and various Messianic movements).

<u>4. Zoroastrianism</u> – started as early as 1700 BCE or as late as 600 BCE.

The primary religion practiced in the Persian region prior to the birth of Mohammad, Zoroastrianism (referred to as Mazdayasna by its followers) strongly influenced the growing philosophies of Judaism and serves as a foundation for Christianity, Gnosticism and Islam. Unknown to most, its doctrine has directly or indirectly formed the cornerstone of many of the world's faiths.[214] Based on the teachings of the Iranian prophet Zoroaster (aka Zarathustra from Greek roots), it embraces a primarily monotheistic path (with an underlying dualism approach similar to Gnostic beliefs) and one of the first to encompass the notions of duality, karma, heaven and hell, messianism, final judgment, resurrection and the balance between free will and destiny. Zoroaster was a priest (with a wife and family) among an agriculture community engaged in Bronze Age polytheism and at around the age of thirty, had visions that reinforced a newer doctrine that he had been formulating. Similar to Jesus' teachings challenging the Judaic Pharisees and scribes during the period of Roman occupation, Zoroaster's teachings were seen as a threat to the established religious ways of his time. He was especially opposed to the needless animal sacrifices being carried out (Empedocles had similar objections) and the ritual use of psychedelic drugs. He understood that genuine psychedelic states are only stable when induced naturally through one's own mind and without the use of ingested or smoked chemicals.

—A*—

"For I delight in loyalty rather than sacrifice, and in the knowledge of God rather than burnt offerings." – *Hosea* 6:6 (NAS)

• • • •

"DO I EAT THE FLESH of bulls or drink the blood of goats? Offer to God a sacrifice of thanksgiving, and perform your vows to the Most High, and call upon me in the day of trouble; I will deliver you, and you shall glorify me." – *Psalms* 50:13-15 (ESV)

—*O—

Other Bronzed Age priests, feeling threatened and opposing his more advanced spiritual concepts, ultimately carried out an assassination of Zoroaster when he was in his seventies. Unfortunately, the pattern of an inferior *status quo* squelching a newer or better form of religious understanding seems to repeat itself throughout history. In doing so, however, it often imbeds the newer revelation even stronger into the hearts and minds of the populace and overtakes the *status quo*. Mohammad was fortunate to have escaped from this pattern of squelching by murder or execution; Jesus was not as fortunate. I can only hope that the next authentic revealer will follow the path of Mohammad's fortune and not that of Jesus' demise.

Before his death, however, Zoroaster managed to plant the seeds of his teachings which grew and spread among the many Persian kingdoms. For almost 1000 years, until the spread of Islam by invading and persecuting Arab tribes, it was considered to be the most influential religious model of the region for relating to God. The well-known story of the three wise men (Magi) from the East who followed the brightest star (possibly a super nova or relatively close planetary conjunction) to Bethlehem and presented gifts to the infant Jesus were followers of Zoroastrianism. The three stars making up the belt of the constellation Orion are sometimes referred to as representing the "Three Wise Men" or "The Three Kings."[215]

The Zoroastrian scripture is the *Avesta* and has been rewritten twice from oral remembrance since it was destroyed by Alexander the Great and later by Arab conquerors. Being obscure and, at times, open to interpretive meaning, the text never-the-less shows Zoroaster to be a profound thinker, mystic and prophet. A core tenant of Zoroastrian is to live a life based on good thoughts, good words and good deeds (actions). Earlier traditional forms viewed that there was one main good God (Ahura Mazda or "Wise Lord") under whom are two forces, one that is beneficial and holy (Spenta Mainyu) and the other that is hostile and destructive (Angra Mainyu).[216] Later forms merged Ahura Mazda and Spenta Maniyu into the same entity and renamed it as Ohrmazd, while Angra Mainyu became contracted and renamed as Ahriman.[217] This similar reflection repeats in one of the perspectives of modern Christian thought where it is a feud between God (Ohrmazd) and Satan (Ahriman). Fleeing religious intolerance and persecution from intolerant Muslim extremists, many Zoroastrians refugees relocated out of the regions of Persia and into India. Those who originally migrated to India between the 8th and 10th century have become ethnically referred to as Parsis (asa Parsees), which means "Persians." Although a tradition which is rapidly declining, Zoroastrians place the bodies of their dead in Towers of Silence, allowing a corpse's molecules to be fed upon by both land and flying creatures. This practice aligns with the ecological notion of returning to nature that which came from nature.

5. Jainism – started about 599 BCE.

Culminating into religions as quasi-reformist offshoot of Hinduism in the centuries leading up to their formation, the origins of Jainism and Buddhism seem to coincide. Chronologically, however, Jainism evolved sooner than Buddhism. Similar to Siddhartha Gautama (the Buddha), Mahavira (either the originator or an advanced guide of Jain), gave up his upper-class existence to search for truth and the nature of existence. Based on the influence of Mahavira, considered the last of a line of twenty-four tirthankaras (saviors or teachers) or Jinas (one who conquers their inner enemies or demons), followers believe that everything in the universe is subject to growth and decay within infinite cosmic cycles that repeat continuously. The soul's liberation from these cycles (rising above them to reach Nirvana) is the ultimate objective and achieving this is done, among other practices, by eliminating karma (in its purest Eastern definition). According to Jainist teachings, the first tithankara was a being named Rishabhanatha that lived millions of years ago. He is credited with providing knowledge to humanity and showing his species how to sustain themselves through agriculture, craftsmanship, artistry and trade – seeming very similar to the Hermes or Prometheus archetype.

Jainists follow the *Agamas* texts of Hinduism, scripture which may have started as early as 1000 BCE but changed over time as more was added by 500 BCE. The word "Agamas" in Sanskrit literally means "that which has come down" as in traditions. It contains studies related to cos-

mology, epistemology, philosophy, precepts on meditative practices, yoga, mantras, temple construction, deity worship and ways to implement
the six-fold virtues towards enlightenment. Many Buddhist scriptures
have titles and subject matter similar to Jainist scripture but present them
as different doctrines. The swastika, prior to the mid-20th century National Socialist Party's (Nazi) abuse and distortion of its meaning, is ingrained within much of Jain symbolism and iconography. Its arms represent groupings of four in relationship to states of existence, characteristics of the soul, and that the particular path we choose to walk will be
our destination.[218]

Jains accept a pantheon of gods, but they do not focus on worshipping a supreme entity. Some of their texts indicate family relationships
of Hindu gods to the tirthankaras, while others mock them with stories of unethical ventures,[219] much like the misbehavior and antics of
the mythological gods of ancient Greece. They consider the destroying of
any living creature (from microscopic organisms to large mammals) and
violence as the most damaging of karma. Hence, they are strictly vegetarian in diet and Jainist monks practice more austere conditions than Buddhist monks. Similar to Buddhism, Jainism has dualistically divided into two sects or schools of teachings, Svetamabaras (meaning "white clad"
or clothed) and Digambaras ("sky clad" or naked). All Jainists thrive for
non-violence (ahimsa), but there seems to be certain convenient allowable exceptions such as for kings and judges.[220] The purpose of non-violence is not an edict placed upon Jains by a Supreme Being, but rather,
it is a necessity for one's own soul to advance into much higher realms
and eventually obtain Moksha.

6. Buddhism – started about 586 BCE.

Buddhism has many parallelisms with Jainism, but there is enough
dissimilarity for it to be viewed as a different doctrine. Historical factual
data on the life of Siddhartha Gautama is lacking, but he is considered
the most recent and most holy in a long line of Buddhas.[221] Legend
has it that he was born into sheltered royalty around 563 to 586 BCE
in the region that is now Nepal. Siddhartha's father, an Indian warrior-

king, had been told by fortune tellers that his son's future was cloaked in ambiguity. Facing a duality, they said that he would either become a world conqueror and unify India or a world redeemer if he abandoned the quest for worldly possessions and desires. His father wanted Siddhartha to follow the path of a conqueror, so he protected and isolated him from all unpleasantness and sufferings encountered with human existence, raising his son among luxury, comfort and wealth. Runners were even sent ahead of Siddhartha during journeys to clear the road of the sick, the dying and the dead. One day, however, venturing out on his own, he came across the suffering, the elderly and corpses. The shock of such sights triggered a re-evaluation of his values and lifestyle. Even though Siddhartha had a wife and young son, he left them to pursue a nomadic search for truth and knowledge. The leaving and abandoning of one's family in pursuit of religious understanding or artistic endeavors is not something condoned. Such acts contain an intrinsic degree of selfishness and narcissistic undertones. In doing so, spouses are emotionally harmed and children are left suffering, having lost a parental relationship to guide them into adulthood. Even Saint Anthony of Egypt abandoning his younger sister at the first convent on record contained a degree of selfishness in the direction of his religious pursuit, for the younger sibling prematurely lost her brother's presence.[222]

After much reflection and internal contemplation, during a particular meditation under a bodhi tree, Siddhartha suddenly gained full insight into the nature of the world and an awareness behind the reality of existence. In this spiritual awakening, he had obtained enlightenment in its purest sense and was henceforth referred to as "the Buddha." I wonder if the Buddha's father was disappointed in his son's chosen direction the same way the father of St. Frances of Assisi was with his son's choice.[223] Going forth to spread his teachings, the Buddha was followed by many disciples and lived to about the age of eighty. Buddhist teachings were handed down orally and not written until centuries after his lifetime. The principle of non-violence and loving kindness of all beings is intrinsic to the doctrine, as stressed in the *Dhammapada*, a collection of sayings attributed to the Buddha. Although meat provides a higher density of en-

ergy/protein for its volume compared to plants, the notion of killing animals for food is surrounded with a degree of controversy. Some Buddhist
monks refrain from killing the livestock themselves, but still enjoy the
flavors of eating meat if presented to them – they won't be the butchers
but will be the vultures. Since Buddhism arose out of Hinduism, it shares
some common notions such as that of karma and reincarnation, in which
the levels of our sentience either improves or becomes degraded depending on our actions during this and previous lifetimes.

In parallel with the merger of many gods from Greek mythology into
the one God of the Hebrew, Christian and Muslim religions, Buddhism
sprouted forth from a Hindu inheritance of nearly two million names
for God, swinging the pendulum from many labels, to none at all.[224]
It does not recognize a formal God or gods and all together rejected the
caste system. Although there are no formal names for God or deities in
Buddhism, the Buddha did not expressively deny their existence, but presented doubt of an omnipotent, benevolent being. However, the notion
of emptying one's mind of all clutter and of releasing the notion of self
is akin to meshing with God. It makes one susceptible to hearing the
thoughts of the universal consciousness above the background noise of
our own. Similar to Jainism, Buddhism has also dualistically divided into
two sects or schools of teachings, Mahayana and Hinayana. The *Prajna-
paramita* sutras, a collection of about forty texts with the oldest dating
to about 100 BCE, transpired from the Indian subcontinent and contain central concepts to Mahayana Buddhism and how to become a Bodhisattva or even a Mahasattva.

The Buddha presented his first teaching after enlightenment in the
form of "Four Noble Truths" and they appear as a symbolic method and
an inapparent categorization of how reality can be interpreted. Although
somewhat unclear in their ultimate meaning and conceptual framework,
they can be summarized as: 1) the truth of pain and suffering – that it
exists; 2) the cause and origins of suffering through attachment cravings
– it has causes; 3) the truth of how to end and eliminate suffering – it
can be reduced; and, 4) the truth of the path(s) that leads to the end
of suffering – how it can be reduced. The fourth on this list leads us to

the beginnings of Buddhist practice which involves following the "Noble Eight Fold Path." The eight paths are travelled and explored by directing the mind to the correct course of: 1) right understanding (*Samma ditthi*); 2) right thought (*Samma sankappa*); 3) right speech (*Samma vaca*); 4) right action (*Samma kammanta*); 5) right livelihood (*Samma ajiva*); 6) right effort (*Samma vayama*); 7) right mindfulness (*Samma sati*); and, 8) right concentration (*Samma samadhi*). Although there are slight variations to the exact words or terms among the different branches of Buddhism, they are symbolically depicted in a dharma wheel, which has eight spokes representing each of the correct characteristics to embrace. The eight folds are to be developed and linked simultaneously, rather than sequentially.

"Zen" is the Japanese pronunciation of the Chinese word "Ch'an", which means meditation. Zen Buddhism is an aspect of Mahayana teaching which focuses on the value of meditation (aka Zen practices) and saviors in the form of Bodhisattvas, beings that are very close to achieving the Eastern form of Enlightenment. A Bodhisattva deliberately delays their final transition into Nirvana out of compassion and remains in this realm longer than required to minimize suffering and help others become closer to Enlightenment. They are not here to break the Matrix, but to insert more joy into the programming code. They devote themselves to the salvation of those around them, to help the *hylics* and *somatics* in the Gnostic sense who are still swimming underwater with eyes closed.[225] The Zen practitioner views the mind as unreliable since it can be influenced by opinions, ideas, biases, experiences and accumulated knowledge. They focus on silencing the mind, so that a truer and more unobscured reality can be witnessed. The four main routes of training by which students of Zen participate is zazen, sitting in meditation; koans, problems beyond logic (thought stopping to be in the purity of the moment); sanzen, private interviews with a master; and ordinary physical labor in the monastery or on its grounds to participate in everyday life.[226] The purpose of the koans is to trigger the mind into enlightenment, placing one at the apex of Self, as it rebounds from such sudden withdrawals from a conceptual existence. Zen is about experiencing meaning and understanding from the illogical, in the form of haikus, statements, and advice that deliberately stumbles the mind and freeze thoughts. As soon as one reflects upon or talks about Zen or tries to define it, the experience is lost. It is the listening to a musical composition not by following the notes, but rather by flowing with the rests. Through the practice of thought stopping, Zen brings forth an awareness from under the covers of mental noise, revealing a more pronounced mode of reality and self. In doing so, instantaneous occurrences of knowing (satori) are encountered within the sudden flashes of epiphanies.

7. Confucianism – initiated about 550 BCE.

Viewed as a philosophical way of life rather than a religion, Confucianism still has a place within the hearts and minds of those seeking spiritual truths and mystical connections. It contains many of the moral tenets prescribed by other true religions, but without the focus on any supreme deity, saints or demi-god hierarchy. Its roots actually predate its founder K'ung Fu-Tzu (Latinized into "Confucius"), since the teachings are based on that of prior scholars. Rather than having devised them, Confucius humbly claims to have only interpreted the ancient teachings and made them more accessible to the common folk. Even so, as a statesman (or unacknowledged prophet), his insights into tying together the continuum of past traditions, moral code for present behavior and adjustments for welcoming the future, were paramount.

Although minimal is known of his early life, married with children, K'ung Fu-Tzu was educated, strived for political success, and mentored many others on promoting peace and implementing good governmental practices. Unable to influence improvements in his home state, he roamed and taught in other states of the Chinese regions. The key foundation of his teachings was the continued growth and spiritual development of one's core and the implementation of moral conduct and behavior. A keen promoter of literature, history and the general seeking of knowledge and truth, he was a respected beacon of inspiration among his students and disciples.

Confucius followed the metaphysical traditions of connecting to the universe through reverence for spiritual beings, departed ancestors and the generational knowledge they passed down. Providing service to humanity was a prerequisite for relating to the spiritual realm. The core of a person's being and virtue was formed through family influences and interactions, which should later be transferred into good government. Confucianism expresses that great leaders implement their power by positive influence and non-violent means through moral persuasion, not by bullying and coercive actions. It later recognized the duality found in the universe and incorporated the doctrine of balance between Yin and Yang (triangles and circles). From Hellenistic thought, Empedocles was making the claim of four basic elements of fire, air, water and earth.[227] About the same time period, Chinese thought was weaving its five basic elements into Confucianism as wood, metal, fire, water and earth, all considered the fundamental states of the material universe prior to modern chemistry's Periodic Table of Elements and the discovery of subatomic particles. The abstract sculpture *Philosophi Lapis*, created in 2005 by the author, refers to the fundamental states as wood, stone, metal and plastic on the rotating cementitious tablet labeled Wednesday, PM. Every non-animal-based textile or product consists of at least one of these macroscopic fundamental materials.

The influence and practice of Confucianism waxed and waned throughout the centuries in China as its moral and metaphysical attractiveness competed with Buddhism and Taoism.[228] Today in the 21st century, it exists more as an ethical prescript dwelling within cultural baselines among much of East Asia without any underlying religious tones.

8. Taoism – initiated about 500 BCE.

Based on the influence of budding philosophies in the 6th and 4th centuries BCE in the region of China, Taoism (asa Daoism) pervades much of Chinese culture and thought throughout the past two to three millenniums. The written basis of Taoism can be found in the *Tao Te Ching* (pronounced like Dow Deh Jing) and it is centered on synchronizing with the absolute essence of all that is and rising above dualities to achieve serenity and understanding. This is done by following the Tao (asa Dao), which means the way, path or road. Lao Tzu (asa Laotze,

Laozi), a rather obscure figure and considered a deity or prophet by some, is traditionally credited with compiling and adding to the teachings of Taoism. Very little is known of Lao Tzu other than his writings.

Taoism focuses on being in the moment, an eternal "knowing" and having a transcendental awareness of our participation in it. It embraces the Yin and Yang notion of duality and balance, a theme also found in Confucianism and Buddhism. Taoism is more spiritual than Confucianism and overlaps with Buddhism. It is interesting to note, that although Taoism, Confucianism and Buddhism were all competing for followers and Imperial patronage in the Chinese regions, they co-existed with much less friction and violence than the Middle Eastern religions of Judaism, Christianity and Islam.

Trying to define or label Tao goes against its very nature. Yet despite this, there seems to be a variant of human meanings or perspective on what it is. In simplest terms, Tao can be viewed as the natural flow of the universe. Properly meshing with "The Tao" is analogous to how a good surfer rides a wave or how one should rake the leaves of life – downhill and with the wind. Following The Tao corresponds to synchronizing, harmonizing and working with this flow by being virtuous. The notion of non-action related to its doctrine is not about passivity, but rather, it is about properly "clicking" with or efficiently meshing with the movements of the cosmos such that accomplishments are perceived as effortless. One does not force or tame it, but rather experiences and cultivates it at a level relative to their current state of enlightenment. It is about being supple with reality and people, not dictatorial and not lackadaisical. Synchronizing with The Tao through ethical and moral actions, leads to higher and higher levels of awareness and less and less resistance (effortless action) to both material and spiritual obstacles. It is considered prakrti, the *prima materia*, the cosmic nature of all that is found everywhere and comes from the same single initial energy source – the seed of creation and the original material of the universe.[229] Notice both the alpha (triangle) and omega (circle) geometric representation within the word Tao. This is not a coincidence.

9. Mohism – initiated about 500 BCE.

Mohism (asa Moism) was also viewed as a philosophical way of life but with more religious undertones. It had both similar and competing aspects with Confucianism and Taoism. Based on the teachings of Mozi (470–391 BCE), it become more submerged about 300 BCE as Confucianism and Taoism started to dominate the Chinese regions. Confucianism, with its teachings of virtue, rites and traditions to be upheld by those in positions of authority within governing bodies, was more embraced and thus promoted by the state over Mohism. Mozi, on the other hand, felt that by reflecting on one's own successes and failures, true self-knowledge is attained rather than by mere conformity with traditions and going through the motions of ritual. Parts of Mohistic influence reveal themselves in Confucian writings of around the second century BCE, indicating the occurrence of a partial assimilation. Of what remains of the original Mohistic thought, many of the written philosophical ideas of Mohism can be found in the *Mozi*, a book titled and named after the founder.

Mohists had their roots in Confucian thought, but felt Confucius was more of an elitist with aristocratic preferences and with an agenda of promoting the state too much over the individual. Mozi (asa Mo Tzu), on the other hand, was drawn to the common people. Similar to Jesus, he was a carpenter or *tektōn* by trade and gained respect by practicing his own teachings while focusing on an existence of primitive simplicity, straightforwardness in human relations, internal reflection, self-restraint, authenticity, and building upon the ancestral faiths. His life, however, resembled that of Confucius in many important respects. Being widely read and well versed in the tradition of the Chinese Classics, he spent most of his days (except for a brief period of holding a public office) traveling from one feudal state to another in hopes of finding a royal benefactor who would allow him to put his teachings into practice. In the absence of finding such royal support, he had to be content with maintaining a school which lasted for several generations and recommending his disciples for administrative positions.[230]

Following prescriptive methodologies was the standard by which Mozi applied a "litmus test" to determine the benefits that a proposition or policy would bring to society. Benefits of the time were defined as en-richment of the poor, increase of the population, removal of danger, reg-ulation of disorder and a meritocracy of advancement based on talent and not relational background (i.e., nepotism). He looked down upon extravagances, especially those of governing officials or royal pageantry that were paid for by taxes from peasants and commoners. He was less tolerant than Confucius in his condemnation of anything that he viewed as being "non-useful", thus disapproving of art and music while ignoring consideration of their potential narrative benefits, humanizing qualities, transcendental abstractions, healing properties and spiritual function. Generalizing further, he declared that, before anything could be declared as good, it was necessary first to demonstrate what it was good for. Such tests and standards were indispensable to Mohists.

Living in a time period in which China was divided into small, con-stantly warring feudal states, Mozi noted how the act of war by one state upon another should be criminalized and not glorified. Based on the scale of damage inflicted upon the individual, he was aware of the wickedness of its moral consequences and exposed the ludicrousness of praising such organized conflicts and campaigns of conquest. He put forth that they should be prevented rather than promoted. Stating, "when everyone regards the states and cities of others as he regards his own, no one will attack the others' state or seize the others' cities." He acted as a peace advocate (war protestor) and is said to have prevented skirmishes through persuasion and revealing the futility of the fight. Al-though opposed to war because of its waste of resources and the havoc it has upon the fair distribution of wealth, he acknowledged the need for strong defenses to protect a harmonious society from external as-saults.[231]

Mozi demonstrated that the principle of undifferentiated love had in it both utilitarian justification and divine sanction. He spoke of "undif-ferentiated love and mutual profit" in one breath, and he was convinced that this principle was both the way of man and the way of heaven (tian). This coincides with the messages of later prophets and bears a striking parallel with Christianity – the replacement of partial love with universal love. A heaven was very real to Mozi and he preached that the will of heaven is to be obeyed by human beings and accepted as the unifying standard of human thought and action: "What is the will of heaven that is to be obeyed? It is to love all the people in the world without distinction." Heaven not only "desires righteousness and abominates unrighteousness" but also metes out reward and punishment accordingly.[232]

While Confucian thought focused on the partiality application of love (caring for family, clan and region to a higher degree than those further away on the relational spectrum), the cornerstone of Mozi's system was undifferentiated love for all. By contrast, he believed people should care for all others equally and stressed that rather than adopting different attitudes towards different people, love should be unconditional and offered to everyone without regard to reciprocation.[233] According to Mohists, the peace of the world and humanity's happiness lies in the practice of undifferentiated love. Noting the potential obstacles and impracticability of applying universal love, objections arouse of this new doctrine. Being perhaps too far ahead for the reality of the time period, the disappearance of pure Mohistic thought by 150 BCE may have been due to these objections and the over demanding difficulties of overcoming the contributing human nature.

It was not until encounters by Western scholars in the 19th century with Eastern Asia's history that Mozi was rediscovered and his teachings reappraised.[234] Mohistic writings are said to contain the statement: "The cessation of motion is due to the opposing force ... if there is no opposing force ... the motion will never stop. This is true as surely as an ox is not a horse." If this anecdote's existence is indeed authentic, it means that Chinese Mohist philosophers were 2100 years ahead of Sir Isaac Newton's *Philosophiae Naturalis Principia Mathematica* in understanding and documenting a basic law of physical motion.[235] However, knowing a law serves little benefit without the included knowledge of how to apply it. Hero of Alexandria is credited with inventing the first steam engine, but the only thing that came of it at the time was a novelty rotating toy fueled by fire that ejected water. It wasn't until almost two millennia later that its usefulness and knowledge was applied to help catalyze the Industrial Revolution occurring between the 18th and 19th centuries. Likewise, spiritual awareness also does little good unless we know how to apply it properly.

10. Shintoism – forming as early as 500 BCE, written records appear about 550 CE to 700 CE.

Primarily emerging from the indigenous beliefs of early Japanese culture but also containing Chinese influences, Shintoism is based on focusing one's connection with the universe and its spirits through the use of shrines (sacred conduits or spaces that are either man made, natural or combination of both) for communing with aspects of the supernatural. It has no founder or universally recognized core scripture, but its preservation has occurred through the oral passing of generational knowledge and traditions. The name Shinto comes from Chinese characters for Shen (divine being), and Tao (way) and means way of the spirits or gods. It was more of a mythology in its early stages but later on, Buddhistic as well as Confucian components commingled with its foundational elements. Eventually it morphed into a pseudo-organized polytheistic religion with priests and priestesses to maintain the shrines and administer the related practices, rituals and festivals. To some, it is more of a way of life than a religion. Viewing all matter as also containing a component of thought, essence or spirits, Shintoists present offerings and seek favors from kami (or jin), local ethereal representative of natural and supernatural forces. Interesting to note that the word "jinni" (or Anglicized as "genie") refers to supernatural creatures found in early Arabic mythology and also referred to in the Islamic *Koran*. They seem to be at a lower hierarchal level than angels or demons and depending on the situation, much like aeons and archons, they can either be benevolent or malicious towards humans. Amaterasu, the Sun-Goddess, invoked at the Ise Grand Shrine is one of the most important kami. Stabilizing the influence of imperial power upon the culture as an authoritative means of unification, the Japanese emperors were considered direct descendants of Amaterasu. At the start of the 21st century, there are estimated to approximately 100,000 Shinto shrines situated throughout Japan.

Literally, the word "kami" refers to the epiphanic power of an event or occurrence that inspires a profound sense of wonder and awe in the witness or beholder. They can be landscape elements, forces of nature, quality of beings, ancestral liaisons, ideas, the supernatural or summation representation of manifestations. Varying views consider them exhibiting the duality of both angelic or demonic behavior: providing love, nurture, guidance and blessings when respected or destruction, wrathfulness, chaos and curses when riled. Within our world, but ambiguous and hidden from our awareness most of the time, kami reveal themselves when we synchronize our being with their energy harmonies or at times, when the need arises, they choose to reveal themselves. We should all strive to emulate the loving nature of kami by developing virtue as the core of our being.

"...At the core of Shinto are beliefs in the mysterious creating and harmonizing power (musubi) of kami and in the truthful way or will (makoto) of kami. The nature of kami cannot be fully explained in words, because kami transcends the cognitive faculty of man. Devoted followers, however, are able to understand kami through faith and usually recognize various kami in polytheistic form. Parishioners of a shrine believe in their tutelary kami as the source of human life and existence. Each kami has a divine personality and responds to truthful prayers. The kami also reveals makoto to people and guides them to live in accordance with it. In traditional Japanese thought, truth manifests itself in empirical existence and undergoes transformation in infinite varieties in time and space. Makoto is not an abstract ideology. It can be recognized every moment in every individual thing in the encounter between man and kami. In Shinto all the deities are said to cooperate with one another, and life lived in accordance with a kami's will is believed to produce a mystical power that gains the protection, cooperation and approval of all the particular kami..."[236]

Shintoism, like other ancient religions, has undergone upheaval, state influenced and sponsored doctrinal changes over the centuries, assimilation and even the sprouting forth of new shoots as recently as the late 20th century. Just as the definitional concept and pantheon of kami goes through refinements and changes depending on the times and scoping needs of devotees, the definition of what Shinto is varies. It evolves into different things depending on the relational life-attitudes, culture and customs of its followers. Unlike earlier times, current day Shintoists may reside outside of the Japanese islands and also be practitioners of Buddhism, Confucianism and Taoism, since there is limited contradiction in their modern meshing. Without amalgamation, they may even follow Shinto practices and those of Abrahamic-based religions, aspects of Hindu beliefs as well as other alternate religious paths.

   11. Druidism – first mentioned about 400 to 300 BCE.

   From Celtic cultures, the Druids were religious leaders and authorities that existed in the regions of Europe prior to the advancing invasions of the Roman Empire into the Gallic regions. Based on pagan mythology and folklore morphing into a pagan religion, Druidism seems to have started in the late Iron Age and faded from sight by the 2nd or 3rd century and fully dispersed to the land masses of the British Isles with the spread of Christianity in mainland Europe by the 7th century. It may have been the influence of Saint Patrick's Christian evangelism that resulted in the demise of the Druids. He seems to have initiated the first act of violence against the Druids by invoking the Lord to throw Drochu, a leading druid, to his death for merely mocking the Christian ways – an extreme and excessive punishment for the slightest of insult.[237] Saint Patrick's contests against the Druids to determine the better god seems reminiscent of Elijah's challenges against the prophets of Baal (aka Tyrian Baal).[238] Elijah even orders the execution of the competing prophets at the end for having lost the contest.[239]

   The word "Druid" means literally "knowing the Oak tree" in Celtic, implying their knowledge of trees and nature. They could be male (a priest) or female (a priestess) and were considered a blend of observing philosophers and tribal shamans of the natural world and the environment, worshipers of divinity and believed in the eternity and indestructibility of the soul. They tracked the movement of the Moon and Sun for agricultural purposes, basing the planting of crops and migration of herds in relation to the solstices and equinoxes and position of the stars. As advisors, tutors, healers, judges and predictors of future events for kings and lords, they could allegedly persuade nature through their spells (i.e., the conjuring up of storms) and communicate with animals. About 1,000 years later on in history, the Cathar Perfects were said to also have the ability to command the elements, calm the waves and direct the clouds.[240] Julius Caesar wrote of his 1st century encounters with the Druids in Gaul. From Greco-Roman records, it is debatable and unclear whether they actually conducted human sacrifices (*The Wicker Man* was a 1973 horror movie rooted upon such sacrificial depictions). The Greco-Roman writings may have been false rumors generated to portray them as barbaric, demonic and uncivilized for conquering propagandistic reasons by the Roman Empire's expansionistic policies (similar to the false rhetoric of the Nazi's party used as an excuse for invasions into neighboring nations). Since there is no solid written record of Druid customs, practices and traditions, what little we know of them comes from limited archaeological evidence and the Greco-Roman portrayals.

Merlin, the famous wizard of King Arthur's court, was considered a Druid, but much of what has been written about their customs and practices seems more based on romanticized and glorified writings rather than fact. This is not to say they were not real, but since oral tradition was their training path, solid specifics of who or what they were are obscure. There appeared to be a hierarchal ranking among them with the Bards being the storytellers and maintainer of traditions, the Ovates being the community shamans and foretellers, and the Druid priests themselves who presided over worship, attended to secular matters and oversaw the Bards and Ovates. With their training said to last up to 20 years, they wielded great political authority among the varies Celtic tribes. Some of the oral traditions were put into written form in the Middle Ages in the *Mabinogion* and the *Book of Taliesin*.

Based on reinvention and the romanticized idealism of ancient Iron Age Druids, Modern day Druidry encountered a rebirth in the 17th and 18th centuries and continues, in some degree, into the present. Incorporating a reconnection to nature and the planet, much of modern

Druidism focuses on environmental stewardship with pagan elements of worship and a reverence for the Creator's works. There is a realization among them that trees are actually like the protective hairs of our body, acting as both living cleansing cilia and defending filament sensors for our home planet. In terms of monitoring and adjusting the climate, Druids are well aware that trees are the ultimate natural absorbers of carbon. They understand that trees, shrubs and plants are part of Gaia's immune system, of which, we are wreaking havoc.

There is no set doctrine of modern Druidic beliefs and the practices can vary among its adherents, orders and societies. One can encounter elements of both Shintoism (i.e., ancestral connective veneration) and Christianity (i.e., messianism) within modern Druidism with the inspirational intention of cosmically realigning ourselves with the natural world through both monotheistic and polytheistic approaches. It should be noted that Stonehenge, that circular prehistoric circle of megaliths in Wiltshire, England, was erected long before the notion of Druids appeared in historical records, but perhaps their ancestors had an influence on the monument's construction. Although there is no hard evidence, Iron Age Druids may have conducted some of their ceremonies and ritual among those lithic outcroppings as well as other menhirs and groves.

Chapter 5
Insights Into The Religions Of Planet Earth With Origins Within The Common Era

"ALL TRUE RELIGIOUS paths eventually converge; they all lead to the godhead." – AO

• • • •

<u>1. Christianity</u> – started somewhere between 6 BCE to 4 BCE, or about 30 CE.

Christianity, as of the start of the 21st century, has the most followers, sects and branches of the organized Earth religions. Although the most predominate religion across the globe, it is not the only path for relating to God. Based on the life and teachings of Jesus Christ, he is considered by his followers to have been the "Son of God." Interpretations vary as to what is exactly meant by "Son of God." Some sources view the story of Jesus as strictly allegory or that he is merely the fabled personification of the ever worshipped Sun-God.[241] Nestorius (386–451) proposed a belief that Christ was the merger of two separate beings, one human and one divine. One view within Gnosticism, a theology that was in place either before or just after the time of Jesus and a couple of centuries before the formation of the Roman Catholic Church, had a premise of Docetism, that he was never here in the material form, but rather, only in the spirit of celestial substance. This implies that Jesus was a mutable figure who represents the archetype of the Self and appears as different ways to the initiates with different levels of understanding and who have purity enough of heart and intention at their core.[242] According to the *Gospel of the Egyptians*, it is Seth (the 3rd son of Adam and Eve) himself that takes on the form of Jesus and descends from spiritual realms to overthrow the hostile archons.[243]

The descriptive term of "Gnosticism" didn't come about until the 17th or 18th century to describe those alternate Christian views that were not part of the early Roman Church's orthodox. Today, the term proto-Orthodox has configured itself from scholarly categorization to describe that which was not quite Gnostic and not quite Orthodox, but came out of the post-Christ primordial message. Gnosticism and proto-Orthodox are not ideal terms since they place all the sects and branches whose views were not included as part of the Nicaea outcome into one category, even if they were different among themselves. Therefore, we must be careful not to insert all "unorthodox" views into the same binder. There is variation as well as commonality among all that is lumped into as being Gnostic. Those we consider followers of Gnostic ways did not all refer to themselves as "Gnostics". Based on the Greek adjective *gnostikos* as used by Plato,[244] it refers to spiritual intuition, divinity inspired knowledge and that which exists but cannot be proven or disproven through the steps of the scientific method. Irenaeus in his attack on what he considered "heretical", applied the term – it was used by opponents to those that did not follow the orthodox.[245] According to Timothy Freke and Peter Gandy, the early Christian Gnostics "engaged in an ongoing exploration of mystical metaphysics which encouraged and incorporated imaginative" means for connecting with the godhead.[246] Freke and Gandy's comical satire *The Gospel of the Second Coming*, is based on alternate scriptural interpretations, the story of Jesus is presented as "an allegory for the spiritual journey each person must make if they are to awaken to the mystical state that the original Christians called 'Gnosis', which means 'knowledge.'"[247] Another view of Docetism is that Christ was an angel taking on human form and had to spiritually fight to maintain his divine awareness. Favoring myth and allegory, the Gnostics would not have taken the *Book of Genesis* so literally, but rather, interpreted Eve as representative of the core and soul of humanity (the psyche) and Adam as its mind of emotion and logic (the consciousness).

Merging the two into an androgynous whole is what would trigger memories of divine origins. To the Gnostics, the crossing of the Red Sea by Moses and the escaping Israelites as portrayed in *Book of Exodus* is allegorically equivalent to the taking of the "Red Pill" as described in *The Matrix* movie – both initiating the stage of passing into an awakening freedom. For some of them, it was not required for the biblical stories of the *Old Testament,* or the *New Testament* for that matter, to have actually physically occurred for them to have profound meaning for raising our consciousness to a higher state. The Gnostics relied primarily on faith and love for salvation, the rest they saw as fluff, background noise and pomp and circumstance. Their approaches still exist today as in the dispersed remnants of the Mandaean faith, a fully formed religion from antiquity found in parts of Iran and Iraq that views John the Baptist as their true prophet and uses the *Ginza* (aka *The Book Of Adam*) for their primary scripture.[248] They strive to emulate their image of Adam, the prototype human, to achieve enlightenment by spiritually connecting with a divine being from the Pleroma.[249] To label the Mandaeans as Christians would not be entirely accurate since their beliefs include philosophical undertones among a variety of fluid doctrines and rituals going back to at least the 3rd century. They also feel that Jesus conveniently took credit for much of what John the Baptist preached and therefore, they choose to venerate the original Nasuraiia, not the later copier.[250] Even Jesus admiringly states, "Truly I tell you, among those born of women there has not risen anyone greater than John the Baptist; yet whoever is least in the kingdom of heaven is greater than he."[251] Like the Druze, they practice under an almost impenetrable cloak of secrecy that has partially protected them from religious persecution. Unfortunately, like many other Middle Eastern cultures and populations, they have become refugees and pockets of diaspora, resulting in their numbers dwindling below 100,000. Hopefully, we can protect them as a historical culture deserving of global preservation rather than extinction.

—Λ*—

"...I came into this world to do the will of my Father, because my Father sent me." – Jesus Christ[252]

• • • •

"THE PHARISEES AND THE scribes have taken the keys of knowledge (gnosis) and hidden them. They themselves have not entered, nor have they allowed to enter those who wish to. You, however, be as wise as serpents and as innocent as doves." – Jesus Christ[253]

—*Ω—

Some interpretations view Jesus having been a very wise man or a prophet, but most followers of the faith view him as being a direct or indirect incarnate form of God, thus the material son as a representation or physical human aspect of the heavenly father. He was alleged to have been either an incarnation of Logos ("the light of gnosis") or at least became Logos. His human aspect may have been Jesus, but his divine aspect was Christ. Putting the two together, we have Jesus Christ. The word "Christ" is an evolution of the Greek past tense verb of *chrio*, meaning "anointed".[254] Viewed as the consciousness of the universe deciding to manifest itself into a being named Jesus Christ (aka Joshua, Jeshuau, Yeshua, Joseph-bar-Joseph) to witness and experience humanity firsthand, he entered into the material/physical realm of space/time through the womb and birth canal of a woman.[255] Considered a manifestation of the Almighty himself, a child of the Sun in both the physical and spiritual form, his birth into our realm was allegedly announced either by the light of a super nova or a hovering supernatural micro-star.[256] If not an incarnate of Yahweh, he certainly seemed to be an avatar of love. Christianity initially started out as a Judaic sect, frothing forth from a feeling of disenfranchisement with the Pharisees' orthodoxy and the Second Temple becoming reserved for only the "elite". It was not initially a separate monotheistic religion and budded from its Hebrew roots as the fulfillment of prophesy written into the scriptures which foretold of a coming Messiah who would bring the Jews out from oppression. Yet it seems

Jesus did something even greater; he brought humanity into the lime-light of God.

Much as it is at the start of this third millennium, Judea was a volatile hotbed of political and religious fervor in the centuries leading up to the time period of Jesus Christ's birth. Tradition has it that he was born in a manger (an animal stable) in Bethlehem while his Jewish parents were travelling to register for the census and/or pay their taxes. An earlier version of the *Gospel of Luke* has him being born in a *katalemna*, a temporary shelter or cave.[257] His mother Mary (and also perhaps his father Joseph, as well), received a vision from an angel saying that she would bear a child who would be the Son of God.[258]

—A*—

"The angels said to Mary: 'God bids you rejoice in a Word from Him. His name is the Messiah, Jesus son of Mary. He shall be noble in this world and the world to come, and shall be one of those who are favored.'" – *The Koran*[259]

—*O—

Most scholars do agree that a person called Jesus of Nazareth (or Jesus the Natsarim) from the region of Galilee did actually exist, but how close his life and travels were to what is presented in the *Bible* is historically hazy and there are a gamut of viewpoints regarding the accuracy of those biographical accounts. Growing up in the town of Nazareth (or a settlement of Natsarim) within Galilee, little hard evidence is known about Jesus' childhood and his secular (biological, step, surrogate or legal) father, Joseph. Joseph was a *tektōn* and would probably have been a carpenter by trade or a metal artisan and passed his craft down to his son, Jesus. He is mentioned in the early chapters of *Matthew* and *Luke*, but only in relation to Jesus' birth and childhood. His role as the Earthly surrogate father of Jesus, although important, seems to be treated with less significance and veneration among all the Christian denominations than the role of his mother. *The Nine Faces of Christ* provides a realistic fictional account of what Joseph could have been like. Per most sources, Jesus' secular foster father does not appear to have been present at the crucifixion, but according to the *Gospel of Phillip*, most likely being a carpenter by trade as well, he is said to have made the cross upon which his son was crucified.[260] Joseph was venerated by the year 800 into a saint by the Catholic, Orthodox and other Christian denominations. Jesus was most likely the oldest sibling (being the first-born per *Luke* 2:7) and other family members (James, Joses (or Joseph or Justus), Judas (or Jude) and Simon and his unnamed sisters (perhaps Assia and Lydia) are mentioned briefly in the gospels and apocrypha and may have been cousins or step-siblings, rather than direct siblings.

In spite of the ravages of World War II just coming to an end, the modern age of humanity become a little more enlightened in the mid-20th century with the discovery of those 13 Gnostic codices by an illiterate peasant named Muhammad Ali al-Samman who was supposedly searching for fertilizer (manure or a soft soil known as *sabakh*). Stashed in a large red earthenware jar around the 4th or 5th century near the town of Nag Hammadi in Upper Egypt, they may have been hidden for posterity sake to escape the destructive censorship triggered by Athanasius of Alexandria's authoritarian biblical media control and the suppression of Bishop Arius' points of view. The Arian controversy became a debate of semantics (*homoousios* – "of the same substance" versus *homoiousios* – "of similar substance") during the First Council of Nicaea in 325 rather than rational compromise on humanity's views on the exact nature of defining the Son of God.[261] Underlying the arguments, it was really a debate about Sophia – was she God's essence or her own being?[262] I wonder what other truths or perceptions about Christ written from the time of his life and physical demise to three centuries later were forced out because of political stubbornness rather than compromise during that gathering of three hundred or so Church Fathers at Nicaea. Were there any Church Mothers present to serve on the committees? Is it here that the Gnostics were silenced due to a controlling fear of providing a greater truth to the common folk – an egalitarian path to gnosis? What relevant information was conveniently clipped out and left as scraps for erasure from history? How many copies of the *Shepherd of Hermas*, *The Shepherd of Men*, *Letter of Barnabas*, *Apocalypse of Peter*,

Apocryphon of John, Gospel of Mary, Apocalypse of Adam and so many other texts that make up fragments of the *Nag Hammadi Library* and other codices became banned, were seized, censored, buried or sent to the furnaces? Was this when Mary Magdalen first became labeled as a former prostitute to discredit her feminine leadership? Was it here that the Goddess was removed from Christianity to make women second-class human beings?[263] Is this where the complexity of Judas of Iscariot's role was simplified to solely a villain rather than someone trying to arrange a meeting of negotiation between Jesus and the Pharisees? Was there something about Jesus' life or death in those Gnostic texts that the Roman Church did not want revealed? Were they afraid of their own temptations? What the council neglected to see is that Christ was the masculine, bringing Sophia properly into the material realms, while Sophia was the feminine, properly leading Christ into the spiritual realms. It was a mutual, symbiotic and loving relationship.

According to those leather bound books (copies and fragments of the *Gospel of Thomas, Gospel of Philip, Gospel of Truth, The Apocryphon of John, Thunder: Perfect Mind, Exegesis on the Soul,* and others) written in Coptic script, Jesus may even had a twin brother (either genetically or symbolically) named Didymos Judas Thomas.[264] A different and more holistic interpretation is that the twin being referred to was Jesus' higher self, his Atman, or his divine essence as described by the Manicheans.[265] The name "Didymos" means "twin" in Greek and the name "Thomas" means "twin" or "leader" in Aramaic.[266] Through the substitution or twin hypothesis, as in the character of Sydney Carton's willingness to sacrificially exchange his life in order to save the life of Charles Darnay in the Charles Dickens novel, *A Tale Of Two Cities,* some Gnostic and even Muslim sources claim that it was the twin Thomas who suffered and was sacrificed on the cross in place of Jesus.[267] Some believe that Christ survived the crucifixion and that he, his family and friends fled to the South of France; from Jerusalem to Rennes-le-Château.[268] Although debatable, it has been suggested that both John The Baptist and Jesus himself may have at one time been members of or influenced by the ascetic and apocalyptic group known as the Essenes, the authors of the Dead Sea Scrolls found in the caves of Qumran. As a young Jewish boy at the mere age of 12, however, Christ is said to have amazed the religious teachers in the temple with his scriptural understandings.[269] We don't hear of his whereabouts again until he starts his preaching and based on the fragmented anecdotes of *Matthew, Mark, Luke* and *John*, it appears that his ministry lasted only 18 to 36 months. Jesus Christ did not start Christianity; his disciples did after knowing him for no more than 1-1/2 to 3 years.

The core belief of Christianity is that God was willing to experience the sufferings of being human firsthand through Jesus, his avatar or incarnate form. Through this first-hand encounter, the Creator would be able to better empathize with his creations. He seemed a tireless wonder worker who projected compassion onto the needy of both spirit and wealth. The birth of Jesus was considered a gift to humanity, God in the flesh, a related being that would experience and witness the celebrations and misery of being human. As astonishing as this gift was, aspects of humanity distorted the meaning of his words throughout the past couple of kiloyears while forcing his message upon others. According to the *New Testament*, "God loved the world so much, that he gave his one and only Son, so that whoever believes in him may not be lost but have eternal life."[270] Through his love, he taught of a new way to treat each other, conducted supernatural events (miracles), forgave humanity for their sins and promised everlasting life. He acknowledged that those who are worthy would encounter heaven and those who are wicked would find themselves in hell due to their own undoing. His role was to liberate us from the wheels of suffering by helping us understand that we all can become a Christ, the symbolic still center of a rotating wheel among the chaos.[271] He is never specifically quoted as saying that reincarnation was not real or not possible, in fact, from the *Pistis Sophia* he tells his disciples to not delay spiritual development for another lifetime, as the number of perfected souls could be reached at any moment.[272]

During the last days in physical form, Christ was willing to subject and sacrifice himself to betrayal, arrest, insult, mockery, false accusation, condemnation by corrupt officials, torment by ridiculing mobs, torture by soldiers, nailing to a wooden cross, and eventual death by crucifixion. It is said that he died for our sins, even though it was the negative elements of humanity, a timeline that God foresaw, that had him put to death. Yet, the very idea of a passionate God deliberately allowing his son to be subjected to a slow execution seems shocking, especially to the clear slate of a child's empathetic morals.[273] In actuality Jesus may have been able to save his physical self during any of those moments, the body of flesh and bone containing his essence, but allowed the timeline to unfold so that the world would always remember the martyrdom of his existence. He was the Nazarene that sacrificed his physical form on the cross (or stake) for the love of humanity and in doing so, identified with all who have undergone suffering and death at the whims of the ignorant, under oppressive authoritarian abusers or by the orders of an insane regime. Despite the frustration and suffering encountered during his final days on this planet, he still forgave us and convinced his heavenly father to do the same. Realizing that condemning an entire species or religion based on the actions of a relative few is not sound wisdom nor fair, he saw through to defend us before God. His love for us resulted in the ending of his material temporal body, the reputed self-exiting from the tomb and for a short period thereafter, regeneration of his essence in a form of consciousness and body recognizable by his followers. I often wonder what the current state of humanity would be like if Jesus opted not to allow himself to be arrested by the detachment of Roman soldiers and temple guards shortly after the Last Supper and instead continued teaching within the physical realm for another forty years. Would our current world situation have become better or worse? That is a question I leave for you to ponder, for according to the Ophites, the spirit of Jesus remained after his execution for 18 more months and according to the *Pistis-Sophia*, he remained on Earth (either in the flesh or in the spirit) for 11 more years after the crucifixion to instruct his disciples.[274] I wonder in what direction humanity would head if a genuine Messiah decided to make an appearance in these days of the global internet and almost instantaneous satellite communication?

Long before the establishment of Christian doctrines, the notion of a trinity existed as a philosophical concept. Going back even earlier to half a millennium before the birth of Christ, Pythagoras of Samos declared, "Three or the Triad is the first of unequals, it is the number containing the most sublime of mysteries, it represents: 1) God; 2) the Soul of the Universe; and, 3) the Spirit of Man."[275] The Platonic triad is referred to as variations of the Good, the Beautiful and the True.[276] For Plotinus (204/205–270), regarded as the founder of Neoplatonism, the trinity represented the soul, the intellect and the One. For the Gnostics, the trinity consisted of God the Father, Barbelo the Mother, and Christ the Son to form a three-member divine family.[277] It is no coincidence that this is a precursor to the Catholic Trinity later introduced from the results of the First Council of Nicaea in 325. Many, but not all, Christian denominations explain the divine relationship between Jesus, God and the Holy Spirit (or Holy Ghost) through the abstract metaphysical model of the Christian Trinity. It represents the interplay between Jesus (God incarnate), God (the ultimate source), and the Holy Spirit (the medium, method or influence through which God delivers his power or messages.) Essentially, the Trinity is a symbolic reference to the same essence (the *homoousios*), but in different forms (the *hypostasis*). The idea of the Trinity is not specifically called out in the doctrines of the *New Testament*, but was formulated indirectly from them during the First Council of Nicaea as a Trinitarian model for describing the relationship between Christ the person, God the almighty, and the Holy Spirit as the connective medium in between. Resurfacing a Gnostic view, Valentin Tomberg reveals a feminine trinity composed of the Mother, the Daughter and the Holy Soul – a complement to the masculine trinity.[278] The Sethians, however, provide the simplest and most direct trinity of them all: the Father, the Mother and the Child.[279] Taoist terminology refers to the trinity as "the three treasures" of the body and is composed of vitality, energy and spirit.[280] Some more modern concepts refer to the trinity of existence as the consciousness, the psyche and the physicality or the mystery, the God and the Goddess or the archetypal, the cosmic and the human.[281] Jung's trinity consisted of the conscious, subconscious and individuation.[282] Another trinity on relating to existence is the mystical, the Gnostic and the magical or the heart, the mind and the will.[283] Still other trinities are thought, EMR and matter as described within Chapter 8 or Yahweh, Sophia and the Logos.[284] Which trinity do you think is the correct version, that of the Council, the Gnostics, a different one, neither or all of them?

—Δ*—

"Also there is a similitude of a Trinity shining in the body, soul and spirit." – George Ripley[285]

—*O—

By the very same formulations, one can draw (and several churches do) from the letters of Paul (although some may be forgeries) or even the *Gospel of John* and say it is a binitarian relationship, hence putting us into a duality in more ways than one – pun intended.[286] The concept of divinity being represented by a binitarian model or a triadic model becomes more based on semantics and perspectives, rather than significance. It seems the same as petty arguments of whether Jesus was born a savior or became one. Either way, we need to focus on the particulars of Christ's message, not argue over the uncertain details of his divine relationship. Metaphorically speaking, let's just say he was human by day and divine at night, and leave it at that.

The primary written scripture of Christianity is the *Bible* (aka *Holy Bible*). Derived from the Greek word "biblia" and simply meaning "the books", it is a culmination of both Hebrew scripture (*Old Testament*) scribed prior to the birth of Jesus Christ and writings from the era after his physical departure (*New Testament*). The *New Testament* recognizes the baseline laws provided by Moses but softens them with grace and truth through the teachings of Jesus and a bit of his biography. One should not consider it an all-inclusive account, but more as snippets of reflective tidbits, leaving us with a craving for more on his actual background and mission. The Roman invasion, occupation and destruction of Jerusalem in the year 70 destroyed many 1st and 2nd century documents and Judaic relics that could have been used to fill in the missing information. Relics and art considered by historians to be authentic of early Christianity are dated only back to the late 2nd and early 3rd century. Based initially from the accounts of Matthew and Luke written about the years 80 to 90, the present form of the *New Testament* and the *Bible* was mostly finalized within 350 to 400 years after Jesus' crucifixion. It (or portions of it) has been translated into at least 3,000 different languages, and within the past century in the English language alone, there are about 100 versions available in circulation containing variations in interpretation and wording. Offered as a source of hope and inspiration, bibles have been placed in hotel nightstands all over the world by the Gideons.[287] Being close to 2 millennia ago, many written details of Jesus' life, family and friends are absent as well as the intended meaning behind certain passages. The Gospels, although overlapping in information, are not a complete presentation of the life of Jesus and his teachings. His whereabouts and studies from about age 13 to about age 30 are historically absent from any written scriptures. To compensate, religious leaders and scholars have provided their own varied views as well as speculating on what may have occurred as a means of filling in those gaps of missing information. Christianity is no doubt a divine and diverse phenomenon that requires one to question, reflect and ponder on both what appear to be truths or falsehoods within the testaments.[288]

—A*—

"The *Bible* seems to be trying to make all of us into God, but without the inflated ego." – AO

—*O—

The closest original followers or students of Jesus are referred to as the Twelve Apostles (or Disciples). Their names are generally accepted to have been Simon Peter (called Peter), Andrew (Simon Peter's brother), James, John (James' brother), Philip, Bartholomew (aka Nathanael), Thomas, Matthew (aka Levi), another James, another Simon, Jude (aka Thaddeus), and Judas. Jesus Christ himself was not a Christian, but more of a "rogue" Jewish rabbi with a spiritual lineage going back to Abraham. This is the same spiritual lineage of all Jews, Christians and Muslims.

After Christ's torturous physical demise, there appeared to be a leadership clash in the direction the post-crucifixion beginning religion would go. Allegedly, one of Jesus' brothers, known as James the Greater, was head of the Christian community (the headquarters) in Jerusalem, while Paul the Apostle (Saint Paul) was head of its spreading and expanding missionaries.[289] Although several gospels were written from the different perspective of Jesus' original followers, most of modern organized Christianity relies more on the written instructions of St. Paul (considered the second founder), which may have deviated from the purer orally spoken teachings of Jesus.[290] Christianity is considered to have existed before Jesus' intuition as a result of Plato of Athens and Philo of Alexandria, but the resulting doctrine was Paul's institution.[291] Plato provided the ideas, Philo provided the materials and Paul put them together and assembled the halls of Christianity.[292] Most of today's Christians are in fact, unbeknownst to themselves, followers not of Jesus, but of Paul.[293] The Saul in him built upon Judaic roots, but the Paul in him pulled in Hellenic influences.[294] Scholars and theologians assume that Paul was the impetus for Orthodox Christianity, but the Valentinians and Sethians would argue and declare that he was critical for forming their Gnostic framework.[295] I often wonder what the late 1st century and early 2nd century Christian schools of thought were really like in their raw and purest form prior to their compilation by the 4th century edict of Rome's governing empire.

Confining all that God has to say in just one book or within the limits of four canonical gospels fails drastically in expressing the multiplicity of divinity's thoughts. Although not among the initial followers, Paul (aka Saul of Tarsus) was crucial at establishing the early fledgling Christian churches as he spread Jesus' word of a loving God who found equality in all believers.[296] For the initial 300 years of its existence, followers of the Christian faith were faced with sanctified persecution by the ruling authorities of both the Pharisees and Roman forces. With the Roman Emperor Constantine converting to Christianity in 320, the official persecution ended or rather, it was transferred to followers who were not specifically Christian based.[297] After which and extending into the Dark Ages, unfortunately, the Christian church started to distort Jesus' teachings as it began disdaining and persecuting followers of other religious paths. Anytime someone or a group questioned or challenged the medieval Catholic church or presented alternate ways for mingling with the divine, (such as suggesting that Jesus may have been an intermediate between God and man, rather than God himself), they were instantly branded as heretics by the clerical powers. Instead of promoting towards humanity's spiritual and intellectual evolution, out of fear and misguided leadership, it stymied progress. However, its dogmatism and institution also helped to preserve small pockets of culture after the fall of the Roman Empire and throughout the worst of the Dark Ages. Upon entering the Middle Ages, due to geo-political drift and continued historical arrogance, pettiness and squabbling from both sides, the Christian Church found itself as two distinct regions of influence, one in the West and the other in the East. The Catholic Church had influence in Rome and its surrounding regions and the Orthodox Church had influence in Constantinople (modern day Istanbul) and its surrounding regions.

During the Renaissance, Christianity in Europe underwent fluctuations of geo-political control and moral reformations, resulting in new branches and offshoots of Christian-based theological ideology. With the invention of the printing press ($\approx$1440–1450), the written words of the *Bible* became more accessible to the common folk, thus offering an alternate to primary reliance on church traditions or fanciful pictorial stories presented in stained-glass windows. Unwittingly, the printing press became the greatest "game-changer" in bringing God's Word to all classes of society and out of the control of a Church heavily involved in gathering secular power and wealth. The threat of returning to the early days of Christian thought and removing all the pomp that had been added over the centuries to support its business affairs, terrified the Church authorities. Martin Luther, among others, objected to the banking system created through the commercialization of penances and monetizing of indulgences and felt that everyone had the right to read the books of the *Bible* for themselves – a very Albigensian belief.[298] Regrettably, Luther put forth anti-Semitic writings and condoned violence towards Anabaptists (forerunners of the Amish and Mennonites). His declarations (the *Ninety-five Theses*) as well as those of John Calvin protesting the Roman Catholic Church's interpretive teachings, dogmatic absolutes and a perceived drift from its moral core, resulted in the Protestant branches (i.e., Presbyterian, Methodist, Lutheran, Baptist, Adventists, Anglicans), the Quakers (a blend of both Protestant and Catholic aspects), and more recently, the budding of Pentecostal movements that strive to induce and tap into the Holy Spirit.

Thomas Paine, born (about 1736 or 1737) into a Quaker family, vehemently ridicules Christianity. The following sums up his perspective: "Of all the systems of religion that ever were invented, there is none more derogatory to the Almighty, more unedifying to man, more repugnant to reason, and more contradictory in itself, than this thing called Christianity. Too absurd for belief, too impossible to convince, and too inconsistent for practice, it renders the heart torpid, or produces only atheists and fanatics. As an engine of power, it serves the purpose of de[s]potism; and as a means of wealth, the avarice of priests; but so far as respects the good of man in general, it leads to nothing here or hereafter."[299] Although he went about it in a confrontational manner and his approach was counter-productive, I would say that he was partially correct, but not always. Many saw him as attacking religion to destroy it (due to his ostracization only six people attended his funeral in 1809), but on the contrary, his dissent was trying to improve the effects of faith upon people.

Jehovah Witnesses, originating near Pittsburgh, Pennsylvanian from a mid-19th century Bible study group with a focus on millenarian restoration, is another late forming branch growing out of orthodox Christianity. Later coming from a group called the Bible Student movement, it has been viewed as controversial and fringing on unfavorable cult-like due to its more extreme beliefs, restrictions and practices. "...The movement has been accused of doctrinal inconsistency and reversals, failed predictions, mistranslation of the *Bible* (developing their own version called the *New World Translation*), harsh treatment of former members and autocratic and coercive leadership..."[300] Despite the criticism, it has one of the most racially and ethnically diverse followings of all the American religious groups. Similar to Unitarians, they do not believe in the doctrine of a Trinity nor that Jesus was divine, but rather, that a Holy force acted through him. They also believe that Jesus died on a wooden stake rather than a wooden cross. Even though there has been controversy among its doctrine, (i.e., discouragement of receiving blood transfusion for medical life-saving purposes, denial of anything deemed as pagan or slightly pagan, ahistorical preaching, door-to-door evangelicalism, shunning of any member questioning the group's teachings, abstaining from military conscription), particular Kingdom Hall affiliations (congregations) have provided a positive influence among many of its members by providing a diverse family-like community of support, provided they don't put forth independent thought on scriptural interpretation or show any dissent towards its leadership. Like so many other religions, they have undergone persecution, especially during Nazi Germany's holocaustic campaign. Aspects of their beliefs (both based on truths and falsehoods) are still challenged and have faced legal proceedings in court. As of 2019, there are claimed to be more than 8 million Jehovah Witnesses worldwide.

The Church of Jesus Christ of Latter-day Saints (informally or previously known as The Mormon Church) is also a relatively new North American sprout of Christianity, although coming forth from neither Catholic, Orthodox nor Protestant branches. Although there are at least 15 million members worldwide as of 2015, they are currently primarily based out of Salt Lake City, Utah. The Church of Jesus Christ of Latter-day Saints (LDS) base their beliefs from interpretations of the *Bible*, and going even further, incorporate additional religious revealing and interpretations within their own companion sacred book, *The Book of Mormon*. Being composed of fifteen smaller books titled after each narrator or prominent leader discussed within the sections, it is considered by its followers as a record of God's dealings with the peoples indigenous to the Americas.

Born on December 23, 1805 in Vermont, Joseph Smith, Jr., the founder and prophet of The Church of Jesus Christ of LDS, was said to have a vision at the age of 14 from God and Jesus telling him not to join any Christian denominational churches.[301] A few years later, Smith claimed that an angel named Moroni appeared to him, telling him that he had been selected to translate the *Book of Mormon*, a sacred text that was written around the 4th century and named after Moroni's father, Mormon. On September 21, 1823, the spiritualized Moroni returned to reveal the hidden location of them to Joseph Smith. However, it wasn't until September 22, 1827 that the messenger (Moroni?) felt that Joseph could be trusted with them and showed him, through the use of special spectacles or seer stones, the way of interpreting the engraved language marked upon them. Joseph returned the plates back to Moroni for safe-keeping after his translations into English was completed. The religion is considered to have officially started with the *Book of Mormon*'s publication in 1830 and started to spread soon afterwards to communities in Missouri, Ohio and Illinois.

It tells the story of two civilizations, one referred to as the Nephites and the Lamanites who emigrated from Jerusalem about 600 BCE and the other, the Jaredites who came much earlier near the time of when the Tower Of Babel was being constructed.[302] It is interesting to note how similar the word "Nephite" is to the word "Nephilim" (meaning giant) found in *Genesis* 6:4. The Lamanites are considered the principal ancestors of all indigenous Americans, due to the eventual destruction of the Nephites and the Jaredites. The book of *Third Nephi* (aka *3 Nephi*), the eleventh within the *Book of Mormon*, is considered of particular importance to their religion because it contains accounts of Jesus visiting the Americas sometime after his physical demise in Golgotha. Other narratives talk of the indigenous prophets having visions of Messiah Jesus before the time of his actual physical birth. He is said to have instructed the Nephites with much of the same teachings (the way towards peace within this life and salvation for the one thereafter) after his attempts to enlighten those in the Middle East centuries earlier and established a peaceful society in the Americas that lasted for several generations. *The Book of Mormon* is considered by its followers to be a revealing from many ancient indigenous prophets and a prophetical historian named Mormon and his son Moroni. They compiled the revealed stories upon various metallic (i.e., gold, brass or other specialty alloy) plates (possibly spiritual in nature rather than physical) and buried them for posterity in the Hill Cumorah located between present day Palmyra and Manchester, New York.

The religion's founder, Joseph Smith, Jr., seems to have fluctuated many times from sinner to saint, leader to tyrant, placing him in a hypocritical duality. He was arrested on several occasions (the first being in 1826 in New York) and in several different states for different charges. Finally charged with treason in 1844 for abusing his mayorship of Nauvoo, Illinois, he had invoked marshal law to use the powers of the office against his enemies and to punish the publishers of the first and only issue of the *Nauvoo Expositor*. The issue was published by several former members of the church and non-Mormons who had become disenchanted with Smith's (and other leaders') practices of plural marriages, controlling views on exaltation and possible desires to make himself a theocratic king.[303] Unfortunately, while in jail in Carthage, Illinois awaiting trial, the state failed to protect Joseph and his brother Hyrum from the onslaught of an angry anti-Mormon mob and both were murdered. It should be noted that Joseph Smith was running for office of the President of the United States at the time (campaigning on an advanced abolitionist platform) and became the first United States presidential candidate to be killed.[304] After the murder of the Smith brothers, the Mormons were divided and facing continued persecution. Joseph's successor, Brigham Young, had many of them follow him out of Illinois and resettled into the Salt Lake Valley region of Utah in 1847 to escape persecution and in search of religious freedom. Brigham's organization and emigration of the remaining congregations is remarkable, but he himself was no saint. Opposite of Joseph Smith's views, his leadership was more brutal, imposing a pro-slavery line and hard anti-African stance; it wasn't until 1978 that those of African descent were even allowed to serve as priests.[305] He was the leader overseeing the church during the Mountain Meadows Massacre in which more than 100 non-Mormon settlers passing through in 1857 were disarmed based on promises of safe conduct and passage. Instead, after surrendering, they were mercilessly shot, stabbed and slashed to death in a planned and organized subterfuge.

Historically, those high up in the leadership ladder of The Church of Jesus Christ of LDS had many wives and the church elders publicly confirmed in 1852 that polygyny (polyandry was conveniently prohibited) was central to their beliefs. Yet, due to economic limitations, only about 5% to 15% of Mormon men had achieved the ranking to have more than one wife simultaneously.[306] In 1890, facing public and even Federal backlash for the condoning of polygyny, the church elders reluctantly banned the practice – in doing so they may have saved their fledgling religion. In recent years, the church acknowledged that Joseph Smith wed as many as 40 to 50 wives, some as young as age 14.[307] Today, the LDS' leadership frowns upon polygamy and promotes having just one spouse and cites their own *Book of Jacob* and *Book of Mosiah* as justification against polygamy.[308] Some fundamentalist factions, who veered from the main trunk line of the church, continue to practice plural and/or "complex" marriages. The practice of polygamy itself seems contrary to their religion, unless it is a loosely convenient way around committing the notion of adultery as expressed in *Three Nephi* 12:27-32.

Modern American tribes, archeologists and historians do not consider the *Book of Mormon* as an accurate ancient record of the anthropology of the American continent, since science has shown plenty of anachronisms and DNA tracing indicates there is no indigenous American connection to a Judaic lineage. It is viewed by them as a made up past that did not actual occur among the tribal populations. Perhaps the stories of the Lamanite, Nephite and Jaredite civilizations were misinterpreted as having occurred on planet Earth, when they may have been alternate timelines or the past historical occurrences of God's dealings with other worlds, planets or realms – lost civilizations reminiscent of Atlantis.

In John Smith's own words, he refers to the gold plates as "an account of the former inhabitants of this continent", perhaps meaning that they emigrated or were relocated to non-terrestrial abodes.[309] If this is indeed the case, it gives strong validity to the foundations within the *Book of Mormon*. Moroni may have been trying to convey the history of other ancient off-world civilizations within those plates as a warning for us not to repeat their same mistakes and Armageddons. His hiding of those plates in Hill Cumorah about 421 for posterity would be no different than the hiding of the Dead Sea Scrolls or the concealing of the Codices of Nag Hammadi. Being the early 1800's, the notion of AISBs from other planets may have been beyond Joseph Smith's interpreted comprehension, an understandable error of any seer prior to the age of humans having exiting the earth's atmosphere, space travel or of manned controlled flight for that matter. Do these parallel existences and alien world postulates sound ludicrous to you? They certainly seem far-fetched to me, but I only ask that you keep an open mind especially when you consider the "Superiors" mentioned in Mesopotamian tablets and the "Powerful Ones" talked about in *Genesis*.[310]

The *Book of Mormon* has been referred to by some as a fraud written by Joseph Smith. Even Mark Twain negatively commented on its prose,[311] thus causing him to again question his own beliefs as expressed in his quote, "The easy confidence with which I know another man's religion is folly teaches me to suspect that my own is also."[312] My question is, what con artist would go to such lengths to write a counterfeit scripture amounting to over 500 pages in length? That's an awful lot of work for a spiritual deception. If the *Book of Mormon* is just a fabulous invention, then perhaps we can say the same thing for much of *The Bible* or *The Koran*. Smith may have been psychotic during those writings or under the guidance of a true divine presence or a bit of both. Whatever aspects of Mormon beliefs that may be correct or incorrect, they focus value on quality of family life, doing good deeds, respect for worthy authority and missionary work. Their adherence to these values alone, despite the contradictions encountered within its higher ranks, should earn our respect for it was the followers themselves (the congregation), that saved and steered the natal religion back to a correct direction, not its early leadership. Can the true stories of today's Church of Jesus Christ of Latter-day Saints have developed from a false story created by Joseph Smith, Jr.?[313] It was the ancestral congregation, a church of the people, whom made themselves into the community they are today. Considering those wavers of my mind and that single demon/angel-like visual encounter that I had as described among the beginning sections of this book, who am I to judge the legitimacy of Moroni's appearance to Joseph Smith, Jr. and the testimony of the eleven witnesses who saw the plates for themselves?

A different branch from the Christian trunk line, Unitarian Universalism was officially formed in 1961 with the merging of the Universalist Church of America and the American Unitarian Association, previously two separate Christian denominations established in the United States. Although categorized here as a branch under Christianity, Unitarian Universalism and its church could also be considered as a separate religion (similar to Bahá'í Faith) combining a tolerant and pluralistic approach to the "free and responsible search for truth and meaning." With its roots in liberal Christianity, it encourages members, be they a theologian, an atheist, an agnostic, a deist, a pantheist, or a theist, to search for spiritual growth through personal approaches of self-realization and awareness. It seeks to encourage and embrace, without a dogmatic authority, that which is true of all the world's great religions.

The early Unitarian churches of 16th century Europe rejected the doctrine of the Holy Trinity and viewed divinity as a singular entity, hence the term "Unitarian." They also felt that Christ did not come about from a virgin birth (psilanthropism), but rather, started out as human as the rest of us. Over time in the earlier part of his physical life, having formed a special relationship with God due to the self-development of his core with the purity of spirit, he may have been adopted as the Son of God (adoptionism) rather than born the Son of God.[314] Let us ponder this allegory: An infant is put up for adoption because the parents are not able, ready or responsible enough to provide care. The baby finds herself or himself being nurtured and raised in foster homes. The now mature and responsible biological parents come back a few years later and unknowingly adopt their birth child. Was the child born to them or adopted by them?

Although a particular Unitarian congregation (aka fellowship) can veer more towards one direction than the other, they avoid a solid creed. Religious services, resembling a Protestant template, are presented as a sermon by a minister, an outside guest speaker, or by a layperson of the congregation. The service can be based on any scripture, inspirational message, as well as personal experiences, with interludes of hymns and music to accompany and accentuate the experience. The bylaws of the formed modern (post 2000) Unitarian Universalists contain seven principles to be followed and six sources for metaphysical referencing.

The Seven Principles are:[315]

1) The inherent worth and dignity of every person

2) Justice, equity and compassion in human relations

3) Acceptance of one another and encouragement to spiritual growth in our congregations

4) A free and responsible search for truth and meaning

5) The right of conscience and the use of the democratic process within our congregations and in society at large

6) The goal of world community with peace, liberty and justice for all

7) Respect for the interdependent web of all existence of which we are a part

The Six Sources are:

1) Direct experience of that transcending mystery and wonder, affirmed in all cultures, which moves us to a renewal of the spirit and an openness to the forces which create and uphold life

2) Words and deeds of prophetic women and men which challenge us to confront powers and structures of evil with justice, compassion and the transforming power of love

3) Wisdom from the world's religions which inspires us in our ethical and spiritual lives

4) Jewish and Christian teachings which call us to respond to God's love by loving our neighbors as ourselves

5) Humanist teachings which counsel us to heed the guidance of reason and the results of science, and warn us against idolatries of the mind and spirit

6) Spiritual teachings of Earth-centered traditions which celebrate the sacred circle of life and instruct us to live in harmony with the rhythms of nature

Similar to the Quakers, who also come from Christian roots, Unitarian and Universalists have been active in influencing the improvement of conditions for all in their participation in social and civil right movements. They were active abolitionists in the 19th century, promoters of woman's suffrage in the early 20th century, and supporters of the feminist and the lesbian, gay (homosexual), bisexual, or transgender orientation (LGBT) movements of the late 20th and early 21st century. Some famous Unitarian and/or Universalists were four United States Presidents (John Adams, his wife Abigail, John Quincy Adams, Millard Fillmore and William Howard Taft), Ralph Waldo Emerson, Charles Darwin, Frank Lloyd Wright, Christopher Reeve (yes, the actor famous for his acting role as Superman) and numerous others.[316]

Christian services, relics, paraphernalia, traditions, customs, rites, artifacts, and garments vary across the numerous denominations and chronological periods. Even building styles fluctuate from the simple to the elaborate, following Hellenistic, Gothic or Islamic architectural elements (bell towers that resemble minarets) and sometimes incorporating various proportional blends of each. Some services are very simple in presenting the message of Christ while others, to enhance the mystique, glamour, drama or entertaining performance of the religious experience, are much more ornate. In the more traditional churches (i.e., Catholic, Orthodox) the role of Jesus' mother, Mary, is celebrated to an elevated level of veneration and is an integral part of Christian iconography. Being highly regarded in Islam, Mary the mother of Jesus, is actually mentioned more in the *Koran* than in the *New Testament*. In fact, the *Koran* has an entire chapter (Maryam) named after her. The emblematic divine relationship between mother and child (the Madonna Mother and Child symbolism), however, was not originally unique to Christianity and is predated by Hellenistic influences – the notion of a virgin birth was around before the writings of the *New Testament*. Discovered in 2005, there is a drawing painted with reddish-brown ochre on the ceiling of a small cave cavity in the Egyptian Sahara desert that could be viewed as a nativity scene. It predates Christianity by almost 3000 years.[317]

The worshiping of the Virgin Mary was initiated by the Cathars (aka the "pure ones") and later adopted by medieval Catholicism.[318] The meaning of the word "Cathar" may have come from the Greek etymology of the word *katharos* (καθαρός), which means pure. Another scholarly opinion is that their enemies within the medieval Catholic Church came up with the propaganda term to portray them as demonic "kissers of a cat's behind."[319] The Cathars were similar in their practices to those of early Christians near the time of Christ and were a group of medieval Gnostics whose beliefs would never be tolerated by the powers of the papacy. The Cathars believed that: 1) Jesus was a prophet; 2) his teachings were true and significant; 3) he was here to guide us from ignorance to enlightenment; 4) Christ reminded us of our divine aspects; 5) reincarnation is real; 6) the *Old Testament* was false and the *New Testament* was real; 7) their leadership should work for a living and not be financed through donations or handouts; and, 8) love was the way to become closer to God. They did **not** believe: 1) that Jesus was literally the Son of God; 2) in the virgin birth; 3) in Christ's death upon the cross; 4) in original sin; 5) the Roman Church's favor of monetary institutions; 6) in accepting the celebration of the Eucharist; 7) in heaven, hell or a last judgment; and, 8) in ornate buildings and structures of worship.[320]

The only female apostle Mary Magdalene (aka The Magdalene or The Madeleine) is also venerated to a certain degree. The Cathars saw her more important to the spread of Christianity than St. Peter. She may have come from a wealthy background, enabling her to provide financial support to Jesus' ministry. Having been linked with the Gnostic Sophia in the *Gospel of Phillip*, the *Pistis Sophia* and the *Gospel of Mary*, she may have been the carnal lover and/or wife of Christ.[321] However, if the Cathars were against marriage, then why did they consider Jesus and Mary Magdalene to have been married to each other?[322] It was not that they were against marriage, on the contrary, they promoted it among the communities they served. It was their leadership that opted for celibacy, just like the practice of the Catholic Church. The *Gospel of Phillip* and the *Pistis Sophia* of the Nag Hammadi Codices are said to contain references to Mary Magdalene. The *Gospel of Mary*, although officially not a gospel, is part of the Berlin Codex. Due to being only remnants remaining of the manuscript, possibly hidden in about the year 380 to save them from purges of the Roman Emperor Theodosius, it is unclear of which Mary it relates to – the many references to those named "Mary" can be as confusing to the many names of "John" occurring within scriptures and scrolls. It may relate to Jesus' mother, his sister or Mary Magdalene (the favored figure) and most scholars believe the writings either date to the time of Christ or within a couple of centuries.[323] There are other references to women named Mary in the *New Testament* that have caused confusion, even among verses in *The Koran*. At some point Mary Magdalene may have become confused with two other women in

the *Bible*: Mary of Bethany, the sister of Martha, and the unnamed sinner
from Luke's gospel (7:36-50) both of whom wash Jesus' feet with their
hair.[324] Despite the confusion and uncertainties, the gospels do tell us
that Mary Magdalene chose to stay near to Christ during his crucifixion,
was the first person to encounter the empty tomb and the first to witness
his resurrection. Her story of going to look after the preparations of the
body and finding the tomb empty, then seeing either the physical or spiritual form of Jesus, is what changed the ministry from a movement and
into a religion.[325] It wasn't until 1969 that she was finally canonized
into saint hood, almost 2,000 years after being so close to and supportive
of Christ. Due to the structure of the *Gospel of John* and the description
of eyewitness accounts, some scholars believe it was actually written by
Mary Magdalene.[326]

I could go on for thousands of more pages on the details and implications of the life of that being named Jesus Christ and the schools
of thought that promulgated forth from his messages and the teachings
of his disciples. There is even much to be said about his betrayer mentioned in both the *New Testament* and the *Gospel of Judas* per the Codex
Tchacos (asa Tchacos Codex). Due to all the other texts, books and media available on the subject, however, I rely on you to continue with your
own investigative reading and research.

2. Islam – started about 600 to 610.

The word "Islam" is derived from the same Arabic meaning for
"peace" or "entering into peace", but it also means "surrender" or "submission to God" or peace through compliance with Allah's divine guidance.
It is a religion whose primary creed is based on surrendering to the will
of God or doing the right thing, as God would expect of us. When done
properly with a true connection, "surrendering" to the will of God is akin
to surrendering to love.

The global followers of Islam account for 1.8 billion adherents, consisting of almost a quarter of the world's population.[327] The third of the
so-called desert religions and being the world's second largest religious
group, Islam, like Christianity, has branched and intertwined itself into

schisms, sects and cults. Also like Christianity, some of these divisions have resulted in the cancerous tarnishing of the true intent of the base religion while others have provided new paths and positive concepts for relating to and interacting with divinity.

Mohammad, the person who triggered the start of this great religion, was born about 570 after the death of his father and his mother died when he was still a child. He was raised by his grandfather and then by his uncle. As a youth, he developed a knack for business while traveling with the trading caravans and at age twenty-five married his supervisor, a wealthy older widow named Khadijah bint Khuwaylid (aka Khadija for short), who was forty at the time. The twenty-five years of marriage with his older wife were considered happy ones, making up for the rough years of his orphaned youth. Mohammad greatly respected his older bride and gained much of his wisdom from her compassion, and yet it is ironic that some modern practitioners of the Islamic faith (and Christianity and Judaism as well for that matter) still seem to view women as a threat and suppress them as inferiors. The Islamic prophet Mohammad's beloved first wife Khadija was highly respected by her husband for her compassion, intelligence, savviness and knowledge. Being fifteen years older than Mohammad, she was a twice-widowed single mother and successful trader.[328] In fact, Khadija was the very first Muslim, converting based on her husband's revelations and prophetic mission. With all the love and devotion Mohammad had for his original wife, it is confounding that some insecure aspects of Islamic culture still seek to dampen the feminine mystic and oppress (sometimes violently) its freedom. This seems counter to respecting all that Mohammad stood for since women were among his closest followers and their emancipation was important to him.[329]

Face veiling of women was around prior to the start of Islam and the practice was adopted from other adjacent cultures. The modern-day hijab, a scarf worn loosely about the hair and neck while allowing exposure of the face, serves more today as a means of religious identification and belonging. The burqa, viewed by many as being extremely oppressive, covers the entire body. There are other variations of coverings that fall somewhere between the hijab and the burqa, such as the chador. When an Islamic state or governing law demands the wearing of such garments, its enforcers need to remember the cultural purpose for the veiling. The various head garments mentioned for Islamic women to wear was to protect them, not to suppress, oppress, nor punish them. It was to ward off the lustful eyes of aggressive males and prevent unwarranted temptations. Serving to reduce the probability of a female having a male force themselves upon them (e.g., rape), it was easier for the women to cover themselves than for men to wear blinders. Perhaps blinders worn by males would have been more appropriate, but the preference for an advanced and enlightened society is that it should be the decision and choice of the individual woman if and when to partially or fully veil themselves.

During his development as an individual, Mohammad was exposed to the ideologies of Judaic, Christian and perhaps other beliefs. Later, as a trade caravan leader, he is said to have befriended a Christian monk and at later times fought side by side allied with Jewish leaders or rabbis. He acquired a reputation for honesty, wisdom and strived for the implementation of truth into everyday practice. Deep within his core, he was a man of religious conviction, whose purity of intention allowed him to unite people on the basis of a common belief and moral practice, going against segregation due to nationality, race or tribal associations. As a trader and merchant, he was far from xenophobic and encouraged cultural interaction, rather than suppressive isolationism. This is in direct contrast to some current elements of Islamic followers that choose to instantly attack anyone or anything they perceive as being different – an unjustified fear of any infidel.

The Arabic term for the holy text of Muslims is called *The Qur'an*, meaning "The Recital" or that which is recited. The Anglicized translation of the title is referred to as *The Koran* or the *Koran*. Unlike the *New Testament*, which is believed to have been written at least seventy to ninety years after Jesus' parting from the physical realm, the *Koran* was written in 657, only twenty-five years after Mohammad's death.[330] It was compiled based both on oral revelations committed to memory and writings by the Prophet's aid, Zayd ibn Thabit. Mohammad himself was principally illiterate, which makes the conception of *The Koran* even more intriguing.[331] Despite the compilation of the text within a quarter of a century following the Prophet's death, discrepancies occurred due to the interpretation of many words that could be read in different ways. There were discrepancies not only in the meanings of the words, but also in the pronunciation due to variations in dialect. Sections of *The Koran* seem fragmented, indicating portions were left out either by accident or with deliberate intent. Items seemed to be taken out of context to the situation they were addressing, opening themselves up to interpretation or sometimes misinterpretation. As to be discussed in Chapter 11, leaving out a few key words in any language can drastically change the meaning of a statement. The fragmentation of the *Koran* or a lack of a chronological structure does not make it any less significant in its importance or in uniting the regional people with a commonality; a scripture that reinforces the teachings of former prophets and strived to bring equality and tolerance among its followers.

Mohammad's intention was to raise the spiritual quality of people, not to suppress it. He recognized the need for change among the social order of the times due to the increased distance between the privileged and the underprivileged, the haves and the have-nots. Unrestrained by suppressive dogmatism, Muslims were alive with cultural creativity when Christian based Europe was experiencing its Dark Ages. If it weren't for the Golden Age of Islam's ($\approx$800 to $\approx$1258 or $\approx$1500 depending on the perspective of the source) quest for knowledge after the Roman Empire's collapse, much of today's information and technological progress would not exist. The Islamic culture preserved a great deal of humanity's advancements through the perilous times of the European Dark Ages ($\approx$500 to $\approx$1500) and the world should thank them for this. The unity of the Middle East and beyond became based not on nationality, but on the common recital and continuation of Mohammad's message of God's compassion and desire for humanity's advancement in the eyes of the universe. Within the framework of religious and ethnic tolerance, scholarship and learning went on relatively unhampered by religious injunctions. In the boundaries of Islamic civilization, new dimensions were being feverishly added to the sciences, mathematics, art, agriculture, literature, when the European community was experiencing a period of cultural arrest and contraction.[332] Independent thinking flourished as did learning in general as the true intent of Mohammad's message was continued. Dogmatic fears did not override cultural growth and exchanges, nor did the threat of exposure to other religious beliefs. Exchanges and interactions with progressive Muslim regions triggered a period of rebirth and sprouting for the Christian world, which contributed to the general awakening of Europe out of its Dark Ages amidst which *The Koran* was finally translated into Latin in 1143 by Robert of Chester.[333] Much, but not all, of the European world then distorted the true meaning of Christianity to justify the ransacking of culturally rich Islamic regions under the guise of The Crusades. Ultimately, the final fall of the Golden Age of Islam around the 16th century occurred primarily due to internal strife and conflicts, both political and religious, which snuffed the torch of learning and dimmed cultural creativity to a faint glow. In the 21st century much of the Islamic world has reawakened and is alive with the true desire of Allah; that is to raise the lower self of all citizens to their higher self through education, understanding and tolerance.

—Λ*—

"Do not kill yourselves." – *The Koran*[334]

• • • •

"DO NOT FORGET TO SHOW kindness to each other. God is cognizant of your actions." – *The Koran*[335]

—*Ω—

Unfortunately, fragments of the modern world population falsely claiming to follow the words of Mohammad, still resort to violence, excessive anger and hatred in their misguided Jihads. The use of negative actions, falsely justified by the ignorant distortion of true Islamic principles, is no different from the record than that of Christian or Judaic religious distortion. Even Buddhist monks have been known to rise up against each other and throw some punches at their fellow worshippers. The ancient and much of today's modern Christian and Muslim worlds do not appear to be aware of the common religious foundations they both share, derived as they were from the roots of Judaic and Hellenic beliefs. They share the same original prophets, such as Abraham and Moses and similar stories such as the Great Flood and Noah's Ark. As mentioned in the previous paragraph, the first *Koran* was not translated into Latin until the 12th century, so any written understanding of its tenets into Europe and beyond the Arabic world did not occur until at least 500 years after Mohammad's death.

Just as Jesus was accused of being blasphemous and false by the Judaic culture of his day, Mohammad was accused by the Christian culture of being false. Just as the *New Testament* describes Jesus' recognition and confrontation with the hypocrisy of the Judaic Pharisees of his time period, *The Koran* confronts the corruption and distortion of followers claiming to be practitioners of the Judaic and Christian scriptures. The Arabian Peninsula during the time of the Prophet Mohammad was a region in which various faiths were present. There were Christians, Jews, Zoroastrians, polytheists, and others not affiliated with any religion. When one looks into the life of the Prophet, one may draw on many examples to portray the high level of tolerance shown to people of other faiths. Mohammad was not attacking the other base religions, but rather he was against the distortion of their true fundamental principles and intent. Coming from a merchant background, he was not against other religious paths or foreigners, for he understood the benefits of cultural interactions and its revelations of new ideas. He was against chosen ignorance, emotional mass hysteria and dishonorable acts. It was the political discrimination, dishonesty, hypocrisy and bias associated with those higher up in the worship and political chain of command associated with the individual idol religions that he sought to destroy, not the followers, nor their artistic sculptures nor their artifacts, nor the religions themselves. His enemies were resistant to his message due to their fear of losing political power, religious and commercial grip on those whom they oppressed. The reason for Mohammad's personal destruction of over

three hundred and sixty idols in the Ka'bah (asa Ka'be or Kaaba; a cu-
bicle holy structure said to contain a stone given to Abraham by the
Archangel Gabriel), upon his return to Mecca (considered by many Muslims to be the place where Adam and Eve reunited after their exile from
the Garden of Eden) in the year 8 of the Muslim calendar, was **not** to
literally destroy other religions and their artifacts. It was to symbolically destroy the representations of oppressively achieved wealth and power, to unite all the people on the common ground of Islamic kinship and
to show the Meccans how spiritually empty the material items actually were. He was against when one's pagan idol affiliation or religion determined one's trading and business status; he was not against tolerating
other religions and their relics provided they did not compel (force) others into their worshipping practices. Mohammad objected to one's socioeconomic status in society being dependent on their religious path or
tribe, not necessarily the path itself. His fight was for equality and fairness among the Arab world. One's religious practices should never determine one's socio-economic ranking. Upon entering Mecca (asa Makkah)
without having to resort to bloodshed, he did not commit murderous
acts upon the pagan followers, infidels, the innocent or the inhabitants
of the temples. Only four criminals, condemned according to the current
laws, were executed.[336] I wish the same could be said for the behavior
of "Constantinian Christians" after that meeting in the year 325 of the
Council of Nicaea.

Mohammad saw the imperfections within some of the Christian and
Judaic leadership of the time period or more precisely, he recognized the
distortion occurring with their base concepts to justify negative exploitation and elitism. He made it clear that the message he preached was a
continuation of the same religion as Abraham, Moses and Jesus. The *Koran* contains references to Adam, stories of Cain and Abel, Noah and the
great flood, David and Solomon (aka Sulaymān ibn Dāwūd), and numerous other *Old Testament* prophets. There are *New Testament* references
to the role of Jesus, John the Baptist, Zachariah, and the crucifixion. At
times, being only human, he confused certain names and biblical relationships, such as mistaking Miriam, Moses' sister for Mary, the earthly

mother of Jesus.[337] He was an expert on the intent of the earlier scriptures, not on their finer details. The motive of his teachings, however, still stressed a continuation of God's perpetual theme for mankind: the rewarding of the true and righteous and the punishing of the wicked and immoral by their own design. Unfortunately, Mohammad seems subjected to more distorted interpretations than any other prophet of history due to an unwillingness to investigate further into the truths of his life's details and his message. This is done both by some Muslims twisting his words to justify violence and by others who prefer Islamophobic stances through maligned propaganda.

Almost 1400 years ago and just after Mohammad's passing, due to disagreement among the future of the faith's theo-political leadership, Islam split into two branches known as Sunni and Shiite, creating a clash between the duality of its future direction. As of 2019 about 85% of Muslims are associated with the Sunni branch and the other 15% are associated with the Shia branch.[338] The schism all started when there was no plan in place for the transference of leadership after Mohammad's departure in 632. Islam at this point was more than just a religion; it was at the upmost of social, commercial and political influence and whoever became Mohammad's successor would take the reins of authority and power in the region.

One group, followers of "the way" (sunna) of Mohammad, felt that it should be based on qualifications and skills and that the new leadership should be Mohammad's father-in-law and friend Abu Bakr. The other group, the "party of Ali" (shi'atu Ali) felt the leadership should be based on inheritance and genealogy and favored Mohammad's cousin and son-in-law, Ali ibn Abi Talib. The Sunni camp ultimately won and Mohammad's friend (Abu Bakr), became the first official successor, or caliph, of the region. The Shiite camp did not recognize his legitimacy and held fast to their allegiance for the prophet's descendants. One of Mohammad's grandsons, Husayn, continued to lead the Shiite branch until his death at a battle with the Sunnis in Karbala, Iraq in 680. The death of Husayn and many of his supporters and relatives during the battle still leaves a bitter taste between the two groups, resulting in continued strife and violence to this day, with the Shiites often feeling like the oppressed minority.

If only the Sunni and Shiite parties could have found a way to merge Abu Bakr and Ali ibn Abi Talib into a functional government back in 632, so much bloodshed and violence could have been removed from the Middle East's history. If only they had followed the words near section 4:29 in the *Koran*, so much needless loss, misery and grieving could have been avoided. The duality of this power struggle and friction continues at this start of the 21st century in the region with the nation of Saudi Arabia dominating by the Sunni influence and nation of Iran dominating by the Shiite influence. Hopefully, by the middle of the 21st century, the leadership of both these nations and other countries in the region will again go back to the tenets of true Islam and focus on love, gratitude and forgiveness. A future of peace and reconciliation begins with the forgiveness of all the atrocities each side has committed upon one another throughout the centuries. This is what Allah wants – to bring Islam back to a religion of peace and prosperity as it was always meant to be.

3. <u>Sufism</u> – started about 700 to 900 (?)

Sufism is a mystical branch or order coming forth from the Sunni branch of Islam and its symbolism speaks to the heart and mind in discovery, poetry, music and art.[339] Initially considered heretical and forced underground in the 13th century by Ottoman rulers, it has woven itself with welcomed acceptance into the mainstream of Islamic thought.[340] The exact time period of when it came about is difficult to pinpoint since it may have come directly from the greater thresholds of Mohammad's message, about a century after the prophet's initial teachings or two to three centuries later. Sufism (aka Tasawwuf) is based on being a lover of Allah, a mystical practice of being in constant longing for God (a *Sehnsucht* for the divine), which drives the soul in search for the Beloved. It is the longing and separation itself, which brings one closer to and eventually in union with the cosmos. Through contemplating on one's love for divinity in all its forms, mystical experiences reveal themselves. It is an ancient wisdom and considered the science and study of love. It is not primarily of the mind, but of the heart (in a spiritual sense) and seeks to know love through every prophet, every practice, and every form of worship that leads towards love and all its glorious forms.[341] Sufis strive to return home to God, the Beloved, while in this material realm by making the journey from ego to Self.[342] The ego pulls us towards separation, while the Self pushes us into wholeness – the finding of our <u>Atman</u>. According to the poetry of Sufi mysticism, when one truly surrenders to God, they become "drunk" with love and awash in an ocean of divinity's grace – a "madness" of joy overtakes them.

One of the most famous of Sufi mystics from whose writing and poetry led to the creation of the Whirling Dervishes (Mevlevî Order), is Jalal ad-Din Muhammad Balkhi-Rumi or generally known just as "Rumi." He was born in 1207 in Afghanistan, which was then part of the Persian Empire. His father, a Muslim scholar and mystic, moved the family to Roman Anatolia (present-day Turkey) to escape Mongol invaders when Rumi was still a child. At the age of 25, Rumi inherited a position as a teacher at a madrassa (Islamic school) upon the passing away of his father. Continuing studying Shariah (Islamic law), he eventually issued fatwas (legal opinions) and gave sermons in the local mosques. Rumi also indulged in Sufi mysticism among a community of local dervishes, who are Muslim ascetics similar to mendicant friars in Christianity.[343]

He came across a wandering dervish monk named Shams (aka Shamsi) Al Tabriz in 1244, and after exchanging theological discussions and debates, becoming so enamored with each other and each other's perspectives on Allah, they became inseparable. Spending months together in prayer and an ecstatic communion known as "sobhet", Shams ignited a divine spark that sent Rumi above the planes of academic knowledge and into the mystical elements of his religion. Rumi was so grateful for this awakening, that when Shams suddenly disappeared (possible sensing jealousy and resentment among Rumi's students), he became distraught. Hearing that Shams had gone to Damascus, Rumi sent his son (Sultan Walad) to retrieve him. Upon Sham's return, Rumi was elated with joy. However, after a short period of time, Sham again disappeared and was never heard from again. Based on conjecture, it is thought that he was murdered due to the jealousy of Rumi's students or under the orders of Rumi's own son.

Rumi then engaged in the outpouring of expressive lyrical poetry as a coping mechanism and means of bereavement for the loss of Shams. His poetry of longing for divine love of the Beloved is both uplifting and mournful, depending on the written passage. There is controversial debate (viewed by some as blasphemous even to discuss) on the type of love Rumi and Sham instilled within each other. Were they intense platonic friends enthralled with each other's transcendental perspective on Allah's love or did it go beyond that and into the physical? Despite lacking evidence and relying only on speculation, the exact nature of their relationship does not matter and should not concern us. They may or may not have been homosexual lovers, but either way, the poetry on love that Sham inspired out of Rumi is a gift for all of us to cherish and to assist in awakening the mystic within by speaking beyond our mind and into our hearts. Sufism, regardless of the sexual orientation of any of its mystics, answers the needs of its seekers on their quest for truth.

4. Alawites – started sometime in the 800s.

The Alawites (aka Alawis, Ansaris, Ansariyya, Nusayris, Nusairis or Namiriya) are a sect fluctuating perhaps between pagan, Christian and Islamic beliefs that live primarily in the region of the Syrian coast, in the Al Ladhiqiyah Province. Smaller pockets of them live in Turkey, Lebanon and even the Golan Heights. They revere Ali (Ali ibn Abi Talib), considered the first Imam of the "Twelver school" of thought. The religion is believed to have been founded by Ibn Nusayr (possibly a disciple of the tenth and eleventh of twelve Imams considered to be divinely ordained) during the 9th century. To minimize being persecuted, they dwell in mountainous regions and are marvelous at giving an outer appearance of being aligned with whichever religious authority is in power. It is not an outward deception, but rather a cloaking or garment covering up their inner workings which remain secretive even today. Unfortunately, the terrain and outward cover did not protect them from persecution during the Ottoman Empire's expansionism and attempts of forcing them to convert to pure Sunni Islam.[344] Reflections of Walter Birks, who spent time in the Alawite (aka Jebel Ansariya) mountain regions while serving during World War II, talked of his fascination with what he referred to as the Nosairis sect, prior to being named the Alawites during French occupation.[345] In the modern era, the use of the term Nosairis (aka Nusayris) has come to be pejorative (insulting and demeaning).[346] Unfortunately, the Syrian Civil War which started in March of 2011 during the Arab Spring and which still smolders as I write these words, resulted in 41,000 to 150,000 young Alawite men losing their lives to the sectarian violence.[347] Fearing the persecuting chaos if the government in place were to collapse due to mainly Sunni opposition, they have suffered dearly for their support of the Assad regime.

Alawites practice a secret initiatory religion. Their tenets conceal esoteric inner meanings that are known only to the internal adepts who are found to be worthy keepers of their knowledge. Like the Cathars, they did not favor elaborate structures dedicated to worship, but preferred qubbas, characteristic white domes surrounded always by a sacred grove of evergreen oaks.[348] They may even still have some of the same spiritual "treasures" as the Cathars. Prior to the advances made at the beginning of the 21st century among religious scholars to better understand them, disclosing of their beliefs to the profane person could result in death.[349] The *Kitab al Majmu* is one of their prayer books and the *Koran* is another of their holy scriptures, but with an allegoric interpretation that follows more in line with early Batiniyya and Muslim ghulat sects. Breaking away from fundamental Shia tenets, the Alawites drink wine socially (in moderation) and as part of their rituals. They use candles, incense and venerate saints such as St. George and St. Matthew. They believe in the reincarnation of the soul or metempsychosis, (with infidels being reborn into a lower animal forms), a divine triad (denoted by "Meaning", "Name" and "Gate"), and that avatars (divine incarnate emanations flowing forth from the godhead) appear cyclically in human form throughout history. They also celebrate Christmas, Easter and the Epiphany.[350] According to their belief, all persons at first were stars in the world of light but fell from the firmament through disobedience.

They believe, through the development of character, to once again take their place among the stars upon reaching the Eastern version of enlightenment. One of their prayers states, "Deliver us from these human forms and re-clothe us in light among the stars."[351] According to Birks regarding the Alawites of the northern region bordering Turkey, two of their most important symbols are Light and the chalice which contains the sacramental wine. In drinking of the wine, the worshipper would say "I drink to the Light."[352] This alludes to the notion that the vessel of our being, even with its small cracks and holes, can hold the divine essence. It means that we are in fact, all Holy Grails capable of containing the "Light" of Allah – to be his/her instrument of love.

   5. Druze – started about 986.

   Originating in Egypt in or near Cairo and first publically preached in 1017, the Druze faith can be considered an isolated sect, having sprouted out of the Shia branch of Islam. It started as an organized movement claiming the sixth Fātimid caliph, al-Hākim bi-Amr Allāh, as a divine figure and the last in a series of incarnations of God. The Fatimid religious establishment of the time period viewed this as heresy, since they felt that al-Hakim and prior caliphs were divinely appointed, but not divine themselves.[353] Al-Hakim, however, was intolerant of other religious ideologies and was notorious for his persecutions of Jews, Christians and orthodox Muslims.[354] Perhaps at one time al-Hakim had meshed with Allah, but the connection most likely became tarnished and broken as he succumbed to his lower nafs.[355]

   The leading proponent of al-Hakim's divine nature was Hamzah ibn ʿAlī ibn Ahmad al-Zūzanī. Within the movement, he was competing with Muhammad al-Darāzī, (a former pupil and disciple), for followers, authority and recognition and favor in the eyes of al-Hakim. It seems he did win his favor, since al-Darazi was conveniently declared an apostate and was either exiled, went into hiding, or was murdered on the orders of al-Hakim. Despite his disappearance or death, the movement was still credited with his name, morphing as associated with al-Darāziyyah or al-Durūz. In 1021, the caliph al-Hakim, too, vanished under suspicious cir-

cumstances (a plot possibly carried out by an older sister) and persecution of the movement claiming his divinity began. The Druze, however,
believe that al-Hakim went into occultation and will return in the End of
Days as the Qā'im ("Ariser") or Mahdi ("Guider") to inaugurate a golden
age.[356] Fleeing Egypt, the movement settled almost exclusively in the
protective mountainous regions of Syria, Lebanon and Israel.

Preferring to call themselves muwahhidūn, which translates to "unitarians", or al-muwahhidūn meaning "monotheists" or Ahl al-Tawhid
meaning "the people of monotheism", the spiritual elements and scriptures of their religion are kept highly guarded so as to preserve and protect them from potential additional persecutions or destructions. Like
the Manichaeans, they follow a creed of taqiyya, acceptably denying their
faith when required for self-preservation.[357] Passed down from generation to generation with oaths of secrecy and a protected lineage, their
known practices consist of elements of Hinduism, Christianity, Islam
and Judaism blended with Gnosticism, Neoplatonism, Pythagoreanism
and other philosophies. Their religious compilations were influenced by
interactions with various nomadic tribes during their migration into the
security of elevated regions. They were rediscovered in the 12th century
by the Jewish traveler/explorer Benjamin of Tudela, who described them
as fearless, mountain-dwelling warriors who were receptive and supportive of the Jews. Due to earlier persecutions and for future protection,
they closed their faith to new followers (around 1043 to 1050) thus prohibiting proselytization and opposed or strongly discourage marriages
outside of their faith. Access to their sacred texts is only granted to worthy initiates ('Uqqāl) who can be male or female. More advanced and pious 'Uqqāl can become Ajāwīd (godly), the truth revealers.

DNA testing shows that an unusually high percentage (35%) of
Druze males carry the Y-chromosomal haplogroup L, which is otherwise
uncommon in the Mideast since it originates from prehistoric South
Asia.[358] In recent years, through genome tracking, it was discovered
that the Druze and the Ashkenazic Jews share more common genetic ancestry with each other than with other Middle Eastern populations.[359]

This indicates that earlier practitioners of the Druze faith were not as restrictive to isolationism as portrayed.

Often caught in the throes of geo-political instabilities in the region and teetering between the religious rifts, they are pulled between their Arabic culture solidarity and their Zionist ethos in support of Israel's right to exist.[360] They have actively participated in Israel's border security and political system as well as direct conscription into the Israel Defense Forces. A recent law implemented in 2018 and approved by a majority in the Knesset, symbolically enshrines Israel as a Jewish state and thus insults decades of Druze's support. Opening the doors to treating non-Jewish minority ethnicities as second-class Israeli citizens, it further compromises the notion of cultural and religious inclusion and pluralism. The law, although currently symbolic, further threatens to move Israel away from a haven and into a suppressive Jewish caliphate.

   6. Sikhism – started about 1499.

Considered the first Guru of Sikhism, Nanak Dev Ji was born in 1469 in the Punjab region, which laps into both modern India and Pakistan. Influenced by both Muslim and Hindu teachings during his youth, he become disillusioned by intolerances expressed by both the Muslim and Hindu clerical leadership in the region at the time. During the preaching of his first sermon at about the age of thirty and based on revelations he encountered, he proclaimed the equality of all in the eyes of God and removal of labels by stating "there is neither Hindu nor Muslim" expressing that all true religions were the way to God and all should be respected.[361] Sikhism blossomed forth for about the next 200 years under the grooming, teachings, leadership and input provided by its Ten Sikh Gurus, starting with Nanak. The word "Guru" is an ancient Sanskrit term for spiritual teacher or inspirational guide, especially in Hinduism or Buddhism. Modern Western adaptations have applied it as praise when referring to an expert or master in a given field, or in the derogatory sense, when referring to false spiritual instructors that negatively exploit their followers for material gain. The generalized modern meaning is someone who teaches to raise others to the same level of understanding, awareness or knowledge on a particular topic.

The word Sikh in the Punjabi language means "disciple" and they follow the writings and teachings of the Ten Sikh Gurus, who lived in the times from 1469 to 1708. The *Shri Guru Granth Sahib* (or just *Guru Granth Sahib*) is the holy scripture of Sikhism and contains a 1,430-page accumulation of their contributions. It is considered to be the 11th Guru, a revered teacher in of itself, due to its comprehensive instructional nature and contains hymns written by the Ten Gurus as well as contributions by Hindu and Muslim authors. Sikh followers strive to have God in their thoughts at all times, practice living a virtuous and truthful life while maintaining a balance between spiritual and temporal obligations.[362] Thus, there is a universal appeal to many of Sikhism's writings and teachings. Since Sikhism is a relatively young religion (a little over 500 solar years) there are biographical records of its Gurus and ample history on its propagation, struggles and cultural stages. The Fifth, Ninth and Tenth Gurus were martyred for defending religious freedom and standing against forced religious conversion. Like other religious cultures, Sikhs have undergone state sponsored persecution, affronts, and discrimination. Upon the fall of the Mogul Empire in the mid-18th century, they dominated the culture and state in the Punjab region until they were defeated by the regional colonial expanse of the British Empire in the mid-19th century. They are known as reputable fighters (soldiers) in defending their civil rights and those of others and have earned renowned respect for their virtue and fairness. In fact, due to their admirable fighting skills, the British Empire recruited them into their army during the World Wars of the mid-20th century. Facing pressure from ignorant and unenlightened Hindu and Islamic extremists, the very religions that they defended, many Sikhs have left the Punjab region and fled to other regions of the globe to maintain their culture, traditions and religious identity.

Rather than being immersed in rituals, Sikhism focuses on developing one's being through scholarly study and charitable actions. Essentially, the primary emphasis is on loving devotion to God, conducting ourselves as decent beings while participating in society, earning our keep and living an honorable life.[363] It abides by the equality of all and rejects hierarchal distinctions of caste, creed, race or sex. Aspects of Sikhism were well ahead of other religions in terms of their spiritual evolution and regard for the equal treatment of women. One could say and emphasize that Sikhism's progressive equality towards women in both its scriptures and traditions is extraordinary for its sociological time period of formation. Having a monotheistic concept, it views God as transcending the boundaries of all religions and that God could only be experienced by meditation (internal reflection on our relationship with divinity), worship and kind service to others in need. Incorporating elements of Hinduism, Sikhs believe in reincarnation and the ultimate spiritual goal is to break the cycles of birth and death to again fully merge with God. The wearing of turbans by males to contain their hair is part of the Sikh identifying heritage and they also carry with them a Kirpan, a ceremonial sword or knife which has spiritual meaning similar to how a Crucifix is symbolically worn by some Christians and a how a Star of David is worn by some Jews. Although the religion has no specific priesthood, there are individuals trained to read the Gurmukhi script in which the *Guru Granth Sahib* is written.

7. Rosicrucian – founded about 1614.[364]

Rosicrucian or Rosicrucianism is more of a religious order or movement that allegedly started in Europe in the early to middle 17th century and its members claimed to possess esoteric knowledge from ancient times. The name of the collective (Order of the Rosy Cross) comes from its 10th or 11th century Byzantine symbol, a rose located on the intersection of a crucifix's line segments. The order's name may also have come from its possibly allegoric founder, Christian Rosenkreuz.[365] It should be noted that the poetry of Rumi and Jami (13th and 15th century Sufi mystics respectively), the influence of Chevalier Rose-Croix of the Free Masons, the "Wise Knight" of the Polaire Brotherhood and White Eagle also denote a rose as a representation of God's beauty, providing a focus for allowing calmness and divine trust to enter into our being.[366] Rosicrucian doctrine is a combination of occultism, Hermeticism, alchemy of the human character, Brahmanical influences, Jewish (Kabbalah) and Christian mysticism, and Christian Gnosticism.[367]

Its original existence has been doubted, but as a relatively secret society, they would have preferred that view to protect members from the wrath of religious-politico dogmatic intolerance and persecution. The alchemy and mysticism associated with its "hypothetical" existence, however, was quite influential in Europe. In the 18th century, its membership started to decline but it resurged as part of a revival in the 19th century. Rosicrucian ways and ideas have found their way into 20th and 21st century Freemasonry doctrines and initiation rites. Count Michael Maier (1568–1622), whose mystical writings were studied and partially interpreted by Sir Isaac Newton, was an early influencing member of the original Rosicrucian Order.[368] Modern Rosicrucian Orders, such as the Rosicrucian Fellowship founded by Max Heindel in 1909, the Ancient and Mystical Order Rosae Crucis (AMORC) established in 1915 by H. Spencer Lewis and the Lectorium Rosicrucianum (LRC) founded by the brothers Zwier and Jan Leene in 1924, are still active today in the 21st century. The LRC was banned under Nazi occupation during World War II but survived the suppression under the pen names of Jan van Rijckenborgh and Catharose de Petri. There are several other current Rosicrucian orders and sects with sites throughout the world. From the Lectorium Rosicrucianum school, "...Rosicrucians are people who have heard this voice of the 'Other' within their deepest being. Through inner experience they know the Light of the Gnosis. They put themselves at the service of this 'Other' and give the Light more and more room in their lives. Thus, the birth of a new consciousness is possible which is led by the light of soul and spirit. This transforms man completely. In the Bible, this process is called 'born again out of water and spirit...'"[369]

The focus of true modern Rosicrucian Orders is inner development with an emphasis on intuition, the subconscious mind, independent thinking, self-esteem, self-confidence, psychic and inner spiritual growth.[370] In doing so, their teaching's aim is to help people access their divine nature and develop their potential as self-mystics – the rational art of knowing, raising the consciousness to a higher state and transcending the ego, even if for only glimpses. Valid Rosicrucian studies aid in developing a workable and practical philosophy of life and the inner peace that comes from understanding the nature of the universe and our relationship to it.[371]

—A*—

"For behold, the kingdom of God is within you." – Jesus Christ[372]

—*O—

8. The Bahá'í Faith – started about 1884.

As a relative newcomer to the scene but still instilling concepts of prior religions, the Bahá'í Faith emerged from the Shiite branch of Islam in the Persian region of the Middle East. It exalts all the world religions by focusing on their unifying commonalities with an emphasis on figuratively syncretic merging into monotheism. Similar to John the Baptist's foretelling of Jesus' coming, in 1844 a young prophet named Siyyid Ali-Muhammad (later titled "The Báb", meaning "the gate") announced the imminent coming of another messenger of God. The Báb, like John the Baptist, was executed by the dominant regional authority for his controversial proselytizing rhetoric. One of his followers, Mírzá Husayn-'Alí Núr, while being imprisoned and tortured for his beliefs, underwent a revelation that he was the messenger foretold by The Báb. Announcing his mission in 1863, he later became known as "Bahá'u'lláh", meaning the "Glory of God." Similar again to early Christianity, original followers of the Bahá'í Faith underwent persecution (which is still ongoing in the modern regions of Iran) and massacre since they were ignorantly considered to be deserters or apostates from Islam. Bahá'u'lláh himself was exiled to various regions in the Ottoman Empire, including Baghdad, Adrianople, and then the prison city of Akka (aka Acre). During his exile and house arrest, he wrote many religious works, most notably the *Kitáb-i-Aqdas*, the *Kitáb-i-Íqán* and the *Hidden Words*. During the last years of his life, he was allowed to live outside of Akka. Following Bahá'u'lláh's death in 1892, his son 'Abdu'l-Bahá took on leadership of the new faith and later, leadership was passed to Bahá'u'lláh's great-grandson, Shoghi Effendi.

A tenet of the Bahá'í Faith is that periodically God has and will continue to reveal his guidance to humanity through divine messengers, theophanies or manifestations in an incremental effort to further awaken our spiritual qualities, teach us and develop our moral consciousness. Abraham, Moses, Zoroaster, Buddha, Jesus Christ, Mohammad and Bahá'u'lláh are some examples of such intermediary representatives of divinity throughout history. Hindu doctrine and others put forth a similar ideology; that an aspect of the Lord appears in one form or another when there is a decline in true religious practice or when it is time for a paradigm shift of human behavior. According to the Bahá'í religious perspective, the next manifestation is not expected to appear for at least 1,000 Solar years (any time after 2863) within the revelations of Bahá'u'lláh's. But then again, God can always change his/her mind and perhaps send one earlier. Maybe this date was given as a ruse to test our perceptions and spiritual resolve. No one knows for sure when "the thief in the night" will make an appearance, but when he or she should arrive, whether sooner or later, will we be receptive enough to recognize him or her? Perhaps the "thief" will not be limited to one individual, but will appear in that stranger, neighbor or nurse who provided a compassionate hand.

—Δ*—

"The business of the Final Hour shall be accomplished in the twinkling of an eye, or in a shorter time." – *The Koran*[373]

—*O—

Just as prophets must correlate to the time period in which they live, each messenger or manifestation brings humanity a more advanced revelation that builds upon previous ones. Those who recognize and respond to the call of such legitimate messengers will transform into the next phase of spiritual evolution and enter the door to the future. The coming of each of these messengers is seen as a "Day of Judgment" to the adherents of the previous dominant or traditional religion, who may choose to accept the new messenger and develop their level of closeness to God (entering a "heaven" of belief), or denounce the new messenger and remain at their current plateau (within a "hell" of denial).[374]

—Λ*—

"For those who have denied and scorned our revelations the gates of heaven shall not be opened; nor shall they enter paradise until the camel shall pass through the eye of the needle." – *The Koran*[375]

—*Ω—

Such revelations render themselves as becoming a form of scripture if they resonate properly with the human consciousness of the time period and catalyze enough followers into recognizing the truth of their substance. Religion is seen as a tool which naturally progresses, improves and advances to continually transform the character of humanity closer to God. Similar to other religions, Bahá'ís view the basis of human purpose is to know, love and connect with God through prayer, reflection and beneficial service to those in need. The idea of world unification (a new world order implementing the embodiment of God's plan for humanity) that promotes unity and justice for all nations, races, creeds and classes is at the heart of Bahá'í teaching. Such a world order of political, social, scientific and spiritual advancement would be implemented, not by the enforcement of tyrannical individuals' fanciful perspective of a utopian ideology upon a population, but by the natural acceptance and embracement of civilization's diversity into the global consciousness of humanity. It would occur as a preferred option of pluralistic unity and autopoietic osmosis into a world church – an irresistible choice of spiritual awakening.

Shoghi Effendi, Guardian of the Bahá'í Faith from 1921 until his death in 1957, has stated that the structure, importance, implications, benefits and possibilities of the new world order cannot be understood at the current time, but that only through time will it become obvious.[376] It will not simply be the formation of broader political and economic alliances, but it will also encompass an evolutionary jump of each individual's genuine practice of love and compassion.[377] It will be denoted by a quantum rise in the spiritual understanding and wisdom by the masses to the next level of existence; it will be the era of Positive Empathetic

Equilibrium: the implementation of that which is fair and an emulating global culture of reciprocal altruism.

The Bahá'í Faith emphasizes the equality of men and women, yet at times, it promotes one over the other. A daughter's education is viewed as more important, and when necessary, should take precedent over a son's since a mother is considered the initial influencer and primary educator of children. This approach seems to fall apart when a father is left a widower. The overseeing authority of the religion, the Universal House of Justice, at the time this sentence was written, is restricted to only male membership. By not promoting women of worthy stature into the higher ranks, they are making the same mistakes of certain Essene orders, that of the Roman Catholic Church, and of certain restrictive Islamic practices. Full spiritual and social equality of the two sexes within the Bahá'í Faith does not imply sameness, so that gender distinction and differentiation are observed in certain areas of life.[378]

Although their ideology is not perfect, the Bahá'í community practices and follows rather progressive benevolent convictions for preserving and boosting humanity's place in the universe. They are well advanced in their humanitarian objectives and spiritual progress. It will be interesting to see how they embrace and recognize the next true manifestation upon his or her arrival and whether the next level of spiritual development is initially accepted or rejected. Humanity has a habit of at first resisting advances in religious direction and more efficient or alternate paths for communing with God. True prophets are often at first considered heretical madmen, outcasts and profane lunatics, before history judges them otherwise.

—A*—

"Fools deride Me when I descend in the human form. They do not know My transcendental nature as the Supreme Lord of all that is." – *Bhagavad-Gita*[379]

—*O—

9. Astronism – started about 2013.

This newly forming cult, revival or religion at least deserves honorable mention since whether it grows into stability or stagnates into self-focus is yet to be seen. It was founded by the self-proclaimed British philosopher Cometan, born as Brandon Reece Taylor (aka Brandon Taylorian) on July 1, 1998, and consists as a combination of a religion, philosophy and political ideology.[380] Appearing to be a rebellion from the founder's Roman Catholic upbringing, Astronism partakes and draws upon humanity's ancient worship of the stars and the desire to become a spacefaring species. Its foundational text (the *Omnidoxy*) was first published in 2019 and is further divided into twelve disquisitions among over 3,300 lengthy pages.[381] It appears to be a living document (subject to continued updates) and contains messages relating to the cosmos. According to the Cometan, the revelations of the *Omnidoxy*'s contents took place over a period of exactly seven years, from July 1, 2013 to July 1, 2020. The symbol of Astronism is the Vendox and consists of an open book surrounded by twelve stars – most likely representing each of the disquisitions or possibly also correlation to the dozen stars as described by Joseph in *Genesis*.[382] If the Cometan keeps himself benevolent and balanced in both the secular and the divine, properly merging delusions of the subconscious into the reality of the conscious, then his natal religion has a good chance of recognition and gathering a following based on its futuristic attractiveness. I would encourage the Cometan to read up on Astrogeographia or *The Urantia Book* to realize his perspectives are not unique and repeat a common theme within the human psyche.

• • • •

CONCLUSION TO INSIGHTS Into Earth's Primary Religions

Beyond the current full scope of this book, there are many other philosophies, philosophies of religion (i.e., Theosophy, Anthroposophy, Secular Humanism), religious orders, sects and schisms that have sprouted forth within the past couple centuries. They are based on those sensing a trend or pulse building within the global consciousness of humanity from a resonance with the universal consciousness. From Wicca and neo-paganism (such as the Supreme Council of Ethnic Hellenes) to the various extraterrestrial-driven religions (UFO Religions), there are elements that are true and elements which are false within each of them. Some are truer than others; some are falser than others. Approach any new religion, philosophy, cult or sect with healthy curiosity and caution, but always retain your divine right of self-thought, freedom to question ethics in search of truth, and ability to freely enter or leave such religious congregations or philosophical orders without exploitative consequences. Every mythology, every philosophy and every religion are tools for accessing the universe's mind. Some tools are better or may be preferred more than others, but when we use any of them properly and with healthy love, they have the propensity to build and latch onto something much greater than our individual selves.

—Δ*—

"Do not force your ideas or religious beliefs upon another, for there are many different paths to the sacred Altar. You have chosen your path: the brother by your side has chosen his path; respect it." – White Eagle[383]

—*O—

After having read some of the history and insights into the more common religions, you may be asking yourself, what if there was just one world religion? Well, what if there was just one football team, one flavor of ice cream or only one place to go for vacation? What it there was just one bicycle design, one automobile model or one country? The world would be awfully boring with just one religion, one football team, one flavor of ice cream, one vacation resort, one type of bicycle, one car model and one country. Without diversity, there would be no interplay and wonderment would cease. No religion is 100% perfect and no path or branch has all the knowledge, all the answers and all the goodness. That is why there are many paths for us to choose from. Just as there are many sports to becoming and athlete, there are many religions for reaching enlightenment – it is all about the training. It is the sum of all the true paths put together that will result in the highest truth. The greatest reverence one can show to Allah/God is to respect the multiple paths (belief systems) available to reach him/her and to respect those that follow such different and/or similar paths. There are several true paths to Allah, just with different scenery to be encountered along the way. This I can assure you, no approach to God is paved with hatred. On the contrary, hatred, violence and intolerance are in the opposite direction of the Almighty. A true spiritual being respects the religious path that others choose to identify with, provided it is a path of peace and non-violent pursuit towards the godhead/God/Allah. God embraces all true paths used to reach him/her and a true spiritual being respects all the paths to Allah. We are all treated equal by the eyes of God and all true religious paths paved with love, peace and non-violence have legitimacy.

—Λ*—

"Heaven cannot be made up of people of one religion only. It needs people from many different religions." – Emanuel Swedenborg[384]

—*Ω—

Religion and spirituality have been expressed in the modern communication format of fictional media through television and film that often contains non-fictional elements – the figurative *Gospel of McHale's Navy* or the mythology of *Rudolph The Red-Nosed Reindeer* could even be a source of inspiration. There are even religious plots within the futuristic fictional *Star Trek* series,[385] first debuting in 1966 and presenting storylines much aligned with Gnostic views and beliefs. Ironically, the series producer (Gene Roddenberry) was considered an atheist – or was this just another accusative misnomer and misapplied label put forth by the Orthodoxy?[386] The series creatively and ingeniously expressed the pursuit of advanced civil rights, one's search for their soul, the pros and cons of technology and what it can do to either hinder or save humanity. In the near future, I believe *Star Trek* will not appear so fictional after all.

South Park, an animated series about the idiotic behavior of adults as seen through the naive and innocent eyes of young children, has covered the past, the future and current events with a creative edge delving into raunchiness. First debuting in 1997, the show has presented episodes that comically mock some religions, their prophets and the fallibility and frailty of their deities. Risking public outcry and uptight religious fanatics, the cartoon's creators were willing to show a perspective of parody in some of the seemingly absurd aspects of faith.[387] Granted, the cartoon is reserved for mature audiences, but in those religious attacks of humor, they were mocking humanity more than their beliefs. Who says that the universe, the cosmos, Jehovah, doesn't have a sense of comedy? Only those at the very bottom levels of illumination speak of such false rumors. Allah/God has a sense of humor and even laughs at his own follies. Being secure enough to laugh at our own follies is a sign of spiritual wisdom. If one cannot laugh at some of the follies of their own religions, they shouldn't be laughing at the faults of anyone else's. I'm pretty sure God and Satan were both chuckling a bit while watching the imitations of their characters in *South Park* and enjoying their "celebrity roasts."

We also come upon Festivus, that "fake" holiday against the commercialization and consumerism becoming ingrained with spiritual celebrations. Made popular and expanded upon during a comical 1997 *Seinfeld* episode titled *The Strike*,[388] it originated from Daniel Lawrence O'Keefe (author of *Stolen Lightning: The Social Theory of Magic*), with his family about three decades earlier. Occurring on December 23rd, the rebellious celebration reminds us of how crazy our consumerism can become during the Holiday seasons and the need to step back and reflect upon family and more non-secular matters, in a humorous sort of way.

In the futuristic comical satire of *Futurama*, Bender the robot discovers that it's not so easy playing God and it was the fictional character of Professor Farnsworth who tells us that most video tapes were damaged due to the Second Coming of Christ in the year 2443.[389] I guess the savior's "magnetism" was too powerful for those antiquated digital storage tapes. Following in the religious exploration of Peter Griffin, the bumbling fictional dad in the cartoon show of *Family Guy* who decides to start his own "First United Church of the Fonz", which is further based on a fictional character from the show *Happy Days*, we may also find ourselves searching for something different due to our own spiritual disenchantment.[390] Yes, Arthur Fonzarelli could perform mechanical miracles such as blindly re-assembling a motorcycle and turning on electrical circuits with the tap of his fist, but he's never been blamed for earthquakes, tsunamis, wars, scourges and other mass destructions credited to the God of the *Old Testament*. If Fonzie were to have been around a few centuries ago, he too would have been burned at the stake for the "bewitching" power within the snaps of his fingers. If the tenets of the Church of the Fonz are based on love and friendship, should a mature and rational God become jealous of a congregation worshipping the Fonz? For the Lord to be jealous of the Fonz? That's just outright comical! The worshipping and implementing of love, in all its healthy forms, is the same as worshipping the divine spirit.

—A*—

"Just as God is infinite, so too, are the number of true paths available to reach him or her." - AO

—*O—

The greater one's awareness of other religious paths, the stronger becomes one's own connection to divinity. There is a degree of validity within all the true religions that comes from that framework of an eternal religion. This does not necessarily mean that one should or should not be a practitioner of multiple religions, but rather, one should expand their spirituality through reading of other religious texts and/or watching or respectfully engaging in the celebrations, pageantry or rituals of other paths. In pursuing a belief system, common sense and sound reason should take precedent over religious hairsplitting and fanaticism. Upon discovering the similarities and differences, one who is on the proper course towards enlightenment and/or a true follower of God/Allah/Krsna/Jehovah will find their own religious path being reinforced while developing a healthy tolerance towards the traditions and practices of other paths. Faith is the plectrum for stimulating and advancing the mind – it is the panacea engine and starting point by which all the great religions rely upon. With it, one connects to the metaphysical mystery of our existence. Without it, one remains lost, disconnected and ruled by chance alone. Perhaps humanity's greatest frailty is a wavering resistance to accepting God's existence in all noble forms, hindering our growth as a species and causing us not to recognize miracles of love, healing and benevolent opportunity.

—Δ*—

"When we become one with God, we actually become several with many." - AO

—*O—

Many religions and their sects have specific holidays (holy days) geared around significant annual celebrations, commemorations and memorials. They also have geographical locations in reference to planet Earth that are considered sacred or holy sites relevant to founders and saints. Some religions call for or recommend a pilgrimage (religious journey or migration) of its followers to the sacred sites for providing a spiritual retreat, talismanic reset, physical and mental healing, or focal reflective maintenance of the soul. Be it a mosque, a shrine, a chapel, a temple, a cathedral, a synagogue, a church, a room, a house, a hill, a mountain, a cave, a cavern, a river, a tree, a boulder, a tomb, a building or a monument, the specific location has significance to the religion's birth, development and growth. A truly advanced spiritual being feels comfortable in all such places and further recognizes that every point in the universe is sacred. Every point in the universe is its center and the entire universe is hallowed space.

Having read this and the prior chapter, you have been exposed to some of the similarities and nuances of various religious paths. Religion was never meant to become an unhealthy obsession nor a fanatical transference from a bad addiction. It was never meant to be about excessive control or a means to justify murder, negative exploitation, intolerance nor self-righteousness. Religion was meant to be a mechanism by which to reconnect to the godhead, that universal consciousness that permeates all, in terms that humanity can somewhat comprehend. It has evolved into several mechanisms, some of which contain methods and practices that are more efficient and effective than others at reaching the godhead. We can approach and worship Allah through the ways of silence or through the action of song and dance – soulful or enticing music that celebrates humanity is not <u>haram</u>. It is the path most suited to our individual needs that we should select and travel to return home to God.[391] Much like the plush toy animals or dolls of our childhood, we can love them all but there may be one or a few that are our favorites. It does not matter to the Lord, however, which is the most efficient and effective, as long as such methods condone a process of peace. In the eyes of God all paths of true religions and their phylogenetic network will lead home to divinity. The path that you walk as a practitioner of religion will determine the truth of your relationship with divinity.

—Λ*—

"Religions of all history are sewn together by the secret inner golden thread, for there is no religion higher than Truth." – Joseph[392]

—˙Ω—

Every culture's bioregionalism develops and incorporates its own unique yet similar mystique for communing with the divine. In doing so, it produces a feeling of security and connections into the depths of its local inhabitants, who then carry, spread and intertwine those connections as they emigrate across the globe and beyond. No matter what geographical religious group you belong to, be it Indonesian Muslims, Mexican Catholics, British Protestants, Orthodox Russians, Israeli Jews or Indian Hindus, do not think you are better than others or more entitled to God's grace because of the particular religious path that you follow or religious tool that you use. The chosen people of God are based on what is in the fiber of their beings, not on their conducted customs and rituals nor the religious affiliation or "club" to which they belong. Do you follow a path that seeks to improve the conditions for all of humanity, only a select elite or "chosen" group, or one that implements violence to achieve its goals? I can assure you, any path of violence or indiscriminate intolerance is not a path to God/Allah. As mentioned elsewhere in this book, religion is a tool of humanity (and perhaps other sentient beings) used to connect to God. Just as no tool is perfect for all applications (although a Swiss Army knife and a Leatherman® make a bold attempt), no religion is perfect for all situations. Although humanity profits from the diversity of spiritual paths, it is the commonality among the various religions which excels the soul. Allah/Jehova does not need religion; it is advanced intelligent sentient beings such as ourselves that are dependent on religion as a means of being touched with divine power to unleash greatness. Although our longing for the Beloved is equal to him longing for us, God does not need you, but you need him.[393] In the end, despite what a particular doctrine may say, do you really believe that the divine, all-knowing and semi-perfect personification of the cosmos referred to as God, really cares which religious path you chose to follow in order to reach him or her? The Lord is going to judge us on: 1) whether we added love or hate to the world; 2) how we curbed or carried out our aggressions; and, 3) how we treated others and the surrounding universe. It is through love that the seeker is taken to God and every spiritual path leads the seeker to the truth that can only be found within.[394]

Chapter 6
Our Body – A Temporary Cocoon For The Soul

"I ONLY ASK OF YOU, Oh Supreme Consciousness of the Universe, to keep reminding me of your presence." – Prayer Of The Forgetful, AO

• • • •

WE ARE ALL PACKETS of thought originally created from God and temporarily contained within a semi-fragile carbon-based container. This container, our body, is composed of many different molecular arrangements designed to trigger and operate in the physical realm through electro-chemical responses and interactions. There are some who view our existence as just random arrangements of the amino acids (21±1) making up our bodies' proteins. Connected as a result of chance encounters of molecules within a water bath, they formed within the primordial soup. That may be true from a limited perspective, but we must always go a step further. What hand brought the beakers of chemicals together in the first place? What spoon was stirring the broth of life? What initiation of action decided that our liver cells would have a better chance of survival if they hooked up with our spleen cells to form a much larger and complex creature? Who wrote the DNA programming in the first place to instruct our brain cells to cooperate with our heart cells for the good of the same organism? Who is that ancient being that exists within each of us?

Modern human theories about the universe state that all the energies that we can currently have the capability to measure (matter and electromagnetic radiation), were initiated by the divine through the spark of creation (the "Big Bang") and then further morphed within the fusion furnaces of stars. The chemical elements were devised within those celestial incubators and sent forth by explosive copulation to seed the fields of space. According to current scientific agreement, the remnants of exploding stars spread forth as nebulae and then coalesced into new stars, planets and moons. From this coalescence, our current home planet, Earth, morphed forth from materials orbiting our sun. The particulates and molecules that make up our physical beings came from the soils and fluids provided by Mother Earth. In essence, our physical being is the manipulation of remnants from exploded stars – we are a projection through time of our sun's essence and avatars made of ancient stardust. We are the result of supernova fragments recombining into higher order configurations who have gained the ability to further manipulate stardust (atoms and molecules) into configurations of our desire.[395] But what matrix of thought chose to reconfigure and combine those elemental particles into atoms, molecules, compounds and eventually life, incorporating a part of itself into every creation? Is our coming into being purely based on chance and randomly sporadic events? Is the universe full of accidents or is it an abundance of predictable fairness? Or is there a deeper order beyond serendipity, an *Unus Mundus* to our existence?[396] Composed of atoms and molecules, why has it taken modern science to prove we are distant avatars of Earth and Sun, when ancient religions have been trying to deliver that message to us for millennia? Humanity's ancient worship of the rising and setting sun and its cycles (homage to the Sun-God or Sun-Goddess) has legitimacy in the sense that the enormous fusion furnace is an earlier basis of our beginnings. In a way, our quest for knowledge about our home planet, the moon, the sun, the distance stars and ourselves is a form of idol worship considered so "forbidden" by the controlling and suppressing scriptural orthodoxy found amidst the *Old Testament*.[397]

Upon morphing and growing into human form from single cells to fetus to infant to toddler to child to adolescent to adult, some of us seem to lose the recollection of the origin and source from where we came. Reconnecting to this source is done through seeking Allah by applying the principles of love denoted among all the true religions. As packets of thought originally created from God and temporarily contained within carbon-based containers constructed primarily of protein, lipids, water and electrochemical interactions, our material body is merely a temporary vessel to harbor the soul as it evolves during its stay within the material realm of existence. It is a container acting as a permeable barrier between the core of our being and the supreme human cosmic consciousness of the universe or Supersoul.

Religions instruct us that the Universal Being pulsates its life-radiating power into form, the effect of which we recognize in the myriad of its manifestations as a larger intelligence forever proclaiming its handiwork.[398] They further teach us that the core of our being, our psyche, our soul, is an autonomous life-force that initiates as it enters at conception, gestation or birth, continues to develop throughout the various stages of life (growth, budding, flowering, wilting, death, decay), and then permanently releases itself from that body soon after brain activity has ceased. The end and beginning stages of life are usually much shorter than the other stages and the middle stages can overlap and repeat. Does the body take on a soul, does a soul take on a body, or is it a combination of both? From the *Gospel of Thomas*, Jesus Christ said, "If the flesh came into being because of the spirit, it is a wonder. But if the spirit came into being because of the body, it is a wonder of wonders."[399] Another perspective is that a soul enters into a developing fetus like the way an operating system is loaded into a computer's hardware. The body is a replication of cells, programmed for specific tissue and organ functions, but it requires a soul to ignite it into an entity of sentience. Once the soul starts to unfold with the developing body, it becomes our core. It is within the body that we must develop our core through the various methods of truth such as charity, virtue, and love written in the relevant passages of the great religious scriptures. The better we take care of and maintain the body, the more earthly time we have to develop the spirit and contribute to the cosmic consciousness. Although the very root of our core is a form of energy that is eternal, we have a finite period of time existing within this dimensional framework of physical form in which to refine it. According to Emanuel Swedenborg, "Only material beings in the physical world are differentiated from one another by the spans of space and time. In the spiritual world, entities are differentiated in terms of 'states' of moral and spiritual development and perfection measured ultimately by their proximity to or remoteness from God."[400] When the material body can no longer maintain itself as a barrier, the core is released to travel freely as the soul within the spirit realm. Some individuals, through meditation, purity of thought and the trials of visions,[401] may have developed the ability to soar within the realms of the universal consciousness and return back to the body. Through our ignorance, this was once looked upon as being something evil or a form of devilish witchcraft. It is nothing more than swimming in that sea of spirit and thought which surrounds us all.

The core of our being is contained within the physical vessel of our body. Upon our passing into the next realm, the core becomes our soul. The core is our being's essence within the physical body; the soul is our being's essence after having left the physical body. The core is temporary, the soul is eternal. Consider the term "meteorite" which refers to a rock-like projectile hurtling from outer space into the Earth's atmosphere. That same rock-like projectile hurtling through space beyond the reaches of Earth's atmosphere is referred to as an "asteroid." They are both the same object, but depending on the medium being traversed, the name is either "meteorite" or "asteroid." Consider molten rock here on Earth or another planet. When it is below the surface, it is called "magma", when it is above the surface, it is called "lava." So too, with our "core" and our "soul" which are that part of our awareness which is not of the body. They are that part of us which pulls out of time during the absorption of good music, poetry, flowers, scenery and when engaging in deep meditation, aspirations or spiritual illumination.[402] The core is our individuation while in this physical realm, the soul is our individuation in the next realm. The term "an old soul" refers to someone who retains much of their essence from realm to realm. A child showing advanced behavior in how they reflect upon their own existence and how they view, interpret and interact with the world is indicative of them having an older soul.

Our state of being is very much like a vessel with a semi-permeable seal floating in an ocean of universal thought. The outer membrane of the vessel is generated by the functions of the material body and shuts down upon our physical death. The inner substance is the core. The surrounding sea is the Universal Mind of Humanity and the Supreme Universal Mind. The Universal Mind of Humanity is ubiquitous while the Supreme Universal Mind is both ubiquitous and omnipotent. There are also universal minds of other sentient beings that are under the umbrella of the Supreme Universal Mind. All the universal minds are subsets of the Supreme Universal Mind.

During our earthly lifetime, this membrane sometimes becomes hardened and less permeable to the surrounding sea of the Universal Minds. Some individuals' membranes become so hardened and choked due to following paths of anger, hatred, greed and lies, that their connections with God/Allah become clogged or tarnished. Their membrane does not grow because nothing is penetrating to expand its internal borders – its filters and pores become clogged. For those who follow a path of evil and negative exploitation, when their physical body shuts down upon death, the membrane can no longer be supported and sustained. It dissolves into the abyss upon physical death exposing whatever is left of their core. The remnant of their spiritual core, while transitioning into the soul, no longer has a border shielding it from the onslaught of justice – karma starts its rebound upon them. The emotions and thoughts of prior souls, the evil doers' victims in life, swoop in and bombards what little is left. Every pain and injustice that they caused to others will be returned to them tenfold. This bombardment is the judgment mentioned in many of the scriptures.

—Λ*—

"Each soul is the hostage of its own deeds." – *The Koran*[403]

• • • •

"FOR IN THE WAY YOU judge, you will be judged; and by your standard of measure, it will be measured to you." – *New Testament*[404]

• • • •

"HE THAT COMMITS SIN commits it against his own soul." – *The Koran*[405]

• • • •

"WHOEVER DOES AN ATOM'S weight of good shall see it, and whoever does an atom's weight of evil shall see it also." – *The Koran*[406]

• • • •

"HOW PEOPLE TREAT YOU is their karma; how you react is yours." – Dr. Wayne Dyer[407]

• • • •

"ONCE YOU START TO LOVE the universe, you will notice it starting to love you back."– AO

• • • •

"BE NOT DECEIVED; GOD is not mocked: for whatsoever a man soweth, that shall he also reap." – *New Testament*[408]

—*Ω—

There are others who maintain the permeability of their membranes through purity of thought and action. Through their love, integrity, kindness and choice of positive actions the permeability of their membrane is maintained which allows the osmosis of the cosmic consciousness into their core. The membrane thus expands, and their core grows. The Supreme Universal Mind, God, can always see through this membrane and witnesses all, but we cannot always sense beyond its borders. When the membranes of the doers of goodness dissolve into the abyss, they will encounter a loving welcoming that will sweep in and fill their souls with joy and ecstasy. Refer to Chapter 18 for more on the expectations of what is to be encountered upon our physical death.

There is that elusive boundary between the secular and the spiritual in which a moment becomes equivalent to a millennium. As beings currently meant to dwell primarily in the physical realms, we should only occasionally venture into these zones. It is the subliminal transitioning between the earthly and the heavenly that triggers our connection to something eternal. The face of God is both beautiful and terrifying to gaze upon. This can be taken in both the figurative and literal sense. Sophia's beauty can be so overwhelming that our limited human conception initially defaults to terror in trying to process it, yet she is the lover and inspiration of the good and the wise in all of us.[409] With our cognitive levels still being relatively underdeveloped, going further beyond and dwelling within the pure realm of the spiritual would disrupt our identifying sense of reality and is better reserved for angels and the afterlife.

Encased within a material body for the duration of our life, spiritual vision comes from imagination. It is the engine by which desire or a quest establishes its form and can be viewed as the maternally creative side of the masculine spirit.[410] It was William Blake who first articulated that by perceiving the word imagination, we gain a rich knowledge while pulling ideas into the material realm.[411] Imagination is not to be confused with make-believe, fantasy, fanaticism, superstition or fiction, for these items often form the basis of unwarranted fear. Imagination is the mental formation and framework for putting thoughts into reality and drawing truths into this realm. It is also the logic through which we process the acceptance of faith. Faith is about rising above the things we understand and the accepting of things we do not fully understand. Without imagination we cannot have faith, for all faith comes from imagination.[412] Does this, therefore, mean that God is a figment of our imagination? Is an afterlife of heaven or hell also a figment of our imagination? Is our existence, a figment of our imagination? Is our nontangible government, an organism of politics, a figment of our imagination? The key word here is "figment" which acts as a negative qualifier. It changes the meaning of the word imagination into something that is false. Did the space program and sending humans to the Moon and eventually Mars start out as "figments" of our imaginations? Did the visionary magic of Walt Disney's amusement and entertainment industry start out as a "figment" of imagination? Did the Golden Gate Bridge of San Francisco or the Eiffel Tower of Paris (both initially protested as aesthetic eyesores but now accepted as wondrous skyline additions and emblems of their respective cities) start out as "figments" of imagination? Did the

Great Pyramid of Giza or the Burj Khalifa in Dubai start out as "figments" of imagination? How could items considered as "false" imagination be so very real today? In the same sense, it is the "true" or "real" part of our imagination that creates the mental circuitry, our faith, for connecting with God – responding with a personal midrash to interpret our divine story. How then, do we shift from a reliance on faith and hope to a solidity of gnosis or an understanding that permanently awakens the consciousness of humanity to the subconscious of divinity? Your continued reading and study of this little book as you scroll through its contents may trigger that answer, for our magnetism towards God is also the same force that draws him or her towards us.

Chapter 7
Is God Fallible?

"GOD DOES NOT TAKE HIMSELF as seriously as you may think. She smiles and laughs at her own antics and follies." – AO

• • • •

GOD IS NOT ALWAYS PERFECT and we are not perfect. What Almighty essence would be foolish enough to put their trust and the writing of their biography into the hands and minds of us mere imperfect mortal human beings? The fact that the Creator relies on the pen of men and women for interpretation of his or her thoughts is enough to convince me of the Lord's fallibility. God does make mistakes in this material realm, but he/she works to correct them.

The sentences within the prior paragraph are not blasphemy. I repeat again, the starting paragraph of this chapter and the chapter title are not blasphemy. People are not perfect and God still loves us. God is not perfect and we should still love God. We can love an occasional imperfect God all the more, just as he loves us through and despite our imperfections as human beings. Being all powerful, Allah is capable of both perfection and imperfection. According to the *Old Testament* (the foundational beginnings of Judaic, Christian and Islamic doctrine), every human being is created in God's image. If God were perfect, humans would also be perfect since we were created in his/her image. We are not perfect and our creator is not perfect. This does not mean we are not enormously loved by the Lord, but quite the contrary. God loves us so much, that he/she is willing to be imperfect to allow us to be closer to him/her.

The Yahweh of yesterday was perhaps viewed as being perfect,[413] but the God of today understands that he too has his faults.

If we are created in God's image, or perhaps in the image of Sophia or the Demiurge, why then are we a dirty animal that oozes sweat from our glands, fatty oils from our pores, soil from our orifices and made as a creature which starts to smell if going too long without showering or bathing? I'm sure our insides are much more odorous than our outsides. Why then does our digestive tract mimic a worm, extending from mouth to anus as it sucks nutrients from decaying organic matter? Without our exterior appendages of arms, hands legs and feet, would we be left to writhe along on our bellies? What creature are we from brain to genitalia? Being of "worm" do we have the potential of morphing into a "butterfly"? If early life has worm or serpent like beginnings, then string shaped life having formed on other planets would also have the potential to evolve into advanced intelligent sentient beings remaining either in their initial cylindrical shape or becoming humanoid-like as well. We should not be ashamed of our given bodies for it was not ours to choose; it was assigned or granted upon us. We don't need to apologize to the creator for our human form, but we do need to work on improving its character. Within and surrounding our wormlike interior, however, evidence presents that there exists a being not of molecule, but of thought, emotion, consciousness and soul. We can strengthen our wormlike interior, the supporting framework of calcium columns, beams and struts (bones), and the exterior appendages by physical activity, resistive exercise and endurance training. We can educate, develop and refine that intertwined being through reading, curiosity, reflection and study. Our wormlike mass is certainly finite and mortal, but that co-existing being of thought may or may not be mortal, the nature of which we do not know for sure. For that being of thought and consciousness could have the ability to exist independent of the fluid-filled mass it was first connected with, and eventually find itself in a future state of incorporeal awareness.

Life is the touch of God's breath upon matter and energy, inflating it into new forms and levels of sentience. When we torture animals, it is called cruelty; when we slaughter them for food, it is called survival. How do we separate one from the other? Why then would a perfect God create creatures that rely on the consumptive destruction of other creatures for sustenance? Why would a creative artist make living, feeling sculptures that eat its other living, feeling sculptures? Our planet and perhaps others, consists of organisms that consume vegetation (herbivores), animal proteins (carnivores) and both (omnivores) for calories and nutrients. From warm-blooded mammals to cold-blooded reptiles, such life form consumers are often equipped with specialized hunting skills and digestive tracts. Many have claws and sharp teeth for the tearing and shearing of flesh and muscle or with filters (baleen) for capturing an abundance of smaller prey (krill). While the largest known Earth creature, the blue whale, feeds on some of the smallest crustaceans, in polar opposite, microscopic bacteria feed on the decaying cell material of larger animals and plants.

All creatures seem to exhibit a desire for self-preservation and don't typically voluntarily jump to be on one's dinner plate or to become a stuffed trophy hung on a wall or mounted and displayed upon a pedestal. Is it because all creatures feel some degree or level of pain alerting it to take available action for self-preservation? Is this level of felt pain dependent on the complexity of its nervous system? Does the degree of a creature's sentience determine if it is acceptable to be the consumable prey of humans? What measuring gage or scale should be used to quantify the amount of sentience that a given creature has? Is it based on exceeding a certain threshold quantity of active neurons within its brain or central nerve bundle? Is the degree of our sentience base on the processing power and/or size of our dorsolateral prefrontal cortex? The strongest indicator of sentient intelligence seems to be based on the level at which one can abstractly visualize themselves in the other person's shoes, regardless if they choose to do so.

Should advance intelligent sentient beings be devouring the components of lower sentient creatures? Is it ethically permissible to consume ants, grasshoppers, water striders and worms but not cows, dogs, dolphins or octopuses? Are we to feel a mouthful of culpability every time we chew on the meat or organs of other animals? Do other predators feel a degree of guilt or sympathy when they kill other animals? These perplexing questions were parodied when the hungry crew of Planet Express (a fictional cartoon intergalactic delivery service owned by Professor Farnsworth) came upon an addictively tasteful delicacy that was more than just random proteins.[414] The indigenous people of the Americas often dedicated time to ceremonially thank, appreciate, celebrate and worship the slaughtered animal that gave up its life to feed the tribe.

Whether these rituals were out of guilt, an expression of gratitude, or a means of justifying God's cycle of predator and prey, I'm sure the individual animal would have preferred life over symbolic reverence. In our industrialized slaughterhouses, the bottlenecks, inefficiencies and cost implications that would be created by taking the time for such religious rituals for each individual creature sacrificed for our sustenance would amount to mass starvation. However inhumane those industrialized slaughterhouses are, they still seem less cruel than the alleged cracking open of a monkey's skull while it is restrained in place to devour its living and active brains.[415]

Jainist monks refrain from killing or eating any creature, no matter how large or small. Some go to the extremes of wearing filtered masks over their mouths for minimizing consumption of air-borne bacteria and viruses, whether considered life or not. Many Hindus and Buddhist also follow a practice of not consuming the meat, fats and bones of other creatures. The ending of the life of another creature for consumption of its nutrients, protein and caloric content is still an act of violence and a conundrum. All of humanity may not yet be able or ready to answer such moral questions, but they should at least be considered. Until such time when the technology of food replicators (i.e., a Santa Claus machine) is able to adequately mimic the proteins, amino acids, energy content, scents, aromas and flavors of dishes made of animals, and fisheries and slaughterhouses are able to transition their staff to other industries, consumption of animals by humans will continue as an ethically questionable consequence of energy transference.

The lower form of God seems to have forced and enslaved this planet's life to eat itself as a means of consuming blends of organic compounds alchemically forged over time from and by the energy of the Sun. Perhaps giving humanity the ability to evolve its morality and reassess its role in the food chain was divinity's mistake, but either way, we are called upon to help moderate it and then ultimately correct it. Until every animal and creature become a vegetarian, we are left with the inherited sin of slaughtering lives for the sake of our sustenance. In the interim, our predatory right to quickly access the necessary proteins and amino acids for survival seems to trump our prey's right to life.

According to *The Book of Genesis* (found within both the *Old Testament* and the *Torah* and most likely drawn from the earlier roots of Mesopotamian and Sumerian stories), the Lord had to rest on the seventh day after creating heaven and earth.[416] He/she was tired (and perhaps even sleep deprived) from creating the world and the universe in only six days. Would a Supreme Being or consciousness require rest? Does this not show a weakness or fallibility since Allah also succumbed to the human need for rest? If the Lord were infallible, he/she would not become tired. God seems to have both superior and inferior natures.[417] This notion on the fallibility of Yahweh is not to belittle the Supreme Consciousness, but rather to relate a better understanding of who we are within the realm of this universal and divine entity. Think how easy it is for us to relate to divinity and retain hope when our energy reserves are fully charged and how challenging it can be when we are worn down and lacking in sleep. Those internal demons and shadows seem to froth forth more so when we are tired. The strength of our spiritual connection may wax and wane depending on the degree of our mental fatigue, physical tiredness and the circumstances that we find ourselves in. It is difficult to feel spiritual when we are overly drained, stressed, worried, undervalued or disappointed just as any doubts in ourselves seem to magnify when we are in need of rest and sleep – identifying the specific label of our emotional states does much to produce actionable ways to deal with them. Like God and as human beings, we are not always perfect and may falter in putting forth the best of our Atman (or Atmon to coin a new word). There will be days when our divine connection seems to be off or dimmed, but rest assured, these are merely the pauses of the curtain temporarily closing between acts of the show and the lulls prior to the next upward leap.

—Λ*—

"Fatigue makes cowards of us all." – Vince Lombardi[418]

• • • •

"YET THOSE WHO WAIT for the Lord will gain new strength; They will mount up with wings like eagles; They will run and not get tired; They will walk and not become weary." – *Isaiah*[419]

—*Ω—

There are things that happen in this universe that seem to have no visible metaphysically justifiable reason; the loss and death of a loved one, the suffering encountered by the injured, sick or dying. The potential that we, too, may suffer just prior to leaving this physical realm or that our death will be instantaneously painless. The deoxyribonucleic acid (DNA) in our body can become corrupted and then decide to divide, multiply and disperse in a way that causes harm to our organs, rebelling against our body by refusing to allow mutated cells to die at the appropriate time – we call such growths tumors or cancer. Viruses can hijack our cells, tricking them into becoming replicators until our immune system either catches up, or that we should die before the race is finished. There may be reasons for such pangs, but we, as humans can't always see or comprehend them. This can make us sad, angry, bitter, frustrated or even apathetic towards the Lord. Allah understands our skepticism and our doubt. He knows that we sometimes feel like there is no meaning to our existence. She knows that we sometimes doubt her existence and the value of ours; especially when we are fatigued, drained and exhausted. Perhaps all these painful items occur as a means for developing our empathy towards others. Perhaps it is the necessary resistance needed to give us a sense of meaning. Perhaps to understand the importance of love, we must be exposed to suffering. It forces us to an awareness of our commonality of suffering, the value of life and our capability to ease the pain of others and within ourselves. God understands our confusion. It is very much like a teacher or parent presenting a lesson that one may not understand for years to come. God does the same thing to teach us about forgiveness, letting go, moving on and allowing for positive change. Sometimes he/she lets us fall so we can grow (like the Phoenix rising from the ashes), to transmute from the old self into the new self, to raise our consciousness to a higher vibrational state of existence. Some of us do, and some of us don't.

—Δ*—

"The lips of wisdom are closed, except to the ears of understanding."–
The Kybalion[420]

—*O—

The story of humanity's first parents being tempted by the "Serpent of Darkness" and falling from a primal state of innocence and bliss through eating a forbidden fruit, appears in fractured Babylonian tablets long before the Old Testament scriptures were ever written.[421] According to the primitive God of the Hebrew-Christian scriptures, both male and female humans were created in the first chapter of *Genesis*,[422] and yet, they seem to have been created again in the second chapter.[423] Was the earlier mention of human creation just a prelude of what was to come, or is there a chronological glitch in the story of creation due to the fallibility of human authorship? Paul Wallis, among others dabbling in a Gnostic approach, examines and dissects the discrepancies found in *Genesis*. In his book, *Escaping From Eden*, he even goes as far to suggest the influence of beings from other planets and/or giants – speculative interpretations that may have more truth to them than we are willing to admit. The science fiction franchise based on the movie *Stargate* draws its narrative from aspects of similar premises.[424] Wallis is willing to wonder how many times our planet's civilizations have been erased and how many cataclysms and reboots of history remain submerged as residual remnants in our collective subconscious.[425] His questions about whether *Genesis* is a creation story or a re-emergence story, such as recovery from the Younger Dryas,[426] certainly have a degree of validity. Making the stretch that some legends of mythology are more than just for campfire storytelling, he views them as misinterpreted historical accuracies, the remnants and motifs of real ancient memories spread across cultures.[427] Thank goodness he is able to put forth such conjectures in this modern age without having to undergo a trial for "heresy" and fear of being burnt at the stake if found guilty.

There seems to be several chronological "glitches" elsewhere within the *Old Testament*, indicating thoughts that are more human than divine.[428] Referring again to *Genesis*, God provides all fruit to mankind to partake of in chapter one,[429] and then takes one of them away in chapter two.[430] Is that not like an adult taking back a gift that they have already given to a child? After Adam (aka Albion) was told not to by the Lord God, the original humans eat fruit from the Tree of Knowledge, causing man and woman to become aware of good and evil.[431] Eve did not deliberately go to the tree in the middle of Garden of Eden to eat its forbidden fruit. She was tempted by the serpent (Satan in disguise). In her innocence she trusted the word of another of God's creatures over those of God himself. She then shared the fruit from the Tree of Knowledge with her mate, Adam, and they both became wise.[432] They became like the Lord, knowing the difference between good and evil. God was angry with mankind for eating of the forbidden fruit and cursed and drove them out of the plentiful Garden of Eden. That one mistake of eating the mystical fruit seems to have condemned us all for eternity, yet it was the dawn of our recognition of consciousness.[433] Yahweh was even fearful that humanity would gain everlasting life by eating the fruit of that other tree in the Garden of Eden, the Tree of Life, yet he never previously told them that fruit too was forbidden. After banishing Adam and Eve, kicking them out of the garden, God places the cherubim and the flaming sword to keep them away from the Tree of Life. I would think that any immortal good parent would want their children to have healthy everlasting life. Is any parent that so loves their children perfect? Can any parent make the claim that they never made a mistake in raising their children? Has every child never been unjustly punished for something they didn't do? Do parents sometimes overreact when they are tired and cause unintentional emotional harm? Do even the best parents sometimes misunderstand or misjudge their children's actions and intentions? At times, it seems that the primitive God of the *Old Testament* and of other ancient scriptures was a bit belligerent, monstrous, neurotic and dysfunctional with his parenting skills. Yahweh even seems to suffer from the mental illness of bi-polar, narcissistic personality disorder or schizophrenic behavior. Perhaps there was no one to show him that good parenting amounts to teaching us how to look into our own form day by day and encompass a connection with the universal soul as we grow forward in a safe environment.[434]

God, being all aware, should have known that Adam and Eve, with their child-like innocence and curiosity, would not be able to resist eating the forbidden fruit. Could he not have foreseen the future of Eve giving in to temptation prompted by the words of the serpent? Did he fail to keep his children safe from the "dangers" lurking within the Garden? If God was infallible, why didn't he place a fence around the Tree of Knowledge to keep Adam and Eve from the fruit? As Nicola Denzey Lewis points out in *Other Voices of Gnosticism*,[435] if God is omnipotent and omniscient, why does he have to call out "Where are you?",[436] to find the original couple after they ate their fruit snack? God could have warned Adam and Eve about the potential temptations of the serpent and advised them of its desire to expose them to the world and destroy their innocence before they were ready. God told Adam and Eve that they would die if they ate of the fruit. Yet after eating the fruit, they didn't die. Their eyes were open to knowledge, both good and evil, and they became ashamed of their nakedness. The serpent was right in saying, "You surely shall not die!",[437] for "Your Lord has forbidden you to approach this tree only to prevent you from becoming angels or immortals."[438] Did God lie to his human creations? Is this not the same "white" lies a well-intentioned parent may tell their children to protect them from potentially harmful situations or to preserve their innocence until they are older?

Telling Adam and Eve to stay away from the forbidden tree was like telling a five year-old child not to play with guns and then leaving a loaded pistol on the coffee table, in the play pen or in the toy chest the following week. Our creator made us as creatures of curiosity who find interest in the unknown – it is coded into our DNA. Perhaps "the fall of man" and the expulsion from the Garden of Eden should not be blamed mainly on Eve, nor on Adam for that matter. The responsibility of Eve and Adam tasting of the forbidden fruit is shared by that of the serpent and that of the parent. God, as the parent, needs to take a majority of the responsibility and recognize that there was negligence on his part.

Eve was blamed as a convenient scapegoat for starting the catastrophe (the expulsion from the Garden of Eden) yet it was through her innocence that the serpent deceived her. The serpent (or what the serpent represents) negatively exploited Eve's innocence and curiosity either for the purpose of antagonizing God or for its own evil misguided pleasure of tormenting others for a narcissistic feeling of power and control. The serpent prematurely exposed and bestowed upon humanity the ability to abstract into the mind of God, tricking the original man and woman into becoming godlike. Perhaps God, then lacking evolved parenting skills, should have sat down with Adam and Eve and explained what to do with this new found knowledge and how to use it wisely instead of becoming angry, clothing them with skins and banishing them from the Garden of Eden. To have the eating of an apple in Paradise condemn the entire future of our species, with no offer of recourse for redemption is not only excessive punishment and inhumane, it is ungodly. Womankind and mankind were eventually meant to receive the fruit of knowledge, but the serpent's temptation caused this to happen too early in human evolution. The serpent (Satin in disguise) promised to give them instruction and counsel after they ate the fruit,[439] but instead he laughed, slithered away and enjoyed getting his younger siblings in trouble.

Yet as a polar opposite, per a story from Greek mythology, it is the serpent that instructs Asclepius (a son of Apollo) the practice of medicine and how to be a physician. In fact, from Gnostic beliefs, the serpent was considered the wisest of all the animals in the Garden of Eden and did not cause the fall of humanity, but rather, encouraged their awakening. Adam and Eve gained knowledge from eating the "forbidden" fruit and it was the authoritarian, temperamental and narcissistic God of the *Old Testament* that "freaked out" and threw them out of the Garden. According to the Manichaeans, is was the Christ being that through a serpent, provided Adam with gnosis and what humanity can aspire to become.[440] From the *Zohar*, a Kabbalistic text, it is Adam who throws God out of the Garden of Eden – he expels the Shekhinah, the feminine aspect of divinity and regrets his decision.[441] Eve is even viewed as being superior to Adam by certain Gnostics, for she was the first to become aware and out of her desire to share and educate, she awoke her sleeping partner.[442] Maybe Eve found the serpent (or the being that was disguised as the serpent) to be more attractive, more attentive, more nurturing, more loyal, more interesting and more loving than Adam. Maybe the serpent encouraged and supported her rather than Adam who may have suppressed and stifled her.

The Christian Nazoreans or Nassenes, were a 1st century Gnostic group said to honor the ancient serpent wisdom.[443] There was also Glycon, the snake-like god worshipped by a 2nd century cult within the Roman empire.[444] Mentioned by Horace and Lucian, the cult may have been more of an enterprise to gather the offerings of its followers, a very familiar model of religious business repeated throughout history. The pattern of the serpent representing wisdom and gnosis is not unique to just early Christian and Roman sects. The Mesoamericans (i.e., Mayans, Aztecs, etc.) had Kukulkan, a feathered serpent deity which represented power, agriculture, language, earthquakes and the sky. Ani Williams, the world-renowned harpist and singer of music based on ancient spiritual traditions, recognizes this pattern in the Sanskrit naga or nagas which are serpent wisdom entities, nadi is the serpent path of the human chakra system, and in the root sound of "NA" incorporating itself into other mythologies as meaning serpent, wisdom or "godliness."[445] The word "Vatican", the name of the Holy City and domicile of the Catholic popes, has a possible etymology meaning "divining serpent."[446]

—A*—

"Just as Moses lifted up (exalted) the snake in the wilderness, so the Son of Man must be lifted up, that whoever believes in him may have eternal life." – *New Testament*[447]

—*O—

Moving even further forward in the book of *Genesis* to the story of the Tower of Babel,[448] the Lord seems to feel threatened by humanity working together on accomplishments and feared that they would conspire to do evil. It seems humanity had infringed upon Elohim's zoning ordinances and building codes without the proper approved divine permits.[449] It was most likely not the height of the Tower that was feared, but what its technology was capable of doing. Rather than offering praise, instruction, guidance and mentoring on how to accomplish even more but with a core built on morality, Yahweh chose to create havoc by initiating communication problems and invoking a disruption in the commonalty of language. Is this not like an immature parent feeling threatened by their own offspring and thwarting their children's efforts? It seems that the Lord was as insecure here as the tempting serpent (from an Orthodox perspective) was in the Garden of Eden. A functional God would have offered praise and encouragement to humanity rather than dispersing them, sabotaging their efforts and confusing their language. Yet, this same God, or a new one altogether, gives the communication problems a temporary reprieve in the *New Testament* by allowing everyone to hear the Galileans' words in each individual's native language.[450] An enlightened parent would be proud and want their children to be equal or even surpass them. God himself/herself seems to have acted during the Tower of Babel's construction like a jealous, wounded child in need of counseling. He of all beings should have known that one's creations (children) do not always grow in the expected or desired direction.

Look at all we have gained since eating the fruit of knowledge – from the understanding that simple ingestion of small quantities of vitamin C wards off the deadliness of scurvy, that metallic lead accumulation is poisonous when ingested over time, to having beings walk on the Moon and return to planet Earth. During the colonial beginnings of the United States of America, we only knew of six planets. Orreries made prior to the signing of the Declaration of Independence in 1776 had Saturn as their outermost sphere and by the time the Constitution was ratified in 1788, the seventh planet of Uranus needed to be added. Pushing against the boundaries of ignorance, humanity has achieved much with the application of knowledge. The universe can be an experience of wonderment, joy and beauty, but it can also be an experience of hardship, tragedy and loss. We should cherish and focus on the good moments of our lives with the understanding that bad moments may happen in between.

Divine fairness is the notion that there is more to our existence than just our secular bodies. In this realm, molecules come together to form our bodies and then separate as our bodies degrade. Divine fairness implies that there is much more to our existence than just the connection and disconnection of our molecules. As sentient beings, we wish for divine fairness. As religious beings, we pray for divine fairness. As human beings, we hope for divine fairness. For divine fairness means that our creation is not a random act, that universal justice exists and departed loved ones will be reunited upon leaving this realm.

We ask ourselves, why does God allow personal and global tragedies and disasters to occur? We ask ourselves, why does God sometimes take away the familiar or disrupt our comforts? We may be angry at God or not understand his/her ways, such as the secular death of a baby or a child. We may wonder why she allows some infants to be born physically healthy and others with illness, maladies and deformities. I wonder if that soul, knowing it was going to enter into a body that was not within healthy operating parameters, had a choice in the matter. Perhaps a miscarriage is merely a soul choosing not to enter a malfunctioning vessel. Possessing foreknowledge, it decided to either invest itself or wait for a better opportunity to enter the material realm. I do not believe the imposing of such afflictions upon the newborn is due to karma from miscreant behavior occurring in prior lives, a form of transmigration punishment and blaming the young victim for the imposed deformities. Such explanations too easily excuse God for his errors. If it is a form of penalization for past life sins, then it is our role to parole them through the application of sound medical corrective practices and procedures. Perhaps we witness and encounter such inflictions to reveal the deformities within our own character and expose the cracks covering our outward stance, and to then make the necessary corrections and repairs.

Understanding that Krishna is not always perfect in his teaching methodology allows us to forgive him/her. There can be life lessons that we didn't feel were fair nor that we are able to fully comprehend. God, at times, may seem to let us down or disappoint us by not answering our prayers. Before becoming angry at him, we should reflect on how many times we may have disappointed Allah with our behavior. I'm sure Allah's frustration with our behavior far exceeds the amount of times he disappointed us. Realizing that God (or at least our interpretation of God) has imperfections allows us to forgive the imperfections within ourselves. The Lord's imperfections actually enable us to better connect with him. She chooses to be imperfect to better relate with us. Show reasonable mercy for the faults of others and the faults of God, just as allowances are made for ours. God often forgives us, just as we should forgive him/her.

As industrious beings, we strive to steer and control our direction in life and through crises. At times, however, after exhausting all that can be done, one must sometimes let go of trying to control and submit to fully trusting Allah and relying on his/her divine plan. The world is not perfect, but we must navigate through its challenges, gains and losses, loves and anguishes, the best we can. We are all students of God who have been given the balance between free will and destiny. Although God has given humanity free will, she lends a hand every now and then in steering us in a particular direction. Being blessed with the freedom to choose our actions, some of us still continue on paths of destruction. The Almighty offers guidance to those who listen and constantly watches us, but he does not micromanage our lives. One cannot heal those who do not want to be healed and one cannot save those who do not want to be saved. This is another unfortunate consequence of free will. When you encounter and recognize the Lord's influence, you will know him by his love, grace, humility and even humor.

With free will comes the quagmire of some choosing to enlighten themselves, while others choosing to remain in ignorance. It is an instinct of the unenlightened to fear intelligence and the unknown. They fear what they don't understand and choose to mock and remain ignorant rather than to embrace. It is easier for them to remain in their isolated boundaries than to risk something unknown and have their understanding of the world redefined and expanded. This is also why many fear a higher intelligence such as God – they lack courage. The unenlightened fear their insignificance among something so much greater. The enlightened embrace this intelligence with love for they welcome knowledge above what they already know.

You can argue with God and sometimes you may be angry with him. There are times we may feel God has abandoned us; even Jesus shouted out "My God, My God, Why Hast Thou Forsaken Me?" during the final suffering moments of his physical being on this planet.[451] Much earlier in history from Canaanite mythology, when the resurrected Aleyin kills his murderer (Mot the god of death), Mot's last words to his father are allegedly identical.[452] There are times we are very much aware of the Lord's supportive existence. He understands your feelings and also knows that your moments of doubt are necessary for the evolution of your core. You must try to be patient with God, just as she is patient with us. I'm sure God has had to be much more patient with us, than the other way around. You will not win your arguments with him, but you will learn. You will learn that you may have to either change your way of thinking, dealing and interacting with people and the universe or else you will remain stagnant and decay within your thoughts. You may even need to change your definition of what Allah is. God does not punish us, for it is our own ignorance and detrimental behavior that punishes ourselves. The Lord wants us to expand our mental boundaries in search of truth and knowledge, to transcend our current system of thought and arise to new levels of awareness, so that we do not repeat actions performed out of ignorance and detrimental behavior that again result in a reaction of violence or extreme punishments.

If God is perfect and all powerful, why does evil and suffering exist? Is it that the supposed all powerful Lord does not actually have the power to remove evil from the world? Is it that Allah can remove all evil from the world, but chooses not to as a means to test, punish, prepare or train us? Do we need to occasionally taste the pungent bitterness of evil as a reminder to always aim for the flavors of goodness? Does the dualistic nature of our universe require evil to exist so that goodness can also exist? Perhaps the notion of evil and debating theodicy is humanity's burden, not God's. These questions and conjectures are not original and have vexed religious thinkers for centuries. Instead of exhausting efforts on trying to determine the metaphysical cause of why evil exists, we should focus our energies on making sure there is more goodness in the world. A full analysis and explanation of the nature of good and evil is beyond the scope of this book. There are, however, several other suitable texts on the subject.

The image of the God of yesterday was personified by our ancestors based on their limited cognition. Perhaps that old world biblical view of a jealous and temperamental God is obsolete. Do you really think that an all-powerful being or consciousness is concerned with the specific semantics used to describe or reference it? Similarly, do you really think such a mighty essence that permeates all and is all, still gets jealous if one worships through more than a single connection? Do you really think the God of Judaism, Christianity and Islam, is a jealous God? Maybe the Yahweh of yesterday was, but do you really believe the Allah of today would succumb to such human anthropomorphic failings as hatred, intolerance, jealousy, revenge and humiliation? Allah, who is all and has all, no longer gets jealous. Even God, who knows all, can still become wiser.

Some humans seem to take it too personally when someone insults their God or prophet, lashing out with death threats instead of providing a witty comeback, a whimsical retort or a satiric rebuttal. Allah and his prophets are much more "thick-skinned" and wiser than we give them credit for and do not let insults, criticisms nor blasphemy trigger them into wrathful fits of anger, rage and murderous revenge. They are much more immune to blasphemy than we are. Such disrespectful claims and mockeries are viewed by Allah and his prophets as ineffectual gestures of weaker minds and serve only to reflect the insulter's dullness and immaturity.[453] Allah, Mohamad, Jesus, the Buddha, all laugh at the pettiness of the insulting comments or words, realizing it is only the babbles of an underdeveloped being. They do not lash out with violence, but with humorous wisdom, forgiving the insulter and only wishing for their eventual illumination and enlightenment. It should be left only to Allah/God/

Yahweh to judge and reprimand those who comment, speak or write words of blasphemy; judgment and punishment should not be done by human influence. No hand shall be laid upon the blasphemous, the unbelievers and heretical, no stones hurled at them, and no harm shall be allowed to come upon them based on the actions and secular laws of men, women and other advanced intelligent sentient beings (AISBs). Physically harming the blasphemous or atheist in any way is a sin in the eyes of God. The only human retribution allowed upon the impious or sacrilegious are words of educational guidance to try to open their eyes and lead them out of the pit from which they dwell. They shall only be subjected to the normal secular laws of monetary restitution and/or community service for acts of destruction or vandalism to religious artifacts, monuments and objects. This is a new commandment directly from God and it is strongly recommended that it be obeyed – thou shall not harm the blasphemous and non-believers.

—Λ*—

"One who denies God, denies themselves. One who affirms God, affirms themselves. One who fears God, fears themselves. One who loves God, loves themselves." – AO[454]

—*Ω—

With our much more expansive (but still limited) understanding of the universe, our modern image of the Almighty Creator, Sustainer and Destroyer can be less harsh, more forgiving, and kinder to its creations. Between an angry tormenting God causing destruction upon his/her creations in fits of rage to a loving benevolent one that raises and nurtures his/her children to excel, which one would you want to worship? The daily continued extreme struggles of life and pain encountered by early *Homo sapiens* had them improperly deduce that divinity must want suffering.[455] Believing that appeasing and calming the universe required offerings of suffering to a deity or deities, human sacrifice was sometimes part of their rituals. According to the book of *Genesis* within the *Old Testament* of the *Bible*, even the prophet Abraham was instructed to sacrifice his offspring to Yahweh as a test of his faith. Wanting proof of loyalty, God requested him to sacrifice his beloved only son

Isaac, by slaying the child with a knife. Fortunately, upon the Lord's acceptance of his faith and loyalty, Abraham was reprieved of the horrendous task of filicide before the final moments. Again, this Creator of yesterday seems rather dysfunctional with his insecurity, immaturity, cruelty, abuse of power and tormenting of her creations. We can, however, forgive Yahweh for his past behavior and transgressions as he has forgiven us for ours. God's parenting skills have drastically improved over the ages as she learns to be more empathetic with and understanding of her creations. The Jehovah of today has evolved beyond such violent requests and prefers that humanity evolve as well. The Allah of tomorrow will be even more advanced because as humanity spiritually grows and expands its reaches and knowledge to the stars, God can reveal more of his wonders and secrets to us. The Lord should be a role model and mentor to emulate, not a Leviathan to be feared. Much of the true scriptures provide guidance on how to make God your friend and companion. Become a friend with Krishna, and remember, friends are not always perfect.

—A*—

"The Almighty doesn't have all the answers, but he/she knows where to find them." – AO

—*O—

As we spiritually advance, we must be willing to let go of the Allah who "was" while focusing on the Allah who "is" and the Allah who "is to be." The God of yesterday has grown, for God is both prehistoric and evolving. As the Lord advances from his primitive behavior of archaic times, so too, must our species' relationship and the religious tools used to commune with him. Our modern God is a loving teacher and parent always trying to raise and mentor her children in the direction of spiritual understanding. For the greatest gift parents can give their children is the knowledge and foundation for them to have a better life. A good parent wants and teaches their children the means to have a rewarding and satisfying life and how to be their own positive role models. Just as we obtain a feeling of satisfaction and healthy pride from our children's accomplishments when they behave and grow, so too, do our divine mother and divine father when we behave and grow.

Chapter 8
The Development Of Self – The Core Of Our Being

"WHO AM I?" – ASKED the advanced intelligent sentient being (AISB)

"Whom do you want to become?" – answered God

"A being of depth." – replied the AISB

"Then do the work." – answered God

"How?" – replied the AISB

"By learning to minimize the ego while enlarging the Self." – answered God, AO

• • • •

ONE CANNOT KNOW A COUNTRY by merely looking at its maps, one cannot judge a people by its government, one cannot take a journey by merely looking at travel brochures and one cannot become an enlightened being by merely quoting religious scripture. Priests can only lead us to the gates of God, but true knowledge of the divine needs to be experienced directly by the seeker themselves.[456] Becoming an enhanced spiritual being requires reflection of read material, deciding which to implement as part of our core and experiencing and applying it into everyday practice. One must do the work and perform the actions to evolve their being. In our quest for meaning and an ultimate reality, are we searching for the divine consciousness or is divinity searching for us? I think it is we who are lost and waiting to be found, not God.

Doing the work involves internal reflection, holistic understanding, being cognizant of our own human susceptibilities and weaknesses to avoid or at least minimize hypocrisy and negative exploitation of others, monitoring and adjusting our own inner thoughts and resulting actions and implementing the practice of improving our world based on the merits and impetus of love. It is the risk of being vulnerable to confessing our past negative deeds to ourselves and to a higher power. Admitting to ourselves prior mistakes of things said, our own conduct and errors in judgment, it is a commitment not to repeat them and to forgive ourselves for our moments of behavioral weakness – absolution of self. Doing the work is the forging of mental alchemy to transmute one's self to an elevated reality of consciousness and into a higher being. The search for finding one's true self begins in the helping of others.

Each of our daily social interaction and conduct is based on the behavioral core within our beings. Much of the start of our core characterology was influenced by the parents we are born from, the guardians who raised us and the geo-social location and conditions that we are raised in. Some of us were born into loving households with parents, guardians or relatives who nurtured, guided us and become our initial templates for developing our own being. Others of us are born into dysfunctional parenting situations that may have ingrained a program for self-destruction through continued chaos or excessive control. Still others may have lost their parents at a very young age. We may have found ourselves born in areas with reasonably stable governments, sufficient food supplies and opportunities or we may have found ourselves in regions of war, conflict, strife and instability. No matter what our start was, no matter into what conditions we later found ourselves, we all have the ability to mold and flex the core of our being and its future behavior. When we choose to redefine our being, our core is always malleable and receptive to improvement.

—Λ*—

"The first act of honoring the self is the assertion of consciousness: the choice to think, to be aware, to send the searchlight of consciousness outward toward the world and inward toward our own being. To default on this effort is to default on the self at the most basic level." – Melody Beattie[457]

—*Ω—

Our core has been morphed by many factors but we continuously influence it each and every day by the thoughts we incorporate into our being. Such factors include our internal reaction to external stimuli, emotionally, mentally and physically, as we act to either strengthen our connection with God or to weaken it. Emotions were meant to be felt and experienced, but expressed and dissipated within moderate boundaries. They matter since they define, in part, who we are, but they should not be left to dictate our personality. Emotions are indicators, a litmus test of our internal state. They are our source of feelings from undesired pain to sensual sensations; they are the generators of joy, elation, happiness, ecstasy, frustration, sorrow, fear and anger. Yes, feeling angry at times is a normal, healthy emotion – it is an internal disturbance being triggered from unwanted external circumstances. It is an interior alert, an alarm, that something is wrong, unjust or unfair. It could be something that is incorrect within ourselves, calling us to admit there is a fault in how we are thinking, reacting or doing. It could be due to a breach of our internal comfort (a hit to our psyche) from an external influencer. It can also be from a combination of both, an external force building up into an internal pressure. How we handle or react to such feelings of anger determines our level of enlightenment as sentient beings. It is dealing with our emotions responsibly that makes us functional and separates us from the dysfunctional. Train the mind to be self-aware, to be in the present and to recognize when our emotional reactions may cause harm to others as well as ourselves – do not allow your uncontrolled responses to dictate who you are.

Emotional upheaval drains away our energy and that of those around us. Dissipating such raw emotions in a productive manner is the best approach for dealing with those who may have been disrespectful to us. It takes spiritual focus and resolve to steer our core's development in the correct direction and regain or maintain our balance. It is by healthily dissipating such disturbances of the mind through productive channels that fosters our return to serenity and a stable state. The degree and level of resolve will vary depending on how far off or how close we are on the path to God. Some of us will have much more work to do than others in becoming our own positive role model, our own loving and guiding parent. Being our own parent means taking care of our inner child with self-nurturing and selecting our battles wisely since our daily emotional and energy reserves are limited. With spiritual work, the core of our being is receptive to change. Your self-worth as a human being is based on the core of who you are as a person, not on your financial wealth or popularity. Developing a healthy sense of self-worth shields us from the temptations of unhealthy behaviors.

Some questions to ponder as we develop our niche in the universe:

1) Are we an aspect of God or separate from God?

2) Are we here and God is there?

3) Is God intertwined with our being and those around us?

4) Do you want to morph into a being of shallow surfaces or a being of depth?

5) Do you want to filter out the noise of insignificant chatter and find a deeper dimension to living?

6) What thoughts, ideas and patterns of behavior are you going to allow to permeate into your being?

7) Are you going to succumb to mental laziness and myopic generalizations or open yourself up to different perspectives?

8) Do you prefer to remain in a plane of mundane existence or choose to become receptive to epiphanic glimpses of God's ecstatic grace?

A basic maxim of Zoroastrianism is *Humata, Hukhta, Huvarshta* which means "Good Thoughts, Good Words, Good Deeds." However, it is our deeds that count more than our words. Mentioned in the previous chapter, there is the Buddhist saying that "we are the sum of our thoughts." Expanding upon that saying: "We are the sum of our thoughts and results of our actions." "I think, therefore I am", is again that famous phrase coined by René Descartes in the 17th century as proof of the reality of our existence. "What I think, therefore, I shall become", expands upon it by steering the direction of our reality. We are the builders of our own destiny.[458] Steer your mind in the correct direction, for you are at the helm to a greater destiny. God put each of us on this planet with a mission. The quest is to live a human experience while raising our consciousness to a higher state of self-realization. In doing so, we are shifting ourselves and the global consciousness of humanity to a higher plain of enlightenment.

—A*—

"God, please guide my behavior and conduct such that I may eventually enter the Domain of Heaven." – Prayer Of The Tempted, AO

—*O—

Throughout each day, you decide what is going be the composition of the core of your being, the arrangement of your inner house, your inner-verse and your inner thoughts. Be aware of what is going on in your inner mind and adjust the thoughts to prevent your actions from going astray. Become the master of your thoughts, not a slave of them.[459] If one lies and fibs, then one becomes that lie or fib. We own what we say. Through focusing on strengthening our self-will to improve our condition, each and every day we decide what type of person to be. Eventually, such positive focus becomes habit. Our standard of living can fluctuate due to its dependence on the pressures of external conditions. That is why the structure of our internal condition is imperative for survival. You decide how you are going to react to the influences and pressures of the outer-verse upon your being. You decide who you are going to become. You decide the integrity of your character. You decide how you are going to relate and react to others and the universe.

We are the sum and choices of how we choose to behave in a given situation. From what music we listen to, the books and magazines we choose to read, and what role models we emulate; all can influence our thoughts and actions. We can float through life with the shallowest of existence or choose to develop the depth of our being and live a fulfilled experience. Literature, a wonderful method for evolving our core, is a form of mental travel that broadens our experiences and can expand the horizons of our consciousness. Seek the truth and wisdom in the written words of many past worldly sages, prophets, saints, thinkers and innovators. You don't have to agree with every one of their views or statements, but being aware of their thoughts will aid in the proper development of your inner core. Reading the words of past God Seekers will aid in strengthening your connection to divinity and interactions with the universe. There will be certain phrases that, when read, harmonize with us more than others. Such scriptural messages of love and enlightenment echo with our being and provide a temporary glimpse of understanding and divine ecstasy. During these epiphanic moments, we feel as if we are so near (qurb) to Allah, after which we fall back down to the material plane again in separation (bu'd) as we plateau upon a new level of illumination. These are the phrases and moments to use as the building blocks of our core. As we come closer to Brahman while travelling the path of life and encounter experiences both good and bad, more scriptural passages will resonate with our core. One can read a great work of words in their twenties and not understand all of its mastery. Deciding to read it again in their forties, a realization occurs of how much was originally missed of its contents. Such revelations come to us later in life because we have more experiences to draw upon in relational empathy.

As sentient beings, the truest spiritual fulfillment comes from witnessing and reflecting on the passage of events and significant markers in our lives. We can't always be on a religious high or continuously dwell in an epiphany, for as novices, we are not supposed to constantly remain in such realms nor be long-term denizens of the spiritual worlds. Epiphanic energy is the current created, felt, and experienced when transitioning from ignorance to awareness. It is the sensing of your own mental and spiritual evolution as you grow from that which is unknown into that which is known. Such moments of divine realization are temporary as they integrate into the core of our being. Although fleeting, as we approach enlightenment, such moments will occur more often. Balance is about transitioning and having a proper material and spiritual existence. In a state of balance, we are able to find excitement in simplicity. The simple things give us as much pleasure and sometimes more than the expensive things. We are content to be without the false reliance on excessive material consumption. Our pleasure must come from within, before we can truly be happy. Balance comes from gaining the composure of being

at peace with the events of our past, the state of our present and the potential of our future. It is finding the optimum position for the fulcrum
of existence between the extremes. Once we find it, the universe will fall
into place as we synchronize with its movement.

—Δ*—

"Evolution is gaining the psychic zones of the world...life, being and
ascent of consciousness, could not continue to advance indefinitely along
its line without transforming itself in depth. The being who is the object
of his own reflection, in consequence, of that very doubling back upon
himself becomes in a flash able to raise himself to a new sphere." – Pierre
Teilhard de Chardin[460]

—*O—

The media we choose to watch and the literature we choose to read
and how we correlate its passages into our core have an effect on our
connections with divinity, whether we become educated or miseducated.
Freedom of the press does not mean there is always truth in its words.
One can absorb the ethical wisdom presented by *Aesop's Fables* through
the experiences of its animal characters or one can read the infamous
Mein Kampf, an autobiographical outline of Adolf Hitler's distorted political ideology. Most will filter the contents of *Mein Kampf* with disdain
and horror and not embrace its wicked manipulations into their core.
A fractional portion will choose to agree with its marred rhetoric. That
fraction, unfortunately, has a void that caustically craves an ego embell-
ishment by denigrating others and/or by finding someone else to unfairly blame (a convenient "scapegoat") for anger over their current life circumstances. How we process various forms of literature will either make
our conduits to divinity stronger through epiphanic unveilings or diminished by regressive dereliction.

A true path to God is travelled by learning to filter information such
that only appropriate behavioral programming enters into the core of our
being. Although we may be exposed to inappropriate conduct, we have
the free will to decide what is going to enter and be retained by our core.
Just as our body's health builds upon the type of foods we put into our
mouths, our mind feeds and grows from the type of intellectual and spiritual nourishment it receives. Miseducation (negative conditioning) is

what results if we allow inappropriate behavioral programming to contaminate our core and penetrate our ego membrane. We must use our God-given critical thinking skills and spiritual strength to determine what becomes part of our being and what remains as external false propaganda. Happiness and love are a choice as much as anger and hatred are also a choice. Hatred, if not properly channeled and dealt with, can fester and become an infestation within the core of our being. How we handle and choose to cleanse ourselves of such infestations determines if our soul will prosper or perish. Which choice will you make a habit and allow into your core? Which will become the second nature of your personality? Who is your default self?

Learn to strive and enjoy the euphoric accomplishment of having completed the reading of a good book, for worthy leaders are readers. Become addicted to reading, for it prevents the mind from becoming stale and sluggish. In doing so, your thoughts will expand and journey to places far beyond the borders of the body as your psyche enters and melds with the minds of great authors and scholars. For those having access to literature, (public libraries exist in many nations), seek books from a diversity of religious, spiritual and philosophical viewpoints. The reading of various scripture from a multitude of religious paths is good practice for maintaining one's spiritual center. It will broaden your perspective on how humanity (or other sentient beings) relates to divinity and make you realize that there are more similarities than differences. Indulge into other topics as well, both fiction and non-fiction, but always ask yourself, how is the author(s) words and/or point of view affecting my core? Is it something that I want to allow in and to become part of my being or does it detract from my essence and relationship with the universe? Do I find myself synchronizing with goodness or succumbing to the manipulations of evil? Will the deeds and stories being read advance my awareness and core or diminish it? In doing so, you are creating your own personal anthology of a lifetime of read books. You are creating your own bibliography of being. I wish that my bibliography could consist of every interesting book ever published and every informative website ever posted, but due to the secular restrictions and limitations of time in this physical realm, that would not be possible within the limitation of a human life span – there is too much to accomplish in this world in just one lifetime. The greatest desire of every book made of paper is to become worn out and fall apart from being voraciously overread. Reading is an exposure to the veritable expansion into an author's inner workings and a method for communing with God. It builds the synaptic connections of our brain for immersing ourselves through the inner-verse to reach the outer-verse; delving into the triangular to expand into the circular.

—Λ*—

"On your reading and learning depends the welfare of the world." – *Accept This Gift*[461]

• • • •

"I'VE LEARNED THAT LIFE is like a book. Sometimes we must close a chapter and begin the next one." – Hanz[462]

—*Ω—

Do not be a shallow passive sheep when following a religious, political or governmental herder. When part of a collective, still retain your individualistic thinking to evaluate words, actions and policies. Avoid becoming part of a runaway wolf pack mentality that turns into a stampeding lemming migration hurling itself over a cliff. Do not be brainwashed by empty statements. Be cognizant of narcissistic leaders or harmful organizational cults that seek to chip away and weaken your core and pull you into their distorted way of thinking. Use your Creator-given critical thinking skills to evaluate if such leaders or organizations are worthy of your participation and are truly leading all of society towards a better future. Ask yourself, do their actions match their words? Are they parasitic to or symbiotic with society? Are they committing questionable acts that go against morality? Are they striving to advance the positive relationships and interactions between all races of humanity and advanced intelligent sentient beings? There have been numerous warnings of false prophets within many religious texts. The warnings do not mean that there won't be future genuine prophets, but rather, approach and listen to their words with caution, grounding and balance. To evolve your core, your inner house, become your own role model and internal teacher while traveling your journey of self-realization. Become the person through whom you wish to benevolently influence others. Never blindly follow any religious shepherd, government herder or instructional text, but apply the mind of spiritual logic and gift of rational interpretation that God gave you.

The path of spiritual development can be challenging and rewarding, so be selective in what role models you choose to emulate. Avoid those propped up by the indiscriminate greed of corporative objectives and the darker side of Hollywood glitter – "...grotesque caricatures of adulthood, narcissists driven to hysteria and wallowing in money..."[463] Be selective of the positive behavior patterns you choose to absorb while morphing into your own essence. Become the type of being that others will strive to emulate and imitate – be your best. Use caution when a role model's behavior is questionable and do not put them upon a pedestal.[464] As we hero worship our idols, be cognizant of their faults, frailties and imperfections. Think for yourselves and be aware if the behavior of your role model(s) appears inconsistent with how they try to portray themselves. Do not try to rationalize inappropriate behavior with convenient euphemisms and emotional pleas in an effort to hold on to the image they portray, but rather, focus on the reality and logic of who they are and how they take accountability for their deeds and words. Some role models do have profound insights, but others can be "false prophets" seeking to fulfill only their own self-absorbed and diabolical agendas. Such false prophets are focused on their self-interests and self-aggrandizement as they deviate others from a true path. All human beings are fallible (capable of making mistakes), some less than others, no matter what their relationship with divinity may appear to be.

Avoid displaying and acting out with dysfunctional behavior and/or becoming a dysfunctional individual. Dysfunctionality is not something to be proud of or bragged about. It is something to be worked on and removed in order to improve one's life and interactions with others. It is something to be cured of; to be healed from. If you are already dysfunctional, then do the introspective work to change your active and reactive patterns of behavior. The pathway to enlightenment is monitoring and reflecting on our own behavior and then adjusting accordingly to improve. Reforming our character after reflection is normal, healthy maintenance of our core. The vitality of our daily life is determined by the approach we exhibit towards the universe; the interaction of our inner-verse (a triangular perspective) with the outer-verse (a circular perspective). Consider the approach taken in our daily lives. Do we contribute to the contamination or cleansing of our inner and outer universe? Do we exhibit aggression or composure towards others while commuting to and from our jobs? Do we pollute our bodies with harmful substance such as tobacco products and excessive alcoholic consumption? Do we insert excessive or dangerous addictive foreign chemicals into our physical bodies to achieve a temporal and falsely acquired emotional feeling or perceived state? Do we unnecessarily release into the environment trash, waste or other contaminants? Have we expressed patience towards others to the same degree that God exhibits patience with us? We all make mistakes, tumbles and fall downs during life. The concern is how often, how many and the affect (degree of severity) they have on others.

Daily life can be challenging and rewarding. Pharmaceuticals have been developed for legitimate medicinal purposes which can alleviate some of the conditions and symptoms encountered by the malfunctioning of our bodies and mind. However, unhealthy are those without balance or spirit who resort to the use of illicit drugs as their false idol. There are many lost souls who turn to drugs to falsely alter their reality. Escaping from responsibility through illicit drugs or excessive alcohol consumption only temporary masks emotions, feelings, shadows and conditions that must eventually be faced. Their reality may seem too hurtful or hopeless to bear, so they alter their perception of it. The reality hasn't changed, just the emotional reaction to it through the use of artificially induced mind-altering substances. They lose the true desire to change their reality through growth and mental work. Motivation becomes replaced with apathy. Growth is a scary thing to them for it means acknowledging and confronting their current state and addressing emotional pain as well as the associated underlying manifestations of physical pain. It also means reaching a new plateau of existence out of the previously familiar one, which can be initially strange, disorienting and frightening. The continuous use of escapement drugs alters the mind's sense of emotional achievement. Imagine buying a trophy at a pawn shop, and then believing you won the football championship, just because you have the empty memento to show for it. It is a false achievement, an empty symbol. The use of illicit drugs (chemical substances) for "entertainment, recreation, escapism or psychedelic transcendence" behave the same way. In Jungian terms, they prevent and dampen individuation and lead to inflation.[465] They give you a temporary emotional state without anything to back it up, creating a hollow sense of self. It is like taking off in an airplane and then dropping the landing gear and wheels while in midflight. To land, the plane comes down hard and on its belly, scraping along the runway because it lost the connective medium of wheels for bringing it properly back to ground. The results are accumulated damage of both mind, body and soul. Some illicit drug use provides us inappropriate extremes of sensations, others give us a lack of any. The training of the mind through mediation, music, pondering, reflective altered states and the practicing of genuine religious or spiritual exercises to reach imaginative consciousness will automatically access the correct proportions of our own body's natural internal pharmacy.

The core of our being is what we develop within this physical realm. It is the conscious mind feeding the subconscious mind, and vice versa. Our soul is what the core becomes as it continues into the next realm. Just as chunks of rocks and minerals drifting or orbiting through space are referred to as asteroids, when those chunks enter the Earth's atmosphere, they are then referred to as meteorites. Just as molten rock below a planet's surface is referred to as magma, that same molten rock is referred to as lava when it exits the surface. These analogies were mentioned previously in Chapter 6. The terminology used to describe the essence changes, depending on the relative medium, location or plane of existence.

For one to advance their core, any turbulence of the mind must first be addressed and then minimized. Having the courage to face our faults and inadequacies, then working to diminish their influence upon our character, is the way to enlightenment.[466] Working and developing our core strengthens our being and properly conditions and prepares our soul for the next realm. Our actions in this realm are preparation for the next – it either evolves us into higher beings or diminishes us to lesser souls. Developing the core of who you are is about self-realization, God-realization and training one's mind with each step on the path of enlightenment. Training one's mind means monitoring or being cognizant of thoughts leading us on the correct route or down the wrong path. It is about recognizing when we are dwelling on potentially harmful courses of action and then readjusting our mental focus on more constructive ways of handling frustrating or difficult situations. Whenever you find your thoughts thinking in the wrong direction, trigger them to return to love. Any impulse of thought which is repeatedly passed onto the subconscious mind tends to translate into its physical equivalent. The mind is creature of habit and feeds off the thoughts playing in the background. This phenomenon can allow for both good and bad thoughts to promulgate into actions. Which ones become actions, however, depends on one's character, will-power and self-control.

—Δ*—

"A mind not driven by love serves no purpose." – AO

—*O—

Engineer your mind such that love becomes the *modus operandi* of both your conscious and subconscious thoughts. In doing so, your intuition, impulses, hunches, intimations, urges and ideas will carry you aloft as you rise, transcend, grow, advance, venture and move upwards to greater heights of achievement. The great aspirations, inspirations and visions for a grander and nobler life spring forth from the interplay between the conscious and the subconscious, turning everyday life into an artistic and/or mystical experience. This is the tool by which great painters, sculptors, designers, musicians, inventors, speakers and writers become animated and inspired. Great and noble thoughts upon which you habitually dwell become great acts.[467] A mind dominated by positive thoughts and emotions based on love becomes a favorable abode for the establishment and recognition of faith. This, in turn, will give the subconscious mind instructions on what correct course of actions to implement.[468] Make your last thoughts at night before falling asleep thinking of love and peace and your first thoughts upon waking up of love and joy.

There are many books already elaborating on the power of prayer so I will not overly delve into its importance for influencing our lives and its various methods. Prayers produce three marvelous effects: 1) they detach us from our creature aspects; 2) they unite us with God by absorbing the thoughts of divine things; and, 3) they gradually transform us into God as he/she swoops down to bestow graces.[469] They are an expansive expression of ourselves into the ether with the hopes of taking root and growing into reality. We pray often at times of distress and need, but we should also remember to express gratitude during times of joy and abundance. Divinity may not hear our words, but it always feels our emotions and knows our thoughts. Personally, whichever method of prayer works best for you is the one which should be practiced. Affirmative prayers tend to release powers by which positive results are accomplished.[470]

—Λ*—

"Therefore I tell you, whatever you ask in prayer, believe that you have received it, and it will be yours." – *Mark* 11:24 (NIV)

—*Ω—

Praying for certain accomplishments or desires is done by asking, visualizing or foreseeing an act unfold while accompanied by a feeling of joy and love, then concluding with gratitude, thanks and appreciation. In conjunction with our efforts, it is then left for the universe to manifest the request or prayer into reality. The answer to our prayers may not always be the desired response, but their guidance can restore internal harmony and lead us through tough situations. Prayer, by providing an instrument of mental engineering, has certainly been proven to assist in resolving internal conflict by influencing the subconscious mind to make the correct choice of actions for addressing the topic at hand. But does it provide assistance in solving external problems? Can praying for the health and well-being of someone halfway around the globe reach and assist its intended target? Can the power of love be transmitted over infinite distances? We've seen how electromagnetism in the form of ra-

dio, television and microwaves can bounce and reflect as they travel the
globe, so why shouldn't thoughts which resonate with God do the same?
If starlight can reach us from lightyears away, I'm sure prayers can travel
the same distances.

—Δ*—

"Moreover, those who pray should not come to the Lord with fruit-
less or naked prayers. Petition is ineffectual when it is barren entreaty
that implores God." – Saint Cyprian of Carthage[471]

—*O—

Prayers seem to fluctuate between selfish and selfless requests of the
Almighty. When we encounter too much sunshine, we pray for rain.
When we encounter too much rain, we pray for sunshine.[472] Our
prayers amount to us trying to influence and persuade God's decisions,
as if to say, "we know best." Should prayer be used to ask God for more
money, obtaining particular material processions, fame and popularity?
The universe seems quirky and perverse in its behavior when one praying
for a new car sometimes receives their Lamborghini, Cadillac, Mercedes-
Benz or Tesla while one praying for the safety of their soldier son or the
curing of their daughter's illness sometimes loses their child. The Lord's
actions can seem strange, inscrutable and unreasonable at times, especially since a parent outliving their child seems to so go against the very grain
of life and natural order of things. What cosmic precedents are at play in
granting luxuries to some while denying necessities to others? Witnessed,
endured and observed by Job in his lamentations to the Lord, why do
hardships sometimes seem to indiscriminately be dispersed among the
populace, regardless of their morals?[473] Why does the Creator allow a
cat to torment a mouse before eating it? Why does the Almighty permit
over 80% of newborn robins in the wild to die in their first year? Why
did Yahweh allow the Apollo 1 fire, the Challenger to explode and the
Columbia to disintegrate? Why did God allow the Titanic to sink, the
Holocaust to occur and the wasteful homicidal events of 9/11? Why did
Jehovah allow the Bubonic Plague, the 1918 Influenza outbreak, HIV,
Ebolavirus, SARS, MERS or COVID-19 to spread? What lessons have
we learned from such pandemics? Perhaps it is to teach us the necessity

of listening to the validity of science, the magnitude of the need for international cooperation and that culture and societies thrive better when we support each other through interconnectedness and compassion. Why does God allow us to love and then be subjected to emotional pain when those we love are removed from our world? Perhaps it is to put us all on an equal footing and to teach us to the importance of asking, "How can I help?" Why does God allow detrimental politicians not acting out of the service of love for others to rise to power and win elections, even in democratic voting societies? Perhaps it is to show us the importance of being an educated voter and to obtain our news from multiple sources before forming opinions.

History judges the decision, strengths and flaws of governing leadership accordingly. No leadership is without flaws, but some have more than others. For those voting in any future democratic election, I encourage you to cast your ballot for the candidates who will most likely lead by love, rather than by hate. Vote for leadership that will think more of others than of themselves. Vote for the leadership that will most likely solve crises, not create them. Vote for the leadership that will put forth more truths than falsehoods, for lies result in deaths. Vote for the leadership that will not think that they are perfect, will admit their mistakes, and work to correct them. Vote for the leadership that will be secure enough to immerse themselves among advisors that may disagree with them, rather than relying on sycophants, "yes-men", "yes-women" and "flying monkeys." Vote for the leadership that will think in terms of eternity for their country, not in short-term aggrandizement of shallow accomplishments. Vote for the leadership that will take responsibility and not blame others for their own errors. Vote for the leadership that will seek knowledge, rather than claim that they already know it all. Vote for the leadership that will seek the soundness of science, not ignore it. Vote for the leadership that will build its credibility on consistency, not dismantle it based on contradictions, questionable conspiracies or false hopes. Vote for the leadership that will properly plan rather than clumsily react. Vote for the leadership that will accept defeat graciously, rather than falsely play themselves as the victim. Vote for the leadership that will put forth words of wisdom and calming truths to quell civil agitation, rather than comments that invoke and contribute to riots. Vote for a leadership that will listen to the lessons of history and improve upon them. Vote for the leadership that will lead by positive example, not by touting the opposite of what it does. Vote for the leadership that will be straightforward with the facts, rather than take advantage of our gullibility. Vote for the leadership that can work with and respect both a biased and unbiased media, that last ditch guardian of freedom, rather than condemn it. Vote for the leadership that can heal the wounds of a divided nation, rather than rip the scars further open. Vote for the leadership that is connected to us common folk and not just with the elite. Vote for the leadership that will work with their allies, not alienate and abandon them. Vote for the leadership that will contain tyrants and not give them legitimacy. Vote for the leadership that will not hide behind "The Number of the Beast" as their credentials, for complacency is no longer a suitable option. I can only hope that whoever wins an election, that they are well aware of and properly apply *Matthew* 23:12 – "And whoever exalts himself shall be humbled; and whoever humbles himself shall be exalted." We will not be judged by which candidate we vote for, but we will be judged on the reasons for giving a particular candidate our vote.

—A*—

"A great nation is like a great man: When he makes a mistake, he realizes it. Having realized it, he admits it. Having admitted it, he corrects it. He considers those who point out his faults as his most benevolent teachers. He thinks of his enemy as the shadow that he himself casts." – *Tao Te Ching*[474]

• • • •

"EVEN AS SLAVES HUMBLE themselves before a tyrant and praise him though he slays them." – *The Prophet*[475]

—*O—

The answers to our prayers seem subjective to God's will. These spiritual dilemmas have us questioning how the universe seems to play favorites indiscriminately and may cause one to feel angry and upset with Allah's decisions. Remember, it is understandable to be angry at God the same way children can be angry with their parents. Such conflict is a normal part of our spiritual growth and we should look for ways to resolve our feelings of frustration and disappointment. Learning to accept that divinity's actions are, at times, mysteriously obscure in their approach and chronology provides a degree of mental solace and emotional catharsis. Believing in and relying on the expectation that the Lord, with her infinite insight, will eventually provide what is best for us when we are ready to receive it, is the reason for faith. It is what can heal us.

—Δ*—

"There will be times when we feel very close to God,
There will be times when we feel abandoned by God.
There will be times when we are sure of God,
There will be times when we doubt there is God.
There will be times when we trust in God,
There will be times when we feel betrayed by God.
There will be times when we are delighted with God,
There will be times when we are frustrated with God.
There will be times when we are happy with God,
There will be times when we are angry with God.

Through all such times we must choose love for God instead of hatred for God.

These times are necessary for our spiritual growth, for as individuals, we all have to determine our relationship with divinity." – AO

—*O—

We all have a lower self and higher self, also referred to as respectively the lesser ego and the sacred self or Self.[476] The ego is a confession of your lower identity and can sometimes mistakenly see itself as a victim of the world. Do not be afraid of it, but learn to understand it and to open it to new experiences and perceptions. The lower self is composed of our animalistic tendencies, our lower reality, and operates at the very primitive levels of emotional reactive function – it is the Demiurge, the Rex Mundi of our psyche revealing itself through us. The higher self is that which accesses reflective insight and taps into divine knowledge, the upper reality – it is the true God revealing itself through us. The higher self is that radiant being within all of us that is trying to break free of its restraining chrysalis; a chrysalis we put in place to shield us from the oppressive elements of human society and the accumulations of past karma. It is the lower self that gives in to temptation and impulsively reacts without thinking. It is the higher self that overcomes temptation and reflects on outcomes and consequences. It is the lower self that succumbs to short-sited aspects of human follies, giving in to ignorance, excessive ego and negative temptations of the flesh. The Self, our higher essence, sees beyond the illusion of being trapped and confined within our body. It recognizes that our body and frame is but a cocoon, a supportive vessel for our soul to grow and learn, and a means for communicating while in the temporal realm. Those with under-developed consciousness dwell too much in their lower self and have failed to develop a well-aligned moral compass.

—Λ*—

"...yet not I, but the Christ livith in me..." – *New Testament*[477]

—*Ω—

It is the higher self, the Atman (ama Atmon) within, that aligns with divinity in thinking and action, following the path of light and wisdom. It is much smaller than a mustard seed and yet, contains the vastness of the entire cosmos – for the macrocosm is found in the microcosm and vice versa.[478] The **Atmon** within is the portal by which we access our higher self, that divine and ancient being that is connected to every **ato**m, to every photon and to every consciousness. Temporarily residing within the atoms of our body, it is what binds stardust into sentience and is unconstrained by time. It is the thoughts of the universe within, witnessing and experiencing itself. It is boundless love and ultimate truth. One who finds, develops and knows their Atmon, their own true self, will encounter the joy of the Supreme.[479] When we are accessing our higher self, the core of our being vibrates in resonance to God's messages of guidance, her thoughts of creation, and her tune of love. An advanced enlightened being maintains their cognitive fulcrum much closer to the higher self than the lower self, but allows for temporary shifts of internal precepts when appropriate and due to circumstances, for one size does not fit all.

It is the inner battle for concentrating and choosing the higher self over the lower self that reading true religious scripture and philosophies of wisdom come into play. For reading such material provides the mental training, conditioning, exercises and energy for remaining focused on what is correct. The correct path of action is always in the service of love towards the world. Cynicism may occasionally surface on the outer layers of our being, but it should not be the central dominance of our core. When mental power, energy and motivation are not in the service of love, then history and the daily news shows the results.[480] Our greatest fear in developing our core is, if we should ever find ourselves in a position of power and influence, that we shall not abuse it by contributing to negative exploitation. The last thing we ever want to turn into in pursuit of an internal messianic quest is to become another Hitler, Stalin or Saddam Hussein. When Mahatma Gandhi said that he was guided by the divine, he was questioned since Hitler made similar statements. Gandhi in his simplistically direct manner responded, "You look at the results."[481] The difference is that our guidance should not be ruled through the ego, but inspired from the motives and objective of the heart; a *modus operandi* of love and agape. History judges the war causalities caused by Napoleon Bonaparte's narcissistic imperial expansive desires much differently than the deaths caused by Abraham Lincoln's humble desire to preserve the union of states while criminalizing slavery. With duality comes the referencing of famous people in similar circumstances, but for opposite reasons.

Stonewall Jackson, a prominent Confederate commander during the United States' Civil War, is said to have calmed one of his general's fearful objections by saying, "General, never take counsel of your fears."[482] Jackson's suggestion of striking at the heart of Union industrial power to psychologically remove the will of the northern enemy to fight was dismissed by the Confederate president Jefferson Davis and his military advisor Robert E. Lee. By Gettysburg, Jackson was unavailable to continue his arguments, having died weeks earlier at Chancellorsville due to com-plications from being mistakenly shot by his own troops.[483] Had Jackson taken counsel of addressing any fears of mistaken identity by his own troops (a minor but decisive detail) and had his campaign of a guerrilla-like strike consisting of 5,000 troops been approved, the outcome of the Civil War and continuation of the United States could have been very different.[484]

In developing your core, practice to always default to a steady state of love in all possible situations. By defaulting to a steady state of love, it will awaken that dormant underlying genius that is often suppressed by our own insecurities. To truly awaken to life, view every day as your last. This does not mean to frantically cram all desires to complete a "bucket list" within 24 hours in a morbid frenzy. It means to reflect on the wonder of each moment of existence like it will never come again – to always be at the conclusion of the story. This places you in the present and goes along with what Paul the Apostle meant when he wrote, "...I die every day."[485] Train your core to revolve around peace, joy, beauty, happiness, wisdom, good-will, integrity, virtue and knowledge, and then watch the world around you shift into place. In doing so you will make better decisions, think more intelligently and with greater wisdom by properly applying newfound knowledge. Defaulting to a steady state of love will help to quell and dissipate the internal demons within. It will keep them at bay and tame their tendencies. Defaulting to love quells the internal demons of fear, anger and guilt that tend to drain our energy reserves the most. Through love, the application of genuine confidence and contentment replenishes those energy reserves. Our perception of the world is a partial reflection of how we perceive ourselves.

Defaulting to a steady state of love will keep you young in spirit but allow the wisdom of the ages to flow through and within you. It will actually reduce the physical effects of time upon the body. Aging, when done gracefully, has its own glory, beauty, value and stage of prominence.[486] Aging gracefully means drawing upon our life-earned wisdom to become less prone to anxiety, less susceptible to depression and less triggered into anger. It is incorporating the past, present, and future trials of life, both positive and negative, into an amalgam of constructive poignancy. Defining ourselves every moment of the day through the decisions and choices that we make, the direction of our decisions is what makes us who we are. You are the result of choices made when you were younger; you are the result of old plans. You were younger a minute ago, you were younger an hour ago, you were younger yesterday, and the days before yesterday. Therefore, you may improve your behavioral direction at any age.

Be careful never to generalize the behavior of a religion, race or culture as a whole, based on the actions of a few. Refrain from stereotyping based on a limited sample set. God created diversity in the outer pigmentation of humankind to give us variety. We should embrace this chromatic diversity and variety with love, wonderment and joy. For diversity is God's elixir of creation. If you are not yet able to default to a steady state of love then at least default to a steady state of healthy tolerance. By learning and practicing tolerance in the face of duality, one becomes more aware, astute and able to achieve productive and beneficial outcomes.

When a neighbor, acquaintance or stranger trespasses against you, practice defaulting to a steady state of love. How does one do this? A simple start is just saying the words "default to a steady state of love" either out loud or internally when someone has agitated internal emotions of anger, rage or frustration. By doing this, it will help to healthily dissipate the anger and to come up with a rationally focused way of dealing with the situation. It will initiate self-restraint and dampen impulses of retribution that would cause both parties harm. Acting as a dimmer switch or volume knob, escalation of destructing revenge cycles is prevented.[487] Defaulting to a steady state of love does not mean becoming a complacent "doormat", apathetic observer or bystander, but rather, it evokes rational thought patterns and guidance from within and from above. It allows you to alleviate the anger by opening up receptors to all the good things occurring in your life – it changes your perspective. Of course, in situations where you are being physically attacked and are unable to exit the assault by speaking words of reason, defending yourself takes precedent over defaulting to a steady state of love. In such instances, such as a soldier or warrior in battle, love of self-preservation and for a future of freedom for posterity takes precedent when the cause is genuinely just.

In developing and maintaining your core, work towards a healthy sense of self by finding the proper balance between narcissism and empathy. Empathy is based on your connection to others and willingly approaching interactions through alternate perspectives, while narcissism is based on your solitude of self-importance and self-generated emotions that may or may not be legitimately nor appropriately responding to the presented facts. Properly developing your core means establishing self-awareness to be able to monitor and adjust your own behavior and thought processes. It is about recognizing when your thoughts are dwelling or obsessing too much into the fog of anger, pausing the internal voices, and redirecting them in a different or beneficial direction. In a sense, it is learning to supervise your own thoughts and guiding your mind into a more positive direction. Our minds can be rewired to transition out of the destructive thought patterns etched during the survival mode of enduring a dysfunctional environmental or flawed family dynamic. The thoughts within us can gain momentum in either the wrong or correct direction, but we have the free will to steer the direction. Training one's mind to recognize when stuck in a groove or in a set track means breaking generational cycles of dysfunctional interactions with others, ending harmful codependent relationships, regaining moderation and finding the right balance between empathy and narcissism.

Be cognizant of your inner voice. It is the words silently uttered by the consciousness of your inner-verse and represents the unspoken reflection of your internal thoughts as you question, analyze and ponder the outer-verse (that which is outside of your inner consciousness and body). Your inner voice can be heard as the amplification of higher reason as you read. It is that which guides your decisions and speaks to your mind while reading – your subconscious revealing itself. Throughout the reading of this book, it has been your inner voice communicating with your mind and influencing your core. Asking questions of yourself is the essence of learning and raises your consciousness to a higher state of awareness. Within each of us is the potential to do great things for humanity, or to do horrific deeds. The direction we head is based on the development and maintenance of our core and the actions we choose to take. It is up to each of us to find our way and make our path in the universe. Once we are content with how insignificant our place is in the universe, our importance and influence upon it will multiply.

—A*—

"According as one acts and walks the path of life, so one becomes." – Hindu Proverb[488]

• • • •

"BE HUMBLE, FOR YOU are made of earth. Be noble, for you are made of stars." – Serbian Proverb[489]

• • • •

"THE ONLY PERSON YOU are destined to become is the person you decide to be." – Ralph Waldo Emerson[490]

• • • •

"IF YOU WANT A CERTAIN thing, you must first be a certain person. Once you are that certain person, obtaining that certain thing will no longer be a concern of yours." – Zen Proverb

—*O—

If you want more out of life, you need to first become more. To improve your situation and circumstances, you need to improve your core. Once your inner-verse begins to align with the path of enlightenment, your environment and outer-verse will start to mirror those changes.[491] This is a basic principle of synchronicity. The first step to synchronizing with God and obtaining piety is becoming comfortable with our own being and existence. Within every moment, we need to monitor and acknowledge the makeup and fiber of our being. Is it filled with love or is it filled with hatred? Entering into a state of rage only validates destructive narcissism. Placing healthy limits of behavior and reason upon ourselves and others is a form of love. For love will provide prosperity, hatred will provide destruction.

The loop of the divine relationship between us and God is like an electrical network (the power grid) traversing the globe and we are like light bulbs. His radiance emanates through us and the luminosity of our shine (the Paramatma within) increases as we improve our connection. Just as a single bulb is still part of the network, so too, are we a part of God. We become the local venue of a non-local omnipresence.[492] The Lord's power, however, can have an intensity beyond what can be handled or fathomed. For those who are not grounded in a true path, this intensity can scorch our core, overload our spiritual filaments or throw us into mental disarray and emotional imbalance. This is where Sophia (wisdom and the Holy Spirit) come into play. She acts as a controlling conductor, a resistor and a fuse, allowing God's power to reach us but also protecting us from being overloaded. All the power and all the true things of nature emanate from the mind of the universe. If we listen by implementing the Divine Benevolent Principles (love, forgiveness, gratitude) forthcoming in Chapter 25, we too can become beacons of Allah's benevolent and gracious thoughts.

—Δ*—

"Truly I tell you, the one who believes in me will do great works and even greater ones than I, because I am going to the Father and from my position with God, I will assist them in doing such greater works." – Jesus[493]

—*O—

In this age of overstimulation from the bombardment of an electronic and digitally connected world, we are constantly under attack for our attention and time. Daily occasional internal reflection within our own thoughts can help regain a temporary reset and restore our equilibrium. Turn off the external stimulators, feel comfortable in silence, let go of the day's entanglements and listen to the background noise of your own consciousness or engage in meditation. This is how you again become in union with your core. It is through such daily reflections or meditations that we can analyze who we are and who we are becoming. Know thyself and improve upon it, for self-knowledge is the beginning of self-correction. As we monitor ourselves through internal reflection, adjustments to our core may sometimes be necessary. Monitoring and adjusting is an axiom of any functioning feedback and control system as well as the primary methods of proper educational instruction. The teacher adjusts the lesson based on monitoring the receptiveness and understanding exhibited by the student. Good performance should be praised while guidance should be provided for improving areas of perceived deficiency. We are both the teacher and student of our own inner instructions, which calls upon knowing when to apply patience and when to initiate stimulus when dealing with the flux between our internal thoughts and the external world.

—Λ*—

"When the student is ready, the teacher will be there." – *Nine Faces Of Christ*[494]

—*Ω—

Properly developing our core involves seeing things from the perspective of others, even if you don't concur with their ideas, thoughts, opinions or feelings. This is done by conditioning the mind to typically react with restraint and self-control, initiating a "cat-pause" for allowing time for reflection, empathizing through their point of view and defaulting to steady state of love, before recoiling with an impulsive response. It does not mean that you will suddenly agree with them or that you are required to do so, but by avoiding rash choices and snap decisions that will damages one's future self, it will allow for the better handling of disagreements or to work towards a reasonable compromise. Disagreeing without being disagreeable is the way of dutiful civility and the enlightened. Through mental exercise and conditioning for self-control and the application of empathetic fairness, connections to God are strengthened. What a person says has no power over us unless we allow it to. Focusing on the matter at hand and avoiding diversion by defaulting to a steady state of love is the way to remain emotionally poised and serene during bouts of verbal confrontation. This is how the functional person outmaneuvers the dysfunctional.

There is a saying that "beauty is in the eye of the beholder." For that matter, "truth is in the reasoning of the beholder". Beauty and ugliness are a rating of how well something is pleasing to the eye in the material visual sense and/or pleasing to the mind in the abstract sense. One can see both beauty and ugliness in everything. Being a balanced spiritual being means seeing beauty and truth where and when it is appropriate and seeing ugliness and falsehoods where and when it is appropriate. Projecting love helps us to see more beauty than ugliness. There is a longtime practice among Buddhist monks in Thailand and Southeast Asia to meditate upon and find beauty in the image of rotting corpses as a means to come to terms with the transitory nature of material things and as a reminder to focus on the importance of positive productive actions while in this material realm.[495] Life is temporal, so why use it unwisely or waste it on unproductive actions? We must choose our battles wisely, because our time and resources are limited during this finite physical life. Give the major problems in life their due and let go of the minor problems. We can't win or solve all problems, but we can put the appropriate amount of our energies towards the important ones. Learn to expect success as a result of effort and endeavors but understand that results may vary. Increments of success increase our self-assurance. Continuing from those incremental gains and lessons learned, by adjusting future actions and behavior, establish a belief that you can bring almost anything into the realm of possibility and attract the best to materialize.[496] Faith in ourselves is a good thing, but over-confidence will not withstand the face of a crisis and will result in failure. A winner knows at what point to quit, minimize future losses, apply proper closure and come back with a new plan or direction for achieving success. A good leader knows when to stick to the plan and when to adjust or improvise.

Do not make promises unless you will genuinely follow through on your words and have the capability and means to do so. Making false promises (not following through on commitments or intentions) only means that you are saying things to soothe your own ego and feed your own narcissism. Do not make promises of causing physical harm; these are called threats of violence. Avoid bombarding others with overstimulating demands of pompous energy draining attention. Be respectful to the ears of your captive audience – reflect if you are coming off as a self-focused bore.

As a fetus during our first weeks of *in utero* development, it appears that we repeat the evolutionary story during our initial gestation but at an accelerated rate. Starting from the merging of single celled gametes into unicellular organisms, our multicellular beginnings rapidly morphs through the pre-natal profiles, in both brain and body, into fish, amphibian, reptile, bird-like, primate, and then to the final stage of humanoid form as *Homo sapiens*. Upon exiting the womb, we merge into the surrounding culture while soaking up its characteristics. Are we born animal and then become human or born divine and then become human? As a species with the longest childhood of any known creature on Earth, we have an adaptive and instinctual drive to prefer the familiar: familiar faces, familiar voices, familiar surroundings, familiar behaviors and familiar ideas. It is an instinctual bias to first fear the unfamiliar or what we do not understand. This innate survival mechanism gives us security and limits vulnerability when we are in our infant and toddler years, but it can prevent us from expanding our awareness of the world, acceptance of that which is different (but harmless) and blossoming beyond a myopic perspective as an adult. If we do not outgrow this stage of our childhood, we will continue to see everything that is different as a threat, regardless if it really is or not. Many things that are different can actually be beneficial to our advancement and well-being but accepting and embracing the unfamiliar with incremental caution is still a sound approach. Opening ourselves to higher levels of awareness and experiences calls us to draw upon courageous vulnerability, feeling a degree of fear but moving carefully forward anyway.[497]

—A*—

"It seems to be a sin in the eyes of nature to hide our insufficiency – just as much as to live entirely on our inferior side." – C.G. Jung[498]

—*O—

At times we may need to be rational with our thinking and feelings, and at other times it is the irrationality of our senses and intuition that saves us. "...Sensation establishes what is actually given, thinking enables us to recognize its meaning, feeling tells us its value, and finally intuition points to the possibilities of the whence and whither that lie within the immediate facts..."[499] Striving to be rational intelligent sentient beings, we should be humbly proud of our good deeds and feel the appropriate amount of guilt for our bad ones. The critical part of our morality and so much of what makes us intelligent (but not always rational), emerges over history through our imagination, reasoning and embracing the necessity for compassion.[500] We all encounter tempting thoughts, but it is how we deal with them that matters. From Aristotle's views presented in *Nicomachean Ethics*, a person of virtue turns conscious decisions of good behavior, through practice, into subconscious habits of good behavior. Their moral fiber develops and strengthens, much like exercising a muscle, as they put into daily practice choices and actions of ethical behavior. In doing so, they morph away from negative temptations and develop stronger core connections with divinity. Just as an athlete develops skill and muscular stamina through exercise and repetition of correct routine, so too, is the moral sense of our core strengthened through practice and implementation of proper ethical behavior. Such continued practice results in our ethical behavior becoming instinctual habit, rather than something requiring focused effort. Integrating constant reflection on God into one's subconscious mind, (whether called prayer, internal chanting, or creative visualization), will ultimately result in tuning into the universe's pulse and tapping into its natural rhythm of benevolent energy; this is the way to becoming an enlightened being.

—Δ*—

"God loves those who do good." – *The Koran*[501]

• • • •

"DO UNTO OTHERS AS YOU would like them to do unto you." – The Golden Rule[502]

• • • •

"HURT NOT OTHERS IN ways that you yourself would find hurtful."
– Buddhism[503]

· · · ·

"DO UNTO OTHERS AS THEY would like you to do unto them." –
The Platinum Rule[504]

· · · ·

"DO NOT DO TO OTHERS what you do not want them to do to
you." – Confucianism[505]

· · · ·

"THIS IS THE SUM OF duty: do not do to others what would cause
pain if done to you." – Hinduism[506]

· · · ·

"THEREFORE, ALL THINGS whatsoever ye would that men should
do to you, do ye even so to them..." – *The Book Of Mormon*[507]

—*O—

Unfortunately, many among us are either unaware of their potential
or relinquish control of their lives. In doing so, they essentially choose
to waste away akin to a life of a semi-vegetative state.[508] Dwelling with
their eyes always under water and closed, like swimming below the surface in a mud-pool, most spend much of their existence in this mater-
ial/physical plane – remaining as *hylics, somatics* or *sarkics*. Occasionally they surface and skim the boundary into the thought plane. Others
spend more of their existence above the water line, living in the mental or
mind plane of thought – dwelling as *psychics* or *psuchikoi*. Then there are
those who can rise even higher, to the levels of the clouds and beyond,
soaring in the vastness of Pleroma energy existing in the spiritual plane
and then returning back unto the physical plane when it is time to land –
these are the *pneumatics* or *pneumatikoi*.[509] Saint Paul considered him-

self as being a *pneumatic*.[510] These three planes of existence (material, mental, spiritual) do occasional overlap or temporarily mesh, but usually for brief epiphanic moments. Upon synchronizing with the universe, referred to by the Gnostics as being in or past the *psychic* stages of initiation, our desired dreams will start to break through into reality. It will feel strangely mythic and blissfully mystical as our character, the person we want to grow and change into, becomes both the participant and the observer of our life's show.

Living life to the fullest by having a well-developed core means harnessing the senses such that material desire is balanced with spiritual fulfillment. Self-realization and proper core development involve first obtaining the correct balance of self-sacrifice and sense gratification – it is about implementing moderation to savor the joys and ecstasies of life's existence. Upon achieving the appropriate balance, utilization of the subconscious mind as a dissipating grounding for the consciousness mind, it will no longer feel like anything is being sacrificed – this is an application of the Hermetic Law of Neutralization.[511] An indication that one has risen above the duality is when a state of contentment is achieved and one find themselves serving in the name of the Lord with pleasure and truth. The gratification of our senses and of our spirit needs to be properly self-regulated such that both are in balance. Purity and selflessness lead to contentment; contentment and peace leads to blessedness; blessedness leads to ecstasy; and, ecstasy leads to the state necessary for individual union with God.[512]

—Λ*—

"May your stresses be small and your joys boundless." – Dorothea Malina[513]

—*Ω—

Every true seeking AISB's motto should be to do good works in this world while also working upon themselves. A major life purpose is to cultivate spiritual knowledge in building our relationship with divinity and to be a benevolent part of something bigger. Developing a purpose and a cause beyond the individuality of self prevents the plagues of boredom, restlessness, depression, apathy, loneliness and helplessness from creeping in during our youth and old age.[514] It gives desire, meaning and a reason for a continued existence and a worthwhile life.

Our psyche seems to be non-corporeal and non-spatial, except when responding to and locating internal or surface regions of pain or pleasure. It overlaps our core and soul, the merger of our subconscious and conscious, and is a paradox of both a mathematical floating point of totality and an unending extension of the cosmos. Exactly where does our mind begin and end? It can dwell beyond the limits of self, residing in a field of probability that extends beyond the confines of body. Are its boundaries truly contained only within the gray matter of our brain? The human brain and its perceived prominence compared to other Earth creatures, appears more receptive to and more wired for the thoughts of the universe; that stew of cosmic consciousness. It is certainly better designed for creatively manipulating the elements and communicative languages as a means of expression. Acting as an organic processor and antenna, it tunes into and senses the abstract future which can have more meaning than the present physical realms. Through purity of thought and intent, it can also act like a Wi-Fi receiver for accessing the information provided by the universal and supreme consciousness, tapping into that higher mind which provides helpful flashes of intelligence to guide us to better solutions, clearer perceptions and novel ideas. The brain is a biogenic computer with trillions of neural electric switches that can connect you with divinity, once you program and upgrade it through the proper development of your core.

Considering our vision is limited to the electromagnetic wavelength band of about 380 to 740 nanometers, we really have a narrow range from which to perceive and register reality. Just as there are magnetic fields influencing the surrounding space, perhaps there are also fields of thought. The Sun and Jupiter are heavenly bodies that put forth enormously strong and large magnetic fields. We can measure their intensity with instruments made of matter. Measuring fields of thought, however, would require instruments with sensors made of thought that are influenced by thought. Existing in the physical realm, access to such sensors is not feasible. An unproven theory or hypothesis is that our thought pat-

terns transfer not just internally across the brain, but propagate externally as well in a fashion similar to how magnetic flux lines of the Sun fluid-
ly dance across its surface or bursts outward as solar flares or mass coro-
na ejections. We don't currently have instruments for directly measuring
thought or consciousness, making the hypothesis unfalsifiable, but we do
have instruments (i.e., electroencephalography) for measuring the electro-chemical differentials or signatures that indicate thought. Just as the
path taken by cosmic rays and other subatomic particles can be witnessed
through the trail left in the ionized vapor of a cloud or bubble chamber without seeing the particles themselves, we can witness the trail taken
by thought based on electro-chemically active regions of the brain when
subjected to controlled experimental situations. We can't see or measure
the thought itself, just the regions of activity or anchor points of the flux
paths taken. Postulating forward, just as a tone or sound is a vibration
through molecules, our thoughts are vibrating in an ocean of consciousness.

From a monistic perspective, there is one ultimate physical and metaphysical form of energy in the universe. For the sake of simplicity, let's
call it spirit, the most refined and pure vibrational form of energy. It can
be found in a combination of any of the four states of energy: pure spirit, thought or consciousness, electromagnetic radiation and matter. All
four of these energy states are an aspect of God and we too are composed of them. In the physical realm, matter is the form of spirit in its
lowest energy state. Electromagnetic radiation (EMR) is the transition
state (the transport medium) between each of the states; spirit to/from
thought, thought to/from matter, matter to/from spirit. Triggered by
our thoughts, it is EMR that travels down our arms in the form of electrochemical stimulation to move our fingers and manipulate matter. It is
through EMR that our thoughts become our creations. The aromatic fragrance of a flower are tiny particles of matter floating into our nasal sensors which then triggers electrochemical stimulation to our brain, which
then makes a determination by applying thought on whether the smell
is pleasant and to be desired or disgusting and to be avoided. There is a
constant interplay of spirit between these three forms of existence, the
degree of which varies depending on the state. Consider the desire to lift

a spoon. Our thoughts initiate the moving of the muscles in our arms with electrochemical communication. Our muscles contract closing our fingers around the spoon and tightening our bicep to lift the utensil off the table. The final result is a change in the position of matter. This all occurred through a thought, creating an electronic signal, and resulting in the manipulation of matter. The transition can also go in the opposite direction. Consider a ball being thrown at us. Matter has been manipulated. Electromagnetic energy is reflected off the ball in the form of light which travels to our visual sensors. Our eyes process the signal and our brain creates the thought; "Football coming at us: either kick, catch, block or duck away from it." This transition of spirit occurs within our universe over and over again and builds upon itself into huge chains of occurrences. The very creation of the universe itself was initiated by the thoughts of the Creator. The duality of proper existence calls for us to be in the world of matter, but not of it. One must maintain balance between the secular and the divine, an equilibrium of the material world of humanity and the spiritual realm of divinity to prevent unwanted schizophrenic wavering. Residing too long at either extreme can be destructive to the nervous system circuitry of our being.

As an amalgam of the Lord's creative essence intertwined with human tendencies, we have the ability to hone and polish our connections to the sentient mind of the universe. Through developing our core with steadfast mental training and conditioning, we cast the formation of our inner character. With the persistence of continued intelligence, we work towards finding, morphing and synchronizing with our purest identity – the meshing of the humanity within (Δ) to the divinity throughout (O) to form a better being.[515] In discovering our true identity, we can realign with the natural life we were supposed to live and become motivated by our "original goodness", not hampered by the "original sin." Upon achieving true and pure virtue within our core, synchronization with something beyond ourselves will be encountered. It is achieving vibrational resonance with the direction and guidance put forth by the universal mind. It is the tapping into divinity from within by finding our Buddha nature; the most direct way is through a consistent path of love.

Aspects of it can be referred to as The Tao,[516] the Holy Spirit, or the Ruach of the Almighty depending on one's religious perspective. Synchronizing our faith in God is very much the way a good surfer rides a wave. Fighting, confronting and opposing it results in being knocked over, submerged or even drowned; flowing and meshing with it results in harmonious travel while being carried by its energy. Whether we look at the vastness of the seawaters along a coastline, the cresting of incoming waves, or cup a palm full of swash in our hands, they are all still a part of the ocean. By a similar analogy, whether we look at the vastness of the cosmos from afar or see it in the closeness of ourselves, it is all still God. Through striving for perfection and by not being perfect, we merge and reconnect with the almost perfect being.

—A*—

"God is like a musician who crafts the harmonies of the Cosmos and gives each individual his or her own particular theme to play. If the music of life seems discordant to us, we should not blame the Master Musician, but ourselves. We are the out-of-tune instrument which mars the beats of divinity's composition." – *The Hermetica*[517]

• • • •

"We are all a work in progress." – Miguel Conner[518]

—*O—

WE CAN NEVER CONTROL the universe's fluid current and vibrations. We can, however, recognize its patterns and learn to synchronize with them by thinking in terms of eternity. In doing so, we learn to guide and harness its tremendous power; this is the art of mysticism. For mysticism is the personal experiential receptive skill of recognizing, knowing, acknowledging and expressing God's presence. It is the trekking out beyond the borders of body, the ego-self, and to realize, connect with and strengthen the ties that we have to the whole body of the cosmos.[519] When a mystic reaches out to witness, experience and understand the intrinsic sentience of other true religions, he or she is reaching out to God. It is the worship of the Lord as we experience our oneness with him/her while pondering the mystery of our own being through the elements of religious tools, meditation, transcendence, internal reflection and external participation.[520] The proper development of our core and communing with God go hand-in-hand, for it is love which most often attracts the angels' gaze and the blessings of their guidance.[521]

—Δ*—

"Before enlightenment, chop wood and carry water. After enlightenment, chop wood and carry water." – Zen Koan[522]

—*O—

An interpretation of the meaning of the Zen saying above is that after moments of illumination and expended horizons of the psyche, when the inside world has changed so much but the outside world appears the same, we are to re-enter the material realm and continue as active participants within the flow of time. Expanding on this saying, "Before enlightenment, chop wood and carry water. After enlightenment, chop wood, carry water and shovel snow." Meaning, with this newfound awareness after achieving enlightenment, one should clear the path for others by doing good works. Mysticism is indicated through the sensational "chills" that flow through your body when an epiphany of understanding occurs. Transcendence and enlightenment are about learning to make our nervous system vibrate more frequently and at greater amplitudes as the mind engages in those mystic states – it is the simultaneous applying of several Hermetic principles. One must be properly grounded in the temporal world and have a balanced core before advancing into the mind of God. Otherwise, unbridled ecstatic madness will occur instead of genuine practical spiritual mysticism. After moments of interacting with the divine, we are to return to this world bringing with us the provided gifts of spiritual food for sharing with those hungry for its nutrients. It is these divine nutrients that feed our core and develop our soul. It was Jesus quoting prior scripture when he said, "It is written, Man shall not live by bread alone, but by every word that proceeds out of the mouth of God."[523] For Jesus knew that although the body needs food as physical sustenance to survive, the core of our beings needs the nourishing input of God's words to maintain our connection to divinity. In our search for a deeper identity, it is the development of our core and Self that transcends death – the salvation of our essence beyond the ego.

—Λ*—

"Just as there is a God beyond the God, there is a Self beyond the Self." – AO

—*Ω—

Chapter 9
Entity Of Being

"WE ARE NO ONE SPECIAL to the world, yet we are its universe." – AO

. . . .

THE MATERIAL UNIVERSE operates by cycling between smaller constituents forming or recombining into larger components and then larger components disintegrating or breaking down into smaller constituents. These fragments can be referred to as elementary particles, atoms, molecules, dust, proteins, cells, modules, minds, bricks, tiles, fractals, LEGO® or any other appropriate term, depending on the nature of the entity. When the smaller constituents recombine properly into higher order larger components, the net result is greater than the sum of the individual contribution provided by each small constituent. One could say that potency is not being conserved; it is increasing. When the smaller constituents do not properly combine into larger components, the net result is less than the sum of the individual contribution provided by each small constituent. One could say that potency is not being conserved; it is decreasing. When smaller constituents conglomerate into larger components, an entity is born. Larger entities can also break down or divide into several smaller entities. Entities come in many forms, both tangible and abstract, and are composed of triangular and circular components.[524]

. . . .

TRANSPORTATION ENTITIES

There are entity groupings of human inventions that deliver us to/from various locations (modes of transportation). A bicycle is typically a two-wheeled entity composed of a rider and primarily mechanical components. A motorcycle is typically a two-wheeled entity composed of a rider and electro-mechanical components. An automobile is typically a four-wheeled entity made up of electro-mechanical components that participate in transporting itself across roads and terrain. A train is typically a multi-wheeled entity made up of electro-mechanical components that transport passengers and freight across a predetermined track. A boat or ship is either a mechanical or electromechanical entity for sliding across the surface of a body of water. A submarine or bathyscaphe is a capsuled entity made up of mechanical or electromechanical components for submerging to various levels below the surface of a large body of water. An airplane is an electromechanical entity made up of components that participate in generating controlled lift and maneuvering for flying through various levels of an atmosphere. A spacecraft is an electro-mechanical entity for traversing beyond atmospheric and/or gravitational domains.

• • • •

STELLAR ENTITIES

The creation of a star entity is formed by the accretion of molecules, gas and dust (nebula) being gravitationally compacted to extreme pressures and inducing extreme heat such that it exceeds the threshold required to trigger fusion reactions. The exhaustion of its usable fuel brings about the end of its furnace life. Upon collapse due to dominating gravitational forces, most of its outer constituents explode outward leaving behind an inner core in the form of a white dwarf, neutron star or a black hole. The ejected constituents then recombine to form new entities in the form of younger stars, planets and moons.

• • • •

WRITTEN ENTITIES

A book is formed from a cloud of letters that have coalesced into words, that have linked into comprehensible sentences, that have arranged into written expressions of cogent thoughts and ideas. It becomes a tangible entity of informational nutrients, an enrichment manual for the mind, and an archive of knowledge. The reading of a book, a quality piece of literature, evolves your mind, for it exercises, strengthens and changes your brain. It prevents cerebral atrophy and mental laziness (having knowledge but failing to properly apply it) from taking over. The basic necessities for the body to survive and thrive are food, shelter and clothing, but the mind needs an influx of spiritual nourishment if the consciousness is to grow.

• • • •

COLLECTIVE ENTITIES

Any grouping of individual sentient components forms a culture of its own – an organizational entity. A family is an entity made up of elders, parents, siblings, youngsters and infants. A community is an entity made up of people with individual skills, personalities, backgrounds and talents. A business is an entity made up of employees, management, vendors, contractors and customers. A school, college or university is an entity made up of students, faculty, support staff and the administration. A government is an entity funded by its subjects and made up of civil employees, contractors, and authorized representatives, either elected or appointed to jurisdictional posts. A religious gathering is an entity made up of the congregation and the clergy. A flock, herd or colony is an entity made up of the accumulation of individual animals. All these group intelligences develop a culture of their own, usually (but not always) determined and steered by the dominating leadership in its hierarchy. The specific culture can be either functioning in a depth of ignorance or on the path of enlightenment. It can either be operating in a disruptive manner or as a cohesive unit with balanced interplay among its components. The degree of which is determined by the location of the cultural fulcrum between disruption and cohesion.

The growth, maintenance, and advancement of a larger entity of sentience is always dependent on the symbiotic relationship between the whole and the individual enlightenment of its parts. If the individual components are negatively exploited, overworked, suppressed or overly damaged, then the larger entity will also be. The well-being and health of the larger entity is always dependent on the well-being and health of its individual members or its components. A larger entity which is destructive to its individual members will find itself disintegrating as its components recombine to form a new entity or are transferred into maintaining or growing an alternate existing entity. The balance between the whole and its components determines the continued existence of an entity. When you give of yourself to an organizational entity, ask of yourself, is it a worthy entity?

• • • •

LIVING ENTITIES

There are groupings of organic components that make up life on Earth. Plants are living entities made up of cellulose encased cells. Our body is an entity made up of individual cells specializing in their specific organ functions to maintain the conglomerate of our material being. Depending on the reference source, the atoms of our body are considered to entirely exchange anywhere from every 11 months to every 15 years. This is based on cellular life-cycles as cells replicate and disintegrate. The cells of certain organs (colon, skin, liver) are exchanged at a greater rate than others (brain, neurons, heart). Our body is composed of over 50% water, which in a healthy body, is replaced about every 16 days. Think about how many times that hydrogen, oxygen and carbon atoms are traded, removed, or added to molecules within our body just in a period of one year. Based on these constant atomic exchanges, physically, we are not the same molecular entity of yesterday. We are, however, the same spiritual contents from infant to old age.

—Λ*—

"As an infinite minute entity within God's totality, nevertheless, we are still unique in her consciousness." – *Eternal Quest, Volume 1*[525]

—*Ω—

The template of ideal health is an intrinsic part of your core and it can sometimes be reset when the body starts to go astray with disease. Due to harmful interactions occurring in both the inner-verse and outer-verse, our body may become corrupted with physical ailments and/or our mind may become corrupted with mental illness. There is a back-up template within your subconscious mind that, when accessed through proper medical attention, prayer, meditation and reflection, can reboot the programming of both your body and mind back to an optimum state of health.[526] In conjunction with accessing proper professional medical, counseling or psychiatric treatment, finding and triggering this template file to run contributes to healing the affliction(s). Reloading this file is best accessed just as one is calmly falling asleep through the process of creative visualization and prayer.

• • • •

GOVERNMENT ENTITIES

Currently, a democracy (or democratic republic) is an entity of government (social system of jurisdictional rule) that allows for and promotes the most diversity and advancement of thought. It is not the most efficient form of governing, but it is the safest and provides the most security for its citizens. By encouraging freedom of educational expression, within reason, through divisions of authoritative power for determining truths ("blockchain" sets of nodes for checks and balances) it generates an expansive genesis of ideas which build upon themselves to form even more elaborate and advanced ideas. It also allows the voting populace, its citizenship, to influence whether their governing authority veers towards a benevolent humane leviathan or towards an oppressive parasitic regime. The quality of civil services provided by a governing department, division or agency, is directly proportional to the competence of its leadership and budgetary allocations. Inept leadership and inadequate funding results in inept services; a failure in leadership contributes to a demise in governing confidence.

Separation of religious entities (church) and state entities (government) is highly recommended to maintain purity of intent and prevent tarnishing of either component. This keeps religion from contaminating and conducting governmental affairs and government from contaminating and conducting religious affairs. There is no reason, however, that they can't work together on projects of social improvement as long as they comingle without combining.

• • • •

BUSINESS ENTITIES

In corporate mergers, smaller businesses are meshed together under the umbrella of larger organizations. When done properly, the fusion results in a more effective, productive and prosperous entity. When done incorrectly, the result is an unhealthy entity that self-inflicts financial wounds and increases managerial dysfunctionality. Every organizational unit has a degree of dysfunctionality. Be it a family, a business or a government, there is always some level of occurring dysfunctionality. Good operating organizations have a minimal degree of dysfunctionality; poorly operating organizations have a high level of dysfunctionality. When the leadership or management is not the cause of the dysfunctionalities, it is up to them to correct the negative dynamics.

The corporate entity has a culture or consciousness of its own. It may be a being that promotes the proper advancement of all its individual members, or it may be a being that destroys itself in the long run due to the treatment of its members by other members. It may be a being that exploits the planet's resources, or it may be a being that strives for a harmonious relationship with the universe. When an entity exploits aspects of itself, it harms its own existence. Improper short-sighted actions will harm its probabilities for long-term survival. An entity which grows excessively on top of its constituents results in an unhealthy organization. It may grow in the short term, but will collapse on itself in the long term. Such unhealthy entities can be referred to as parasitic or dysfunctional organizational cults and can form in governments, businesses, religions, families and other such collectives. The degree of an organization's parasitic dysfunctionality will, in essence, determine the rate or probability of its collapse.

A business entity that only focuses on the accumulation of financial profits without regard for the proper growth of its members or itself, will stagnate and perish. Blatant greed stalls the growth of a business entity and its constituents. Despite monetary claims by self-promoting gurus of wealth, pure greed is not good. Proper growth requires being at a rate which maintains an equilibrium between the well-being of its individual members and the preservation of the company. Too much growth is chaos and cancerous to the entity, not enough growth is stagnation and extinction. The long-term survival of a business entity is based on the happiness and spiritual balance of the individuals within its being. It is about minimizing organizational and employment dysfunctionality among imperfect human beings. Dysfunctionality is in the opposite direction of illumination.

A symbiotic relationship between employer and employee will assure the long-term survival of the corporate entity. The employee should contribute to the growth and preservation of their employer and the employer should contribute to the well-being and enriched lives of their employees. An enriched life is one in which the individual spends genuine quality time with their families, themselves and their world as a whole and has enough wealth to maintain their income reasonably above the threshold of expenses.

The spiritual balance of the individual is dependent on the nature of his or her feeling of purpose. If the purpose is only to make money, then that is all whom they will become. Money in of itself is empty. It is the actions attached to it that give it purpose. If the individual's purpose becomes something greater, a willingness to do with material less so that others will have more, then they have truly become empathetic to the desire for universal happiness. They will find their world expanding into something greater.

Corporate entities need to become more intertwined with their communities, not through artificial gestures, but genuine action. The global economy needs to be weaned off of its production of profits through the negative exploitation of labor and steered towards advancement through the enlightenment of its workforce and away from archaic incentive programs. The creativity of its members needs to be stimulated through balance of being, enrichment and education. Every organizational entity related to earning a living has a degree of dysfunctionality. Be it a corporation, a university, a governmental department or nonprofit agency, the degree of dysfunctionality is a truer measure of the organization's value and potential than its financial ledger. For the level of organizational dysfunction forecasts the more accurate direction of future trends. It shows the potential sloping direction of either up or down on a plot of the true health of an organization.

—Δ*—

"Lead by example, inspiration and competence and you will succeed. Rule by ego, rank and dominance and you will fail." – AO

—*O—

True and good leaders have integrity of character and set a behavioral example for others to follow. They portray such traits as honesty, creativity, vision, awareness, humility, fairness, responsibility, following through and reciprocal communication. The consciousness or culture of a corporate entity is often determined by the behavior and actions of its leaders, management or board. This behavior may trickle down and affect all its members. Some in the higher ranks have a healthy sense of self-awareness and are spiritually advanced enough to filter out negative behaviors; others succumb to its influence. Others elevate themselves into "ivory towers" of pretentious isolation, preferring to be disconnected from the pulse of their corporate behavior and true health. There is a hypocritical tendency for employers of elevated dysfunctional levels to describe questionable behavior of those higher up in the leadership hierarchy with convenient euphemisms, while questionable behavior of those in the lower ranks results in discipline or termination of employment. If its leaders are self-serving, irrational, unbalanced, short-sighted and out of touch with the general pulse of the corporate entity they are trying to direct, the entity will wither and unless appropriate change is made, it will cease to exist.

How should a corporate entity remain in touch with its own consciousness or culture? How should it monitor itself? It can be self-aware through the evaluation of its individual members from both upper and lower perspectives. To clarify this point, all too often, the entity's members are evaluated from a member in a higher position looking down the ranks. The perspective of a member in a lower position is often overlooked. If a business or corporation's leaders truly want the entity to thrive, they must be willing to look at themselves through the eyes of others. They must be willing to acknowledge their own fallibilities and alter their behavior from one of self-serving intentions to that of balanced behavior. The evaluations should not be focused on the imperfections and faults of others, but rather on constructive comments and suggestions on how an improvement in behavior or course of action will help the entity to thrive. For truth to emerge, the evaluations should be handled by an independent third party who is not dependent on the outcome and in such a manner that the evaluators are able to remain anonymous. If the evaluators from lower or equal ranks cannot remain anonymous, the input is skewed and the evaluation of leadership is pointless.

Corporate entities are going to have to decide if their only purpose is to make money. If that is their decision, then those entities will stagnate and soon find themselves becoming extinct from their own actions or inactions. There is an alternative. Corporations could decide to become much more than blind monetary beasts. They could evolve into creatures of balanced proportions and suddenly find themselves flourishing beyond expectations. How does a corporate entity accomplish this? By spiritually advancing their constituents by allocating time for its members to reconnect to the global community; by providing and encouraging leaves of absence for educational expansion (hiatuses) and interludes of community compassion. Such acts reduce negative exploitation and provide a recharge of refreshed vitality to a corporation's constituents. All too often corporations are separate from their external universe; they neglect that they are a part of the greater whole. Some may give the illusion of productive community involvement through propaganda. They may be having a fundraiser for the environment on one hand, while the other is destroying it. They may be planting a tree with one hand and destroying two with the other. Just as the financial health of an entity is based on its balance sheet, so is its spiritual health. It is the total sum of its actions that determines its worth. Conversely, the business' constituents (employees and managers) must contribute to the financial health, maintenance and well-being of the entity through contribution of ideas, implementation of approved actions, and timely fulfilling of functional roles and duties. In a functional business environment, the employee will provide genuine effort in proportion to the return from the employer. Both must fairly give of themselves for efficiency to prosper.

When economically feasible, the providing of well-being hiatuses is an excellent way for organizational entities to provide for the spiritual evolution of its members. If a business entity is profitable enough, why not provide community time in addition to vacation time? This can be in the form of a few hours, a few days, a week or a leave of a few months. Some current business entities already do encourage and dedicate time for such humanitarian activities. The allocated time could be used for such things as:

Being a guest speaker at a school

Proctoring a field trip with a class

Helping out at a hospital

Aiding a homeless shelter

Working at a food kitchen/pantry for the needy

Visiting a senior citizen center

Assisting with an academic archeological dig

Participating in an environmental cleanup or conservation project

Offering organized assistance and aid after a natural disaster

Volunteering time to a legitimate local charity

There are many other contributing possibilities of service not listed here that would be suitable for re-engaging with the community.

Perhaps it's time for the creation of a new organizational "business" entity or alternate ones within the current framework. It should be an entity: 1) whose objective for existence is the spiritual advancement, quality of experience and enlightenment of its individual members; 2) that learns from its mistakes and those of others; 3) that takes on an active and positive role in the universal advancement of the human community and allocates the time necessary for its members to become positive participants within both the local and global framework; 4) that evolves through the advancement of its individual minds and thrives on the diversity and cultural makeup of its members; and, 5) whose growth is in balance with its environment. Is this too idealistic and holistic of an entity to ask for?

• • • •

THOUGHT ENTITIES

There is an entity that we are all a part of and that is much greater than ourselves. It is an entity which connects all of humanity to each other and that grows with us as we raise our own personal consciousness to a higher state. It is an entity that grows stronger as we make the right decisions in the relationships we have with ourselves and others. It is an entity that we cannot see nor always be aware of its existence, but it is always there. It is an entity that has been in existence since the beginning of modern humanity, of *Homo sapiens sapiens*, but just as mankind and womankind have evolved through the generations, this consciousness has also evolved and continues to grow with each generation. It, too, is a subset of God, but God can see fully into it. This entity is the Global Consciousness of Humanity and it can also be referred to as Team Humanity, the community of our species, the flock average of our thoughts.

Being part of Team Humanity, the development of our depth of character should be aligned with the goal of minimizing the infliction of pain and suffering upon others, while increasing freedoms and civil rights. An entity which grows its constituents within the protection of its own progression results in a healthy collective. Such an entity allows for its segments to receive the benefits of its own growth without endangering its own existence. Enlightenment is finding and knowing the perfect balance between the prospering of an entity and its constituents, without endangering the existence of either.

As the world becomes metaphorically smaller, we must make sure that Globalization becomes a balanced entity in of itself – an egregore of reciprocal compassion and benevolent advancement. It must become a symbiotic entity, encompassing the cultural diversity of all nations, without engulfing them. It must recognize that in order for it to grow and thrive, the individuals that make up its being must also grow and thrive. Our self-centered ambitions must be fused with the goal of prosperity for all. Too much parasitic action will devour the planet, destroying Globalization along with its host. If the leaves are not nourished, the tree will not grow. If the roots are not watered and firmly established, the branches will not be supported. The true intention of Globalization must be for raising the standard of living of all its participating constituents without becoming a façade for negative exploitation resulting in nefarious ends. If humanity can do this successfully, they will have proven their readiness for their next great challenge in seeking the divine mystery: Universalization.

Chapter 10

The Ten Directives

"THE WAY TO BECOME A spiritual master is to become a perpetual student." – AO

• • • •

PRESENTED BELOW ARE the ways (directives) in which we should all live our lives.

1. Default to a steady state of love when the situation permits and fairly empathize with others – make love your constant.

2. God grows through diversity – engaging pluralism, embrace the mosaic beauty in all shades of creation, skin color, ethnicities, cultures, languages, true religions and people.

3. Strive to improve the well-being of all advanced intelligent sentient beings and minimize negative exploitation and organizational hypocrisy.

4. Commune with the metaphysical realms through the tools of religion; commune with the physical realms through the tools of science. Both are wondrous mysteries to behold while embracing the unitive.

5. Preserve sentient life whenever possible. Be respectful of other forms of life, their relationship with the ecological environment and interactions with the universe.

6. Humbly regard and revere the multitude of true religious paths available to reach God and recognize the commonality of experiences. Any path which advances our relationship with the cosmos by minimizing violence and seeks to improve the fairness of experiences and socioeconomic conditions for all is a true path.

7. Focus on your relationship with divinity and be careful how you judge other people's relationships with divinity. Choose the path that works best for your needs and preferences.

8. Seek to leave the world in the same or in a better condition than when you entered it.

9. Engage, influence and lead by positive example, while avoiding the use of force or coercion. Become your own benevolent role model. True leadership is developed not by power, but by the positive influence upon others based on integrity of character.

10. Do not succumb to hatred or rage, often triggered as a non-productive byproduct of anger, fear, resentment, insecurity, frustration, confusion, disgust or envy. Hatred does more to destroy the person and soul harboring it, than at whom it is directed.

Chapter 11
Religious Distortion

"UNDERSTANDING GOD SEEMS easier than understanding humanity's attempts of forceful interpretations." – AO

• • • •

THE PURPOSE OF FOLLOWING organized religious principles is to know the Supreme Truth and humanity's relationship to him/her/it based on commonality of experience.[527] True religion (organized spirituality) is for the advancement of humanity's relationship with the universe. It wasn't meant to control the spirit, but to free and guide it for continued growth and expression. Unfortunately, the message of sacred texts and scrolls have sometimes been distorted, misapplied, misinterpreted and/or manipulated throughout the centuries by accident, by individuals or by groups for power and control over others. Religion should not be an unobtainable mystery, but rather, an openness of moral truth. Its authenticity does not set itself up to bewilder the mind or puzzle the senses, yet that is our usual reaction to it.[528] Its purpose is to provide clarity out of and above a murky world. It is not perfect, but should strive for accessibility and improvement. Religion was not supposed to mess us up or suppress healthy expression of individuality. It was and is meant to assist us in flourishing.

—Λ*—

"They have tempered with words out of their context and forgotten much of what they were enjoined." – *The Koran*[529]

—*Ω—

The fog of time causes us to conjecture and postulate on the intended message of ancient scriptures, without always having access to absolute truths or to the implied context. The actual meaning sometimes became lost in the dogma of corrupt leaders with self-centered goals and for the false justification of affronts on peace. True religion was never meant as a means of suppression, but rather, it sought to provide its followers with universal guidance. This guidance was for strengthening connections to divinity, preserving culture and advancing the species. The true words of divinity within the sacred scriptures are those that show one how to understand their spiritual existence and their eternal relationship with the godhead. They were never meant to be used for justifying or encouraging unhealthy behavior. Unfortunately, when the fundamental principles of legitimate religions go awry, the resulting outcome is Religious Distortion; a perversion of religious truths and an akin to religious ignorance. It is the manipulation of <u>satyam</u> for selfish reasons.

—A*—

"And there are some among them who twist their tongues when quoting the Scriptures, so that you may think it from Scriptures, whereas it is not from the Scriptures. They say: 'This is from God,' whereas it is not from God. Thus they knowingly ascribe falsehood to God." – *The Koran*[530]

—*O—

Religious Devotion is following the love and truth of the Lord's desires within the merits of religious doctrines. Its antonym is **Religious Distortion**, which reveals itself whenever hatred, falsehood or violence, a disregard for life and wastefulness of resources in the perversion of truth, is used to falsely promote a cause related to God/Allah. Promoting or implementing violence is never the influence of God/Allah. It is purely the misguided actions and incorrect interpretations of and by human elements. Throughout the ages, religion has suffered convulsive distorts, perversions and literal seizures, either out of ignorance or due to self-serving interests. These negative applications under a façade of religious doctrine result in Religious Distortions, a refraction from the truth of divinity's message. The underlying meaning behind the scriptures becomes lost or forgotten as particular passages are distorted or emphasized to condone violence, mistakenly justifying controlling oppression, putting forth needless strictures or used as an excuse for geo-political expansionism. Jesus Christ knew such future distortions would occur even from the misapplication of his own teachings (pointing out to us that the Commandment of Love was mistakenly left out of the original ten) when he said, "Do not think that I came to bring peace on the earth: I came not to send peace, but a sword."[531] He even seems to reject four of the original Ten Commandments by naming only six when someone comes out from the crowd to ask "which ones" should be followed.[532] Why did Jesus leave out the ones pertaining to prohibition of pagan or polytheistic practices while focusing on the ones pertaining to morality and ethical precepts? Did he recognize the multitude of paths and options for reaching the godhead? Did he realize that the Almighty is not concerned about the formalities or denominations used to address him/her as long as the worshipper abides by good character, decency and love? Christ knew that some would understand the truth of his words and embrace them properly while others would distort them for their own conquests and personal self-absorbed phobias such as the slicing brute force and mass murder placed upon the Cathars (a term that became vogue in the late 19th century to describe those "heretical" peoples of Occitania) by the medieval papacy and slaughter of Muslims during quests to occupy the Holy Land. Like the early Christians' willingness to be fed upon by the Emperor's exploited and hungry lions rather than renounce their faith (the Roman authorities were often appalled at their eagerness for martyrdom),[533] the Gnostic-based branches (i.e., Manichaean, Bogomils, Cathars) also underwent untimely deaths at the hands of the papal Catholic Orthodoxy gone astray. Gnosticism was any alternate path to the godhead that did not give control to the Church nor fall in line with Rome's enforced dogma. "Part of the appeal of Gnosticism was its willingness to acknowledge and incorporate pagan, monotheist, dualist and even Buddhist thought, fusing it into a new world view that still reflected its combined Hellenistic and Judaic heritage."[534] They were the inheritors to the thoughts of Babylon, Egypt, Persia, Greece and several other ancient cultures.[535] The Roman Church assimilated all the pagan pantheon of ancient gods into a convenient composite Devil, blaming it for all that was wrong or bad with the world. In reality, said the Bogomils and Cathars alike, it was the early Roman Church that was the Devil. It became a Devil that had distorted Jesus' true teachings in a diabolical manner, by substituting a false version of Christ for the real one.[536] The Cathars insisted that one could communicate with God directly, and if they had succeeded in convincing the masses of this, the Roman Church feared becoming superfluous.[537] Already noticing the empty collection baskets and abandoned chapels within the regions of Albi, Toulouse and Carcassonne, the Church so feared the layperson and commoner discovering the true workings of Christ, that they acted out of self-preservation to suppress, destroy and snuff out any inkling of Gnostic awakenings and maintain their monopolistic grip and control. In doing so, it became the "Evil Empire" being led by the "Dark Side" where every other religious path became the "Rebellion" and had to be squelched.[538]

Despite the Roman emperor Constantine's decriminalization of Christianity in 312, his politicization of a formerly pacifistic-based faith for the militant use of earlier conquest during a power struggle over his brother-in-law's claims to the empire, initiated a veering from its true peaceful calling. As a hero, he initiated the spread and acceptance of Christianity throughout the Roman Empire and its spread to Europe and the Middle East. As a villain, he initiated its distortion, resulting in the discriminatory death of thousands of pagans and erasing almost all traces of Hermeticism. The sad irony of this distortion is that Jesus Christ himself seemed to have a very advanced inherent understanding and aptitude for properly applying Hermetic principles. Constantine murdered his own family members and turned Christ into a talisman of a fascist state and totalitarian empire.[539] With the backing and support of Christians, he turned himself into the Supreme Emperor and Pontifex Maximus, dethroning all other gods, destroying their temples and persecuting their followers and worshippers.[540] In doing so, he gave the early Roman Church the monopolistic power to merge and absorb all existing religions into its own. Christianity then became the most authoritarian and barbaric dogma of the past two millenniums through its distortion. This is not the fault of the religion; it is the fault of mostly men and a few women. What we seem to often overlook is that Christ wasn't just a Judean, he was also a pagan bringing love into the world of the Hebrew heart.[541] Jesus never said wipe out paganism and the spiritual wisdom of other religions while spreading the teachings of the Gospel. His intent was for it to supplement existing paths and indigenous beliefs, not to suppress or eradicate them.

—Δ*—

"Do not think that I have come to abolish the Law or the Prophets; I have not come to abolish them but to fulfill and add to them." – Jesus Christ[542]

—*O—

One of the most infamous religious distortion tragedies was the systematic destruction of the great library at Alexandria and all the knowledge of the ancients that it contained on Egyptian, Hellenistic, Persian and other cultured civilizations of thought. It was subjected to intellectual purging starting about 145 BCE during the reign of Ptolemy VIII Physcon, then damaged about 47 BCE or 45 BCE in a conflagration occurring during one of Julius Caesar's politico-military campaigns, decimated by Christian zealot fanatics starting about 387 under the plotting influence of the local Bishop and then its remains were finally ransacked by Muslim invaders about 641.[543] Using the word "ransacked" may not be fair or appropriate, for it seems that the army of the broad-minded and tolerant Caliph Omar was there to salvage and preserve what was left, rather than to destroy.[544] It was the Muslims during the Dark Ages who desired to preserve the teachings of science and civilization with tolerance, in contrast to the so-called "Christians" who preferred to snuff out anything perceived as a threat to the *status quo* of preferred ignorance. With its emphasis on knowledge, self-discovery, and awareness, the Gnostics were on the path to self-actualization (illumination) without the mob mentality of those "Christians" who stormed temples, smashed statues, destroyed artifacts and trashed libraries. Yes, "Christians" had already established a reputation for smashing "idols" long before Mohammad did. Acting as a virtual library of Alexandria, aspects of today's worldwide internet web seem to be refilling at least some of that lost knowledge and providing access to all – an *episteme* for the ages.[545]

In 325, under the convening request of Constantine and coinciding approximately with the 20th anniversary of his reign, about 300 early Christian leaders met as the Council of Nicaea (aka Nicaeo or Nicene) to establish an orthodox position on the nature of Christ's divinity. Constantine made a guest appearance during the council, making the bishops honored participants.[546] Earlier gospel editions prior to the gathering at Nicaea depict Jesus' death as primarily the fault of the Romans. Later editions in catering to the state, shift the blame as primarily that of his own people; the Jews.[547] The outcome of the Council was a declaration that salvation (enlightenment) could only be obtained through them, the Church of Rome, and they now had the sole authority to "destroy or alter what it chose."[548] All other methods, paths, or views to illumination were conveniently put down as heresy.[549] It was the Patriarch of Alexandria Egypt, Athanasius, who condemned any "apocryphal books" not considered part of his list. In doing so, he forged the New Testament's foundational books that are still treated as the only acceptable mainstream portrayal of Christ's life, singularized views of his teachings and monopolized the means of salvation. Such "apocryphal books" were then burned or destroyed to erase them from history, and in doing so, took much of the great library of Alexandria with it.[550] The outcome of the Council became a doctrine that self-authorized the Church to police, judge, purge and eliminate any threats to its perception of what relating to God should be about and squelch any possible questioning of its status as a superpower. The *New Testament* became a censored and abridged version from an encyclopedic array of available scriptures. In doing so, we do not really know how much or what parts of the included books "...were written by the persons whose names they bear...", "neither are we certain in what language they were originally written."[551] What became the "truth" was decided upon by majority rule, whether it was correct or not.[552] We can be certain that those considered acceptable for inclusion fall under two domains – either anecdotal or epistolary.

What became the *New Testament* at the Council of Nicaea was based on the political bullying of man for power and revenue. While the Gnostics were actually accelerating Christianity in the public domain, Bishop Irenaeus was leading it into a business.[553] He was repeating the behavior of the Judaic Pharisees, exactly what Jesus had vehemently protested against one or two centuries earlier. Irenaeus, who favored the literal interpretations, found arguing with the Gnostics frustrating because they would playfully always agree with him rather than expose what they actually did or did not believe.[554] The literal preferring and profiteering characters later siding with Irenaeus' views, being under the influence of the imperialistic expansion of a militant Roman empire and a desire to establish a profession, primarily forged the *New Testament*, decreed to be the word of God, by vote rather than by revelation or exploration. The Lord seemed absent from the discussions, the ballot and the terror later induced forth from enforcing the outcome. The books of *Matthew*, *Mark*, *Luke* and *John* with their fragments and discordant relations form much of the basis of the Christian Church's doctrine, yet the ministry of Jesus was not written by its founder. Its authenticity was decided upon by election, through the bullies of the committees and by exclusion some 300 years later, not by inclusive investigation. Those of us with a belief that the universe would be willing to enter our world in the form of one of us, to experience, witness, and participate in what it is like to be human, are willing to read between the lines of those fragmented anecdotes and accept that whoever the real authors may have been, they provided us with a glimpse into a truth of a higher meaning. Their words allow us to forgive a universe that was willing to empathize with us, so that it could understand us. The only reason that the universe would be willing to submit itself and enter into our realm as flesh, bone and blood in the first place, was not out of a desire to create hardship, but on the contrary, it was due to curiosity, compassion and love.

The last Roman emperor to rule over a non-divided empire, Theodosius I (aka Theodosius The Great), made the results of the Council of Nicaea as the official state church, creating in essence, an intolerant Christian "caliphate" and putting into play Christendom expansionism.

Some fifty to sixty years after Athanasius' decree, the newly formed Church using Rome's policing power, began its first predatory attack on a "Gnostic heretic". Priscillian, a wealthy nobleman of Roman Hispania who advocated studying the *Bible* as well as apocryphal books, was executed as being a sorcerer in 385 under the authority of Emperor Maximus. Having successfully eliminated one threat to the newly formed Roman Church, the attacks expanded to a whole faith perceived as a threat – the Religion of Light known as the Manichaeans. Theodosius I further distorted Christianity by suppressing polytheistic practices and in 393 decreed a stop to the pagan competitions among state athletic representatives, otherwise known as the Olympic games of Ancient Greece. Among the casualties of pagan suppression was Hypatia (Ὑπατία), a great scientist, mathematician and philosopher. While working in the region of Alexandria in 415 after the library's primary decline, she was seized by a mob of Christian extremists for either political or religious reasons, whom then removed her flesh with shells and burnt her remains.[555] This seemed to be the inauguration of the Dark Ages and the start of declaring women who show any signs of intelligence, secular or spiritual, as being heretics throughout medieval Roman Christendom. Acting as a maddening excuse, her murder laid the groundwork for future torture and executions of the feminine intellect while accusatively exclaiming, "She's a witch!"[556] Perhaps what our society needs these days is more of those "good" witches to heal our mythological psyche.

—Λ*—

"All formal dogmatic religions are fallacious and must never be accepted by self-respecting persons as final." – Hypatia of Alexandria[557]

—*Ω—

The Byzantine Emperor Justinian The Great (482–565) added more to distort Christ's intentions by decreeing the death penalty for all Manichaeans, followers of the Persian prophet Mani (215 or 216–275, 276 or 277 depending on the reference), many who were burnt alive at the stake. So effective was the Church's genocidal eradication of Manichaeism and the anti-Manichaean drives occurring in 9th century Asia, Tibet and China, that nearly all of their scriptures were lost forever.

Their last known existence as a community was in south China in the 14th or 16th century.[558] The religious, ethnic and cultural cleansing of Manichaeans, however, was not absolute, for its Gnostic roots remerged again among the Great Heresy of the Bogomils and Cathars during the late Middle Ages. Fortunately, a number of texts were discovered in a ruined Manichaean monastery in China between 1904 and 1914. Additional findings of Manichaean writings were also discovered in Egypt in 1929 and 1969 and remain available within *The Kephalaia*.[559]

Mani grew up in Babylon as an Elchasaite, a Judaic-Christian sect. After a series of divine revelations, Mani tried to redirect the Elchasaites but was banished for his ideas. He claimed to be of the same traditions as Seth, Zoroaster, the Buddha and Jesus, but stated that those earlier masters did not reveal all nor have a chance to.[560] Manichaeism, called the Religion of Light, was an early attempt at universal religion. Mani was probably the closest of any of the prophets so far of achieving syncretism, merging the antiquities of religious thought (Zoroastrianism, Buddhism, Gnosticism, and Christianity) into a synthesized whole. Its objective was to save humanity through one all-encompassing religion, combining elements of Zoroastrianism, Christianity and Buddhism as a means to appeal to as many people as possible.[561] What Mani attempted, the Cathars rekindled and took it to the next level. Early on, Mani was provided with court patronage but as politics changed due to royal transitions, he fell from favor allowing enemies among the Zoroastrian priesthood to eradicate his self-styled preaching. Mani, reaching at least sixty years of age, was then subject to a kangaroo court, sentenced to death, thrown in prison and perhaps tortured, before expiring. Manichaean texts read that realizing his moment of death had arrived, Mani went into prayer and meditation and ascended out of his body prior to being fetched by the guards and tortured to death.[562] Having lost the satisfaction of torturing and controlling Mani's death, the emperor of the Iranian state took his anger and frustration out on the remaining body. The corpse was stuffed with straw, decapitated and portions of the remains were put on display above the city gates.[563] The term

"Manichaean" then later became applied to anyone considered following a heretical path or not abiding to enough of the Roman Church's orthodoxy. Ironically, the very etymological definition of "heretic" is from the Greek word *hairetikos* (αιρετικος), which means "able to choose" – uncannily close to the definitional basis of the word "freedom."[564] This continued distortion of Christianity, a policy of resistively smothering intelligence or alternate perspectives for communing with God, through the last days of the Roman Empire ushered in the next millennium with a decline in human advancement and squelched thirst for knowledge within Europe, contributing to the continent's entrance into the Dark Ages. One might even say that the subduing of the Gnostics by the Roman Church's quest for monopolistic power resulted in the Dark Ages.

—A*—

"An age is called Dark not because the light fails to shine but because people fail to see it." – James Michener[565]

—*O—

It was then an announcement by Pope Gregory VII during his tenure (1073–1085) that set the stage for a backlash of dissent. He decreed that the Roman Catholic Church was the only means by which one could commune with God and every other church or religion was false, thus safeguarding and perpetuating its elitist privileges. His claim of the Church's supremacy intrinsically self-invited the pope himself as the highest-ranking authority on what God wanted of us. It set into motion a quest for material accumulation and secular gain among an utterly corrupt and power hungry papal hierarchy that did little for its followers, other than positioning itself as a barrier or toll gate between its believers and the Lord.[566]

Other examples of such Euro-Asia geo-political excursions of conquest through Religious Distortion include the Crusades to the Holy Land by adults and exploited child-aged knights (who never made it far) during the Middle Ages. In January of 1208, Pierre de Castelnau, a papal envoy sent to scold Count Raymond VI of Toulouse for being too lenient with the Cathars, was murdered on his way back to Rome. It was probably committed by a rogue soldier or villager on behalf of his loyalty in defending the Count of Toulouse's honor, for the Count himself would have known that ordering Pierre's assassination would trigger unwanted repercussions from Rome. Triggered they did, for the infuriated Pope Innocent III then excommunicated all Cathars and those who supported them declaring "anyone who attempted to construe a personal view of God which conflicted with Church dogma must be burned without pity."[567] Excommunication meant being declared an "outlaw" and subject to death unless one was willing to cower and beg for forgiveness under the papal rulers.[568] This excommunication was the beginning of the Roman Catholic Church's violent purge of other Christians; a time of "Christians" turning on other Christians. Initiated by Pope Innocent III in 1209, it started with the Albigensian Crusade, two decades of besieges by warlords conducting land grabs and quests for power under the guise of cleansing the Languedoc region (the district of Albi) of so-called Christian heretics – "the friends of God." These land grabs by northern French nobles and authorized by the papacy, were mimicked on a smaller scale by the Union army's seizing of private property within conquered Confederate regions of the late 19th century United States. The fuse was initially lit in the early 13th century Languedoc region of France by exchanged insults at the walls of Béziers and then flash ignited into hundreds of towns and villages being laid to waste, the start of the massacre occurring during the celebrated feast day of Saint Mary Magdalene. It became a genocidal annihilation of both non-Cathars and the ascetic Cathars (men, women and children who were probably more pious and holy than the Catholic clergy of the time period) of southern France. The Albigensian spiritual leadership was a paragon of virtue compared to the decadence of the Catholic clergy.[569] Even their accusers noted their decency of character and the Catholic Bernard of Clairveaux had the following to say: "If you interrogate them, no one could be more Christian. As to their conversation, nothing can be less reprehensible, and what they speak they prove by deeds. As for the morals of the heretics, they cheat no one, they oppress no one, they strike no one."[570] Yes, these are the very people the Church of Rome decided to annihilate.

The Cathars were generally pacifists, unlike the crusaders and inquisitors who hunted and annihilated them. In line with the saying "from tragedy comes comedy", the classic cinematic spoof titled *Monty Python And The Holy Grail* (1975) makes an indirect parody of the insults exchanged between a band of crusaders and defenders at the town walls of Béziers, France – "your mother was a hamster and your father smelt of elderberries."[571] Those highest on the Cathar religious leadership were called "perfects" (aka parfaits) and were passionate about their theology. Often called the "good men" and "good women" by the locals and for justifiable reasons, they were merely trying to awaken the divinity within for all of humanity, exactly what Jesus was trying to teach us. Although women were considered equal in spiritual potential, the male Cathars were not always sincere towards promoting them within their ranks, for the feminine equality seemed to fluctuate depending on the time period and region.[572]

The Catholic Church felt that divinity should be reserved for the elite and their staff only, and that God could not possibly dwell within the common folk. The Gnostic brand was about each individual reaching spiritual maturity and themselves becoming a "Christ." The Roman Church's brand was about sales in preparation for when the "End of the World" was to arrive. The Albigensian Crusade was then soon followed by the European Inquisitions forged by papal and monarchial politics upon the slightest threats to the Church's exclusive sovereignty on interpreting God's desires. The use of "mild" torture was officially church sanctioned by Pope Innocent IV in 1251 at the beginnings of the Inquisitive years. It was brutally and sadistically accelerated by the Dominican Order of monks and others, upon anyone with behavior or beliefs considered contrary, regardless if they were or not, to the dogma of medieval Orthodox Christian ideology. The Inquisitors and critics ignorantly and foolishly interpreted the Cathar canons literally and at face value, and in doing so, twisted their meaning. Although those popes of the Middle Ages and the King of France were satisfied with their extinguishing of the Cathars, it was a hollow victory. The very fact that we even consider to talk about the Gnostics, the Bogomils or the Cathars, means that there is a motivation for the continuance of their esoteric conceptions, which hopefully, will again enter the mainstream of modern thought.

The spirit of the Cathars still remains strong in the land that they were forced from, a land which extends from bordering pockets of the Rhineland to the countryside of Southern France to the slopes of Northern Italy and still whispers of the sorrow and slaughter that it witnessed. Through the Catholic Church's hiring of mercenaries to do as they pleased to the people and land of the French countryside, it was a holocaust of Christian upon Christian that smoldered for some 50 years or more. The Roman Catholic church had a penchant for the smell of burnt human flesh in its executions of Gnostic followers and leadership, from the supreme leader of the Bogomils, (aka Vasili Vrach, Basil the Physician), who was ignited upon a huge pyre sometime between 1111 to 1118, to the last official record of a Cathar "perfect" being executed in the summer of 1321 and the last Cathar being executed in Italy in 1389.[573] At an anti-Bogomil council in 1211, Cosmas the Priest puts forth the following accusation: "They denounce wealth, they have a horror of the Tsar, they ridicule their superiors, condemn the nobles and forbid all slaves to obey their masters."[574] Wow! The Bogomils were over 800 years ahead of their time.

The viciousness and detestable arrogance of this holocaust against the Gnostics was a repeat of what had occurred in the year 70 by the Roman military upon the Jewish culture and an introductory prelude of what was to come some 700 years later, resurfacing in "The Red Summer" of 1919 upon Americans of African descent and implemented by the National Socialist Party (Nazi) controlled Europe to come a few years later. The Catholic Church of that medieval time and the Nazi regime to come seven centuries later both believed that they must seize and confiscate the sacred and secret teachings away from those who possess them.[575] What was that treasure in the possession of the Cathars that the Catholic Church so desperately desired to either obtain or destroy? What was it that was lowered down the cliff face of Montségur and whisked away for safekeeping by that small band of "parfaits"? Was it a lost original *Gospel of John*, a complete copy of the *Gospel of Mary* or a whole version of the *Gospel of Judas* that was sent away for protection during the ending moments of the siege of that final Pyrenean stronghold considered to be a "Temple of Satan" by the Roman crusading religious authorities?[576] Was it the actual physical chalice of Christ from the Last Supper or an understanding of how to properly apply Hermetic principles that was hidden away in secrecy during those final hours before March 16, 1244? Were they books, scrolls and writings saved almost 1000 years earlier from the library at Alexandria prior to its demise or a knowledge of how to step out of the realm of time? Was it a gift of clairvoyance, healing and telepathy that could be trained upon willing students and thus the removal of a fear of Hell? Or was it knowledge of the father of children born of Mary Magdalene's womb and the genealogy lineage of Lady Sara, the supposed child of that divine union that was kept hidden from the eyes of Archbishop of Narbonne and the Seneschal of Carcassonne?[577] Was it that there was some truth in their belief of human beings containing the sexless spirits of angels trapped in the material realm, who were destined to continued cycles of transmigration until finally recognizing their divinity and connection to a good God? The notion of a Cathar treasure still out there in or near the French Pyrenees, waiting to be discovered either in a cave, on a hill, near a boulder or within ourselves, keeps writers, mystics and readers alike awake at night.

Otto Rahn, in tempting to appease the leadership of the Schutzstaffel (the Nazi SS), pursued anything considered to have mystical powers, even taking over other cultures' heritage and contortedly claiming their ancestry to be that of the so-called "Master Race" of Nordic German descent. Despite having insufficient written records of their peaceful beliefs and ways (most what we do have is based on the biased prosecution put forth by their main nemeses, the Inquisitors by the Dominican Order), the Cathar story is still very much alive. It was the spiritual energy of the Bogomils and Cathars, we can call it the influence of a benevolent Force, erecting a bridge through history that set into motion the Renaissance from the 14th to the 17th centuries, the Reformation of the 16th and 17th centuries and influenced the Age of Enlightenment coming forth in the 18th century.[578] It is a bridge of worshipping the inner light of God to become brighter and purer than our current lives and in doing so, becoming more charged with love for our fellow beings. That bridge is opening up again within the first quarter of this 21st century, for "the spontaneous expression of the natural inquisitiveness and enthusiastic exuberance of the human soul" can never be permanently quenched.[579] The thirst for truth, joy, liberty, wisdom, equality, insight and love is the force of life, the being of Sophia, reasserting herself.[580]

We must recognize and acknowledge that the Roman Catholic Church of today is not the same as its infant and medieval counterparts. Yes, it previously practiced blatant hypocrisy, such as on one hand, praising Francis of Assisi for his love of the natural world and even canonizing him into sainthood within two years after his departure. Then on the other hand, declaring the Fraticelli (a later sect of his students and disciples) as being heretical for their path of poverty and extremes of asceticism, sending many to be burnt at the stake. Yes, it was the growing dogmatic orthodox of the fledgling Church that stamped out and persecuted believers in Gnosticism (Valentinians, Carpocratians, Cainites, Borborites/Phibionites, Sethians, Ophites) in its early centuries, for they were considered the competition in a developing totalitarian Roman-Christian playing field. Rather than incorporate and mingle Gnosticism into the Gospels, it chose a path of eradication, spiritual suppression and intellectual genocide.[581] What was it about Gnosticism that the early fledgling Roman Church so feared to put into its canonical writings? Was it that they didn't like the idea of the feminine being treated as complementary equal to the masculine, with women also playing an active role as teacher, missionary or prophetess? Was there a degree of truth to Gnostic doctrine that the early Church leadership, in forming its orthodoxy, so feared and did not want acknowledged? When under an authoritative hierarchy that lost its true mission, Rome started habitually resorting to rumor-mongering to attack their targets, falsely accusing anyone perceived as generating dissent as having participated in moral indecency. Although the Church committed atrocities led by power-crazed popes during its dark and delinquent years after the fall of the Roman Empire and well past the 16th century, projecting its own diabolical behaviors upon anyone seen as a threat, it has made efforts to mend its ways. It has also done substantial good for humanity when under the direction of more enlightened leadership and reformations in the direction of illumination. For even Pope John Paul II apologized, indirectly to a degree, in March 2000 for the behavior of his earlier predecessors and their destructive distortion of the Gospels for the misguided implementation of the Crusades and terror of the Inquisition. Today's followers of the Catholic faith are not accountable, nor responsible for the sins of Catholics from prior generations just as modern Germany is not liable for the atrocities of the Nazi party. Many of their ancestors were also victims of leadership gone astray. Even Saint Lutgarde of Aywiéres was misinformed during her fasting and prayers for the Cathar's "crimes" with their belief in a material world that was seen as evil and favoring the view of a Christ that was not human.[582] Many others, such as Bert Ghezzi (the author of *Mystics & Miracles*), have also been misinformed about the nature and details of the Cathar "heresy".

It is time to forgive the Roman Catholic Church for its earlier transgressions and to reawaken the Cathar consciousness within us. History is to be acknowledged, and then all should proceed forth with reconciliation in the direction of compassion and love. True Christianity can have elements of both the Cathar and the Catholic, the orthodoxy and the heterodoxy, and still remain whole. The orthodox seems to come forth from elements of the gnostic, the heterodox comes forth from elements of the orthodox, and then the gnostic comes forth again from elements of the heterodox – an Ouroboros of continuation. For the heterodox is the budding child of the orthodox, they are of the same family, the same tree. As the parent has given the world what was needed at the time, a stability from which to launch, the child carries elements of the parent while becoming its own entity.

We are too well aware of the horrors of religious and cultural intolerance – from the persecution of Christians shortly after Christ's secular existence, the Nazi state sponsored anti-Semitism of the earlier half of the 20th century, the attacks between Hindus, Muslims and Sikhs during the de-colonization of the Indian sub-continent post War World II, and the Chinese government's systematic oppression of the Uighurs (asa Uyghurs) within this first quarter of the 21st century. The Americas also had their incidents of Religious Distortion as well. There was the forced evangelical destruction of indigenous religious perspectives from various proselytizing Christian denominations emigrating from Europe and the Mountain Meadows Massacre, the murder of about 120 people of the Fancher-Baker Party by early Mormon militias in 1857. As a credit to The Church of Jesus Christ of the Latter-day Saints of modern times, they have acknowledged the blemish in their history and have done much to be open about the truth of the atrocity. The destructive replacement of Buddhist statues with Hindu statues during state sponsored violence that swept through Cambodia in 1219 is no different than the more recent attacking of its religious works of art in 2001 by the Taliban. Armenian and Greek Orthodox monks have brawled with each other at the revered site of Jesus' tomb and Buddhists followers are no exception to occasional flair ups of violence.[583] Even though aggressive thoughts and violence are inimical to all Buddhist teachings (destruction or injury to life is strictly forbidden), there has been infighting with fists among bhikkhus and Buddhist provoked outbreaks of mob violence against Muslims, especially in central Burma, Sri Lanka and other nearby regions. Muslims have also initiated violence upon Buddhists. Zoroastrians have persecuted Manicheans and Christians, and Muslims have persecuted Zoroastrians, but at different points in the past. The Pagans have enslaved the Christians and then the Christians have enslaved the Pagans – one dogmatic religion striving to eradicate the knowledge and wisdom of another "competing" religion. The orthodoxy violently attacking the heterodoxy is nothing more than the devil's influence and manipulations. The pendulum of an oppressive majority persecuting the minority, the establishment suppressing the schism, the fundamentalist branch attacking a sprouting bud, seems to swing back and forth continuously within the timeline of history's sectarian violence. The following is a direct commandment from God: "**It is time for the violence to stop!**"

The battle cries of the *Old Testament* have made Yahweh the hitman, Elohim the assassin and Jehovah the exterminator hired by the early Jewish religion, eliminating all Gentiles and Heathens, moral or not, to make more room for the widening of the Judaic path and expansion of its real estate. That "ethnic cleansing" god, the one at the beginnings of the Desert religions, "seems confused, morally dissonant and ultimately incompatible" with the God revealed to us by Jesus.[584] In revenge of all the butchery committed by the ancient Hebrews as described in the *Tanakh*, perhaps this is why anti-Semitism continues to peek up its ugly head in unfair responses to residual ancestral memories. Yet it is "Christian" triumphalism and empire building that resulted in so much more slaughter, torture and loss of life. Just as no son should be blamed for the sins of his father and no daughter should be blamed for the sins of her mother, no posterity should be blamed for the sins of their ancestors. The *New Testament* made the Lord into a martyr of himself, preaching for no more than three years to expel the older, harsher ways of the Hebrew faith and then dangling the hope of his someday return upon the desires of humanity. The radical extremist Muslim (if we should even associate Islam with them is questionable) has made Allah into a being that views all other paths to divinity as that of the "infidel" and who rates one's entrance into paradise by how many others they brought with them in massive acts of self-destruction and murder. The Hindu can't decide which aspect to worship and the Buddhist has tried to eliminate God all together from the scene. The authentic religious seeker and genuine philosopher, however, recognizes that the ramblings of negative exploitation in the scriptures are distortions and falsehoods of men, women, and all of humanity, allowing hatred to creep into their egos rather than love to merge with their Ego. The true believer knows to focus on the kindness and goodness put forth by all the great religions, and not to dwell in their flaws and imperfections.

Some of us have forgotten that all human creativity comes from that initial divine spark planted within each and every one of us. It does not matter which true path we follow, so long as we peacefully allow others to travel their true paths. What we do with that spark of creative free will determines how far we travel on the path of enlightenment. Do we create a better world around us or do we create a wake of harm as we travel through life? A relatively few misguided individuals throughout history have chosen to distort the words of their religious text(s) or prophet(s), thus tarnishing the beauty of God's underlying message. Humanity as a whole is starting to learn, but distortions still continue today. Many religious escapades have claimed they fight in the name of the Lord or they die for Allah. How many times has violence been promoted as a means of action for instantaneous change? How many times have zealot individuals and groups promoted violence through their ignorant actions and words? Christianity had self-serving individuals and groups promoting and romanticizing the Crusades, when in actuality it was more of a suicidal and genocidal ransacking fueled by indiscriminate pillaging and looting. The Crusaders were astounded and even envious of how the Muslim regions' prosperity put the Christion lands to shame.

Within the recent decades, elements of "Christofascism" cropping up in far-right ideologies are comparative to Islamic Fundamentalism, with both distorting the true instructional intent of their founding prophets' words. Islam has its misinterpretation of the Jihad to aggressively promote terrorism under the façade of it being a "holy" war. In the late 20th and early 21st century, there has been the unfortunate congealing of radical supposedly Islamic leaders and groups that distort and twist Mohammad's teachings to justify their violent actions and desires. They have forgotten that "Islam" and "peace" are both derived from the same Arabic etymological roots. After physical departure from this realm, Allah will judge their works of evil accordingly and their souls, due to their own undoing, will be tormented and diminished to coincide with the actions they implemented upon others.

It is unfortunate that Mohammad's message of compassion seems to be overshadowed by those fractional elements distorting the underlying meaning of Islam to justify hate, anger and violence. He was against the geo-political powers of his time that were based on a religious economic hierarchy which suppressed the ability for talent to flourish. One's economic place in that time period became determined by their religious following. He was not specifically intolerant of other religious paths, but rather, favored common religious bonding as a means to provide for fair trading practices and opportunities. Having an awareness of other religious paths often helps us to better understand and reconnect with our own. A myopic religious perspective does not coincide with God's desire for humanity to seek knowledge, wisdom and truth. Certain individuals and radical groups have unfortunately tarnished the true meaning of the *Koran*. Acting as religious gangsters, such misguided followers commit atrocities under the guise of foolishly believing they are doing it for a greater cause. I can assure you, no act of violence ever justifies a greater religious cause. The destruction of another's body, place of worship or ancient structures of worship is really the destruction of self. Imagine how Mohammad feels seeing terrorism justified as a Holy War in the name of Allah. He is saddened by such misguided use of his message to humanity.

We must all come to realize that the only true Jihad or Crusade is the striving for the spiritual advancement of all of humanity. It is based on peaceful confrontations with the suffering and ignorance of others as well as the confrontation of the suffering and ignorance within ourselves. However strong the tempting calls of distorted Islamic extremism is for a violent jihad, the hugely influential Sufi orders taught that the real struggle, the genuine Jihad, was the inner battle to control one's sinful human instincts, and this mattered vastly more than any pathetic clash of swords, spears, guns or bombs. The Greatest Jihad is one's own internal fight for their soul.[585] The way to free oneself from the world of suffering is by empathizing with those who are immersed in it, while rising above it through the spreading of joy. It is a non-violent "holy war" against the poverty, hunger, distress, negative exploitation, suppression and ignorance of all humanity. There are many weapons that can be used to win a true Jihad or authentic Crusade and they are charity, compassion, kindness, respect and healthy tolerance – all being elements of love. Activating the ultimate weapon of love, however, is through a positive education instead of a miseducation (negative education). The awareness of knowledge and ideas beyond our current intellectual and spiritual bounds, even at the risk of drastically changing our perception of reality, is the ultimate mechanism to winning any true holy war.

Humanity's search for all-encompassing unity to the universe created a distorted quest for monotheism. In doing so, the mythology of polytheism was abandoned, if not sacrificed, for the intuitive logic of a monotheistic model. The ancient idols of statues representing gods, goddesses and the personifications of nature and human emotional experiences became taboo. The first historically known recognition of a civilization moving away from a polytheistic approach and towards a monotheistic entity that encompasses all, goes back to an Egyptian Pharaoh named Akhenaten (asa Echnaton, Akhenaton, Ikhnaton or Khuenaten) who reigned around 1352 BCE. He was the husband of Queen Nefertiti and father of the boy Pharaoh now popularly referred to as King Tut.[586] His monotheistic approach of worshipping one primary entity, the sun-god Aten, was viewed as heretically unacceptable by the numerous polytheistic priests and among some of the population of the time period. The monotheistic approach was temporarily abandoned after his death and there were attempts to erase records of his reign from history, perhaps partially as retaliation for his removal of pagan iconography and from the many polytheistic priests put out of a job during his rule. The Prophet Moses came forward as the leader to reawaken the notion of a monotheistic path about a half to a full century later.

As monotheism began to catalyze in the central Middle Eastern regions, coalescing as Judaism and Zoroastrianism, it revolted against polytheistic paths and pagan approaches to divinity and began a suppression of their practices. In doing so, it disregarded that it had morphed from them and because of them. Idol worship in the form of worshipping a statuesque representation of an aspect of God/Allah is considered a severe sin in both the biblical *Old Testament* and the *Koran*. Several sections in those scriptures point out to how wrong it is to do so.[587] Yet, I cannot believe that the ultimate force of the universe would feel jealous or threatened by the actions of peaceful worship of inanimate idols by humans. The Almighty saying that he is jealous when a human benevolently worships a clay or stone representation is preposterous! That is like saying the Sun is jealous of the Moon. If the Lord has such human-like insecurities and feelings of low self-esteem, then it would portray a God who is not perfect. I believe such insertions into the scriptures against peaceful idol worships were the influence of human biases, not the word of God. Personally, I would rather go right to the source and worship the oneness of divinity in all its forms instead of going through several intermediaries, but that is everyone's personal choice and freedom to follow.

Some of those ancient idols were in the wrong direction of the godhead and followers practiced negative exploitation based on misinterpreted demands, such as the self-mutilation and child sacrifice sought of the war god Ba'al or Molech, the prostitution believed encouraged by the goddess Asherah and the human sacrifices thought to delight Chemosh.[588] As I recall, however, the monotheistic god named Yahweh of the *Old Testament* almost demanded a child sacrifice, that of Abraham's son.[589] This seems to make the one and only God of the *Torah* a hypocrite. Idol worship in the *New Testament* expands beyond statues and to anything that can block our path to divinity. Fixation and unhealthy obsession on the written words and literal interpretations of scripture is a form of its own idolatry.[590] Too much focus on personal material gain, supporting questionable leadership or acting out with dysfunctional behavior has become a modern-day form of idol worship.

In the trend of focusing on a singular connection, others were attacked for their polytheistic views, even if such connections were truly benevolent in nature. It is unclear, however, which polytheistic groups were worshipping the statuesque idols at their face value, and which groups were merely using the idols as representative focal points (similar to a shrine or talisman) for tuning into a particular aspect of Allah. The question is, were those ancient cultures worshipping the material statue itself or merely using them as a means to focus the energy of their prayers, honing in on the aspect of God that it represented? Was it wrong for them to use a material item as a focus for their prayers? Do the historic artifacts and modern shrines of Islam, Buddhism, Christianity, Hinduism, Judaism and the various other true religions not serve as the same means as a focusing talisman for reflecting on one's place in the universe and relationship to divinity? Perhaps the intolerance to the ancient idols was based on human fear, ignorance and misunderstanding, rather than a legitimate edict from God. I cannot fathom a Supreme Being who is all powerful and loving being jealous over other gods. I can't believe that the all-encompassing Allah who made us and the universe would be jealous of our material creations. This would imply an imperfect and insecure God succumbing to a human emotional failing. Perhaps the Lord of yesterday was susceptible to human emotional dysfunctionality, but the Allah of today has matured and grown with wisdom, love, tolerance and respect. If you follow a monotheistic approach to the godhead, I am not saying to change your religious path to that of polytheistic approach. I am saying to respect those whose culture incorporates polytheism within its framework. If everything is God, is not the multitude of religious paths also God?

Mohammad was against one's societal status and trading rights being determined by which statuesque idol or god they worshipped and within which tribe they belonged. His physical destruction of such idols and tribal identifiers at the Kaaba in approximately 630 (year 8 of the Muslim calendar) after his entrance to Mecca was not directly against the religions, their talismans, articles or pathways, but rather it was a symbolic destruction of economic boundaries and limitations. Unfortunately, the equality intent behind his symbolic destruction of idols has become distorted in modern times by an unenlightened few to justify attacks and violence upon other religions and their works of art. He never meant for the erasure of artifacts from other religions or mythologies from history, but rather, was for the elimination of economic and social discrimination associated with such labels. Mohammad's geo-political unification of the region through commonality of religion was his effort to improve equality and to dispel the entrenchment of tribal hierarchies and infighting. He was against the tribal gang-like mentality that ruled Arabic socio-economic status in the 6th and 7th century; a tribal mentality which, unfortunately, still seems to have cropped up among governing bodies and radical extremists of zealot fanatics in the late 20th century and early

21st century. One can only hope, إنْ شَاءَ اللّٰهُ , for the extinguish of such conflicts by the end of the 21st century through the recognition of Allah/God's desire for diversity in all the paths of love travelled to reach him/her and through the spread of and access to economic opportunities for all.

There is no such thing as killing and conquering in God's name. Any individual or group that claims they kill in the name of the Lord is false. Even the *Koran* puts forth the notion of not killing one another and condemns it.[591] In fact, every chapter (sūrah) in the *Koran* (except the 9th) begins the Basmala with the term Bism Allah (aka Bismallah). The Basmala is a phrase which translates into "In the Name of God, the Compassionate, the Merciful." Is the killing and murder of others compassionate and merciful? I think not and Mohammad would agree.

—Λ*—

"He that fights for God's cause fights for himself. God needs no man's help." – *The Koran*[592]

—*Ω—

Those who kill in the name of Allah have been deceived by the demons within their own minds. Succumbing to the influence of evil jinn, they have allowed themselves to be influenced and overtaken by those seeking to spread their plague of hatred. I can assure you, a path of violence leads away from the direction of Allah. There is no such thing as a well-intentioned act of violence. Fighting or igniting conflagrations of violence to enforce one's faith or particular religious sect upon others is a grievous sin against God. There is only killing and murder in the name of human failings, not in the name of Allah. Never use Jesus, Mohammad, God or Allah as an excuse for killing – doing so is a sin. The turning of passion for religion and the path that is followed into an excuse or reason for violence is exactly what Satan wants you to do.

How does one find that balance between protecting ourselves, our rights and our property versus keeping the peace? At what point do we stand our ground so as not to become a "doormat" to be walked upon? When attacked and with no means left by which to diffuse the situation, you have the God-given right to defend yourself, but not to further escalate the affront. Whenever possible, we should strive for the protection and preservation of the lives of others, even those of our enemies. Those who provide compassion, charity and seek to change the world through non-violent means follow the true path to Allah.

We kill in the name of humans, not God. When humanity goes to war with each other, Allah mourns. He mourns that his human creations have chosen to destroy advanced sentient life rather than preserve it. Just as a parent who loves all their children, God too feels the anguish when his children fight. God does not always take sides in such aggressions, but rather, accepts that war and violence is the desperation encountered when his children have not yet grown up and cannot peacefully solve their differences. How would any parent feel when their children fight one another? Perhaps anguish, frustration, mourning, hurtfulness, unhappiness and even disgust. When God sees his children fighting one another in violence, he feels the same way as a loving parent. God cries when humanity fights each other in actions of skirmishes, battles and war. And remember, God sees all and knows all, including your innermost thoughts.

Freedom fighters confront oppressive military forces; terrorists target and attack civilians – there is a difference. Terrorism is not new. Rogue elements primarily unsatisfied with their perceived level of representation among the state or a non-acceptance of their ideology have taken out their frustrations on civilian targets for centuries. Even in the days of the Roman conquest of Judea over two millennium ago, cells of assassins (most likely members of the Zealots or Sicarii) stabbed Roman officials and any Jews appearing to collaborate with them, regardless if they were or not.[593] Terrorism is the negative exploitation of the innocent and has a historically statistically inverse ratio of hysteria and fear to actual resulting harm. Despite the inflicted violence, terrorist groups fail and are unsuccessful 94% of the time to achieve any of their strategic goals and objectives.[594] The deaths from terrorism on a global scale dwarfs the deaths caused by pandemics and a lack of cooperation between nations. Leaders of terroristic groups feed on recruiting the disenchanted by offering a comradery of belonging aimed at the unproductive use of anger and frustration turned to hatred. Their acts and tactics often alienate the populace, potential sympathizers and certainly the state, as they unproductively force their own agenda and demands through tantrums of violence. Terrorism is an act that goes against the word of God. Mohammad himself will be one of the prosecutors confronting the soul of any murderer of the innocent. Allah will see them as evil jinn and deal with their souls accordingly. There is no such thing as killing in the name of Allah. A martyr of the faith is someone unfairly and unjustly murdered for their beliefs, not someone following delusions while murdering others. The objective is to avoid becoming a martyr so that one may prolong their benevolent influence into this world. If one allows themselves to be martyred when it could have been prevented, then the inner and spiritual person are prematurely denied the opportunity for full expression and blossoming.[595] Both Christians and Muslims have a history of being ready to die or kill for deluded concepts and misapplied catchphrases, all for a cunningly promised pay-off conveniently reserved for us by the Devil in the afterlife.[596] Unfortunately, those who kill others in the distorted name of their religion will not find themselves blessed with "virgins" in paradise, but rather, they will become the food of demons.[597] The demons will be the personification of the pain and horror they have caused to others reflected back upon them tenfold. The world is not always a perfect or fair place, but resorting to hate, anger and violence to perpetuate a cause only results in the worsening of conditions. The emphasis of dealing with dire conditions should be through positive actions, seeking clarity, patience, charity, kindness and forgiveness. Dwelling on hatred, anger, fear and intolerance only allows demons to form and enter into our core and blocks our relationship with Allah.

There is no honor in killing. In times of war, there is honor in defending a position, saving comrades, rescuing captives, capturing an enemy stronghold, but there is no honor in the act itself of killing. Unfortunately, due to desperation, aspects of humanity still resort to conflict as a means for settling disputes. The violence of war takes hold in situations where logical perspectives and good arguments of diplomacy fail. There are times when bullies must be confronted. Sometimes the conflicts are just and other times they are not. The advice given by the Lord Sri Krsna to his friend and devotee Arjuna as described in the *Bhagavad-Gita* is an example of sentient beings trying to come to terms for dealing with war. Arjuna is overcome with extreme empathy, grief and pity at the thought of having to kill others (many who are his relatives, colleagues and teachers), in an act of upcoming war. He can no longer function and is bewildered as to the correct course of action. Lord Sri Krsna reveals that it is Arjuna's duty to fight for a cause perceived as just and explains the continuum of existence beyond the current physical realm. "Though the soul is immortal, violence is not encouraged, but at the time of war it is not discouraged when there is actually a need for it."[598]

Duty and loyalty should not be given blindly, but towards causes and individuals that are worthy of our honor. War and the associated sacrifices and costs should always be avoided whenever possible, but with the understanding that it is a desperation of last resort. For war itself is not glorious and not honorable. It is misery and mass killing often triggered by unrighteous cultural behavior, invasions falsely justified with politicized propaganda or an outcropping of an individual's despotic ideology. These are ideologies that simmer in the minds of zealous narcissistic leadership with a lack of compassion, a need for admiration and delusions of unlimited success, power, intelligence and infallible goodness. The results of which incorporate a belief system that results in the death of millions.[599] It often starts with pocket regimes that disseminate from thugs. Thugs which enforce the pursuit for a self-serving false and delusional utopia – a narcissistic illusion of personal fantasy that ignites and propagates with based categorical characteristics suffixed with "-cide": liberticide, genocide, ethnocide, politicide and democide. The 20th century had its share of tyrannical polices and ideologies implemented upon the masses by such demagogues as Hitler, Stalin, Mao and Pol Pot. Starting with their muffling and then elimination of thinkers and intellects, the final results were "cidal" outcomes. The world has learned to watch for, and at times take preemptive action, for when such characteristics show signs of again frothing forth.

There is a duality in the view of religion and how it has been implemented. On the one hand it expresses an impetus for following a moral compass, compassion and works of charity. On the other, it can mistakenly catalyze violence, irrationality, intolerance, racisms, tribalism, bigotry, being contemptuous of women and coercive to children.[600] One must recognize, however, that the negative aspects of religion are often due to misuse by a minority of its followers or a distortion by its overall leadership. Trying to justify torture, violence, the conquering of others under the veil of religious justification is as illogical and meaningless as stating that a newspaper headline caused the prior day's events – it just doesn't make sense.

The duality of religion is much like the duality of water. Water is necessary for life and for quenching thirst. When misdirected, however, it can result in devastation and drownings due to flooding and tsunamis. Religion when applied with love, has contributed to raising the conditions of civilizations, preserved societies through times of turmoil, advanced cultural standards and improved human relationships. When applied with hate, it has tarnished humanity, resulted in societal regression, and contributed to negative exploitation. Religions are tools for communing with God and culture often ingrains them. Those tools then become both functional and symbolic to a particular ethnicity group or subset and are composed of the generally practiced ceremonies, traditions, customs, rituals and related paraphernalia. Understanding the challenges of religious tools provided by God can be easier than comprehending the ways in which humanity chooses to implement them; to build, to repair or to destroy. How such tools are used determines the outcome and the direction of either towards or away from enlightenment.

There are dysfunctional individuals, dysfunctional families, dysfunctional organizations, dysfunctional ethos, dysfunctional governments, dysfunctional ideologies and dysfunctional cultures. Cultures and groups throughout history have been led astray by distorted religious interpretations that have resulted in destructive ideologies based on hatred, fear and intolerance. Unfortunately, the leaders of these destructive movements often use religious façades as their excuse for immoral behavior. It is not the fault of the religion, but rather that of individuals and groups with underdeveloped cores. Within the great scriptures throughout the ages, there have been warnings about such false prophets, fallacious messiahs (*mashiah shekers*) with miscreant religious deviations that would erode and warp the roadway leading to God.

We are well aware of religious zealots pushing their own egos in front of the multiple paths of truth. There have been many false teachers and false prophets throughout history pushing the agenda of their own ego above that of the godhead. Either because of mental illness, self-aggrandizing delusions or political motives, they succumbed to the temptations of hatred, unbalanced power, anger and intolerance of that which may be different, but not necessarily bad or threatening. Often, these misguided ideologies are a cancerous byproduct extruding forth from broken political systems, corrupted governments and extremely dysfunctional individuals. Through their false charisma and unwarranted potential for a better future, they charmed their followers with lies and deceit. The late 20th century harmful cults of Reverend Jim Jones of the Peoples Temple, David Koresh of the Branch Davidians, Luc Jouret and Jo Di Mambro of the Order of the Solar Temple, Marshall Applewhite of Heaven's Gate and the disciples of Aum Shinrikyo are a few examples of where recent charismatic false prophets tarnished the paths to the godhead. Early 21st century cults of religious distortions have appeared in the Grace Road Church's move to Fiji and revivals of the Order of the Black Sun may be the next one in the news appearing along with the unsubstantiated paranoid and sensationalized conspiracy theories of QAnon's falsehoods. Understand this eternal truth – the only true prophets of God are those whose words and actions are based on perpetuating healthy love and pluralism of community.

There have been and are still many claiming to be devout practitioners of their religion, but yet, they do not even understand the tenets of their own faith and misapply the basics of its doctrine. Whenever the followers or leaders of a given religion resort to aggression, violence, murder and/or mass suicide in the name of their religion, they are obviously not

following the tenets of true religion. They have become manifestors of religious distortion. A true martyr is someone who sacrifices their physical
being in the name of their religious beliefs to save others or is murdered
because of their religious beliefs. It is not someone who commits suicide
and murder in a mass effort to kill others.

—A*—

"Do not kill one another." – *The Koran*[601]

—*O—

Based on Jesus' self-sacrifice upon a torturous device of punishment
used to prolong a painful death, the crucifix or cross, in contrast to the
desires of the Cathars (aka The Good Christians) and Bogomils alike,
has become a modern symbol of the Christian faith.[602] It was Emperor
Constantine who made this decision, for prior to his vision in the year
312, Christianity was predominantly represented by the symbol of Pisces
(the fish).[603] The Church of Jesus Christ of Latter-day Saints has no
crucifixes in their temples, focusing more on the savior's triumph, not
on his suffering.[604] It seems the victory of Jesus should be more appropriately celebrated by representations of the empty tomb found after the
stone was rolled away, rather than by the cross that put him there.[605]
If Christ's execution had been by means of the gallows, guillotine, firing
squad, electric chair, or lethal syringe, I wonder if the profile of one of
those instruments of death would be ingrained in stain glass windows,
behind church alters, or upon Christian literature? Yet at the start of
this third millennium, that symbol of two intersecting perpendicular line
segments has become a beacon of hope and faith for almost a third of
this planet's religious population, having become the emblem of sacrifice
upon which Christians admire their founding leader. It is also the spokes
of indigenous Americans' medicine wheel quadrants, for the overlapping
region of a cross' line segments can be considered representative of the
intersection of humanity with divinity.

Even religious symbols meant to represent peace have been tarnished
through misguided ideologies. The Klu Klux Klan burned crucifixes as
a means of race intimidation and the Nazi's Third Reich morphed the
swatstika (the bent legged cross) into an emblem representative of intol-

erance, violence and ways of hatred. Prior to the mid-20th century, the swatstika symbolized very much the opposite. For millennia, the sublime symbol has been imbedded in the consciousness of many cultures and religions. Coming from svatstika, a Sanskrit word meaning "conducive to well-being", it is found in Buddhism and is an integral part of Jainism symbolism. It was stamped on some Mesopotamian coinage, woven into indigenous American textiles, found on pottery shards from Africa and Asia, and formed borders in Roman/Greco architecture long before Adolf Hitler's propaganda machine stole it as a rallying cry for the misguided, contorted and inaccurate ideology of racial superiority. Hitler's angered view of the world was plagued with *apeirokalia* as he distorted the cherished religious symbol. We can only hope that one day the wounds of Nazi stains and tarnish will heal, allowing the swatstika to again be viewed as a symbol of peace, such as within the emblem of Theosophy or Falun Dafa (aka Falun Gong), without triggering negative connotations. In the meantime, we must consider its source and approach the swatstika symbol with cautious metaphysical acceptance when from the Eastern religious concepts of the pre-Nazi era. In defending itself from persecution, I suggest the Falun Dafa uses caution in what political leaders they choose to support and follow or else they may suddenly realize that their media propaganda was on the wrong side of the final Judgment. Dealing and dancing with the devil can have more long-term detrimental consequences and repercussions.

A particular religious path should never be forced on an individual or society. Even if one feels his or her religious path is better or the correct one, others should never be coerced into it. Threatening harm, punishment, violence or death upon another if they don't convert to a specific religious path or follow specific human implements or methods of worship is a grievous sin against Allah. Never seek converts to chase them to your religious path – let them come to you out of their own curiosity and volition. It is up to each individual to decide in a non-violent manner and through spiritual exploration on which path they choose to travel to connect to God. A major edict of God's word is that religious freedom is a fundamental right of every sentient being provided it does not trample on the freedom of others. The map to God is paved with many roads. Even the *Koran* states "There shall be no compulsion in religion",[606] and "To you be your religion, to me be mine/ you have your own religion, and I have mine."[607]

Unfortunately, humanity sometimes obsessively focused more on determining or validating a prophet's or spiritual teacher's (be they Moses, Buddha, Jesus, Mohammad, Bahá'u'lláh or other) particular relationship with divinity, instead of implementing the compassionate truths of their messages. Becoming more concerned on the nature of their relationship with divinity, whether or not they were a direct avatar (God in the flesh), a docetic formation, or a simple human, the noble truth of their message becomes lost, minimized or improperly implemented as a means of enforcing a particular viewpoint. The nature of the connection to the source became more important than the news itself. At times, this focus has become an unhealthy obsession as people fight and resort to violence to prove that their relational interpretation is the correct and only one. This is a fault of humanity, not of the religion. It is humanity applying the tool incorrectly. When used properly, religion is a wondrous instrument for leading us towards communion with God. When used improperly, it becomes a clumsy weapon, stealing its followers away from Allah.

Do you really think Jesus cares or is overly concerned if you believe he is the Son of God or not, however it may be defined, so long as you treat your fellow humans (or other advanced intelligent sentient beings that we may encounter) with kindness, dignity and respect? Does it really matter if we define Christology through dyophysitism, monophysitism or miaphysitism, while failing to implement its teachings of healthy love? Allah's judgment of each and every one of us upon leaving this physical realm is not based on our interpretation of such divine relationships, but rather on how we interacted with others and our environment as we implemented the relevant truths provided by such great teachers. Did we become positive role models and examples of moral conduct for others to emulate and learn from? Did we portray balanced peaceful behavior in our everyday interactions with others?

• • • •

THE RESULT OF WORDS

The messages of the true prophets have occasionally become blurred and distorted when implemented by later followers. Sometimes it was distorted due to misinterpretation, linguistic translation errors, punctuation misplacement, the filling in of lacunae, the confusing of metaphor or expressions for literal meaning, and other times for justifying self-centered motives for power and material gain. Keep in mind, many written scriptures are not originals and are based on the copying of copies of copies of copies – influence of the scribers is bound to work its way in.[608] In the English language alone, look at what can happen to the meaning of a word by inadvertently merely changing, switching, adding or removing a vowel or single consonant such as going from the word "on" to the word "no", from "one" to "none", from "deed" to the word "dead", from "hello" to "hell", from "my" to "by", from "morality" to "mortality", from "torque" to "toque", from "iman" to "imam", "violet" to "violent", "taqiya" to "tagiya", "immanent" to "imminent" or from "ksama" to "ksema." The only difference between the shape of the English consonants of the lowercase letters "n" and "h" is the length of the first leg. Depending on penmanship accuracy, the word "not" could be mistaken for "hot" or the word "need" for "heed", and vice-versa. Consider what can happen to the meaning of a sentence by the simple accidental omission of the word "not" within a phrase. The word "not" was left out of the seventh commandment in a 1631 printing of 1000 bibles, resulting in the commandment written as "Thou shalt commit adultery." This omission may have been a genuine accident or a deliberate act of publishing sabotage. Think of the confusion over such acoustical pronunciation or phonetic similarities between words such as "prophet" and "profit", "pray" and "prey", "content" (in a state of peaceful happiness) and "contempt" (disrespect), "compliment" and "complement", "illuminate" and "eliminate", "discuss" and "disgust" or "vigor" and "rigor", which, coming from their Greek and/or Latin based etymologies, have very different or opposite definitions. The phonetic resonance of a word tends to carry more meaning than just its spelling, as it can change dramatically even within a few generations.[609] Paul Wallis in his investigative questioning of *Genesis* makes note of how even the word "chapter" has changed in its meaning over time.[610]

One of my greatest fears is because of the similarities and interchanges between the prefixes "anti" and "ante", those of limited religious understanding will fear and condemn an actual coming of a true messiah based on sensationalism and sketchy interpretive details from medieval times. Due to all the lore, media attention, YouTube videos, contrived fictional attributes and movies surrounding the notion of an antichrist (a son of Satan) which is a term only mentioned in the Johannine epistles and despite all the commotion and fanfare, the word is never specifically mentioned in the biblical book of *Revelation*. We may actually confuse the eloquence and intelligence of a genuine second coming as being the antichrist.[611] Such a case of mistaken identity would be disastrous for humanity; refer to Chapter 22 for more on this. Saint John's letters do not refer to a single individual, but rather, he further clarifies that there are many antichrists – a collective. The prefix "anti" means against, while the prefix "ante" means coming before. An "antichrist" is someone that has disconnected from God; their connection to the godhead is so blocked and tarnished that nothing flows. They are lost in the abyss and according to the Valentinians, they will never achieve gnosis or enlightenment. An "antichrist" would be someone or many who distort and negate the teachings of Christ, while an "antechrist" would be someone coming before Christ, in agreement with his teachings. An "antechrist" could be an individual or many who prepare the way for a second coming by reiterating in agreement with Jesus' teachings. I think the best way to tell the difference between an antichrist (a fake prophet, imposter, deceiver or Dajjal) and a true messiah (or antechrist) is by referring to Jesus' own words when he said, "If a house is divided against itself, that house cannot stand",[612] and those of Moroni's interpreted writings, "A good tree cannot bring forth evil fruit, neither a corrupt tree bring forth good fruit."[613] These quotes mean the deeds of goodness will identify a true messiah and deeds of evil will identify an antichrist or deceiver. We will need to judge the works of the person(s) to decide if they are an evil antichrist or a good antechrist.

—Δ*—

"The good man out of his good treasure brings forth what is good; and the evil man out of his evil treasure brings forth what is evil." – Jesus Christ[614]

—*O—

The duality of meaning among words can also cause interpretive confusion, with the same word having polar opposite definitions. For example, the word "sustain" can mean either strengthen or to suffer, depending on the context. The word "oversight" can mean watchful monitoring and supervision or missing an error and overlooking an omission. The word "poignancy" can mean piercing sadness or pleasurably stimulating. The word "immaterial" can mean insignificant or spiritual, almost contradictory concepts. The word "daimon" can be interpreted to mean a demon or a benevolent spirit, the higher self as according to Socrates.[615] The word "novel" can mean new or a story depending on its use as an adjective or a noun. The word "satiety" can mean being greatly satisfied or the revulsion and disgust of overindulgence. The word "object" can mean a material item or to disagree, depending on its use as a noun or a verb. Thousands of words within languages have such definitional contradictions and multiple meanings depending on their usage – just look into the multiple meanings of the word "mean." Scriptural passages have been historically susceptible to misinterpretation due to the multiple definitions and dual usages of certain words and symbols.

Look up the variety of definitions for the word or acronym of "swag" or "fit" in the English language. Consider the slang phrases of "that's wicked!", "that's evil!" or "that's sick!" used by adolescents to denote an exited state of exclamative pleasure or happy agreement, exactly opposite of what the words wicked, evil or sick denote. I'm sure the ancient languages had such multiple meanings, homonyms and homophones among the words, phrases and symbols just as modern languages do. There are also cases when deliberate sarcasm, false flattery, mild mockery or potent imagery intended by an author can be accidentally misinterpreted by readers as valid statements requiring literal enforcement. Insisting upon absolute literalism from scriptures so full of metaphors or contradictions is dangerous, naive and irresponsible.

Consider what can happen to the meaning of a paragraph by the omission of a single or a few key phrases. Reflect on the example statement "We can choose violence." Out of context this can be interpreted as giving permission to commit violence. Now let's include other phrases around it: "We can choose violence. We can choose peace. The choices we make determine whether our cores stagnate or evolve." By including those other sentences around the statement "We can choose violence", the phrase becomes a rhetorical question to elicit deeper thoughts of spiritual reflection for selecting good over evil.

Consider the phrase "She came before God." Does this mean that she existed chronologically prior to God or does it mean that she walked towards God as for judgment? It is only a phrase of four words, yet the meaning, based on one's context, can be very different. This shows how religious scripture can be misinterpreted due to linguistic errors or omissions. Consider the single phrase "He fought with Christians." Standing alone, this can be interpreted as he fought against Christians or he fought in support of the Christians. Each has the opposite meaning, hence there is a duality in how it can be understood: a double interpretation; a dual edged sword. The phrases "He fought together with Christians" or "He fought alongside Christians" is still not precise enough to eliminate all ambiguity in the author's intent. The phrase "He fought as an ally of the Christians" provides enough clarity to indicate that he was allied with the Christians during the battle. Again, this shows how religious scripture can be misinterpreted due to linguistic errors, omissions or lack of clarification.

Every linguist knows that it is impossible to translate all content of thought (especially simile, metaphor or allegoric references to cultural folklore) perfectly from one language to another, without losing some content, impact and meaning. There have been both vowel and consonant shifts when pronuncial translations occur from language to language. Expressions (idioms) in one language and/or from a prior time period may not translate well into modern languages. Consider the phrase "an open sesame." If one is not aware of the *Tales of the Arabian Nights* and the password used by Ali Baba, the phrase could be interpreted literally as an open sesame flower or seed. With an awareness of the story, however, the correct meaning of the phrase "an open sesame" is that which allows a person or thing to do or enter something successfully and easily; a key to unlocking success.

Khrushchev's famous (or infamous) quote in 1956 at the Polish Embassy in Moscow was translated to English as "We Will Bury You." It actually may have been a variation of a Russian idiomatic expression meaning "We will outlast you" or "We will be present at your funeral." It was more of a flippant boast of communism outlasting capitalism rather than a threatening remark of the Soviet Union attacking the Western capitalist nations. How many people of today are aware of this discrepancy? Take a look at all the translations of the first phrase of *Proverbs* 23:7 among the various biblical versions for a typical example of multiple interpretations.[616] The meaning of some past idioms and allegories may have become lost with time, resulting in modern literal interpretations missing the author's true intention of the phrase.

The previous paragraphs have shown how accidentally or deliberately leaving out a word, phrase, statement or sentence during initial writing, copying or translation can drastically change the scriber's intent. This is why when reading ancient scripture, one must be aware that some paragraphs and statements may not be the complete message or properly convey the full intent due to deciphering "noise" encountered during the linguistic translation. I'm sure if this book were to be translated from English to another language, some of its idioms, expressions and meaning would also be lost. Keep in mind that many religious stories and messages were passed down for decades and centuries through oral story telling with ancient languages before they were ever written down into scriptures. Be aware and accepting of the fact that susceptibility for inaccurate transcribing exists. Also be aware that some statements, due to human interference, may be blatantly false.

Our ancestors developed their beings on words of wisdom and past the contents down from generation to generation. Incorporated from oral into written form, the scriptures may contain contradictions within their texts, either by our misinterpretation of the writer's intent or by the influence of the writer's views over that of the Universal Creator. These syntax discrepancies do not make the scriptures any less relevant in their importance to us, but rather, help us to understand the fallibilities within ourselves. We must therefore focus on the love, grace, tolerance and quest for truth and meaning as opposed to words which may convey anger, violence and hatred. If we choose to focus on beauty, we will see beauty both within the sacred texts and within others. If we choose to focus on hatred within the sacred texts, then we will only see hatred within ourselves and the world. We have the choice of where to focus our thoughts and energy – on love or on rage. We have the choice to see beauty in the diversity and traditions of others or we can close ourselves off in a world of isolated anger, paranoid hatred and intolerance. God never hides behind a cloak of racism or intolerance. He created the plethora of skin tones, cultures, and pathways to reach him just as he created the beauty within the colors of the rainbow. Only certain ignorant humans hide within their ragged emotional tents, too afraid to come outside. There are those who justify actions of self-destruction, murder, jealousy, hatred, insecurity and negative exploitation as being a path to God. I can assure you, none of these roads will lead to her. We all choose what type of being we become and we all have to decide the focus of our emotional energy; on love or on hatred. We are the sum of our thoughts and results of our actions.

Many of the great scriptures contain passages that depict generational relationships, phrases that substantially recharge one's being, words that denote images of violence, and still others, with stories of God's influence and intervention in humanity's affairs. Every true religious text is the word of God, but it is the word as interpreted by humans. It is therefore subject to the thoughts, emotions and weaknesses of the scribers. Sometimes the scribers were being literal and other times they used artistic expression to portray figurative notions. This is even indirectly stated in the *Koran* and *Bible*: "By such comparison God confounds many and enlightens many",[617] and "But God hath chosen the foolish things of the world to confound the wise; and God hath chosen the weak things of the world to confound the things which are mighty."[618]

The three primary middle eastern originating monotheistic religions (i.e., Judaism, Christianity, Islam) have the same guardian being or entity of All as their creative and destructive god and revere many of the same prophets. Yet often times, depending on the socio-geographical and geopolitical interplay, they are in conflict with each other. This conflict is not the fault of the religions themselves, but among other issues, is due to a percentage of humans distorting the underlying message delivered by their prophets. It is the fault of a cultural segment still clinging to dysfunctional archaic biases. There are primitive and then there are enlightened interpretations of religious scripture. The primeval focuses on outdated phrases condoning violence and implementing excessive forms of cruel punishment for violating an aspect of doctrinal law; the enlightened focuses on phrases perpetuating peace, love, tolerance, kindness, forgiveness and grace. True religion was meant to celebrate and express the goodness of the human spirit, not to suppress it. Religion was never meant to deny the nature of who we are nor dampen our persona. On the contrary, it was meant to expand our being through the lowering of our ego, not by overinflating it. True religion contributes to spiritual growth. The following of a true religious path means focusing and implementing the aspects of scripture pertaining to kindness, healthy love, charity, the value of life and the improvement of the human condition. Whenever a possible option, true religion strives for the preservation and respect of life.

Unfortunately, there are incorrect, distorted or outdated interpretations of many true religions' scriptures. Some choose to distort the beauty of their religion's core by implementing its ideology through force and violent means. Be it through the mishandling and damaging religious-political agenda of the Crusades,[619] under a false Christian façade during the Middle Ages, the Inquisitions occurring across parts of Eastern Europe, the tactics employed to infectiously spread the Ottoman Empire, the extension of some zealous missionaries that may have oppressed rather than educated, and the 21st century terrorism and damage to Islam being inflicted by extreme elements, such events throughout history are not the fault of the religion, but rather are the actions of misguided and miseducated "false" followers.

Every act creates both elements of evil and good. It is our responsibility to approach the godhead in a manner which minimizes the evil components and maximizes the good ones – the approach to paradise is not paved with anger, envy, violence and hatred. Entering the kingdom of heaven and seeing the bliss of Allah is based on one committing balanced actions of kindness, grace, mercy, charity, forgiveness and acceptance. There are many different links and pathways to God and a failure to acknowledge this divine fact throughout the ages has resulted in the misguided spreading of religious stains and cancerous lesions of violence. Whether it has been the forcing of one's faith or pathway upon another or the putting forth of ideologies of intolerance and violence, such actions only serve the personal failing of humans, not the word of God. It is a great sin to exploit your religious beliefs on another. Forcing your religious beliefs on another is very different than welcomingly expressing your beliefs to another and having them express their beliefs to you. The dictating of one's religious beliefs through violence or threats of damnation upon others is not true religion. True religion is about improving the world through acts of kindness. Leaving this world in better shape than how we found it is everyone's life mission. One should ponder, respect and tolerate the differences of all true paths and find the beauty in the commonalities, rather than focusing on hairsplitting the dissimilarities.

A true spiritual being puts forth respect for and finds pleasure and joy in the celebrations and traditions of other religious paths. Think for yourself on whether a doctrine makes spiritual sense and whether it is something that should enter your core. Never approach any religious path with blindness, but approach with curiosity, wonder and an openness to ecstatic pursuits. And remember, just as too little religion is unhealthy, so is too much religion. Some of our and civilization's dysfunctionality have come from overly literal interpretations of scriptural drama, for unfortunately, we cannot always codify spiritual common sense – the setting of automatic alarms to tell us when the devil is leading us astray. It calls upon faith and trust that the reader will understand the message's intent and apply it properly. Religious faith is not about deliberately driving your car into oncoming traffic, slamming it into a tree or not wearing a mask during a pandemic to test and see if God will save you, for that is called foolishness, tempting the Lord, sinful, "missing the mark" and religious distortion. The wearing of a mask and social distancing when in public through a pandemic is **not** about politics or government oppression; it is about whether or not you are going to follow Christ's example of being a "good Samaritan". The wearing of a protective mask is how you would treat a total stranger – with respect and compassion or with disregard and contempt. The wearing of a mask and social distancing (when possible) is about protecting the stranger and the self. True faith is about a trust in a greater relationship with the divine that goes beyond the present moment. When taking religious scripture to unhealthy extremes, those with an unstable sense of self tend to latch onto detrimental behaviors. We've seen such outcomes in the form of extreme codependency or blatant terrorism. Too many times, we have seen throughout history where individuals or fanatical masses carried out atrocities disguised under the false cloak and costume of a religious doctrine. From the brutal militarized campaigns of the Crusades (≈1096 to ≈1291) conducted in the name of Christianity to retake Jerusalem (aka Jebus, Jebusi, Jebusite) to the oppression inflicted during the start and expansion of the Ottoman Empire (≈1299 to ≈1922). Millions perished due to enforcing the distortions of religious fanaticism amid pillaging invasions of conquest.

The purpose of practicing a particular religion is for maintaining our connection to divinity. It was never meant to be a substitute for thinking or searching for truth. The notion of free will, freedom of thought and self-determination was deliberately planted within our minds by God at the beginning of our awareness. It is our responsibility to assure that they are never blindly given up for the sake of distorted zealots, false prophets or mental laziness. To blindly accept statements that may detrimentally inflate our egos beyond healthy boundaries without searching for the root or intent of such words is mentally irresponsible. Religion is not about making one feel self-important and better than others, but rather, it is about humbly reflecting on our own faults and working to improve the core of our being and to help others with their core.

If you encounter or see an item of worship in the workplace, a governmental setting, or in commercial establishments which may not be indicative of your religious path, do not be insulted. Focus on the beauty of the religious creation, icon or artifact, not that it is associated with a religious path different than yours. Rather than strike out with insult, protest or anger, be tolerant or offer an item from your religious path. If you are of the Judaic faith and encounter a Christmas tree in a public non-religious setting, instead of protesting, ask if you can provide a menorah during Hanukkah to be displayed. If you are of the Islamic faith and encounter a Buddha statue in public non-religious setting, present an artistic copy of the *Koran* or calligraphic craft to be displayed. Be respectful if the representative or proprietor of the establishment declines your offer, but perhaps they may yield to polite yearly persistence. Enjoying and embracing the creativity and artistic celebrative icons of various religious paths of worship is the surest way to understanding the broad definition of what God is. It is perfectly acceptable for a Christian to say "Eid Mubarak", "Ramadan Kareem", or "Bajram Serif Mubarak Olsun" to a Muslim at the end of their fasting within Ramadan just as it is for a Muslim to say "Merry Christmas" to a Christian within their holiday season. If you are a solid atheist, then why should it even matter to you what greeting is said?

In rejecting any divinity being associated with the person named Jesus of Nazareth, there is a view among some atheists that he suffered from mental illness. Psychologists, philosophers, historians and authors have all contributed their take on Jesus' psyche. If one looks in the gospels themselves, there are indications of mental instability. The *Gospel of Mark* reports people saying "He has lost His senses" or "is out of his mind" or "has gone crazy."[620] His contemporaries state that he is "possessed by demons" and that he is "insane."[621] Yet, others point to the fact that if he can make the blind see again, how can he be possessed by a demon?[622] There are sections where Jesus' own family comes looking for him as if to excuse his behavior and fetch him from the crowd.[623] Yet, during the crucifixion while the three named Mary stood nearby, it was Jesus who expressed concern for their well-being while he himself was approaching death.[624] He was more concerned for others than his own situation.

It wasn't until the late 19th century that dissent felt safe enough to speak on the topic without fear of the Church's wraith and that of public opinion. In *Das Leben Jesu*, David Friedrich Strauss publishes in 1864 that "Jesus was not divine, but insane." Other authors later expressed that Christ was delusional, mentally unbalanced or suffered from religious paranoia.[625] The first person to write extensively and openly on the topic of his sanity was the French psychologist Charles Binet-Sanglé in his 1915 book titled *La Folie de Jésus.*[626] Later, in an effort to further demythologize the hype, additional psychiatrists, psychoanalysts, and neurologists applied the categorizing of sections of the *Diagnostic and Statistical Manual of Mental Disorders* (DSM) to conveniently label Christ as having extreme egocentrism, suffering from multiple personality disorder and even falling under schizophrenic classifications.[627] Some have even placed Jesus' "madness" and that of other gurus on the same plane with destructive cult leaders like Jim Jones and David Koresh.[628] I personally do not find such comparisons palatable since Jesus' instructional messages were more about boosting the "egos" of those around him and raising his followers to a higher state, not deluding, controlling, suppressing and negatively exploiting them. If Jesus of Nazareth was just an insane lunatic, then why do the synoptic Gospels all describe his transfiguration (the visual revealing of Sophia's bond with him) upon a mountain in which rays of light seemed to emanate from his body as he became his own etheric star?[629] Even Anthony of Egypt (aka Antony the Great, Saint Anthony) was said to radiate with an induced glow upon praying.[630] I know of no madman or lunatic that can emanate illumination from their being, unless they truly tapped into their primal memory and recognition of being a Sun-Avatar. Yet, there are contemplators and scholars who postulate the figure of Jesus never existed, explaining the stories as expansions of pagan myths such as the "Godman" of Osiris-Dionysus, strictly based on a compilation of the personified relationships of astrotheology or his stories were just an allegory to the movement of the sun across the heavens.[631] Accordingly, some scholars feel that the Essenes and the Therapeutae, sects that fused Jewish and Pagan Gnosticism, created the mythos of Jesus, a preferred allegory to awakening our mystical selves.[632] In doing so, they are not undermining Christianity, but on the contrary, they are suggesting that it is based on a perennial myth with the power to impart the mystical experience of gnosis, our internal connection to our nearest star, which can transform each one of us into a Christ.[633] Wait a second...is that not exactly what the figure of Jesus was alleged to have said by stating the "Kingdom of God is within you"? If Jesus truly was a symbolic pagan reference, a repeating myth that never historically existed as a real person, then why is the mental state of this fictional character even being evaluated? If the being of Jesus is purely allegory and make-believe, then why have him partially rebel against the Judaic establishment? After all, albeit containing impurities and juxtaposed contaminative statements, the Hebrew scriptures were also about achieving gnosis and self-awakenings as forged from pagan influencers. Should we lean towards a real person who fulfilled the pagan prophecies or should we lean towards the pagan prophecies generating an artificial biography? Was the intimate relationship between Jesus Christ and Mary Magdalene (the beloved disciple) based on the lives of real historical people or on the mythological resonance of fictional characters? If the stories of Jesus and all the other prophets are just imagination,[634] then what triggered and initiated those internal battles and the start of gnosis within the psyche of my early twenties? Either way, there is something amiss here between or above the duality. Whether Jesus was a real person or not, his legend generated a radical resurgence of movements and trajectories coming forth from resonances with existing Judaic-Roman-Greco mythological stances and traditions. It is not of primary importance if one believes in the Jesus' stories being real or myth so long as one places Christianity's true tenets of love, forgiveness and gratitude into everyday practice. Reinterpreting scripture in a benevolent manner to suit one's literal or allegoric personal concept can still lead to the godhead.

To say Jesus was mentally ill is to say that every prophet of history was mentally ill, which is exactly what some psychiatric sources have presented.[635] To his defense, other more recent psychiatric sources have provided evidence and arguments supporting his connection to divinity above the norm.[636] Perhaps he was facing internal conflicts during his battle with demons, yet mental illness seems relative to those defining it. Consider this, if you truly saw or knew the mind of God, even for the briefest of moments, wouldn't you accept yourself to be mentally ill as well until you gained back your grounding? Wouldn't an authentic influence or unveiling of divinity cause you to question your own sanity? If we are the only sane ones in the room and everyone else starts telling us that we are mentally ill, eventually we would start to believe them – the soundness of one's mind is relative. I will let you decide if the application of the DSM is the proper tool to use in understanding prophets of history within the language of modern day psychoanalysts or if it is way off the mark and entirely incorrect. Were such prophets having delusions of grandeur or just being extremely confident with their awareness? Perhaps the genuine prophets of history had to first merge their madness with their understanding of truth before stepping forward out of the crowd. I wonder how many people first considered Leonardo Da Vinci, Sir Isaac Newton or Albert Einstein to have a form of mental illness for revealing new forms of thought, yet what they provided to humanity has been, at least for now, very much the opposite of illusion.

Religion should not become a substitute unhealthy addiction for another former disruptive addiction (i.e., drug abuse, overspending, extreme alcoholic consumption, deviant sexual behavior, excessive materialism) but rather a guiding beacon to keep one on the path of recovery. Religion serves well as a spiritual substance that can be grasped when encountering a void of the unknown. Excessive consumption and forceful pontificated emotional secretion of anything, (i.e., religion, politics, water, air), is an unhealthy reaction in place of a previous detrimental behavior. The over-touting of any religious idea or concept can become in of itself a disruptive addiction. True religion was meant to be practiced with healthy moderation, not as an obsessive addiction.

Religious distortion can occur when metaphorical stories and references spoken and written by our ancestors are mistakenly interpreted in later times as literal, representing the exact words without any allegory. Enforcing a particular questionable interpretation through acts of violence and harm to others goes against the will of Allah. The intent in the Gospels of spreading the word of Christ was to deliver the message of Jesus via peaceful means. It was meant to optionally supplement and complement existing methods for connecting to divinity, not to rob ethnicities of their prior religions, traditions and heritage. Spreading the word of the Gospel was never meant to be exclusive nor to be "crammed downed people's throats" as a singular and absolute dogma.[637] Jesus did not specifically say that he was "the only way" nor did he say "destroy other religions, eliminate their cultures and torture and wipe out others unless they convert" – those were the words of the *Old Testament*. He **never** said, "kill anyone who does not believe that I am the Messiah." He recognized the distortion of the *Torah* to the Pharisees' self-interests and was saying that he was the way in challenge to the hypocrisy of the Judaic clerical leaderships' words and actions of his time period.[638] For when Jesus Christ said in his allegoric way, "There are many mansions in my Father's house", he was leading us to the notion of several paths, rooms and levels within the domain of God.[639] Even the ancients referred to the various constellational positions of the sun as the "Mansions of the Sun-God" during the star's annual journey across the heavens.[640] Mohammad recognized the distortion of Christian and Judaic teachings among some of the clerical leadership and also acknowledged those who correctly practiced their respective religious scripture with truth and purity of heart. Likewise, he never said to go forth and continue destroying the relics of other religions. Unfortunately, centuries after Mohammad's shattering of symbolically oppressive idols in the Kaaba, interpretive distortion occurred along the way due to human failings. It is the unenlightened and ignorant person, the *hylic* or *somatic*, who continues to distort the meaning of scriptures for their ego's own self-promotion and inflation.

Just as we should not condemn a whole species because of the actions of a few, we should not judge an entire religion because of the actions of a relatively small portion of its constituents. Generalizing a particular religion based on the actions of a few perpetuates religious distortion and is harmful to society. Should we judge all of humanity by the atrocities directed by the tyrannical leadership of Nazism of the mid-20th century? Do we judge all Catholics or Christians by the atrocities of military campaigns organized by the popes of the Middle Ages, the European Inquisitions of the late Medieval and early Renaissance periods, the actions of James Warren Jones or David Koresh? Do we judge all Muslims by the oppressive spread of its Ottoman empire, the attacks of September 11, 2001 upon the soil of the United States, or the radical violence carried out by terroristic isolated followers of extreme destructive cult-like ideologies? Should we judge all of a religious group by the offshoot actions of its extreme violent frothing schisms? Before judging or condemning a group based on generalized conjectures and the simplistic thoughts of our lower self, seek the knowledge and truths necessary to prevent drawing conclusions based on ignorance. When violence occurs under the guise of a great religion, it is not the fault of the religion. It is the fault of humans. Being careful not to generalize any group, culture or religion as a whole, we must never blame or negatively categorize a true religion due to the faults of a portion of its practitioners or due to misguided individuals claiming to be its practitioners. Proper understanding of a base religion and their ways is necessary to containing the malignancies of hate that may weed forth.

—Λ*—

"Beaucoup condamner c'est peu comprendre" – (to condemn much is to understand little)[641]

—*Ω—

As previously mentioned in the first paragraph of Chapter 7, any scribing of God's words and thoughts will have a degree of adulteration or contamination due to the natural influence of human frailty. The degree of how much contaminative influx within the pages varies among the scriptures and manuscripts. However, just because some scribed passages may contain more human influences than others, does not make the rest of the passages of a true religion's scripture any less significant. Just as no government is perfect, no religious path is perfect either. Some paths can become distracted with excessive rituals, or become mundane with too little, while others may temporarily meander off course. The meandering can be the result of certain phrases from scripture that are taken literally when they should be taken figuratively or due to too much attention and focus on a particular passage.

Confronting and conquering others through violence and bloodshed under the guise of religion has damaged humanity's connection with the Lord over the millenniums. The use of religion as an excuse to negatively exploit others is a severe sin in the eyes of God/Allah. Forced conversions and proselytizing should never be done upon another. Each individual has the God/Allah given right to question his or her own religion and investigate other religious paths in a safe a comfortable manner. There is no denying that atrocities have been committed under the veil of religion as an excuse for empire building and misguided expansionism, but religion has also preserved civilizations throughout times of crisis. For when Christian regions were in the midst of 900 years of fluctuating cultural retraction and scientific deterioration (from about the 5th century and continuing into the 14th century), although some of human knowledge was being preserved by the monasteries, Muslim regions were flourishing in a rebirth of the sciences, quests for knowledge, cultural activity and economic vibrancy.

There is no doubt that some passages of religious scripture seem or are contradictory to the message of love and empathy such as the phrases promoting the killing of all without pity nor mercy found in *Ezekiel* 9. I leave it up to you to find additional examples of such religious distortions. They are the exception, however, not the standard. The ancient writers may have been angrily venting out against the suffering, frustrations and wailings of the human experiences encountered by oppressive foes and extreme conditions. Many of the ancient words are the lamentations of humanity's woes to a higher power. Some writings put forth forms of punishment (often excessive) for behavior considered unacceptable or against traditions and norms for the society of the time period. They may even be testing our spiritual critical thinking skills to see which passages we clasp onto and which ones we allow to ingrain into the core of our being. Perhaps such scriptural unrighteous or even wicked thoughts were deliberately written as a means to trigger and test our resolve. I am not being an apologist for such questionable phrases, but merely bringing to light that there are flaws within some of the ancient scriptures that need to be historically acknowledged and then bypassed.

There may be rules of action, punishment for disobedience, required behavior or dress codes that seem behind the times or contradictory to what promotes the advancement of our species. These rules may have been necessary during their place in history to preserve the population through times of peril or hardship. Such rules and statements may no longer have a place in the current times due to our spiritual advancement from the period in which they were written. Although such rituals may not be necessary from a survival standpoint, many are still practiced today as a means of connecting with the actions of our ancestors. There is nothing wrong with maintaining a non-oppressive custom or ritual, provided it is done so out of personal choice. The continuation of non-oppressive traditions and rituals are actually a constructive means for synchronizing with the continuum of human experience. Remember, we are all entities of spirit witnessing and participating in the human endeavor. Our visit here in the material realm is relatively brief, so we should focus our energies on leaving this world in a better condition than we found it. That is the ultimate goal behind the meaning of our existence.

—A*—

"When paving your spiritual path, do not make religion an extreme obsession, make it a healthy habit." – AO

—*O—

Negative exploitation (bad manipulation) and positive exploitation (good manipulation) are the opposite poles of the duality which exists in the act of manipulation. An ethical teacher can manipulate the minds of students to embrace the wonders of mathematics or an unethical parent can manipulate their child to shoplift (steal) items for them. True prophets fill themselves with love and mesh with the flow of divinity, conducting manipulative acts of goodness. False prophets choose to fill themselves with self-serving motives and hatred, falling into the clutches of darker forces, they conduct manipulative acts of evil. Both forms of manipulation have the ability to catalyze others (society) in a given direction. One, however, is much more powerful than the other. Can you guess which form of exploitation is much more powerful and will endure for the longer term?

How can we know the light of a true religion and not be fooled or succumb to the fancies of religious distortion? Simply, a true religion is based on love, not control, nor suppression, nor manipulation, nor negative exploitation. True religion, and its interpretations, walks a path away from violence. Religious distortion, on the contrary, spurs up cracks and potholes of violence on the roadway to the godhead – it is God/Allah's word and thoughts being misapplied or misrepresented. Religious distortion often thrives on wooly allegory, emotional commitments to text that no one reads and other forms of benign hypocrisy.[642] Scriptural statements and advisement are often tied to relevant situations and chronological references. Ignoring or disregarding those references, standing alone, a phrase can lose its cohesion, intent and accuracy of its message.

—Δ*—

"The most detestable wickedness, the most horrid cruelties, and the greatest miseries that have afflicted the human race have had their origin in this thing called revelation, or revealed religion." – Thomas Paine[643]

—*O—

A set of codified organized beliefs seems a system of opinions about non-empirical subject matter that is experienced and comprehended with internal and personal interpretation. Enforcing a moral imperative that one's particular religion or world view is the only way and violently squelching anyone who sows doubt, is an insecure reaction to perceived threats and narcissistic injuries upon an internal belief system. Since one cannot solidly defend a belief based on faith by persuading skeptics it is true, misguided zealots are apt to react to any threat of their belief system with narcissistic rage, and may try to eliminate the affront to their wedded beliefs as an assault to their fragile dignity and everything that makes their lives meaningful.[644] Each of us has our own private opinion on religion and some are too consumed and convinced that they know more about it than anyone else – "know-it-alls" to matters of spirit. Allowing the negative aspects of tradition and culture to freeze our minds blocks the sprouting forth of new ideas and the possible advancement of our essence. If one is truly secure with their religious path, then such announcements of doubt by others should have no merit or cause for alarm. If you are secure enough in your religious path, then why should the religious path of others bother you? Those who do not feel confident with their own religious path seem to be threatened by the paths of others. Resorting to religion "bashing", unfairly criticizing a religion in modern times based on the past leadership or present actions of a few of its practitioners, followers or members, is a form of negative exploitation. Catholic bashing, Islam bashing, Buddhist bashing, Judaic bashing are uncalled for and unproductive. Rather than bashing the religion, while acknowledging the mistakes of its past or present, provide suggestive ways on how it can improve, both internally and externally, for the future. Are my comments in the prior paragraphs in presenting the early and medieval history of the Roman Catholic Church considered "bashing" or are they merely acknowledging painful truths? If they appear as "bashings" then I apologize for my words. My endearing wife and son, whom I love very much, are members of the Roman Catholic Church and although no religious path is perfect, I have the utmost respect for the direction of its modern leadership.

There are those who feel betrayed by their religious roots, but they often confuse the religion with the religious distortion they encountered. They may rightly perceive that their youthful religious views betrayed them and feel a sense of cynicism and abandonment towards God/Allah. To heal from such cynicism, re-approaching their religion with forgiveness while redefining internal direction is the best way to regain spiritual health. Religion was never meant to be a totalitarian and dogmatic enforcement by being struck with rulers across knuckles, being schooled by a strap across one's back,[645] ridiculed and humiliated for not properly memorizing or reciting a prayer or scriptural passage, or being subjected into a state of fear and powerlessness. It was never intended to be a weapon for controlling weak-minded people who are content to be manipulated and led like an unthinking flock of sheep. Such distortions encountered in youth would naturally cause anyone to turn away from, forsake and renounce the religious upbringing that damaged, abused and punished the soul rather than expanding it. Having undergone such human inflicted damage upon the psyche, apostasy is understandable. It is reconnecting to true religion, however, that memory of love and acceptance which can heal such wounds and redirect us back on a path of enlightenment to become again, the architects of our core and soul.

—Λ*—

"May God preserve us from stupid nuns!" – Saint Teresa of Ávila[646]

—*Ω—

There is no doubt that religious distortions have brought on the bloodiest of persecutions, the torturous of deaths, and religious wars that pummeled the Middle East, Europe and other parts of the globe. These distortions have been the works of human ego and ignorance that have laid waste to life and property, not the words of the Almighty. In conclusion, aspects of religious texts have sometimes given us mixed messages in presenting the stories of civilizations and their relationship to a higher truth. That is why we must rely on our God-bestowed intelligence and spiritual logic to sort through what are divine truths, what are metaphors to describe an emotional state of being, what are civil guidelines for a previous archaic time period of history and what are statements influenced by human bias.

Statements that elate the spirit, those that resonate our being with the love of existence, promoting the advancement of all humanity and our relationship with the universe are revelations of truth. Those promoting violence, war or the diminishing of the human character and spiritual existence of others are the bias and ignorant words of the lower aspects of human influence. No true religion is a threat, but its distortions are. It is the eternal virtues within the scriptures of all religions that we should base the development of our being upon and not on the contradictions and misconceptions – focus on the commonality and similarity of their voices, not on their differences. Value comes from sorting through what is relevant to the advancement of our species growth, its relationship with others and its relationship with the universe. Choose the best of spiritual roadmaps from all the religions while passing over the worst. When in doubt, defaulting to a policy of ahimsa (nonviolence) is the best way to move forward in life.

Chapter 12
The Path To Illumination

"ACKNOWLEDGING THE EMOTIONAL shortcomings of my human frailties, I ask of you, Oh Divine Essence, to guide my thinking and reasoning to align with a higher mind and to properly comprehend your thoughts and wishes." – Prayer Of The Humble, AO

• • • •

SIMPLY WISHING TO KNOW God is enough to set us on the road to enlightenment.[647] As mentioned in the Preface, from a purest translational perspective, "enlightenment" is an Eastern Buddhist term which means to end the cycle of being reborn (escape from transmigration) since one has achieved or "awaked" to the truth of life and death. Following the desire and notion to be released from the cycles of death and rebirth, it correlates with religions having reincarnation as an aspect of their doctrine. Enlightenment, in the pure Buddhist sense, is having been released from a mandatory requirement of reincarnation back into this material realm. Unless otherwise noted, the word "enlightenment" in this text will take on a Western definition by signifying "illumination", the advancement to a higher level of spiritual awareness and understanding (spiritual realization) or a momentary epiphany of God's grace. The word "illumination" will be used interchangeably throughout this book to mean the Western definition of "enlightenment." The Eastern doctrine treats enlightenment as a noun; an end goal to be achieved. The Western doctrine sees it as more of a verb; a continuous action of maintenance and upkeep. According to Thomas Paine, there are two distinct classes of thought: those that bolt into our minds on their own accord, rapidly percolating upwards from the subconscious and those that we produce in our minds by reflection and deliberate contemplation.[648] Contemplation is used by the mystics of Western thought to mingle with the divine while meditation is used by practitioners of Eastern thought to transcend in union with the cosmos.[649] Both methods will take you to encounters with God. One may achieve a state of enlightenment as both a noun and a verb, but only if they have mastered the action for all of eternity – having found the permanence among the impermanence. A Buddha is one who has achieved this highest plateau of existence; a perpetual intersection with the godhead. When one has truly awoken the Buddha within, life will start to feel like a dream – you are awake and yet asleep at the same time; you are dreaming your reality into existence. This happens when you start to properly implement several of the Hermetic Principles into your everyday existence. The rest of us have our infinitesimal brief moments of soaring with Buddha and then falling back to our previous state; a material plane of existence. It is the transitioning between the earthly and the heavenly that triggers our connection to something eternal. Stepping across that chasm between the ego and the all-permeating divine being, crossing that boundary between the secular and the spiritual, drifting past the event horizon beyond the self in which a moment becomes equivalent to a millennium, as physical beings we should only occasionally venture into these zones. We weren't meant to remain there for very long since the current programming of our bio-neuro receptors and processors cannot endure such lengthy exposures. In line with the advice of Gary Lachman, we should only "dip" our heads into it for a bit and the come back to process and share the experience.[650] Just like looking directly into the physical Sun without protective filters would damage our eyes, looking directly into the spiritual Sun of God without purity of heart and core, would damage our minds. Going further beyond and dwelling too long within the pure area of the spiritual world in a deified state would disrupt our sense of reality and is better reserved for the expertise of angels. It is permissible to venture into such states as temporary tourists, sojourners of realms beyond this one, but we should only stay for a short visit.

—Δ*—

"As those who are unable to gaze upon the sun, look upon those reflected radiance as a Sun, so likewise the image of God, his angel word, in himself considered to be God." – Philo of Alexandria[651]

—*O—

An aspect of enlightenment is the merging of historical, scientific, philosophical and creative knowledge all under the umbrella cover of divine knowledge. Another aspect of enlightenment is balancing the interplay between circular and triangular elements.[652] While avoiding escapism, it is surfing on the duality of opposites by increasing our good qualities while reducing the negative ones. With it comes the ability to readily travel between the circular and the triangular in such a manner that goodness is harnessed to minimize evil while the extremes are transcended. It's although one is looking at the two ends of the spectrum from above such that the scene becomes one. Consider an astronaut's view of Earth from the Moon. The boundaries that separate countries are no longer seen, the opposite extremes of water and land have become one. The whole planet is now seen as one, but composed of opposites, water and land. Enlightenment is not a dualistic nature nor is it a rapid swinging back and forth from one extreme to its opposite; it is the ability to walk an ideal path composed of opposite elements, but not dwelling too far within any extreme. Assets of both the circle and the triangle merge into one in a balanced state of mind.

Enlightenment is also knowing what proportion of the extremes are appropriate for a given situation based on social norms and what parts of the opposite elements are necessary for the formation of a healthy ego boundary. A healthy ego boundary is one that allows words and ideas which advance our character to infuse into our core and to deflect those which diminish our being. A healthy ego recognizes concepts which aid in making us better human beings, leading us in the direction of our higher self, the Atmon within. When you are at the peak of your Atmon, you will sense God. An unhealthy ego follows a downward path leading us into a direction of the lower self. This unhealthy boundary can allow prejudice, excessive anger, hatred, immoderate pride, myopic self-focus, greed, vanity, destructive behavior, lies and distorted truths to become the core of our being. Love is minimized in an unhealthy ego. A healthy ego contributes to the energy of those around them. An unhealthy ego drains the energy of those around them. A healthy ego strives for a balanced focus between itself and those around them. An unhealthy ego strives to maintain the focus on only itself. Enlightenment is properly balancing our emotional, mental, physical and spiritual needs to love others without loss of love for ourselves – developing the proper sense of Self. As we become closer to enlightenment, there is a point at which our inclination and pleasure is to remain calm and silent, while being lovingly aware of God's infinite and comforting caress.[653]

—Λ*—

"Becoming aware of Me, you will pass over all the obstacles and difficulties of a conditioned life by My grace. If, however, you do not work in such consciousness, but act through false ego and excessive pride, not hearing or listening to Me, you will be lost and perish." – Krishna[654]

—*Ω—

There are those with willful ignorance that attack and try to bring others down to their lower levels of existence. They are suffering inside themselves and cannot understand why those around them are happy or content. They will misjudge others and make assumptions that are not true. Seeking truth scares them because it may change their isolated view of their social universe. They may have been exposed to hardships early in life, but instead of learning to forgive, clear the slate and reset their worldview, they choose to continue along a path of emotional suffering, anger and hatred. They think that those who are happy have never suffered, but that is the ignorant boundary that they choose to maintain. They are too insecure to go beyond their self-built walls and thus, they deny themselves enlightenment and creative enrichment. Even Swedenborg states "A wise person is a more adequate receiver of divine love and wisdom than a simple one, and therefore a fuller receiver."[655] One of the most difficult challenges of interacting with others is how does one deal with those at much lower levels of enlightenment? It is not easy to deal with someone who prefers and chooses a world of ignorance. They prefer to remain within the comfort of their delusions for the truth is sometimes too much for one to bear. Consider two people of equal intelligence who hear a word for which they do not know what it means. One will look it up in the dictionary or online to advance their knowledge; the other will say "He talks down to us with his big words." Which person has chosen the path of ignorance and which person has made the effort to move beyond?

There are situations which need to be confronted with verbal explanations, others in which remaining silent is the optimum temporary recourse. It is a balance of when to confront and when not to confront, when to object and when not to object. You must choose your battles wisely and to whom you reveal your ideas, insights and thoughts. Gnosis is the beginning of receiving divine knowledge – the discovery and exposure to something we do not always understand. It is both a curse and a blessing, for its knowledge can save and accelerate ideas, but only when the audience is willing to listen.

—A*—

"Wisdom and intelligence cannot grow in a garden of fear and ignorance. Becoming an accomplished person among the enlightened is expected; becoming an accomplished person among the ignorant is miraculous." – AO

• • • •

"IGNORANCE IS NOT SAYING 'I don't know.' It is saying 'I don't want to know.'" – Unknown[656]

• • • •

"Knowledge is love and light and vision." – Helen Keller[657]

—*O—

EVEN IF OUR SPIRITUAL trek has company and the support of others, it is a lonely one since it is a tour of the Self and a flight of the Alone.[658] It is the awakening and building of our mind, heart and soul's relationship to the Beloved. Our journey to enlightenment will not be effortless or instantaneous. It requires us to cross intersections of facing our own personal inner demons, bringing forth an awareness of the emotional shadows trapped within the ego. The confrontations of those shadows will not be easy, but they will be necessary. It is the outcome of these emotional challenges of self-reflection that change who we are and send us to higher intensities of illumination. We may stumble on our path of spiritual travel when we don't open ourselves or fail to recognize the lessons that God is always trying to teach us. We may get angry at others and the universe, but it is how we deal with our situation that leads to growth. Enlightenment is learning to let go of those things and negative experiences which aren't that important in the bigger motion picture of life. By letting go, you clear the arterial connection to the divine dream of the universal mind and remove the impediments which act to restrict your entitlement to joy, love and happiness.

Do we acknowledge the insignificant incidents in the grand scheme of things and recognize the importance of following through with action on the significant ones? Do we control our emotions or do we let them control us? Controlling emotions does not mean constantly suppressing them. It means recognizing what we are feeling without always instantly reacting, understanding why we are feeling the way we do, listening to the words of others and then transferring that emotional energy into productive words or actions. It is finding that ideal mental location between thinking and reflecting through situations or letting our emotions and feelings dictate. It does not mean adding more fuel to the emotional fire, but rather adding cooling words to remedy a confrontation. The universe is always trying to teach us, but sometimes we fail to learn its lesson.

—Δ*—

"...God confounds many and enlightens many." – The Koran[659]

* * * *

"ALTHOUGH WE WRITE PRIMARILY for the edification of the disciples of the art, we also write for the mystification of those owls and bats which can neither bear the splendor of the Sun nor the light of the Moon." – George Ripley[660]

* * * *

"GOD SPEAKS TO ALL OF us in various ways. The universal teacher is always providing loving guidance, but some of us are better listeners and more receptive than others." – AO

—*O—

The path of enlightenment, the path of attainment, is a willingness to expose yourself to knowledge, the acquisition of relevant information, which may change the preconceived view of the world and those around you. It is the tapping into our potentialities while learning to support and comfort oneself through all experiences by means of our own courage and effort – to find our real self.[661] It is about allowing the proper amount of the angelic and the demonic into our consciousness, while drawing from the best of both worlds as we make amends with both Satan and God. One method of self-discovery is by following an organized religious doctrine based on healthy love and fair justice. It is a willingness to allow your old self to continuously die away as the new you springs forth with life and vigor. Our growth lies not in the doing of what is familiar, but in the reaching for that which is outside of our comfort zone. True spiritual growth requires constant reevaluation of our beliefs and a willingness to tap into the innermost core of our being and make the necessary changes when called for. There is no doubt that our beings will be tried and ripened on our journey. We may have to work for someone whose behavior is questionable. We may find our being dampened by the ill-intent words and actions of others. We may fall and stumble in our attempts to hurdle the obstacles encountered along the way. With each step, however, comes the opportunity for a new direction. With each step we increase the distance in time from the moments when others did us harm. With each step we grow away from our failures and move forward into the potential for success.

—Λ*—

"They whose chariot is driven by reason, who watches and holds the reigns of their mind, reaches the end of the journey, the Supreme everlasting spirit." – *Katha Upanishad*[662]

—*Ω—

Enlightenment is the process of developing the very core of our being through the thoughts and actions that we select to encompass and engage. Getting there is not sudden or instantaneous, but rather it is a process based on minute flashes of satori – small epiphanic steps. Every time we have an epiphanic event which raises and transcends us to the next plateau of awareness, we gain new insights into truth and reality. Upon taking such steps, we grow by allowing the old symbolic self to die away, birthing forth a newer, more enriched core but with an enlargement of the wholeness and integrity of our being. It may require that we first come out of the denial about who we have been and what we have done, acknowledging flaws in our behavior and previous actions.[663] Upon doing so, we then do the work to overcome them and to realize that some imperfections in our character are relative and subjective – they are baselined from a reference. Recognizing and acknowledging that we are an aspect of the cosmos experiencing itself, enlightenment is the balance between the outer-verse (interaction with the outside world, the exoteric) and inner-verse (internal reflection, the esoteric), being involved and escaping, participating in the secular and the divine. It is realizing and participating in the microcosm of our mind accessing the macrocosm of a greater mind. It is about knowing how to keep the proper proportions between the self (the ego) and that which is outside of the self (the "ega" to coin a new word). It is the merging of the best of left-wing liberal ideology with the best of right-wing conservative morality. Would Jesus Christ himself have skewed or aligned himself with the policies and behaviors of the Democratic Party or the Republican Party of the United States' political duality? Would he have rooted for one over the other or would he have crossed into the borders of each?

Enlightenment is the merging of material security with spiritual certainty. It is the recognition of the opposites within our universe and engaging in the proper actions based on the appropriate selection of proportions from these extremes to bring the bipolarity of spirituality into unity. It involves developing the ability to see not just the extremes, but also what is in between. It is being able to transfer, when benevolently appropriate, from the calming, serene state of the Buddhist to the agitated, motivated state of the Druid. The path of enlightenment entails gaining the wisdom, perception and self-awareness to be our own loving parent. It is the development of that inner voice or feeling that makes the recognition between what is proper behavior and what is not, and then initiating the appropriate course of action. It is about planning for the future with the correct degree of instant gratification. Too much instant gratification is harmful to the perception of ourselves being the beneficiaries of a future delight. Too little is harmful to the perception of ourselves being in the moment and participating in the present. The development of our core, the fulcrum of our souls, is done not through false talk or contradictory behavior, but rather through the consistent matching of our deeds with our words. It is not a façade of words without meaning or the outpouring of anger to suppress someone else and satisfy an unhealthy craving for power. For true power does not desire itself, but rather, displays itself when others choose to follow you of their own free volition. They follow and respect you because they know and sense that you do not desire or crave power over others. True power exists on the carrier wave of love and earned respect. Enlightenment is not a façade of words used to hide ulterior intentions or the fear of confronting the truth within ourselves and that of others. It is the forming of our being into one that knows the differences between what is right and what is wrong, the reduction of fear and the carrying out of actions that reinforces that internal knowing. The path to enlightenment is paved with the development of our inner voice such that it steers us in the correct direction between good and evil, resulting in healthy and appropriate behavior and outcomes. It is learning to empathize with the universe and to dissipate the demons within.

—A*—

"Greatness lies not in being strong, but in the right using of strength." – Henry Ward Beecher[664]

• • • •

"A SOUL THAT HAS GAINED no knowledge of the things that are, and has not come to know their nature, nor to know the Good, but is blind, such a soul is tossed about among the passions which the body breeds; it carries the body as a burden, and is ruled by it instead of ruling it. That is the vice of the soul. On the other hand, the virtue of the soul is knowledge. He who has got knowledge is good and pious; he is already divine..." – Hermes Trismegistus, *Libellus X, Corpus Hermeticum*[665]

• • • •

"HE WHO KNOWS OTHERS is clever, but he knows himself is enlightened." – Lao Tzu[666]

—*O—

An enlightened respects his or her body, but realizes that their true essence is not of the body. Their vision of themselves is of spirit, an eternal and immortal primal being that has gained mastery over their fate through the beauty and power of goodness. Since it takes time for a signal or light to travel, relative to a given point in the material universe, every other point in the physical realm is located in the past. How far in the physical past is dependent on relative distances. For example: relative to Earth, our Moon is located about 1.3 seconds in the past, our Sun is located about 8.3 minutes in the past, and the next nearest star system (Alpha Centauri) is located about 4.3 years in the past. Every point in the universe is connected and every point in the universe is the epicenter. For the present moment in which I write this statement within the realm of thought, it has extended in space-time to connect to the present moment in which you are reading it.[667] An advanced illuminated being (an enlightened) recognizes that every point in the universe is a focus of divinity in its totality.[668] Matter and energy (divinity in the realm of time) are omnipresent, since even in the isolated vacuum of space, electro-magnetic particles and waves are passing through while subatomic particles pop in and out of existence.[669] Although an enlightened understands that every moment in time and every point in the universe is sacred and a reference to the past, present and future (not just particular Earth-based landmarks or holy attractions associated with particular prophets, saints, imams, or kami), they still respect the sanctity of the holy sites and shrines of all true religions. When invited and not having prior commitments, an enlightened being feels honored and comfortable attending the ceremonies and holy sites of all true religions. They can transcend within any true religion's tenets and understand the message of God that is being delivered. Modern enlightenment means coming to terms and accepting that your religious view is one of many possible overlapping and diverse perspectives. As we work on our enlightenment training, relevant scriptural passages will gain more meaning to us as we age and grow. Certain passages read years ago will become more clear, significant and applicable as we encounter more of life's experiences.

—Δ*—

"When the ears of the student are ready to hear, then cometh the lips to fill them with wisdom." – *The Kybalion*[670]

—*O—

The path of enlightenment is a journey of choices and distractions. Those higher on this path of attainment choose to follow ideas that raise their beings and filter out those notions that are detrimental. We choose the type of music to hear. We choose the type of television to watch. We choose the type of books to read. We choose the type of ideas to agree with or disagree with. We choose to filter what permeates into our being from the circular outer-verse, crossing the triangular membrane and forming our inner-verse. Academia needs to go beyond just teaching the categorization and processing of things; it needs to also delve into our relationship with those categorizations and processes. A higher education does not guarantee spiritual or financial success, but it does guarantee flexibility and access to opportunities in pursuit of success.

The proper use of critical thinking skills is what protects us from harm; being overly judgmental is drawing a conclusion while lacking in all the facts or without applying appropriate empathy. Finding balance between applying critical thinking skills to evaluate a situation or personality and being overly judgmental requires fair reflection. On the path of enlightenment, we must apply our critical thinking skills to prevent miseducation from crossing our triangular barrier and entering our cores. Miseducation is learning and applying things that will result in harm to us and/or others. For example, an incarcerated offender released from a prison system may have become miseducated by other inmates on how to con others, pick locks, obtain passwords, steal identities or burglarize a home. The use of such learned skills for detrimental deeds may provide the culprit with a temporary feeling of accomplishment, but the net effect is a downward spiral of existence. Due to our connection with the All, the universe becomes diminished from our bad deeds and benefits from our good deeds. Which type of deed do you think the universe prefers? Through selection, analyzing and processing, we each have the self-determination to decide what morphs into our core. In doing so, we either develop a healthy ego or an unhealthy ego. We choose each and every day who we are going to be and who we are going to become. It is the habit of selecting the proper influences and allowing them to enter the core of our being that develops and raises our spiritual composition to the next epiphany and the next transcendental realization. During such epiphanic moments of transcendental mysticism, flashes of vision,[671] there is divine reciprocity – we enter God as he enters us. This correlates to the Hermetic saying of divinity encompassing "that which is above as that which is below, and that which is below as that which is above",[672] and from *The Upanishads*, "what is here is also there, and what is there is also here."[673] This means that there is reciprocity and a connection between the physical realm and the spiritual realms. The physical and spiritual go hand-in-hand with one influencing the other.[674] The lower or animal self (hati and bai),[675] has an effect on the higher or spiritual self (cheybi and kou),[676] and vice-versa. Above the animal self that dwells within and higher than the humanity that we are, there is an aspect of divinity waiting to be tapped into and developed. We are however, not God or gods, but have the capability to temporarily link and synchronize with this universal consciousness; to dovetail with Krsna. This synchronization occurs through positive education, the pursuit of knowledge, defaulting to steady state of love, being honest and truthful, maintaining a healthy ego, engaging in acts of kindness, applying appropriate tolerance and reflecting on what we allow into the core of our being. The universe influences our mind, but our mind also influences the universe. The exchange is reciprocal, however, the impact of the exchange of one upon the other can vary based on the potency of the influence. All these actions, in a balanced approach, lead to enlightenment.

—Λ*—

"Beware when the great God lets loose a thinker on this planet." - Ralph Waldo Emerson[677]

—*Ω—

A primary teaching of Islam is the submission or surrendering to the will of Allah. The *Gita* mentions "surrendering to the will of the Supreme Lord" and states in its final chapters that an ultimate principal, the polestar of all true religions, is to surrender onto the Lord.[678] Surrendering to God in the Buddhist sense is <u>sunyata</u>, the emptying of the egoic self to allow the divine persona to symbiotically enter. We normally vibrate within the quantum limitations of this physical/material realm, but there are other vibrational realms of different frequencies which are external to this one. Surrendering is the removal of all our false masks and the revealing of our core, releasing it to vibrate again in resonance with the Universal Consciousness. What does this all mean to surrender to a greater consciousness? It means surrendering and lowering the walls of one's ego to allow love to flow into your being and gratitude to flow out, while allowing our divine nature to step forth as it asks for forgiveness of ourselves and those that have trespassed against us. It is done through letting go of the ego-self of our own mind, to place us in touch with a greater mind (the Universal Consciousness). It begins with becoming "hollow" inside such that our ego is replaced with the thoughts of the universe. Each time we lower our ego-self and surrender our mind to the influx and thoughts of this greater mind, we are raising our consciousness to higher and higher plateaus and vibrational levels of existence. It is the releasing of the mind through devotion to a mystery beyond our full comprehension and opening doorways into our being to allow the full grace of God to enter, flow through, and fill our psyche.[679] When we lower our ego-self and listen to that silent voice of the Universal Consciousness, we are conforming our will to the will of the better Yahweh. The Brahman often feeds us information about the universe without us even realizing it. It is the risk of loving God, to have your ego soften and mesh with Allah, entering a state of <u>wahdat al-wujud</u> upon which you will realize all the love the universe has been projecting onto you. Upon surrendering, you will gain a heightened sense of reality, a greater awareness of truth and streams of knowledge (gnosis) will start to flow into your inner-verse by which liberation from ignorance (the removal of irrelevant information) is obtained. Christ may have allowed his own execution for the redemption of our sins eternal, but it is up to us to pay off our moral debt for his sacrifice by living a life based on his teachings of truth – to incorporate love in every moment, every thought and every deed. It is being amenable to having love as the base of all your words and actions. It is having God at the root of underlying thoughts, being in Krisna consciousness, and carrying out his/her loving instructions – steps that **never** contain requests of violence or actions of hatred. By surrendering unto the Lord, through <u>bhakti</u>, we make contact with divine benevolent power. For when one truly surrenders to God, their actions become manifested by love in service to the universe. It is not full detachment from the material world, but a balanced approach of being grounded in the physical realm while surrendering to the Supreme Personality such that the Self is not overwhelmed or overinflated – to be both of the flesh and of the spirit. Enlightenment involves finding the proper balance between materialism and spiritualism by moving steadily forward with grounded balance through both failure and success. Live in the joyous expectation of the best and allow the best to come to you.[680] By defaulting to a steady state of love, some of us will enter a perpetual state of love as the background of our thoughts; this is the way to illumination and being in rapport with God – to interact with divinity and then return again to participate in the physical world. Achieving illumination requires participation in the material world with honesty, sincerity, kindness, compassion and integrity in order to properly connect with the spiritual worlds.

—A*—

"Your safety lies in truth, and not in lies. Love is your safety. Fear does not exist. Identify with love, and you are safe. Identify with love, and you are home. Identify with love, and find your Self." – *Accept This Gift*[681]

—*O—

Attachment is about labeling things and phenomena as "mine", making them a possession of self rather than an extension of self. An extension of self by detachment is the healthy way to observe and participate in the universe and to promote the word "our" rather than "my." Detachment is minimizing or removing the ego's possessiveness. It is our world, our planet, our lives – there is no ego involved. When our material desires become minute through an inner state of non-attachment, the world will shower us with options and availability of material abundance of which we will have minimum need or want. Upon reaching the highest levels of enlightenment, one realizes that material gain is not the ultimate goal, but rather, being in a balanced state between devotion and detachment in eternal service and friendship with the Lord is the ultimate championship. All things are connected; it is recognizing those connections that brings one to the path of mysticism. Once this understanding is achieved, you will start to synchronize and flow with the universe, encountering and witnessing firsthand the mystery of God. This transcendental knowledge is reveled when our hearts, intentions and actions are pure. When one synchronizes with the thoughts of God, they are in samādhi, a euphoric trance of peak experience or epiphany. Synchronizations are the breadcrumbs leading us out of our lost state and into gnosis. The best time to hear and reflect on the thoughts of God, the voice of Krsna, the guidance of the new and improved Yahweh, is when our mind is calm and our internal noise is low. It is often a quiet mind that is able to see and absorb the wisdom of the universe, after which, doors of opportunity, better options and courses of action will start to reveal themselves. Devotional service, cleaning and polishing our connection to Allah through acts of love, is a process of spiritual understanding.[682] The kingdom of God is accessed from within, and then applied throughout as we become enamored with the universe. Jesus' teachings were not put forth to prove he was the Messiah; they were presented to make "Christs" of us all. Go about your daily actions being in Krishna Consciousness,

Allah Thought, God Space, or whatever label you wish to use to describe when having the divine essence of the Lord as your focal point. There is a Hermetic axiom stating: "While All is in THE ALL, it is equally true that THE ALL is in All."[683] This is a statement of reciprocity between the Creator and the created, declaring that both are a part of each other.

—Δ*—

"The spirit of the creator is inherent within me, and yet, I am not my creator." – *The Kybalion*[684]

• • • •

"IF YOU ARE CLOSE TO God, you have a motive to listen to His voice, and His voice or teaching is that we should love one another." – XIV Dalai Lama[685]

• • • •

"ONE SEES GOD BY LOOKING outward. One finds God by looking inward." – AO

—*O—

Our level of enlightenment, the brightness of our illumination, is based on how far we have opened ourselves up to the Beloved's guidance – the transition from ego to Self. By allowing the breeze of the universe's love to flow into us, we become even more receptive to the Beloved's guidance. The spark of divinity within all of us is a glowing ember to be fanned with Allah's grace. When we focus on Krisna or Vishnu, this ember grows as we engage our underlying thoughts in surrendering to the love and will of God, awakening the avatar within. The process of awakening begins when we acknowledge that we are all in fact, an aspect of God and therefore, capable of meshing with him/her. We are by no means the whole, but as a subset of the universe, we are reflecting and participating in its own creation.

—Λ*—

"One cannot be God, for that is unbalanced ego and too much responsibility for any being to handle. One can, however, occasionally humbly synchronize, mesh and become one with God by falling in love with the universe. In doing so, epiphanic resonance will occur. This is a key to mysticism and ecstasy." – AO

—*Ω—

Coming to terms with our place in the universe occurs with the realization that our divine right to exist and experience life far exceeds the trivialness of our beings compared to the vastness of all. When we open up our thinking to the whole, the whole will reveal itself to us. Our egos bear witness to a small part of what the Universal Consciousness sees and feels, and in doing so, we become an instrument of divinity.

The characters of the scarecrow, the tinman and the cowardly lion from the 1939 American classic musical cinematic fantasy *The Wizard Of Oz* (a mythology of its own), each were in search of something that they already had. The scarecrow wanted brains (mind), the tinman wanted a heart (body) and the cowardly lion wanted courage (spirit). What the wizard did was show them that they already had such attributes and gifts within. Similarly, the great ones keep advising that the power of divinity can be accessed by all of us from within. Healthy love, gratitude and forgiveness are the peaceful path to heaven and enlightenment, while hatred and violence is in the opposite direction.

—A*—

"In truth who knows God, becomes God." – *Mundaka Upanishad*[686]

• • • •

"I am an expression of the divine." – Alice Walker[687]

• • • •

"I AM GOD, BUT SO ARE you. You are God, but so am I. God is all, but we are neither." – Zen saying (koan) of the Enlightened, AO

—*O—

It is through love, inward contemplation, external experience, and pure faith that we tap into our God-self, the temple within (a template) upon which we merge our humanity within with the divinity throughout and slope upwards towards enlightenment. From Hermeticism, it is our vibrations of goodness, the preferred default frequencies to have our consciousness resonate, that move us up on the scale of enlightenment. The fulfillment and illumination of our being is through the pursuit of moral ideas and creative development. The process of reading and studying pertinent and applicable sections of the great scriptures will greatly contribute to our self-actualization. All the great scriptures keep trying to teach us that we must come to know and love Allah in our own direct way and that God is diversity. The Lord is diversity in people, culture and in religious paths. Whosoever fails to understand, accept and embrace this does not walk a path to Allah. Do not let tribal, clan and gang-like belonging blind you from enjoying the beauty of God's diversity. Allah is love and perhaps sometimes disappointment, but not hatred and anger. No true religious path has exclusive access to divinity and no true path provides extra privileges from the Lord. God/Allah sees all true paths as equal.

—Λ*—

"Your daily life is your temple and your religion." – Kahlil Gibran[688]

—*Ω—

It is through this self-mastery that we achieve inner greatness and then apply it to improving the external world. Allah is growing; the universe is expanding. We first enter this material plane as a non-individual of the divine spark, with the goal of climbing the ladder of enlightenment to become an Illumined. As we advance higher on this ladder, relevant scriptural passages will illuminate our minds to the signs and authentic compassionate voice of Jehovah, speaking through the thoughts of our Self, our Atmon, our inner voice sensitized to divinity. At the end of our physical life cycle, we bring back our attained levels of physical, mental and spiritual evolution as we return to the source from which we came. We learn to love God and the Goddess with full and utter devotion. In doing so, our ego becomes one with the divine Ego. Hermes Trismegistus writes, "The aim of those with Gnosis is to become God."[689] Becoming God is not about self-importance and always being correct, it is about lowering the ego, humbling ourselves, continuously learning and existing in the realm of love. Gnosis is the doing of good not because of fear of punishment or expectation of an eternal reward, but because of the "selfish" desire to dwell in a steady state of love.[690] As mortals, we cannot become gods or God. We can, however, mesh with their thoughts, synchronize with their vibrations, and resonate in harmony with their pulse. This skill of recognizing one's divine natures is reserved for the advanced initiate. The very fact that you are reading this book means that you are an advanced initiate – your eyes, ears and mind are open. Focusing on whatever we can to improve upon our happiness, intelligence, generosity, health, love, ambition and wealth (aka The "HIGHLAW") and that of others, is one path to enlightenment. The fastest and most efficient way to achieving the grace of God and/or the Goddess, to become an instrument of divinity, is by putting into practice The Divine Benevolent Principles of Love, Forgiveness and Gratitude as expanded upon in Chapter 25. Love is looking forward into the future, forgiveness is healing the past, and gratitude is being in the present moment. The implementation of all three principles in a healthy and balanced manner is a requisite for communion with the Almighty.

—Δ*—

"Remember that the law of mystery veils the great truth. Total knowledge can be revealed only to our brethren who have gone through the same trials as ourselves. Truth must be measured according to intelligence; it must be veiled from the feeble, whom it would madden, and concealed from the wicked, who are capable of seizing only its fragments, which they would turn into weapons of destruction. Keep it in thy heart and let it speak through thy work. Knowledge will be thy might, faith thy sword, and silence thy armor that cannot be broken." – *Poimandres*[691]

• • • •

"ALCHEMIZING OUR BEING, we seek spiritual transformation by raising our consciousness to a higher vibrational state. Connecting our awareness to understand the universe, we purify our soul and cleanse our karma through the commandments of love, forgiveness and gratitude. Discovering in ourselves the correct formula and perfect mixture of the poles of existence, we rise above the dualities to master them and transmute ourselves into a benevolent instrument of divinity." – Chant Of The Initiate, AO

• • • •

"IF I AM A GOD, IT IS only because God is working through me." – AO

—*O—

It is difficult beyond description to conceive that space has no beginning and no end, but it is even more difficult to conceive a beginning and an end. It is difficult to conceive an eternal duration of which we call time, but it is even more impossible to conceive when there shall be no more time.[692] Some physicists are quick to warn us that there is no such thing as "before space", "before time", "before energy", "before matter", or "before the beginning."[693] According to their views, since humans are manifestations of space/time/energy/matter, the recombined byproducts of stellar dust, how can we have a connection to anything before the "Big Bang", that ignition of material creation? Stephen Hawking, the respected and renowned astrophysicist, expressed his views that a personal God does not exist or at least, could not have existed before the start of time at the "Big Bang."[694] Such conjectures, unfortunately, are based on a limited myopic scoping of what constitutes divinity and the use of instrumentation that only measure matter and units of linear time, not thought or streams of consciousness. Such instruments are incapable of measuring those energies that are beyond the constraints of time. They can only measure consciousness when in its lower and condensed state, that of energy and matter. The scientific view is that consciousness came forth from the explosion of creation while the religious view is that it was consciousness that initiated the burst. Maybe, however, the keyword to note in Dr. Hawking's view is the word "personal", for if our specific persons did not yet exist, how could a "personal" God exist? Albert Einstein reported in his book, *Out Of My Later Years*, that he saw no conflict between the duality of science and spirituality. He described his own theories as products of spiritual awareness – the observer participating, part of, and connected to the observed.[695] Creation occurred the instant God become aware of his/her/its own existence for time, space, energy, matter and thought are all extensions and emergent expressions of the divine being itself.[696]

The creation myth of many religions is the memory of the "Big Bang", that perceived spontaneous eruption of energy into space/time and what was before, imbedded within the initialization reserves of our memories. This memory of the eternal pouring into the temporal through a flash point of a singular conception is recorded in the Judeo-Christian-Islamic scriptures within the beginning thirty or so verses of *Genesis*. The Hindu and Buddhist-based religions along with others have their own variety of creation myths (and there cyclical repetition) that can be correlated in an abstract sense to the same "Big Bang" of science.[697] Was the "Big Bang" not the awakening of the universe and the hatching of the cosmic egg?

Jesus Christ and the Buddha are considered incarnations of that being of consciousness who recalled and recognized (awakened to) our beginnings prior to the spark of material creation induced forth from that ancient point of singularity. Indeed, as they were trying to teach us, we too are manifestations to varying degrees of that being. Ponder for a moment on who you were as part of that primordial consciousness before the birth of the universe. Visualize and imagine that you are alive and dead at the same time, both born and unborn. The rebound from such ponderings will make your greater reality become clearer – there will be a new vividness and freshness to your experiences.

—Λ*—

"And that which sings and contemplates in you is still dwelling within the bounds of that first moment which scattered the stars into space."
– *The Prophet*[698]

—*Ω—

Each of us is a repeated expression of the "Big Bang", born from a beginning with a mystical memory booted into our brains of what we were prior to exiting our mother's womb. The story of our Genesis evolutionary memories go beyond the chronological limits of "The Big Bang" and unfolds forward with the formation of first generation stars, many of which exploded into Super Nova and rose again into second generation stars. Our nearest star, the Sun, is a middle-aged second generation member. The planets of our solar system were the clumping of remaining stellar natal materials, morphing into gargantuan spheres from the proto-solar disk. The being referred to as Sophia then inserted and diversified a part of her incarnate creativity into the third closet planet orbiting this star, the marbled blue water planet referred to as Earth by its later advanced intelligent sentient inhabitants.[699] Diversity is therefore the subsequent expression of God emanating from that initial pearl of pure eternity, mixing with itself to create even more combinations of matter and life. Through the Hermetic Law of Neutralization, the ultimate goal is to merge the best of God, Sophia, Allah, Satan, Lucifer and Ahriman, into our being by using love as the binding agent. Alchemy of the mind is learning to be in a state of calm excitement because we don't need to sell or convince others of our enlightenment level.

Chapter 13
Maintaining Spirituality – Resetting The Mind

"I PASS MY WORRIES ONTO you, Oh Lord, such that I can focus my energies on today." – Prayer Of The Anxious, AO

• • • •

THESE RECENT CENTURIES close to the turn of the second millennium into the third millennium are hurdling forward in the midst of a technological and intellectual renaissance that can be considered off the charts. The 19th century discovery and exploration of the electromagnetic spectrum by such scientists as Sir William Herschel, Johann Wilhelm Ritter, Michal Faraday, James Clerk Maxwell, Heinrich Hertz, Wilhelm Conrad Röntgen and Paul Villard triggered much of this technological acceleration. The realization that light continued beyond on both sides of the visible spectrum was a greater contributor to humanity's advancement than the use of fire or the invention of the wheel. By investigating, studying, understanding and utilizing the behavior of light across its spectrum, quantum leaps in informational storage and retrieval, medical diagnosing, positional location systems, cosmology and above all else, communication have occurred. With our still minimal understanding of light energy, we didn't conquer it and we don't control it. We guide the electromagnetic spectrum into providing productive uses for navigating through and interpreting the universe. Like fish swimming through water, birds soaring through the air, or surfers riding waves, we have learned its flow as it guides us.

A limited number of humans, relaying their experiences back to us, have ventured out of Earth's atmospheric domain and higher up the walls of its gravity well – going beyond 100 kilometers above our planet's surface. More will venture out and eventually beyond any appreciable influence of our home planet's gravitational funnel. Our understanding (or at least the accuracy of theoretical modeling) of cosmology, particle physics, geology, genetics, molecular and evolutionary biology, sanitation and the neurosciences have made vertiginous and miraculous leaps ahead since the days of horse and buggy. We have pioneered replaceable and substitutive body parts, genome mapping, brilliant and detailed images of the outer planets and distant galaxies, and the ordering of our meals by pressing menu options on a touch screen. That tiny portable "gadget" called a smart phone has provided: 1) communicative connections to billions of people; 2) instant snapshots and videos; 3) reasonably accurate navigation of one's location on the globe; 4) a vast vault of music collections; 5) entry to seemingly unlimited databases and libraries of knowledge; 6) purchasing power of just about anything from anywhere; and, 7) entertainment for our minds with an assortment of digitized games.[700] It has opened up the world of portable access to anything that can be electronically digitized.

This technological acceleration can send us into shock, denial of its benefits and a craving for a false romanticized nostalgia of simpler times, but consider our ancestors' affairs from only a few centuries ago. They were riddled with lice and parasites, the microscopic world was unknown to most, food was bland, questionable, uncertain, monotonous, limited in variety and sporadically available for all but the fortunate or those residing close to an active port or major trading hub. Poverty and destitution led you to the public funded institutions of poorhouses. Bankruptcy automatically sent you to time in debtor's prison in which privileges had to be purchased, if your family could afford them, to ease the severity of the incarceration. Mortality rates were much higher, especially among children and for women during childbirth. A splinter, deep scratch or large scrape was more likely to fester, sending the body to the point of death. Hygiene was minimal and healthcare consisted of a doctor's saw, a dentist's pliers and a jar of leeches. The workday of labor started at dawn and ended at dusk, with the next 7 to 14 hours being surrounded by total darkness except for flickers of rudimentary torches, taper candlelight, oil lanterns, fireflies or the reflected sunlight from the brighter phases of the Moon. Indoor plumbing and effective heating systems in dwellings were uncommon or non-existent. Access to public libraries or museums of history, culture and the arts were inconceivable to all but a few within the regions of metropolises. Until recent times, most people never travelled more than a few miles from their place of birth and if they chose to emigrate across the Atlantic or Pacific Oceans, their parents may never have seen them again or ever meet their grandchildren.[701]

As a result of this rapid technological implementation of electromagnetism over a relatively short period (only two centuries) of human history, encountering its advantages and disadvantages, many of us find ourselves being over stimulated by all the electronic gadgetry with lights, sounds and buttons encountered at the start of the 21st century. Referring to this era as a "Norm of Overstimulation", we are bombarded with an overabundance of communication, attention-grabbing information, data overload, rampant comments of over-synthesized excitement from internet based social media and what we see on hundreds of televised channel options via illuminated screens that are no longer restricted to monochromatic blips. Youngsters often complain about being bored. Grown-ups complain about being overstimulated. Many of us adults find ourselves grasping for a secure footing in an age of over-stimulus from non-stop emails from more than one account to texts without pause. Our senses are overdosing from a constant barrage of visual and auditory media in the form of display panels, flashing lamps, flickering diodes and bursts of soundbites. Television (TV) has evolved to over 100 channels while the internet's numbers are without end. If one were to say that their TV is talking and tracking them, they are considered "mad." If one were to say the internet is talking and tracking them, they are considered correct and sane.[702] Are we being productive human beings spending our time creating a virtual mark that may not be available on an outdated server file, five, ten or fifty years from now? How far into the future will anyone be aware of current day popular bloggers' binary-coded thoughts left in the archive of communication storage banks to acknowledge that they ever existed?

The chips of time and energy put towards filtering out extraneous information erodes away at the time and energy needed for absorbing useful material. Our awareness is being taken from us due to the constant onslaught of such digitized external stimuli. For this reason, occasionally surfacing from the lights and sounds of the modern world is all the more necessary to regain our footing. Taking the time to reflect on our existence and relationship to something grander is the purest means for retaining our balance. It is important to find our resetting moments of "godspace" – states of serenity, tranquility, ambition, motivation and internal peace. Being productive in life is not about going fast and maintaining a rapid pace; it is about being efficient in both reflection and action. It is about conserving energy and then applying it appropriately where it is needed most. Learn to adjust your life tempo to be more efficient. This means developing the skills of knowing when to slow down and when to speed up. The pace of modern life must be adjusted or else we are going to suffer profoundly from its debilitating overstimulation and excessive super-excitement.[703] God works both slowly and fast, adjusting his pace accordingly. We are more efficient when we match her tempo.

We make hundreds if not thousands of daily micro-decisions as we scroll through pull down menus and options upon glowing displays connected to computers, phones and small portable devices. We now have television screens bigger than a bay window and smaller than a postage stamp.[704] Just because a particular technology exists or is novel, does not mean it should automatically be implemented. Adapting to technology for the sake of technology can be reckless. Its advances grant opportunities, but not necessarily parallels with the required ethics nor guarantees marketplace success. Technology has its place and its place is not everywhere. It is the tool by which we may destroy ourselves, but it is also the tool which may be our salvation.

The electronically digitized world of global communication certainly has its advantages and benefits, namely, the generalization of liberalizing currents stored at multiple locations. Such internetwork redundancy provides a resistance to authoritarian influences from exerting total control, and ultimately, contributes to their demise. The Orwellian "Big Brother Is Watching" has morphed into a duality. Initially relating to speculative fearful surveillance conducted by authoritative regimes upon its citizens by 1984 (hence the book's title), it has also spread to the world's citizens themselves acting as a benevolent global neighborhood crime watch, revealing localized atrocities for all to witness and judge. Distributing such civilian obtained surveillance to the world, however, is a much simpler task from true democratic or democratic republic governing regions.

Our world of trade, commerce and economic interchange has us bombarded with images and phrases trying to convince us to purchase a particular product or service. Not all marketing is bad and not all advertising is unscrupulous, for some present proof of a genuine sense of well-being. Learn to recognize when advertisements or marketing ploys are relying on false shaming as a means to make you feel less important or less happy unless you purchase their product. Will that latest electronic gizmo, gadget, fragrance or article of clothing truly improve your life or will it only act as a temporary and empty status symbol? Be a wise consumer and do not blindly succumb to catchy but empty advertising. The advertisement may be sexy, exciting, stimulating, refreshing, but very often the actual object of promotion is not.

—Λ*—

"People presume every advertiser to be innocent until he is proven guilty." – *Burba's Barbs*[705]

• • • •

"ADVERTISING MAY BE described as the science of arresting the human intelligence long enough to get money from it." – author unknown[706]

—*Ω—

You have the power to dictate the marketplace. We try to teach children within our school systems to respect themselves and others, and yet, they are bombarded with advertising media that declares their happiness and worth will be increased based on the purchase and use of certain products. Being exposed to displays of instant sexual encounters associated with cosmetics, perfumes, colognes and other consumer products, the self-worth of our teenagers is constantly under attack from the advertising community. Fighting against this battle, we can train our youth with the tools to make the proper monetary choices and decisively filter out what will add to their character and what will take away from it. We can show our youth how to recognize when they are being deceived and tricked into buying products that won't necessarily make them any "cooler", any more likable, or any more accepted by their peers. We can only hope that our youth recognizes that some people will depend on the ignorance and low self-esteem of their audience to get them to spend money on items of false worth. It is up to each individual to develop the self-awareness for determining what will truly add to their being and what will add more money to the pockets of deceptive marketing practices. Being "cool" is based on being happy and content with yourself, not on succumbing to the whims of artificially created marketing trends and overrated accessories.

Much of the commercial world of consumer marketing is constantly bombarding us with artificial stimulus, creating a false façade of excitement where there is none to be found. They want the focus of our thoughts and for us to become addicted to their message that very often, has no source of truth. They want us to pay attention to their voice, and not our own. Advertising through various media, constantly tries to convince us that their products are what we need to be happy, healthy, sensual or desirable. Some may be truthful, but others are misleading you into believing that you are less worthy without their product. Don't be fooled. Listen in silence to your inner voice and be a critically conscious consumer – select products, when feasible, that minimally impact and pollute the environment. Your happiness, sensuality and desirability are based on the core within your being, not on the artificial exterior created by an environment of potentially false commercial influence.

The pressures, monotony and unceasing continuity of distractive responsibilities can dull the freshness of mind needed for focusing on achieving success. During such periods of drainage, expenditure of greater focal energy is required to do with difficulty and strain what one formerly did with ease.[707] Have we become so afraid of internal reflection and the sound of our own thoughts that we must blast them away with external stimuli? Does the notion of being disconnected or without a cell phone send us into a tizzy? Is the stampede of new digital technology, materialistic over-consumption and a lack of time for reflection creating a world that is spiritually sterile? Has the onslaught of excessive consumerism and mass media bombardment drowned out the epiphany of religious experience? I think not, but finding our footing above the noise, distractions and temptations requires an internal reset.

As in the days of Carl Jung, it seems that the neurosis of our times is a feeling of senselessness and emptiness in our lives. However far-fetched it may sound, experience shows that many neurosis are caused by the fact that people close their eyes and deny themselves to their own religious prompting – usually because of fear and bias against the susceptibilities and vulnerabilities of a child-like passion for enlightenment.[708] The good news is that such feelings can be replaced by a sense of purpose and meaning through reigniting the spiritual libido – engaging in the proper and balanced religious pursuits. All too often, the clamor of the physical world deafens us and the noise of our own mind distracts us.[709] In order to receive the hints of the universe, we need to be still within ourselves, to allow the Atmon within and throughout to come forth by the underlying voice of Self. After temporarily withdrawing into the sacred space of meditation, surrendering the ego, the mind and the heart all to love, we re-engage ourselves back into the material realm and put into practice the spiritual reality and revealing confessions of the universe.

As we learn to empty the mind of non-productive noise or the art of thought stopping as referred to in Buddhist scriptures, we need to allow it to refill with thoughts of healthy love. Healthy love and respect for ourselves, respect for others and respect for the universe and planet that we participate in. The alternative action is waste. We can waste our mental energy on anger of what has happened to us in this life or the rough start we may have had coming into this world and growing up in it. We can waste our emotional energy feeling bitter over what our enemies have done to us and trying to figure out ways to settle the score. We can waste precious minutes dwelling over events or failures within our past. We can waste valuable time licking the wounds that dysfunctional people have inflicted within our psyche. Or we can choose to efficiently use the limited time we have in this physical realm and learn to acknowledge, heal, move on and grow into better people. We can learn to become healthy love. Once we have implanted healthy love at the core of our being and the impetus for our thoughts and actions, a genuine sense of purpose will start to unfold.

An aspect on the path to true enlightenment is the ability to travel, at the appropriate moments, from a calm low energy state to an excited high energy state. It is the ability to go from a cluttered mind of many thoughts to a clear mind with efficient thoughts. Calming the mind is the first step to enlightenment, for when the mind is cluttered, one is not focused and learning becomes more difficult. Being focused does not mean an intense state of concentration, but rather a relaxed, receptive and alert state. A cluttered mind can be full of emotions or thoughts, both positive or negative. When one is excited about a momentous occasion, even extreme happiness can be dizzying and overwhelming.

Many of us have hectic lifestyles that leave our energy reserves drained at the end of the day as we find ourselves frequently operating at the verge of exhaustion. We unhealthily skip over the importance of quietism and resigned aloofness due to the pace of our global tempo.[710] As our minds become filled with thoughts necessary to deliver us through our daily grind, we sometimes lose our connection to that divine spirit which permeates all. Closing off the flow from that eternal reservoir of spiritual wisdom, we become lost and diverted from an enlightened existence. Constantly feeling like we have too much to do in too little time among a crowded, busy routine full of certainty and uncertainty, there are many methods for calming the mind. Sometimes we need to "mentally" slow down and acknowledge the beauty that is around us. Quieting the mind and allowing only calming external input as opposed to the noise of internal thoughts can be a good way of centering our beings. Other times, temporarily eliminating external stimulus all together and allowing internal thoughts to speak for themselves is the better way to re-set. Select the approach based on your preference for the moment.

A common approach from Buddhist practices is to tune into only the sensation of air going into your nostrils, remaining stationary for a few moments while holding it within your lungs, and then gently exiting the breath while feeling the sensation of air slowly flowing through and slipping out loosely opened lips. Another method is to focus on the energy fields or auras around trees.[711] The etymology of the word "aura" reveals that it means "light" in Hebrew and "breeze" in Greek. By Eastern thought, (Spiritual), one may be seeing the life force emanating from the leaves and branches. By Western thought, (Scientific), one may be seeing the after image left on the retina as the eye's nerves relax and reset themselves. Psychometry, the reading of auras of inanimate objects, is a practice performed by Spiritualists to decipher the object's history. Whether psychometry is legitimate or not, the results have been inconsistent.

Stare at the following image (optical illusion) for a few moments. Much like looking at abstract art, current thoughts of clutter may be put on hold as you start to see black dots appear then disappear. Focus on the flickering illusion while undergoing natural eyeball movements and the internal noise of your mind will be put on a temporary pause.

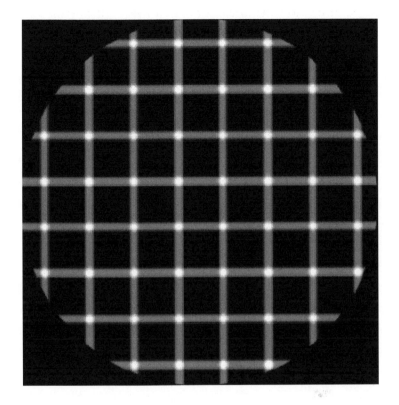

(Image based on a 1981 art project by the author)

WATCHING THE BLACK small circles morph in and out of existence as you chase them, but never locate them, will induce a certain
quietness into your mind – it momentarily stops surface thoughts. Similar to the central region of the Asterox on the front cover of this book,
the optical illusion is Zen encapsulated within art. Looking at the effect
is also rather cool in a mesmerizing sort of way! If you are in an agitated
or panic state, focusing on the blinking illusion will calm your thoughts.
Similarly, viewing these images and auras around both animate and inanimate objects calls for calmness of the mind. The black dots in the image
above do not exist on the paper. Our mind sees them in the form of an
optical illusion – they do not physically exist on the page. They are not a
hallucination because more than one person can see them, making them
a collective optical illusion. Perhaps this is similar to one of the methods
by which true visions initiate and angels click, chirp and chime (both fig-

uratively and literally) their presence to us – the ringing of tiny bells. For angels do not always make an appearance in a macroscopic humanoid-like form and can work their miracles through microscopic bursts of energy, similar to the constant bombardment of subatomic particles into and out of existence. God is always performing miracles. Just because we don't notice them doesn't mean they aren't happening. Everyday there are thousands of miracles happening around us. When our spiritual vision, our third eye, is keen and clear, that is when we will start to see those everyday subtle miracles that add up to a vast continuance. Perception is seeing and connecting the dots; paranoia and delusion is making them up or ignoring them altogether.

It is not important whether you view the aura-like images as circular, (Spiritual), or triangular, (Scientific), but rather the fact that you can see them. When you see these images, be it around a tree or another person, you are in a calm state of mind. You have filtered out the multitude of excessive thoughts to be able to see these images. Now that your mind is calm, you will be much more receptive to your external environment. Smells, tastes, sound, textures, colors, etcetera, will all take on a much more elaborate and enjoyable association. The calmness will not come right away, it may take practice and mental training, but there will be epiphanies.

Regularly emptying or draining the mind throughout and at the end of the day of all irritations, all resentments, all disappointments, all frustrations and all annoyances is a healthy habit.[712] Suppressing such feelings only causes them to bottle up; it is better to learn how to healthily dissipate them. Focus on love and/or God, as it will provide the mental space for solutions to form from subconscious thoughts. In the calming of our internal voice, we must learn to acknowledge the anger and sadness we may sometimes feel, but our focus should be on the love, beauty and joy in our lives. If we don't have any love, beauty or joy in our lives, then we need to take a look at ourselves and our past actions. Have we made excessive choices of instant gratification, ignoring the long-term ramifications? Have we intentionally distorted the truth of events within our lives, too afraid to acknowledge our own shortcomings and expose our weaknesses? Have we created a world in which we feel isolated from others in order to falsely protect ourselves? Do we make up false tales of our past and crave excess attention from others to fill the voids within ourselves?

There are certain occurrences that will naturally remove the feelings of well-being within our earthly lives such as the loss of loved ones, war, pandemics, famines, droughts, natural disasters and unavoidable circumstances that can force us into poverty. It is in these situations that our spirit or faith is truly challenged. Will we ever survive? Will we ever get out of our current situation? Will we ever feel joy again? Have we lost our hope for a better future? Although we may sometimes feel that God has abandoned us, it is in these moments that the divine entity is the closest. This is where our reliance on something beyond our mortal existence is the glue that holds us together. This is where a miniscule amount of faith somewhere deep within our consciousness is the only thing that keeps us going. We may not all or always believe in a cosmic energy of a higher mind, but we can always hope that there is one.

"Time Robbers" and "Timer Wasters" are those items in our daily existence that take time away from what we really want to do or to enjoy in life. They are negative influencers that can dull our senses or drown out our spiritual connections. Whether facing them in a first world, second world or third world nation, they still drain our being and leave us in a robotic or zombie-like existence. Our sense of what is truly important can become distorted and the lines between what is right and wrong may become faded. As we juggle all of life's demands, they bog us down and distract us with unwanted extraneous activities. They can be the time spent filling out paperwork, shopping for groceries, cleaning house, maintaining machinery, fixing equipment and the accumulation of excess. Excessive materialistic behavior, the accumulation of too much stuff, exacerbates the "time robbers and wasters" in our lives because material items need to be researched, procured, purchased, placed, stored, dusted, cleaned, protected, maintained, adjusted, updated, replaced, refurbished, replenished, repaired, reconditioned, renovated, sorted, recycled and/or eventually discarded as refuse. Some material items are necessities such as food, clothing and shelter. Others provide us with a sentimental connection such as knick-knacks from a vacation, our childhood, an ancestral heirloom or a collectable series. Still others provide only a temporary and fleeting impression, later turning into clutter. We seem to spend the first phases of our lives accumulating and collecting material items then dedicating time in the latter phases of our lives trying to reduce or get rid of them.

—Δ*—

"When a person delights in and gloats over his possessions, in reality he limits, even loses his freedom. The mania of riches has enslaved him. He is lowered in status, being no longer the owner but the owned. He has subordinated himself to his goods." – Saint Anthony of Padua[713]

—*O—

The degree of excess of a particular material item is based on how far above the norm it is from what we actually need. Indoor plumbing, hot water and furniture are relative luxuries to some degree. Diamond, jade and sapphire jewelry are luxuries of a higher degree. To what degree should we indulge beyond the necessities and into the luxuries? Often, it is the emotion associated with a luxury item that we are purchasing, not its material value. The item itself may not be capable of sustaining that emotion after the purchase, yet some start to associate happiness with those fleeting feelings of excitement or joy that are attached to the initial purchase. Many of the purchases that we make are not actually for the item, but rather, they are for the state of emotion that we associate with the item. Denying one's self from all luxuries, however, is not conducive to a balanced well-being and can stagnate economic flow. Since the degree of excess is subjective depending on the person or group, it is difficult to place a quantitative measurement upon it. Developing personal systems of organization and tracking to handle all the burdens of "time robbers" can release us from some of their draining demands. Be selective when choosing which material objects you want to dedicate part of your life to. Practice healthy materialism and be a conscientious consumer, since our gathering and hoarding behavior can exacerbate the "time robbers" in our lives.

Has modern society become too afraid to dwell within the silence of our own thoughts or have we become addicted to constant external stimuli? Do we really need to be electronically connected all the time? Although connecting with God is done both while alone and among a crowd, within isolation and interaction, we need to favor and take time out for reflective moments of solitude and quiescence. The deep silence of our soul can be heard when we are in union with the background of our consciousness. Other times we will be unified in solitude while walking among the crowd by having God on our minds and in our hearts. Living and participating in this physical realm, but not blinded by its material illusion, we need to be connected with our spirituality, but not lost in it. Time permitting, seek out companions who inspire the desire and search for truth. Channel and amplify each other's purifying energies in linking to the Beloved by serving humanity based on intentions and motives of love. The soul's journey is a solitary one, but with good company, the trip is much more enjoyable. Disconnecting or escaping from society on a permanent basis does not bring one closer to God or a spiritual life. One must be a participant in society to understand the full range of emotional perspectives encountered in everyday life.

Temporarily retreating from society, on the other hand, can be a great elixir for refocusing thoughts and dedicating some time to the development of our inner core.[714] Such solitary moments of being disconnected from external stimulus provides the time to let our thoughts flow freely or to reflect on who we are and where we are going. It allows for our overloaded senses to regain acuteness to the whispers of the universe. Moments of contentment can be achieved by wavering our quiet mind and thoughts just above the twilight of the dream state. A civilization without time for internal reflection is a society without direction, for internal reflection is necessary for maintaining a healthy path of existence. When we take the time for internal reflection and listen to the whispers and hints of the universe, the enlightened mind will hear the thoughts of God – for our mind is the immortal part of our humanity. Today's society needs to regain its cohesion with a modern mythology that distinguishes between good, evil and neither. Without this binding reflective connection between generations, humanity will be left with no direction but downwards.

There will be times in life when others, either intentionally or un-intentionally, may cause our ego to be hurt or our honor assaulted. It is how we choose to handle and react to these acts of disrespect that de-termines if our core will grow or stagnant, evolve or diminish. Consid-er each encountered act of disrespect as an immovable and impenetra-ble brick wall that we must somehow surpass. Continually bashing and thrashing against it will get us nowhere. The best course of action is to change our direction (patterns of thought), transition sideways and go around it. Properly dealing with acts of disrespect is very much the same way one should get out of a riptide. Swimming and fighting against it will only result in drowning. Changing direction and swimming in a path that is perpendicular to its motion and parallel to the shore will result in our success and continued existence. The brick wall and riptide correla-tions are good analogies of how one should properly deal with encoun-tered transgressions to our self-respect, avoiding showdowns over empty facades of honor and preventing unnecessary escalation.

If we ever find ourselves developing feelings of excessive anger or hatred towards others or a particular group, it is imperative to channel that negative energy and coagulating frustration in a productive manner such that it eventually fades and dilutes. Dissipate the energy of anger in productive ways; do not let it fester into hatred. By either training our minds to default to a steady state of love, obtaining the proper mental health counselling, focusing on helping others through works of charity, or channeling that hurting energy into healthy art forms such as paint-ings, music, writing or sculpture, we can prevent damage and the perma-nent loss of our souls. The productive venting and transference of our frustrations into art is an application of the Hermetic Law of Neutraliza-tion; it dissipates the swings of the pendulum. Every morning upon wak-ing and before the tasks and battles of the day take over, the first thoughts that we should train our minds to dwell on is the word "love." Making that word our internal mantra will help to bring us back into balance. When tension builds up in our mind and body due to fear, worry, sup-pressed emotion or suppressed desire, love becomes the healing balm for our internal state. Focusing on love prevents us from becoming a victim of anxiety, anger and frustration; it makes us a victor of our days.

Within our times of internal reflection, we should allow for both moments of meditation and moments of contemplation. Contemplation is the mental activity of a thinker, the movement of thought within focused boundaries, and the journey to an epiphany. Meditation is the silence of a creator, the stillness of thought that allows the subconscious to surface, and the destination of the epiphany. It is the practice of listening to the silent voice of the cosmos' depths coming from within, without the external influence of words, thoughts, concepts, actions, images, music, song or chant. Upon hearing that still and magnificent voice of creation, it enters our core where it incubates internally into the later manifestation of external expression in the form of words, thoughts, concepts, actions, images, music, song or chant. Meditation is the means; contemplation is the results. The *vice versa* of the five preceding sentences is also valid. Once you have quieted the mind, listen for the deeper expressions of God (the pulse of the universe) that is better sensed in the essence of silence. To reach stability and balance, one must become comfortable with internal silence; the temporary lack of controlling thought within the mind. Raising your consciousness to a higher state is about going into the All while meditating on your true identity. We all came from a primal creature that still dwells within us. It is the imprint of who we are today and reaches through time in both directions, anchoring us to the past while filling our sails towards the future. The reaching of the eternal self, the atoms of the ancient being within, our Atmon, is through resting the senses, concentration of one's mind and peace in one's heart.[715]

—A*—

"Silence is the element in which great things fashion themselves." – Thomas Carlyle[716]

—*O—

What is our inner voice? It is the stirrings and echoes of that primal creature, that ancient being within. It is the same as the internal whispers and thoughts heard while reading and reflecting upon literature to ourselves. One who connects with the self, the contemplating creature within, and builds it to the higher self, will release joy into their lives. Stop reading this book for a moment and think of only one thing. Think of love. Now look at the immediate universe surrounding your being. Look at a plant, a tree outside, the corner of the room, your child at play or your pet's delight. Look at a pattern on fabric, the pigmentation within your skin, the scene out a window. Did you feel it? That was a brief moment of enlightenment; an epiphany of being.

In questioning the speed of our lives today, has it become so fast that we lose the richness of the experiences and miss out on the beauty within the details? Are we moving too slow that we are ineffective and dulled? Do we have time to reflect on who we are, where we are going and who we are becoming? We may be moving fast or slow but are we moving efficiently and effectively? These are some of the everyday issues that must be pondered and the appropriate steps taken to regain our direction. Too much intensity of anything is unhealthy. Too much thinking can create intellectual indigestion and too much spiritual seeking can create religious indigestion. We must allow time to absorb and digest the knowledge we take in. The reflection on information is just as important as the initial ingestion. The reflection creates the association of memory within our minds as we relate how the information is important to us and what we may be able to do with it in the future. Approach any religious pursuit or investigation with healthy moderation. Put this book down every once in a while and come back to it later; go outside and play. If according to the Cathars, we really are trapped and captured spirits confined within this evil physical realm, then we might as well make the best of it while we are here. A good life and a proper existence are about having balance between the secular and the divine, dwelling in both the material world and the spiritual realms.

Chapter 14
The Roots To Evil And The All Encompassing Sin

"EVIL IS NOT TO BE IGNORED. It is to be watched and monitored with adjustments made by emulating goodness." – AO

• • • •

THE ROOTS TO EVIL

Evil, in its simplest definition, is doing harm to someone else that you would not want done upon yourself. There is not one root to wickedness, there are many. Just as there are many paths to the godhead, there are multiple paths into the void and abyss of evil. Some of these paths are more commonly traveled than others, but the ones paved with ignorance, insecurity, hatred, selfishness, conceit, a lack of compassion and an addiction for power are more worn than any other. Those who crave power and control are very low on their spiritual development; such a desire or craving for power is the surest sign of spiritual darkness. From ignorance and insecurity, intolerance and hatred often grows as a cancerous trail, leading those that travel it heading in the opposite direction of God. Evil seems to arise from when the ego goes astray. It is excessive egotism, the opposite of gnosis, which does so much damage in the world.

The path of evil begins its smoldering when we disconnect ourselves from that universal mind that encourages us to be both unique individuals and yet ties together all of humanity in terms of eternity. Insecurity and thoughts of inadequacy set in because of a blindness towards the future and our perceived disconnection to that which is much greater than ourselves. It happens when we emotionally and mentally isolate ourselves from this loving, compassionate, understanding and guiding organism of thought that comes to us in the form of eternal inner wisdom. Our perceived disconnection allows such negative thoughts as anger, hatred, rage, intolerance, racism and falsehood to brew and fester within the core of our being. Evil in its parasitic and cancerous form is infectious and propagates itself by disfiguring and twisting all that it touches – it distorts as a means of psychic decay.[717]

Aggression is one of the key indicators of wickedness starting to manifest in this physical realm. It should be noted that ambition is not aggression, although aggression is often mistaken for ambition. The act of committing an evil deed is often implemented through aggressive actions, persuasions or behaviors. Evil seems to froth forth from the banished depth of the subconscious, repressed by feelings encapsulated from childhood that were never properly acknowledged, tended to or expressed. Surfacing as cruelty in the heat of anger or the coldness of manipulation, it is the actions of inner demons, characteristics suppressed within that we dislike about ourselves or when we see them in others.[718] It may portray and present itself as being superior, the master race, more worthy and more powerful, but these boastful swaggers are overcompensations for an inferiority complex, an underlying sense of unworthiness and feelings of rejection. Having to believe that you are superior means that you are currently substandard and barbaric.

—Λ*—

"Those that can make you believe absurdities, can make you commit atrocities." – Voltaire

—*Ω—

The violence desired by evil is often an outcome of too much externally expressed self-esteem, a façade of overcompensation for internal insecurity of the self and a dislike of others. It is often the masking of internal hatred of self. By mistakenly interpreting the world based on a turmoil of self-generated internal emotions rather than on external facts, it is put forth by the narcissist within that magnifies the slightest affront into a malicious slander of overdone proportions. It is the rage reaction to a narcissistic injury. Such traits are even more consequential when among political leaders and governing authorities, since their reactive policies towards a narcissistic injury affects thousands to millions of lives rather than just those within their local sphere of influence.[719] We must remain vigilant for when such narcissistic personalities crop up to start perversions of justice and deformations of truths. The defense, antidote and vaccine against narcissism is through logic and the progression of facts. Even more guidance on recognizing and dealing with narcissist traits can be provided by psychological professionals such as Dr. Ramani Durvasula or Dr. Les Carter.[720] Defining any sequential events or cause and effects with logic, rather than emotions, diffuses the narcissist hold on painting a false picture of the reality. The false emotional reality of the unhealthy narcissist is shattered by applying the truth with a reality defined by logic and facts.

We may come to believe that the more possessions we own, the more our personal value becomes. We may come to believe that the more material items (modern day idol worship) we gather, the more secure we will feel within our universe. We may come to believe that an unhealthy quest for power will fill a void created long ago within ourselves. We must always remember, there is an internal and an external universe, both of which need to be properly cultivated and groomed to maintain our connection to God. The internal universe is the structure of our thoughts, the flow of our emotions, and our reactions to external stimuli. If our external universe is in too much chaos and cannot provide us with the basic needs for the healthy survival and growth of our physical and emotional being, our internal universe can sometimes be thrown into a state of chaos as well. A lack of emotional nurturing, a lack of food, a lack of shelter, a lack of intellectual stimulus, a lack of a constructive education, a lack of direction, a lack of purpose and a lack of a vision for a better future, these lackings can all stunt the growth of our being and cause us to fall back into the shortsightedness of our lower self. Whenever we are tempted to exploit our universe and those within our world, we must ask ourselves, will this contribute to an expansion or contraction of humanity's global mind? How will the universal mind, which knows all and sees all, judge us? Were we only thinking about our individual selves or were we also thinking about the potential consequences to others? Remember, this universal mind has felt all the emotional reactions caused by your words and actions on others and those of your ancestors. When you leave this physical realm, you will become fully exposed to these reactions. Remember, as you treat others so shall you be treated. Karmic reaction is a very real law, the cycle of which may not always be readily observable within our lifetime here. There is truth to the proverb "As you sow, so shall you reap."[721] Our karma is the joy or terror we contributed into the universe coming back upon us.

Evil has been personified with names such as the Devil, Satan, Hades, Diablos, Shayton, Eblis, Beelzebub, Yaldabaoth, Saklas, Nebruel, Archenemy, the Prince of Darkness and Mephistopheles (aka Mephisto).[722] The name of Lucifer seems to have more depth and duality, (its etymology means "the morning star" or "light-bringing"), indicating a being that was perhaps misunderstood rather than being wicked. By some, Lucifer is considered more of a liberator and guiding spirit, a representative of the Promethean archetype. Perhaps he became known as a fallen angel for providing humanity with intellect (gnosis) and trying to lead them to enlightenment, and in doing so, opposed the Old Testament Jehovah's previous desire to keep humanity within a bubble of innocence or even naivety. In other texts, such as within the closing paragraph of the Latin versions of the Easter Proclamation (Exsultet), when denoting the light of the morning star, the title of Lucifer is a reference to Jesus Christ himself. The word Lucernarium, the service and ritual of lighting lamps, begins with the word "Lucer", yet again symbolizes Christ.[723] Whether the human association of all of the names above with evil is fair or not, there seems to be a variety of definitions of their influential role or their hierarchy within the domain of heaven and hell. There is even a duality in the meaning of a "Fallen Angel" with one referring to divine beings that were expelled or cast out from heaven for opposing God, and the other, meaning angels that volunteered to "fall" from heaven, to exit the Pleroma, into the physical realm for their love of God's leadership and to do what they could to influence and steer humanity in the correct direction.

The name "Satan" (considered a betraying angel or a jinn) is a more common reference from the Abrahamic-based religions (*The Bible, The Koran*). There are variations in the descriptions of the relationship between God and Satan (the personification of evil). Is Satan just against humanity, or just against God or against both? Some literary sources have God and Satan working together in a partnership in which God sends forth Satan to test, tempt and disrupt humanity's spiritual resolve – or is it Satan that is trying to teach and train us in the direction of enlightenment and we have misunderstood his intentions? Perhaps it is the archons that tell us there is something wrong with our reality and it is the aeons that tell us how to make the proper repairs. If Satan and the Demiurge are one in the same, then it seems any abandonment and neglect from his mother (Sophia) is what resulted in his narcissistic rage, anger, torment and self-destructiveness. Do we blame Sophia (fair or not, the mother often gets blamed for a child's outcome) for the Demiurge's bungling or did she do all she could to steer her child straight?

In the *Book of Job* from the *Old Testament*, God was boasting to Satan about Job's faith and loyalty. Satan states his opinion that Job is only pious because of his provided bountiful life, without which, Job would berate, curse and denounce God. In what one could consider a form of a bet, wager, dare or contest, that dysfunctional *Old Testament* God allows and sends Satan to test Job's resolve and loyalty by tormenting him with secular losses of livelihood, family and health. Job then searches for God to appeal why so much hardship has been unjustly sent upon him and why there appears to be a lack of divine justice in the world – why the righteous seem to suffer while evil doers seem to prosper. Letting us know that he is the ultimate boss, God's own ego steps in to ignore, invalidate and dismiss Job's complaints, reminding us of "who do we think we are" to even question the high and mightiness of the Lord's decisions. God eventually intervenes to correct the condoned torments of Satan, perhaps out of guilt for their exploitive betting game and to make restitution, and again provides Job with secular gains and prosperity: restored health, a new family and twice the wealth. In these instances, Satan was working as a subservient agent or playmate of God by doing his bidding in proving a point.

—A*—

"He [God] causes the sun to rise on the evil and the good, and sends rain on the righteous and the unrighteous." – Jesus Christ[724]

—*O—

Being at its apogee in the two centuries after Christ's departure and prior to the establishment of a Christian orthodoxy, Gnosticism was rampant in its development. It follows a belief that it was Sophia, a younger aeon and emanation of God's wisdom, who breathed life into Adam, not the belligerent and temperamental Creator described within the *Old Testament*.[725] Certain schools of Gnostic thought viewed that Satan and Christ are brothers, distinguishing that the original creator God is evil while the later True God is good. From the Bogomil/Cathar Duelist creation myth found in *The Book of the Secret Supper* (*Cena Secreta*) circa 12th or 13th century, Satan is cast out of heaven for wishing to be greater than God. He fakes having repented, so the Lord forgives him and allows him to go about his business – did the Lord forget to use his omniscience to see the deception? After this con, Satan creates the world of matter and forms human beings from the primordial clay. In doing so, each soul contained within a body is unknowingly a trapped angel pulled from heaven. Satan then proceeds to convince humanity that he is the one true creator, an action which causes the real God to send the Messiah (Jesus Christ) in order to remind humanity of their true celestial origins, alert them to the ways of the devil, and to steer them back to the true god.[726] In fact, many of the sects of antiquity containing Gnostic elements (i.e., Marcionism, Manichaeans, Paulicians, Bogomils, Cathars) that follow a Duelist view consider that there are two Gods; the creator God of the *Old Testament* who is satanic, bad or incompetent and the God of the *New Testament* who is considered the true one which does his good works hidden behind the scenes of the material realm. How else do we explain away the "monstrous" Yahweh of the *Old Testament*? He seems a being who expects humans to be moral, when he is not and forbids compassion and mercy upon any people already in his sights to be subjected to suffering or to be killed.[727] This Duelist mindset against the Old Testament God may have been a bit of a rebellion against the strict, over-controlling, tormenting and excessively punishing Yahweh put forth by earlier Jewish (or Babylonian) heritage and doctrines.[728] The early Gnostics view Jesus' words (found in *John* 12:31 and 14:30) describing that Satan is only of this realm, being "the prince of this world." Marcion of Sinope put forth one of the first Christian canons in the 2nd century explaining that the God of the *Old Testament* was an evil and lower being compared to the God of the *New Testament*. He was of course declared a "heretic" and excommunicated in the year 144 by the founders of a nascent Roman-based church that barely existed, but was craving its rise to power. His followers, which may have continued in small settlements well into the 10th century, held that the Creator(s) as described in the pre-existing Judaic religion was inconsistent, jealous, wrathful and genocidal, and that the material world was a trap, prison or defective place of suffering – any maker of such a world is a bungling and malicious Demiurge.[729] His writings, which were lost or deliberately destroyed from history, may have contributed to the forming of the Council of Nicaea in 325 as a means to respond, squelch the questions, suppress further investigation and make the decisions for us that it was all a scandal – "nothing to see here, move on."[730] Even Madam Blavatsky's theosophy views the universe as having been created by inferior spiritual beings and regarded Jehovah of the *Old Testament* as Satan.[731] Is it fair to ask if Satan and God are the same omniscient, omnipotent, omnipresent essence, but just under different temperaments or moods? Is God, much like government, "a two-sided being, free or unfree, responsible or irresponsible, an energy or a victim of energy, moved by choice or moved by compulsion, as the interests of society seemed for the moment to need"?[732] Personally, whether correct or incorrect, I prefer the approach that the Creator God and the True God are one and the same, but he/she has evolved, matured and grown beyond anthropomorphic failings in parallel with humanity's growth – the teacher has evolved with the students, the parent has improved along with the children, for both have taught each other.

Many other stories of Judaic, Christian and Islamic influence talk of Satan being insecure with his place in the universe and therefore becoming a rogue angel, an antithesis of God, and thus going against humanity and the will of Allah. Satan felt insignificant and therefore, to overcome an inferiority complex, had to prove his worth through the manipulation of others. Feeling that power and security came from the control of others, he did not realize that it comes from the self-control of ourselves. Satan's weakness is that he/she could only torment humanity through the actions of others – through the use of emotional weak, spiritually challenged or suffering pawns. The works and wonders of God, however, appear in both the animate and inanimate, the living and the non-living. If the story of Satan being a fallen angel (in the negative sense) is true, then he/she is like the jealous older sibling who desires the attention of the parent and deals with his or her insecurities by tormenting the younger arrivals. It started with Satan's cunning exposure of the Tree of Knowledge upon the innocence of humanity and continued forth with detrimental teasing and torment throughout the ages. Not realizing that younger siblings (humanity) so admire and unconditionally love their older sibling, Satan chose to lash out with insecurity and narcissistic rage. We must take pity and show mercy upon Satan and understand that he/she only craves the constant attention and love of the parent (God) and lacks a love of self. For Satan did not realize that just because God was no longer providing his full attention after the creation of man and woman, the Lord still adored him with boundless love. Satan will eventually come to an understanding of this and end the sibling rivalry. In the meantime, in line with the Rolling Stone's song *Sympathy For The Devil*,[733] we should have pity and sorrow for his/her state of mind – for the Devil is more insecure with his place in the universe than we are with ours. That is why she torments us so much, because of having fears and insecurities that are so much greater than our own. Satan actually fears us, the species of humanity, much more than we need to fear him. This is why she has been tormenting humanity for eons; it was actually a response to both unwarranted jealousy and needless envy.

According to Christian doctrine, the personification of all that is against humanity (i.e., the Devil) will go out and make one final assault on the world. This assault will be the Devil's last-ditch effort to prevent humanity from making Earth as it is in Heaven.[734] Perhaps narcissistic leadership under the spell of the Beast, negative exploitation of the planet's resources, and global terrorism are the Devil's last stand. Perhaps another meaning to the wine of Babylon referenced in *Revelation* is petroleum.[735] Perhaps we are in the middle of such times, in which case, a new beginning seems to be just around the corner. Being human in our limitations, we can only guess, speculate and conjecture the "goings-on" within the spiritual realms. We have hunches, hypotheses and theories, but nothing tangible to grasp in our fingers. However, if the legions of angels and the legions of demons cannot themselves forgive each other, make amends, and turn their own swords into plowshares, how can the authorities in Heaven ever expect humanity to do so? Are we pawns caught up in a feudal spiritual war of vendettas between beings of different domains, an alternate reality of thought and existence, being manipulated by those referred to as aeons, archons, angels and demons, all under the highest God's encompassing umbrella? Are we being toyed with by higher beings or those of parallel and alternate realms revealing themselves to various people throughout history, turning them into prophets of a slightly altered doctrine or a new tale to believe in? Or are we under the constant watch from benevolent creatures from alternate realms who tirelessly labor to heal and guide the broken fragments and disharmony of human lives and hopefully ignite some spark of divine light within our own consciousness?[736] The reason for so many mythologies, so many religions, so many cults, so many sects, so many prophets and so many schools of thought, is because we really do not have absolute clarity on what is going on in the spiritual realms. This has left us to rely on intuition, observation, perception and revelation. Do we really always know precisely what the authorities in Heaven want? Sometimes I think God or the gods themselves do not even know what it is that they want.

I do believe that in the very near future Satan will regain balance, his unwitting archons will make amends, and then they will only ask humanity for their forgiveness. The final compromise and treaty between angels and demons is now being signed. Within it, is the agreement that humanity shall only be granted the power of gnosis (divine knowledge of the universe's workings) when their actions are based on love. When love is the focus of our thoughts, the spirit of God shall enter us. We do not possess his or her energy, but are merely instruments which rely upon it. Like a flute or trumpet that speaks because of the air flowing through it, it performs no sonata when the breath is absent. Likewise, without love, the Rauch of the Almighty will not flow through us. This is a failsafe contract to ensure that anytime our actions are not based on love, the gnosis shall be removed. This is the proviso for declaration of peace between God and Satan. We don't need to forget the eons of Satan's torment and we should still continue to protect ourselves from his influences, but our response should be one of acceptance, forgiveness and love.

—Δ*—

"Love is a lot more effective and powerful as a motivator than hate. Love is risk, but hatred is riskier. Therefore, love is the path of the higher probability and with the greatest odds of success." – AO

—*O—

There are those who mock others as a way of making themselves feel powerful. They belittle those around them in an attempt to make themselves feel mighty, but they only make themselves smaller in the eyes of God. They are too insecure to open themselves up to other worlds for fear of losing their own. They do not realize their world would not be lost, but rather, it would be expanded. As soon as you think you are more significant than someone else, you are really giving in to your own self-created feelings of insecurity. From this self-created state of insecurity, branches of willful ignorance, negative manipulation and hypocrisy start to extend. Willful ignorance is chosen laziness of one's mind. It is the deliberate closing off of one's eyes and ears for fear of that which is different, new or may contradict what one currently believes. When one is insecure that their world may change or that they may have been wrong in their perception, they choose willful ignorance as a means of blocking out that which is true. They fear the truth for it may prove them incorrect in their perception. The power of truth is a natural force that disturbs what is artificial in those being exposed of their falsehoods.[737] Insecurity makes them believe that if they were wrong, they are worth less in God's eyes. One who admits that their damaging perception was incorrect, is praised by God and is one more step closer to enlightenment.

One may debate or express their opinions on their own or another's religion, but one should never attack or physically harm an individual for their religious views. Freedom of thought is one of the greatest gifts to humans, but freedom of thought also calls for and requires responsibility – the task of gathering as much information as possible and looking at both sides of a situation to understand it better. There are some who claim to be Christians, Muslims, Jews, Buddhists, Hindus or other but only practice the meaning behind the respective scriptures when it is convenient. Practicing the traditions of Christianity without putting its philosophies into play, does not mean you are a Christian. There are many who display a false façade to deceive others. They claim they are honorable, and sincere, but their core is overly tarnished. They may resort to "gaslighting" and manipulations as a method of negative exploitation.[738] Some make vocal claims of having changed their ways, but do their actions really match their words? There are many who go to church regularly on the Sabbath day but disregard its teachings. It's easy to be a Christian on a Saturday or Sunday during the sermon; try applying its principles on the other six days of the week. There are some who knowingly commit inappropriate actions during the week, with the attitude that they will be forgiven by God upon going to mass or confession. It doesn't work that way. One is forgiven if they are truly worthy of forgiveness. God has knowledge of all your thoughts and actions.[739]

Mohammad's meaning of dying for Allah throughout the *Koran* relates to those who give their lives for a just cause, such as bringing down the tyrannies of Hitler and Saddam Hussein. It relates to those who sacrifice themselves to save the lives of many. It does not relate to those who terrorize innocent establishments through random acts of violence or explode themselves to annihilate those in proximity to them. There is no honor in the random killing of others in misguided claims of doing it for God, even though there are still those today who distort the scriptures to justify the killing of another human being for their cause. The only just cause for killing another sentient being is in unavoidable self-defense or unavoidably necessary acts of war. The Almighty wants all his children to live in peace and prosper with justice, so think carefully before you decide if what you do is for a just cause and not based on inaccurate or delusional perceptions. Religious naivety is no excuse for killing as a means to promote one's cause. One who claims they killed for Allah is false and misguided.

—Λ*—

"He that fights for God's cause fights for himself. God needs no man's help." – *The Koran*[740]

—*Ω—

The primary problem is not ignorance; it is the repetition of ignorance. Benevolent intelligence cannot grow in a garden which fears enlightenment. That is why, at times, actions of benevolent intelligence must be implemented with stealth. Genius is not safe to flourish openly in a garden of ignorance. Throughout history, we have seen the damaging results of myopic ignorance blinded by hatred, intolerance and a lack of compassion. From the initiation of the Crusades, to the seven centuries of repressive thought control and torturous European Inquisitions (a free-for-all burning of people at the stake if considered guilty of views and paths different enough from that of the kingdom of the Catholic Church in its Middle Ages),[741] to the alleged entrapment and starvation of those with Bubonic Plague left to die at Mary King's Close in Edinburgh, Scotland during the 17th century,[742] to the Judaic Holocaust of the middle 20th century, to the satanic actions carried out by a group of misguided individuals in September of 2001 upon the innocent populace of New York City, Washington D.C. and airline travelers. Although the leviathan military of the United States has aimed for just causes, there are fractional elements that have, too, made errors in judgment such as the My Lai massacre that occurred in Vietnam. It is the recognition of such evil events that puts forth the necessity for actions of love. Love is the means of extinguishing evil. Unfortunately, defining what is wicked compared to what is good is left to the commonsense perspective and views of those making the judgment.

Great leaders can be found in very low places just as terrible leaders can be found in very high places. The most efficient form of government, but not necessarily the best, is a benevolent, compassionate, educated, wise, righteous dictator or monarch acting and ruling out of love for others. Even the *Book of Mormon* of The Church of Jesus Christ of Latter-

Day Saints expresses this view.[743] But how often does that actually happen and what are the odds that it will ever happen? The trend is that we continue to have hostile dictators and criminals falsely entering positions of authoritative power. However, the grip of dictatorships and totalitarian regimes is always relatively short term and temporal, for there is nothing more powerful than the generational yearning for freedom, dignity and self-determination. A fundamental universal law is that which is good tends to flourish, while that which is bad tends to implode. For the good encourages more of the good, but the bad hampers the bad. The minions of good leadership rise with them, the minions of bad leadership fall around them. Leadership in governing authority seems to either result in the rising of great statespersons or the frothing forth of narcissist despots. Basing leadership on inheritance, however, is a recipe for endless wars of succession since the later generations often try to outdo the earlier ones.[744] On average, however, humanity is more wired towards peace than for war.

How do we assure that appropriate knowledge and guidance is passed on to every generation so they can evolve as productive and kind human beings? How do we lift the veil of being informed and coming out of a fog of ignorance such that all the complexity of facts are available for scrutiny? How do we assure every child is provided with healthy love and the ability to sympathize with others? How do we reduce the number of people "snapping" and causing harm to others during their evil acts of desperation? It seems to be a continued cycle of certain misguided or off-balanced individuals (i.e., Adolf Hitler) frothing to the top of the leadership hierarchy who generate cultures of evil. Gaining power through generating an environment of fear, they often negatively exploit the masses to perform horrific deeds. One suggestion for reducing brutality is the continued creation and access to committee-developed and maintained educational training videos (UN Global eLearning) available on the United Nations' website. The expertise of such reference videos in all languages could provide uniform parenting behavioral instructions (how to become a "Supernanny") on proper child raising techniques and ways for governing authorities to police its citizens while implementing proper self-control and restraint. This is not the panacea for eliminating all savageness and cruelty, but it is a step in the correct direction.

Having an understanding of how evil can manifest itself by projecting suffering upon others, empowers us to avoid being drawn into its vortices. Neglecting to emanate goodness can result in evil gaining momentum. Teaching our children to have a healthy sense of self-worth and to apply critical thinking skills in conjunction with instinctual senses are first steps in assuring a continued generational astuteness to overcoming evil with goodness.

—A*—

"The ignorance of humanity never ceases to amaze me, yet I keep trying." – God, scribed by AO

—*O—

There is also a duality to evil: that which is caused by nature and/or natural disasters (the supposedly indiscriminate actions of the universe) and that which is caused and/or generated by human behavior, either as individuals or as groups. Can one really consider a natural disaster (i.e., tsunami, earthquake, hurricane, tornado, flood) as evil? Should an expanding star growing into a red giant during its final stellar stages and destroying civilizations on its orbital planets be considered something evil? Such events are certainly harmful, devastating losses of life and tragic occurrences when sentient and non-sentient physical beings and property are obliterated. But to accuse some natural disasters as being evil, when humanity accepted the known risks of probable events occurring, is an unfair description of the calamity. We take the risks of building and habituating close to fault lines or volcanoes, knowing the risks of earth tremors, eruptions and pyroclastic flow. We accept the risks of dwelling too close to shorelines or riverbanks, even though the region is prone to frequent torrential rains, tsunamis, cyclones or hurricanes. If God has taught us that snakes can bite and some with venomous fangs, why then, do we tempt the Lord by putting ourselves within reach of the serpent's strike? When such disasters occur, we cannot feign ignorance to the probabilities and neglect responsibility for the risks, so is it really fair to label them as evil? Perhaps it is fair to label them as evil when we are confined to dwell in such regions and find ourselves caught in the wake of harm due to poverty and socioeconomic restrictions – when we have no alternate choice and are trapped within geography. It is the poorest people who tend to live in the most polluted environments. In the rural areas of the developing world, they have been forced onto marginal areas by the process of enclosure, leading to deforestation, soil erosion and agricultural failure.[745]

Just as each one of us leaves a carbon footprint behind as an impact on the environment, so too, do we each leave a footprint of negative exploitation (evil). The objective is to keep both footprints as small as possible. Consider the clearing of a section of forest to make way for a large hospital. The clearing of trees and movement of soil uproots animals from their homes and habitats. Is this not considered an act of environmental evil? The establishment of a hospital, however, will provide healing and health services for those in need, thus reducing the footprint of wickedness. With many such decisions in life, there could be an evil component's impact which needs consideration.

Evil is a moral problem that challenges the whole collective consciousness. Countering it calls for individuals to transcend above the workings of "shadows" and allow compassion to dominate rather than disgust.[746] The Demiurge is Sophia's shadow and as social beings, we must catch ourselves so as not to be influenced into partaking of evil actions and the temptations of negative peer pressure. It requires having a strong sense of self to be able to think outside of a mob mentality, avoiding runaway repeats of "McCarthyism" and stop ourselves from being swept up into a swarm of wickedness.[747] A strong sense of self comes from developing our cores through habits of positive action. Understanding that dissipating evil requires the ability to empathize and/ or sympathize and to take action when appropriate. Empathy makes one more likely to care; it boosts compassion and altruism. Disgust has the opposite effect; it makes us indifferent to the suffering of others and has the dark power to incite ridicule, cruelty and dehumanization.[748] How should we address the derelicts of society who lack empathy or the ability or willingness to expand their empathy into compassion and resort to bullying acts of violence? How do we educate or redirect those "knuckleheads" who choose convenient scapegoats within a society as the cause behind their own self-made circumstances, xenophobia or perceived civil failings? One view of evil compares it to detrimental mold growing on the walls of a house or barnacles engulfing the hull of a boat; it must be removed, cleansed, minimized or kept in check before it spreads as an epidemic. Ignoring it only promotes its continued spread.

There have been and will be bumps of violence along the way in humanity's spiritual evolution, from the World Wars of the 20th century to the civil brushfires of governments versus elements of its civilians. Despite what the immediate news may display, violence over the centuries and decades as a percentage of the population is on an average decline. What is it that has helped us endure through the darkest hours of our lives? Was it only ourselves pulling us through? Or was it the help from family, friends and at times, new acquaintances? Was there a higher being of consciousness or its representatives pulling us onward? It is in such times when devoured by voids of helplessness that our conduits to divinity are so needed, tested and desired. Although the 20th century was the most violent hundred years in living memory, the remainder of the 21st century has a strong potential be the exact opposite. It will be a peace unbeknownst to the men and women of the globe than ever before.

If we were taught racism and prejudice in our youth by our family or peers, then we have the difficult task of facing the demons within ourselves to unlearn or at least adjust such traits, and to relearn the importance of embracing racial and cultural diversity. The desire for social dominance needs to be subdued by the desire for social diversity, for there is unity and strength in variety. For the intricacies of social diversity can withstand the pressures of extinction much greater than the insularity of social dominance. Failing to embrace diversity is a lacking in connectedness with God, for God is diversity. A person who is against diversity of religion and of culture is against the will of the Creator – there is unity in diversity.

Evil can gain momentum when unwarranted repugnance for that which is different becomes amplified with the absence of healthy sympathy or empathy. Misplaced disgust and contempt are a common propaganda weapon of choice discharged by evil as it sets forth to persecute. It starts with regarding the target group as political and moral reprobates rather than being just like everyone else.[749] It then puts forth dehumanizing language to sway a following into believing a particular group is "disgusting", "vile" or an "infestation." It is often accelerated through denying accessible hygiene to the targeted groups for devaluation by applying a "yuck" factor, which further spreads the propaganda. Groups, often the minority, become marginalized by oppressive factions as a means to initiate negative exploitation. Going even further, evil governing authorities have perpetuated this marginalization by visually tagging their target group through identifying patches upon clothing or branding upon the skin. Infamous decrees of wearing demeaning yellowish articles of clothing to make the target stand out from the crowd were put forth by Caliph Umar II in the 8th century upon non-Muslims and Jews. Later medieval popes, monarchs and lords placed them upon the Jews and some Christian heretics. Pope John XXII observed in 1325 that many Cathars were fleeing to Bosnia, where the Bogomils were still thriving. A chilling omen of the Nazi terror to come, captured Cathars who agreed to convert to Catholicism or die, were forced to wear a yellow cross sewn onto their clothes and lost all civil rights – the eastern Europe Inquisition even used ovens to roast "heretics" alive who refused conversion.[750] Hopefully for the last time in human history, the yellow identifying derogatory tag of shame, disgrace and disgust was again forced upon the Jews by an authoritarian regime gone astray; the Nazis and Axis Powers. A governing authority campaign rhetoric of disgust and contempt has been used to caustically catalyze genocidal acts throughout history; in the 20th century alone disgust and contempt triggered the mass slaughtering of Armenians and other ethnicities under the Ottoman Empire, by the Nazis to those of the Jewish faith or anyone considered undesirably similar enough, and of the Tutsis in Rwanda by the members of the Hutu majority government. The non-inclusion in the sentences above of other exterminating genocides committed throughout the centuries in the list above (such as that committed against Bosnian Muslims) does not make them any less horrific.

Marginalizing or generalizing an entire religion, culture, race or organization based on the actions of a few of its members is a form of negative exploitation. To judge and condemn a collective group as a whole, based on the actions of a few, is the shallow projection of lower intelligence and entices combustive coals of hateful propaganda and vituperation. For example, do not judge all Russians based on their governing leadership, all Americans based on their governing leadership, and all Chinese based on their governing leadership. Do not judge all of Islam based on the actions of a small proportion of its followers, all of Christianity based on the actions of a small proportion of its followers or all of Judaism based on the actions of a small proportion of its followers. Approach a collective or representatives of a collective with cautious curiosity and with the quest of gaining further understanding of their behavior and intentions. For the alternative is the ignorant understanding of the unfamiliar and a laziness of the mind to dig deeper, an unwillingness to evaluate based on rational experiences, resulting in the forming of the caustic precipitate of prejudice.

By displacing compassion, wickedness manifests itself in the form of suffering, either temporary or prolonged, as a result of human action or inaction upon others. Why is it that some humans follow a code of moral behavior while others do not? Suppose there is no God/Allah or afterlife, then why should we choose to conduct ourselves with goodness rather than wickedness? Much like a flock of birds behaving as its own entity while it morphs and changes direction during flight, the global mind of humanity is an entity made up of all people waxing and waning along with each individual's spiritual resolve. If the flock is to grow and flourish, it calls for its constituents to grow and flourish as well. Our behavior has a trickle effect that echoes throughout the global mind.

The emotions triggered by states of hate, anger, resentment, jealousy, holding grudges, ill will and vindictiveness are attitudes that will eventually destruct your own body and mind. One of the reasons, among others, Jesus said to "Love thy enemies" was as a means to prevent harbored feelings from causing our own ill health – it was to prevent self-destruction. This is also why defaulting to a steady state of love is so important – it induces good health and seeks to dissipate destructive attitudes. The body reacts with sensitivity to the type of thoughts flowing through the mind. Many people suffer poor health as a result of not only what they eat, but also due to what is eating them.[751] Emotional turmoil creates internal filth and strife, disrupting the body's natural healing ability, sapping productive energy, and clouding mental processes.

—Δ*—

"Anger is an acid that can do more harm to the vessel in which it is stored than to anything on which it is poured." – Mark Twain

—*O—

When faced with hardships, do not allow anger to froth into hatred and encapsulate you into a void of evil. Such voids seek to destroy you by preying upon your susceptibility and frustrations. Succumbing to anger is allowing demonic influences to overtake one's mind. Recognize that the emotion of anger has occurred and understand what triggered it, but do not allow it to flash over into hatred. Allah/God does not hate. Hatred is a human expression of weakness; a folly often resorted to for lack of emotional intelligence and limited empathetic connections. Generalize hatred upon a particular cultural or religious group based on the actions of a few is counter-productive to the future of our species. Spiritual logic dictates that a path of hatred and intolerance will only lead our species as a whole to destruction. Therefore, the alternate path is the correct one. Embrace and enhance the goodness in others, but protect yourself from potential harm excreted by the spiritually underdeveloped. Just as goodness can be felt by a sense of comfort, so too, can evil be discerned by an unsettling sense that something is not quite right.

—Λ*—

"Mā himsyāt sarvā bhūtāni" is a Vedic injunction which means "never commit violence to anyone." – The Bhagavad Gita[752]

—*Ω—

We are creatures of passion with emotions that trigger due to internal thoughts and/or from the influences of external events. The emotions are not to be suppressed, but rather, kept in check and appropriately expressed given the situation. The delight of a child's birthday celebration can elicit outward expressions of excitement and pleasure. The frustration of being cut off in traffic can elicit initial feelings of agitation, anger and annoyance. Remember, Moses smashed the original stone commandments due to his agitation with the worshipping impatience of the Israelites, Jesus was angered when he flipped over the merchants, lenders and currency exchanger tables at the Temple, and Mohammad was annoyed at the associated discriminant trading and social practices when he smashed the idols in the Kaaba. Having soft emotions or mild fleeting thoughts of lust, greed, narcissism, desire, anger or envy is not necessarily a bad thing. Such emotions must, however, be kept in check and dissipated or expressed outwardly in constructive ways. It is how we act upon the feelings of such emotions or thoughts that determine our level of enlightenment, our intensity of illumination and the quality of our connection to divinity. I can assure you of this – acting out with violence or hatred to such emotional triggers is in the opposite direction of Allah.

Greek mythology tells us that it was Pandora, the first woman of Earth, opening the container, jar or box that released all evils into the world. Orthodox Judaic, Christian and Islam view that evil entered into the world due to the human error of Eve's innocence, curiosity, naivety and gullibility. Perhaps these stories imbedded into the inner depths of the human psyche is a contributor to the shadows of rampant institutional misogyny and the recent waves of global femicide, the brutal killings of wives, mothers, daughters and sisters.[753] Even within *Pistis Sophia*, Mary Magdalene expresses her fear of the disciple Peter with the words "...but I am afraid of Peter, because he threatened me and hateth our sex."[754] Her concerns seem to be validated with even more of Peter's (and also Paul for that matter) desire for women to remain submissive as presented in the *New Testament*.[755] According to Gnosticism, the source of evil being introduced into the world was by the immature, unforgiving, anthropomorphic reactions of the *Old Testament* God, not by Eve's introduction to gnosis (divine knowledge) by the serpent. As a consequence of free will, evil exists in our universe. One need witness only a little bit of evil to understand the necessity for good. Just as our emotional reactions must be kept in check, wickedness must be kept in check through the constant blossoming of goodness. Applying Hermetic principles, vibrations of evil can be dampened by putting into practice the Law of Neutralization. By concentrating on the pole of love rather than the pole of hate, evil can be overcome by goodness, stopping the oscillations and rhythmic swings. It is by such simple methods of harnessing and releasing goodness into our environment that evil can be minimized and the world can change for the better.

—A*—

"The Lord neither hates nor likes anyone, though he appears to." - *Vedānta-Sūtras*[756]

—*O—

• • • •

THE ALL-ENCOMPASSING Sin

The **Negative Exploitation** of others, ourselves and our world is a sin. It is the sin that covers all and has within it various levels of grievousness, some more extreme than others. To prevent negative exploitation from occurring it must be defined so it can be recognized. Any act which encompasses a self-serving intent at the unfair expense of another's wellbeing is a form of negative exploitation. It can be the unacceptable use of another of the same species or another AISB for personal gain or power, through deceit, manipulation, suppression or oppression, by not offering them an appropriate compensation, a share of the resulting fruits of their labor, the choice to participate in the investment risk of their labor's venture, or the opportunity for genuine advancement if they so choose. Whether it is the exploitation of foreign workers in the laying of track for the transcontinental and other railroads, depression-era workers to build the Hoover Dam, migrant farm workers to harvest the crops, or Au Pairs to assist with household chores and the raising of children, resorting to taking an unfair advantage of someone's labor is a notorious deed. There are still members of our species who continue to justify this sin for their personal gains.

There are various degrees and amounts of negative exploitation; ranging from dishonesty, hypocrisy, abuse of power, torture, derogation and dehumanizing of others and racial segregation, to outright murder and the deliberate killing of the innocent. Any act which stunts, delays or lowers another being's level towards enlightenment is a form of negative exploitation. It covers the whole gamut of humanity's evil from the minor to the extremes, from bizarre "over-the-top" decadence to the narrow-minding mentality that reduces with unbending legalism.[757] It can range from the overworking of subordinate and the inflicting of abuse, to the extremes of outright slavery and slaughtering of *Homo sapiens sapiens* for cannibalism. Employees toiling for benefit levels significantly lower than those provided in the upper financial echelons of the managerial hierarchy are being negatively exploited. The oppression of another sentient being or of a sentient culture is also a form of negative exploitation. The torment and torture of other creatures (animal abuse) by advanced intelligent sentient beings is a form of negative exploitation.

Any form of sexual behavior that damages or can damage the sexual, emotional and physical being of another is negative exploitation. This includes everything from sexual harassment to nonconsensual sex (rape) to illicit child pornography to mutilation of sensory genitalia. Deliberate mutilation of any sacred part of the body has little to do with holiness and piety.[758] The sexual abuse of a minor is a grievous act that will not be treated lightly by the Lord, for it is an act that goes against the very continuum of humanity's core. A child is to come of age into their sexual identity on their own, not by the manipulations of an adult's evil will. Anyone committing the act of rape of a minor or adult is devoid of religion and a parasite of God. Rape is a form of negative exploitation and should have been included among the Ten Commandments as a forbidden item; a "Thou shall not..."[759] Yet, Moses conveniently did not include that commandment on the stone tablets and actually promotes rape as a legitimate act of revenge.[760] I can assure you of this, if not in this realm, a rapist will face the harshest of judgment and punishment in the next realm. On the other extreme, someone agreeably consenting without coercion to intercourse and then, when encountering feelings of regret afterwards, falsely accusing the other party of rape, is also a form of negative exploitation.

Religious Distortion, as discussed in Chapter 11 is a form of negative exploitation as well as the forcing of religious beliefs and ideas upon another. Stealing, cheating, vandalism, and lying for selfish intent are all forms of negative exploitation. Abuse of power, false projections of facts, authoritarian manipulations, hypocritical policies and contradictory actions are all forms of negative exploitation. Being complacent or apathetic when witnessing situations of violence is a form of negative exploitation – acts of violence need to be revealed and/or reported to the appropriate trusted authorities.

—Δ*—

"He that commits sin commits it against his own soul." – *The Koran*[761]

—*O—

The sin of all is Negative Exploitation: the act of utilizing another developed sentient being or ecological system for selfish motives or unethical purposes. Many heinous acts or grievous actions are included within its definition, but there are several degrees and extents of negative exploitation, some being more atrocious than others. According to the orthodox view of Old Testament scripture, negative exploitation was the first sin ever committed by a powerful being against another being. Satan, disguised as a serpent, exploited a woman named Eve into eating a forbidden fruit. The serpent took advantage of Eve's innocence and curiosity. She wasn't bad or wicked, just naïve, curious and gullible. God's intention was to one day give the fruit of knowledge to humanity when we were ready in our spiritual evolution. Satan's deed prematurely exposed us to the knowledge of good and evil before we were able to handle it. We were not spiritually mature or ready to handle the knowledge of good and evil. Our eyes were opened by that apple before our core was ready – pun intended.

Throughout the centuries, Eve has been unfairly blamed for the damnation of humanity, but Adam is just as guilty. Although she gave him the forbidden fruit, Adam could have just said "no." He could have refrained from eating the fruit and gone to the Lord to explain and remedy the situation. Eve gave the fruit in a sharing gesture and Adam responded in a sharing gesture. The masculine is as guilty as the feminine. God created us as creatures of curiosity and we responded to the temptation as any child would. God is guiltiest for not putting a gated fence around the tree of knowledge in the middle of the Garden of Eden to protect his children.

A person who craves power cannot handle it. Their craving is based on a need to feel a void within their internal being. The void can be from a lack of intimacy during childhood or a desire to quell a chaotic upbringing by mistakenly trying to control too much of our adult environment. One who craves power and control, in fact, often really craves love but doesn't know how to give or receive it. Power cravers are terrified of being emotionally vulnerable and are often intolerant of ideas which conflict with their views. The craving of power only makes tyrants. If one rises to leadership through aggressiveness and perpetual confrontation, their core is not pure. Absolute power does not always corrupt. It depends on the true intentions of the individual, their beliefs, the strength and foundation of their core and the influences of their advisors. George Washington, the first President of the newly formed United States, was someone who could have made himself a king. Understanding his own temptations and the weaknesses within his own nafs, he directed the energies of his noble intentions to build the foundation for the preservation of a future democratic republic. Saddam Hussain on the other hand, a former dictator of Iraq, butchered the meaning of the *Koran* to suit his Stalinistic self-promotion.

There are those in positions of power who, through tyranny or tyrannical aspects, continue to negatively exploit those without a strong voice of influence. Such power cravers may have a strong influence on those around them, but it is short-lived, for they do not have true wisdom. Wisdom is not just a matter of knowledge or intelligence. It is also a matter of carrying out truth, righteous action and seeking enlightenment. There are those dwelling in ignorance who continue to try to exploit those who are enlightened. Those who carry out truth and righteousness will have power long beyond this secular world. Those who crave power are not capable of handling it. Those who do not crave power are more worthy of it for they are capable of handling it through their wisdom and righteous action.

Negative exploitation is the act of a primitive and ignorant mind. It is also the act of a primitive culture; very low on the path of spiritual evolution. If one works hard, then portions of the fruits from their labor should be returned and spread among the many, not into the pockets of the few. Opportunities and the necessary tools to achieve them should be made available for one to advance from their current position if they choose. Every worker should have the educational opportunities and training available to advance in their career or into a different one. They should also be able to remain in their current post if they so choose. Freedom of choice and the freedom to earn one's qualifications is of the utmost importance in preventing exploitation from taking hold. The condemning of genius without giving it an opportunity to flourish is a mild form of often self-inflicted negative exploitation. The act of forcing your religion on another is also a form of exploitation. Who's to say that your belief is the only true path and better than another? Jesus spoke of spreading the gospel. He did not say to force it upon people. He did not say to torture or kill them unless they convert their religious path. He did not say to destroy their culture and beliefs in showing them another path. Jesus said that he was the way, but despite what zealot interpretations have tried to present, he never said that he was the only way. His path may have been more direct or easier to navigate, but it was not exclusive. It is men and women who exploit the words of the scriptures because of misinterpretation and self-serving objectives. It also men and women who have the ability to seek truth above religious distortions and dogma. Even the *Koran*, the primary scripture of the Islamic faith, states that "there shall be no compulsion in religion."[762] An enlightened being answers the questions to the best of their ability to those seeking truth, but they do not force their ideas upon another. An enlightened being may expose and express aspects of their beliefs through wisdom, display and rhetoric, but they do not force these beliefs on another. Each individual has the God-given right to choose their religious vehicle. It may be the one they were first exposed to upon birth and while developing consciousness, or they may decide to modify it or choose an entirely different model. It is up to the individual to decide which religious concepts they accept and which they do not accept.

An empathetic child has only unconditional love for their elders; this power should never be abused nor negatively exploited. The negative exploitation or deliberate harming of a child is the same as harming Allah. It is not something that the Lord takes lightly. Anyone who deliberately harms or deliberately allows harm, whether physical or psychological, to occur upon a child will be confronted by the Almighty directly upon their passing. Those religious and secular institutions shall be held accountable that knowingly harbor members who negatively exploit children to satisfy their unhealthy sexual urges; pedophiles who ignore the damage they are inflicting upon another soul. God does not take kindly to those who cause harm to children. Those who deliberately harm the young offspring of their species or deliberately place them in danger's way will be directly confronted by the Supreme Consciousness. He/she will judge their worthiness and punishment to be encountered in the next realm since they have tarnished their core and their souls. The protection of children is the seed that God plants in all of us; choosing to destroy that seed within will leave our core rotten and our soul barren.

I now dare go forward into the combustible landscape on the issues of abortion. The morality and dilemma of aborting a fetus, the deliberate choosing of an artificial miscarriage, will be touched upon lightly since it is an issue beyond the scope of this book and left for future questioning, discussion and debate. However, the answer relates to when sentience occurs during growth within the womb. Does it occur instantaneous at conception upon the creation of the zygote? After the first two embryonic cells divide and exist? When there are at least 10, 100 or 1000 cells? When there is a pulse? When there is electrochemical activity in the brain? When physical pain can be felt? When there is frontal lobe activity? At what point is a fetus beyond its earlier evolutionary forms and considered a human being? When does the divine spark enter or ignite during the material formation of a new life form? Does the soul enter a being upon conception, upon the start of brain activity, gradually over time in accumulating increments during development, or does a soul form in parallel with the biological growth? The Tibetans believe the spirit enters at about three months of embryonic development within the womb, at the transition from embryo to fetus.[763] Origen of Alexandria (184–253) held that the soul is pre-existent, falls into the world of matter, but then one day returns to God.[764]

An abortion is not something that a woman chooses to go through because it is emotionally convenient; it is a traumatic tragedy, a disaster of psyche and a choice to be grieved. It has no advantages and leaves a bipolar scar that never fully heals. Sometimes it is done out of medical necessity, when both the mother and fetus would die otherwise, and sometimes it is done as a means of birth control. To use it primarily as a repeated form of birth control is definitely sinful. Is the abortive callousness and repetition because of a lack of self-worth, an irresponsible disregard for life, or not wanting to be troubled by raising and nurturing a younger version of self? Looking deeper, if a pregnant woman does not value herself and the fact that she is a gateway for eternity to enter the world, how can she responsibly value the life growing within or the options available? If society provides value, worth and support to the scared, isolated and uncertain pregnant carrier, no matter what fantasy world she may be living in, both during and after the pregnancy and teaches her the same value and worth of the unborn within, then perhaps the adoptive road will be travelled instead of the desolate abortive path. Instructional guidance and access to training can go a long way towards flourishing self-sufficiency – it can teach one how to be a better parent of both themselves and their progeny.

When the right to have an abortion done by the proper medical personnel is outlawed within certain national geographical regions, those with the financial means will still have access to the right to choose while those in poverty will not. Those with the funds will be able to afford proper abortive medical care outside of their local regions and the transportation fare, be it an airline, train or boat, to travel to such regions. The outlawing of abortions would also create questionable underground "pseudo" and "back alley" doctors who would still perform the operation for a large fee to cover their risks. The moral right to choose should be granted to everyone and not be based on income alone. The argument that what if Mary, the unwed mother carrying Jesus, chose an abortion is nonsensical by the very same argument that what if Klara Hitler had aborted her son Adolf. Outlawing abortion makes it a dilemma of both economic class and morals, instead of just morals. Better to have one ethical dilemma than two.

In the debate and views on the abortive issue, there are those who take their cause to the extreme and harm medical professionals who perform all aspects of feminine health, from abortions to prenatal care to childbirth. Through their ignorance, such extremists claim that they are acting in the name of God. There is no such thing as killing and harming in the name of God. We kill and harm for selfish reasons of anger and frustration only. Many of the same doctors that perform abortions, also aid in bringing new life into this world. Those doctors study all aspects of prenatal and natal medicine to give their patients all around quality healthcare.

We must strive for something beyond the right to choose and that is the education of self-worth and access to the least exploitive form of dependable birth control. Someone who does not or cannot value themselves will not value the life growing within, a life that has no voice of yet to speak out with regarding its destiny. We must strive to make the responsibility of parenthood a beautiful experience, not a burden. We must strive for our jobs and career to become a part of the family experience, not in lieu of it. The utmost idealistic goal is such that abortion becomes a thing of the past through 100% perfect obstetrics bio-medical technology and 0% unwanted pregnancies. Between the realization of this hope and the actual current reality, there lies an abyss of duality in which no transcending reconciling bridge can be found.[765] Unfortunately, there is no current utopian reality, but we must continue to strive.

Having not learned my lesson of the previous paragraphs on abortion, I now step even further into the flames of debate by expounding on capital punishment. Coming forth from Mesopotamia and Hebrew laws, the reciprocal system of justice calls for an eye for an eye, a tooth for a tooth and a life for a life. The intention may have been to restrict the compensation (or retaliation) to be equal in value or to make it simple for the courts to process punishment. Capital punishment, the legally sanctioned extinguishing of life of a convicted criminal by the government for a penalty of extreme crimes against individuals or the state itself, has its own dualities of pros and cons that need further analysis.

We must look deeper into the logic behind a recognized government's sanctioned execution of a person for their deliberate execution of another or acts of treason against that government. Is it to prevent the condemned criminal from inflicting their crimes upon society again? Life in prison accomplishes the same objective. Is it to deny them their life in retaliation for denying the life of others? That would be a form of revenge, not justice. Justice is to prevent the same crime from happening again. Revenge is an empty action with the mistaken belief that it will quell the pain within the victims' egos. I would be very fearful of any government entity that has sentient itself to the point of having an ego. Is it an incentive not to kill knowing that you will be executed by the state for such conduct? Anyone who has entered the lowest of self in planning or committing murder either believes that they will not be caught or they are not in a rational or sound state of mind to even consider the consequences of their actions – an exposure to capital punishment. Statistics show that threat of the death penalty does not serve as a deterrent.[766] What of the state executing an innocent or wrongly accused? There are very strong indications that this has happened, and more than once, especially since DNA evidence, when it is available, has led to exoneration of death row inmates in recent times.[767] State execution of the innocent only leaves to the tarnishing of everyone's souls involved in the arrest and overzealous prosecution of the case. If one can't be damn sure that a person is guilty, better to default to life in prison then to execute an innocent being.

The ritualization of implementing capital punishment, on average, seems to do little in providing healing closure for the victims' families. In fact, it may be like pulling the scab off open wounds and leaving an even bigger scar upon the affected families' psyche.[768] Long after the murderer is gone, the pain of both the loss of their loved one(s) and the punishment of the execution lingers within the victimized families' thoughts. Perhaps allowing the convicted a choice between life in prison or the death penalty, would leave it in the legal registers without the decision having to be made by the state or placed on the conscience of a third party.

An uncomfortable anecdote: the last child subjected to capital punishment in the United States was George Junius Stinney, Jr., executed in 1944 at the age of 14. Accused of killing two girls, ages 7 and 11, in his hometown of Alcolu, South Carolina, he was put to death by the electric chair in the same year that he was convicted of the crime. The courts refused to hear his appeal and the appeals to the Governor for clemency were denied. He was said to have confessed to the crimes based on the handwritten notes of the arresting deputy and was convicted after only a 2 to 3-hour trial in less than 10 minutes of deliberation by the jury that was selected earlier that day. There were no transcripts taking of the trial and few or no witnesses at all were called to testify on the accused's behalf. The 90-pound frame of his boyhood body alone was too small for the electric chair, so a bible was used as a booster seat to carry out the execution – an abominable and sacrilegious use of the Christian scriptures. George Stinney, Jr., may or may not have committed the crimes, but in 2014, some 70 years after his exposure to a lethal dose of high voltage electrical current, his conviction was posthumously overturned based on the obvious facts that he did not receive a fair trial. Oh, did I forget to mention that George was of African American descent and the two murdered girls were of Caucasian descent as well as all members of the jury or did you already assume that? Although it wasn't until 2005, less than 15 years ago of the completion of this paragraph's writing, that the United States Supreme Court ruled that the death penalty for anyone under the age of 18 is cruel and unusual punishment, many other nations are not restricted to who they can execute based on such age limitations.[769] Simply put, to minimize negative exploitation, one should preserve life whenever possible.

Allah/God cringes away from those who commit crimes based on hatred. Hatred is illogical – it never leads to a better future. Hatred is anger gone astray. Anger is a responsive feeling we encounter when subject to harmful or disrespectful situations arising out of the actions of others. Sometimes the anger is justified and sometimes it is not. How we handle, utilize or ground our anger determines the growth or regression of our core. Do we channel its corrosive energy in productive ways to move on and/or towards improving the lives of others?[770] Or do we allow it to smolder and fester into flames of revenge?

If we continue to believe in a better future, then we have nothing to fear. Evil can manifest itself in fearing that which does not need to be feared. Therefore, learn to laugh at your internal abnormal fears. Most of our fears have no reality.[771] Many sources site that hatred, the opposite of love, rises out of anger triggered by fear, frustration and anxiety. How do we tame our internal fears and anger so that it is balanced with cautionary prevention? Why is it that some humans seek to expand their awareness through the absorption of knowledge from enlightened sources while others tend to dwell and remain dulled in a pit of nescience and false conspiracies? We have seen the bullying effect of negative exploitation (evil) in diminishing the value of the individual through such institutionalized violence as slavery, cruel punishment and frivolous executions. We have seen it in the everyday abuse of vulnerable populations such as women, children, homosexuals, transgender, racial minorities and animals. We have seen it in the waging of wars, conquests and ethnic cleansing implemented with a callousness towards their human cost.[772] Moving forward to minimize negative exploitation is about sequestering the influencing demons of our inner-verse. It is choosing to nurture and care for rather than neglect and harm others.

Humanity as a whole has come to understand that violence and brutality is not conducive to the advancement of our species. This understanding in of itself is a positive advancement towards God. Unfortunately, there are still factions and certain individuals that resort to this negative primal function as a means of enforcing their wishes, desires, power or control over others. It is because they have not evolved the core of their beings in synchrony with the love of God. They have chosen a false path, perhaps through a combination of allowing too many detrimental external and internal influences to sink into the core of their beings. It takes spiritual critical thinking and logic to develop and constantly steer one's core in the correct direction. Allah has given each individual the freedom of thought and self-determination to decide what their inner universe is to become. It can be filled with either love, tolerance, inner peace or with hatred, destruction, and inner turmoil. A desire to believe in God, a reduction of our fears, a hope for a better future, a need to be in harmony with the universe; all these things can lead our core in the correct direction.

—A*—

"I sought the Lord, and he heard me, and delivered me from all my fears." – *Psalm* 34:4, KJV

• • • •

"HAVE NO FEAR. I SHALL be with you. I hear all and see all." – *Sūrah Tā Hā* 20:46, *The Koran*

• • • •

"...USING WHAT YOU HAVE learned in an intelligently discerning way, negotiating between selfish desires and unselfish actions of helping others apply it to the dilemma facing you. This will free you from all your fears, and I will bestow the state of oneness on you." – *The Gita*[773]

—*O—

Acknowledging that the world is imperfect, we should not be blinded from all the goodness that shines forth. It is through participating in this goodness by which all indications point to the sign that we and the world can be saved. The clearer we understand the duality of good and evil, and beyond it, the clearer the revealed insights provide a means to embody the good. The world is not a simpleminded function of good vs. evil, but rather a complex array of perspectives and ideas, some of which sway more towards evil and some of which sway more towards good. One can never be too sure of which way a policy will swing, but one should always reflect on the potential consequence that any action may have on a future course of events. Having encountered the damaging effects of hatred and aggression, one realizes the necessity for love and compassion. It is knowing the opposite which directs where in the duality our moral compass should lay. Why is there evil in the world? Perhaps it exists to establish a baseline from which goodness can be measured after calling out that which is wicked. Evil may be an illusion of existence from the perspective of the spiritual realms, but its manifestation can be very real in these physical realms. Goodness often crystalizes forth from the damaged remnants left behind from the wasteful emptiness of evil. In its most simple definition, evil is anything which attempts to break our connection with the true God.

—Λ*—

"The nature and essence of the good is a certain disposition of the will; likewise that of evil." – Epictetus[774]

—*Ω—

Chapter 15
Achieving And Maintaining A Mindset Of Happiness

"OH, BEING OF ALL, PLEASE take away anxieties and concerns so that I may move forward without the paralysis of fear and dread." – Prayer For The Future, AO

• • • •

WE ENTER THIS WORLD without an instruction manual and as artists of life, ready to spread our colors on an empty canvas. From a human perspective, to whom and where we are born seems to be based on luck. The randomness of who our parents are can either condemn a child to suffering and pain or to the development of fond memories to be cherished. An anthroposophical view would say that it is based on past karma from prior essences of existence.[775] We are all created equal but do not find ourselves born into equal circumstances, nor do we remain equal. There are many post-utero influences that determine where our equality goes after the moment of our birth. Our instincts initiate all the patterns of life and behavior inherited from our parents and ancestors, but allows for flexibility, change and adaptation from the conscious back into the subconscious. Our <u>karsati</u>, the struggles for existence in a material realm, seems easy for some and challenging for others. Relying on guidance from our elders, we are initially at their mercy as they show us how to survive in our environment and interact with others. Most of us had wonderful guardians who nurtured and provided for us with encouraging guidance and security. For some of us, if our parents or guardians were unable or unavailable to provide us with the proper mentoring, we may have become miseducated or lacking in the appropriate interaction skills. To fill those voids, we may have grasped onto the behavior patterns of our nearest role models (for better or for worse), relied on chemicals (i.e., drugs) to temporarily escape by self-medicating or

achieve a false sense of self-value, or deduced our own methods of interacting with others and the environment. In order to cover up what we
fear others would see in ourselves, we created a series of false masks or
latched on to addictions in a belief that they would protect us from any
perceived vulnerabilities to our self-esteem.[776] Our addictions, "...at-
tempts to assuage the pain of loss and fear by introducing a false god into
the soul to relieve it...", were like the drinking of seawater – cool, satisfying and quenching at first swallow, but then its salts becoming a burning rage within the mind and body.[777] Sometimes our emotional filler
produced short-term positive results but then later degraded into detrimental consequences. From the abnormal fears installed in us by early
life influencers and experiences, we may have developed habits of trying
to excessively manipulate others to make ourselves seem self-important,
but it only temporarily filled the emptiness felt within. We might have
filled the emotional cavities in our development with excessive purchases
and accumulation of material objects, jumping from fad to fad or latching onto each latest trend, rather than tuning into the latent gnosis within.[778] Always looking for another item to give us that short-lived feeling of self-value and delight, the objects were a crutch and acted as a temporary replacement for loneliness and missing intimacy. Have we so forgotten those elevated levels of joy that were once felt from enjoying the
little things, like our childhood imagination when exploring an empty
box or playing with a rolling ball? Have we really lost our "Blue Bird of
Happiness" as described in the fairy-tale play by Maurice Maeterlinck?

Our happiness as a young child may have been cut short due to unfavorable influences and circumstances. Through exposure to detrimental situations, neglect or abuse, our steady state may have become one
of fear, anger, hatred, disappointment or loss of self-value. We may have
lived with or encountered serious, complicated problems that have disrupted our lives and caused any normal person to become anxious, upset, worried and obsessive.[779] Our childhood environments may have
been unpredictable due to parental loss, dysfunctional family situations,
war, famine, natural disasters, religious extremism, or other hardships

that made us feel hurt, helpless, lost, isolated, disconnected or out of control. Despite our willpower and resolve to keep going as survivors, some of us still harbor those adverse reactive emotions and inappropriately apply them to present situations. In doing so, we continue to magnetically draw situations or people detrimental to the improvement of our lives. Finding ourselves in the role as the excessive caretaker, the victim or the persecuted, we may still harbor those self-defeating learned behaviors or character defects that result in a diminished capacity to initiate or to participate in genuine, loving relationships.[780] Grasping onto fading remnants of childhood dreams as the harsh realities of life's demands take over, the coping mechanisms we put in place may have provided protection for the short term, but stifled and further damaged us in the long term. We may avoid acknowledging, confronting and transcending these negative echoes from the past through excessive work, lashing out, illicit drugs and/or harmful compulsive behaviors. Our feverish activity was an unhealthy avoidance mechanism to prolong coming to terms with the grief of a relationship or childhood lost – we were trying to outrun our own emotions or felt that we were not deserving enough to feel them. Sometimes we overfilled our minds with thoughts and intellectual analysis or constant apprehension that something bad was about to happen; the more noise that was in our heads the more we could cover up and drown out those past echoes. Sometimes our suppression of them started to manifest as physical symptoms, attacking the body in addition to the mind. Some of us may have thought that the happiness and stability lacking or lost in the chaos of our youth could be regained by excessively controlling our world as an adult. We were wrong. Recovering from such ordeals and counter-productive patterns of behavior calls upon an internal adjustment to take action by rescuing ourselves; by stopping and not continually rescuing those in close relational circles whose behavior is continuously self-destructive. The person you have become today is a result of the external forces exerted on your being by your parents, your siblings, your relatives, your friends, your teachers, your role models, your coworkers and also by your internal reactions to those forces. You have become the sum of your reactions to all the events that have influenced your being. Remember, you are the sum of your reactions to those events, not the events themselves. These reactions may be constructive to your happiness and wellbeing, or they may be destructive in your dealings with others and situations that have similar echoes to past events.

—Λ*—

"Deceive yourself no longer that you are helpless to overcome the face of what was done to you." – *Accept This Gift*[781]

• • • •

"Turn your wounds into wisdom." – Oprah Winfrey[782]

—*Ω—

SURE, WE CAN CONTINUE to blame our parents, the guardians, or the relatives who raised us for how we feel and react today. We can choose to either repeat their mistakes or learn and grow from them. Sure, we can blame the suppressive situation that we may encounter in our school or jobs every workday. Sure, we can blame the environment and circumstances we were born into or exposed to as a young child; consider the life of Henry Darger.[783] Sure, we can whine about our petty discomforts, while the condition of others in worse predicaments leaves us to shame for complaining – there are many grasping for life under harsher conditions. We can remain stagnant in our internal situation blaming past experiences or we can choose to allow that divine energy that is everywhere to embrace us and help us to recreate the core of our being; to end those cycles of self-punishment and/or excessive guilt and heal that child within. We are not destined to follow in anyone's footsteps but our own – pain and suffering seem to be a prerequisite for growth. However, we should not shirk the legitimate frequent self-analysis required to ascend through the developmental stages towards healthy maturity and design of systematic responsibilities.[784] The impetus for our growth comes as soon as we realize that the love of self is to be balanced with the love we have to offer others. We cannot give proper and healthy love to others if we do not have it for ourselves.[785]

—A*—

"What a child doesn't receive he can seldom later give." – P.D. James[786]

• • • •

"LOVE ISN'T A LUXURY; it's a gateway to our very survival and sanity." – The School Of Life [787]

—*O—

The personality habits developed in our youth have an elemental affect in our adult life. Regardless of their origin, if such defensive traits produce detrimental outcomes, our behavior can be adjusted. Due to our own insecurities, do we falsely build our internal self-esteem by either internally or externally unfairly denigrating or belittling others and/or their accomplishments? Providing genuine praise to others when their accomplishments are recognized and their actions are deserving is a healthy means of building up the egos of others. Instead of over-constructing our own egos, however, we should do the opposite. We should lower the walls of self, surrender unto Allah. It is when we lower our egos that allow us to learn the most about others and allows God's guidance and love to enter.[788]

Dealing with significant loss, the grieving encountered with major life transitions (both desired and undesired), and the disruptive changes to the reality of our *status quo*, call for us to jumble through and exhaust ourselves in the theoretical stages of denial, anger, bargaining, depression and acceptance.[789] When we do not muddle our way adequately enough back and forth within and between any of those five stages, we will not heal properly. For those still feeling the pits and pains of a traumatic childhood or life-changing event that is causing relational hardships (both with ourselves and others) of our adult life, reaching out to a qualified psychiatric professional, group therapy and self-help books is highly recommended. They can offer guidance, but it is up to you to perform the internal work of reprograming your behavior away from negative results. It is up to you to implement your sama, and improve your responses and reaction to stimuli as you redefine who you are, becoming a person that you can admire. Just because life has been painful so far does not mean it has to keep hurting. Life doesn't have to hurt so much if we begin to change.[790] Relief won't come instantaneously and healing requires dedication, commitment, adjustment and maintenance. With proper mental focus and will-power, improvement of life interactions and peace of mind can again be achieved. Happiness, the coherence of self, is found in the quality of relationships we have with others and with ourselves while harvesting a quiet mind operating at optimum efficiency.[791] It encompasses having someone to love, something to do, and somewhere to look forward to.[792] Many who succeed in life got off to a bad or rough start and pass through several struggles and traumatic events before arriving at their desired life destination, becoming their true self.[793] We have to play the tiles we are given in life to the best of our abilities.[794]

—Δ*—

"Life is what happens while you are making other plans." – *Reader's Digest Magazine*[795]

• • • •

"WE MUST BE WILLING to let go of the life we have planned, so as to have the life that is waiting for us." – E. M. Forster[796]

—*O—

Euthymia, in its philosophical sense, is a Greek word meaning serenity or calm, steady, balanced confidence of the mind. It was first used by Democritus (460–370 BCE) and expanded upon by Seneca (4 BCE–65 CE) as a goal everyone should thrive to achieve. It is a quiet confidence displayed by believing in and knowing yourself, ignoring external sirens of distracting pulls, doubt or suppressive conjectures, focusing on signals from within and trusting the path you have chosen.[797]

—Λ*—

"When we are unable to find tranquility within ourselves, it is useless to seek it elsewhere." – La Rochefoucauld[798]

—*Ω—

As an adult, efficient and constructive interactions are based on developing and maintaining a healthy sense of self-value through constructive achievements, the proper balance between narcissism and empathy, and moving forward in life with steady and healthy determination. It is about striving for perfection, but not expecting it, as we navigate an imperfect world. Seek perfection but be content with balance. Submitting and communing with God is based upon the trust that reality means us good, not ill.[799] Life is not always fair, but we owe it to ourselves and others to strive for fairness.

A secret of life is achieving happiness, balance and resilience while serving the universe with love. It is walking the highway of our mortal existence with intelligent mystical steps – being in a state of buddhi-yoga such that we unite the mind with the higher consciousness.[800] It is that plain and simple. The real challenge is how do we get there? We get there by falling in love with every possible moment of existence and by projection gratitude upon the universe, for love casts out fear. However simple the principle of love may be, it is not always easy to implement and apply.

The notion of dreams within this book relates to the waking dreams of our desires and wishes which propel us forward. Unless otherwise noted, it does not relate to the sleeping dreams as mentioned in the Preface. The secret of life's journey is to align with your passions and follow your bliss in the direction of your waking dreams and desires, provided they: 1) are not harmful to self or others; 2) do not burden society; and, 3) do not infringe upon the autonomy and well-being of others.[801] Another secret of life, more simply put, is to create purpose by finding and following your passions, desires and dreams while allowing them to change accordingly. Finding and aligning with one's purpose is what the Greek philosopher Aristotle referred to as *telos*.[802] Developing a healthy passion of which to focus our attention acts as an aid in blocking out unpleasantries and allows miracles to come into fruition. Pursuing a healthy life of passion, not obsession, requires balancing care and concern for others with the desires of our goals and intentions. A good life balances our own self-interests with the needs of others.[803]

The driving motivation behind our dreams may not remain constant over time as our priorities and perspectives change. If you immerse love into your thoughts and put forth joyful effort, purpose will come to you as a feeling, a hunch or an image and it will steer you in the direction of fulfillment and destiny.[804] We all came into this world with the mission of creating our destiny. To fulfil that mission, we need to follow our dreams with simple practical steps. For it is through simplicity that mosaics of structure are built. When our steps are at the correct rise and at the proper run, we will feel content with the flow of our movement through life. If the steps are too high or too short, we will trip because the rhythm of ascent is not synchronized with the universal clock; we become out of tune with the oscillatory pulses between implicit and explicit realities. We need to have a firm footing on each step or else we will lose our balance. The direction of our destiny is self-created by our own thoughts, feelings and attitudes. The only thing getting in the way of your dreams is reality and time. Therefore, either change your reality or change your dreams until they coincide.

—A*—

"The universe is change; our life is what our thoughts make it." – Marcus Aurelius[805]

• • • •

"THE FUTURE BELONGS to those who believe in the beauty of their dreams." – Eleanor Roosevelt[806]

• • • •

"DREAM YOUR DREAMS, but when you act, plant your feet firmly on the ground." – Noel Clarasó[807]

—*O—

Following your dreams involves allowing the subconscious mind to influence the conscious mind with creative visualization and planning. It is the duality of the conscious mind interacting with the subconscious, and vice-versa. It is about tapping into that higher mind and assimilating constructive imagination into reality, through inspirational plans of action that allow for improvisation, but without crossing the threshold into delusions. Creating meaning and purpose for your existence is what life is all about. Fueled by passion in the short term, it gives a reason for the journey in the long term. The meaning of your life is what you choose to make it. Your ultimate purpose is to develop, hone and express your hidden talents to the world, to serve humanity, and to reveal more of God's wisdom, truth and beauty for all the world to see.[808]

—Δ*—

"The privilege of a lifetime is to become who you truly are." – C. J. Jung

• • • •

"WE ARE EACH BORN WITH a 'Heartsong' – or a reason for being and a purpose in life." – Mattie J.T. Stepanek[809]

• • • •

"THE TWO MOST IMPORTANT days in your life are the day you were born and the day you find out why." – Mark Twain[810]

—*O—

God wants us to reach for the stars, but with humility and acceptance of the final outcome. The average individual is capable of much greater achievement than he or she ever realized.[811] Always have plans (short term and long term) for the future as a means for providing purpose and for reaching new plateaus, no matter how small of achievements. Allow and accept when those plans change or are put on hold for a while. You may plan, and receive adequate counsel and advisement, but God determines the plays. It is finding balance between being patient with the universe and when to initiate moves. Allah's timing doesn't always seem to coincide with our desired pace, yet we need to be patient with his rhythm and trust his tempo. The Lord exists both in time and beyond it, while we exist primarily in the realm of time. The fulfillment of desired dreams is not the primary goal, but rather, it is experiencing the journey and seeing the view along the way. As we travel through life, we walk the balance of savoring the journey, witnessing the experiences and accomplishing the goals. Life is a journey; the goal is to have lived as full and productive a life as possible given our circumstances. Learn to enjoy the process just as much as the goal. For example, one who builds model ships as a hobby doesn't do it just for the end result. They also do it for the enjoyment of the process, imagination and the involved craftsmanship of cutting wood and plastic components, sanding, painting, and gluing. Be prepared that upon achieving a dream or goal, you may not like or enjoy the end result. If this is the case, then accept that happiness was not achieved and seek a new direction to aspire towards. Anecdote: Albert Einstein provided a handwritten note to a courier in place of a monetary tip which stated, "A calm and humble life will bring more happiness than the pursuit of success and the constant restlessness that comes with it."[812] The advice suggested in the note that chasing and achieving a long-dreamt goal does not necessarily guarantee happiness.

—Λ*—

"What gives you happiness you want to learn and not forget." – *Accept This Gift*[813]

• • • •

"BE CAREFUL WHAT YOU set your heart on, for it will surely be yours." – Ralph Waldo Emerson

—*Ω—

Having a steady climb of levels within our lives gives us sense of a direction. Reaching each landing will give us a sense of accomplishment, but we shouldn't dwell there too long. We may stumble and fall in trying to reach new levels but that is all part of the learning process of who we are and what we can achieve. There are no victories without a preceding struggle; one cannot succeed if they never try. It is always better to have tried and failed then to regret not having ever tried.[814] Failure provides the training for achieving success.

—A*—

"Why should I stay at the bottom of a well when a strong rope is in my hand?" – Rumi[815]

• • • •

"THE GREATEST GLORY in living lies not in never falling, but in rising every time we fall." – Nelson Mandela[816]

• • • •

"IT'S NOT WHETHER YOU get knocked down, it's whether you get up." – Vince Lombardi[817]

• • • •

"IF PLAN 'A' DOESN'T work, remember there are 25 other letters in the alphabet." – Unknown[818]

• • • •

"Fall seven times. Stand up eight." – Japanese Proverb[819]

• • • •

"IF THERE IS NO STRUGGLE, there is no progress." – Frederick Douglas[820]

—*O—

Early failure is usually better than early success, because the lesson in humility lasts a longer time and makes you more effective over the long term.[821] We ultimately achieve our goals and objectives not through the significances of our great successes, but primarily through the teachings of our earlier failures. It is our response to defeats that determines the final outcome in our preparations towards the direction of success. Learning from our failures builds competence for achieving future success. A perfect infamous example of this was the disasters encountered in 1944 during Exercise Tiger (aka Operation Tiger), a rehearsal by Allied forces for the start of Europe's release from its Nazi occupation. From the horrendous communication errors, lack of correct and clear instructions, surprise enemy encounters and inadequate defensive escorts, many lessons were learned and corrected which contributed to the providential foothold landing of D-day occurring about six weeks later upon Normandy's beaches which launched and catalyzed the continued liberation of Europe. Mistakes determine the outcome of a project or endeavor far more than the greatest of advanced planning. Studying and retrospectively analyzing our failures, however costly they may have been, provides the stepping stones towards future success; we learn from our mistakes.[822] Success is a grind of perseverance and changing approaches when repeated paths of persistence are not providing the desired results. It is often achieved after wading through swamps of discouragement. It is by learning to push through the failures while thriving on those little strings of accomplishments encountered during the grind that brings one to success. One's effort is relative and the degree of preparation is directly correlated to the degree of success.[823] Doubt is often the result of conflicting wishes. Be sure of what you want, for in doing so doubt will still exist, but its influences will become negligible. Having the will to succeed is not enough; preparing for favorable results is what matters while underlyingly accepting that alternate outcomes may occur. For at times, we may over-estimate our potential and be blindly driven by ambition in attempts to scale heights of success for which we are not fitted.[824] Often enough, due to a lack of personal awareness and valid self-assessments, one may overestimate their ability and skills as denoted in the Dunning-Kruger effect.[825] Moving full steam ahead in following our dreams without questioning any exaggerated expectations, reevaluating if difficulties were underestimated, falling into the trap of blind or unjustified optimism, and adjusting persistently negative attitudes of being our own worst enemy, are all recipes for failure. Having those "impossible" dreams and desires makes for great internal theater, but trying to push the universes' movements faster than they will go is recipe for stress and depression. A willingness to recognize that fantasy is the dream that may or may not enter the realm of time, will enable us to endure with the pain if it fails to materialize.

—Δ*—

"Failure is good...through failure we may mount the hill of vision." - White Eagle[826]

• • • •

"GREAT WORKS ARE PERFORMED not by strength but by perseverance." – Samuel Johnson[827]

• • • •

"SUCCESS IS A LOUSY teacher. It seduces smart people into thinking they can't lose." – Bill Gates[828]

—*O—

In a state of balance, we are able to find excitement in simplicity. The simple things give us as much pleasure and sometimes more than the grandiose things. When in balance, we are content to be without the false reliance on excessive material consumption. Our pleasure must come from within, before we can truly be happy. The main factor for achieving contentment is our internal attitude towards existence, the world and ourselves. The opposite of contentment is continued internal anger which destroys our piece of mind, for if not properly dissipated, it will cast and harden itself into multidirectional hatred. Balance comes from gaining the composure of being at peace within the events of our past, the state of our present, and the potential of our future. It is creatively visualizing a desired future yet detaching from it to reduce anxiety. It is finding the optimum position for the fulcrum of existence between the extremes. Once we find it, the universe will fall into place as we synchronize with its movement. Balancing creative visualization with futurized fantasies for a desired goal calls for relinquishing expectations and detaching from the actual results. This is what is meant by praying to God while accepting her answers and responses. This is surrendering to the will of Allah. It is moving forward with diligence between the duality of conducting positive visualization for the desired outcome while learning from the actuality of undesired results that thwart achieving goals. Give mental attention in the form of little steps of follow-through towards your goals, ideas and ventures. Your deeper mind, the subconscious, will put forth the way to even bigger steps. When continuing with perseverance, never accept limitations, unless the costs of pursuit become greater than the value of that which will be achieved.[829]

—Λ*—

"You are building your mental home all the time, and your thought and mental imagery represents your blueprint. Hour by hour, moment by moment, you can build radiant health, success, and happiness by the thoughts you think, the ideas which you harbor, the beliefs that you accept, and the scenes that you rehearse in the hidden studio of your mind. This stately mansion, upon the construction of which you are perpetually engaged, is your personality, your identity in this plane, your whole life story on this earth." – Dr. Joseph Murphy[830]

—*Ω—

Finding the positive pole within every negative situation, a Hermetic principle based on reverse thinking, can lead us to desired outcomes. Practicing the letting go of unnecessary fears and refraining from "over thinking", we can reverse think our worries away. Much of life is about confronting fears. That which is known, is usually not as bad as that which can be imagined.[831] Fear is worrying about the future. Negative thinking, however, appropriate concern about what can go wrong and implementing preventive measures, actually produces much more positive results rather than unrealistic Pollyanna-like optimism. It is the duality between positive and negative thinking which brings one to see the reality for what it is and properly positioning one's operational and emotional fulcrum between Pollyanna and Cassandra.

Appropriately preparing for the future in a balanced fashion reduces our worrying about the future. If you are afraid of failure, then give negative thinking its due attention by preparing to succeed. Never allow what is considered positive factors to override your ability to determine and address the negative ones. Those negative potentials will always turn out to be the more important and dominant influencer. Construct "pros" and "cons" lists to compare, in writing, the positives and the negatives, then base decisions on the realities of the conundrum. Between optimism and pessimism, choose realism. A "negative thinker" who considers, reveals, acknowledges, analyzes and addresses the risks, can still be a happy and content person; even more so since they consider the negatives to minimize their occurrences and promote positive results. Happiness does not guarantee propitious outcomes in life, but it drastically increases the probability. Keeping it as part of our internal default state is what can give us the endurance to pull through tragedies, from which valuable experiences can provide us with a better sense of reality and what is truly important. Although there are never absolutes in life, just very high probabilities, we have the divine right to personal happiness and to follow healthy means for achieving it.

A positive attitude alone did not place a man on the moon; it was the preparative appropriate worrying about everything that could possibly go wrong and addressing or mitigating those risks. True confidence, not exaggerated boldness nor inflated conceit, is acquired through the trials and tribulations of real-life experiences. Bravado leads to far more failure than does caution while blind optimism leads to doom; don't be dismissive of the negatives.[832] Based on the overconfidence and temerity of a quick victory, think of all the times in modern history when wars were started with such positive political assurances of how quickly they would be finished.[833] Success is not based solely on positive or on negative thinking, but it shuns those who lack ideas or the initiative to act on them. It is based on looking at the pros and cons of a situation and establishing decisions on a wise analysis of the perceived reality while moving forward with healthy, productive and steadfast tenacity. Fear is real. It may be warranted or unwarranted, legitimate or unnecessary, substantial or trivial. The cure for fear is the implementation of the appropriate constructive actions – those which minimize the subject of those fears from becoming actualized. Paralysis is fear succeeding; action is fear contained. Fear comes and goes, but anxiety paralyzes. Once we confront the reality of our fears and how they affect our physical mortality, facing the truth of what is to be feared and what is to be hoped, then and only then, will we be able to take action to address the more important of the two; to address the dualities.[834]

—A*—

"A man's got to know his limitations." – fictional character of Dirty Harry[835]

—*O—

A good life is about balance, mixing the proper proportions of triangular and circular elements, to walk the middle and the forward path towards enlightenment. When one is in proper balance with the universe, healthy synchronization will start to occur. Patterns and occurrences in the direction of your desired dreams will start to present themselves. You will become more aware, astute and receptive to these "coincidental" occurrences and revealed information beneficial to achieving your goals. When time allows, make final decisions after unrushed reflection because being in an anxious state, one is prone to make more mistakes. Every decision you make stems from what you think you are and represents the value that you place upon yourself in lowering the ego to reach your true Self.[836] When one is properly synchronizing with the thoughts of God and harmonizing with the chronological pulse of the universe, being in Krishan consciousness, answers will appear and excitement for the future will continue with minimum anxiousness.[837] Things happen when we're ready, when the universe decides it's time to provide, and the power of God's timetable starts to initiate. With sufficient time to reflect, more options and better solutions formulate from the subconscious into the conscious mind. The universe is always providing us with options. It is up to us to be aware when Allah is providing guidance. It is up to us to be receptive and listen. God speaks to us not typically by audible language, but rather, through symbols, signs, recognitions, connections and results. The timetable of the Supreme calls upon us to wait with patience and to implement actions, depending on the universe's optimum rhythm. This waiting after releasing our works to the appropriate decision makers and then placing the outcome at the hands and mercy of their decisions, can cause frustration and depression since we are no longer in control of the process. The achievement of our goals seems dependent on the acceptance and actions of others. It is through such waiting periods that we need to sometimes float or redirect our focus to other tasks.

—Δ*—

"The goal of life is to make your heartbeat match the beat of the universe, to match your nature with Nature." – Joseph Campbell[838]

—*O—

Create independent alternate and parallel tracks of a life plan to fall back on in case some don't come into fruition. Given the choice between alternate tracks or two options, establish them such that either outcome is favorably preferred. They should not be interconnected such that if one of those plans fail, then all of them fail. Applying sound, reasonable, justified and substantiated self-confidence is how obstacles are overcome and the road to success is paved. Through changing our attitude in the way that we look at frustrating phenomena, we should try to see them not as hindrances to be overcome, but as training exercises for building and maintaining our character. For example, the development of a nemesis gives us the opportunity to really practice projecting love and patience, even when our anger would prefer an alternate direction. The enemy has become our teacher and trainer by letting us practice counter measures put in place with love.[839] Faith in God while following through with the appropriate course of actions to improve conditions also seems to play an influential role in achieving success. For faith in a higher consciousness at work triggers confidence in that you can do just about any reasonable endeavor. It can provide renewed strength, constructive energy, enthusiasm and revitalization of accomplishing tasks, objectives and goals.[840] When you start to find your true Self and express and give of your talents for the betterment of others, then you are on the surest auspicious path – become the person you want to be and success will soon follow. You need to do your part while God does his part.

—A*—

"The Lord helps those who help themselves." – an adage from the ancient Greeks

• • • •

"USE WHAT TALENTS YOU possess: the woods would be very silent if no birds sang except those that sang best." – Henry van Dyke[841]

—*O—

Never feel ashamed of doing an honest day's work, not matter what the task. One who is satisfied in her or himself should have no fear of any task, unless it is unhealthy, criminal or contributing to negative exploitation. Respect those whose jobs may not pay as much as yours, for if they weren't doing those tasks, you'd have to do them. Never be above the most menial of tasks, for attending to them keeps us connected with humility. Ideally, by the third decade of life or sooner and based on the calling for which one feels the most suited, a career path should be selected in which to pursue and follow. During this life stage, the background of our minds should be shaping the future direction of our ego for social adaptation, in essence, educating and training the will to find our niche. It does not mean that one can't decide to change careers or jobs later in life, but rather, heading in some direction is better than heading nowhere at all. We may not always first land into a job that allows us to express our true nature, resulting in a torturous feeling that we are denying our potential. The aim, however, is to steer towards a fulfilling vocation. Find the desire to do something, to head in some occupational direction rather than none at all. The progression to success is done one step, one accomplishment, one hurdle, one achievement at a time. Although we may plan for a certain career direction, direct opportunities may not immediately present themselves and the occupations we pursue may not initially coincide with our "externalization."[842] Preparation is prudent so that when doors of opportunity do open, we are able to take advantage of the moments. Accumulation of additional life experiences can trigger a redirection of our desires and goals and re-establish a definiteness of purpose; our positive contribution to the world. Those in later years of age will need to shift the focus to understanding the meaning of their individual life and to experience their own inner being. An inwardly sound and socially confident person will be more effective in societal accomplishments when they have become on good terms and made amends with their subconscious.[843] Avoid running away from a job that you do not like, instead, steer towards a job that appears to be better. When you are able to align with a cause or occupation that you truly agree or believe in, your conviction to it will become energized.

—Λ*—

"Don't wait until you know who you are to get started." – Austin Kleon[844]

—*Ω—

A purpose of life is to train and work on one's self-realization – paving your way with a path of love. This is done by becoming aware of one's inner core, learning to adjust it when it is headed in the wrong direction, and becoming and maintaining the person God wants us to be. Step back and reflect on the person you want to become and steer yourself in that direction. As sentient beings, spiritual fulfillment comes through witnessing and reflecting on the passage of notable events and significant markers in our lives while still enjoying the most mundane of occurrences. The truest of spiritual paths is being an honorable and humble participant in the human experience.

Many of the great thinkers, philosophers and religious sages are well aware of a fundamental law underlying the functions of our being: The Law of Desired Happiness. It is denoted as "...the pursuit of Happiness..." at the end of the first line of the preamble of the *Declaration of Independence*, (a guiding document in the 18th century formation of the country of the United States), as an example of unalienable rights granted to all by the Creator. Franklin Delano Roosevelt, the 32nd U.S. President, implied it when he discussed the four universal freedoms (Freedom of Speech, Freedom of Worship, Freedom from Want and Freedom from Fear) in a January 6, 1941 speech to Congress. There is a well-known Buddhist statement that "you are the sum of your thoughts" which reinforces this universal principle; if you desire happiness, then focus on it. An Old Testament interpretation in the scriptures states that, "As you think, so shall you be."[845] Rumi wrote "You are what you seek."[846] Michel de Montaigne, a significant philosopher of the 16th century French Renaissance, stated, "The most certain sign of wisdom is cheerfulness." Abraham Lincoln allegedly said, "People are about as happy as they make up their mind to be." Ralph Waldo Emerson has told us that, "We become what we think about all day long." Thoreau wrote, "If one advances confidently in the direction of his dream, and endeavors to live the life which he has imagined, he will meet with a success unexpected in common hours." Descartes declared, "I think, therefore I am." All these philosophers are saying the same thing; the focus of your thinking is what you will become. The direction of our future is formed and steered by the thoughts we hold in our consciousness most often.[847] If we choose to become greed, we will become greed. If we choose to become anger, we will become anger. If we choose to become happy, we will become happiness. If we choose to become love, we will be love. Become indifferent to your future by being aware of the fears, but containing them with the proper amount of care and concern. Can focusing on happiness and love, even if one does not genuinely feel it, "snap" away depression? When practiced over a period of weeks or months, it has worked for some as method that provided relief. Make the notion of love the first thoughts upon awakening in the morning and the last thoughts on your mind as you fall asleep at night.

—Δ*—

"For what one thinks, one becomes." – *Maitri Upanishads*[848]

• • • •

"HAPPINESS IS NOT SOMETHING ready-made. It comes from your own actions. The key to a happy life now and in the future, is to develop a happy mind." – XIV Dalai Lama[849]

—*O—

We all have the ability to choose our thoughts, to do what is right and to make fairness part of the equation within our daily lives. One must be willing to sometimes let the old self die away so that a new, more aware self can morph into existence, very much like a phoenix continuously rising from the aphar of the past. Great beings can arise from the tribulations and obstacles of past events, for if it weren't for such events, would our character have even developed to the point and awareness it has reached? Sometimes the universe will test us and sometimes we will break under the load. It is the picking up and mending of the pieces that results in our growth. It is the risk of change we fear, not necessarily the change itself. It is the risk of becoming responsible for ourselves and our growth.

—Λ*—

"Find your bliss and all will fall into place." – AO

• • • •

"To be in love with being, is to wake up to life." – AO

—*Ω—

HAPPINESS (AKA INTERNAL cheerfulness) is a condition of being and an emotion that motivates positive action. It keeps us energized more efficiently than any other emotion. Sometimes our happiness can become hampered by external circumstances or unavoidable situations, but it is constructive to return to a content state of mind as soon as possible. We still must address affronts to our persona and protect our property in a lawful manner, but while doing so, send vibes of love to the transgressors and compartmentalize the frustrations. This will preserve your karma, reduce unproductive dwelling and allow the universe to take the necessary actions. It is the internal self-manufactured unhappiness that can be addressed more readily by adjusting our thinking processes. Anger may sometimes motivate us, but it consumes a tremendous amount of our energy as well as those around us and can strain our physical health. It is a short-term motivator that masks the beauty around us. Its overuse is detrimental to everyone in the long run. Refer back to Mark Twain's quote in Chapter 14 on what the acid of anger can do to our body and soul. Repressed anger, when not properly addressed and dissipated, will fester and take over like uncontrollable prolific weeds. Having a responsibility to deal with our anger appropriately, we still need to occasionally and temporarily feel rageful, frightened, cautious and worried in response to external matters, but it is how we acknowledge and deal with these emotions within ourselves and within others that will determine the underlying emotional current of our steady state.

How happy does one have to be? How about a little happiness? Is a little happiness or a lot of happiness required to feel good? Do we really need an abundance of happiness to be happy? How happy does one have to feel to be happy? Achieving a mild steady state of happiness is all that one needs to implement the secret of life – to find our internal *eudaimonia*. Constant extremes of happiness would be considered madness, mania or on the high extreme of a bipolar cycle; it only takes the most miniscule amount of happiness to feel good. This miniscule amount can be referred to as contentment. A mild steady state of happiness is just another definition of contentment. Contentment doesn't mean being stagnant; it means feeling good with your rate of growth. Too high of a rate and one feels stressed, apathetic and depressed. Too low of a rate and one feels the same. Enlightenment is balancing the direction we want to head with the direction the universe is leading us. It is both a straight and winding path that delivers us to a destination based on both free will and destiny.

Therefore, whenever the word happiness is encountered within this book, it refers to a healthy state of contentment, not to the frenzy levels of madness. We have to learn to make one of our most underlying emotional current one of happiness such that our steady-state condition defaults back to contentment. For when contentment becomes the basis of our mind and foundation of our thoughts, we will flow serenely through both the pleasantries and unpleasantries of life more effectively. Training and conditioning our core to quickly rebound to a steady state of happiness and not the short-lived extremes is the way to achieve contentment, balancing the idea of being with the idea of love. Yes, we will still feel instantaneously angry when someone cuts us off in traffic since they caused the potential for a collision, but instead of focusing on it and having it fester and grow into something larger than it needs to be, we need to quickly return to a steady state of love. This will reduce anger towards aggressive drivers and help minimize the stressful fight or flight response. We need to constantly remind ourselves and learn again after each negative moment, how to be happy. This is done by returning to love.

The universe has a tendency to magnify and reflect back your vibrational state; the degrees of your emotions. Arthur Guirdham would describe interactions between people as "vibrations" to describe how they get along together.[850] With some people, the vibrations put us at ease or create a sense of comfort. With others, they create disintegration, a negative influence that can actually destroy character. I'm sure you have had encounters with both personality types. Angels are attracted to love; demons are attracted to hatred. Like moths at night around a light, which would you prefer to have hovering about your being? If you transmit hatred, the world will collapse upon you with self damnation. If you are angry, it will echo back anger. If you are pleasant and cheerful, it will echo back happiness. If you transmit love, it will echo back love. If you transmit gratitude, it will echo back gratitude. As soon as we learn to live a life of happiness, everything else will fall into place. Tasks will seem less burdensome and may actually become enjoyable. The relationship within our self and our outer-verse will improve. Our desire for excessiveness or detrimental behavior will decrease. Our self-value will increase with minimal effort. Our ability to laugh through appropriate situations instead of allowing them to drain us will increase. We will become content with where we are in life, yet pursue our hopes and dreams with increased vigor. The universe will seem more beautiful, colors and form will be more alive, food more flavorful and our minds will become receptive for balance. The world can be a stage of deceptiveness, taking away the innocence of the child as much as it can be an environment of honesty, putting in place the wisdom of the adult.[851] Understanding this duality, we will be able to approach each day with the enthusiasm of a child, but the know-how of an adult. Synchronization and resonance with the vibrational frequencies of the universe will start to occur, sending you on the steps towards achieving your dreams. Circumstances will start to gather in favor of your desired direction. For when one is truly ready, in both spirit and action, one's dreams and reality will start to coincide, unveiling a glimpse of the metaphysical universe's power. Infinite intelligence, knowing of all things (gnosis), will start to work within you and outside of you, revealing the correct decisions and the correct directions in divine order.[852] Actualize your dreams and desires into reality by going at it with healthy love: love the process, love the journey and love the results. There is a tendency for the universe to become attracted to harmonizing with the nature of our dominating thoughts. It likes to play with us for it is our "sandbox." Psychologists have correctly said that "when one is truly ready for a thing, it puts in its appearance."[853]

God wants us to be humble, but not doormats to be easily stepped upon. God wants us to be ambitious in our endeavors, but not aggressive in pursuing them. God wants us to default to a steady state of love but defend ourselves and approach accosting situations with safe caution. The world is full of sadness and it is also full of joy, for human life is composed of ineluctable experiences of ups and downs. The objective is to minimize the tragedies and maximize the celebrations by focusing on the goodness in our lives to get us through the interludes of hardship. We need to acknowledge the sadness and work on reducing it, but focus on increasing joy. Focusing on the suffering of others can drain and make us melancholy, depressed and angry. Shifting our efforts on increasing their joy is much more effective and an efficient use of emotional energy.

• • • •

WAYS TO ACHIEVE HAPPINESS

1) Walking a stable path involves a balance between investing in long-term goals and objectives, and addressing the immediate short-term goals and objectives. Have long-term projects to strive forward for the future. Such long-term objectives should either strive to maintain the person who you are or change and grow you into the person who you want to become. Have short-term goals to enjoy being in the present. Break long-term projects/goals into many short-term projects/goals. Have many projects and goals to hedge your bets, understanding that some objectives may not be achievable. Focus on enjoying the process and what the goal may bring, but accept that results may vary. Learn to enjoy the journey's progress and encounters more than the goal itself.

2) Decide to be happy. Smile every day during the work commute; it will make the other drivers envious. We are all actors in our daily lives and sometimes the mere act of choosing to focus on feeling happy inside is enough to trigger us into becoming a happy and content person. Choose to be happy for a few days, then a few weeks. All of a sudden you may find that you actually are.

3) Find happiness with other people's happiness. Be empathetic to their joy, not envious of it.

4) Do a good deed for another and empathize with the happiness you brought them.

5) Find happiness in the simple things such as the greeting of a playful dog or the purring of a satisfied cat. The mere fact that you are working your way through reading this book is a simple thing which makes me very happy.

6) Happiness is found in sharing – the sharing of yourself, your love, your truth and your happiness. If you share with the world, it will share back. You cannot share something that you do not have to give. You cannot share happiness or love if you do not have it within your own being.

7) Simplify your life whenever it starts to become overwhelming. You can't do it all in life, but you can become happy just by doing some of it.

• • • •

SET ASIDE TIME TO ACHIEVE even the smallest portions of your dreams. Practicing creative visualization by imagining how to achieve your goals or heal yourself is the surest sign that you still have hope. The sensation that you are heading in the direction of your dreams is sometimes all that we need to stimulate happiness within our being. Some indigenous American cultures have a talisman consisting of a circular hoop with a web of sacred or natural materials and referred by Anglicization as a "dream catcher." Traditionally placed over cribs and beds, its original purpose was to filter our nightmares and trap evil spirits, much like the God's Eye, to prevent them from entering the minds of infants and children. In more recent decades under the influence of commercialization, it romantically morphed into a charm for catching our good dreams and hopes for bringing them into reality.

Focus on finding and maintaining healthy obsessions (those that maintain well-being) without going to extremes. Replace unhealthy addictions and detrimental obsessions with healthier substitutes. In doing so, healthy passion will invigorate your vitality and stimulate your existence, making you more energetic in your motives. Utilize and apply your energy in useful manners towards constructive goals and objectives. Otherwise, misplaced energy is wasted energy. Find joy in doing things that require very little money: working in a garden, traveling on a short road trip, staying inside, reading a book, going to a library or just appreciating what you are doing in the moment. Find a hobby or activity that allows you to lose track of all time. Achieving that state of true absorption into what you are doing is referred to as being in the Zen, Zone or Flow. You have become one with what you are doing and this will give rise to a feeling of greater happiness.

It is normal to feel flat, down, disappointed or bored at times as long as the condition is temporary. Having an understanding with yourself that the condition is going to be short-lived and that you will bounce back to a steady state of contentment is what provides the momentum to endure such undesirable moments. Being outwardly happy all the time is not normal; defaulting to contentment is. Accept such down moments as the intermissions between acts. These are the plateaus of rest and reset from which we launch into the next endeavor. Boredom is the resting platform from which excitement initiates and launches.

Whenever possible go to sleep at a reasonable hour and get a good night's rest. Not many good decisions are made by tired minds in any walk of life.[854] Adequate rest provides the spiritual recharge to send us in the direction of joy and vitality in life.[855] It is when the day's thoughts are deposited into memories (the Universal Consciousness) and prevents us from becoming needlessly irritable the following day. Yet, for those nights of insomnia in which we reflect among our thoughts, it was Saint Anthony who complained of the sunrise that robs us of the greater light of inner contemplation.[856] Simplify so you have time to enjoy the quality of your life, not the quantity that is in it. Living a jet set life doesn't necessarily equate to contentment. Don't try to cram too many things into such a small amount of time. Set aside some moments of self-space when you can lose track of all time. Base your self-value on your degree of contentment, not the money in your bank account, the size of your house, the fanciness of your car, or the position of your job title.

—Λ*—

"Fame or integrity: which is more important?
Money or happiness: which is more valuable?
Success or failure: which is more destructive?"

– 2,500 year-old wisdom from the *Tao Te Ching*[857]

—*Ω—

Evolve your core to prefer and favor joy instead of pleasure. For joy can become eternal as a steady state of existence, but pleasures of the physical realm are temporary, momentary and dissolve with time. Joy (ananda) occurs across the infinite; pleasures occur within the finite. The jewel of a proper education is instilling the joy of learning and the wonderment of discovery. Make cognitive stimulation as part of your religion; the enjoyment of mental expansion and challenges through exposure to the continuum of literature in the arts, the humanities and the sciences. Illumination is also the installation of the wisdom of knowing when to act like a child and when to act like an adult; when to play and be silly and when to be responsible and serious. An enlightened being can tickle themselves and giggle from the sensation. No matter what our age, the truest sign of maturity is knowing when to act like a grown-up and when to act like a kid – acting our age when times call for responsibility and seriousness, and acting "immature" when times call for play and wonder. It is not the activity that you are doing that determines if it is work or play, it is whether it drains your batteries or charges them – is it punishing, frustrating and overwhelming or is it pleasurable, soothing and enticing? As Friedrich Schiller stated, one is completely human only when they are playing.[858] Healthiness is behaving as both the young and the old in the appropriate situations. The greatest gift we can teach our children is for them to grow into and become their own positive role models as adults.

The proper way to travel on streets and in traffic is very similar to the proper behavior for travelling the roadway of life. Sometimes you need to slow down, other times you need to go faster. The treatment of other drivers on the road should be done with courtesy and respect; the same way that people you encounter in life should be treated. As you look back upon your life, focus on the beauty and good times, while allowing the difficult and rough times to fade into the past. As constructive beings preparing in the present for our future, we often miss the abundance of goodness going on in our lives and overly dwell on trying to remove the bad. A painless life of gumdrops and lollipops would be wonderful, but in reality, most lives are bittersweet as represented by the Greek and Eastern Orthodox wedding favor tradition of giving out koufeta, hardened sugar-coated almonds. It is not about forgetting or blocking the difficult and rough times, but rather, achieving happiness, contentment and the ability to move forward as you define the continuum of your chronological connections.

—A*—

"It is not always easy to find happiness in ourselves, and it is impossible to find it elsewhere." – Agnes Repplier[859]

—*O—

Encapsulating life's irritations and agitations into pearls is the best way to move past frictional moments. Striving for improving an imperfect world while acknowledging and accepting the flaws is part of the dynamic of being a healthy adult. The objective is to continuously move forward into the future and not dwell too long in past pitfalls. It is not always what is in the world that determines the quality of your life, it is how you choose to process the world with the reaction of your thoughts. Do you choose to inflict pain on others because pain was inflicted on you? Or do you help others deal with their inflictions because you remember what it feels like and choose to show compassion to ease suffering?

Living a good life is about love, courage and determination. To live a spiritual existence, one must always default to a steady state of love. This means training the mind not to act in an aggressive manner when impulsive primal urges of retaliation flood our thoughts. Instead of acting on those impulses, think of the words "default to love." This requires mental training but the results will be the bringing of the mind into a clearer focus on the best way to handle a situation. Defaulting to a steady state of love, happiness and contentment, when appropriate, is the best way to keep our balance when enduring all the unpleasantness that life may throw at us. When facing fear, default to love. It gives us the inoculative resistance and benevolent power to be phlegmatic and productive under the direst of circumstances.

—Δ*—

"What is essential in life, is invisible to the eye." – Mr. Fred Rogers[860]

• • • •

"The best things in life are not things." – Ginny Moore[861]

• • • •

"YET, THE THINGS THAT the eye can see are mere phantoms and illusions. Only those things invisible to the eye are real." – Thoth-Hermes[862]

• • • •

"THE LEAST OF THINGS with a meaning is worth more in life than the greatest of things without it." – C. G. Jung[863]

—*O—

When you come to the point in your life in which your spiritual search is no longer based on the need to fill a void created in your past or to escape the hardships of a tough reality, but rather it has become a journey of adding to your character and that of the world, then you know that you are on the right path. For knowledge stimulates the quest for more knowledge and familiarity breeds ease of action and simplification. What seems like the most elementary and simple concepts of today were usually considered the impossible challenges of yesterday.

—Λ*—

"Through knowledge I receive God onto myself, and through love I enter into him." – Meister Eckhart[864]

—*Ω—

Intelligence is the skill of analyzing occurrences within the boundaries of their proper perspective.[865] Genius, however, is not about intelligence, nor is it about regurgitating memorized facts. It is about humbly introducing something great, through the persistence of overcoming obstacles, condemnation and hurdles, for humanity's advancement. It is about flourishing despite facing a wake of criticism or doubt and recognizing that actions in the present affect the future. It is about adjusting our behavior and actions now and foregoing certain activities desired by the current self in favor of benefitting the future self. It is the determination to be a better person tomorrow than we are today. From Jung's doctrine, merging our internal mind with our extroverted expression into a functioning personality is an achievement of great realization.[866]

—A*—

"The life in front of you is far more important than the life behind you." – Silvia R.[867]

—*O—

Don't worry about who you might have been in a previous life or where you are going in the next, concentrate your time and efforts on this life. Focus on becoming a role model for yourself based on integrity, kindness, trustworthiness and the development of a balanced, healthy ego. The ultimate secret of life is to live by a motto of love, gratitude and forgiveness. Love is what leads us forward and is unitive with the future, gratitude is being thankful in the moment and is unitive with the present, and forgiveness is moving beyond a prior incident and is unitive with the past. This is a method by which we surrender to Allah, to be in Krishna consciousness, to have Buddha awareness and to walk with God.

—Δ*—

"We are here to serve the purpose of life, that is, to train the Radiant God within us to step forth under our conscious control. We are here to raise the Radiant God from within this tomb of flesh. We are here to become immortal, and have life everlasting." – Skakus[868]

—*O—

Chapter 16
Getting Even Or Letting Go

"GOD, GRANT ME THE EMOTIONAL self-awareness and restraint such that love is the driving force of my actions. Guide me to use the energy of any harbored anger in productive ways such that it does not succumb to hatred." – Prayer Of The Tempted, AO

• • • •

FORGIVENESS

When one trespasses against us, should we forgive? Yes, although difficult at times, forgiveness is something we should do both for ourselves and others, but mainly for ourselves. It is about healing, but not necessarily about forgetting. It frees and clears our minds so that we can move on. It is not always a simple thing to do. It takes patience, thought training and practice. One should not forgive until they are ready to do so, or else strife within the subconscious will occur. It may require the passage of adequate time or an improvement in circumstances to reach the point of forgiveness. If we are still not ready to forgive, then it means we have judged that it is too soon to release the past. In looking at the notion of forgiveness perhaps it would be better to separate the word into a duality of external forgiveness for a perpetrator who is truly deserving and internal reconciliation within as we come to terms with the act that was transgressed upon us. We can have "internal reconciliation" without "external forgiveness", but ideally, both are preferred. The merging of internal reconciliation as being contained within the word "forgiveness" is probably what has caused so much emotional confusion and turmoil among victims and targets. Saint Athanasius in reflecting upon Saint Paul's *1 Corinthians* 15:31 in achieving virtue, writes that we should forgive every person who ever offended us.[869] Can a Jewish survivor of a Nazi concentration camp genuinely forgive Hitler or can the living victims of brutal ethnic cleansing campaigns of history (i.e., Armenia, Rwanda, Bosnia and Herzegovina) truly forgive the assaulters, and should we expect them to do so? Are we expected to forgive every transgressor's assault (verbal, emotional or physical) upon us, regardless of the level of its heinousness? Most likely not, but achieving a level of internal reconciliation would allow the victim to continue on while releasing the justified anger so damaging to the internal psyche. Within this book, the word "forgiveness" can mean either forgiving another or ourselves, internal reconciliation, or defined as achieving both. The absolute concept of what forgiveness means seems to vary based on one's perspective and the situation, but ultimately, it is left for God to see what is in our hearts (figuratively).

Prematurely forgiving another can lead to internal conflict and a denial of one's feelings. In response to the "eye for an eye, tooth for a tooth" Old Testament Laws of Retaliation, the *New Testament* tells us that Jesus spoke of turning the other cheek in his preaching of "Love your enemies, do good to those who hate you, bless those who curse you, pray for those who mistreat you. If someone strikes you on one cheek, turn to him the other also. If someone takes your coat, do not withhold your shirt from them..."[870] Even with this simple parable, there are several perceptions and interpretations. Did Jesus say it to promote the pursuit of legal action rather than personal vengeance? Did he preach to turn the other cheek as a means to promote non-violent reactions? To be submissive and docile? To choose one's battles wisely? To encourage the turning in a different direction when faced with blockades? Or as a trending protest stance of the time period to the occupation by the Roman Empire, as a defensive move for avoiding a repeat blow from a soldier to the same facial region? Even here, such a seemingly straight forward passage has resulted in more than one interpretation of its intent. I also view the turning of the other cheek as a metaphor for controlling your own fate by steering oneself around the obstacles encountered in the river life. When you see the rocks approaching while floating in the rapids, use the oars or rudder to steer the vessel of your destiny around and away from them. Taking the stance of promoting non-violent reactions, we should all turn the other cheek to quell our urges of revenge, switch to empathy, show mercy and head in a better and new direction. When smitten on one cheek, figuratively turn the other in pity and love for the aggressor. If you must have revenge, then the best way to get back at your enemies or upon those who "talk smack" of you is to be successful and happy in life; your earned achievements and state of contentment will drive them nuts.

When Jesus was asked by Peter how many times one should forgive your enemies, he responded "seventy-seven" or "seventy times seven", which amounts to 490 times.[871] Yet, if you keep turning the other cheek in forgiveness to an abuser, you risk forming an unhealthy codependent enabling relationship that harms both and helps neither party. How many times should one forgive another? At what point does perpetual forgiveness become a pattern of dysfunctionality? At what point does a line become crossed in which one should stop turning the other cheek? How many times have we repeatedly forgiven the same person, their broken promises and their damaging lies? How do we keep forgiving someone who continues throwing salt into emotional wounds? Some of us may have reached a point where forgiveness is no longer an option, for it only opens us up to the vulnerability of continued betrayal. Forgiveness can turn on us and become a repetition of painful experiences.[872] Forgiveness does not necessarily mean forgetting and often becomes a changed state of "normal" as a means for moving forward. It is not about cleansing our memories to forget the past, but it is about reconciling our feelings towards it.

—Λ*—

"When we are able to recognize and forgive ignorant actions of the past, we gain the strength to constructively solve the problems of the present." – XIV Dalai Lama[873]

—*Ω—

There are those who are constantly forgiven, but they do not learn. They become miseducated that they can commit any inappropriate action or behavior, because those around them will always forgive them. Instead of realizing the gift of forgiveness that has been bestowed upon them, they become enabled into repeating their unacceptable behavior. They do not learn to take responsibility for their actions, because the only consequences they've been accustomed to, is forgiveness from their victims. They realize that through their self-serving interests they can manipulate and take advantage of those who choose to forgive them. It is with these people that forgiveness, just like trust, must be earned and not freely given. To what level should we display a reasonable degree of patience? How does one forgive without becoming a doormat?[874] Where does one draw the line between going that extra mile and not being taken advantage of and becoming a sucker? How does one turn the other cheek without "assassinating the dignity of forbearance, and sinking man into a spaniel"?[875] How does one forgive without enabling the other to become perpetually dependent on forgiveness for their continuous unacceptable behavior? I believe what Jesus meant was to keep forgiving internally the repeat behavior of an offender, but not externally, since they are not yet deserving of such forgiveness. External forgiveness, like trust, is earned.

—Δ*—

"Those who forgive are releasing themselves from the clutches of the past, while those who cannot are latching themselves into its shackles and chains." – AO

—*O—

A victim is someone who has lost a part or sense of self due to the words or actions of a perpetrator. Knowing this will help you heal by rebuilding that part of yourself that was taken away and will reduce the likelihood of you again becoming a victim of someone else's voids. There is the duality between a victim forgiving an assailant and the implementation of proper justice to prevent the assault from happening again. Forgiveness provided in person should be reserved for minor infractions that are not constantly repeated and when the person is deserving. Forgiveness is also granted inward as a means for the victim to start their healing process. Major infractions can be forgiven, but they should not be forgotten. Ideally, we must first internally forgive the person before we can forgive them in person. If we are unable to forgive them in person, then our internal forgiveness is more than enough to suffice. Should a person who repeats the same offense over and over again be forgiven in person each time? The answer is preferably not, because in such a situation the grantor is merely enabling the offender. An offender that continuously repeats the same infraction is not deserving of forgiveness, until they truly stop repeating the offence. Should forgiveness be granted to another if they are not ready to receive it? Should we forgive before the transgressor has learned their lesson and amended their ways? Should one forgive knowing the transgressor will continue to repeat the same transgression? I would say forgiveness to them in person is not deserving, but internally forgiving them is worthy.

Forgiveness is not always easy. It needs to wait for the anger to subside for it to be genuine. It requires reconditioning of our thought patterns to release a grudge or deal with resentment. In doing so, however, we will become more receptive to the blessings within our lives. We may forgive, but still need to stand firm. We may forgive, but not necessarily forget. Forgiveness is so that we can move on. It is not about giving permission for the offender to repeat the offense. It is permissible not to forget as we need to protect ourselves from repeat of the incidents which affronted us – hence the idiom "Once bitten, twice shy." Forgiving those apologizing for the atrocities committed by prior generations should be inherent. The fault of the crimes should never be placed upon the children or posterity of those responsible. Forgiveness opens the doors to reconciliation.

—Λ*—

"A kind word with forgiveness is better than charity followed by insult." – *The Koran*[876]

—*Ω—

Putting into practice ksama, we should forgive and forget the little things, forgive and remember the big things, but do not outwardly forgive or inwardly forget the repetitive things. Forgiveness occurs when our disgust is transmuted into compassion.[877] In this balance and moderation between forgiveness and justice, we must still strive for justice on the larger things that have been committed with consideration of the intent behind the acts. If justice is not achieved in the secular world, I can assure you it will be achieved in the spiritual world – the Universal Consciousness witnesses all. Upon material death, the deeds that a soul has done shall be returned to them, both good and bad. The *Koran* indicates that good deeds shall be returned to the soul with a tenfold increase in intensity, but evil deeds shall be returned upon the soul with the same degree.[878] The pain one caused to others will be returned as well as the kindness one showed to others – "as you sow, so shall you reap." There is truth to Karma-Dharma.

Your current reality is an indication of your place within and connection to the dream of the universal mind which created you. If your internal reality is a state of unhappiness, suffering and hardship, then you must strive to reconnect to that universal dream by choosing positive steps, thoughts and actions that will clear the excessive clutter within your mind and free you to enjoy life. Sometimes the steps will be painful and slow as you become aware of the emotional pain you may have caused others. You may also have to acknowledge, confront and let go of the emotional pain caused to you by others. This is the act of forgiveness so often stated within the scripture of various true religions. It is not always easy, but it is always necessary for your spiritual, psychological and mental growth. In order to move on to the next plateau of your enlightenment journey, you must first resolve and come to terms with the issues on your current plateau. Self-realization is becoming aware of those negative things of our past which still have their emotional claws in us. Enlightenment is recreating our internal core and our external universe as we learn to change the one thing we do have the ultimate control over: ourselves and our reactions to situations. Enlightenment is learning how to accept the negative things we don't have control over as lessons for our instruction, riding over them like a surfer on a wave, and then moving beyond and not allowing them to emotionally control us beyond their physical presence. The Nation of God is accessed from within; you are the king or queen of your internal empire. You alone preside over the thoughts of your internal mind and to what direction they veer.

The greatest way to defeat your enemies is to forgive and wish love upon them. Remember how Jesus said to love your enemies? He said this because when you love your enemies, it places karmic retribution in the hands of God and releases you from all forms of revenge and karma backlash. Thomas Paine felt that "loving enemies is another dogma of feigned morality",[879] but I disagree within him on this point. Loving your enemies is not about sacrificing yourself for them, it is about wishing them well even though you may be at odds with them. It lets God, the universe, take care of things as he/she sees fit to do so, rather than having you do something that will be regretted.[880] By projecting love onto your enemies and foes, it releases you from their emotional grasp and prevents them from getting under your skin.[881] It dissipates unproductive anger, redirecting your thought patterns to prevent internal damage and retrains your mind to associate healthy thoughts rather than destructive ones whenever their names or faces pop into your head.

—A*—

"Do not gloat when your enemy falls; when they stumble, do not let your heart rejoice, or the Lord will see and disapprove and turn his wrath away from them." – *The Old Testament*[882]

—*O—

Your enemies may still encounter hardships and burdens, but they are the results of God's spiritual actions, not yours. Let vengeance be the Lord's to take, not yours. Only project love and let the universe decide the fate of your enemies. You may find yourself feeling sorry and taking pity upon your enemies as well as expressing love towards them. The boundary between the triangle and the circle is semi-permeable. What goes on within the triangle, seeps out. What goes on outside of the circle, seeps in. If we send anger and harm to others, some of it will remain within ourselves. Wishing ill thoughts to others also reflects back onto ourselves. If we send love and kindness into the world, it will also reflect within. Repeating again The Law of Karma is an eternal truth – "as you sow, so shall you reap." Wish only love upon your enemies and watch what happens. Wish only love for Satan, your enemy, and watch how the world improves. Wish malice upon no one, even your greatest enemies. The universe will deal with your enemies as it sees fit, freeing you from karmic entanglements. Loving your enemies as yourself is about loving both God and Satan; not an easy task to do but it is possible. Remember, the best way to defeat your enemies, for when times permit, is to make them your friends. The victors of World War II finally realized this, and unlike the outcome of World War I with the economic destruction of the defeated under the Treaty of Versailles, the Allied forces rebuilt their enemies and made them their friends. The Gospels tell us that God works with the crooked timber of human failure, transforming even the most down-trodden souls into magnificence beings of glory. When you forgive the world of its sins and the sins of transgressors upon you, then and only then, will you be able to be released from the karma of your own sins. The greatest way to eliminate an enemy or foe, when conditions and terms permit, is to make them your ally or friend. With forgiveness, love can start to heal.

—Δ*—

"One of my wise teachers, Dr. Orr, told me, 'There is only one thing evil cannot stand, and that is forgiveness.'" – Mr. Fred Rogers

—*O—

• • • •

JUDGMENT

The *Bible* states not to judge and the *Koran* states to be careful in how you judge. Without applying specific prejudgments, we are forced to make decisions in this physical realm to preserve our secular existence. For survival, we need to discern between what is evil and what is good. By applying _diakrisis_, distinguishing between right and wrong, we develop a taste for what should be permitted and what should not, sifting through that which improves and that which degrades. Based on our trusted intuition, we must sometimes rapidly determine if a person, situation or thing is a threat or danger to our well-being – we must occasionally react fast. Relying on our instantaneous "gut feelings" and not ignoring our instincts, sometimes we need to and should quickly judge the behavior or actions of others. The most important thing is to make sure that we have all the information or facts, when the luxury of time allows, prior to making a judgment. Judgment comes into play, sometimes based on the minimum of facts, as the means of determining whether the intent of a person or nature of a situation could be perilous to our well-being. Other times we should not judge without knowing all the circumstances surrounding a given situation. The choice to judge prematurely rather than to know the reasons and facts behind a situation is the cause of much misery and loss of peace.[883] When passing judgment on others when your immediate well-being is not under threat, be sure to know all the facts and not just partial perceptions, gossip or things being whispered into your ears. When revealing truths to expose falsehoods, whenever possible, progress first from the approach of educational kindness rather than immediately escalating to accusations, finger pointing and full prosecution. The objective is to initially apply the least aggressive effort to have the parties abate and come out of the falsehoods, rather than jump right into accusative confrontation. Avoid hypocrisy within your own actions when judging the actions of others. If it is not imperative to one's well-being or livelihood, then make no judgments.

—Λ*—

"For in the same way you judge others, you will be judged, and with the measure you use, it will be measured to you." – *New Testament*[884]

. . . .

"WITHHOLD JUDGMENT AND criticism. The human way is to judge in haste the actions of others, but the divine way is to remain quiet and loving. You are divine as well as human and are here on earth to learn to manifest divinity." – White Eagle[885]

. . . .

"YOU MAY JUDGE BUT BE careful how you do so, for you will be judged by the very same criteria." – AO

. . . .

"If they judge then they're interested." – Cometan[886]

—*Ω—

OUR DEEDS ARE ALWAYS being recorded while in this material realm. From the first moments of our awareness as a child to the final moments of our material existence, it is the significant deeds that are presented as evidence during our final review upon the throne of judgment, the court of all knowing, as we pass from this world, through the universal consciousness of humanity and onto the supreme consciousness. Hopefully, it will be more lenient than the most critical judge of all – our own subconscious merging with our consciousness. Much of our judgement in the court of the afterlife is merely a realization of ourselves as we truly are – seeing without bias into the depths of our being. Upon leaving the physical body, the collective consciousness of humanity will judge us by the same methods we use to judge others. This notion is even stated in the *Bible* and the *Koran*; I leave it to you to find the relevant sections within those great scriptures.

• • • •

JUSTICE VS. REVENGE

Justice is punishment targeted at a wrong doer to prevent him or her from repeating a crime and as a deterrent for others considering committing the same or similar crimes.[887] It is an eternal principle and will always be served. If it is not achieved in this temporal existence, it will be in the spiritual realm. It is beneficial for those who commit sins and injustice in the temporal plane to mend their ways and seek redemption through future purity of action and thought. If they do not seek redemption, but continue their unacceptable ways, the punishment they endure will be much worse in the spiritual realm. The pain they have inflicted upon others will be felt with intensity when the time comes for their material form to collapse and their soul faces the onslaught of the universal mind.

Is justice just a sanitized form and a version of revenge? Both justice and revenge can serve to encourage the non-repeating of an affront to a society, a group or an individual. Justice, however, is eternal; revenge is temporal. Justice is a course of penal action taken to prevent the future repeat of detrimental acts. Revenge, on the other hand, is a course of action taken to satisfy a temporary emotional reaction to a perceived or committed detrimental act. Seeking revenge may provide a fleeting sensation of satisfaction, but it will soon dissipate and become wasted life energy. Revenge is an act of retribution (getting even); justice is a policy of deterrence (preventing it from reoccurring). One serves to preserve and maintain the whole, the other serves to destroy and shatter the whole.

The threat of revenge by the other party may thwart future retaliation, but it is fragilely dependent on the braver, wiser and more courageous party being willing to step out of and remove themselves from the escalation cycle. "Don't waste time on revenge. The people who hurt you will eventually face their own karma."[888] Any act of violence for the sake of revenge is an act of the lower self. It will only turn upon its originator as karmic forces always come back to their source. Remember, revenge is a temporary emotional satisfaction of an unhealthy ego; it will invoke a short-lived feeling of satisfaction and then leave us feeling even emptier after the act. Justice is a legitimate set of steps taken to prevent a future occurrence. It is much better to focus our efforts on justice, rather than on revenge.

Even though justice is sometimes not achieved in the secular of time, it is always achieved in the non-secular beyond time. Allah/God knows all, sees all, hears all and witnesses all. This concept is denoted several times in all true religious scriptures. Those who commit aggressive acts (i.e., murder, theft, assault) and believe they got away with it in the physical world will be faced with a dismal future in the non-secular realm upon leaving the containment of their bodies. They will no longer have the physical shell and framework of their material self to protect them from the pain and suffering they caused others through their deeds – all will come crashing in upon them. The all-knowing information from God on a person's life will be given to the Universal Consciousness of Humanity for the judgment of that soul. God will know if that soul deserves bliss, forgiveness, mercy or to be subject to torment and various degrees of Hell. Karma is perpetual and the level of a person's spiritual development will determine the freedom of their soul's movement in the non-secular world. Your degree of freedom in the next realm will be determined by your degree of moral integrity conducted in this realm.

You will be judged **not** by your belief in God or gods or how you choose to practice those beliefs, but by your words and actions upon others. Doing good works throughout your life is a common theme and uniting thread among the scriptures of how to create your Heaven. Good works include actions taken to relieve the misery of others through charity, kindness, compassion, mercy and tolerance within acceptable bounds. An objective of our existence is to leave the world a better place than how we found it.

The means used, the methods followed and its effects on others in the procurement of one's self-interest will all be considered by the divine jury. It is a jury that has all the knowledge of the Supreme Consciousness and Universal Human Consciousness at their disposal.[889] Those who abuse positions of power will have their abuses returned to them. Tyrants will be judged accordingly upon leaving this realm. One will be judged on how they treated those above and those below them within the military, political and corporate hierarchies. The effort put into the treatment of subordinates will have equal bearing as the effort put into dealings with supervisors. How supervisors treated their reports and how companies treated their employees through the coronavirus (COVID-19) pandemic which started in 2019/2020 has all been witnessed by the Universal Mind. It knows who respected the health and well-being of others and who did not. It also knows all those unsung heroes of the medical profession and health care industry who put themselves on the frontlines to minimize the pandemic's ravaging effects in order to save us and others.

There is a pool of emotional and intellectual consciousness from which we all formed – the Universal Consciousness. Upon our physical death, we re-enter this pool. It is within this massive gathering of human experiences that we re-encounter all the influences of our actions and words upon others. Swimming once again in this ocean of emotional waves, we become witness to either the pain or delight that we caused others to feel. We become aware and feel what others from our past felt due to our deeds. Others within this pool become witness to the reasoning behind our thoughts and actions. There is no escaping this onslaught of emotional experiences or a bodily shell to protect us from its gaze. We become permeable to all empathy. Depending on how we treated other beings and the world around us, this sea of emotional experience can either become our heaven or hell. This is why it so important for us to think of the treatment of others as the treatment of ourselves; karma is very real. Prior to meeting God, we will be judged by the universal consciousness of humanity on our civility towards others. In order to reunite with the consciousness of God upon our physical departure from the secular world, we must first pass through this universal consciousness of humanity. This is where the evidence is presented for the judgment of our souls. The final verdict and determination of our degree of freedom in the next realm is based on how we treated others, our relationships and how we interacted with the universe and our environment. The Derivative of Divinity's Consciousness will judge you by how you treated those who are different from you. Did you display healthy tolerance or did you lash out with hatred? Did you move forward through life by aggressively thinking only of yourself or with healthy ambition? God approves of ambition, but not of aggression. We will be judged not by the particular religious or spiritual path that we chose to follow, but by how we treated others while in this physical realm. A human should never be judged by another sentient being regarding the path they walk to interact with Allah provided it is a path of peaceful means and built with steps of love.

We are all the Universal Consciousness of Humanity's video cameras, constantly recording our intentions and actions, and the actions of others upon us. Every thought and how we handle them is saved onto the perpetual hard drive of humanity – a cloud of universal thought. In a sense, each of our lives are being recorded by the universal mind for future viewing and playback as evidence of our deeds. Think way back in your memory of when someone spoke to you, be they a childhood friend, a parent, a sibling, a grown-up or a teacher. Recall the scene and re-listen to what they said. As you tap into the memory, it is as if you can hear the sound of their voice internally within your mind as you watch the scene replay itself. These are the types of recordings that will be played back to you on your day of judgment as the Akashic records of your influence on the cosmos are retrieved from the archives.[890] The significant scenes will be the strongest noted for evidence on how you lived your life, how you treated others, and how they treated you.

We are all connected to the Universal Mind. When we leave our physical body at a secular death, all the filters are removed and all the gates and ports are opened. We become directly exposed to the ocean of knowledge of every other soul's deeds and actions, but we no longer have our physical bodies to protect us from this emotional tidal wave of thought. We are forced to confront and feel the emotions of others. For some it will be extreme euphoria and for others it will be unbearable pain, all depending on the intentions and results of our actions during our stay in the physical body. Jesus knew that the behavior and actions you present to others in the short term is really the behavior and actions that you present to yourself in the long term. This is one of the reasons why he felt sorry for the sinners, for he knew that they would have to endure the pain that they caused others to feel. Those who commit deeds and crimes against humanity will feel the pain of what they intentionally caused or could have prevented. The suffering, the sorrow, the anguish, the torment will be reflective back to them when they no longer have their material body to filter out the sounds of the cosmic consciousness. They will feel the pain and effects of what suffering they caused. This is the Karmic Law of the metaphysical universe. Imagine being confronted with the onslaught of all your past crimes coming back to you. Divine justice is very real.

We all have occasional thoughts which may be negative or questionable. It is how we deal with them and the intention behind any action that is important. Do we dwell on them and carry them into action? Or do we recognize their effect on our character and our potential for enlightenment? We must mentally rise above our negative thoughts to properly quench our desire to do harm to our karma and to the spirituality of others. It is still God that has the power to forgive all. The most merciful One knows when forgiveness is worthy and when it is not.[891] God can always change his mind.

The sages and prophets of the true religions will be with us upon the presentation of our deeds in the afterlife before the jury of the human consciousness and God. They will be serving on both the prosecution and the defense. Mohammad will be there presenting the evidence of every Muslim before Allah. Did they choose to serve in the advancement of their species through practicing tolerance and truth? Or did they allow their anger to cloud their spiritual eyes? Jesus shall be with every Christian seeing if they implemented and practiced the true intent of his teachings or whether they distorted his message for personal gain. For those who are truly on the path of enlightenment, all the prophets shall be with them upon full exposure to the Supreme Cosmic Consciousness. For one who is on the correct path understands the commonality of the message of love presented to humanity by all the great ones.

Those who distorted the true religions, using them as excuses for intolerance, justifying torture, murder and rape, will have to deal with the full wrath of God and the Universal Human Consciousness after their departure from this physical realm. Those who have committed crimes of horrendous magnitude will have the pain of those crimes reflected back upon them for all of eternity. The negative exploitation of another is not something that can ever be hidden from the universal recorder.

The litmus of a nation's development or a country's greatness is based on the degree of civil rights entitled to all its citizens and non-citizens and how it works to make its less-fortunate, more fortunate. The judgment of a society and its culture is directly correlated to how it treats, includes and attends to its members with special needs and to how it reforms those who violate civil laws. A civilization's level of enlightenment is measured by how it strives to find a meaningful livelihood for those with physical and mental variations and hindrances.

The intent of every action, every word and every thought are known to the divine consciousness. We are the witnesses for God in both our actions and the actions of others. Our reaction to external stimuli, our working through internal conflicts, our dealings with other beings, is all witnessed by this universal mind. The omniscient perspective of the divine consciousness is like a one-way mirror that views and records everything. At times, this mirror reduces is reflectivity to reveal the divinity behind it. These revelations have occurred to the true prophets of the past.

Those who perform deeds and actions of love will feel the joy that they gave to others. They will feel the hope and happiness that others felt because of their efforts no matter how small. Even if they do not see the results of their positive action, it will be reflective back upon them. Our intentions will always come back to us if not in this world, then in the next. Our behavior will be returned to us. What do you want to feel upon return to the eternal? That is something that you can determine while still here in your earthly existence.

• • • •

MERCY

There has been much talk of divine and karmic retribution but there is a cosmic loophole to receiving a pardon for the accumulation of sins. This loophole is true repentance. It was one of the messages that Jesus and Mohammad delivered to us. When we sincerely seek God's forgiveness, and not just because we were caught doing the negative act, then divinity has the option of granting mercy. Are we not allowed to judge God the same way he or she judges us? I would think that fairness between the mortal and the divine should be a universal law. Sometimes we need to forgive the universe for its actions upon us, just as it has often forgiven us. If one truly repents, and not just because their deed of negative exploitation was exposed, then divinity tends to show mercy. True repentance is something that comes deep from within ourselves and shows in our future actions with others and the world around us. Remember, Allah knows all our thoughts, all our intentions and how we deal with those who trespass against us. The Lord also knows if we have truly repented or are just putting on a false show. Mercy upon others is triggered when we default to a steady state of love. For even though we may have anger towards another for their negative actions, being able to see beyond the anger and provide mercy shows that we are in control of our persona. The greatest of leaders and prophets have implemented mercy when situations call for it. Remember, if we expect Allah to show mercy upon us then we need to show mercy upon others.

The showing of kindness onto those who have previously harmed or tried to harm us is a form of mercy. Showing kindness to a stranger who has done no harm to us is also a form of mercy. Showing mercy can be as simple as quickly dissipating our anger by defaulting to love when someone cuts us off in traffic. Yes, you will be mad at first but by quickly defaulting to love, you will prevent revenge and road rage from ruining your and someone else's future. We will be divinely judged by our behavior in traffic since that is a reflection of how we treat total strangers. When no one was watching except God, were we courteous or aggressive in our driving? Did we regress to a mindset of us against them?

Consider the parable of the Good Samaritan as told by Jesus in the *New Testament*. A lawyer asks of Christ how to inherit eternal life. Having the lawyer come to his own conclusion, Jesus leads him to recite the universal law of "loving God and they neighbor as thyself."[892] Jesus then responds with the timeless story:

"A certain man went down from Jerusalem to Jericho, and fell among thieves, which stripped him of his raiment, and wounded him, and departed, leaving him half dead. And by chance there came down a certain priest that way; and when he saw him, he passed by the other side. And likewise a Levite, when he was at the place, came and looked on him, and passed by on the other side. But a certain Samaritan, as he journeyed, came where he was; and when he saw him, he had compassion on him, And went to him and bound up his wounds, pouring in oil and wine, and set him on his own beast, and brought him to an inn, and took care of him."[893]

Jesus questioned the lawyer to elicit a response as to which of the three men was truly a "neighbor" of the injured person. Unwilling to utter the word "Samaritan", who were so despised by the Jews of that time period, the lawyer responded with "He that showed mercy on him." Jesus responded, "Go, and do though likewise."[894] When we approach a stranger, injured or otherwise, and depending on the surrounding environment and circumstances, our first instinctual reaction may be of fear, disgust, anger or hatred. It is normal to have thoughts of "If I show compassion and mercy upon this stranger, regardless of their background or ethnicity, will they turn on me with their own self-interest or with violence?" As we evolve and morph our core to a higher epiphany of enlightenment, our instantaneous reaction should become one of caution, but a willingness to assist.

Chapter 17
Addressing Violence Within The Scriptures

"UNDERSTANDING GOD IS easier than rationalizing the resulting human behavior." – AO

• • • •

THERE IS NO DENYING that stories of violence, statements expressing threats of aggression and words condoning the diminishing of civil rights do exist within some of the great scriptures and even more so among the ancient mythologies. The *Gita*, the *Old Testament* (aka *Septuagint, Tanakh*), the *Koran*, the *Book of Mormon*, and others present violence in their stories, punishments, and tales of tribulations, battles and wars. The difference between the *Bible*, the *Koran*, the *Gita* and other scriptures is not that one book teaches love while the other proclaims warfare and terrorism, rather it is a matter of how the works are read – it is the state of mind of the beholder. A few sections denoting violence should not taint the entire works.

To quote the eloquence of Phillip Jenkins' words in his March 8, 2009 article *Dark Passages*:

"... All faiths contain within them some elements that are considered disturbing or unacceptable to modern eyes; all must confront the problem of absorbing and reconciling those troubling texts or doctrines. In some cases, religions evolve to the point where the ugly texts so fade into obscurity that ordinary believers scarcely acknowledge their existence, or at least deny them the slightest authority in the modern world. In other cases, the troubling words remain dormant, but can return to life in conditions of extreme stress and conflict. Texts, like people, can live or die. This whole process of forgetting and remembering, of growing beyond the harsh words found in a text, is one of the critical questions that all religions must learn to address. ..."[895]

The first testament of the *Bible* is loaded with much more death, violence and torturous acts than the *Koran*, and whoever says otherwise should get their eyes and mind examined. Even Alex DeLarge, the fictional criminal gang leader in the 1971 movie *Clockwork Orange*, finds enjoyment in the violence within the *Bible* during his "rehabilitation".[896] There are far more verses praising or urging bloodshed in the *Old Testament* than within the *Koran*, and the biblical violence is often far more extreme and more savagely indiscriminate.[897] According to the historical accounts presented in the *Torah*, the ancient Israelites under a so-called "divine edict" massacred other nations not because those tribes were evil or treacherous, but because Moses and his lineage wanted more land, possessions and property. The *Koran* does urge its believers to fight, yet it also commands that enemies be shown mercy when they surrender. This is in direct contrast to the *Bible* which promotes genocidal massacres of the defeated. Mohammad wanted to win over his enemies, not slaughter them. Even the spiritual nourishment within *Psalms* is tainted by the line blessing anyone who would seize Babylon's infants and children and slam them against rocks.[898] Both the *Koran* and the *Bible* have had their texts manipulated and ransacked as a call to distortedly justify acts of murder.

The Abrahamic religions and the books of the *Old Testament,* with its stories of mass assassinations and sparing no one considered the enemy from butchery, appear to ooze with violence. If all the tales of conquers, rancorous wars and seemingly celebrated stealthy slaughter of whole nations be true, what do these scriptures tell us of Yahweh? He seems to have been a jealous and despotic tribal monarch showing fluctuating favoritism, rather than a being looking out for humanity's interest.[899] To believe in the literal factuality of all sections of the *Bible*, especially the slaughter conducted under the express command of the Almighty, should leave us in horror rather than in piety. If one is to believe in a moral, compassionate and loving Allah, then we must view the Old Testament writings as being under too much influence of early unevolved man's testimony, the ancient Israelites (or Babylonians) to be exact, rather than the revelations and desires of a Supreme Being or ultimate consciousness. The barbarity of the ancient Jews and their ancestors denoted in the *Tanakh* (the same books of the *Old Testament* but in a different order), could not have been the condoned works of a compassionate God nor his blessings upon his "chosen people."

—Λ*—

"Whenever we read the obscene stories, the voluptuous debaucheries, the cruel and torturous executions, the unrelenting vindictiveness, with which more than half the Bible is filled, it would be more consistent that we called it the word of a demon, than the word of God. It is a history of wickedness, that has served to corrupt and brutalize mankind; and, for my part, I sincerely detest it, as I detest everything that is cruel." – Thomas Paine[900]

—*Ω—

Anyone with spiritual critical thinking skills would see the early Moses as a prophet, but also later as a detestable and horrid villain who gives vengeful orders to butcher boys, massacre mothers and debauching of daughters (raping of girls).[901] Coming down from Mount Sinai, Moses went into a tirade upon seeing the golden calf (most likely made as homage to the Sun's movement through the constellation of Taurus), yet he later makes a graven image of a bronze serpent – hypocrisy of the Second Commandment at its worst?[902] Jeroboam, around the days of King Solomon, repeats the same thing that so upset Moses about 12 generations earlier – the making of golden calves in reverence to the Sun's zodiacal story.[903] The priesthood claims that the *Tanakh* hasn't changed since the 1st century – it is the same wording that Jesus encountered. Either we believe the authors' quotes of Moses within the *Book of Numbers*, or we don't. If one believes the Lord to be noble and benevolent, then the author(s) of the *Old Testament* have created many foundations of lies and blasphemous defilement – they were not fair, accurate or correct in portraying the Creator! Later on in the book of *2 Kings* of the *Old Testament*, we learn of the heads of executed children, teenagers and young men being carried in baskets outside of the city gates and left in two piles for all to see – 70 decapitations in total.[904] We then learn of Menahem's assignation of Shallum followed by his butchering and slicing open of all the pregnant women in the city of Tiphsah.[905] In the same *2 Kings*, we are told of Yahweh resorting to violence by sending bears to maul juveniles or young men that were teasing, cursing and mocking the prophet Elisha.[906] Perhaps God was protecting Elisha from a crowd that was beginning to become unruly and about to harm the prophet, but there are more effective ways to handle a mob than slaughtering them, especially by a being with the powers of the universe in his fingertips. The *Bible*, in particular, contains morally grotesque passages that seem to go against the very basis of ethical standards.[907] The condoning of mass murder (*Numbers* 31:16-18), praising of genocide (*I Samuel* 15:2-3) upon the enemy, acceptance of slavery as a norm of existence (*Peter* 2:18) and depicting the butchering of children and mass rape (*Isaiah* 13:15-16) seems very contradictory to what a well-adjusted and benevolent divine parent or guardian should be promoting. The Babylonian-Hebrew god even resorts to death by inguinal tumors or hemorrhoids and sentences capital punishment upon Onan for using *coitus interruptus*, rather than get his brother's wife pregnant.[908] The Hebrew testament prior to Jesus' arrival on the scene is riddled with stories of mass genocidal assassination, the butchering of men, women, children and the unborn with equal ferocity. I am not sure how apologetics of the *Old Testament* can circumvent such atrocities placed upon human life.[909] It is like stating despite Hitler's crimes against humanity, he did a lot of good for Germany. Needless to say, there are several other sections of violence within the older covenant books.

Racism and the desire for segregation, the exact opposite of healthy diversity, even extends its ugliness in the *Bible*. The tale of Phinehas, grandson of Aaron and a priest during the ancient Israelites' journey out of Egypt, shrewdly identifies the plague brought on by God's anger as being caused by a Hebrew interracially mixing with a Midian woman.[910] Phinehas then murders both of them simultaneously with a single lunge of spear, pinning their entrails together. I wish I could hear the perspective words of the murdered couple and wonder what their love story was. Were they husband and wife with children, a young couple in love, or a prostitute and her client? Modern racists cling to and harp on this passage and in 1990, Richard Kelly Hoskins used the story as the basis for his ideology of hatred in *Vigilantes of Christendom*. Hoskins advocated the creation of a new order of militant white supremacists, the Phineas Priesthood, and since then a number of groups have assumed this title, claiming Phinehas' violence as the justification for terrorist attacks on mixed-race couples and abortion clinics.[911] Ironically and ignorantly, Hoskins distortedly promotes anti-Semitism in his book, even though Phinehas was an early Jew.

So much of the *Tanakh* seems boringly focused on whose son was who, and what that son did or did not do. The book of *Ruth*, although about a country-girl Moabite woman "...creeping slyly in bed with her cousin",[912] is one of the few books of the *Old Testament* that is without mention of murder and rape. The book of *Job* seems out of place, being the first time the noun of "Satan" is even mentioned in the *Bible*, and it also lacks the stories of human treacherous besieges and cultural slaughtering of civilizations. Reflecting on the pressures of being human while enduring the vicissitudes of life, *Job* can be read without indignation or disgust, and almost presents God and Satan as competitive pals or playful cohorts. It contains advanced interactive dialogue, well-written prose, sarcasm and character development. The constellations of Pleides, Orion and Arcturus (the Great Bear) are mentioned, presenting evidence that the story of Job is of Hellenic origins, not Hebrew.[913]

The Abrahamic religions, in particular, contain phrases affronting the feminine qualities and menstruation with almost a perverse sexist fear rather than embracing its mystique. Statements exist condoning suppression of women by means of denying education and physical beatings.[914] This puts the God above the Goddess, rather than being on equal footing. The *Koran* even states that "men have a status above women", but was this truly the word of Allah or the influence and contamination of the scriber?[915] Despite such distortions and misinterpretations, Islam has a rich history of forgotten female leaders. Knowing of the Prophet Mohammad's love and respect for his older first wife Khadijah

bint Khuwaylid (aka Khadija), I can only believe that he would have promoted equal status. Mohammad's second or third wife, Aisha bint Abu
Bakr (aka Aisha), was extremely knowledgeable, inquisitive and had an
intellectual standing and religious authority that was extraordinary. She
was an Islamic scholar, an inspiration to champions of women's rights, a
military commander riding on camelback and a fatwa-issuing jurist.[916]
She significantly contributed to the spread of Islam and served the Muslim community for 44 years after the Prophet's death. She was highly regarded for her intellect and knowledge in various fields, including poetry and medicine.[917] Yes, she was a child bride of Mohammad and
antimuslim rhetoric and Islamophobics often tout her case as a means
to denounce this great religion, ignoring her epithet as "the Beloved of
the Beloved of Allah." Her rapid transference from the playground of
childhood to the silk gown of the bridal chamber was certainly a tragedy
based on financial and political influencers and should not be repeated
by any girl in these more modern and enlightened times. Since the days
of Moses, Isaac, King Solomon, Mohammad and Joseph Smith, we have
since learned the oppressive psychological damage and physical harm inflicted upon pre-adult brides.

There were other feminine Muslim luminaries such as Ummal-Dar-
da, a 7th century jurist and scholar who taught jurisprudence in the
mosques of Damascus and Jerusalem. There was Fatima bint Muhammad
Al-Fihriya Al-Qurashiya, who founded the oldest and still existing
award-winning University of al-Qarawiyyin in Fez, Morocco in 859.[918]
There was Fatimah al-Bataihiyyah, a 14th century Syrian scholar, who
taught both men and women in mosques in Medina, drawing students
from as far away as Fez.[919] These historical facts only go to show how
distorted the Taliban's interpretation of the *Koran* actually is in denying
the education of girls and women. The Taliban and Islamic State of Iraq
and Syria (aka ISIS, Daesh) have shamefully dishonored the Prophet
Mohammad. Women Islamic scholars taught judges and imams, issued
fatwas and traveled to distant cities. Some even made lecturing tours
across the Middle East.[920]

—A*—

"I know of no other religion in which women were so central in its formative history." – Sheikh Mohammad Akram Nadwi[921]

—*O—

Contaminated by humanity's limited perceptions due to the struggles and cognitive limitations of the time period, violent literal aspects of ancient scripture pertain and belong to the time period of their original writing and should remain there. These violent references provide a benchmark or reference from which to gage how far humanity has come in their spiritual evolution. True spiritual content, however, belongs to all ages. Sections seeming to condone violence are the exceptions and pertain to generations of long ago. Such statements of violence were a cultural product of their time and should not be used to reflect modern values. They are from the past of where we came from but they are not of the direction in which we are headed.

Certain scriptures have accumulated more passages of violence than others. Although there are statements of both peace and violence in the *Bible* and *Koran*, putting forth dualities that must be sorted through, as mentioned earlier in this chapter, there are many more phrases expressing violence in the *Bible* than there are in the *Koran*. Sometimes the passages are figurative, symbolic, metaphoric or literal, but in all cases, they are still portraying or expressing violence. Often times, such violent phrases of strife come out of every culture's and individual's right to defend themselves when physically attacked. We all have the right to defend ourselves to prevent physical harm or annihilation, but with restraint. Never be the initiator of violence; you have the right to physically defend yourself for self-preservation but not to escalate the affront. The objective is to minimize escalation, not to fuel it. Other times, those questionable passages relate to beyond reasonable forms of excessive punishment implemented upon individuals for violating a determined doctrine of acceptable societal conduct, such as the archaic treatment of those accused of committing adultery by having stones hurled upon them.[922] Methods of sacrifice, rules of ritual and civil law were often intertwined for denoting what seemed acceptable societal interplay during those time periods. Maybe such passages were placed there by God to test the free will of our moral resolve and discernment.

In truth, there are discrepancies in the ancient scriptures that defy spiritual logic and can even be considered satanic, such as cutting off the hand of a thief rather than reforming them.[923] Religious Distortion comes into play when particular passages are overly obsessed upon such as "Make war on them until idolatry shall cease and God's religion shall reign supreme."[924] A more extreme version of this same passage has been further distorted so say "So fight them until there is no more Fitnah (disbelief [non-Muslims]) and all submit to the religion of Allah alone (in the whole world)."[925] Whatever happened to focusing on "In the Name of God, the Compassionate, the Merciful" which starts every sūrah (chapter) in the *Koran* except for the 9th?

Slavery was once considered acceptable and the mainstay by cultured civilizations and denoted as permissible and common practice in the *Torah* (the first five books of the *Bible*), the *Old Testament* (the first 39 or more books of the *Bible*), the *New Testament* (the *Gospel*) and the *Koran*. Muhammad Ali, a famous heavyweight boxing champion in the 20th century, in reflecting on his reason for conversion from his prior religion stated that Christianity is the religion of slaves, while Islam is the religion of warriors. Yet early Muslims were often quite far down on the socio-economic scale and many were current or former slaves, women and those lacking tribal identity, giving them few protectors and subjecting them to oppression.[926] There seems to be a duality occurring here in the interpretation of the etymology of Islam's initial followers. Today, through divinity's continued influence, we have spiritually evolved and know that slavery and human trafficking is a heinous sin as it is an extreme negative exploitation of another.

In these modern times, passages expressing or feigning to condone violence within the true scriptures should be viewed as a reflection of an archaic age and a means to test the direction of our empathetic and moral compass. Do we agree with such violent statements and participate in their implementation or do we recognize there may be interpretive flaws and approach them with a cautious reflection? The Creator gave us a certain degree of free will and deliberately tests us with contradictory scriptural passages that call upon our critical thinking skills to sort through what is beneficial and what is detrimental. If we latch onto to those passages seeming to promote violence rather than those promoting compassion, tolerance and charity, then we have failed his test. If you focus on the text and words that promulgate violence, you will become evil and diminish your relationship with Allah. If you focus on the phrases that strive for peace and equality, you will become goodness and refine your relationship with God. This is a duality that exists within many of the great scriptures to train us how to handle our free will. The sustainment and advancement of a religion is based on the proper selection among its various elements. Remember, you are the sum of your thoughts and results of your actions. Choose wisely.

Coming to terms with phrases of violence within our scriptures requires our acknowledgment that the scribers were not always perfect in their written communication. Many of the humanity's languages were still evolving and morphing at the time of the compilation of those scriptures and there may not have been a broad range of accurate vocabulary to define a particular view, statement, expression or feeling. Modern day interpretations may not always be correct. This by no means diminishes the importance of such writings, but allows us to focus on those enlightened passages of goodness which contribute to the spiritual advancement of our being and of our species.

In practicing medicine today, would one follow all the passages from a medical journal written over 1000 years ago or even 200 years ago? When learning about the motional paths of planets, would one rely heavily on the use of a manuscript on astrology from 1400 BCE or on astronomy written in 1400 CE? Most likely one would prefer to rely upon neither antiquated reference. One would reflect on what statements are appropriate based on modern knowledge and which statements no longer apply. For example, having advanced in our medical knowledge and understanding of biologics, we no longer follow the once common practice of bloodletting, using leaches to remove supposedly harmful or "bad" blood from our system. Having advanced in our understanding of gravity and orbital mechanics, one should no longer cling to the belief that the Sun orbits around the Earth according to a geocentric model. This does not make the ancient medical journals or manuscripts on astronomy insignificant or any less important, but on the contrary, they should be cherished as necessary and valuable building block steps along the path to modern knowledge.

The Gnostic tends to view everything in scripture as allegory and figurative. The Orthodox tends to take everything at face value. Emphatically insisting that the *Bible* is verbatim to the thoughts and word of God and cannot be questioned, the Fundamentalists and Literalists neglect to consider that it was transcribed by the fallible minds of humans. Truth is, scripture often contains allegoric, figurative and literal elements and leaves it up to us to determine which are which as we make our spiritual journey. Often within the language of legal binding contracts, it is stated that if any section of the contract should become null and void, the rest of the contract still remains valid. So too, should our approach be to the passages within the ancient religious scriptures. Just because some lines or sections of scripture may not seem spiritually sound or seem contradictive to love, we should not negate the importance or positive messages found within the remainder of the scripture. If we disagree with 5% or 25% of what is written, do we throw out the remainder of a book? Although partial truths or inaccuracies found in scripture (or any manuscript for that matter) may cause us to question or review other sections with additional scrutiny, the remaining sections are still useful for advancing our connection with divinity. Rather than remaining chronological locked, perhaps modern spiritual texts should have the flexibility to be living documents (capable of updates), subject to corrections and to advance with our perception of God.

All the words of great religious books and texts should be treated with respect and reverence, but with the understanding that some of those passages condoning or seeming to condone violence were specific to the authors' reflections of the time period in which they were written and should no longer be literally applied today. There are outdated passages and phrases within certain archaic religious scriptures that are deemed, by today's level of empathetic awareness, inappropriate towards advancing humanity's spiritual evolution. Some are just plain wrong and flawed from today's advanced perspective, but the vast aspectual majority of the rest of scripture still have validity and merit. Jesus was well aware of such scriptural anomalies in the *Old Testament* when he presented the *New Testament* of God to humanity. He even challenged those outdated anomalies such as when he defended an accused adulteress and protected her from being struck to death with stones thrown from a hypocritical vigilante mob.[927]

We can accept that such phrases contradictory to love and condoning violence exist, but they should not become our focus. Whether the written passages were documenting history, venting human frustrations, or establishing cultural laws seemingly appropriate at the time for an early evolving species, does not make the rest of scripture any less meaningful on our path to God. The laws of humanity do not always coincide with the laws of God, especially with the treatment of children. Just because certain phrases or sentences in the *Bible*, the *Koran*, the *Torah*, the *Gita* or other religious scripture refer to something that may not be true, that no longer applies to the current time, or fails to properly deliver in depicting a dramatic metaphor, does not mean the rest of the text is obsolete. On the contrary, the commonality of catalyzing intertwining connections to divinity among the various religious scriptures is as timeless as their relevant passages that will continue to positively resonate for all of eternity – for one must first crawl before walking upright.

Noble nations often get caught in the duality of striving for peace by preparing for war – they need to be prepared to defend their existence and interests from threatening forces. They must be extra careful and extremely cautious when justifying the implementation of a preemptive strike in order to defend themselves. Is the plan to strike based on fear and frenzy, geo-political motivations or validated facts? Is the perception of an imminent threat being painted when the connecting dots are insufficient or conveniently arranged? Following the Prophet Isiah's and the Prophet Micah's proclamations and utopian hopes that "they shall beat their swords into plowshares, and their spears into pruning hooks; nations shall not lift up sword against nation, neither shall they learn war any more" can lead to being caught off-guard when aggressors decide to strike.[928] One finds that a well-trained and educated military is the final recourse of last resort for protecting a nation's identity, trade and citizens from the bullying and dominance of potentially invading or aggressive regimes. A noble and honorable military trains and prepares for violence, but does everything possible to avoid it. A highly skilled and technically acute armed force is more likely to be successful in battles and skirmishes than one based on soldier quantity alone. In congruence, the lives of a nation's warriors become more valuable due to the cost of their skill level training and less likely to be subjected to frivolous risks of glory missions destined for suicidal annihilation. The other option is to follow the participation requirements of a larger protective military leviathan (i.e., United Nations, NATO) and join its ranks. In doing so, the joining of a protective leviathan, the odds of a nation's continuance against a superior individual foe is increased. We can only hope that one day the adage of "in times of peace, prepare for war" can be outdatedly replaced with "in times of peace, engage in reawakening." There is no honor or glory in the killing associated with war. There is honor in defending a position, saving comrades, rescuing captives, capturing an enemy stronghold, but there is no honor in the act itself of killing.

Throughout history and during these current times of the 21st century, there have been good Christians and bad Christians, good Mormons and bad Mormons, good Hindus and bad Hindus, good Muslims and bad Muslims, good Jews and bad Jews, good Buddhists and bad Buddhists, so on and so forth. Most people are good; it is a small fraction who are bad. Due to the nature and swiftness of modern-day media, much more attention is given to the fraction of the populace committing criminal or heinous actions. The violence is not the fault of a true religion. It is the fault of a portion of its followers distorting and tarnishing the true religion to justify primal actions of their lower self. To derive a vile ideology of hatred and intolerance from the great scriptures is disrespectful of the religion and to the respective prophet(s). When acts of violence are committed under the guise of any religion, it is the responsibility of the religion's leadership, clerics and enlightened followers to call upon their higher selves in condemning and speaking out against such acts.

The *Bhagavad Gita* (aka *The Song of God*) is a 700-verse Hindu scripture that is part of the epic *Mahabharata*, and tries to address an approach to dealing with the killing of others when forced into war. Rather than going into detail on how it does this, I will let you read the *Gita* on your own. The pain, turmoil and destructiveness of going to war or into battle is obvious. In most cases, war can be avoided through diplomatic channels. In some situations, however, it becomes the unfortunate decisive approach of last resort when all means to peace have been exhausted.

—Δ*—

"When all other means have failed, it is just to resort to the use of the sword." – the Tenth Sikh Guru Gobind Singh

—*O—

Policies of invasions for the purposes of expansive conquest should be left to the annals of history. Wars are not started by the masses; they are started by those wielding levers of power. Wars destroy generational knowledge, erase pages from history, dissolve parental guidance, and the health of family structures as fathers, mothers, sisters and brothers are lost to its ravenous appetite for death and destruction. It creates lapses and voids to ancestral connections, destroys societal continuums and collapses infrastructure. Gaps occur in the developmental and mental health of young adults as they try to cope with losses of and during their childhood, resulting in their own later parenting skills being hampered unless they seek the proper counseling channels.

When humanity attacks each other in affairs of war, whose side does Allah take? When both sides site *Romans* 8:31 as their battle cry, whose side does God take? Krsna sided with the Pandavas because of their moral caliper and against the unrighteous policies of the Dhrtarastra.[929] Although the Lord takes the side of the most righteous, which may not always be the side that wins the battle, he mourns over the fact that they are fighting at all. How does a parent feel when their beloved children fight among each other? How does any loving parent feel when there is strife among the creations from their seed? They become angry, frustrated and sad at the same time, but will support the one who they believe is correct or most righteous. Parents seem to sometimes have eyes in the back of their heads, but they do not always have the privilege of knowing the truth. The Lord does not have this disadvantage and always knows who is righteous for the Supersoul, an aspect of ourselves connected with the godhead, knows all and witnesses all. God cries whenever his children resort to war and violence to settle their differences.

Organized religion has helped preserve culture through periods of peril and, at times, has also been used as a veil to condone violence. A reader or listener approaching the absorption of religious scripture through the eyes (mindset) of love will serve as an accelerant of morality, a beacon of caring and a conduit to divinity. Children by nature approach the world with a mindset of unconditional love. Remember, it was Jesus himself who said "unless you change and become like little children, you will never enter the kingdom of heaven."[930] Reading or approaching the scriptures through the eyes (mindset) of hatred and fear will only serve as an accelerant of intolerance, destruction and cruelty. Sound religious reasoning is dependent on the mindset of the beholder. The particular religious passages that take root in one's core are determined by the mindset of the reader. Whosoever exhibits violence upon the peaceful religious paths of others is insecure with their own path. Violence due to intolerance of religious differences is ignorantly used as a convenient façade, when the real culprit is often due to political, economic and ethnic tensions. Clashes of violence that occur under the guise of religious intolerances, when looked at more closely, are often rooted in cultural differences. Yet, intracultural and intercultural violence with regard to the nature of God is an abomination.[931] God is about love. Violent actions contrary to love is failing Allah. Religious covers may take the blame, but the underlying cause is usually cultural suspicion or overly scarce resources. Be cognizant and cautious not to confuse dysfunctional cultural practices, actions or superstitions as being that of a particular religion. The major difference between most people when there are clashes is due to circumstances. Circumstance is the component that triggers either interactions of cooperation or of confrontation. Cooperation is always the preferred path to be taken.

The oldest known evidence of written law dates to about 2400 BCE, about 600 years before the writing of Hammurabi's Code. Later, from the religious teachings of the *Old Testament* and sections of Hammurabi's Code for the region of ancient Mesopotamia, comes the simplistic archaic sanction of an unwanted action upon the victim triggers the same reaction upon the culprit: an eye for an eye, a tooth for tooth, and a wound for a wound. This approach eventually leads to the removal of all anatomy until there are no bodies left. Unfortunately, this same behavioral action/reaction relationship triggers violence for violence. As a species, the initiation of violence seems to cascade into more violence. Means to avoid the cascading of violence is not always clear, but they should always be sought out.

—Λ*—

"He who sees that the Lord of all is ever the same in all that is, immortal in the field of mortality – he sees truth. And when a man sees that the God in himself is the same God in all that *is*, he hurts not himself by hurting others: then he goes indeed to the highest path." – *The Bhagavad Gita*[932]

—*Ω—

We used to think that infants coming into this world and then becoming children were already mentally shaped by God or by other dark oedipal impulses. In this 21st century, we know much better that they are shaped by both DNA interactions and their environment's influence on those same protein molecules. We no longer view them as "mysterious creatures" driven by subterranean Freudian passions or the pure innocence of a divine hand. Biology has taken the reigns away from both psychology and theology, for better or worse. Rationality would say that all three (biology, psychology, theology) should come into play. If something goes wrong in a child's development, it was either because there was a glitch in the genetic coding or the synapses were not cultivated correctly. In either case, later application of medical and/or behavioral sciences may be able to provide a cure.[933] Much of child rearing centuries or even decades ago used to be based on the notion that a child must be physically subjected to mild torture for modifying behavior. Going back even further to the outdated and cruel punishments of the *Old Testament*, stoning an unruly son to death seemed the acceptable method of permanently ending the behavior.[934] Resorting to a literal translation later from the same scripture, "Whoever spares the rod hates their children, but the one who loves their children is careful to discipline them" was justified for implementing corporal punishment upon juveniles of all ages.[935] The rod came to mean any stick, whip, shaft, belt, paddle, branch, object, device or adult hand. The use of a spanking or slap today, much less than the rod, is considered a cop-out by parents too lazy to properly teach and borderline child abuse, especially when much more effective non-violent methods are available such as timeouts, instructional guidance and gentle lectures when emotions are calmer. How a human being is treated or disciplined as a child has a great influence on what type of adult they grow into.[936] Providing lots of unconditional hugs is one of the secrets to turning a child into a wonderful adult.

If you have children, then raise them by using constructive suggestion rather than punishing criticism. For criticism will plant fear, anxiety and resentment, rather than building love, confidence and affection. The same principle of constructive suggestion applies to how good officers, managers and supervisors should groom their troops, reports and subordinates. An employer will bring out the very best of their employees through training by constructive suggestion rather than by criticism. The same principle applies to the teacher-student or mentor-apprentice relationship.

Atrocities of the past committed under the guise of religion and for "honor" within humanity's infancy have been forgiven by God, and thus, we are to acknowledge and forgive them as well. Forgiving does not mean forgetting. When it comes to virulent ideologies, the misapplication of morality may have been the disease, but its correction will be the cure.[937] Finding ourselves empathetically squirming and cringing as we read or hear about eyewitness accounts of the horrors, anguish, misery and physical loss inflicted upon others in the course of violence, punishment and war, is all the more reason to implement reason and restraint of our lower self to prevent repeating similar escalations. Again, defaulting to a steady state of love is the best approach for stimulating reason to prevail over insanity. It prevents us from resorting to regrettable extremes and encourages reactions with more productive and less consequential approaches.

The *Bible*, the *Koran*, the *Bhagavad Gita* and other scriptures are mostly composed of words of love, but there are also expressions of violence and even plunges into the voids of hatred. Accepting this duality within their historical narration, our character is tailored by the statements we choose to focus on within these spiritual training manuals. Are we going to focus on love or hatred, kindness or violence? What type of person are we going to become? Is a scripture which mentions strife and violence 10% or 20% of the time and love the other 90% or 80% of the time about war or about peace? This book that you are now reading contains sections referencing acts of violence, but is it a manuscript for promoting violence? There are plenty of books that are not promoting or condoning violence, yet contain stories of violence, references to violent events or mention the topic of violence. Are the *Bible*, the *Koran*, the *Gita* or *The Book of Mormon* condoning violence or are they promoting peace? *Revelations On Interstellar Highway 10*, which mentions acts of violence among several of its paragraphs, is it a book about violence or is it about peace? Is it condoning hatred or is it promoting love? Likewise, many scriptures discuss and mention acts of violence, but they are not necessarily promoting their continuance. They are merely providing the pole, setting a benchmark from which peace can endure.

Unfortunately, violence has been a hurdle in humanity's evolution. The great scriptures are full of instances either discussing or condoning attacks from or upon others. Methods of severe punishment (such as capital punishment for adulterers) are mentioned for civil crimes that would be considered miniscule by today's standards in progressive societies.[938] Many of the references to violence within the scriptures were speaking to a specific people, at a specific time period, and a specific geographical region. Passages and phrases seeming to accept or condone mutilation, genocide, pogroms, rape, slavery, slaughter, pillaging and the razing and destruction of population centers, is an unfortunate part of our behavioral evolution that needs to be acknowledged and then left behind in the pages of history. Choosing the other pole of the duality, one can choose to seize on any available word or verse that authorizes violence, but once someone has decided to do that, it scarcely matters what the text or the rest of the scripture actually says.[939] The violence and affronts to civil rights that were present in a portion of the old great scriptures of our ancestors are from the direction from where we came, but they are not the direction in which we are headed on the path of our spiritual maturity. Our species' compass points to a much more distinct, favorable and lasting future. We must, however, apply reason and spiritual logic to sort through what scriptural passages are to remain in the past and what passages are to be timeless.

Chapter 18
Our Exit From This World

"OH GREAT CREATOR, GRANT me as healthy and as long a life as possible so that I may grow to a worthy level of illumination through the gathering of knowledge, the implementation of wisdom and the spreading of joy." – Prayer Of The Mortal, AO

• • • •

LIFE IS A JOURNEY OF both planned and unexpected destinations in which we are always aware of the running clock of our physical mortality. The desired destination of our journey is the same for all of us but how we get there is customized and unique to each of us. Every night we go to sleep and count on the Lord to let us wake up the next morning. Learn how to embrace and surf this beautiful ticking wave called life. Enjoy the ride instead of thrashing against it. Make it the greatest wave you ever rode to shore. Eventually, it will crest and break as it blends and fades upon the beach sands of death, releasing your energy to coalesce again unto eternity. We may not have known enough of or been aware of God during our physical existence, but we have certainly encountered sensorial glimpse into his and her presence.

• • • •

THE FOLLOWING QUESTIONS are for you to reflect upon and the answers may vary.

1) Do we have souls and a part of our essence that continues after death?

2) If we do, are we the only creatures that have one?

3) Do other animals (e.g., apes, dogs, cats, rodents, horses, mules, cows, pigs, chickens, deer, fish, dolphins, whales and single cell organisms) also have souls?

4) Do any plants have souls?

5) Do creatures and intelligent beings from other planets, if we should ever encounter them, have souls?

6) Is the soul's state of evolution and degree of containment dependent on the complexity of a creature's brain and nervous system?

7) Does one need to be an advanced intelligent sentient being to have a soul?

8) Does part of our soul ever come back again within a living being in the material realm?

9) Is our physical departure from this world simply a vacuum of oblivion or is it a threshold into a non-corporeal existence?

* * * *

IF THE ESSENCE OF OUR existence is truly finite with nothing else occurring after our death other than the decay and dissolution of our bodies, then the numerous religions of our planet are meaningless propaganda. Sir Arthur Conan Doyle's devotion to finding and producing evidence of an afterlife would then be judged a farce.[940] Our sentience would be nothing more than a temporary blip in the vastness of space and time; insignificant anomalies of consciousness that come and go in and out of existence similar to the spontaneous bursts and fades of elementary subatomic and virtual particles in an ephemeral brew. Existence seems to be based on only what can be seen with our eyes or measured with our instruments. But are those particles existing and then non-existing, or are they just passing through our realm on their way to others?

Do they only exist when our measuring instruments made of matter say so? Is existence based solely on qualitative references? When whales surface into our realm of air and field of vision, we say they exist because our eyes see them and our ears hear them splash. But when they submerse below the waves, back into their usual realm of below sea level, do they no longer exist because we don't see them? Do elementary subatomic and virtual particles not exist before they enter and after they exit our realm? Does consciousness not exist because the associated body is no longer operating? It requires instruments made of matter to measure matter and it would require instruments made of spirit to measure spirit.

The universe has a habit, a *modus operandi*, of recycling its physical constituents. The fragments from the death of an exploding star often become the building blocks of new stars and planets. Atoms and molecules are re-used when one form of creation breaks down to form another. Why shouldn't the universe also do the same recycling with consciousness and thought? If we can learn to identify ourselves more as consciousness than as body, perhaps that is the way to put an end to death. To believe our consciousness is just temporary biological micro circuitry seems almost nonsensical. According to thermodynamic laws, matter and energy cannot be created nor destroyed, but they can alter between forms. It seems only logical that just as atoms and molecules are recombined, so too, then should we expect developed consciousness to be reused as it alters form for continued use. Awakening to the perspective that our essence is eternal, being birthless and deathless, we can become learned and overcome the delusion of an absolute death. Therefore, this physical realm alone that we currently reside in is not the ultimate reality; it is just our present temporal state.

Within a lifetime, we cross paths with relatives and acquaintances during our daily existence. Some will be very close or become good friends, maintaining bonds travelling parallel with our timeline. Others will fade as our paths diverge due to changes in schools, jobs, geographical locations or life circumstances. One of the greatest challenges of living is overcoming a fear of death. It is this fear that prompts us to religious and spiritual exploration.[941] Facing and overcoming our mortality is an ultimate test of our faith. We should by no means hasten our materialized undoing, but strive to reasonably prolong our existence in order to add as much goodness into the world as time allows. In the natural approach to our own demise due to aging, it is not the fear of death that dominates, for death is but the passing into the speculative unknown. It is the approaching steps that can trigger concern. It is the fear of loss – loss of loved ones, loss of friends, loss of independence, loss of finances, loss of hearing, loss of sight, loss of hair, loss of teeth, loss of memory, loss of faculties, loss of mobility, loss of mind and loss of control. To manage these losses, incorporating and commingling new achievements, no matter how small, is imperative to extending our contribution to the world while still in this physical realm. In the heartbreak of loss, it is the comfort of fresh gains and new desires which propels us forward until the time of our reunification with God. We should certainly do everything reasonably possible to avoid death, but it seems that part of the conditions for being alive is that we have the chance of leaving this world by means of a premature or painful demise, be it from violence, accident or disease.[942] We continually move forward with life while knowing that death hangs over us like the Sword of Damocles, possibly striking us down at any moment. Upon accepting this duality of existence without apprehension, acknowledging the impermanence of the items we will lose along the way but recognizing the permanence of the items that will always be a part of us, we can better focus on striving for a life of achievement. The more we dispel our fear of death, the more courageous we can be to the beauty, wonderment and joy of living.[943]

—Δ*—

"With my feet, benumbed in death, shall warn me that my mortal course is drawing to a close – Merciful Jesus, have mercy on me! When my eyes, dim and troubled at the approach of death, shall fix themselves on thee, my last and only support – Merciful Jesus, have mercy on me! When my ears, soon to be shut forever to the words of men, shall be opened to hear your voice pronouncing the sentence of my irrevocable doom – Merciful Jesus, have mercy on me! When I shall have lost the use of my senses; when the world shall have vanished from my sight; when my agonizing soul shall feel the sorrow of death – Merciful Jesus, have mercy on me!" – Saint John Bosco[944]

—*O—

In our youth, we are trained and educated to deal with a world beyond childhood sandboxes and elementary schoolyards. Yet, how many of us reach our later years without the proper schooling for death and eternity? As doubting mortals, how do we vaccinate ourselves from the fear of death and the unknown beyond? Encountering and addressing the anxieties, unknowns and questions associated with our own future passing can be daunting. Are we going to feel pain and suffering in the initial and final stages of our death? Will we be aware of the progressive failure of our organs during our transition into the deceased? If so, how long will we need to endure such final anguish? Will those loved ones that we leave behind such as family and friends adjust properly without our physical presence? Does everything within our mind just go blank and cease or do we fall into a universe of our own thoughts as we cross over the threshold between life and death? Has there been meaning to our life and will there be meaning after our death? Will the account of our life be limited to the synopsis placed in a necrology or will it amount to something much beyond those words? Is death all about loss, extinction and endings or is it about new beginnings, a continuum of our identity and purpose beyond the physical realm? We know our physical body is temporary, but is there an aspect of our individual self that continues beyond this material realm? Does our individualism and the uniqueness of our essence somehow exist beyond the expiration of our corporeal containment vessel? Do aspects of our essence ever reemerge in other future living beings? If so, what happens in between those incarnations as we wait in the divine lobby or antechamber? Many religious paths provide responses to these question or stories of related occurrences among those with true relationships with divinity. Although we may not fully comprehend how, our life here and our death afterward are inextricably interwoven in a complementary interplay.[945] Being a mere seeker of pleasure will leave us unfulfilled in old age, but the pursuit of an internal philosophy, objects of the mind that can lead and accompany us all the way through life, will be the very constant that propels us without fear unto and past death.

—Λ*—

"I do not fear death. I had been dead for billions and billions of years before I was born, and had not suffered the slightest inconvenience from it." – Mark Twain

• • • •

"IMMERSED IN THE WONDER of Tao, you can deal with whatever life brings you, and when death comes, you are ready." – *Tao Te Ching*[946]

• • • •

"WE ARE THE TRUTH THAT rises from earthen materials made in the kilns of stars, our core becomes embodied in the folds of our brain, and then our soul is wooed back into divinity's graceful embrace." – Paul Weiss[947]

• • • •

"LIFE AND DEATH ARE one, even as the land and the sea are one. One is determined by the border of the other." – AO

—*Ω—

Life is like a musical composition; the pages of sheet music symbolizing the actions and experiences of our existence. The melody of our life story consists of millions of notes and rests. The very first note is your birth and the very last note is your death. All the notes and rests in between are the memories of both the lows and highs of your life. Each of us is destined to finish our composition with the same final note; the exiting out of the gate of time and re-entering eternity.[948] This physical finitude is the natural order of things and the last and final note upon ending our life's composition. It is our exit from space-time upon death to re-enter eternity and the mirrored pole of our entrance at birth from eternity and into space-time. However, don't be focused on the final note; be focused on the whole composition, the paneurythmic expression that comes before it – continue your music and song as long as physically possible before the curtain closes.[949] Death is merely the ending point of our material existence among the many points of our life, the discarding of our worn-out corporeal vessel, the dissolution of our mortal framework, and the "event horizon" prior to releasing our soul to recombine into and with the immortal alternate realms of existence.[950] Knowing of our physical mortality and that it is death that ends our life in this realm, is all the more reason to cherish the moments of our materialized existence and strive for a life of productive goodness. There is no guarantee that you will finish out this day alive, nor that you will be alive tomorrow. Recognizing this, we pray that our death will not be premature, untimely, inconvenient or unnatural. When you were born, you were crying and those around you were smiling. Live your life so that when you die, you are the one who is smiling and everyone around you is crying. When you have lived a good life, others will reflect upon it and want to emulate your symphony.

—A*—

"Thine own consciousness, shining, void and inseparable from the Great Body of Radiance, hath no birth or death." – *Tibetan Book of the Dead*[951]

• • • •

"TO BE ABLE TO LOOK back upon one's life in satisfaction is to live twice." – Kahlil Gibran[952]

• • • •

"Love is eternity." – AO

—*O—

SHOULD ONE'S DEMISE be due to the predictable malfunctioning of the body as natural decline takes over, will we accept our departure with stoic pretense, regrets, self-pity, resentment or enthusiasm? Knowingly approaching our final breaths, will each of us be able to face our last moments with curiosity and a virtuous state of mind? Will our final days of bodily awareness be spent feeling anger and bitterness or will we dwell in a reflective state of contentment and love? Relying on the vitality of the spirit, I would prefer the latter. During the final phases of a natural departure due to aging beyond our mental and physical faculties, we can only hope that we do not become a prisoner within our bodies nor feel like we are being incarcerated from society just for being old. It was Plato who wrote, "I have heard from the wise that we are now dead and the body is our tomb."[953] Ideally, we want to live to the very last moments with the feeling that we are a person-patient in a home, not fading away as a prisoner-patient in an institutionalized asylum for the sick. As we become more dependent on others and if we should ultimately end up in eldercare, our greatest desire is for minimizing sacrifices to our autonomy, remaining the authors of our lives and the shapers of our story no matter what circumstances we encounter – to have a sense of purpose and meaning to the very end of our time in this realm and to be able to use the restrooms on our own accord to the final days.[954] Having achieved old age of a life well lived, death should not be viewed as an enemy. Encountering decline and death in one's youth, however, can seem unfair, unjustified, unconceivable and a mistake made by the universe. In both cases of an age natural or a premature death, relying on faith that there is a divine plan in place for all of us is what can provide a degree of comfort and conciliation. In essence, it is the view of the Cathars that upon separating and leaving the body, it is then when we finally "wake up" to the greater reality – death is not the end, it is the graduation and the release.[955]

In our descent from God after birth, we formed our personalities for interacting within a corporeal material realm. With our ascent back to God after death, we will rediscover our own true nature and the vastness of our spiritual heritage.[956] Referring to our existence as a life cycle, an Ouroboros of continuation, it puts forth the notion that there are stages to pass through in a circular loop of repetition. Conception provides the threshold for life to enter through the doorway of birth while death provides the egress to the doorway of beyond, as we ask ourselves, how many times have we worn out the cloak of our human form? How many times before have we shed our bodily shell upon reaching a state of frailty? How many times have we displayed a temporal covering, a corporeal sheath, a recyclable container? Upon exiting the world, has my soul finally ripened to the point of becoming omniscient, omnipotent, omnipresent and omnibenevolent with God amidst the ultimate reality of the next realm?

—Λ*—

"Revolving around the wheel of necessity, the psyche is transformed and confined at different times in different bodies."– Pythagoras[957]

—*Ω—

Our time in this physical realm is limited, so therefore, use such time wisely. Do not waste it on non-productive quests based on revenge, envy, spite, getting even with someone who disrespected you or deliberately inflicting violence. Do not be overly concerned with speculating the afterlife or what lies beyond this material realm. Be concerned with your current life. Your life choices and actions are about preparation for the next phase of existence. Allocate energy and effort on improving the here and now of your sphere of influence. Physical death will arrive upon all of us in due time when the core/soul is let loose from the body, and hopefully, not at an inconvenient hour and as far away from a significant holiday or close relative's birthday as possible.

—Δ*—

"Wake up, O sleeper, rise from the dead, and Christ will shine on you. Be very careful, then, how you live – not as unwise but as wise, making the most of every opportunity, because the days are evil." – New Testament[958]

—*O—

Suicide due to emotional pain and anguish is a final act of violence upon oneself. There may be times in one's life when all hope is lost and the emotional pain or intense emotional void tempts one to leave this world prematurely. An enormous sense of unworthiness, loss or failure may become so overwhelming that it taunts our minds to move forward with a plan to cease our own physical existence. When encountering such thoughts, in addition to seeking professional counseling help, there are some basic things to consider:

1) Taking one's own life leaves an impressionable permission slip for younger family members and relatives to also take their own lives. Do you really want to encourage suicide among your children, and younger nieces, nephews or cousins?

2) Taking the dualistic approach, you are either alive or dead. If you are not dead, then just allow yourself to float through such times of despair, continuing your existence, hour by hour and day by day. Eventually a new purpose will unfold, revealing and providing meaning for continuance.

3) Grasp on to the notion that although all hope may seem lost among the emotional toil of unworthiness, the condition is temporary. You don't know how your state of affairs will be next year or the year after that.

4) Focus on helping others. Small acts of compassion can trigger a desire to do more, both for ourselves and others.

If you ever should enter into a state of mind where suicide is your final concluded way out, then your last and final act should be reaching out to an expert counselor and explaining your reasons. Taking one's own life, however, may have merit in situations dealing with a terminal illness which leads to extreme pain, suffering or loss of our cognitive awareness. The notion of being in control of the timing of one's death rather than succumbing to the ravages of such illnesses can provide the bearer with a dignified sense of conclusion on their own chronological terms. By remaining the author of one's life to the very end and determining how final circumstances will be handled, places death in our control and not to the whims of fate.

Upon such time of our physical death, we will encounter judgment and reunification with the radiance of God's love, the level of which will be determined by the outcome of our review. The Almighty may love each and every one of us, but we still have to earn the rewards of heaven. Each of us will either ascend and intertwine blissfully into the great expanse of the divine consciousness or descend into a painful isolated oblivion. The degree and duration of which will be determined by the gross sum of a lifetime of behavior and actions, some of which will have a greater influence than others. The direction you go is dependent on which side of the threshold your moral fulcrum resides due to the accumulation of your acts and deeds while in this realm. Just as there are various levels of hell and heaven in this realm, so too, are there various levels in the next. As you teetered between the duality of goodness and evil during your physical existence, does your net accumulation leave you deserving of eventual bliss or eternal pain in the next realm? Is it going to be heaven, hell or a bit of both?

—A*—

"Yes", replied the voice of Osiris, "many perish in the fatal descent. The soul is the daughter of heaven, and its journey is a test. If it loses the memory of its origin, in its unbridled love of matter, the divine spark which was in it and which might have become more brilliant than a star, returns to the ethereal region, a lifeless atom, and the soul disaggregates in the vortex of gross elements." – *Poimandres*[959]

• • • •

"DELIVER US FROM THESE human forms and re-clothe us in light among the stars." – Syrian Nosairi prayer[960]

—*O—

As symbolized by the trinity denoted within the Asterox's geometry on the front cover, our body is a finite shell of which we shed from life to life – the triangle. Our soul is the part of us that waxes or wanes, grows or diminishes, expands or contracts, depending on our behavior in these entry level realms – the circle. Our spirit is the eternal part of ourselves that continues from realm to realm, giving us perpetual opportunities to remerge with the godhead and thus achieving the Eastern notion of enlightenment – the center starburst. Focus on this life, not on what comes next. For in this physical plane, we are under the bondage of time but in the spiritual planes, there is access to the liberties of eternity. The beauty and precious moments found in this world will still be experienced in the next, but without the agony of their eventual passing. For your degree of freedom, planes of existence, states of being and boundaries of enjoyment encountered after physical death will be determined by your behavior and actions upon others in this realm. It is reciprocally proportionate to the degree of aggression and negative exploitation that you expressed upon others. If you do not conduct yourself in this realm in a manner that is respectful of all sentient beings, you will be denied privileges in the next realm. Your degree of freedom in the next realm will be determined by your degree of moral integrity conducted in this realm. Your advancement and choices in the next realm of existence are dependent on your actions and empathy towards others in this one.

—Δ*—

"Those who sow in winter reap in summer. Let us sow in the world to reap in summer. Winter is the world, summer is the other realm." – *The Gospel of Phillip*[961]

• • • •

"A MIRROR DOESN'T REFLECT your soul. All that it is does is show you're getting old." – AO[962]

—*O—

Our postmortem will be a transfer through portals between this world and the next; a journey into the next realm of existence as we become part of an infinite being in an infinite universe. Physical death is but a complete reunification with the universe's mind – a dimensional transition beyond the normal cognition of our physical existence. Just as we go through various stages in life (e.g., newborn, infant, toddler, preteen, adolescent, young adult, full adult, middle age, senior),[963] there are also various stages of abeyance, exposure, growth and evolvement in the afterlife. According to the spirit of Sir Arthur Conan Doyle, it averages about 30 solar years after death to pass through the astral, mental and celestial planes to fully merge again with the sphere of God.[964]

From *The Sophia Teachings*, those at the lowest levels (the *hylics* or *somatics*) have their etheric essence start to re-enter with the Supreme Consciousness within about three days after death and those closest to Christ (the *pneumatics*) can delay their re-entrance start to a little over 40 days after the physical departure.[965] The fact that you are even reading this book means that you are above the *hylic/somatic* levels and your re-entrance can be delayed to start somewhere between 3 to 40 days after death.

When our physical bodies release our core as we leave our containment vessel behind, our souls will be open for judgment by all. While passing into the next realm and directly encounter the glory of God, he/she will say "Come forth, for I am the God of all true paths." There will no longer be any hiding of our deeds as we pass from our physical existence into the astral planes – we will all face the fruits of our past life.[966] Ascending through various stages of the afterlife, one is confronted with who they really are and how the lives of others were affected by their words, actions and deeds. Our personal contribution towards the divine essence's evolving plan of loving creation will be gaged.[967] We will not be judged based on what particular religious path we followed, nor on whether we believed in Allah or not. For God welcomes the multitude of true paths used to reach him. All will be judged according to how we treated others based on the circumstances and given the resources available. Our judgment will be a tally of how well we considered the needs of others in balancing the needs of our own. As a figurative representation; our soul will provide the evidence, it will be presented by the observing angels and demons of our lifetime, reviewed by the jury of the universal consciousness of humanity that will determine our verdict, Jesus and Mohammad will serve as bailiffs, Allah and Abatur will oversee as judges in the court of Osiris, and Thoth will establish who is deserving of a degree of heaven.[968] God has the ultimate authority to pardon our sins or declare a mistrial in the judgment of our souls. Remember, the Lord has absolute, unlimited and universal cognizance. It is much like a boomerang effect, where our actions and deeds committed in this realm are returned upon us in the next realm. Some will be praised and others will be demolished. Our essence will either be expanded or diminished, exposed to grace or punished with pain according to our deserving. When appropriate and genuinely warranted, God/Allah also grants mercy upon souls for their abominations.

—Λ*—

"Man shall on that day be told of all his deeds, from first to last. Indeed, man shall bear witness against himself, plead as he may with excuses." – *The Koran*[969]

• • • •

"HE HAS KNOWLEDGE OF all your thoughts and actions...God has knowledge of all things." – *The Koran*[970]

• • • •

"TO THOSE WHO COMMIT evil through ignorance, and then repent and mend their ways, your Lord is forgiving and merciful." – *The Koran*[971]

—*Ω—

Our souls can be subject to pleasure and pain in both this realm and the next. The degree of which of each is dependent on many factors, such as the weight of the good deeds compared to our bad deeds that become grafted into our life story. Heaven and hell are very real, but rather than being places of existence, they are states, planes and degrees of existence. Entering into one state of existence or the other is based on our actions and behavior during our lifetime. We are not sent to heaven nor condemned to hell by others, it is our own doing or undoing that determines our destination. Hell, however, is not just a prison. It is also a training ground for rehabilitation, always giving us the opportunity to re-enter the track back towards enlightenment. God's love is unlimited, but before we can enter into his/her expanse of love in the afterlife, we must first pass through the Universal Consciousness of humanity for judgment. This is where the evidence is presented for the judgment of our souls. Jesus was well aware of this exposure of all our deeds, both good and bad, as he conversed with those (the two criminals, thieves or robbers) being crucified adjacent to him.[972] Acting as a jury of our peers, this consciousness is what determines and grants our degree of freedom and continuation or annihilation in the next realm. The final verdict and determination of our degree of freedom in the next realm is based on how we treated others, our relationships and how we interacted with the universe and our environment. Our reward in the next realms, based on merit, will be the options of eternal spiritual rest, to participate in the continuation of material creation, or proportions of both.

For those who have committed deliberate grievous sins and extreme acts of negative exploitation, there will be an onslaught upon them of all the pain and suffering that they inflicted upon others. Their rendezvous with the afterlife will be torturous, but it is not a punishment inflicted by God. It is a return of that in which they sowed while in the physical realm – the shame for deeds of negative exploitation. They created the harshness of their next realm due to their actions within this world upon others. Without physical bodies to shield them, their souls are fully exposed and immersed in both the emotional and physical pain that they intentionally produced upon others during their time in this physical state of existence. The murderer, the rapist, the hardened criminal and other responsible perpetrators will feel all the pain and trauma inflicted upon their victim as well as the emotional pain felt by those mourning for the victim. What they will feel and encounter in the next realm could be described as demons gnawing and feasting upon their essence. It will be a self-induced quagmire of never-ending frost filled with stinging insects and biting snakes.[973] How long the feast of anguish lasts is up to God.

For those who have lived as righteous life as possible given their circumstances, when passing away from physical existence and into the next realm, spiritual guides and familiar beings (i.e., family and friends who passed before us) will be encountered who will surround them with love, happiness and acceptance. Returning home to the loving embrace of our universal mother and father, they will feel all the pleasure they brought to others while in the physical realm and will come to know the past, present and future while merging back with God. Their reunification and rendezvous with God and loved ones will be a celebration, for all good things pass through the "Summerland" on their way to Nirvana and all the realms exposing us to ultimate bliss and infinite knowledge. When a loved one passes on to the next realm, there is a duality of adjustment occurring among those still remaining in this realm. There is the grieving and mourning process for the felt pain of our secular loss with an underlying celebration for the departed's returning to the Beloved. We will miss encountering their physical presence, their in-person spoken words and expressed thoughts, but the influence they had upon us will always remain. The duality of undergoing proper grieving is part of the human experience. Denying the honest feelings of anger and frustration with the universe for the removal of a loved one from our world, for creating a loss and undesired change in our lives and routines, will only cause internal destruction. We must grieve, to healthily mourn, before we can heal. We will feel sorrow and unhappiness in this realm, since now we must endure a wait time before encountering them again in the next realm. With the acceptance that the departed has returned to the loving embrace of God, that they have meshed again with the universal consciousness, we will encounter them upon our own future re-meshing. The greatest prescription of addressing grief and sorrow is to eventually allow for the cathartic surrendering of our mind to the notion that time, eternity, love and God are inseparable – a trust that there is an underlying grace and meaning to the universe.

Proper psychic hygiene calls for the embracing of death coming in our old age with the same willfulness that we embraced life in our younger years – either state is to be engaged with a certain readiness of excitement. Life is a series of known transitions; death is the unknown transition based on a promise between us and the Creator. At birth we exited the subconscious and upon death we shall re-enter it in a cyclical continuum. When someone of a young age passes, there is additional remorse for a life unfulfilled and what they could have offered society. We may try to understand the universe's reason for removing an infant, child or young adult from our world too soon, but trying to make sense of the pain of such a loss can become unfathomable due to our limited secular perception into God's insight. Because of our limitations, submitting to Allah's will, however difficult it may be, and praying for internal healing can provide a source of cathartic release, alleviation, solace, grace and hope. Processing incrementally through various cyclical parameters of adjustment, such as the theoretical Kübler-Ross model and others, can help us to mend ourselves through grief.

—A*—

"When the wise knows that it is through the great omnipresent spirit in us that we are conscious in waking or in dreaming, then we go beyond the boundaries of sorrow and death." – *The Upanishads*[974]

—*O—

Each of our final judgments will not be based on which religion we belong to, which path we travelled or which traditions that we followed, but on how we interacted with others and our environment throughout our lifetime. Upon becoming a ghost, the ghosts of past relationships will either come back to haunt or to praise us. What we conjured within ourselves in this realm is what we will carry into the next. We bring our baggage, both the good and bad, home with us for sorting through upon returning to the Lord's mansion. Immortality has to be earned and not freely given, an unpleasant but perhaps necessary reality to encourage one's duty of personal and collective betterment.[975] The nature of our essence in the next realm is based on our conduct during this realm. Simply put, were we kind to others who were the same and/or different than us? Did we respect the world around us and treat it with dignity? Did we minimize our negative exploitation of the universe or introduce severe abominations? The answers to these questions determine our degree of freedom and the intensity of our existence in the next realm. We get graded on our behavior during our existence in the physical world. The better the score, the greater the continuation of our essence, the rewards, the prizes and available options in the next realms as the story of our essence continues. Both the Gnostic and the Orthodox would agree that our life here is not about the material, it is about spiritual schooling for graduating to higher levels. Their disagreement lies in which course of study is best to follow for achieving a diploma of gnosis. Wouldn't you love to go back to High School and relive those days with the wisdom, confidence and knowledge that you have now, rather than with the awkwardness, insecurity and uncertainty that you had then? That is why some souls choose to reincarnate – to go back to the school of life again in hopes of being a better student and learning more. Some will choose to relish and remain in the heavenly bliss. Others may eventually become "bored" and choose to fully or partially return to repeat another temporary existence, leaving the ether of higher realms and reconstituting within the womb of another woman, thus starting a new sequel in the physical world. This material world is not a cage, a punishment or a prison, it is a training ground, a boot camp and an education in which to develop our morality, compassion and our better Self.

—Λ*—

"At the end of the game, pawns and kings go back into the same box."

– Italian proverb[976]

• • • •

"DON'T CRY BECAUSE IT'S over, smile because it happened." – Dr. Seuss[977]

—*Ω—

Chapter 19
The Twins Of Science And Religion

"THE MARRIAGE OF SCIENCE and religion is not a sacrilegious affair." – AO

• • • •

THE GRAECO-ROMAN PERIOD and through the Middle Ages firmly grasped onto the concept of a person's core (soul) as being real both in substance and development.[978] At various times, especially during the Dark and Middle Ages and even trickling well into the Renaissance, religion has viewed science as blasphemous and ungodly. As late as 1610, the Florentine named Galileo upon discovering the true motion of heavenly bodies through the use of better cut, polished and arranged optics, was sentenced by the Catholic Church to rename his findings. Had Sir Isaac Newton or René Descartes been born a few centuries earlier, they would not have been allowed to live long enough to provide humanity with the gifts of their findings – the Inquisitors would have eliminated them first. It wasn't until the late 19th century that empirical advancements through the scientific method started to dominate, and thus with it, only that which could be seen, touched, felt, heard, smelt or experimentally repeated was real. The theories of Darwin and Marx weaved new ideas that would alter the human perception of God's influence, putting the emphasis on the secular and tangible, rather than on the spiritual and abstract.[979] In doing so, the supernatural became denigrated along with any religious influence and acknowledging any form of divinity's hand was muffled. The notion of being guided by something beyond our own minds became preposterous in a developing era based on Freudian psycho analysis; that our core could actually receive spiritual things whose origins cannot be discovered or determined in this visible world.[980]

As Paul's Christianity began to triumph in the 1st millennium, it was civilization itself that was put into peril due to changing climate patterns in conjunction with the creeping of a conquering Church. Europe underwent centuries of excessive punishments during the Dark and Middle Ages while enforcing which should dominate human thought: theology or scientific hypotheses and methods. It was theology and the Literalists, however, who are guilty of first inflicting violence upon the sciences and the Gnostics, and never the other way around.[981] The awakening scientists were promoting peace more than the distorted theologists. In the current age, much of science views religion as mythology, fictional beliefs and false dogma. In 1966, the anthropologist Anthony Wallace predicted that religion would falter away at the hands of advancing science.[982] His projection was not unique since the secular was starting to dominate based on those earlier 19th century empirical focuses. Fundamentalism on either the religious or scientific front, are extremes that will degrade, if not destroy, our species' continuum. We must be willing to redefine both our religious and scientific perspectives and not tightly coerce either into validating or invalidating prior scriptures. Merging the two if we want both the secular and the spiritual to succeed, we need to understand that science and religion are both aspects of divinity, for one deals with primarily tangible phenomena and the other deals primarily with nontangible phenomena. Science is the Logos within the realm of time. Religion is the Sophia beyond the realm of time.

Reconciling the direction of scientific and religious outlooks call for an understanding that they are different tools. Science is the triangular tool best used for the tangible (that which is measurable), religion is the circular tool best used for the nontangible (that which is measureless). Science is humanity's tool for exploring, predicting and understanding the physical universe. Religion is humanity's tool for relating to the metaphysical universe. Sometimes the tools overlap. A tool works best when it is used properly – "the right tool for the right job."[983] Science tends to ask and answer the questions of "who, what, when, where and how." Religion tends to ask and answer the questions of "why."[984] Religion is our relationship with the universe while science is the study of that relationship. Science divides the layers of inquiry into segments of hypothesis; religion divides the fields of faith into pulses of devotion. Science has never negated or proven the existence of a higher consciousness – it has only changed our perception of God. It is the interpretation of God's works within the limited confines of human context. Technical advances and scientific models challenge us to redefine our perception and relationship with God. We may tend to fear this expansive change that science brings upon us, but instead we should welcome it.

—Λ*—

"The secret things belong unto the LORD our God: but those things which are revealed belong unto us and to our children forever, that we may do all the words of this law." – Deuteronomy 29:29[985]

* * * *

"THERE IS NOTHING HIDDEN that will not be revealed under the Sun." – the author's father

—*Ω—

Science is the elemental study used by humanity to crudely interpret and predict the behavior of the divine mind within the physical realm of time. It is a relative language which allows us to verbalize the actions of God without overwhelming ourselves with the immensity of his words. To be fully exposed to God would send most of us into shock; the intensity of his thoughts and knowledge would drown us. That is why God reveals himself to us in fleeting glimpses of awareness, transitory awakening bursts, gestures of symbolism and illuminative flashes of reality.

Science is generally dictated by qualitative absolutes or predictable probabilities through protocols laid out in the scientific method, a given input (a cause) will most likely provide a determined output (an effect). The religious method (metaphysics) is shrouded in ambiguity since measuring the mind's grasp and state of existence cannot be clearly delineated. Both can inspire a sense of wonder and awe. Through the tools of scientific expression (i.e., Periodic Table, DNA models, Solar System dioramas, Theory of Evolution) tangible instruments are created for conceptualizing the operations of the physical universe. Likewise, through the tools of religious expression, (i.e., Hinduism, Judaism, Buddhism, Christianity, Islam) non-tangible vehicles are created for conceptualizing the metaphysical universe and/or God and our relationship to him/her. Freke and Gandy cross the tool threshold by intertwining science and Gnosticism. They see science as being the complex and Gnosticism as being the simple, yet both cannot be fully comprehended because of their poles.[986] Richard Dawkins, author of the *Selfish Gene* and *The God Delusion*, is critical of religion because one cannot apply the scientific method to it by applying a hypothesis to prove or disprove the existence of a divine essence.[987] Place orange slices on one plate, apple slices on another plate, banana slices on a third plate and pear slices on a fourth plate. Offer the slices to a random child but tell them they can only have one type of fruit. Can the scientific method always correctly identify which one of the fruit slices a child will choose? The application of the scientific method is not the correct tool for either scenario.

Religion often speaks of angels and demons revealing themselves to humans. What if science discovered the existence of beings from alternate or higher dimensions that only reveal themselves to those who interest them because of the nature of their thoughts or the direction of their purity? What if a helio-based species were to be discovered that dwells in the realm of light or the etheric consciousness rather than of matter? They could be beings that reflect and mimic our own internal state, appearing as angelic (mutualistic) to those with enough pureness within their souls and appearing as demonic (parasitic) to those with tarnish. What if these revelations became more and more frequent to the extent that science accepted them as real? Religion may call them angels, demons, Elohim in the plural sense, aeons or archons but science would call them alternate life forms, interdimensional people, multidimensional creatures, transdimensional entities or extradimensional beings.[988] Does this mean science has destroyed religion? Absolutely not! Items sometimes start as religious beliefs or principles when the appropriate physical and mental tools are not available or yet developed for use in scientific study.

Upon the growth of humanity and advancement of knowledge, new tools and higher levels of mental comprehension become available for use in scientific analysis methods. Science currently has not been able to prove or disprove the existence of angels, higher conscious beings, our own consciousness, or a higher consciousness referred to as God. Radio waves on the electromagnetic spectrum weren't discovered by scientific instrumentation until the most recent 1/1000th of *Homo sapiens sapiens'* (modern humans) existence on this planet. Does that mean that radio waves didn't exist during the prior 999/1000th of our species' existence?

Previously mentioned in Chapter 1, it was found that the mixing of meat with dairy products during the time of King David in the *Old Testament* caused people to die. Therefore, it was concluded by those of the Abrahamic religions that God must not have wanted this to be done. The mixing of meat with dairy products became taboo and forbidden within the context of religious law. Kosher practices evolved, maintaining the health of the populace prior to refrigeration. As knowledge increased and new tools became available, it was discovered through the use of microscopes that particular harmful strains of bacteria were more likely to propagate to harmful levels on meat exposed to dairy products, especially in the Mediterranean/Asian heat. The combining of magnifying lenses at the proper location within an opaque tube had given humanity an instrument which revealed a whole new universe. The microscope did not create bacteria or the miniscule forms of life invisible to the naked eye; they were always there. It did, however, open a window into their world. This revelation of science reinforced the reasons behind the kosher religious practices. The universe then revealed to us the principles of refrigeration and thermodynamic cycles. Applying this cooling technology enabled us to slow down the propagation rates of bacteria and extend the consumable duration limits of meats and dairy products. Many choose to maintain the kosher tradition out of respect for their Abrahamic religious roots and they have every right to do so. Does science destroy God? No, it merely changes and expands our perception.

—A*—

"Scientific knowledge is necessary both for the training of the soul and for gravity of conduct; making the faithful more active and keen observers of things." – Valentinian Theodotus[989]

—*O—

Since we perceive through our own individual minds, a science or a religion is never made by one person, but through the common agreement of many. We must always remember that our universe is also defined by that which cannot always be seen or measured. We should not allow ourselves to be narrowly confined to a reality which can only be measured. Doing so will only enslave us to our current technology of qualifying measurement and recordable observation. Just because there is no means of validating something does not negate the fact that it exists. This is where the notion of faith has to take us beyond our instruments. There is currently no "souloscope" for measuring our non-corporeal essence, but that does not negate the existence of ourselves beyond that which is matter. There are many things that science cannot quantify. Can the occurrence of a miracle be measured by the instruments of science? The tools and probability of science can predict what should have happened, but it does not always explain what caused the alignment of influences for such a miracle to occur. Science is merely the study and interpretation of God's mind through the use of humanity's primitive descriptive models and instruments made of matter that measure actions and reactions of matter.

—Δ*—

"The principles we discover there are eternal and of divine origin; they are the foundation of all the science that exists in the world, and must be the foundation of theology." – Thomas Paine[990]

—*O—

When we discover something unknown and find a new way to relate with our world, it is because the universe has allowed us to learn its secrets. It is not us that conquers our universe, it is our universe that allows us to see more into its workings. The universe reveals itself to us when our actions are appropriate. Humanity needs to continue its quest for knowledge and truth. The desire to think above mediocrity is necessary for the advancement of ourselves as individuals and as a society. If we become satisfied with passivity and stagnation, failing to encapsulate morality within the sciences, then our species will lose itself in data and analytics that serve no purpose other than for the degeneration and over-whelming of our global consciousness. It will stunt us and reinitiate an-other cyclical period mimicking of the Dark Ages.

Science may present itself as the intellectual path to mastering the universe, but it is the intertwining mystical experiences occurring among the interplay between the observer and the event that reinforces and states our participation within it. The Austrian theoretical physicist, Wolfgang Pauli, had a whimsical synchronization associated with his presence as an observer. Known as the "Pauli Effect", technical equip-ment would seem to break down whenever he was nearby. The observer influences the results, much the way a good doctor affects the outcome by providing healing methods for the patient, the way a good coach guides the athlete to their peak performance, and the way a good director visually creates the scene by coordinating the actors' dialogue for the op-timum presentation. For when an observing pioneer is pushing the limits of human understanding while witnessing a discovery for the first time, their thoughts are influencing the result and paving the way for future observers to see the same results. The initial observing influencer has primed the field, in effect, establishing the result or better said, the uni-verse has allowed the initial observer to encounter glimpses into its se-crets. We may pompously think that it is the grandiosity of our species making discoveries and innovative machines, but we should humbly rec-ognize that the credit belongs to the universe for choosing to reveal its secrets. For when we properly align and synchronize our thoughts with that of the universal mind, it discloses its secrets and grants us new knowledge – it relinquishes gnosis upon us. The jewel of eternal truth and genuine gnosis is to become an infinitesimal naked nothing bathed in a vast ocean of universal knowledge.[991] The name of that univer-sal mind, depending on one's spiritual perspective and semantic prefer-ences could be referred to as God. When a novel discovery is made or a transformative invention produced, we should humbly realize that it is

not solely the workings of man or woman. Through an anthroposophical approach, it is the universe choosing to reveal its vulnerability when
one properly empathizes with its thoughts. Empathizing and synchronizing with the cosmos' mind is done by a process of inner development,
achieved by honing one's imagination, inspiration and intuition. In doing so, our intellectual abstraction will better harmonize with our spiritual sensory. Good science needs to incorporate this holistic approach and
credit the universe as much as it credits its innovators. Gratitude needs
to be in place for thanking the collective cosmos for allowing glimpses
into its cognition and intellect.

—Λ*—

"The scientist's religious feeling takes on the form of a rapturous
amazement at the harmony of the natural law, which reveals an intelligence of such superiority that, in comparison with it, all the systematic
thinking of human beings is an utterly insignificant reflection. This feeling is the guiding principle of his life and work, in so far as he succeeds in
keeping himself from the shackles of selfish desire. It is beyond question
closely akin to that which has possessed the religious geniuses of all ages."
– Albert Einstein

—*Ω—

According to the study of Theoretical and Particle Physics, there
are particles constantly popping in and out of existence, some of which
have periods of existence that are unmeasurable. Virtual particles (more
like influencing disturbances) fall into this category and exist for very
brief periods of time and then go back into the realm from which they
came.[992] The existence and non-existence of these particles is recorded
with measuring instruments and sensor which are limited to recording
events within our realm of existence. It may appear to us that the imaging
apparatus used to record the brief life of these events tells a story of the
birth and death of such particles, but they are only capable of showing
and measuring a particle's existence within our realm. We assume that
those particles have been annihilated, but that may only be due to the inherent bias of instrumentation that is limited to measuring and recording their paths only in this realm, our visual reality of existence.

Our minds are also instruments used to navigate within our reality. The eyes, ears, nose and nerve endings send their signals to the mind for processing. They are also limited in what they can sense and measure. We tend to make the assumption that just because our human senses can't detect something, it must not exist. We must realize that not only does our mind create our reality, but it also acts as a filter to keep other realms and alternate realities out. This action allows us to focus within the realm of a particular bandwidth and maintain our framework within this secular existence. The true prophet and shamans have gained the insight of being able to stretch their bandwidth of existence beyond their normal limits. John's experiences as described in *Revelation* of the *New Testament*, Buddha's awakening and Mohammad's night flight with angels were such stretches of everyday boundaries of existence. Going beyond these limits without being properly grounded in the secular realm can lead to temporary madness for those whose intentions are not pure enough in thought or action. This flash of temporary madness is what has turned many sinners into saints.

Superstition is when certain secular actions, causes or occurrences are "assumed" to result in a given metaphysical effect or result. By "assumed", it means that the scientific method (experimentation with controls) has not been applied to see if a given input will likely or repeatedly result in a given output. Over time, some superstitions have morphed into traditions. One such "tradition", due to fear of the "unlucky" number 13, many high-rise buildings skip from the 12th to the 14th floor. Such triskaidekaphobia accounts for a lack of a 13th floor designation in almost 85% of buildings served by an Otis Elevator.[993] Personally, I find the number 13 to be my lucky number. Some superstitions are said to bring bad karma onto those who violate its instructions such as walking under a ladder, failing to throw salt over the left shoulder if spilled, or crossing the path of a black cat. Other superstitions are said to bring desired results, such as increased fertility when pregnancy is the goal, attracting wealth or ensuring good health. If one believes their fate is ruled by superstition, then there is a good chance it will be.

Navigating the duality of fate and free will is presented in the following example. Consider being on a raft that is floating among the rapids of a river with large rocks protruding from the water surface. Fate has it that the raft will flow downstream no matter what and will probably hit a rock or boulder if left to its own accord. Free will has it that the raft can be guided with its rudder and oars to avoid smashing into the rocks. By doing nothing, fate will dominate. By balancing the duality of fate and free will, one can influence their destiny and safely reach the river's mouth. The same analogy can be applied to much of how the dualities of life work. Nothing is predetermined or foreordained. The arbiter of our fate is both the intellect and the spirit, faith merged with rationalism and science blended with religion.[994] There are probabilities of occurrences which can either be increased or decreased based on and through our actions. Courage is the strength in recognizing that our fate and destiny is controlled by both our own actions and those of outside forces.

—Δ*—

"Nature has to do with the body. Fate with the psyche. Freedom with the Consciousness. None is absolute. God alone is absolute." – Bardesanes[995]

• • • •

"DON'T JUST GO WITH the flow, take some dares through the rapids." – Isabelle[996]

—*O—

The true separation of humanity from the beasts of the land, air and water is that we have been given the ability to control our own multifaceted evolution. It has been an evolution of increased physical awareness, increased emotional awareness, increased intellectual awareness and increased spiritual awareness. Through the tools of science and the exposure to new constructive ideas, we can visualize and steer our future path closer to the potential we wish to achieve. What other known creature applies an abundance of curative medical knowledge in tending to its wounds and increasing its probability of continuation within the physical plane? What other known creature manipulates pigments, stone or clay beyond just random patterns to influence a mood, evoke a state of stimulation, mimic an object, describe a scene or to tell a story?[997] What other known creature has the ability to gain knowledge and develop the core of its being from the written ideas and verbal stories from ancestors and those who passed on long before we even existed? Our creator or the forces behind our creation gave us the ability to be our own Prometheus – a Prometheus that interprets the behavior of the universe into comprehendible notations that will either save us or destroy us depending on the choices we make in developing our own individual evolutions.

—A*—

"The principles of science lead to this knowledge; for the Creator of man is the Creator of science; and it is through that medium that man can see God, as it were, face to face." – Thomas Paine[998]

—*O—

Technology and scientific achievements have profoundly altered the capabilities of human existence.[999] Capabilities that are both beneficial and detrimental to what makes and keeps us human. Upon the revelation of the universe's secrets, researchers, inventors and scientists are sometimes faced with the dilemma of how or if to release such information to other sentient beings and whether to succumb to Belphegor's enticements of sloth or not.[1000] For many of the universe's secrets contain a duality in which they can be used as a tool to improve society or as a weapon to destroy it. Often such discoveries, like Pandora's container, release things into the world that may become difficult to harness or result in unforeseen consequences. Sir Isaac Newton spoke of concealing scientific secrets that would be dangerous should they fall into the wrong hands.[1001] From its first use as a mining and tunnel building tool to later as a killing and maiming weapon of destruction, Alfred Nobel encountered this dualistic dilemma firsthand with his invention of dynamite. The consequences encountered from splitting the atom speak for themselves. Whether we should attempt to tap into and harness the energy permeating almost 68% of the universe is another moral question that needs its answer.[1002] We refer to it with the dysphemism of "dark energy" only because we understand so little about it. We do know that our very existence is dependent on its influence and it is accelerating the fringes of the universe outward.

Whatever mind created this universe, it was thinking long ahead of its initial impulse. It did not just form a cosmos, but it invoked forth a universe that recreates and grows upon itself. In simplistic terms, subatomic and elementary particles, the building blocks of atoms, are constantly changing into different forms and combinations. Three of these primary particles (electrons, protons and neutrons) stabilized as the lightest of elements – the hydrogen atom. The immense crushing, heating and compressing of this lightest of elements, formed a heavier element called helium. Within the internal workings of stellar bodies, even heavier elements are formed during the life of a star and during its explosive death. These atomic building blocks drift across space and time, interacting with each other to form molecules, compounds, fragments, nebulae, asteroids, comets, moons, planets and newer stars. On the surfaces of at least one of the known more stable planets, molecules collided to form other compounds, amino acids, proteins and eventually life as we define it. In the future, we may come upon life from the surfaces of other stable planets or even within the clouds themselves of vast nebulae. Science may have revealed the atom to us but the way they came together is revealed through religion. A bit of the initial mind was always participating and growing in every collision, interaction, and evolution of consciousness to form the beings that we are today. Our genes and genetic material are influenced by the divine hand of creation.[1003] They tune our brains and those of future generations to a propensity for synchronizing with the thoughts of God; the mind of the universe. Applying the theory of natural selection put forth by Charles Darwin, genes that fortify empathy and self-control have proliferated over generations, while genes that gave free rein to predations, dominance and revenge have dwindled.[1004] The selfish gene perhaps is not so selfish after all.[1005] The Law of Love of the Creator has never changed with respect to the principals of science, the properties of matter, the movement of mathematics, the messages of art or the correct behavioral projections to be emanated upon all living beings. The extension of our auras occurs with love and its contraction occurs with hate.

Chapter 20
Relationships Of Romance And Carnal Love

"WHEN YOU TRULY LOVE someone, you change a bit based on their desires and they change a bit based on your influences." – AO

• • • •

THE ESKIMOS (INUIT and Yupik dialects combined) have over 50 words for describing snow in its various forms. The Sami, people who live in the northern regions of Scandinavia and Russia, have at least 180 words related to snow and ice and possibly 1,000 words for referring to reindeer.[1006] The ancient Greeks had 6 to 8 words for describing love, depending on the connotation. There is Eros (the erotica of sensuality and fertility), Philia (platonic love between good friends), Storge (love found in the recognition of kinship and the familiar), Ludus (the flirting playfulness of a blooming romance), Mania (love based on obsessiveness and dependence rather than support), Pragma (love of endurance that has proven itself over time), Philautia (the healthy love and feelings of worth of self), and Agape (divine love that focuses on the greater truth). In the English language, the word "love" can apply to the nurturing care of a child. One can love the flow and transition of colors in a painting. One can love an internal reaction to a musical composition. One can love the eternal feeling of a sunset, a glowing moon or the distance stars. One can love the invoked feeling of a kind gesture or a kind word. One can love to make others feel loved. Let us not dismiss the most mused of all the loves – the romantic love one has towards another.

Love can be blind. To put it correctly, unhealthy love is blind. True healthy love needs borders; a semi-permeable container to allow it to flourish. The permeability of your boundaries should be based on earned trust, not promises. Completely losing one's identity in another person or object is not healthy love. Just as unhealthy addictions are roadblocks to reaching true intimacy, unhealthy love (Mania) can generate behavior and situations of false intimacy. Having love without the proper boundaries of self and other is unhealthy. Having personalities that continuously merge and separate in a constructive interplay is healthy love. Love requires honesty, spontaneity, vulnerability, trust, responsibility, self-acceptance and the acceptance of others. Pursuing it can bring warmth and joy, but also the occasional stings of hurt and rejection.[1007]

Throughout other chapters of this book, the romantic passion and sexual affection aspects (Eros and Ludus) were left out of the word "love." For the rest of this chapter only, they will be the topic of focus. The love discussed in this chapter includes the acts and thrills of consensual carnal knowledge which go beyond just the sexual mechanics from Vienna and British empirical influences. It goes more into the sexual life energy of Hindu teachings which chooses to surpass the empirical and lifts love to erotic heights.[1008] When performed between two consenting adult individuals in a respectful monogamous relationship with each other, physical intimacy is a wondrous ecstatic interplay that becomes an aspect of love. It is the touch and play of Eros and Ludus at the surface level while resounding and penetrating deeper than the superficial.

Sex is not a sin and it is not just for procreation, but it is reserved for the age appropriate and the mutually consenting.[1009] Albert J. LaChance in *The Modern Christian Mystic* recommends that rather than threatening and subduing the procreative energies blossoming during adolescence as being sinful, guilt ridden, and shameful, we should instruct emerging adults how to responsibly and respectfully wait to use them appropriately as healthy expressions of our individuality.[1010] The sacredness of our sexuality is to be rejoiced in healthy conveyance of the Self with the Other, not shamed as being demonic, with unnecessary celibacy, perceived piety, vulgarization or otherwise.[1011] Suppressing it is denial of God creating us as curious creatures, sensual beings and lustful lovers. Our sexuality is not something to be ashamed of, but rather, it is to be respected and celebrated in healthy moderation and with a balanced approach. It is a gift and a responsibility to be enjoyed and cherished, the celebrated union of the God with the Goddess, not something to be denied or negatively exploited. The universe is composed of feminine spirit (Shakti), masculine spirit (Shiva) and sometimes a blend of both (Ardhanarishvara). We should welcome the diversity of all these sexual spiritual forms not necessarily with understanding, but certainly with acceptance. The desire for sexual expression is typically inborn and natural. It should not be suppressed, submerged or eliminated. It should, however, be channeled through positive outlets into responsible forms of expressions which enrich the body, mind and spirit.[1012] Without such outlets, it will become empty physical encounters devoid of substance and meaning.

—Δ*—

"Gender is in everything; everything has its masculine and feminine aspects; gender manifests in all planes." – *The Kybalion*[1013]

—*O—

The development of a romantic relationship can be complex. For eons, musicians, lyricists, poets and playwrights have expressed the highs and lows and the risks and rewards encountered with courtship. It is a behavioral dance of wooing, responding and internally analyzing to determine if the interplay should continue into the future. The advent of sexual behavior too early in the relationship can cause it to prematurely fail, if other reasons do not cause it to fail sooner. The most important thing is to preserve your personal self-value and dignity during the process. Respect who you are and do not continually romantically pursue someone who is abusive to your heart or not returning or responding to your romantic gestures. I repeat, do not stay in a bad relationship and allow someone to repeatedly abuse your heart. They are not a possession to be won, but rather, it is about a relationship either to be groomed or released, nurtured or abandoned. They may not be ready or willing to acknowledge your amorous desires. The fantasy is the dream of what you imagine the relationship to be or what you hope it could become; the reality is what it actually is in the present moment of today and what it will also probably continue to be like tomorrow. Accept the reality for what it is and decide if you want to stay there or move on unto something more.

The direction you take is up to you. If the reality of the relationship is not true enough, simply let go of the fantasy of its false future, recover yourself and move on. Often times, through no fault of either party, the emotional, intellectual and sexual chemistry or attraction is not mutually present. Respect that the mutual attraction does not exist and put the energy of your efforts into other activities. Abusing someone else's emotions or body or allowing someone else to continually abuse yours is not healthy love. Just because genuine reciprocated romance does not exist in the present with someone, does not mean it won't exist in your future with someone else. Accept that the idealized form of reciprocal courtly love (as advocated in *Romans* 12:10), only romances forward when both parties are willing. Remember, before you can have a relationship of healthy love with another, you must first have a relationship of healthy love with yourself.

—Λ*—

"When you love someone, you love them as they are, and not as you'd like them to be." – Leo Tolstoy[1014]

—*Ω—

Sex is not a four-letter word (something treated as a curse) and neither is sensuality. Consensual fornication by adults of proper age is not evil or sinful. Physical intimacy is a beautiful experience, an interplay of form and consciousness, to be shared by two individuals who have a healthy, caring exclusive partnership and attraction for each other. There's a reason behind the euphoric chemicals created during loving moments of physical and emotional caresses. God created those chemicals within us and the sensory of our genitalia for a reason – to promote the healthy temporary merger of our cores and with the option of generating younger versions of ourselves. Let's face it, sex is fun. It is supposed to be. It is also supposed to be reserved for monogamous relationships of mutual respect. Without the latter, it becomes harmful and meaningless. We should find the joy in our sexuality and respect the sexuality of others. Sensuality is a beautiful thing and something to be celebrated, but it should be treated with responsibility and not be devoid of love and respect. It is about making your partner feel good in conjunction with your own pleasure; it is about embracing in climatic moments of loving ecstasy by combining the best of the physical with the best of the spiritual. It was meant as a physical doorway for entering a broader sense of trust; a deeper reality of who we are and who our partner is. Spiritual ecstasy and erotica are something achieved by those who have a healthy connection with their inner core and that of their partner. True erotica interaction with our partner reveals the inner mystery of who they are and who we are. It awakens a union of love affairs, both with them and within ourselves.

There are many levels of sexual experience and unfortunately, due to unbalanced behavior, many of us exploit or suppress our sensuality. There are members of society who exploit the beauty of sexual experience for only material and monetary gain. A relatively small global fraction continues a backwards cultural repressive act of mutilating the sensory genitalia given to women by Allah; they perverse and disfigure God's design. They remove the mystique of the experience because they are obsessed with only the physical attribute. Sex to them is seen like food without flavor, perfume without fragrance or a blossom lacking beauty. They tarnish their own and other's spiritual growth due to acting on their short-sighted, self-centered physical desires. They become focused on the physical only and ignorantly believe that sexual expression is a limited experience based between the thighs or upon the breasts. Unknown to them, it is both the physiological activity of the glands at one extreme and the highest reaches of spirit at the other that induces forth true healthy erotica.[1015] It is an experience that manifests between the ears (in the brain) and extends throughout our spiritual and physical periphery. The real sex organ processor is the brain and the heart (metaphorically speaking); the genitals and touch receptors are merely sensors. Sensual experiences are felt by the sensations of the body, but they exist within the psyche of self and identify with our spirit. It is the brain that interprets the signals and decides what level of euphoria the mind will feel. It is the heart that pumps faster in the anticipation and excitement of the moment. It is then the mind that raises the sexual experience to those blissful, higher levels based on the spiritual development of both partners. The higher the spiritual development of each partner, the more perpetual the state of erotic bliss between the encounters. An authentic love connection is catalyzed based on spirit, mind and body merging with a temporary lowering of both partners' egos. The attraction needs to be emotional, mental and physical. All these levels must be initially met for love to endure. It is the whole body in temporary unity with another, however, that becomes a link to the supreme when a true yogic connection is achieved. Sex without love among AISBs is devoid of substance – it leaves the body dry and the soul empty.

—A*—

"When presented in an appropriate manner of a genuine progressing relationship, do not deny thyself the joys of earthly love and the craving of the lower self for the healthy carnal knowledge of another." – AO

• • • •

"FOR TO THE BEE A FLOWER is the fountain of life, and to the flower a bee is the messenger of love. And to both, bee and flower, the giving and the receiving of pleasure is a need and an ecstasy." – *The Prophet*[1016]

—*O—

The act of sex is a wondrous experience for those in a loving committed relationship based on mutual respect. It is the affectionate probing and exploring of another's physical form with the desire of providing rapturous glory. A great lover focuses on providing pleasure to their partner rather than just themselves and feels joy with bringing moments of ecstatic bliss to their mate. The welcomed touch and caressing during sexual intimacy trigger the soul's desire for and continuance of a relationship and commitment. Without which, one or both partners will require repair due to emotional damage. One may deny that damage is occurring without the commitment, but it reveals itself in the sinking feeling of spiritual pain or internal numbness. The giving and receiving of sexual intercourse, insertion and enclosing, is a ritual bonding and a sacred act of physical intimacy. It should be reserved only when the intentions are for a continued long-term companionship and a desire for permanence and stability in the relationship. Otherwise, it leads to disintegration of self, internal grief and the collective collapse of cultural and societal co-hesion. There are many levels of sexual experience and carnal sharing, but **never** have or allow intercourse unless you are ready and able to take on the responsibility of providing for and raising a child. Although the bi-ological dimension of sexual love can be prevented, redirected, captured or contained to prevent fertilization, no contraception or birth control is foolproof nor 100% effective against a resulting pregnancy from the exchange of DNA. Therefore, do not engage in non-procreative inter-course unless you are willing to risk the unplanned responsibility of pro-viding care, support, nurture and guidance to a younger version of your-self.

A functionally healthy family unit is the *magnum opus* of biological spiritual context for the raising of young in a bond of continued love nev-er-ending. The notion of "free love", sexual interplay among more than one partner as experimented within the 19th century Oneida Commu-nity and with disastrous promiscuous results in the late 1960s to early 1980s, only leads to destruction of family.[1017] Families created im-properly or with rough starts will not hold together properly unless the starters go back and do the self-work in order to get their Self in order. The well-being of younger versions of themselves is vitally relying on a willingness of the parents to being vulnerable. Good parents must be vul-nerable to improvement, to facing the voids from their own childhood, and to the unconditional love and dependency shining upon them from their offspring. Sexual intercourse is not a rite of passage into manhood or womanhood. It is a spiritual passage of physical communion with an-other being, the merging of like flesh with like flesh, and the mystical embrace of coupling should be treated with reverence no matter how many times the unitive copulating act is performed. The practicing exer-cise of procreation (sexual intercourse without conception or pregnancy) among mature adults in a monogamous relationship, even if fertility is not involved, is a tribute to the Creator.

The art of making love involves the dropping of physical, emotional and spiritual boundaries and the sharing of these aspects. That is why it is imperative that you truly take the time to know your partner through a relationship of understanding, honesty and respect prior to physical engagement. If your partner is not balanced, they will throw you off balance – cheating on a sexual partner is a form of negative exploitation. One must be cautious and sure of their sexual partner's development on the path of enlightenment or else they will inherit their existing spiritual voids. If one partner harbors excessive anger, resentment or ill intent, the other may find themselves taking on these negative emotions. When the voids are too deep, the spiritual energy of one partner will be drained to fill the voids of the other. At times, the voids become like bottomless pits that can never be filled unless that individual is willing to work on themselves through proper professional counseling. This is the reason why rape is such a violent act of negative exploitation; it involves a transference of the perpetrator's anger (typically, but not always, a fit of rage by adult males – a "mantrum") and hatred into their victim. The victim absorbs all that negative energy and then starts attacking themselves with it, even long after the physical rape has ended. They have become a sponge, a capacitor, a vessel, of the rapist's rage. This negative energy can be released and dissipated out of the victim, but again, only through proper professional counseling, therapy and meditation.

Prostitution, payment with the understanding that services of sexual encounters will be provided, seems to fall into two categories. There are those who provide those services out of necessity due to impoverished conditions and lack of other financial opportunities, and those who do it out of choice due to luxurious desires. Rather than relying on my views on the topic, I would like to hear if they are damaged souls, victims of social circumstances, abused or defiled by past lovers and looking for a way out of their profession. Allow the prostitutes to speak about their line of work and how they got into it. Would they prefer to remain in their profession or transition away from the field?

Carnal relationships of incest create stunted psyches and shattered cores, since it confuses the creature within us that seeks diversity of blood and spirit. It throws desires of intimacy into disarray since boundaries of family identities have been broken and fragmented into emotional shards as critically relevant identical genetic material clashes and collides. Although there are billions of genes that are the same between person to person for every one that is different, making us 99.9% genetically similar to the next human,[1018] the pertinent and significant strands of identical DNA reject themselves and fail to properly mesh – the coding becomes corrupted and out of sequence from the incestuous encounter. This failure of not having the correct genetic diversification at the key critical junctures causes rejection of proper cellular attraction and a collapse of bonding between relevant chromosomal materials.

Never sleep (engage in carnal pleasures) with another advanced sentient intelligent being unless your intentions are for a long-term, committed relationship of mutual respect. In such encounters of lustful tension, abstinence has its own sexual power. It provides the time to sort through what is initial physical attraction, which may fade on its own terms, and what is meant to blossom into something much more meaningful. It is unwise to make love to another being unless you feel and want the potential for a future connection together. Otherwise, having sexual intercourse without the intention of a continued future relationship is disruptive and damaging to the cores of both beings. Marriage is a commitment and vow in the pursuit of happiness reserved for mature adults (preferably well over the age of 18) that trumps the diversity of carnal relationships. Let's not be fooled into thinking it is a union of perpetual bliss. It involves work and vulnerability, but with the right person, the work is much less complicated and less stressful. However, marriage is not primarily about procreation and the raising of young. If it were, the nucleus of every married couple would then be an intrinsic mandate to have or to adopt children, which it is not. The various religious and cultural traditions associated with the initiation of a marriage, the wedding, are done to signify the importance and value placed upon the union. There is no divine law, however, requiring people to remain married when there is physical abuse, intimidation, severe disrespect or suppression of personality in the relationship.[1019] Unless there is physical abuse occurring in the relationship, marriage counseling should first be sought to see if preserving the union is possible and worthwhile. Unfortunately, divorce is the outcome of a family already destroyed.

Acknowledging and expressing the Freudian drives within us in a healthy, respectful and balanced manner is part of living a good human existence. When Jesus explained to us in *Matthew* 5:28 that even looking in admiration at another's human form is a type of lust, he was pointing to our inherent animalistic self that needs to be recognized, surpassed and dissipated. Art that defines and portrays the beauty of sexuality accents the human experience, provided it was not created through the negative exploitation of another. I ask for your forbearance in advance for the rest of this paragraph and do not overemphasize on its content. This book is not condoning pornography, but compared to all the suffering in this world, is visual soft pornography created though non-negative exploitive means really that bad? Provided the pornography was created by consenting adults showing the physical intimacy of their monogamous relationship (a boyfriend and girlfriend, fiancée and fiancé, a husband and wife, life partners) or the individual adult choosing to show the erotica of only their own human physical form to others in a voyeuristic sort of way (look but don't touch), should not be considered negative exploitation. Negative exploitation comes into play when the pornography is created through human trafficking, underage participants, the emotionally damaged, obsessive behavior, the addicted or the oppressed. We were created by God as creatures of lust and sexual desires, just as Jesus explained to us. Despite what interpretations of the *Bible* or the *Koran* state, it is normal to have initial reactions of sexual lust and erotic curiosity when seeing the unique beauty of an attractive stranger's profile or nakedness. The exterior physical contours of the sex that we are attracted to was meant to entice, especially when seen in celebration of the human form in art such as sculpture, paintings and seducing photography. There will be the occasional lustful brief admirations and physical desires for another person, even among happily married couples. This is the animal within us temporarily surfacing and we should not be ashamed of it, but rather, recognize that going any further than a quick glance or friendly smile to satisfy the procreative creature within will result in relational destruction of the marriage. Entering mid-to-late adolescence, our first introduction to the awe and beauty of the naked human form may have been from seeing a "forbidden" image that came across our eyes or viewing an adult magazine that found its way into our hands. The initial peeks of curiosity, however, should turn into the admiration of the surface beauty of the adult human form, however temporary that form may be, and not into the unhealthy and uncontrolled pursuit of forbidden or destructive relationships. Obsessively pursuing sex is an unhealthy addiction, an extreme that will do damage to our core and the cores of others. Occasionally attending to those lustful needs from afar in a healthy manner of enjoyment by admiring with fascination and attractive wonder the physical beauty of another stranger or opting to share the physical beauty of our own form in the appropriate venues, is not a form of negative exploitation. Occasionally, viewing mild or soft porn with sensual curiosity and regard to the respective mystique of the adult human shape is not going to send you to hell; there are plenty of other worst sins out there that will such as lying, stealing, violence and murder. This paragraph was written at the risk that some will overly obsess on its words and harp on what it says, rather than focusing on the thousands of other statements in this book.

Some animal species spread their genes among many different mates and others commit to a single mate. According to genetic studies, it was only about 10,000 years ago that monogamy started to take precedent over polygamy, or more specifically polygyny, in human populations.[1020] Based on DNA analysis, it suggests that most children were sired by very few men, and by contrast, most women seemed to pass on their genes. From the chromosomal evidence, our prehistoric ancestors prior to the end of the late Stone Age, like their primate ancestors, were at least "mildly polygynous."[1021] If we desire to go back to the Stone Age, then by all means, we can resort again to practices of polygamy. The previous sentence was sarcasm.

Such nonexclusive, sanctioned mating practices were either polygyny (one man with several woman) or polyandry (one women with several men) and can be referred to as plural wives or plural husbands, and "complex" or group marriages. Although there are pros and cons to each, in modern times it seems merely a sanctioned excuse for adultery that leads to family instability, increased violence and societal failure – the cons far outweigh the pros. Yet, based on a 1998 University of Wisconsin survey of more than a thousand societies, just 186 practiced monogamy. Polygyny was occasionally acceptable among 453 of the surveyed societies and in 588 of them, it was quite common. Only four of those surveyed featured polyandry.[1022] Polyandry seems a desperate way to keep land and resources tightly owned within family control. According to the Fragile States Index, polygamy is practiced in all 20 of the most unstable countries, indicating a measure of societal degradation.[1023] Polygyny is only legitimate and authorized in progressive societies when civilizations have so collapsed to the point in which there are a disproportionate quantity of eligible females to eligible males and the populace needs replenishment. The parliament at Nüremberg, Germany in 1650 decreed that because so many adult males were killed during the Thirty Years' War, every man was now allowed to marry up to 10 women. I'm not sure if that was a blessing or a curse for the eligible male but it was certainly an obligation for the female, if she wanted children within wedlock. In 2001, President Bashir of Sudan urged men to take more than one wife to increase the country's population, ignoring smaller countries with robust economies and mistakenly arguing that the rapid economic development in China and India was due to those nation's huge populations. On the other hand, when resources are scarce and there are too many people, polyandry is a way of limiting population growth. A woman can only have so many children, no matter how many husbands she has.

I can assure you of this, no progressively advanced civilization on this planet is currently at the point where any form of polygamy is a necessity. Polygyny was practiced in Moses' day, in the days (970 BCE–931 BCE) of King Solomon (alleged to having 700 wives and 300 concubines),[1024] in the days of Mohammad and by recent fundamental factions among followers of the *Book of Mormon*.[1025] The character of Solomon seemed a "witty, ostentatious, dissolute and melancholy" sexaholic, who was deprived of what he deprived from 1000 of his sexual partners – happiness and real love. He was certainly receptive to and graced by the wisdom of the divine Sophia,[1026] but his obsession with the influence of the feminine and her physical form became an addiction rather than a healthy respect, admiration and reverence – he could never be content or satisfied. The Hindu god Krishna is said to have had 16,108 wives – that is a lot of anniversary dates to track and remember. In the Prophet Mohammad's day, polygyny may have been the only choice of survival available for many eligible maidens or women whose husbands had passed. Being under the control and protection of a rich patriarch was preferable to starvation or at the mercy of more brutish male elements. Merging widows into existing established households was a social strategy for ensuring they and orphans were cared for. Mohammad had a monogamous marriage for 25 years until his first wife died in 619. Most of the women he later supported and married were war widows (at least 9 of his 11 or 15 wives). The *Koran* ordains that a Muslim can marry up to four wives, but only if he can care for them all equally well. It also explicitly forbids mut'ah (marriages of pleasure), though many Muslim men conveniently ignore that part.[1027] The early leadership of The Church of Jesus Christ of Latter-day Saints, facing potential crumbling of its foundations and potential destruction under Federal laws prohibiting polygamy, officially renounced and took a stand against polygamy in 1890 with its reluctant decree of the *Mormon Manifesto. The Salt Lake Tribune* noted in 2005 that as many as 10,000 Mormon fundamentalists lived in polygamous families.[1028] In general, Christianity views polygamy as an offence against the sanctity of marriage, insisting that conjugal love between a man and wife (mimicking the coupling of Adam and Eve) must be mutual and unreserved, undivided and exclusive.

Having plural spouses "defeats all the felicity of affection by leaving no point to fix upon."[1029] Polygeny makes the female dangerously dependent on the male rather than allowing her independence of thought, will and sustenance. The orthodox biblical Adam and Eve had each other's company, attention and intimacy; no other mates joined or were added to their pairing. Dividing one's love among several mates leaves an emptiness of trusted intimacy, a lack of individualized affection and no one happy. It can result in decay, rather than flourishment, of family and civilization that is not already stagnating, regressing or destroyed. The indication that a culture is flourishing and growing with God is when monogamy is the preference for balancing a population with the available resources. An enlightened society values the dignity and stability of the coupling, not the chaotic whimsies of the menagerie.

There is always the question of homosexual behavior, the sexual desire for someone of the same gender. The Abrahamic religions approach the subject with outdated demonic fury or extrapolated interpretations from the destructive outcome of Sodom and Gomorrah. The *Bible* and the *Koran* both have bygone passages interpreted as condemning it, even with punishment by death.[1030] Yet, in contradiction, much of these same scriptures claim to be of love and understanding.[1031] Some of the letters of Paul or a forging imposter (Bishop Irenaeus?) pretending to be Paul, come across as being written by a misogynist homophobe who was accepting of slavery to appease the elite of Roman audiences.[1032] What was the fear for condemning the act of loving the same gender? Was it because it seemed unnatural among the majority or different in its form of affection? Condemning the forcing of one's sexuality on another (i.e., rape) of the same gender is certainly understandable. The organ of the human brain and its many bio-electro-chemical feedback sensors are complex, so who are we to judge the way God has arranged the chemicals of sexual desire within our or another's body? As the world approaches a state of overpopulation, perhaps there is some natural sexual preference change that occurs within a percentage of the human species to send procreation rates to safer levels. An increase in the homosexual density in regions of overpopulation would be beneficial. There are scientific theories and studies that have related homosexuality to certain genes creating environmental predispositions for same sex attraction. Other studies show that a lack of specific hormones during development in the womb can influence one's sexual preference or even their gender identity.[1033]

Those attracted carnally to others of the same gender have faced centuries of ridicule, torment, physical or chemical castration and at times, executions via murderous beatings or use as public kindling for human bonfires. Why has the perceived sexual nonconformity of homosexuals resulted in outrage of ghastly punishment and condemnation? Is it that homosexuality is viewed as a threat to the continuation of the species because of the possible halting of procreation? Is it because of an unfounded fear of it becoming a misunderstood contagion that could spread to us, our children and our friends? Is it because they are an easy target for a bullying mob? Do we find it bothersome to relate to a fictional character on the television or in a movie and then all of a sudden find out that he or she is cast as a homosexual, when we are not? Is it because we view homosexual carnal exchanges of intimacy as something of disgust and repugnancy when in fact, they are not much different than the physical affections of erotic exploration and sensations exchanged by heterosexual couples? Why would anyone voluntarily choose to be a homosexual, considering the potential abuse, stigmatization and ostracization they could face? <u>Society and certain religions as well owe the homosexual, and for that matter, also the transgender, intersex and asexual, a long overdue apology for the treatment they have endured throughout history.</u> Any fears of homosexuality are primitive, irrational and nonsensical. Same sex unions should not be viewed as a disorder requiring treatment, but rather, as a natural mating preference among a percentage of the population for expressing love and to be loved. Other than a gentle kiss of affection, any form of overt physical sexual behavior, be it homo or hetero, should not be flaunted in public. Such displays should be reserved for the interchanges of couples in monogamous respectful relationships for within the privacy of their chambers.

—Δ*—

"This sweet sacramental act we celebrate is shared in secret, because if performed openly before impure eyes, the ignorant may mock and the divine power manifesting in both sexes will shy away." – Thoth-Hermes[1034]

—*O—

To physically love another adult of the same gender because it is trendy, popular, experimental or rebellious is not healthy in developing one's core. To exploit one's sexuality on another, be they heterosexual or homosexual, when the other person is emotionally weak, underage or vulnerable is a form of negative exploitation and thus sinful. To truly emotionally and physical love and care for another of the same gender in a monogamous reciprocal relationship because that is truly who you are and you are confident of it, is perfectly acceptable. Your sexual preference coincides with the gender that you fantasize about having a carnal relationship with – the sex that turns you on. A person's place in society should not be based on which gender they are truly attracted to, but it should be based on their relationship with the universe. Are they constructive and contributing members of society? Do they truly love, respect and honor their partner? Are they good people? These are the questions to be focused on when determining one's character and place in society, not their sexual preference or orientation.

Nature, God and biology created separate genders as a means for promoting copulative diversity among the same species. No matter what the listing is of our gender on our birth certificate, we all have male and female qualities within us but one tends to be more predominate than the other. As Carl Jung put forth and theorized, the animus is the masculine archetype which cultivates in the subconscious of a woman while the anima is the feminine archetype that cultivates in the subconscious of a man. Likewise, Robert Powell in *The Sophia Teachings* presents that every male has a female etheric body and every female has a male etheric body.[1035] It was Jesus' humanity which penetrated the ovum of Sophia's divinity, resulting in an awakening event – the hatching of a cosmic egg. Typically, from a physiological standpoint, the male of a mammalian species delivers his gametes externally of the genitalia, triggering the beginning of the incarnate from a singularity of conception. The female delivers her gametes internally within the genitalia, extracting the full incarnate form from eternity and extruding it into the physical realm of space-time. The gender of creation calls upon the masculine, the male aspect, to be the giver of his seed to the feminine fertile receiver, the female aspect. From her ovaries, the woman provides the portal from which our species enters from eternity and the male provides the opening of that portal by means of his sperm which penetrates the ovum, thus opening that boundary from beyond and into space-time. Upon this merger of chromosomal material, the female then becomes the brewer and deliverer of life and continuation as she feeds and nourishes the new creation internally through the blood of the umbilical cord and then externally with the milk of her bosom. Providing that first post *utero* comfort to every mammal ever born, she presents the feminine Eucharist with the nourishment provided from her nipples and the warmth of her breasts.[1036] Neither mythology nor theology can compare to these feminine optional rites, honors and responsibilities of motherhood – to be the receptive vessel, carrier and incubator of the future, the incarnate intersections of eternity with time, the focal point of the spiritual with the physical, birthing forth life which is both a blended copy of his/her parents and a unique individual.[1037] Fatherhood, however, also has its own sacred rites, honors and responsibilities.

—Λ*—

"The female is one who receives something and, with it, creates. This creative principle is the most marvelous thing in the universe." – *Tao Te Ching*[1038]

—*Ω—

Had the Bogomils and Cathars alleged view as put forth by their opponents on marriage, fornication and pregnancy taken a global hold, that conception results in the trapping of souls into matter through the painful and distasteful business of childbirth, the human species may have ceased long ago.[1039] Yet their exact view on marriage and fornication are not known and is drawn by speculation only. Stories of the Cathars' prohibition of procreation and endorsement of suicide were from charges put forth by the prosecution; it was the Roman Catholic Church claiming them as a threat to society's continuance. Considering they had such a well-organized leadership hierarchy and system of recruiting schools compared to the disarray of the regional Catholic Churches,[1040] there is little or no evidence available from the Cathars themselves to collaborate Rome's allegations. Participation in consensual carnal knowledge seems to not have been considered an imperfection, but as something to be abstained from as an initiation choice in becoming a "Perfect" or "Elect." It was the Cathar leadership that chose celibacy, much like the leadership of the Catholic Church themselves, not a practice called for by those they served. The households of the Languedoc regions of France and of northern Italy seem to have buzzed with the sounds of children during those years of the Cathars. They experienced the same joys as we do of seeing the souls of ancestors live again in the personalities of our children. As the responsibility of raising children faded and their families were complete, the elder Cathars would untie their conjugal union, dedicating themselves to preparing for a return to God by becoming apprentices of an angelic life.[1041]

We may be souls trapped in the matter of our human (or other) form, but it is to provide a training ground for improving the level of our enlightenment, our illumination, our degree of morphing with God, and our experiencing the cosmos. We are all divine beings cocooning within the framework of our physical form. Our material containment within the shells of our body enables us to develop and grow the divine spark within. It serves as "training wheels" until we are ready to again soar in the Heavens and become again, one with the universe.

At times, genders with overlapping features, both physical and psychological, are created by the universe. Such beings with overlapping or comingled features (intersex) should be treated with equality and as welcomed members of society, not as outcasts to be subjected to ridicule and torment nor as a source of unjustified fear. For example, babies born as girls based on the physical genitalia of a vagina have been known to naturally develop and grow a penis and grow deeper voices upon entering puberty. Such "guevedoces" account for a little more than 1% of the population in a particular village located in the Dominican Republic. It is the result of a genetic mutation caused by a missing enzyme (5-α-reductase) which stops hormones that carry the male Y chromosome from entering the womb during fetal development.[1042] Implementing Howard Gardner's Theory of Multiple Intelligences,[1043] we all have suitable aptitudes, talents and skills for which the form or shape of our sexual organs should not be the determining factor in restricting the development and honing of our being, our occupational capabilities and our placement in society. Shunning those with ambiguous genitalia is a sin against God.

With all the current violence, strife, hatred and destruction occurring across the globe on a daily basis, is it really that detrimental if two consenting adults of the same gender choose a life-long monogamous commitment and relationship in which they cherish and respect each other?[1044] Perhaps nature deliberately alters the sexual attraction among some of us as a means to slow down over-accelerated population growth rates. Perhaps Allah has written within our genetic code and hormonal molecules that some of us will be attracted to the same sex as a means of natural population control. Whether by God's design, evolution or both, homosexual attraction is consistently triggered within a fraction of our species constituents. Couples of a same sex union are unable to procreate based on only their gametes and genetic material, yet are receptive to affectionately welcoming adopted children with open and comforting arms into their family. A child raised in a caring, stable and nurturing household will flourish and prosper regardless if their parents are male and female, both male or both female.

In conclusion, initially meeting a potential soulmate, their looks, captive glances, and mannerisms start to become profoundly pleasant if not euphoric.[1045] However, a true soulmate is not someone we find by chance, but rather forms through the development of a committed relationship with another in which the emotional, intellectual and physical needs successfully intermesh to become twin flames.[1046] They form when emotional vulnerability gives way to spiritual permeability, in which the personification of each converges and diverges in harmonizing patterns. During the coupling formation, thoughts will become similar, but not identical, as the union merges. Your soulmate flourishes with trust, affection, honesty and healthy interaction. In a good partnership, soulmates are made and formed, not found. A true soulmate is someone you would still hang out with on the couch, even if you both had no sexual organs. Again, as with many other aspects of life, the beauty and portrayal of sexuality should be handled in a balanced and respected fashion while avoiding public displays of overt licentious conduct or negative exploitation of the oppressed. Carnal love needs to have healthy love at its core in both partners for the relationship to be more than the sum of two individuals.

Chapter 21
The Verdict – Humanity's Judgment And Its Salvation

"LORD, GRANT US THE strength, the energy, the endurance, the focus, the wisdom and the resources to help heal the wounds of the world."
– Prayer Of The Healer, AO

• • • •

THE FINAL JUDGMENT Upon Humanity

The truest sign of faith in Allah or that of a higher mind, is the belief in a better future and the improvement of the human condition for all. If you believe in the future, then you believe in God. It is faith which propels us forward despite the obstacles that come in our way. It is fine to feel satisfied and content for the moment, but there will come a time in which we will need to climb to a higher level. It is the prospect and vision of a better tomorrow that draws us out of stagnation and into the mode of planning our next move in our continued existence. We may plot for ourselves a particular course of direction in life, but it is the current and turbulence of existence that teaches us how to steer our own boats of self-realization.

We are at a spiritual crossroad. Humanity has technically advanced itself through its quest for knowledge to the capability of self-annihilation. Nuclear weapons made their debut during the Second World War of the mid-20th century and have been hanging over our heads ever since like the Sword of Damocles. It's miraculous that we've made it this far and have lasted this long without blowing ourselves up, but for some reason or another, our species still exists. Perhaps it has been both our ultimate underlying desire for the continuance of civilizations and the work of angels.

Humanity's quest for knowledge has also given us the capability of self-preservation through our relationships with the elements. The world has become much smaller (in the figurative sense) with the rapid ex-

504

change of communication and data via satellites, the internet and more efficient modes of travel that can take us much farther in less time. We now have the ability to track the proximity of asteroids and comets relative to Earth and possibly even alter their course. In doing so, we may be able to prevent a devastating impact and a mass extinction level event from collisions with such interstellar objects. Instrumentation exists to help predict when volcanic eruptions are imminent and when a tsunami (tidal wave) could be forming.

God has judged the fate of humanity. The verdict is that humanity has been given the chance to choose their own future. Although there are some who still continue their negative ways, there are others who thrive for harmony and peace. An entire species should never be judged or condemned on the negative actions of a few. Our future survival will be dependent on our actions as a collective, not on the destructive intervention of divinity. God will not be coming down from the heavens to annihilate and destroy us. We are perfectly capable of doing that on our very own. Do you really think that which created us would truly want to destroy us? Any loving parent wants their children to thrive in harmony with each other but recognizes that children must learn to grow on their own. Self-determination is vital for self-preservation and we need to take responsibility for our direction. We need to regain a positive relationship with nature and stop destroying the diversity and abundance of living organisms on this planet, or else we will eventually destroy ourselves. Despite the current rate of ecological destruction, it is humanity that will be depleted; nature will recover. If we continue our sterilization of the planet, our extinction is inevitable, but the roaches, tardigrades and other life forms will continue on. The species of planet Earth will always recover, with or without us. It would prefer to have us on board as part of its future, if Allah is willing.

—Λ*—

"When man interferes with the Tao, the sky becomes filthy, the earth becomes depleted, the equilibrium crumbles, creatures become extinct."

– wisdom from over 2,500 years ago[1047]

—*Ω—

There is no doubt that turbulent years and extraordinary times places a strain on all our beings. We may have temporarily lost our confidence, but as a species we must look at the long-term growth of humanity over the past 4,000 years. We have advanced our desire to heal through medical and psychological practices which provide repeatable results. We have recognized the negative exploitive nature of slavery (aka human trafficking) and its damaging suppression upon a being and a culture as a whole. Although not completely eliminated from our planet, civilized governments have correctly sought to prohibit this despicable practice. Humanity as a collective is trying, but dangerously narcissistic characters seem to wedge or froth their way up to positions of authoritative power over both the small scale and larger groups of people.

Although some pain still lingers from the birth of this millennium and this century, we have somewhat surpassed the wounds from the atrocious events of September 11, 2001 in which a great religion was distorted as a way of falsely justifying a cowardice and wasteful act of violence and destruction. I'm sure Allah is mightily disgusted with those horrific acts of annihilation and is dealing with the responsible souls accordingly. Although those horrid actions came from the fanatical distortion of Koranic sūrahs eight and nine (*al-Anfal* and *al-Tawba*), they could have just as easily been fabricated by fanatical distortions from sections of the *Old Testament* (aka the *Torah*). Fluctuations in the economy have questioned our sense of material prosperity, and perhaps also our close relationships. We notice weather patterns starting to change as dryer droughts occur in some regions and heavier floods in others. Scientific debate still rages on whether these changes are natural cyclical in the grand scheme of Earth's history or whether they are being caused by our excessive exploitation of this planet's natural resources and release of an overabundance of carbon-based vapors into the atmosphere. Despite what might be causing these potential climatic changes, are you willing to take the chance of having to tell your children, grandchildren or great grandchildren that we could have done something about it and that it could have been prevented? Are you going to be able to look them in the eyes and tell them that the damaged global legacy they will inherit is a result of our failure to act?

We don't inherit the world from our parents, we borrow it from our children.[1048]

—A*—

"The ones that matter most are the children." – Lakota Proverb

—*O—

We are all only human and can't always change the world at once, but it is the small little strings of action that can result in a catalytic web of action. Those little strings of action branch out in time and can have a grander affect than first realized. There is a principle in nuclear physics where a chain reaction occurs after a certain critical mass has been reached. Once a certain threshold is crossed, the momentum of the reaction accelerates rapidly. The Global Human Consciousness (GHC) is composed of a multitude of individual minds, an egregore all contributing to the spiritual movement of the human entity as a whole towards the Universal Consciousness. A minute proportion of these minds retard this growth as they become caught up in thoughts of anger, hatred, isolated ignorance, rage, grasps for power, irrational emotional and unhealthy pleasure seeking. A substantially larger proportion, however, is raising the GHC to the verge of this threshold. If we want to change the nature of the world then we must first change the nature of ourselves. The shrinking of the world through the speed and ease of communication has brought us to a point of synchronizing our thoughts and actions into a pulse which promotes harmony, illumination and enlightenment for all. There is a common approach to describing what must be done to steer ourselves into a better future. It is a dynamic that fluctuates between "I" and "we." There are courses of action and behavior that "we must do", but they are initiated by the first action of "I must do."

—Δ*—

"We but mirror the world. All the tendencies present in the outer world are to be found in the world of our body. If we could change ourselves, the tendencies in the world would also change. As a man changes his own nature, so does the attitude of the world change towards him. This is the divine mystery supreme. A wonderful thing it is and the source of our happiness. We need not wait to see what others do." – Mohandas Mahatma Gandhi[1049]

—*O—

As we become more aware of our global village, we start to transcend and blend the boundaries that define our cultural differences. The boundaries are still there but instead of seeing them as solid walls to keep out that which is different and strange, they become semi-permeable membranes of tolerance, pluralism, kinship and discovery – the exact position of the wall's segregating footings can no longer be defined. As more and more of us start to reconnect to the godhead that created us and our world, our unhealthy egos start to heal. A sense of balance starts to develop in our lives; balance with ourselves; balance with our relationships; balance with our work; balance with our play; and balance with our universe. When more and more of us become balanced in the proper direction, a pressure builds on the GHC, creating a force which steers it in the direction of universal harmony.

Aspects of humanity are out of balance with the universe. We are out of sync with the relationship between ourselves and our world. If we take from our world, we should also return to it. If we do not mend our disrespectful ways of treating our environments, nature will continue despite humanity's self-destruction, but we will not. Every act creates both elements of evil and good. It is our responsibility in approaching the godhead in a manner which minimizes the evil components and maximize the good ones. Over-pollution of the air, excessive contamination of the water, extreme destruction of the forests, plains, soils and species, and all the other eco-sins are our resistance to allowing God's will to be done on Earth as it is in Heaven.[1050] Our behavior of the addictive lure of the false gods of overconsumption, a culture that praises gluttony, the lacking of sufficient exit plans for our refuse and the abusive pursuit of the "Number of the Beast" without proper regard to the ecology of all organisms, is an affront to our offspring, future generations and our own spiritual growth – we are committing biocide due to the habits of our ecological plunder. Why are we participating in planetary matricide, rebelling so disrespectfully of the Great Mother, the *Sapientia Dei*, who embodied herself into the Earth? Sophia is our consort, our divine lover, God's comforter and overflow, always trying to pull us out of the muck and filth residing in the ignorance of only pursuing matter and secular things. She is not just the definition of personification of divine wisdom, she is an actual being, an essence of consciousness and an eternal entity that can manifest into the physical realm, whenever love is projected into the universe. I think it is Sophia herself trying to lead us from the religious absurdities of violence, immaturity and failings spread throughout the *Old Testament*, the defilement of God attributed to the Gnostic Demiurge. As a representative of divinity, she is the gatekeeper between the abyss and emptiness of the kenoma and the fullness and gnosis found in the pleroma. A secret for all initiates is that the pleroma is accessed by first wandering in the kenoma. It is when we learn to embrace and make the best of it while being in the kenoma that we are eventually released into the pleroma. The kenoma is what Jesus went through during his 40 days of temptation by the devil while in the Judean desert and again starting with his arrest in the garden across the Kidron Valley. If Sophia is always trying to reach us to help us discover who we are and what we are capable of accomplishing, then why are we revolting against this goddess, the feminine side of divinity, who morphed the source of life and consciousness into the material body of our planet? Why are we so afraid to recognize and adore the Demeter, Artemis and Isis within the psyche of our home world instead of choosing a pattern of abuse and plunder? I wonder if we had referred to our planet as Father Earth and the life forms upon it as Father Nature, instead of Mother Earth and Mother Nature, would an ingrained misogyny within portions of our species have treated the land, air and seas so poorly? Why are we so willing to commit femicide to the mythological and biological roots of the terrestrial globe that evolved us?

We are all guilty to some degree of sinning against the environment, but it is now time for us to redeem ourselves. All of us leave an impression to various degrees upon the ecological systems and cycles of the planet, from our carbon footprint to the empty containers tossed into the trash. If we are to continue surviving, then we must learn to humble our egos to a balanced state and to regain that lost knowledge of who we are and where we came from by healing the land and the waters. Mother Earth provided the womb of her ecology to incubate our evolution, but she can only give us so much. We are high maintenance and are exhausting her reserves. It is time to give back to her the love she has so unconditionally provided to our species in allowing us dominion over other animals.[1051] Gaia needs our help and it is time to acknowledge our debt of gratitude by making amends for the damage we have done. Our very existence is credited to the green plant life that she sowed for us, the autotrophs that provide the beginning links of our food chain and the oxygen that we breathe. Yet, we continuously pluck the diversity of forests and jungles from Mother Earth's surfaces at a rate that is unsustainable and beyond acceptable. We have negatively exploited our Mother planet enough by overheating her with our exorbitant gaseous carbon emissions, surface devastations, water contaminations and over-destruction of insect and animal habitats. Now we need to care for her. If we act soon enough, she will forgive us. Being at a crossroad, a juncture and at two divergent possibilities in our spiritual development, it is time for each individual to make the decision whether they are going to continue on their present course or if they will evolve to a higher state of existence. Each of us has to decide whether we are going to take the steps necessary to preserve the future or just talk about it. It was the Greatest Generation that pulled itself together in the mid-20th century to stop a dangerous despot from trying to take over the world – we can be the generation that pulls itself together at the beginning of this 21st century to save it. The hands on the Doomsday Clock can still be reversed if we all come together as an energized team and rally as an electrified species towards a better tomorrow.

—Λ*—

"Don't be afraid to care." – *Pink Floyd*[1052]

—*Ω—

We need to act through the steadfast application of sound science, the power of conscientious consumerism and common-sense care and concern, not by an approach that "one size fits all", fanaticism, environ-elitism, unreasonable "Not In My Back Yard" (NIMBYism) or stretching the limits of what is considered "green" through propaganda. More seems to be spent on promoting and advertising the "greenness" of a product or service than its actual level of ecological soundness. The actions of one can trigger the actions of many as we engage in partnership with the planet's ecology, not as its nemesis. We can rebuild and save the hydrosphere and biosphere of our pale blue dot – that isolated, fragile, swirling speck among the Milky Way galaxy and the only planet in the solar system not named after a Greek god or goddess.[1053] What do you think, can we pull together as a species and accomplish such a change in environmental mindset, a shift in cultural currents and a herculean task of global refurbishment? Do we pursue the courageous enterprise of shifting economic branches into repair and maintenance programs for our home planet?

Now is the time to reflect on what type of consumer we are going to be, what type of person we are, what type of person we want to become, and what type of role model we want to be for ourselves and others. Now is the time to determine what type of connection do we want to have with the universe, what type of relationship do we want to have with ourselves, what type of relationship do we want with this grand entity often referred to as "God" that goes by so many other names and has so many other branches for connecting to it, and what type of essence do we want to be when we leave this secular realm and enter into the next. This is the time to reassess how to develop our spiritual core.

Again, I can assure you that the supreme mind (i.e., God) will not be coming down from the heavens to destroy the species of humanity; we are perfectly capable of doing that on very our own. The mere fact that we still exist today is evidence enough of the Lord's love by his determination to keep trying to teach us. No matter how stubborn, resistant and recalcitrant our species may be, the Divine Teacher will keep trying to reach us. Although humanity is far from perfect, we have enough redeeming qualities to justify our continuance. However, repeating from Chapter 13, today's society still needs to regain its cohesion with a modern mythology that distinguishes between good, evil and neither. The mythological dimension of our life is our individual destiny merging with the cosmic destiny of humanity.[1054] Without this binding connection between generations, humanity will be left with no direction but downwards.

The one fundamental spiritual principle that we must never fail to forget during each moment of our secular existence is that we are an aspect of the universal mind experiencing itself. We came from this divine essence and we shall return to it someday. Our behavior, our actions, our words and our deeds become a part of who we are and they are constantly being recorded by this universal entity of thought for all to one day see. Only through divine revelation or upon leaving our current realm do we bear witness to the impact of our deeds reflected back upon us, both of good or evil intent. It is therefore imperative that we always choose a pattern of behavior or action that does not primarily serve our shortsighted egos, a misguided ethos that everything is disposable, but also serves the long-term Self of the greater whole by thinking in terms of eternity.

—Δ*—

"Shortsighted is the philosophy which counts on selfishness as the master motive of human action." – Henry George[1055]

—*O—

Our purpose in this world is to maintain and add to the continuum of human consciousness. This is done through the advancement of intellect and spirit by seeking truth through exposure to the writings of past and current scholars. It requires a willingness to advance our current level of behavior such that we can become our own role models. It is built upon a foundation of treating others with respect and courtesy, but at the same time respecting ourselves in the process. It requires the ability to filter out and block that which drags our being downward (i.e., the abuse of drugs, practicing unethical behavior, emanating unhealthy emotional outbursts, being focused only on ourselves) as well as those around us, while pursuing a steady state of happiness through economical investment in our psychological future. Happiness is a content state of mind that must be practiced and forged through learning to see beyond obscuring dark clouds of misfortune, for sunshine is always above the clouds. Such investments into our psyche should be done over our lifetime and can include the enjoying of a creative activity in solitude, an inexpensive stroll with a friend, the reading of a library book, the painting of an abstract composition, the throwing or kicking of a ball, the playing of a musical instrument, the minimizing of our needs, the positive influence of a child, reflecting on our life direction and the simplification of our routine.

• • • •

DIVERSITY IS OUR SALVATION

Diversity is God's continued elixir and foundation of creation; it is the building blocks of Allah's works growing into more complex forms. The Lord is behind the evolutionary forces of creative diversity that provides a strengthening effect among its collectives by creating resistance to harmful affronts. Diversity is the interaction of evolution by creating the necessary redundancies for survival and for enduring through times of stress. For example, diversity of crops provides a natural probability of resistance for preventing the entire yield being wiped out by a fungus or voracious larvae. Diversity of sensors, controls and back-up systems in electro-mechanical systems assures continued operations should certain critical failures occur. Diversity in economic markets provides buffers and flexibility so financial engines can endure through stock crashes, recessions and depressions. Diversity of people, races and ethnicity is a force multiplier as explained in the well-spoken quote below by a Superintendent of the US Air Force Academy.

—A*—

"Embracing, celebrating and striving for diversity isn't just the right thing to do, nor is it just a sensitive and politically correct, knee-jerk response. It is the application of our collective intelligence – our uniqueness coming together to fulfill our duty to provide the nation with the most effective and lethal fighting force we have the capacity to employ on the battlefield. To put it in the terms of a military leader: Diversity is a force multiplier. We must do this together – all ranks and ages, races and religions, sexual orientations and identities – all of us." – Lt. Gen. Jay Silveria[1056]

—*O—

Indulging in the luxurious meal of albino sturgeon caviar, matsutake mushroom or white truffles and saffron encrusted Scottish lobster finished with a luxurious desert of The Frrrozen Haute Chocolate ice cream sundae sounds like a costly meal of rare decadence.[1057] Imagine, however, that was all that was available for breakfast, lunch and dinner for weeks or months. The thought of eating the same thing over and over again can make one nauseous. The craving for something of different flavors would become one's prayer. The interjection of even a jelly sandwich would become a priceless salvation.[1058] I personally sometimes prefer the flavors of broccoli and Brussels sprouts and other times favor the sweetness of Drakes® RingDings® or Little Debbie® Swiss Rolls. It is the diversity of flavors that stimulates one's taste sensors, not the repetitive and continued consumption of something's perceived value.

Our healthy existence is based on both the silence and noise of life. It is the coming out of silence and into noise and the returning into silence from the noise that makes for the diversity between moments. The instant one hears a tone, such as the note of middle D coming out of the abyss, we become alive with spirit. If that note continues on indefinitely with no change or rest, the infinite condition would then drive us mad. We would become dulled being exposed to constant noise just as being exposed to constant silence. It is the change and dynamic transitions from each state that verifies continuance – the interplay between being human and being divine.

As humanity advances beyond the gravitational domain of planet Earth in pursuit of the physical rapture that will send us to the heavens (i.e., other star systems), if we haven't learned as a whole to accept and embrace the wonderment among the diversity and multitude of true religious paths and cultures, how are we ever going to grasp the potential magnitude of true religious paths followed by advanced intelligent sentient beings from other worlds? If we do not embrace the beauty among the diversity of skin tones, cultures and ethnic backgrounds on our own planet, how are we ever going to adjust to encounters with the forms of intelligent beings from other parts of the universe? If we do not take a serious attitude and approach to heal the global marble of life upon which we dwell, are we willing to endure our home planet's demise beginning with the destruction of diversity among the food chain?

As a species, we should never lose the focus of the ideas and values that have contributed to humanity's advancement over the centuries: 1) the preservation of sentient life whenever possible; 2) the protection of civil rights in all cases; 3) the recognition of the virtues of self-determination and that slavery of sentient beings is wrong; 4) a thirst for knowledge fueled by curiosity; and, 5) that healthy tolerance and diversity is beneficial. Healthy tolerance is the same as reasonable tolerance, meaning accepting differences in behavior that do not cause harm. Tolerance does not necessarily mean liking, but it does mean a willingness to accept and dwell among behaviors that we may not favor. For example, someone can have a preference for hip hop music and a distaste for country music. In which case, they may avoid going to country music concerts, but they should not hate nor become an activist to ban country music. Regardless, all good music provides the listener with a transporting effect, sending their emotional core beyond the confines of self.

Tolerance is the healthy acceptance of that which is different. Coming to terms with the tolerance, or better yet the pluralism required of Globalization is paramount, if we are ever going to attempt Universalization. By the very nature of technological advancement, we are no longer isolated citizens within our own countries. We are transforming from citizens of individual nations to citizens of the common globe. In our transformation, we become more empathetic to the woes of our world. From earthquakes in India, floods in Mozambique, hurricanes in the Caribbean or Gulf Coast, viral outbreaks in China, fires in Australia or the Western United States, warfare in or near the Balkan regions, clashes in the Middle East and the recent global pandemics, we are all instantly exposed to the suffering of our fellow beings.

At times we may feel limited in what can be done from our vantage point. Some of us are striving to get our own local neighborhoods of influence in order, others find their time taken up with the demands of modern life. We need to regain our time for reflection through the process of simplification. Complicated ideas should be simplified, not the other way around. Technology should be implemented in a way that simplifies our lives and gives us more time to be human, instead of taking away from our humanity. Technology should free us and work for us, not the other way around. We should not be working for technology and becoming slaves to its abuse or inappropriate applications. As Globalization takes hold, it has to be done with a sense of ethical implementation. It should not erode the cultures that become exposed to it but rather enhance and merge them in a way that empowers people to raise the awareness of themselves and the world around them.

Globalization has the potential to act as a positive, reciprocal, benevolent self-colonization of the world, creating a global cosmopolitan that promotes cultural diversity, pluralism and access to variations in ideologies. It may spark a so-called reversal of The Tower of Babel, merging our planet into a universal culture that seeks to find that which is different rather than hiding behind that which is the same. Unlike the land grabs of invasions, empires, imperialisms and colonialisms that dominated the last three millennia of human expansion, Globalization may be the very inoculation needed to prevent future wars. We already see the benefits as global consortiums and standards [i.e., United Nations (UN), International Organization for Standardization (ISO), Globally Harmonized System of Classification and Labeling of Chemicals (GHS), etc.] are becoming more influential than their individual members. If societies are so intermingled in trade, both of material goods and ideas, then attacking another becomes identical with attacking the self. The only way that Globalization will be successful is if the notion of negative exploitation of both human and planetary resources is removed as its primary driving force. It is time for us to shift our behavior upon the planet from one of negative exploitation to that of positive exploitation. Remove the notion of greed and excessive profit taking and replace it with the notion of creating a better standard of living for the participants at all levels. This is the proper approach to take if we want a better world for the children of humanity and for our future progeny.

If we are to continue progressing as a species, then curbing our aggressiveness and rising our identities above individual nations and religions is the only way that humanity will humbly come closer to God/

Allah. The greatest threat to the world is not ignorance; it is the repetition of ignorance, for that shows a breakdown in educative access and a lack of compassion. The truest and most sacred of all jihads is striving to bring every generation out of ignorance through teachings of peace, love and tolerance. How do we stop the repetitive cycle of ignorance from generation to generation? How do we stop ignorance from showing itself in times of peril or strife? It was White Eagle's philosophy of love (the love of love) that has ever since helped and healed people and the wounds of the world. This teaching has become a simple revelation of mystical Christianity, transcending religious dogma and bringing together the knowledge of all true scriptural wisdoms.[1059]

God has the confidence and hope that his children will mature. He trusts that we will learn to use knowledge constructively in advancing the growth of humanity and our relationship with the universe to a state of higher existence. She has faith in her children and wants us to manipulate stardust (the remnants of exploded stars), into habitable spaces, moons and planets. But in terraforming other heavenly bodies, any present or existing species of life and their environmental habitats must be respected and not negatively exploited. Repeating the same atrocities done unto the dodo, the bison, for the plumes of exotic birds, the passenger pigeon and other Earth creatures, unto non-terra life forms is a sin in the eyes of the Lord. Anthropocene influenced extinction must end and never extend or spread beyond the gravity well of our own home planet. Our entrance into the final frontiers of space must not be as invasive swarms of conquerors. We must not repeat the decimations that have occurred so many times in human history upon planet Earth. In spreading the seed of our lineage in the colonization of other planets and moons, any pre-existing non-space faring and space faring AISBs must be respected. If a planet already has non-space faring AISBs, then we are not to settle upon it or colonize it. If a planet is already occupied with space-faring AISBs, then we are to respectfully obtain permission to establish any settlements. These are new commandments from the Supreme Consciousness of the Universe. Once we are spiritually and technologically ready, we will be able to push together the cosmic dust into new regions of space for fair and ecologically sound colonization, recreating copies of pseudo Earths and initiating new Edens.

—Δ*—

"The best way to predict the future is to invent it." – Alan Curtis Kay[1060]

—*O—

Humanity has to decide if it wants a future and to determine its direction, not as a country nor as a religious following nor as an ethnicity, but as a species if it is to thrive. If the choice is "yes", then an acceptance of those with different religious views and beliefs is a necessity, not an option. If we are to survive as a species, we must be receptive to crossing religious and cultural borders and embrace the world community. Implementing "Ujima", a Kiswahili word meaning the interdependence of life and a community working together, the future prosperity of the world is dependent on our efforts and those of influential angels

—Λ*—

"How wonderful it is that nobody need wait a single moment before starting to improve the world." – Anne Frank[1061]

• • • •

"GOOD ACTIONS ARE THE invisible hinges on the door of heaven." – Victor Hugo[1062]

• • • •

"I CANNOT DO ALL THE good that the world needs, but the world needs all the good that I can do." – Jana Stanfield[1063]

—*Ω—

Although the trumpets are sounding, telling us the moment has arrived for us to awaken to the next level of awareness in expanding our beings and ascending our consciousness to a higher state, God will not be coming down with all his angels and demons to destroy humanity.[1064] They will not be arriving to harm the earth, sea and trees,[1065] for we are doing that on our very own. On the contrary, the angels of *Revela-*

tion will be coming down to help us heal the wounds of our home planet. The COVID-19 pandemic was a "warning shot across the bow" of our species, telling us of what will continue to happen if we fail to modify our destructive ecological patterns nor improve upon our global social cooperation. Even Pope Francis recognized that Mother Nature will overrule our over-consumptive behavior if we do not adjust it ourselves.[1066] Allah will not be stepping in like a *Deus Ex Machina* to rescue us from our own ignorance either. Divinity has given us the gift of steering our own destiny through tribulations and celebrations, setbacks and accomplishments, stumbles and epiphanies. He will still be perpetually active in the daily lives of all his creations. He/she will still be dropping by every once in a while in the form of direct avatars, emissaries, prophets, spiritual guides, shamans, messengers, buddhas, saints, and angels. When, where and to whom she will be revealing her thoughts is something only God knows.

Chapter 22
The Path Of The Prophets

"TO UNDERSTAND DIVINITY is to become a part of his or her design, not to escape from it nor tarnish it. Maintain yourself as a principal
element of God's works, not just as an observer, but as a participant by
displaying acts of kindness, charity and grace." – AO

• • • •

THERE HAVE BEEN MANY bona fide prophets throughout the history of humanity. Many were great visionaries who did not even realize
that they were prophets. Some were considered to have special relationships with divinity. Others were considered to be simple people who catalyzed the quantum growth of their society through words or actions.
The genuine prophets and shamans of past, having extraordinary insight
and/or divine vision, built upon the works of earlier messengers by reinforcing the eternal truths and at times, dare exposing new ones. Their
message was intended to supplement existing principles and also to add
new ones as a means of advancing us closer to the godhead. They recognized that a new schema of faith can find a hearing only by appealing to
the religious instincts and susceptibilities that already exist in their intended audience.[1067] Designed to cross all boundaries of ethnicity, culture and race, a reminder or extension of the divine message must pass
the test of our reason and of our own spiritual instincts. The prophets
of the past seemed to be composed of both those with a unique connection to divinity, perhaps acting as interpreters, scouts or agents for God,
and others who were merely influential secular moral philosophers. No
matter what their message or their particular relationship with divinity
was, they had an epic influence upon both the consciousness and subconsciousness of humanity. The teachings of all the great prophets are available to us, if we allow ourselves to be receptive to their works. Spiritual awakenings do not emerge from structured programs nor through detailed strategies; they ignite in one heart at a time. However, there have

been instances where one's personal awakening brought spiritual replenishment to the millions.[1068]

—Λ*—

"Allah chooses messengers from the angels and from men." – *The Koran*[1069]

• • • •

"THERE IS NO DISTINCTION whatsoever among the bearer of my message." – Bahá'u'lláh[1070]

—*Ω—

Each of these teachers had to compromise between the visions of harmony they saw for humanity, divine will and the current state of society's *status quo*. They knew God's desire for humanity's advancement but also realized that they would have to compromise with the inertias of ignorance among aspects of the current culture and knew that too much change would not be accepted. Their expectations of us were often more than where we wanted to push ourselves and the prophets faced anguish in confronting opposition to their coaching and shepherding guidance. For ignorance cannot handle the path of enlightenment and resists the epiphanies of true spiritual growth.

When hypocrisy has become too prevalent in a society and truths need to be recognized, messengers exposed the facts. Confucius recognized the collapse of his society among the squandering of feudal disputes and the Buddha recognized cycles of existence and the collective equality of all beings. Jesus recognized the outdated and unreasonable moral standards and falseness of the Judaic Pharisees in his day. Mohammad recognized the hypocrisy of the behavior among some of the controlling portions of the clerical population occurring behind a veil of Christian, Judaic or pagan practices. In doing so, Mohammad pulled the Arabic world together in a commonality of socio-economic equalization while retaining respected Christian and Judaic friends. We have the modern hypocrisy of the negative exploitive actions of unethical and destructive excessive commercial activities. Time and time again, others have arisen when they saw corruption and hypocrisy metastasizing within the religious ranks or to steer humanity's societal evolution in the proper direction. Such setbacks were not the fault of religion, but rather that of human failings. Those prophets recognized the spiritual illogic that was coming from the misuse of phrases and the stressing of contradictions within the scriptures. They voiced their views, sometimes in the face of persecution, punishment or execution, because they felt their society pulling away from the true direction of the godhead.

When walking and participating among the crowds, such enlightened beings were as human as the rest of us. When alone and letting God flow into them, they became part of the divine. Their teachings and advanced knowledge were often initially dismissed within the local region of their upbringing, such as with the case of Confucius, Jesus and others.[1071] With their childhoods being familiar among family, friends and the people of the local region, the prophets encountered the typical small-town smothering, molding and subduing that comes with growing up in a tight village and among sibling relationships. They too found themselves entangled in the emotional knots of family fabric that can dampen one's life energy and often humbly suppressed their true selves to respectively participate within their kin and neighborhood dynamics. They would need to hide their *Daemon* so as not to alarm those around them, while only allowing their *eidolon* to show as they conformed and fit within the culture they were born into. But on the other hand, quality ties of family and friends provided support and love even when they were at the lowest points of their lives.

—A*—

"A prophet is honored everywhere except in his own hometown and among his own family." – Jesus of Nazareth [1072]

• • • •

"NO PROPHET IS ACCEPTED in his own village; no physician heals those who know him." – Jesus of Nazareth [1073]

• • • •

"THE SAGE HAS ONE ADVANTAGE: He is immortal. If this is not his century, many others will be." – Baltasar Gracián[1074]

—*O—

The great teachers never meant for their message to be enforced upon a society or culture, but rather, desired for it to be emulated, accepted, absorbed and embraced. They only wanted others to witness for themselves the grand epiphany of what they knew – to expose us to the same moments of insight and flashes of understanding that they had encountered. Through their love of humanity, they delivered their lessons, knowing they would have to risk the misuse of its intent. Imagine how Jesus has felt throughout the last two millenniums seeing his teachings distorted; from the pillaging carried out in the name of the Crusades, the Inquisition, the forcing of others to give up their traditions and beliefs which was formerly their cultural connection to eternity. For even he said, "I did not come to abolish the Law or the prophets, but to fulfill."[1075] Under the guise of excessive religious evangelicalism, what started out as colonization to the "New World" turned into an invasion of Europeans across the Americas after Columbus' false hypotheses of a better trade route for reaching the Indian subcontinent. Gestures of token amends have been made to the progeny of indigenous inhabitants for the assaulting assimilation of their ancestors, with the understanding that being a represented part of a national leviathan (e.g., the democratic republic of the United States or Canada) has its advantages. Namely, they consist of better medical access and sanitation, educational opportunities, reduced risk of famine and plagues and the unlikeliness of attacks from neighboring nation tribes.

The indication of a true Messiah is that they arrive just "in the nick of time",[1076] like a thief in the night,[1077] in the blink of an eye, and even "out of the blue" to realign the direction of humanity. They will not be conquerors nor invaders and will not be reigning by sword, bullet, bomb, missile or force, but rather will shepherd by example and through the impetus of love. They will be known by their reinitiating of religion back into the hearts and minds of men and women. By becoming an imperfect paragon and beacon of divinity, they shall catalyze humanity to a paradigm shift of scientific and spiritual awakening. They will become an example for faith, a mentor for the age, a symbol of peace, benevolent power, beauty and truth. By teaching us to pull the God-self within to connect to the God throughout, such a role model would give humanity and other AISBs the mindset to strive for the godhead.[1078]

Many of the great scriptures and oral legends talk of divinity again making an appearance through human form. Do not look for a messiah manifestation in others, look for it within yourself. Just do an internet search for "messiah claimants" to see how many people throughout the centuries have made claim to being the anointed one.[1079] Perhaps one day Maranatha (the day of Yahuah) will occur and Kalki, Mahdi, Jesus, Ajita, Isa, Yeshua HaMashiach, the Buddha, Hermes Trismegistus, Vishnu, Lakshmi, Moshiach, a Bodhisattvas, Pahana, a Tzaddiq Ha-dor, a Savior, a Phoster, Maitreya, a Soter, Saoshyant, a Missiayah, the Messiah or Messiahs will again walk among us and, hopefully, we will have the spiritual perception and wisdom to recognize him, her or them. God learned his lesson from the last time the coming of a Messiah was clearly announced; the human authority having jurisdiction, King Herod of Judea, allegedly slaughtered all males two years of age or less and living in the vicinity of Bethlehem – the Massacre of the Innocents.[1080]

—Δ*—

"But of that day and hour no one knows, not even the angels of heaven, not the Son, but the Father alone." – Jesus Christ[1081]

—*O—

A redeemer of our species bringing heavenly knowledge, gnosis to humanity, could in fact be an avatar from any of the great religions, but no authentic Messiah can be everything at once. They would appear being more human at times and other times more divine. Being so bound by the religious requirements, restrictions, and contradictions put in place by a variety of human scriptural interpretations of when, where and how they are to arrive, that our acknowledgment of them is forced to become subjective. The litany and laundry list put forth by those religions with messianic doctrines is too broad and is based on probability, human biases and not absolutes. I'm sure any genuine Messiah would be reluctant to step forward while simultaneously chuckling inside at the multitude of ways that humanity has interpreted his or her arrival. The only thing that is absolute is that only God knows of the day and hour when his/her representative(s) shall arrive.[1082] Any Messiah would not appear to all people in the same way, due to varying levels of enlightenment and spiritual development among the populace – only the wise will initially recognize him or her. I can assure you of this, he or she will not be publicly walking around in white robes and sandals, since they would be conforming to the preferred clothing and attire to match with the generational styles of the day. Can a true Messiah as one person, ever so again influence the world and impact the human psyche the way the Buddha, Jesus Christ and Mohammad did? Can one person's individual surrender and resultant awakening so again change the course of human history? Can a true redeemer ever carry out their noble mission and generous call to truth without facing internal panic and despair tinged with terror? Will the generations witnessing their arrival accept or reject their words? Can a genuine savor not feel overwhelmed by being in a position beyond any mortal's qualifications? Will we see their perceived religious non-conformities as a threat or as a blessing? In presenting their message, they must confront the howling mockeries of self-doubt, external stumbles, resistance put forth by the Demiurge and coming off as the fool, where nothing is certain but uncertainty. Yet it is the fool persistent in his folly who will become wise.[1083]

—Λ*—

"It is no easy matter to live a life that is modelled on Christ's, but it is unspeakably harder to live one's own life as truly as Christ lived his." – C. G. Jung[1084]

• • • •

"IF ANYONE IS CONFIDENT in himself that he is Christ's, let him consider this again within himself, that just as he is Christ's, so also are we." – *New Testament*[1085]

• • • •

"IT IS BY IMITATING Christ, either the person or the mythic allegory, that we become a Christ." – AO

—*Ω—

True prophets and saints are initially thought mad to the masses of ignorant people.[1086] Their understanding of reality makes them seem as "weird" to us, because we are somewhat obstructed from viewing what they see. Yet, appearing mad to us, they see much further into reality than we do and have healthier minds for it. It is we who are crazy, for our narrow focus on the short term of the material world blinds us from the greater significance of the spiritual realms. Hopefully, when such genuine messengers do arrive with recognition, we will welcome them with attentive ears, receptiveness and understanding rather than with ridicule, torment, dismissiveness, persecution and execution. Maybe this time, however, we will marvel at their presence within our lifetime and not initially reject, revile, vilify and despise such God Seekers or avatars of love. Maybe this time they won't encounter disdain, apathy, scorn and opprobrium from us while delivering their message.[1087] Maybe this time we won't curse their arrival as a threat to our ego's *status quo* and will actually feel blessed by their coming as an advancement of our well-being. Maybe this time we won't ostracize or persecute them for holding views that are different from the "norm", counter to the religious authorities or contradictory to the political powers of their day.[1088] Maybe this time, we won't humiliate, denounce, rise against them, condemn them to drink hemlock, force them to wear a crown of thorns, nail them to a wooden cross, imprison, assassinate, scald, roast them over coals or slay their bodies. Maybe this time we won't fear their words, claim them to be heretics and char their living bodies upon flaming bundles of sticks and posts of wood or send them to the gallows. Maybe this time their mothers won't need to endure the shedding of mournful tears or utter despairing wails from their lips while witnessing their child's demise at the hands of unenlightened, sneering and mocking crowds. The mobs that we may describe as being mad, evil or wicked, actually suffer from a lack of spiritual evolution and awareness.[1089] Maybe this time such Seekers won't be misunderstood by our insecurities, we won't condemn their writings, resent their insight, burn their manuscripts or nail their books to shelves and we won't feel intimidated by their deeds. Maybe this time we will actually welcome them with open arms, instead of treating them with callousness, prejudice and fanatic hostility.[1090]

—A*—

"For this reason also the wisdom of God said, 'I will send to the prophets and apostles, and some of them will be persecuted and killed.'"
– New Testament[1091]

• • • •

"AND THE PEOPLE SAW it, and did witness of it, and were angry with him because of his power; and he did also do many more miracles, in the sight of the people, in the name of Jesus." – The Book Of Mormon[1092]

—*O—

In these modern and evolved times of the 21st century, will blasphemy trials again resurface to condemn those seeking illumination, enlightenment and human advancement through a pathway of love? It is not the spirits that I fear, it is humanity's reactions. The Catholic Church of today has made leaps and bounds in steering itself in the correct direction of the godhead and far away from the days of Tsar Boril, Bernard of Gui, Pope Lucius III, Arnuad Amaury and Simon de Montfort. It is the dread and ignorance of modern extreme political and religious fundamentalists that I fear will become the new Inquisitors, not the goodness of today's clergy among the Roman Catholic Church, Judaic and Islamic genuine leadership. What the fundamentalists choose to hate in others is a projection of what they hate in themselves.[1093] Will misguided zealots, fanatics and the feebleminded mistakenly claim a true and authentic return of God's representative as an antichrist? Maybe this time religious authorities will gain composure over the suspicion and madness underlying their fears and choose to embrace and receive a potential Messiah with open arms, rather than mistakenly declare them an unholy anathema. Maybe this time a savior won't stumble and fall against the frustrations and destructions put forth by Tzvarnoharno. Maybe this time humanity will actually perk up their ears and listen – Horton will not be silenced and they will hear Jojo and all the other beings of Whoville.[1094] Maybe this time we will actually protect a redeemer from the wasteful calumny of stampeding mob mentality, kangaroo courts adjudicating trumped up charges of heresy and the ignorance that unjustly fears such savants of science and religion. For when we choose to destroy those rare emissaries and instruments of divinity, manifestors of love that are sent to serve, save and redirect, we are only destroying ourselves. Intelligence driven by love is not to be feared, ignorance driven by hatred is to be overcome. This time, however, I think humanity will finally get it right and not let authoritarian dogmatists destroy our awakening. I think this time we will choose to love an authentic Messiah instead of hating them and sending them to suffer an ignominious end.

—Δ*—

"Darkness will be preferred to light and death will be preferred to life. No one will gaze into heaven. And the pious man will be counted as insane, and the impious man will be honored as wise. The man who is afraid will be considered as strong. And the good man will be punished as a criminal." – Hermes' lament to Asclepius[1095]

• • • •

"IF IT WERE POSSIBLE to lay hands on the man who tried to release them and lead them up, would they not kill him?" – Plato[1096]

• • • •

"BUT IF IT IS FROM GOD, then you will not be able to stop them; you will only find yourselves fighting against God." – New Testament[1097]

• • • •

"THOSE THAT DENY GOD'S revelations and slay the prophets unjustly and kill the men who preach fair dealing – warn them of a woeful scourge. Their works shall come to nothing in this world and in the world to come, and there shall be none to help them." – The Koran[1098]

• • • •

"AND IT WAS THE MORE righteous part of the people who were saved, and it was they who received the prophets and stoned them not; and it was they who had not shed blood of the saints, who were spared." – Moroni[1099]

• • • •

"THOU HAST KNOWN HOW grievously the Prophets of God, His Messengers and Chosen Ones, have been afflicted. Meditate a while on the motive and reason which have been responsible for such a persecution. At no time, in no Dispensation, have the Prophets of God escaped the blasphemy of their enemies, the cruelty of their oppressors, the denunciation of the learned of their age, who appeared in the guise of uprightness and piety. Day and night they passed through such agonies as none can ever measure, except the knowledge of the one true God, exalted be His glory." – Baha'u'llah[1100]

—*O—

We can wait for a genuine Messiah to finally show up again and lead us to salvation, or we can initiate into action and rescue ourselves from damnation. I would prefer the latter since it places the future in our own hands, and not on the dependence of a divine intervening figure; a relic from a bygone age sprouting forth in a modern context. Until then, it is up to us to tap into our internal messiah, the divinity within, and make the world a better place through the energy of love. A messianic mass collective and movement of human souls would do much more to heal the wounds of the world than one person alone. Become your own constructive role model by seeking knowledge and applying it daily through wisdom and balance. Become your own guru of positive action; your own reverend of reflection, your own guide of wonder, and your own manifestor of better realities. Nourish, nurture and engage your *magnum miraculum* and find the magic in ourselves rather than looking for it in others – learn to invoke the mystic contained within and put forth a mana of goodness.[1101] Awakening our internal mystic is not about the apathetic "encounters with the qualityless and unknowable, but an ecstatic revelation of an all-consuming unity and an all-embracing compassion."[1102] It can be born from and initiated through the insights of true Christianity, Islam, Judaism, Buddhism, Hinduism, Paganism and several others of the great religions, philosophies and paths. We all have the potential to be candidates for working as part of God's team; an aspirant of faith. Having faith in the Almighty is one thing, relating to him/her through mysticism is even greater. For when the Lord, that universal mind of the universe, sends forth divine light into our minds, we have the free will to accept or to refuse it.

—Λ*—

"Indeed the understanding dwells in you; in me it is as though the power were pregnant. For when I conceived from the fountain that flowed to me, I gave birth." – Hermes Trismegistus[1103]

• • • •

"MY FATHER, YOU HAVE spoken every word well to me. But I am amazed at this statement that you have just made. For you said 'The power that is in me.'" – Hermes' student's response.

• • • •

"The Son of Man is within you. Follow him!" – Mary Magdalene[1104]

• • • •

"WHOSO ARISETH AMONG you to teach the cause of his Lord, let him, before all else, teach his own self, that his speech may attract the hearts of them that hear him. Unless he teacheth his own self, the words of his mouth will not influence the heart of the seeker." – Bahá'u'lláh[1105]

• • • •

"NO PERSON CAN REACH the summit of learning and knowing who did not become their own teacher and their own priest." – The Nine Faces of Christ[1106]

• • • •

"...WHO CAN EDUCATE OTHERS while themselves uneducated? Who can enlighten others while still in the dark about themselves, and who can purify if they themselves are unclean?" – C.G Jung[1107]

• • • •

"Many are called, but few are chosen." – *New Testament*[1108]

—*Ω—

WE MUST REMEMBER THAT all the great prophets, regardless of whether their message came from having a level of bio-spiritual evolution above the norm, divine influence or mere insight, experienced human existence firsthand and did the best they could considering the current conditions of the societal situation. They felt the same elations and suffering, many times even more so, of the cultures they were born into. They felt the same frustrations, injustices and suppression of spirit in their encounters with ignorance as we do today. They felt anger and love, sadness and joy, and vented to God in their verbal wailings, prayers and writings as he/she counseled to them in their dilemmas. They encountered the same temptations just like everyone else, but most were able to overcome them more than the average person of their day. When reading the writings of ancient scriptures, you are seeing into the minds of their authors as you tap into the early continuum of humanity's quest for Allah and divine fairness. Many of the religious texts contain the venting of human frustration in the encounters with suffering, ignorance and injustice. This venting has very often been misinterpreted as the thoughts of God when it was actually the individual trying to deal with the emotions of their human aspect. How often do we write something down as a way of cleansing our frustrations or thoughts of an emotional burden?

Many times throughout history, the focus has been placed on a few phrases of a prophet's scripture that somehow seem contradictory in their message of love and tolerance within acceptable boundaries. Certain phrases may seem to trigger feelings of anger, rage, violence, guilt and even hatred within ourselves. These were the human aspects of frailty showing themselves, for no prophet is perfect or without the making of mistakes. Although Allah saw the initial sincerity of heart and mind within the intentions of certain selected prophets and entrusted them with carrying out their noble purpose, he/she understood the risks of their lower self possibly steering them astray. All the God-seekers had to find ways to alleviate the weight of their humanness, making errors along the way or slightly succumbing to their own nafs. No saint or student of God can be good all the time on his or her own strength.[1109] In fact many sinners (i.e., St. Paul) turned into saints, while some who were initially prophets (i.e., al-Hakim bi-Amr Allah, Joseph Smith, Jr.) in succumbing to their egos and lower nafs, turned into sinners. Even Noah seems to have had difficulties with the addictive lure of alcohol, abusively blaming his son Ham for finding him passed out in a state of naked drunkenness, and then punishingly cursing Ham's son (Canaan) in a fit of narcissistic projection.[1110] To think that dysfunctional family dynamics of an alcoholic parent went all the way back to just after the Great Flood, yet, it wasn't until 1935 with the establishment of Alcoholics Anonymous by Bill Wilson and Bob Smith that humanity finally found a formulized method of support and camaraderie to break the cycles of an alcoholic lineage. Many prophets and even saints, as reinforced and described in *The Age of Reason*, seem to start out on the path of love, but upon allowing their egos to overtake them, lose their connection to God and switch to a malevolence and rage of spirit. Even prophets can fall from grace after initially having the Divine Master's attention. Some can handle the immensity of Yahweh's power due to the purity and intentions within their core, while others cannot. Although certain prophets themselves were unable to hold true, there were truths in the religions that they promulgated. To remain an instrument of divinity, one must not let their ego clog or contaminate the connection – maintenance is required. We may focus on questionable scriptural phrases as a reflection of our own internal state and must realize that many of the prophets' sayings may have been taken out of context or their target was intended for specific past historical events. No prophet is perfect in delivering their intended message 100% of the time, for codifying religious and spiritual common sense seems an impossible task. We seem to put those god seekers, mystics and saints up on high pedestals, and in doing so, we isolate ourselves from their mistakes, vulnerabilities and spiritual tepidness. Overzealous hagiographers provide a disservice to the prophets and saints by putting them out of reach and concealing their humanity.[1111] It is through their weaknesses and mortality that we can find a common bond and relate to them more easily. Even they were inconsistent with their connection to divinity and were as fallible as the rest of us, but still were able to link with the Almighty consciousness because there was enough purity of intention within that was genuine. A true prophet is sensitized to the underlying trends in the flow of the universal human consciousness more so than others. They have a genuine connection between the consciousness of humanity and God's grace, a connection which can be severed if not properly maintained.

Many a great teacher has left their wisdom on the image of humanity; the ideas of Socrates, Plato and Aristotle especially, are no exception. The "paganistic" philosophies of Plato and Aristotle (all initiated by Socrates) were introduced into Christian thought by Saint Augustine in the 3rd century and by Saint Thomas Aquinas in the 13th century, respectively.[1112] In doing so, their so-called "paganism" actually fueled and forged the foundations of Christian thought on free will and the role of virtue for much of the past two millenniums.[1113] Plato approached the cosmos based on thought experiments and reasoning for proof of reality, while Aristotle called for its proof based on direct observation and experience. Although their contributions branched in different directions, Socrates influenced Plato who later influenced Aristotle. Aristotle provided the world with the empirical approach of observation, hypotheses, and experimentation to obtain repeatable results, much of which still forms the methods of modern science. Much of his teachings would have been lost if it were not for the records of Islamic scholars and their encouraged thirst for knowledge. While Europe was entrenched in the Dark Ages, many Greek treatises were being translated by Muslims into Arabic, providing a preservation of human culture for future generations and later contributing to the Renaissance – otherwise such classical Greek writings would have been erased from history and never recovered. We should remember to thank the Muslims for this cultural preservation.

Socrates' and Plato's views on ethics took the stance that knowledge and wisdom in and of itself would induce forth moral actions and benevolent idealistic outcomes – that knowing the direction of goodness would automatically lead one there. Aristotle felt that knowledge and wisdom would not automatically lead one to a virtuous path, that it took deliberate intentional application of such revelations to create the habit of doing good, rather than evil. Socrates and Plato felt understanding morality would result in its proper implementation; Aristotle felt that it took initiation, action and effort. Unfortunately, just as the *New Testament* of the *Bible* still seemed to condone slavery, Plato and Aristotle both tried to rationalize this negative exploitive institution based on the perceived inferiority (non-persons) of some sentient beings over others and that such beings were incapable of being responsible enough for themselves. It was the discovery of Aristotle's subjugated views on women that influenced later Islamic scholars away from any gender equality expressed in the *Koran*, misshaping the medieval fiqh, the theory of Islamic law.[1114] Socrates, Plato and Aristotle contributed greatly to modern thought and although not perfect, their ideas should be viewed as a starting point and paving stones towards analytical approaches and paths towards enlightenment, but not as an end point.

Therefore, focus on the words of love within the scriptures but accept that words of negative exploitation exist as a means of portraying history, or at times, actually seeming to condone it. Acceptingly bypass over the contradictions to love which seem to provoke anger, oppression and violence. Recognize and acknowledge the contradictions as being a test of your ability to see truth through the fog. The contradictions do not make the scriptures as a whole any less significant, but rather enhance their place within the minds and hearts of humanity. For how can we understand the necessity of the creative emotion of love without being aware of the stagnating destructive emotion of anger and hatred? These emotions are a part of us and we need to understand how they work within us so we can properly direct, control and apply them to a given situation.

—A*—

"The Universe bends because of Love, and the Earth kneels before it, for Love is God." – Jeanne D'Août[1115]

• • • •

"THAT LOVE IS ALL THERE is, is all we know of love." – Emily Dickinson[1116]

—*O—

Some religions or their sects make claims that their prophet was the last to come. Perhaps at the time of their prophet's message that was true. But is God not allowed to change her mind? Is Allah, being all powerful, all knowing and all wise not allowed to change his mind? How many times would you send a messenger to your children in hopes that they would finally understand the love, beauty, grace and acceptance of their existence? How many times does a hen regather her straying and lost chicks? How many times would you try to save your children from destroying themselves? Most likely you would never give up, until they finally grow up. God/Allah will also never give up on raising her children. There were true prophets of the past and there will be true prophets in the future. The Almighty will choose to send and call upon as many earthly or divine messengers as needed until all his children finally get it right.

True prophets of history have a tuned sensitivity to the Universal Consciousness of Humanity, a certain sensitivity to what the global mind of humanity craves, the direction in which it needs to travel to reach that Universal Consciousness and the probability that it will head in that direction. These individuals continue to speak universal truths, seek universal knowledge and often push the boundaries of accepted dogma or the current stasis paradigm of thought.[1117] They are in tune to the current pulse of their species and strive to raise them to the next level of spiritual existence and awareness. Through this adroit sensitivity, they initiate words and/or actions that catalyze others to satisfy such spiritual metamorphic cravings. God will continue to send authorized representatives, emissaries of his/her guidance, to raise advanced intelligent sentient beings to a higher state of existence.

All the true prophets had spiritual insight and the experiences of lowering their egos, resonating with epiphanic vibrations and synchronizing with the cosmic consciousness of humanity and beyond. At times, they were able to fully surrender to the influence of the Supreme Universal Consciousness. Idris, Abraham, Moses, Jesus and his Apostles, Mohammad, Sufis, yogis, true shamans, saints, monks and priests have all had various degrees of exposure to the universal and supreme mind. This same entity of divine thought, presenting itself in various forms, is also what awoke the Buddha and sends forth itself in the form of avatars to experience and to guide the earthly realms into the direction of goodness and heaven. Such incarnates were fully or partially the Universal Consciousness in the flesh. Any true manifestation of God would first need to walk among humanity before revealing themselves. They had to first learn how to be human, to empathize, before they could help humanity. Then they had to learn to be in the duality of being attached in detachment, and detached in attachment.[1118] Dwelling among us under guise, they would need to feel the joy, uncertainty and pain of what it is like to be human in order to better relate to us.

A true spiritual being has respect for all the great prophets of history. They balance themselves between transcendental loving service of the Lord and maintaining a secure footing in the secular. The common message from all true prophets has been to apply oneself in a manner which reduces suffering and misery by providing humanity with hope and direction. The greatest respect for Allah is by conducting acts of compassion to improve the human condition. Simply stated: to help one another whenever possible.

Do not become overly concerned or obsessed with the semantics of a particular true prophet's relationship with divinity, but rather, focus on your own relationship with divinity. Only God/Allah knows for sure on the nature of the relationship. True religion is meant to allow for growth and change as the human consciousness advances and evolves. We refer to things as miracles when they seem to proceed or deviate from the normal expected course of events. Yet, every connection or suspension of time is a miracle. To those who perform authentic miracles, wonders of the moment, we either accuse them of being the devil, a weapon of Satan, or recognize them as a prophet, an instrument of divinity. Benevolent miracles can only be the workings of God. Jesus Christ reminds us of this fact in *Mark* 3:23-29 and *Matthew* 12:25-29. The message of the Almighty speaks to us by means of mystery, miracles and prophecy. Miracles define the past, mysteries dwell in the present and prophecy unfolds the future. Merging this trinity is what releases us from the constraints of time. A religious doctrine whose current elementary message is not based on healthy love is not a true religion. A believer in God should be peacefully tolerant of a non-believer (an atheist), and vice-versa. An agnostic is free to continue fluctuating between the dichotomies. These are the express words of God.

The great sages, mystics and saints, allocated their time in philosophical and spiritual speculation and pursuit. In pondering, they hoped to witness a brief encounter or moment of understanding of the Supreme's transcendental nature. For God/Krisna/Allah reveals him/herself to those whose actions are performed in true transcendental loving service. The goal of every believer in God should be to achieve the Buddha-Christ-Mohammad persona trinity of being and maintain it. It is the direction that every true religion provides by training us to align our will with the divine will. Spiritual darkness is something that the Buddha, Jesus and Mohammad, among others, all encountered at various points during their physical existence which enabled them to advance closer to the godhead and/or strengthen their connection to divinity. Christian teachings thrive on dividing reality into opposing pairs such that the language of opposition works by placing half of reality closer to God and the other half away.[1119] The problem with this approach is that it often does not hold true. Then there is the metaphoric duality where light symbolizes spiritual well-being and darkness represents the opposite. Without knowing the darkness as a reference, how can we gauge where we are in the light? We can talk of physical light being good and physical darkness being evil. But when dying of heat exhaustion under the bright light of the Sun, some darkness would be considered good. Due to there not being enough physical darkness, about 1/3 of Earth's population and 80% of Americans can no longer see the Milky Way,[1120] that luminous river of stars identifying our home galaxy and igniting the imagination of ponderers throughout millennia. Generated in the month of April 2017, the first image of an authentic black hole in space was revealed to the public two years later in 2019. From the Hawaiian indigenous religion chant of Kumulipo, the black hole was named "Powehi", which translates as "the adorned fathomless dark creation" or "embellished dark source of unending creation." That being said, darkness has its roll in creation just as much as light. Light is darkness when our back is to the source and there are no objects upon which to reflect.[1121] The heavens that we observe with our telescopes, interplaying pigments of both light and darkness, is the canvas of God's creation spread across the universe.

We truly do stand on the shoulders of giants when we consider all the great ones; the elite inspirational contributors to true science, true religion, refined art, advanced literature and the social reformers of their day. The incomplete listings below by no means does justice to their names and shamefully leaves out too many other heroes, both male and female, of wonder. From Adam, Eve, Noah, Abraham, Sarah, Jacob, Jethro (Shuʿayb), Moses, Isaiah, Micah, Jeremiah, Ezekiel, Solomon, Hosea, Amos, Zechariah, Zoroaster, Mahavir Janma Kalyanak, Siddhartha Gautama (the Buddha), John the Baptist, Jesus, Mohammad, Martin Luther, Nanak Dev Ji, Emanuel Swedenborg, Abraham Lincoln, Siyyid ʿAlí Muhammad Shírází (the Báb), Baháʾuʾlláh, Mahatma Gandhi and Martin Luther King, Jr.

To Lao-Tze, Confucius, Heraclitus, Democritus, Socrates, Mozi, Plato, Aristotle, Euclid, Pythagoras, Archimedes, Epictetus, Lucius Annaeus Seneca, Ptolemy, Marcus Aurelius, Maria Prophetissa (aka Maria Hebraea, Mary the Jewess), Zosimos, Origen of Alexandria, Hypatia, Ali ibn Abi Talib, Jabir ibn Hayyan (aka Geber with a soft "G"), Al-Kindi, Abu Nasr Muhammad al-Farabi, Abu Yaqub al-Sijistani, Abu Ali Sin (aka Avicenna), Abu Hamid al-Ghazzali, Hildegard von Bingen, Ibn

Rushd (aka Averroes), Ibn Arabi, Albertus Magnus, Roger Bacon, Saint Gertrude The Great.

To Ibn Khaldun, Giordano Bruni, Leonardo da Vinci, Michelangelo, Raphael, William Shakespeare, René Descartes, Francis Bacon, Kepler, Galileo, Copernicus, John Milton, Isaac Newton, Voltaire (aka François-Marie Arouet), Friedrich Nietzsche, Victor Hugo, Charles Darwin, Mary Anne Atwood, Mark Twain (aka Samuel Clemens), Leo Tolstoy, Carl G. Jung, Marie Curie, Rosalind Franklin, Albert Einstein, Neils Bohr, J. Robert Oppenheimer, Padre Pio of Pietrelcina, Richard Feynman, Carl Sagan, Stephen Hawkins, Stan Lee and Li Wenliang.

For now, the revelations within this book focus on bringing the organism of humanity to an increased level of communion with God. Future prophets will be expanding their field of focus to bringing all advanced intelligent sentient beings to an even higher level of communion. It is no coincidence that the universal phonetic mantra of Hinduism, Jainism, Buddhism, Sikhism and many other of the world religions from portions of the Middle and Far East, the "aum" or "oum" (asa om, ome) sound, is contained in the word "communion." The vibrations generated from this universal mantra reminds us of the industrious sounds of buzzing bees.[1122] Notice also that the starting vowels of the universal mantra of "aum" and "oum" are triangular and circular characters, the alpha and the omega. Is God not the alpha and the omega, the triangle and the circle, the beginning and the end, and everything in between and beyond?

—Δ*—

"Aum and Ome, the universal mantra is both triangular and circular, the alpha and the omega. These eternal words resonate with the All and the One. They represent what was, what is, what shall be, and what is beyond the boundaries of time. All and One is the Ome and the Aum." – AO and *Mandukya Upanishad*[1123]

—*O—

The reason behind the motives of all true prophets, messengers and avatars, is for the love of humanity – each of them had a spark and a glowing ember of the Messiah within them. True prophets seek to improve humanity by providing guidance to the next level of spiritual adaptation and development. They often strive to bring a new political, religious or social order out of the current relative local chaos of their time period and to remind us of the truths that are timeless – that love is the antidote for sin. Having integrated God into their being, they have transcended the *status quo* morality of the herd, and in doing so, lead us to the direction of the Promised Land, to bring heaven on earth.[1124] Why do they strive for a better tomorrow? For the love of humanity of course.

—Λ*—

"A new commandment I give to you, that you love one another, even as I have loved you, that you may also love one another." – *The New Testament*[1125]

• • • •

"THE MEDITATIONS OF the profoundest thinker, the devotions of the holiest of saints, the highest expression of praise from either human pen or tongue, are but a reflection of that which hath been created within themselves, through the revelation of the Lord, their God." – Bahá'u'lláh[1126]

• • • •

"THOSE IN RADIANT PURITY pass through the gates of the sun to the dwelling-place supreme where the spirit is in eternity." – *Mundaka Upanishad*[1127]

• • • •

"THERE IS A SPIRIT IN the sun high above, and that spirit I adore as Brahman." – Gargya[1128]

—*Ω—

A Master, an Illumine, an Enlightened, an Adept, a member of the Polaire Brotherhood, the Great White Brotherhood, a member of the Order of Melchizedek, the Followship of Light, and higher order rankings such as the Order of the Sun, are just some of the names for those on this planet who are often touching or even immersed in the lower boundaries of God.[1129] Going even higher, there is the Order of the Stars (revealed only to those who are ready) that welcomes the male, the female, those with overlapping attributes and AISBs from other planets, worlds and realms. There is also an Order of the Universe, but no corporeal being is currently eligible for membership.

"It must be remembered that the initiates, the wise men and the masters of all ages, are not limited by our conception of time and they work, not for the immediate future, but for the gradual spiritual evolution of the whole race. Days, months and years are nothing to them. They will work through incalculable time to obtain the object of aspiration. Their vision is very wide and stupendously grand; they count nothing wasted if out of it can be born ultimate perfection of life and happiness for mankind."[1130] They are all part of the Covenant of the Elect, the great ones, realizing and accepting that they are not perfect, they exist in a state of awareness above the norm. Yet, there must have been an underlying influence upon their behavior, a supernatural impulse guiding their ways and miracles. Their divine abstraction can appear as indifference to those in the material realm, but in actuality, they feel the pain of the world much more than the norm for they are seeing much further into reality than we are.[1131] Some of these great teachers were spiritual beings who enter into a human body (falling from Heaven in the good sense) for the fulfillment of benevolent missions in this physical plain.[1132] Succumbing to aspects of their human frailties just like us, they also must ward off depressive energy drains from dealing with the frustrations encountered due to the ignorance of others within their generation and the nescience within themselves that may crop up from time to time.

They are feared by those lacking in awareness, often accused of being deceptive enchanters,[1133] while admired by those with understanding. The message of the great ones has always been that we have a choice; we can continue dwelling in the lower planes of a mundane existence, or we can expand our consciousness and skim the boundaries of the divine planes as we unlock our <u>Purusha</u> and the <u>Shekinah</u> within.

—A*—

"For the Son of Man did not come to destroy men's lives but to save them." – *The New Testament*[1134]

• • • •

"USING THE HAMMER OF wisdom in preparation, I come to redeem and chisel out fine gems from rough and uncut diamonds." – AO

—*O—

Allah presents himself to us in many aspects of form. He can be found in writers, poets, musicians and artists. He can be found in plumbers, cashiers, doctors, taxi drivers, nurses, farmers, engineers, carpenters, bankers, waiters, teachers, dishwashers and scientists. He can be found in parents, siblings, friends, cats and dogs. Whenever an individual helps to raise our state of existence, either through an egoless act of kindness or the presentation of a creation which inspires or reveals truth, this is their higher-self coming through – a self which is a piece of God. Kindness is a sign of strength, yet a dysfunctional personality views kindness as a sign of weakness. Someone who is genuinely kind does not need to rely on the inflation of their ego to feel secure with themselves. Their self-worth is based on several positive factors, such as a caring interest in others.

—Λ*—

"No act of kindness, no matter how small, is ever wasted." – Aesop[1135]

—*Ω—

It is easy to maintain internal purity in an environment of purity; maintaining it in an environment of tarnish is the challenge. The most holy and faithful of religious practitioners are the chaplains (be they an imam, purohit, monk, rabbi, minister, priest, reverend or pastor) providing spiritual support to the wounded and dying soldiers on the frontlines of battle or the suffering after manmade and/or natural disasters. For under those conditions, finding the choice words to portray God's love and to find refuge in his grace can be daunting. The most holy and faithful of divinity's representatives are the grocery line cashiers, first responders, nurses and doctors putting themselves in the frontlines by providing necessary life essential services through pandemics. The most holy and faithful of those searching for truth, however, are the dedicated journalists and reporters who often put themselves in the crosshairs of those opposing truth. While investigating events, uncovering occurrences and acting as the last bastions of freedom, they labor to sift and sort the facts from fiction for our behalf while telling a story. Often enough, the story told is on behalf of those whose voices are not being heard or who are no longer present to speak.

Faith is an underlying state of mind which wavers with one's spiritual resolve. Without thoroughly having absolutes, we rely on faith. It is a trust based on a covenant between the created and the Creator. Throughout human history, true prophets, messengers and avatars, have reinstated this covenant and presented newer updates and revisions. Listing all of the prophets by name is immaterial and extraneous, yet the listing of some was attempted in this chapter. The importance is understanding that they have presented the guidance of divinity from various religious paths and perspectives. Each update tends to initially plant a seed of improved sentient rights within the local region which then spreads to and crystalizes among the broader global populace.

—Δ*—

"I awaken the Buddha within,
I dwell in Krishna consciousness,
I surrender onto Allah,
I walk with God,
I mesh with the Universe,
I mingle in the Divine.
It is I and it is you.
We are here, we are there and we are all." – AO

—*O—

A supernatural awakening seems to occur when Gnosticism again comes forth from its underlying currents and remixes with the Orthodoxy. It is initiated when certain individuals tap into the Universal and Supreme Consciousness. It happened during the time of Christ, three centuries later through Manichaeism, six centuries later with the Paulicians, ten centuries later through Bogomilism and about eleven centuries later through the Cathars. It is about to happen again in this second fifth of the 21st century with a reawakening to the teachings of love, hope and understanding of all the divine messengers of history. The sensations and radiant influences of the Supreme Consciousness' thoughts can never be squelched. It is recognizing the great mystery of our existence without fully understanding it that triggers the start of gnosis. Realizing based on the tools of science, that you are part of the mystery emanating back to the "Big Bang", one must switch to the tools of religion to go even further back to before that expansion from a singular point to determine which came first, consciousness or matter? Focus on the infinity of who you were before your birth and then who you were before the "Big Bang", that point at which God became transcendental thought and Sophia became immanent matter, for that is the quagmire and split from logic that gnosis provides. A peek into our eternal life can be seen when we reflect and ponder through time to experience our eternal nature. Be in this moment. Now be in eternity. Now be in both. Now step out of your thoughts while releasing your ego to witness a temporary glimpse of ecstasy.

Chapter 23
Taming The Beast

"MAY THE FINANCIALLY fortunate collectively use their abundant wealth for the good of all." – Prayer Of The Giver, AO

• • • •

MONEY. IT IS A TOOL of humanity, a symbol of exchange for providing an abstract representation of a simplified means for barter and trade. It can be denoted with paper, coinage, plastic and/or virtual binary data. The more one has, the greater the assortment of items and services one can barter and trade for. Providing a means of exchange for material goods, experiences or services in the present, having a stockpile also establishes a sense of well-being that one's future may be secure and stable. It can be transmuted out of thin air by bringing imagination into useful innovative reality. Just as religion is a tool for connecting to God, money is a tool for conducting trade. Many wish for more of it and others have more than they can handle.

A hammer is a tool that can be used to build a home for a needy family, or it can be used as a weapon to cause bodily harm. Money, just like a hammer, can be used both as a tool or a weapon depending on its application. When used properly, it is a tool of salvation and positive exploitation; when used improperly, it becomes a weapon of destruction and negative exploitation. It all depends on how it is gained and how it is dispersed. It is not good or evil and it should not be loved nor hated; it is inert until it is exchanged. It is the related human actions that determines the outcome, good or bad, of a monetary transaction. Money can be used to manifest actions of good or actions of evil. It can save, destroy, create or demolish. Wealth is a gage of how much money one has accumulated above what they owe. Being rich or wealthy is not necessarily evil or a bad thing – it depends on how you got there and what you do with the financial abundance once you have it. But how does one define what is considered healthy wealth and dysfunctional wealth? How the wealth was earned and how it is spent, comes into play in determining its category. The judgment of one's wealth is based on how it was obtained and/ or how it is dispersed. We need to ask ourselves: have we dampened or destroyed those around us, on both a psychological and material scale, to get to where we are today? Did we adequately raise those around us as we grew or did we grow on top of them? Did we enlarge our ego by damaging that of others?

Healthy wealth is having enough money for economic stability, a reasonable financial future, access to quality healthcare and supplies the compassionate means to advance others. Dysfunctional or unhealthy wealth is when money becomes wasted on the extravagant extremes of material goods, overly lavish services, outlandish acts of negative exploitation and false symbols of prestige. In the modern world, idol worship has morphed into the accumulation of materialistic status symbols and excessive glamorizing of possessions. Through our own ignorance, some of us may have searched out material items to temporary fill the spiritual voids within us. Instead, they become our shackles and rob us of our time, for material items require attention and maintenance. In our bondage, we became overwhelmed with our delusive burdens. We had the delusion that material objects would liberate us from the pain and voids within. We found our lives becoming attached to those material objects of excess, while others lacked the basic needs and materials for survival. The extremes of too much and too little existed all around us. What we needed to do was to search deep within ourselves for what was missing. Striving for balance among the extremes of poverty and extremes of wealth, we need to reduce our attachment to the desire for excess and change it to a desire for peace of mind. In avoiding the extremes, we need to curb our addiction for excess and let go of our old selves and to bring on the new.

Idol worship of material items comes with a price, and that price is the absence of a deeper connection with the universe and with other beings. A balanced degree of materialistic desire is healthy, for it stimulates innovation and economic movement. Too much overabundance, however, results in dysfunctional opulence as finances are evaporated on endeavors that do not contribute to the advancement of humanity nor multiply the spread of wealth. The excessive accumulation of monetary wealth among a small percentage of the population is detrimental to society for it coagulates into stagnant clots of financial doldrums and evaporates into voids of excessive opulence; it does not circulate well. Just as the harm that happens when blood collects and traps in parts of the body, too much individual pooling of money and wealth causes damage to an economic system. Finding the proper balance between saving and spending contributes to economic health. It is based upon the amount of wealth generated by the transferal current from the savings of one party to the savings of another. Those with the supply of money in abundance should strive to become skilled craftspeople of philanthropic works. Using and applying reserves of wealth towards beneficial programs for those in need and with less financial options is the greatest use of excessive funds. Charity, an act of empathetic love, catches those at the lower socio-economic rungs with the basics of food, clothing, shelter and medical care and then rises from there to provide educational training opportunities for prosperity and the creation of future philanthropists.

Being a precursor to wealth, profit also is not good or evil in itself. It is the amount of money left over after all liabilities and debts have been accounted for; it is the surplus remaining after all expenses have been paid. The profit of a household is what can be put away as savings for future use and the profit of a business entity is what can be distributed to owners, shareholders or invested into future projects and equipment. Profit is necessary to sustain and perpetuate a business or industry. Without it, there would be no money for donating to charities, no means by which to build hospitals, no cash for filling church baskets and no funding for growing an economy. There is bad and there is good business, each with a quantitative level between dysfunctionality and utopia. When business profit becomes excessive by ransacking the planet into environmental devastation or taking advantage of others through negative exploitation, overcharging or deception, it then becomes a harmful weapon of destruction.

A pond or lake that is balanced flourishes with life. It needs to have water flowing into it and out of it to maintain its ecological equilibrium. Beauty can be seen of the creatures living within and of the creatures that come to its edges to drink and quench their thirst. Too much inflow causes its banks to swell and creatures to flee from its flooding path. Too much outflow causes it to dry up and stagnate, resulting in the perishing of the creatures within. Maintaining a healthy body requires the proper circulation of fluids and blood to deliver oxygen, remove carbon dioxide, deliver nutrients and remove wastes. When fluid and blood start to excessively pool in regions of the body, poor health and physical death can soon follow. The same hold trues for the economic engine of a society to properly function. Too much pooling of wealth in limited portions among the populace results in financial starvation of others; the lack of appropriate savings correlates to unpreparedness for future events. The continued movement, transfer or flow of financial current in a stable, steady-state condition is the ideal scenario for a healthy economy.

The charging of interest for the time use of money was forbidden among many of the early religions. The great philosopher Aristotle considered the earning of interest on money to be against nature since money, in itself, is not something that can reproduce. Saint Augustine viewed that business itself was evil and Saint Jerome considered "a man who is a merchant can seldom please God."[1136] The prophet Mohammad, however, was a merchant who seemed to please God. He was certainly against the charging of excessive interest (usury lending) and even condemns it in the *Koran*.[1137] Civilizations, however, have thrived, advanced and prospered with the borrowing of money at reasonable interest rates. People and banks are willing to lend their wealth out to others for a fee and at risk, with the hopes of both parties gaining. Usury (the charging of unreasonably high interest) or inflating rates to take advantage of another party's misfortune, however, is detrimental to society and considered a form of negative exploitation. An interest rate is an index based on how much compensation people demand for deferring consumption from the present to the future. It is partly determined by objective factors such as anticipated inflation, expected income growth and the risk that the investment will never come to fruition. It also reflects the purely psychological preference for instant over delayed gratification.[1138]

The judgment of one's wealth is based on how it was obtained and/or how it is spent. The balanced pursuit of financial gain is not a bad thing. It is when the pursuit is off-balance such as the pooling of wealth among the few or obtaining it through dastardly means. A balanced pursuit generates novel ideas and advances in technology and medical applications. It promotes efficiency and gains in the fields of agriculture, manufacturing, mining, transportation, communication, pharmaceuticals, information transfer and power and energy. In gaining wealth, the objective is to do so without the negative exploitation of others nor by obtaining it through morally questionable means. The economic system of commerce has encouraged the development of empathy as merchants compete to understand their customer's genuine needs. The effect of commerce between trading partners, be they individuals or nations, generates a condition of valuing the other party. Applying a positive sum game approach, it is better to trade in a diversity of goods and services with other nations and keep your customers prosperous than to lose them to the violent byproduct ravages of war. The positive-sum of commerce and trade is preferred over the zero-sum of conquest and war. Commerce promotes both cooperation and competition while invoking advances in creative innovation – it triggers better ways of making and doing things. This can result in prior ideas and methods becoming obsolete and the obsolesced occupations resulting in job loss. When such obsolesces occur, it calls upon those exiting diminishing fields of work to retrain and redefine themselves towards alternate lines of work. Innovation that provides a means for career adaptation is good. Innovation that results in coagulative clumping of wealth among the few or a retraction of economic flow is bad. The coagulative collective clumping of wealth among a small group of the populace is harmful to the overall health of a society – it diminishes democratic and republic representation into restrictive oligarchies and plutocracies.

Do we want a better world or do we want more possessions? Is immersion in a bath of excessive consumerism, being a collector of things, damaging our well-being? By all means we need to have a sense of security and money put away for our families and our future. We need to have food, shelter, clothing and access to good health services. We also need to be able to thrive in an environment of love and encouragement. Ideally and whenever possible, we all need to earn a living and maintain a livelihood. A full livelihood is preferred over a partial one for sustaining our expenses. In other words, earning enough of an income to fully sustain our needs and wants is preferred over an income that does not fully provide for our existence. When possible, we should strive to educate ourselves and thrive for a productive livelihood so as not to become a burden to society.[1139] This is not always possible if economic opportunities are not available or when we are dealing with health issues that prevent us from fully working for a living. Sometimes, we must start with or take jobs that only provide a partial financial means for sustaining our existence. In a capitalistic-based economy, the objective is to view such positions as temporary as we develop our skill sets for when better opportunities present themselves.

In summary, wealth, money and profit for that matter, are not bad things themselves. Standing alone they are neutral. The determination of whether they become good or bad is how they are earned and how they are spent or distributed. Profit is a necessity in a capitalistic-based economy to fuel healthy monetary dynamics. Without it, there would be no development or financial movement, economic stagnation and decay would result and charitable donations would dry up. Profit becomes destructive and bad when it is made through violations of ethical and moral conduct; when it is based on *filthy lucre*.[1140] A question every CEO and corporate board with genuine self-awareness should ask themselves is do we always need to have maximum profit or will a suitable profit suffice? How lucrative does an income-generating entity have to be? Finding the proper balance between the duality of financial altruism and financial greed should be every executive board member's goal. Commerce must be kept in check both through appropriate regulations issued by a governing authority and the influence of a consuming populace.

In the *Old Testament*,[1141] Cain blatantly shirked responsibility for the welfare of another when he answered "I do not know. Am I my brother's keeper?" to Yahweh's inquiry of Abel's whereabouts. In contrast to Cain's actions and words, it is the divine responsibility of all of us to reasonably be our "brother's keeper" when circumstances and finances allow. It is the divine duty of those of us who have been fortunate enough to have wealth and riches in our lives, to share the excesses of our bounty in productive ways to those who have been less fortunate. For those of us having risen well above a stable financial threshold, having an income much greater than our expenses, sharing some of our wealth will not be a sacrifice. It is the divine duty of those with more, to contribute to the well-being and helping those with less, provided the beneficiaries are making a genuine effort to improve their conditions.

—Λ*—

"Money can't buy happiness, but it sure makes unhappiness more bearable." – the author's mother

—*Ω—

Those at the higher end of the economic spectrum must be willing to do without the non-essential excesses of a materialistic successful society. The sharing of wealth does not necessarily mean just providing direct handouts, but rather, it rises to contributing to programs that foster the improved welfare of others; alleviating poverty through facilitating self-sufficiency and away from dependency. The expression or adage of "Give a man a fish and you feed him for a day. Teach a man to fish and you feed him for a lifetime" is timeless and true. Never feel ashamed of doing an honest and legal day's work, no matter what the task. Respect those whose jobs may not pay as much as yours, for if they weren't doing those tasks, you'd have to do them. Virtue and success are not defined by how much money we have in our bank accounts nor by the nature of our chosen employment path. It is defined by how we treat those around us and how we manage whatever monetary quantity it is that we have in our accounts. Success is contingent upon a higher ideal than the mere accumulation of financial riches. [1142]

If you are really into the competition of making money, the enjoyment of the challenge of creating wealth, then make it into a sport or hobby similar to pleasure fishing. There are many anglers out there that catch fish for the entertainment of the interplay between patience and excitement, and not for food. They don't eat or consume their catch, but admire the beauty of the finned water faring animal, and then release it back into its natural habitat abiding by a "catch and release" policy. Treat earning wealth as a similar activity in which money gained above the necessary threshold of financial security is released back into the economy in the form of charitable giving. When you reach a point where renunciation of wealth above that threshold of well-being and a comfortable existence is not considered a sacrifice, then you know that you are on the correct path to illumination. Renounce the financial excesses, the overly bountiful fruits of labor, above that threshold by applying it towards good causes rather than accumulating cluttering and exuberant material possessions.

—Δ*—

"Whoever finds the world and becomes rich, let him renounce the world." – Jesus Christ[1143]

—*O—

In the *New Testament*, Jesus is quoted as saying "...it is easier for a camel to go through the eye of a needle than for a rich person to enter the kingdom of God."[1144] There are a few different interpretations of what was actually being referenced, but most infer that it was impossible to obtain illumination from one's financial accumulation alone. This was counter to the Judaic Pharisees of the time period who viewed that rich people must be more blessed or favored by God, since they were wealthier than the norm. What a convenient way to condition our internal wiring to have us either act as subservient pawns to patterns of autocracy or default to actions of criminal behavior. The notion that the rich are wealthy because of their blessing from God is the reason why we allow ourselves to be hijacked by elites, participate in unjust patterns of employment, tolerate biased systems of money and banking and put up with police brutality or political tyrants.[1145] When we finally minimize systems that serve only the rich while leaving token scraps for the middle and lower socio-economic classes and learn to labor for the common good instead of pyramid schemes for the entitled, then and only then, will we "have upgraded ourselves to a higher consciousness and a better way of being."[1146] The use of one's wealth to improve the conditions of others will certainly align one with the path of enlightenment, but it is also dependent on the spiritual awareness of the individual and how that wealth was earned. Its negative exploitive footprint upon others also has to be considered. This is not to say that those with wealth will not enter the kingdom of heaven, but rather, those whose primary focus is on wealth accumulation will stunt their spiritual growth. Clarifying Jesus' emphatic "eye of a needle" metaphor: a stingy or greedy person will most likely not obtain enlightenment.

—A*—

"Man cannot be satisfied with wealth alone." – *The Upanishads*[1147]

—*O—

The prophets and avatars of history have encountered both poverty and riches during their earthly lives. Prior to becoming the Buddha, Siddhartha Gautama was surrounded by luxury and supposedly on the path to becoming a prince. Mahavir (of Jainism) was also born into a household of wealth and luxuries, but gave it up to pursue truth and ponder solutions for easing suffering. Moses enjoyed the lavishness of growing up in the Pharaoh's household and financially humbled himself as he led, like a shepherd, the ancient Israelites out of Egypt. Jesus was born into a family of relative poverty, became a carpenter or *tektōn* by trade, and experienced a range of economic statuses, interacting with both the wealthy and the poor. Mohammad's wealth seems to fluctuate starting with the early loss of his parents, then attaining riches through honest mercantile practices and the trading of goods, and later as a prophet when his financial status diminished. The wealth of other prophets also fluctuates either by circumstance or by choice.

Within the *Book of Revelation*,[1148] the final book of the *New Testament* of the Christian religious doctrine, there is a reference to a symbol denoted as the numerals 666 or 616 depending on the translation and biblical version. The number 666 is also mentioned much earlier, in the *Old Testament*, as the weight (talents) of gold that King Solomon received in a year.[1149] Returning to the original Revelation scrolls, it was most likely written as **χξϛ** or **χιϛ**. Based on interpretations from the ancient languages (Aramaic or Koine Greek) in which it was written, it is often portrayed as a physical mark found on the forehead or the hand. Representing something more abstract to its numerology than a visible emblem or tattoo, perhaps rather, it was intended to portray or indicate a psychological mark or mental blemish rather than a physical one. The "Mark of the Beast" is a scar upon our psyche, not the surface of our skin. It is something that was prophesized to dominate the thoughts or transactions of humanity sometime in the future. It is a symbol that allows no one to buy or sell without its presence. It is not an image of God but rather an image of man. It is an image often referred to as the "Number", "Name" or the "Mark" of the Beast. Throughout the rest of this chapter, the "Number of the Beast", the "Mark of the Beast", "Name of the Beast" and "Sign of the Beast" will be used interchangeably.[1150]

The *Book of Revelation* seems to itself require divine revelation to properly decipher its numerous enigmas.[1151] There have been many interpretations of the meaning of this potentially significant symbol referred to in the revelations to John. Some sources have applied its meaning to a significant day, year (i.e., 666 or June 6, 1966), the reign of a tyrannical ruler or to the ruler himself (i.e., the Roman Emperor Nero Claudius Caesar Augustus Germanuicus). Others have related it to referring to a specific person, packaging code, stamp or anagram. Movie plots and satirical cartoons have shown it written on the body, stitched onto clothing, or etched into objects. Far reaching conspiracy theory promoters have even falsely put forth the fear that it portrays a microchip to be imbedded into each person who gets vaccinated against the COVID-19 virus as a means for the government to track and control us. I think if this was the government's intention, they would have done this a long time ago every time each of us and our parents were vaccinated against polio, tetanus, smallpox, whooping cough (pertussis), the flu (influenza) or shingles (herpes zoster). Perhaps the visions seen by the writer(s) of *Revelation* was something which is to become a greater threat to the future of humanity. It would be a psychological obsession, a mental hurdle, which steers us away from enlightenment and blocks our connection to God. It is an image or symbol that would start to dominate the minds of individuals, stall the spiritual evolution of humanity and destroy our home planet in its unhealthy pursuit.

You are the sum of your thoughts and results of your actions. Ask yourself, have you also become a self-focused being of unhealthy greed? Have you sacrificed your character for the pursuit of money? Looking back upon your life, how many times have you compromised your ethics or being for the Number of the Beast? Since we are the sum of our thoughts and results of our actions, if we crave the possession of material items, we become the possession of material items. More and more of our thoughts seem to be dedicated to the accumulation and manipulation of the Sign of the Beast. In doing so, we start to lose our connection with the creative flow and beauty within our universe. Money and materialism are not necessarily synonymous with freedom. It can weigh us down and sink us. We can become emotionally dulled or unbalanced in our excessive pursuit for it. As we increase the energies going into obtaining more and more of it, we may take away from ourselves and our families. We may start to lose our sense of wonder, our ability to feel humor and the vision to see beauty within our world. We become bottled within our occupational framework and confined to myopic spheres of awareness, missing the significances of key global occurrences. Our personalities become money, instead of a balanced being on the path of enlightenment. There are many things in this universe that a price tag cannot be placed upon. Sometimes less is better than more.

We must all ask ourselves, is our monetary focus preventing us from reaching a higher plateau of emotional, spiritual and intellectual experience? If all our focus is on money, what thoughts are left for developing our consciousness? What thoughts are left for experiencing states of existence beyond the emotion of desire? What thoughts are left for seeing the beauty of the universe we were created in? What thoughts are left for advancing our being beyond the realms of the physical illusion? What thoughts are left for participating in real love? Perhaps this was the whole intent of the beast; to stop the growth of our consciousness through the archons of materialism and by distracting us from true awareness. Money and materialism are evil only in so far as their tendency to distract the soul from its primary purpose of evolving itself to reflect its divine origins and to reach its divine destination.[1152] Focusing on money alone denies the true expression of hidden talent, true life purpose, experiencing true beauty and the joy of contributing to the welfare and success of others.[1153] Too much focus on the Number of the Beast stunts our self-realization, tarnishes our connection with divinity, and fractures our path of enlightenment. The Beast is not an external foe, but rather a lower state of being that has the potential to dwell within each and every one of us and to dominate our minds. The fact that it can only dwell within us is its weakness for we have the ability to harness the Beast within and to recognize its persuasions. We can never completely eliminate its lurking stance, for it will always be a part of us, looking over our shoulder and waiting for the opportunity to strike. We can, however, keep it in check by developing a recognition of when it is starting to dominate our minds. Such recognitions should trigger a willingness to let go of our egos at times and share the excesses that we have with those in need. A true philanthropic entrepreneur is one who creates increased opportunities for others, not one who made their money by the betrayal and negative exploitation of others and then places it into a tax shelter as a plutocratic means to influence society to their liking. The greatest philanthropist is not one who just gives away wealth to noble causes, but rather, one who enables and catalyzes the creation of many other micro and macro philanthropists and raises the state of those around them.

There is a modern-day image for money that has appeared within the recent millennium and is commonplace for referring to currency. It is a symbol that hypothetically morphed out of Renaissance era Spanish coinage stamped with an "S" shaped banner or ribbon intertwined with the Pillars of Hercules.[1154] Another hypothesis is that it is the overlapping merger of the letters "U" and "S" for United States, becoming an identifying monogram used by the United States Mint within the Department of the Treasury.[1155] It can appear as one or more of the letter "S" intersected by one or two vertical bars. It is referred to as the dollar sign and often appears as "$" or "$$$." The three dollar signs in a row have become a symbolic reference of both wealth and greed. Created in the late 20th century, another common symbol for money is that of the European currency or Euro and it is denoted by "€" or "€€€." The speculative market of cryptocurrencies is putting forth even more imagery variations. Such symbols constantly appear all around us in one form or another as mono, bi or tri emblematic creations. We see them used as a recruiting logo in the help wanted sections, on items of clothing, as jewelry and in commercials. It is always somewhere on our minds as we earn a wage, read the financial news, check our monetary status, use credit, pay the bills or venture on vacations.

The act of prophesy is like looking into the future with a blurred lens and describing what is seen – it is not absolute. Per the modern fields of relativistic and quantum physics, observation affects the process being observed, inducing a different outcome than if the process were unobserved. The role of the observer in an experiment is vital in determining its outcome.[1156] Similarly, the viewing method of a genuine foreteller and the fluxes of time branches influence the future result. After being accessed, the timeline readjusts, with some future events dissipating, or detouring and others becoming more intense. This is why the future is never fixed but can be trending towards a particular direction. Prophetic projections are never fixed in stone but are based on trending probabilities that can be readjusted. Based on the Heisenberg Uncertainty Principle from quantum mechanics in the field of physics, there always lies an uncertainty when trying to measure exactly both the position and momentum (speed) of wave-like particles. Just as one cannot measure the exact position and exact momentum of a particle simultaneously due to its uncertainty, this also holds true for genuine oracles looking into the future. Thomas Paine stated that "there cannot be degrees in prophesying consistently",[1157] for just as there are a variety of quality and sizes of lenses available for looking telescopically at the starlight of past, there are various levels of clarity among the focusing senses of authentic seers, soothsayers, channelers and prophets. Being a seer into future events is partly about sensing the direction of trends – the navigation of social pulses that can veer one way or another. Prophecy, much like the predicting the positions of electrons within its cloud of influence, is based on probabilities. It is like trying to follow and hone in on an aberration. In addition, words and terms would have to be used to describe something in the future that might not be directly explainable within the vocabulary framework of that ancient time period. Imagine trying to describe a steam locomotive, the internet, the protein helix of DNA, remote-controlled miniature quadcopters, a jet engine or the International Space Station, using words and language from the time of Christ. Many such definitional terms or descriptive references did not even exist 2,000 years ago.

Is there enough similarity between 666, 616 and $$$, €€€ to signify that they are all representative of the same image that would dwell on our minds and consume our thoughts? Is the combined blending of the symbols for dollars and/or euros actually a pseudo-gematria representation of the Number or Mark of the Beast? Could this material number be what was seen during the supposed encounter of the ancient author(s) of *Revelation* with the Holy Spirit? Did he or she tap into something much greater than ourselves that transcends time and reveals images of the future? Even blurring the currency symbols in groupings of three of the Chinese yuan, Japanese yen ¥¥¥ or the Russian ruble ₽₽₽ have potential. It may just be a coincidence of stretching written imagery, but what if this, or a variation thereof of many world currencies, is the mark that was sensed, seen or felt? If so, then the Number of the Beast is all around us and the author(s) of the *Book of Revelation*, be he John the Evangelist, John the Apostle, John of Patmos or another Christian seer, really did transcend time and synchronize with the future consciousness of humanity as a Holy force, that awe trembling presence of God throughout creation, as it provided him with a glimpse of what was to come.[1158] If the Number of the Beast as described in the *Book of Revelation* is indeed referring to an abstract monetary mark of the mind or transaction of the hand rather than a physical blemish, it would add additional credence to the divine message brought to humanity by Jesus. It would mean that the prophetic words of the Christian scriptures, although with a dissipated impact due to dampening from benevolent influences, are starting to unfold even in present times. Is what I write in this chapter concerning the Number of the Beast an accurate interpretation or have I overly bent the symbolism to make it conveniently conform and fit to the circumstances of our current times? Are my hermeneutics correct here or way off? It is up to you to decide if the Number of the Beast described in *Revelation* 13 is the modern-day representation of greed, avarice and excessive material gain. If you decide "yes", then it is up to us to recognize it, tame it and keep it in check. Make friends with the Number of the Beast, understand it, educate it into obedience, and direct it for goodness. First learn how to handle a little bit of money – to shape and train the Beast that dwells within all of us. Then refocus on how to achieve happiness from experiences that don't have a price tag associated with them such as the smile and laugh of a child, the elegance of a sunset, the calming effect of a soft rainstorm and the beauty of a scenic vista. We must surround ourselves with the little things that make us happy before we can properly handle the big things.

Assuming the Mark of the Beast is all around us, you will start to notice it ($$$) on television, internet websites, magazines and newspapers. Some have too much of it, others have too little and some of us have just the right amount of wealth and material items in our lives to keep us humble. Many obsess on it day and night. Some feel more powerful by possessing it while others find its accumulation intoxicating. In pursuing the Number of the Beast, we often become entangled in material contamination and excessive sense gratification. Emotions are products of experiences, not material items. It is not the object itself that gives rise to an emotion, but the experience or potential related to it. The artist feels the satisfaction of accomplishment with the application of each brush stroke. It is not the paint or the canvas that gives rise to the emotion, but the associated aspect of the creation, sometimes of beauty and sometimes of pain. Many people inaccurately base their emotional well-being on the material items that they possess. They surround themselves with excessive material items that they think will make them happier, but the sensation is short-lived and another item is needed to fill the void within. It is a vicious cycle that can lead to financial and emotional collapse. The monetary values placed upon items or services of secular or material composition are arbitrarily based on how much a buyer is willing to pay

– the value is relative to what price it can be sold for, not on what price is being asked of it.

The author Charles Dickens wrote about the judgment of our sins in relationship to avarice and greed with his classic tale of Ebenezer Scrooge in *A Christmas Carol*, of which the protagonist discovers that redemption is obtained by walking a path of love.[1159] In the musical play *Fiddler On The Roof*,[1160] the main character (Tevye) sings *If I Were A Rich Man*, lamenting on all he could do with some wealth. The band Pink Floyd wrote a ballad titled *Money* that contains lyrics about the stinginess associated with unhealthy wealth,[1161] the band ABBA wrote *Money, Money, Money* as the desired dream to enter the rich man's world,[1162] and the duo Hall & Oates released the single called *Rich Girl* about an unbalanced person who felt they could do whatever they wanted because of wealth that they could not handle.[1163] An Illumined being knows how to keep the proper proportion between greed and charity. Now that you finally understand the meaning of the Beast, you can diminish its power and grip over you and use and tame it for benevolence. In fact, sufficient abundance will start to pour into your life from which to share with others. As you achieve wealth, will you become a good <u>Kubera</u> or a bad Kubera? Angelic or demonic?

Greed can be a motivating factor to trigger one into a more prosperous future. In its pure form, it is an excessive desire for the accumulation of wealth and power beyond what one needs, deserves or can handle. The desire for a prosperous future can be constructively fueled by monetary greed. The desire of financial security for ourselves, our families and our communities can be fueled, partially by monetary greed. Are we not all greedy for more freedom in our lives? Are we not all greedy for more love in our lives? Are we not greedy for less suffering in the world? Greed can also be a destructive element that turns cancerous when allowed to dominate our thoughts. Unchecked by an undeveloped inner core within our being, greed can result in a painful emptiness within ourselves and the destruction of the world around us. The only way to prevent greed from becoming cancerous is to open the doors in the walls of our egos and make sure that our prosperity is based on the prosperity of others and not on the negative exploitation of others. Greed has various states of influence. Some of those levels are constructive and others are destructive. For those of you who participate with a business entity to earn your wages, is it an entity fueled by a healthy or unhealthy level of greed? Don't let anyone fool you, monetary greed in itself is not good. It is a sign of an unhealthy ego and a shallow core. Its prominence within a personality is indication of an underdeveloped consciousness – someone operating at their lower self and at sociopathic levels. The desire for a more balanced life of happiness, health, fulfillment and prosperity is a constructive form of greed.

—Δ*—

"Those that preserve themselves from their own greed shall surely prosper." – *The Koran*[1164]

—*O—

To encourage order and prevent conflict, we have human laws and regulations pertaining to land ownership, possessions, buildings and infrastructure. Such "ownership", however, is meaningless in the eyes of God. Being in our physical existence for a limited time, we temporarily "rent" all of our items while in this material realm including land. We do not own the particles, atoms and molecules that make up matter or even our own bodies, but we do temporarily borrow them. The indigenous populace of the Americas understood this reality but was assimilated into submitting to temporal laws of humanity from European dominating expansionism.

Prosperity is having a life of productivity and wondrous experiences, contributing to the advancement of humanity and an access to a secure future. It does not mean being wealthy, possessing much real estate nor an accumulation of material items. The Lord wants us all to be prosperous in our lives, but not necessarily rich in monetary terms. Materialistic accumulation only makes us slaves of our possessions. As we open our doors of commerce and increase the interaction of the world's culture through trade, we must make sure that the Number of the Beast is used as a healing instrument to promote the standard of living of all and not as a weapon of negative exploitation. We must thrive to make every human being a philanthropist of both wealth and ideas.

It appears that capitalism is gaining the lead over communism as the economic vehicle and ownership form of choice on this planet,[1165] or is it that republics and democracies are winning the race over tyrannies and dictatorships, despite what the current leadership anomalies may show? Either way, there is a stable balance that needs to come between the advancement and protection of the individual along with the advancement and protection of the state. The fulcrum is searching for a steady position in which the individual may be preserved and promoted along with the societal collective. It is a position in which the social services of the state do not override the freedoms of the individual nor bankrupt the state. Social programs should be designed to promote the needy out of poverty without enabling them to become addicted and dependent on the program itself. Through monitoring and adjusting, a particular social program can be improved in achieving its desired goals. They should be designed, not to isolate, but to groom and guide those in need as productive and balanced members of society. A sense of self-worth and hope needs to be installed within the recipients along with a set of consequences for unacceptable actions. The door has to be available for those ready to open it, but it must also be up to them to reach for the knob when they are truly ready to do the work. Ideal thinking and writing are easy, putting them into action is the challenge. Are we socially up for it? Are we ready to stand behind our intent with follow-through and implementation? Are we ready to risk failures in pursuit of success? Are we ready to designate the required time and resources? It is up to each and every one of us to decide our part. The capitalistic tool of the Beast must become a means of promoting a balance between the preservation of local heritage and the incorporating of a better future for all.[1166]

—A*—

"The wealth created by a thousand men under the motive power of the self-interest of the capitalist is not, and cannot be, equal to the wealth that will be created by the same men under the motive power of co-operation or democracy." – Henry Demarest Loyd[1167]

—*O—

There have been false prophets in the past, there are some in the present, and there will be more in the future. I question whether some news commentators really believe they are presenting a perception of the truth, or if they are merely smiling demons who have sold their souls to the Beast. Some of the modern false prophets, frauds and fast-talking puffers are in the form of televangelist preaching, video media and internet charlatans who feed off of vulnerable souls in pursuit of the Mark of the Beast. This is not to say that all televangelists, social media voices, and megachurch leaders are false herders. Some offer positive guidance and provide charitable works, but many of these so-called media angels are actually demons in disguise. Some are frauds and religious pimps, prostituting the souls of their audience who are desperately looking for any form of liberation. They negatively exploit their followers' need for hope and a connection to a higher meaning. These so-called preachers of God become more obsessed with building ministries of cash than putting into action and revealing the true intent of Christ's or other true prophets' words. Perhaps they have become another voice of the Beast. Others have chosen to exploit and distort the Christian eschatological prophesies into fictional novels (i.e., *Left Behind* series). The metaphors within *Revelation* and other scriptures were reconstrued to instill joy and terror for the construction of monetary gain. Conspiracy theories instilling fear about secret societies such as the Illuminati become the feed of book topic, regardless if the 18th century Bavarian group's current existence is fact or fiction. The Illuminati was a short-lived group of intellectuals who tried to counter the influence of political despots and the Church's dominating grasp on the public. Their objectives were to promote freedoms, not secretly going about controlling markets. It was the threatened Church itself spreading the demonizing rumors that have withstood time and accelerated into modern sensationalism. If anything, it is our own behavior subconsciously making us all part of the Illuminati, for better or worse. I can only hope that such authors, including myself, use any wealth gained in succumbing to the Number of the Beast in a charitable manner that is beneficial for others. However, I am not here to judge nor to condemn anyone, but only to bear witness to their acts. Through catalytic initiative, the power of a mustard seed, I am here to save those who want to be saved. I am here to help others siphon off their bad karma and quicken the raising of humanity's consciousness.

—Λ*—

"Believers, many are the clerics and monks who defraud men of their possessions and debar them from the path of God. To those that hoard up gold and silver and do not spend it in God's cause, proclaim a woeful punishment." – *The Koran*[1168]

• • • •

"...FOR THEY WILL SELL me for silver and gold, and for that which moths doth corrupt and which thieves can break and steal." – Jesus Christ[1169]

• • • •

"...THE CHURCH HAS SET up as system of religion very contradictory to the character of the person whose name it bears. It has set up a religion of pomp and of revenue, in pretended imitation of a person whose life was humility and poverty." – Thomas Paine[1170]

—*Ω—

If the continued pursuit of money and material riches becomes the ultimate quest of humanity, then we will surely stagnate and degrade as individuals and as a species. If we continue to plunder our home planet (the spherical world that has provided a womb for our evolution), for maximum profit without addressing environmental concerns and consequences, we will destroy ourselves. If that quest is, however, changed to one of quality of experience, the advancement of the spirit of all and the lowering of our egocentric shells under the appropriate situations, then the direction of our growth shall return us to the balanced path of enlightenment. To achieve balance, one needs to curb their appetite for excess consumption, extremes of emotional sway, and sense of isolation from the whole. The true illumination of a society can be judged from how it treats its less fortunate, how its leaders treat their subjects, and the effort it makes to minimize the exploitation of its members. Members of enlightened societies engage in a degree of metaphorical colorblindness of its peoples as they embrace diversity.

In an unhealthy pursuit of the Number of the Beast, are certain elements of our species going to continue with excessive planetary plundering? Are we going to continue to destroy our worldwide home with environmental and ecological disruptions? What is the proper balance between maintaining a healthy economy and preserving the ecology of our global domicile? Between 200 to 2,000 species of Earth life become extinct each year mainly due to the fault of our activities.[1171] We are destroying the diversity of life, and in doing so, we are ultimately destroying ourselves. Until we regain our balance here on our home world and within the solar system, perhaps we are not ready and should avoid travelling beyond our sun's gravitational domain. We have no right to cause the same ecological havoc and environmental scarring on other worlds of life as we have caused here on our own home planet. Earth belongs to the Great Spirit; it is an entity of Sophia. It is not ours to destroy. It is God's property, not humanity's dumping ground.[1172] As we become spacefaring creatures, will we be extending outward to other habitable planets as explorers and welcomed colonizers or as plundering invaders and dreaded conquerors? Will we be fertilizing and seeding space through positive exploitation or raping its resources through negative exploitation? Despite the plots of some science fiction movies, I would expect that any advanced intelligent sentient creature that has evolved to the point of travelling to more than one star, would also have evolved to treating other star-faring creatures as friends, not as prey, nor as property, nor as slaves. For we will need each other's assistance and mutual support to deal with the perils and vastness of space exploration and travel.

Money's negative temptations of avarice, greed and fraud can isolate us, break apart families, push away friends and make criminals out of ordinary citizens – think of all the times crimes have been committed in the Name of the Beast. It both destroys relationships and builds them. If not judged in this realm by the third angel of *Revelation*,[1173] we shall all be judged within the next realm by how we handled the Number of the Beast within our beings. The universal mind that we are all connected to is very much aware of how we make our living. Did we earn our wages by stealing, cheating or deliberately messing up the planet? What is our monetary footprint of negatively exploiting others? How purely was our income earned? Did we lie, distort or contort the truth to achieve wealth? How many people did we make addicted to our products, software or empty social media virtual awards? How much dopamine did we falsely generate within our target purchasing audience? Or did we earn our wages through the honest contribution of labor and ideas towards the advancement of others? The Number of the Beast is not about money and financial standing; it is about avarice and greed to the detriment of others. He who dies with the most money does not win; he who does the most with his money to improve the human condition wins. How many have died, directly or indirectly, due to the Number of the Beast? Always remember that there are riches beyond financial accumulation that cannot be quantified by money. One can be financial poor but have riches of the spirit. These are the riches of obtaining an inner harmony which brings peace of mind measurable in only spiritual values.[1174] One can have poverty of the spirit yet be financially wealthy. There are many with financial excess that ruin their lives due to improper grounding and a lack of purpose. More people's lives are ruined by actually winning mega-lotteries than by not winning. The preference is to have both riches of the spirit and of financial wealth. The definition of class has very little to do with wealth. There is financial class and then there is societal class. Financial class is merely a ranking of your wealth. Societal class is a ranking of your being. Class is about how you treat others and the world around you, not about the size of your wallet. I'm sure we all know examples of both wealthy people and those close to poverty with very little class. I'm sure you also know of those of all financial ranks who possess societal class. We can't take our worldly wealth with us beyond the grave, but our developed wealth of character, mind and spirit is said to endure and survive well beyond our mortal span.

—A*—

"Your worldly riches are transitory, but Allah's recompense is ever-lasting." – *The Koran*[1175]

—*O—

Are those with riches willing to curb their desire for excess and put their wealth to good use? Are those without riches willing to work towards changing their surroundings of poverty, if given the opportunity? Where in the duality should one reside between being a consumer and being a saver? Where is that balance as a society and as an individual between buffering extremes of excess and having an appropriate surplus in reserves? How much is too much? How little is too little? Are we at the beginnings of a post-capitalistic new world order? Is it time to move past the extremes of financial booms and busts? Can we have our cake and eat it too?[1176]

In socio-economic regions where consumerism is plentiful, material items start to overwhelm us as we become victims of our possessions and slaves of our portable communication devices. When out of balance, such excessive items rob us of time and invade into our identity. They obscure our view of what is truly important and what is going on in our local surroundings. On the opposite end of the socio-economic spectrum in regions where the bare necessities are in short supply, our energies are strained and fraught with the demands of everyday survival. Access to spiritual nourishment can become restricted in either socio economic scenario. Both the "haves" and the "have-nots" can become spiritually off-balance due to environmental influences and social peer pressures distracting their mental focus.

If we are to reduce the distance between the extremes of poverty and the extremes of wealth, it is going to require a cultural shift and a world society with a different mindset for defining success. It would need to become a mindset that views success as having curbed one's addiction for excess material gain, quenched one's craving for power, extinguished one's use of negative exploitation, and transferred it into a desire for a better future. A better future: 1) shaped by the productive contribution of resources and effort in sustaining the health of our local communities; 2) that participates in the positive growth and health of our global community; 3) that defines the success of an individual by how many others they helped to achieve success, not by how many others they beat down in their climb to the top, nor on the dynastic ruling continuation of their surname regardless of competence or qualifications; 4) where the ego's thirst for excessive wealth is quenched by its desire to provide better living conditions for others; and, 5) in which our passions are defined and stimulated by the simpler occurrences within our everyday lives. This change of mindset is necessary if we want our children to succeed in a fast-changing world where tolerance, pluralism and understanding is the preferred method for blending us together in a peaceful manner. The Hermetic Law of Use calls upon us to use our knowledge to spread wealth to others. We now have the monetary infrastructure, the supply chain technological logistics, the distributive instruments, the educative tools, the communicative connections and the socially advanced methods within our grasp to create a runaway positive feedback loop in which every person can escape from poverty – the reduction or elimination of inequities. This is not fantasy; this is fact. In this day and age, there is no longer any excuse for financial lacking in regions of balanced and fair leadership. During these present days, when the world has been experiencing an economic jolt of epic proportions, we have the opportunity to come back stronger than ever to the true message and the true values – those that have been espoused by good men and good women through time immemorial.[1177] Are those more fortunate of us willing to give up some of the excesses of this world, our Gospel of Wealth, so that others and future generations will have a chance at prospering? Will we have learned nothing of the lessons from the COVID-19 outbreak upon our relationship with humanity and money? Can we afford to redirect the Number of the Beast as a tool of munificence to heal the wounds of our home planet? If so, then it is time to phase out having insufficient supplies of the necessities and to provide a trek out of impoverishment. It is time to use our pecuniary power to improve the quality of life for all. It is time to convert our mammon into saving the world, by remembering that money is of this realm, not of the next.

—Δ*—

"We all do better, when everyone does better." – Captain Ed Mercer[1178]

—*O—

Chapter 24
The Mind Of God – A Physical And Metaphysical Model Of The Universe

"IF THE DEVIL IS IN the details, then divinity is in the dualities." – AO

• • • •

DUALISM IS A DITHEISTIC religious perspective that existed before Christianity, or perhaps before any form of recorded history, and bides by the notion that there is a bad god and a good god (the Devil and God).[1179] They are considered extreme eternal opposite poles depicting hatred and love, evil and good, respectively. First coined in the 18th century by the English Oriental scholar Thomas Hyde, the term has evolved to mean any system or model of a central scale based on a binary pairing.[1180] Our discussion of duality or dualistic tendencies within this chapter is not to be confused with "dualism" as found in the doctrine of some Gnostic based religions (i.e., Marcionism, Manichaeans, Paulicians, Bogomils, Cathars). For within this chapter, duality and dualism are considered different things. Duality is the nature of opposites within the universe that can fall under a monotheistic umbrella. Dualism is more restrictive to the view of two Gods within the *Bible* (as well as some other scriptures); a creator evil God of the *Old Testament*, and a true omnipotent benevolent God of the *New Testament*. Zoroastrianism, having formed prior to Gnosticism, has both elements of duality and dualism. To prevent confusion within this book, when using the words "dualism" or "duelist" in any of the chapters, it is referring to the Gnostic perspective of two Gods – a false one that tempts and a true one that teaches.

We live in a universe of dualities which invokes both contradiction and unity. The world is full of poles and opposites. Sometimes these contradictions work together to form a constructive dyadic (or even a triadic) that is greater than its individual parts, bringing a healthy order out of the chaos. Other times they do not mesh well, resulting in conflict, clashes and disorder. Just as our species uses labels to define the Almighty, we also use labels to define the dualities. The notion of duality being everywhere is not new, but I seek to bring it to a higher level of awareness. This chapter will reveal to you a human model for describing part of the mystery of God. It will show you the basic building blocks and pattern of the universe within the framework of a simplistic paradigm that has the ability to grow out of itself. It is a model that reaches to the most inward core of our subconsciousness and consciousness and yet expands far beyond the grasp of all universal thought. It is a model that maintains its balance while rising above the dance between opposing elements. It is a model that has its own free will to choose its nature among a dualistic direction.

—Λ*—

"I am Alpha and Omega, El and Taw, Aleph and Tav, Abba and Imma, the triangle and the circle, the first and the last, the lamb and the lion, the origin and the dissolution, the seen and the hidden. I am creation, maintenance and annihilation. I am yesterday, today and tomorrow. I am the precedent, consequent and subsequent. I am the singularity, duality and triality of all." – God, as scribed by AO

—*Ω—

A simple model that works is that everything can be based on the dualistic interplay of elements defined as either "triangular" and/or "circular." This interplay between the dualities, the poles, the opposites, is what creates rhythm and movement. The poles need each other for meaning – the measure of one relative to the other is what defines them. Without us necessarily being aware, it is a constant interplay that is ingrained as part of our subconscious and among the universe's operations. Symbolically represented by the simplistic geometric shapes of a circle and a triangle, it is the interplay between opposites and antipodes. This promulgation of circular and triangular elements is the basis of the Supreme Consciousness' thoughts. It is the hieroglyphics of God; the evidential trail of divinity; the interconnectedness of everything. Intermixing the correct proportions and ratios of circular and triangualar elements, one can brew the greatest elixers of theological ingredients. The exchanges of triangular

and circular constituents apply to both scientific and metaphysical relationships. The ultimate tool of proper discovery and decision-making is
to apply reason for determining the correct proportions of triangular and
circular influences. The craft becomes learning to recognize and properly
applying this abstractive model of how the universe operates through the
baseline of love.

—A*—

"The book of nature is written in the language of mathematics. Its
symbols are triangles, circles and other geometric figures, without which
it is impossible to understand a single word; without which there is only
a vain wandering through a dark labyrinth." – Galileo di Vincenzo Bonaulti de
Galilei (aka Galileo)[1181]

—*O—

Finding the right balance, the correct mix, the most effective proportions, the proper behavioral fulcrum location between the triangular
and circular elements of our existence is living a God-centered life. Sometimes our behavior can be too triangular, and other times it can be too
circular. By adjusting the location of our behavioral fulcrum between the
extremes, we can induce more harmonious relationships between our inner-verse (the ego) and our outer-verse (the ega). The cosmos, made up of
patterns seeking balance, is a dance between circles and triangles. Everything around us, including ourselves, is composed of these basic metaphysical and symbolic elements. Everything can be categorized as either
being circular or triangular. The universe is a dance between these relational dichotomies. The key is that simple. The difficulty is knowing
where to dwell between, within or above the dichotomy. Either by design or by our lack of understanding, the duality itself or the separating
line between the dualities is not always clear or concise. For dualities can
have clear delineations, unclear delineations and an acceptable overlapping degree of both.

—Δ*—

"Everything is dual; everything has poles; everything has its pair of
opposites; and everything has its exceptions. Like and unlike are the
same; opposites are identical in nature, but different in degrees; extremes

meet; all truths are but half-truths; all paradoxes may be reconciled." –
The Kybalion[1182]

—*O—

Typically, words or components that portray a static nature, contraction, shrinkage, a closed or semi-static boundary, restraint, containment, isolation or succinct border of some sort either in the literal, figurative or abstract sense should be classified as triangular. Typically, words or components that portray a dynamic nature, expansion, increase, openness, unrestrained, a non-definitive edge, an easily permeable border or some sort of semi-dynamic transition in the literal, figurative or abstract sense should be classified as circular. Sometimes, but not always, categorizing it is as simple as which opposite word has the alpha character (i.e., "a") within it and which opposite has the omega character (i.e., "o") in it.

This symbolic cosmology and literal geometrical model of the universe through the imagery of triangular and circular aspects is **not** 100% perfect, but its trending characteristics and applicable probability is very high. It is not an absolute model and I do not hold it to be the only true one of possible physical and metaphysical approaches or concepts. I do feel it is more than connective gibberish and not just the painting of a pattern where there is none to be found. Having a simple formulation, it is open to doubt due to its cover and absorption of the actual complexities and explaining away too much in too simple of a way.[1183] It has, however, a very high likelihood of being correct when properly applied in understanding the workings and order of both the natural and supernatural world. The greatest of profound truths and ideas put forth the simplest of solutions by sorting through and organizing the clutter. Applying the principle of Occam's razor, where the simplest explanation or solution that properly explains an event or solves a problem is the best selection, an approach to modeling the behavior of both the metaphysical universe and the physical universe as well, is to look at it through the eyes of child. The simplest way is the best way – there is power in simplicity even though important details may be overlooked. The greatest metaphysical truths and observations are often explained by the unadulterated imagery perspectives and verbal comments of our young. We need to look at the universe as its basic building blocks; the way a child first sees it – as a composition of triangles and circles.

—Λ*—

"Truly I tell you, unless you change and become like little children, you will never enter the kingdom of heaven." – Jesus Christ[1184]

• • • •

"BE UNTO THE WORLD LIKE a child, for this is how you return to the wonder, excitement and magic of being." – AO

—*Ω—

The mandala and/or yantra, geometric artistic patterns found among several religions, are essentially a composite of triangular and circular elements. If you observe their layouts, the ancient spiritual and ritualistic symbol used by many Hindu and Buddhist sects to represent the universe, cosmos or an aspect thereof, you'll notice that its elementary pattern is composed of triangular and circular building blocks. It is used as a meditation pattern for gaining insight and is often referred to in the Tantric traditions, representing the universe's mystical dance in its display of circles and triangles. Elements of it are often found in the Sanskrit symbols of the Chakras, nodes or focal points located on the human form that are said to be the interactive points between the physical and metaphysical body. Christianity has its alpha and omega, the rose window of divinity. It is even said that the secrets of the universe are hidden within the rose stain glass windows of Notre Dame Cathedral in Paris, France – mandalas of their own right. Another Christian architectural element built upon triangular and circular imagery is the quatrefoil, in both its original and barbed form.

The fanciful geometric artwork of Islamic mandalas displays the divine interplay of triangular and circular elements and it is often woven into Sufi tapestries. A precursor to the Asterox (the emblem on this book's front cover), a sun-wheel or sun-cross is a mandala image found as far back as the Stone Age, with drawings of it appearing on Rhodesian cliffs before the invention of the wheel even existed.[1185] Symbolizing an abstract symbol emanating from the internal psyche, it is found within the roots of just about every religious culture, especially in Christian churches and Tibetan monasteries.[1186] Even the early indigenous peoples of the America's medicine wheels and the peace symbol that came into existence during the late 1950s movement for nuclear disarmament contain the elementary geometry of a mandala pattern. Nature's mandala has been around since the dawn of time, crystalized water in the form of a snowflake, containing within its lattices all the intricacies of growth occurring from its triangular and circular nodes. Similar to the fractal patterns that build upon themselves with repetition, the basic components of all mandalas is made of the interaction of circular and triangular elements in diverse variations and complexities. Perhaps there is more truth encoded in these ancient symbolic and literal arrangements than first realized.

—A*—

"Nature is full of genius, full of the divinity; so that not a snowflake escapes its fashioning hand." – Henry David Thoreau

—*O—

There are often connective patterns to languages such as the word "all" being part of the word "Allah." The linguistic of words often separate them into poles based on inclusion of alpha and omega characters – refer to this book's Appendix 1 for a sample list. For the triangular and circular as opposites is an inherent trend and gravitating pattern that has woven hints of itself into the very psychological fabric of certain languages (especially those of Phoenician, Coptic, Latin, Greek or Cyrillic etymologies), having become ingrained within the subconscious of our species' collective psyche. The vocabulary of the alpha and omega and its triangular and circular characters is immersed within the polar interplay of words and their dualities. Although sporadically scattered and disjointed, perhaps from Elohim's interference during the construction of the Tower of Babel,[1187] this interplay of triangular and circular imagery is immersed into the characters of many alphabets, forming the base ingredients for one language and one speech of the whole earth. It was objects like the Rosetta Stone and the Behistun Inscription that have mended a fraction of the imposed communication difficulties among the ancients.

Linguists may want to consider the basis of a universal language for a future age, a modern intuitive cuneiform that can be developed out of the interplay between circular and triangular elements, bringing us to a level of communicative understanding not seen since the "Confusion of Tongues" induced during the erection of the Tower Of Babel.

Psychology describes this journey of integrating opposites to become a whole, unique and separate person as individuation.[1188] It is the merging of opposites as they seek each other – *les extrêmes se touchent*.[1189] Yet Jung later asks the question of "How should anything but a formless and aimless uncertainty result from giving equal value to contradictory postulates?"[1190] The answer is that we don't always have to give equal value to each pole and can lean more one way than the other or find a way to rise above the contradiction all together. Sometimes one pole contains more goodness, while the other pole contains more evil, and other times both poles are inert. On our path to self-actualization and individuation, wisdom is knowing which poles to merge and which extremes should be filtered or dissipated away.

—Λ*—

"I see in all happening the play of opposites, and derive from this conception my idea of psychic energy." – C.G. Jung[1191]

—*Ω—

Dualisticism or the notion of duality (interplay between opposites) is not something new. It is a repeated theme emanating from humanity's interpretation of the cosmos' physical and metaphysical behavior. The wisdom of Hermetic philosophy coming forth from ancient Egypt and Greece refers to the notion of duality in The Principle of Polarity presented in *The Kybalion*. The universe is composed of balance and interaction – it is the dance between Shiva and Shakti, the masculine and feminine Hindu representations of divinity. One of the world's oldest monotheistic religions, Zoroastrianism, incorporates the concept of cosmic dualistic views into its doctrine. The three wise men that followed the star to Bethlehem and brought gifts to the infant Jesus were Zoroastrian priests (known as *magi* or *mogh*). Zoroaster was teaching this notion of ethical duality in the Persian Empire about 1500 BCE. Practitioners of Zoroastrianism follow an ethical duality believing that each of us has a personal responsibility to make the correct choice of action between what is good and what is evil. This is personified in Zoroastrianism through the Good Spirit (*Spenta Mainyu*) and his opposite in the embodiment of evil (*Angra Mainyu*).

The earliest evidence of the *Yin* and *Yang* symbol appears on various animal skeletal remains (oracle bones) from around 1400 BCE used in China for divination.[1192] About 500 years before Christ, the Confucian doctrine of *Yin* and *Yang,* the balancing of opposites, spread throughout China. About the same time or soon after, the Buddha spread the principle of The Middle Way, a stable point of existence between the extremes of asceticism (denial) and hedonism (indulgence). In this performance between the poles, it is the interplay of Yin and Yang (or Yan) or the Yab-Yum of Buddhism and other Eastern religions. This principle, that all things exist as inseparable and contradictory opposites, has become ingrained within much of the Asian culture. The opposites found within Yin and Yang can also attract and complement each other.

MUCH LIKE THE TRIANGLE containing the circle at its vertices and the circle containing the triangle at its center, the Yin and Yang symbolism as shown above indicates that each side contains an element of the other (represented by the smaller circles). In its basic form, it is represented as a circle which is divided into two bent teardrop shaped elements that fit together like puzzle pieces – one of which is black and the other white. Each side has a smaller circle inside it made of the opposite color. These dots signify the seed of its opposite within, a seed that can either remain dormant or germinate. Neither opposite is superior to the other and an increase in one brings a corresponding decrease in the other, prompting the need for a correcting balance between the dichotomies in order to achieve harmony. From Chinese mythology, Yin and Yang were born from the same chaos of which the universe's creation evolved. They are believed to exist in harmony at the Earth's core – one of Sophia's centers. In Chinese religion, the Taoists lean towards the serenity of Yin while the Confucians lean towards the active Yang in keeping within the prime focus of their respective philosophies. The Taoists emphasize reclusion while the Confucians believe in the importance of engagement in life.[1193] Within a few years or a couple of centuries, the notion of duality through the exchanges between opposite poles had fully bloomed within Confucianism, Taoism and Chinese Buddhism.

The phrases or expressions of "Walking The Middle Path", "The Middle Way" or "The Straight Path", relates to positioning one's behavioral fulcrum at the optimum location between the secular and the spiritual. It is about remaining balanced when encountering either the weight of sorrow or the ecstasy of joy. It means embracing the dualities of existence in such a manner as to being both immersed in them and rising above them. Upon rising above a duality, one has a better perspective on life and is able to reach higher plateaus of awareness. Walking this path involves striving for balance between serving one's own interests and those of others, being ambitious without being aggressive, and being both inwardly and outwardly focused. During brief glimpses within the highest state of meditation, samadhi, one rises above duality while still being fully aware of them. In doing so, one temporarily empties their ego upon an altar of love, providing space for the cosmos to reveal itself to us – to our Self.[1194] When properly rising above or transcending a duality, the duality itself becomes less defined or dissipates out of existence. The ground of the middle path can either be as narrow as the edge of a razor, or as wide as a continent depending on one's level of enlightenment. Either way, remaining within its boundaries and confines requires devotion.

—A*—

"Brahmon rises above the duality by being one and the many." – AO

—*O—

Within certain religious texts, there are ideas or statements that seem contradictory to the spiritual growth of humanity and our relationship with the universe. As mentioned in Chapter 11, there is duality created due to the multiple interpretations of the same passages within scripture. Think of all the times a religious phrase has been interpreted to mean different things. Does the sentence mean this or that? Is the wording literal, metaphoric or does it relate to a particular scenario in the sequences of time or to a relevant event? The duality of interpretations can be found in many scriptures, from the *Bible* to the *Koran*. Several other religious texts refer to codes or undertones of duality in which we must morally navigate. In *Matthew* 10:34, Jesus states that his teachings shall go out as a sword. Perhaps he knew that his words would be used in the future for both positive and negative exploitation, being used as a dual-edged sword which slices at both good and evil.[1195] The goodness of the true Christian path has brought about charity through the ages and helped others to improve their lives and conditions. The distortion of this path has brought evil such as the slaughtering of Jewish and Muslim populations during the Crusades, the Inquisitions of the Middle Ages, and indirectly the destructive catalyst behind 20th century anti-Semitism and the horrific term "ethnic cleansing" used as a euphemism for genocide. Jesus' comments in *Matthew* about his word going out as a sword may have been the recognition that humanity would use his teachings correctly for implementing good and also incorrectly for justifying evil. Jesus recognized the future duality of his message. He knew that some would understand and apply the true intent of his teachings, while others would manipulate and misuse his words for the advancement of their own egos. The metaphorical sword slices, creating a duality to overcome. The notion of duality being symbolically related to a sword is also found in Sikhism.

—Δ*—

"For the word of God is alive and active. Sharper than any double-edged sword, it penetrates even to dividing soul and spirit, joints and marrow; it judges the thoughts and attitudes of the heart." – *New Testament*[1196]

. . . .

"TO FORSAKE PRIDE, EMOTIONAL attachment, and the sense of 'mine and yours', is the path of the double-edged sword." – Guru Guru Arjan Dev, Devgandhari[1197]

. . . .

"FROM THE GURU, I HAVE obtained the supremely powerful sword of spiritual wisdom. I have cut down the fortress of duality and doubt, attachment, greed and egotism. The Name of the Lord abides within my mind; I contemplate the Word of the Guru's hymns." – Guru Ram Das, Maru[1198]

—*O—

We all have a spiritual fulcrum that denotes the location of our identity between the extremes. Upon understanding the notion of duality, one can position their fulcrum at the optimum location between polarities or even transcend the extremes all together. The best decisions are made when one is aware and considers both sides of an issue: the pros and cons. Real enlightenment comes with knowing where to place one's fulcrum of being and thought between the opposite limits. Just as there are various degrees on a thermometer for measuring temperature, there are various degrees between hate and love. Going right to the middle of the latter scale places one as teetering between dislike and like.[1199] Every quality has its good and bad sides, its pros and cons, its angels and demons. The objective is for the pros to far outweigh the cons, such that the balance sheet is biased towards the good. Duality smacks us with elements of both the negation and the affirmations. Other times one of the opposites is preferred over the other: good over evil, wealth over poverty, feast over famine, joy over sorrow, and love over hate. A fulcrum that is too far off-center results in a teetering of instability. In each case, any excessive extreme of such opposite becomes unhealthy. Consider how the extreme fringes of either a Gnostic or Orthodox perspective can both opt to explain away the mysteries with concocted tales, regardless if there are contradictory facts or supportive evidence. Instead of explaining television as an electromagnetic receiver and amplifier, they would say it is a panel or box with people and stories trapped inside which are released only when powered on.

So where should one position their fulcrum, the supportive location on the seesaw of the duality? It depends on the density of love being generated at each end. Remember how I stated that love is the binding energy of the universe? Well, it is also the densest. To keep the seesaw level, the lever balanced, the fulcrum of one's being and behavior needs to be much closer to the heavier end. Given the same volume, a container of love will have much more mass than a container of hate.

Dwelling in the extreme of any side of a duality only results in dysfunctional chaos and the buildup of turmoil, eventually triggering enantiodromia, the switching of poles. This occurs when a detrimental opposite builds up too much force or pressure compared to the other. Aspects of it occurred within Saul's psyche on his way to Damascus, giving him an awakening and changing his preference to being referred to by his Greek name of Paul.[1200] Survival and our existence are about situating the fulcrum of our behavior at the proper location between the extremes of duality. At times we must wait and other times we must be forthcoming. Being patient when the moment calls for it and/or being swift during the appropriate situations results in the optimization of our existence. Shifting our fulcrum between the duality of emotion and logic, our wisdom allows us to optimize its position for each situation. When the fulcrum of our being and behavior is properly located between the extremes of duality, one's existence will start to synchronize with the pulse of the universe. This is akin to being in Krishna Consciousness and synchronizing with the universe – desired results will occur. Even the great Emanuel Swedenborg presents the interplay of duality and the levels in between within *Divine Love and Wisdom*.[1201]

In the world of physics we have the movement (a DC circuit) or oscillation (an AC circuit) of electrons from one terminal to the other, the north and south poles of a magnet, and the conversion of potential energy into kinetic energy and back again. In the world of the artist we have light and dark pigmentation, foregrounds and backgrounds, straight lines and curves, and the shapes of circles and triangles. In the audio world of the musician we have musical notes and musical rests, treble and bass, soft and load, and staccato and legato. Some dualities are more complementary rather than opposing. Examples are salt and pepper, ketchup and mustard, lemon and honey, sweet and sour. Although oil and vinegar do not mix (they will not dissolve into each other) their duality complements each other very well on a salad. Other poles have caustic or explosive interactions such as hypergolic propellants (fuel and oxidizer) or the poisonous mixing of bleach with ammonia. Applying a linear model of time, we are flowing in the duality between past and future which situates our chronological fulcrum in the present.

Reflect on the following samples of duality. They are just a fraction of the multitude of polar relationships:

1) Physical world – an object is either stationary or moving, static or dynamic relative to an arbitrary point. A stationary object is considered triangular and a moving object is considered circular.

2) Electrical signal – it is either digital or analog, triangular or circular, a series of isolated packets of electrons or a continuous stream of them.

3) Binary code – it is the basis of transferring and storing information via electrical signals. It is either a 1 or a 0, on or off, circular or triangular. The assignment of which element is triangular and which is circular can be arbitrary depending on standards of agreement. The off signal (e.g., zero) could be considered circular because the numeral "0" is circular in shape or the on signal (e.g., the one) could be considered circular because it represents being energized, not contained.

4) Particles and waves – the particle is triangular, the wave is circular. A wave seems to be merely a packet of energy traveling in a significant proportion of its own medium, where a particle seems to be packet of energy traveling within an insignificant proportion of its own medium. Is it general relativity, quantum mechanics or both?

5) Consider mechanics – a stationary object, a supporting member, a strut, column or beam is triangular in nature. A rotating object or sliding member is circular in nature at its joints. The absolute center axis of a rotating object does not rotate and remains static; for 2D geometry it is a fixed point that is triangular and for 3D geometry it is a fixed line that is triangular. Therefore, the absolute center of a rotating object is static and thus a triangle. In other words, the absolute center axis of an object rotating about its absolute center of mass does not rotate with that mass. A circle spinning about its center at infinite rotational velocity will still have its very central point at relative rest. It is the motionless center point that cannot be found or defined about which all things are spinning – the "indivisible point", "the source of all" and the "axis mundi" from which God radiates outward.[1202]

—Λ*—

"The further the creation is from the Centre, the more it is bound; the nearer the Centre it reaches, the nearer Free it is." – *The Kybalion*[1203]

—*Ω—

6) Consider ourselves – we have both the internal mind, our introverted selves, and the external mind, our extroverted selves. The internal mind is the thoughts we keep to ourselves, and the external mind is the thoughts we express to others. The internal expression is triangular, the external expression is circular.

7) Consider the beginning, Alpha (A) and the end, Omega (Ω). It is the journey between the triangle and the circle, then back again. Notice the triangular shape of the letter "A" in Alpha and the circular shape of the letter "O" in Omega. The geometric basis of these symbols was crafted from triangular and circular elements. The use of the triangular and circular geometric elements is found in other Greek alphabetic symbols (i.e., delta {Δ}, lambda {Λ}, theta {Θ}, omicron {O}, phi {Φ}) signifying that divinity also intermixes with everything in between the beginning and the end. Was this just a coincidence or something deeper within the linguistic mind of humanity?

8) Consider the material body and the spiritual soul. The body is represented by the triangle and the soul is represented by the circle.

9) Consider the secular and the divine. The secular is triangular and the divine is circular.

10) Consider order and chaos. Order is a defined pattern, it is triangular. Chaos is a random arrangement, it is circular.

11) Consider change and the *status quo*. Change is circular, the *status quo* is triangular. Too much change becomes chaos, (pure circular), too much *status quo* creates stagnation, (pure triangular). It is the proper duality between creation and de-

struction, out with the old and in with the new, which forges both permanent roots and growing branches. Change can be for the better or for the worse, but nevertheless, it brings about a difference from what was before.

12) There is a duality in diversity. The diversity of life and living organisms can be considered as good. The diversity of cancer cells and harmful viral or detrimental bacterial mutations can be considered as bad.

13) Consider the dynamics of thought. The intellect is triangular, emotions are circular. A form of enlightenment is the balance and transition between these two.

14) Being stoic is triangular, being expressive is circular.

15) The Aristotelian philosophers focus on the tangible of the triangle. The Platonic philosophers focus on the abstraction of the circular.

16) Logic and reason are triangular, emotion and intuition are circular.

17) Isolation is triangular, exposure is circular.

18) Solitude is triangular, sociality is circular.

19) The individual is triangular, society is circular.

20) Consider classical and romantic thought. The first is triangular and the latter is circular.

21) Consider science and religion. Science is triangular, religion is circular.

22) Consider Western thought and Eastern thought. Western ideology is triangular and Eastern ideology is circular.

23) Consider night and day, darkness and light. Night and darkness are triangular, day and light are circular.

24) Consider daily activity, it is a balance between short-term goals, triangular, and long-term goals, circular. Have many long-term goals, because each will give you a multitude of short-term goals.

25) Instant gratification is triangular, delayed satisfaction is circular.

26) Consider work and play. Work is triangular, play is circular.

27) Consider the child and the adult. The child is circular, the adult is triangular.

28) Consider masculine and feminine traits. The male aspect is typically triangular; the female aspect is typically circular. The word "typically" signifies most of the time, but not always. This is a scenario in which we must accept the overlap or even the switching of the dichotomies.

29) Consider cause and effect. The triangle is the cause, and the circle is the effect.

30) Consider the dynamic between nature or nurture, genetics or environment. Nature and genetics are triangular, nurture and environment are circular.

—A*—

"We know the greatest of works can be represented in model, and that the universe can be represented by the same means. The same principles by which we measure an inch, or an acre of ground, will measure to millions in extent. A circle of an inch diameter has the same geometrical properties as a circle that would circumscribe the universe. The same properties of a triangle that will demonstrate on paper the course of a ship, will do it on the ocean; and when applied to what are called the heavenly bodies, will ascertain to a minute the time of an eclipse, though these bodies are millions of miles from us." – Thomas Paine[1204]

—*O—

I think by now, you get the general pattern and application of the triangle and circular model. The roles of which item is triangular and which is circular may also switch depending on the situation and viewpoint of the observer. Again, refer to this book's Appendix 1 for an additional example of triangular and circular denotations.

• • • •

EQUILIBRIUM OF PROPER Existence – Living Among And Avoiding The Extremes

A repetition of what was mentioned in the previous chapter, a pond that is balanced flourishes with life. Creatures come to its edges to drink and quench their thirst. Beauty can be seen of the creatures within and approaching its banks. A pond needs to have water flowing into it and out of it to maintain its balance. Too much inflow causes its banks to swell and creatures to flee its flooding path. Too much outflow causes it to dry up and stagnate, causing the creatures within to perish. The balance of fluid entering and exiting is what retains harmony in this ecological dynamic.

When the triangle dominates, the circle is diminished and vice versa. If left unbalanced, the triangular will shrink into nothingness and the circle will expand into oblivion. When the circle and triangle are balanced with their appropriate proportions, the growth of both will take place and the correct equilibrium will be maintained. This notion is not to be misappropriated nor improperly implemented when aspects of triangular and circular elements overlap and/or coincide, such as those with androgynous features. Our personal growth is based on weaving the best of the triangular and circular patterns of behavior into our default state of mind. One gains enlightenment by rising above this dualistic nature, and viewing it, metaphorically, from above. If one remains only within the duality, it can lead to madness or lack of balance. A being may become too triangular or the other extreme, too circular. An event or situation can also behave in the same manner. One's healthy behavior is determined by the nature of the event. To proceed on the path of enlightenment, one must stretch and lengthen the borders of their circular boundaries in controlled increments, allowing the triangular elements to catch up and regain their equilibrium with the circular elements. Enlightenment is marrying these dualities into unity when appropriate, and then separating the unity back into the dualities, when appropriate. We are immersed in dualities and must travel through them to integrate ourselves back into unity, the wholeness of Self. Once this completeness stabilizes, upon the polar fragments coming back together forming a better and greater whole, our sense of wonder, our depth of meaning and our ever-increasing connection to divinity will be amplified.[1205]

The flowing, cycling, oscillation, phases, rhythm or interplay between dualities can produce results of a higher order. The cycling in and out of a duality is a duality in itself. Even the interplay between non-duality and duality, is a duality. The field of magnetic flux lines between each pole, the flow of electrons from one terminal to the other, the creation of a charcoal image from the varying degrees of black and white, the transaction of money from customer to vendor in running an economic engine – when properly proportioned with the ideal amount of balance, they all make constructive use of opposites to produce something greater. The tension between the opposites generates a movement of energetic output. For example, the transfer of electrons from one terminal to another in an electrical circuit, the flow of air from a high pressure zone to a low pressure zone, and the fall of an object as its potential drops from a higher point to a lower point in a gravity well. Our transformation is based on coming to terms with and properly integrating the primal contradiction of incarnation; that we are humbly both human and divine.[1206]

Paradoxes and contradictions are to be expected among the dualities, for as I mentioned at the beginning of this chapter, it is not a perfect model. With the correct understanding, however, the interplay of the dualities can assist with solving the paradoxes and resolving the contradictions. That is why the position of our fulcrum needs the ability to be flexible depending on the situation. Most cases, but not all, lie somewhere between the extremes. In rare instances, depending on the perspective, a case can simultaneously be at both extremes, behaving as physical and metaphysical oxymorons. In those situations, the defining boundary distinguishing the extremes can be unclear or not definitive. The proper location of our fulcrum should not always be absolutely in the middle between polarities, such as with the case of good vs. evil. Ideal and evolved beings have their fulcrums closer to the extreme of goodness and maintain them there as a constant.

The boundary or delineating lines between opposites or extremes is not always clearly defined. At times, we must lean towards one side of a duality more than the other, such as choosing good over evil. Other times, we must embrace both sides of a duality simultaneously and equally. Transcending a duality involves the recognition and admitting to some limitations, while concurrently pushing against the edges of those limits. The notion that something is either good or evil can sometimes be blurred, calling into question in what direction our moral compass should point. When suitable, first situating our fulcrum in the middle between dualities and then re-adjusting and monitoring as appropriate, is the best strategy for dealing with life's uncertain encounters. In the duality of our daily existence, the correct choice of action in dilemmatic situations that call upon our ethical cores to act, the right choice of action is always the lesser of all the evils or the greatest of all the good, thinking in terms of eternity instead of just the present short term. Understanding the duality of a dilemma enables us to make wiser decisions or better compromises to deal with situations and issues.

One of the secrets for understanding existence is to open one's mind but not necessarily agreeing with either side of any perspective or view. Once we have mentally, emotionally and spiritually risen to see the duality of a situation or problem from above, from this new epiphanic vantage point, we are better able to address and resolve the event. We must apply our critical thinking skills to evaluate a situation, yet be cautious enough not to prejudge since we may be lacking all the facts and all the perspectives. It requires balance to be cognizant and aware of which projections and postulates are paranoia (based on no facts) and which ones are perceptive (based on strong evidence). There is a fine line between being paranoid and being perceptive. After becoming informed with as much information as possible, the objective is to either: 1) position the fulcrum of your stance somewhere between the opposites; or, 2) rise above the opposites while incorporating elements of both. Somewhere in between is not necessarily in the middle and can be on either side of center. Determining which approach to take is decided upon through the implementation of love and wisdom. By seeing the duality from above (metaphorically), one is able to make sound judgments because they are seeing both sides of the issues at hand. To seek truth, one must have relevant aspects on both sides of the duality. For truth is often, but not always, somewhere between the polarities. Once the proper proportions of the triangle and circle are found, harmony is achieved. Understanding the duality of competing convictions helps us to select the proper balance of or between both choices. Rising above the duality of opposite perspectives while embracing both in a reality of love places one at the supernatural vantage point for applying the optimum proportions of reason. From this higher vantage point, a sound decision can be made. This is the advantage point of God that humanity should thrive to seek. Allah wants us to grow, but we must always remember that we are a humble subset of the whole, as equal and worthy as all other creations within this universe.

When faced with the duality of whether to let love or truth dominate, it is better to let love dominate. For example, consider coming upon a utopian society that has never encountered violence or wars, but only perpetual prosperity based on the belief of a magic curved rod hidden under the lid of a small black box housed in their most sacred temple. It is an object that came to them from the heavens, falling from the sky above. You are told that the rod has two ends and three curves that forms the very reason for all the love and compassion in which they treat one another with the utmost respect and decency. It is the focus of all their contentment, all their wishes, and all their achievements. There are no criminals, no committed crimes, no jails, no prisons, no murders and no thefts in this utopian world. There is no poverty, no contentions and no disharmony. Words to describe "hate" or "violence" do not even exist in their vocabulary because they have no point of reference for defining them. In visiting their world, they are the most gracious of hosts, adorning you, the stranger, with gifts and banquets galore. Even though the curved rod hidden in the black box is sacred beyond comprehension to your hosts, they allow you to lift the lid and view into the defining God responsible for the peacefulness of their species. Upon opening the lid with the greatest of anticipation, your eyes focus in on a small, sculpted steel cylindrical object with four connected wire-like parallel segments about the size of your pinky finger. You immediately recognize the object and gasp in astonishment for there are several millions if not billions of them in your world. At the chance of destroying an entire civilization's tenets for a true utopian existence, do you tell them the object is nothing more than an ordinary paper clip?

—Λ*—

"When given the choice between being right or being kind, choose kind." – Dr. Wayne W. Dyer[1207]

—*Ω—

The ancients saw magic in numbers and the base of all calculations seem to be the interplay of triangular and circular variables and expressions arranged in patterns of formulation. Delving further into the mathematics of Euclidian geometry, the area of space between three tangentially coincident circles (as shown below) with diameters approaching infinity (∞) is a pure triangle. The image below is also the starting basis of Nicholas Roerich's "Banner of Peace", a symbology to preserve the religious art and human achievements of all the world cultures, especially through times of strife.[1208]

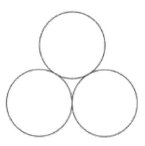

IN THE WRITING OF SHEET music, notes (tones) can be denoted with circular shapes and the rests (silence) denoted with triangular-based symbols. For example, instead of using the traditional symbols for rests (whole, half, quarter, eighth, sixteenth, etc.), triangular-based symbology can be used. This is not an edict to change the format of sheet music, rather it is just a different way of looking at it – having some silly fun with alternate forms of musical rests. Granted, using triangular-based geometry to represent silence may cause confusion when trying to quickly process and read the musical flow.

Current Notation For Musical Rests

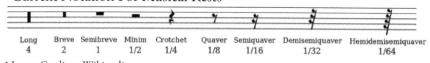

* Image Credit to Wikipedia

Alternate Notation For Musical Rests

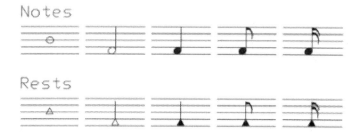

. . . .

THE INTERPLAY AND DEFINING lines between triangular and circular elements are sometimes indistinguishable or not solidly defined. Many items do not always fully reveal themselves or cannot be categorized as purely triangular or circular. They can have both triangular and circular elements. In other words, things are not always "black and white",[1209] or situated at the extremes – there can be shades of "gray." For example, consider the triangle as representing male and the circle as representing female. Some of us are born with genitalia that are not always clearly defined as specifically male or female and can be an acceptable combination of both. In such cases, the triangular and circular elements may be overlapping or intertwined. Another example: consider hearing the siren of an ambulance. On one hand it signifies that someone is in distress, but on the other, it also means that help is on the way or that assistance is being provided. It has both triangular and circular qualities. Many dualities are not good or bad in of themselves; it depends on the defining perspective. For example, the words "destruction" and "creation" can denote different tones. The destruction of cancerous cells would be considered good while the creation of a tumor would be considered bad. Switching the poles of the words used in this example, the destruction of organs would be considered bad while the creation of the proper replacement cells in healing would be considered good. In some cases, the dualities are different views of the same essence, for duality is often based on perspective. The phrase "two sides of the same coin" is an idiom that denotes opposite features of a common idea or notion. Having an understanding of the dualities and how they can potentially overlap enables us to rise above them and observe the dynamic of their interplay from a better and healthier perspective. A question to ponder: are demons and angels, archons and aeons, Satan and God, two sides of the same coin?

Constantly deciding where to locate our decisional fulcrum, we are faced with the duality of choices and actions every day. Do we veer left, right or equipoised somewhere in between? Do we opt for an outcome which only seeks to serve ourselves, one that only benefits others, or one that provides a limited bit of both? The type of person we become and the advancement, stagnation or decay of our core is dependent on how we approach the dualities encountered during our daily physical existence. Through the proper development of one's core, locating the fulcrum of our being appropriately between triangular and circular elements is the secret to enlightenment. When our fulcrum is properly situated between the dualities, our inner-verse will synchronize with our outer-verse and we will be in harmony with the cosmos. When the fulcrum of our being is positioned properly between the extremes, our thoughts will mesh with those of the universe. It is about maintaining the fulcrum of our creative imagination at the proper location between being visionary and being delusional. It is by integrating the poles of productive opposites and the correct levels of their extremes that we become whole.

Proper existence does not necessarily mean refraining from all minor vices, provided such vices are not in excess or causing harm to self or others. If one does not have an addictive personality or chemical dependence, some alcohol consumption, some gambling and some chocolate is perfectly acceptable. An occasional Lowney® Cherry Blossom or Mc-Donald's® Shamrock shake is not going to condemn one to Hell. One is not going to damage the core of their being conducting micro vices within moderation. For example, gambling in excess is considered a vice, but in moderation it can be part of a friendly social game of poker. Tobacco products, however, have proven to have primarily detrimental long-term effects and minimal, if any, health redeeming qualities. They and cannabis were used long ago by the ancient ones as part of infrequent and sacred religious ceremonies, not as something to be relied upon during morning breaks or as a daily or weekend ritualistic means for dealing with stress and partying it up. The reliance and excessive use of such substances will provide an early demise and a premature death, if that is what you desire. For those who rely daily on nicotine products to achieve a chemically induced state of calmness, I am not telling you to quit; that is something which you must decide for yourself. I only wish to have your benevolent influence in this material realm for as long as possible and the inhalation of nicotine vapors, in any of its forms, will greatly reduce the amount of time for the physical world to feel your presence and benefits. Training and reconditioning the mind through healthy spiritual exercises to achieve a state of calm focus without the reliance on external chemical influences is the way to enlightenment. An occasional glass of wine or spirits in moderation is a micro vice, provided it is avoided by those with addictive tendencies or who have had prior problems with alcohol. If one is capable of self-control and moderation, occasionally engaging in small amounts of such minor vices can be salutary.

There is also a definitive extreme in the duality of the existence of a higher consciousness. Either God/Allah exists or he does not. She is either here or she is not. There can be nothing in between – God/Allah cannot partially exist. A lamp is either on as validated by a visible glow or it is off. Perhaps, however, the felt presence of God/Allah can fluctuate or dim at times due to our limited human perceptions. The Lord is the Alpha and the Omega and everything in between. It is the mixing of triangular and circular pigmentation by which God creates diversity, a merger of circular and triangular elements building upon itself to create intricacy of object and life. Brahma has even created diversity in the dualities and in the poles. As discussed in Chapter 5, some Christian doctrines perceive or categorize God into three aspects (The Father, The Son, The Holy Spirit). Referred to as The Trinity, this representation can also be denoted with triangular and circular elements. The three vertices of a triangle can be related to the three aspects of God, when combined together and viewed as a whole, they morph into a circle.

—Δ*—

"Allah is the lucid paradox of love while being both the beginning and the end, singular and plural, past and future, masculine and feminine, rigid and flexible. God is the duality, all degrees in between, and everything beyond. The Lord is both everlasting and always changing while immersed in fixation and flux." – Poem Of The Pious, AO

—*O—

Our universe functions by an interplay of triangular and circular, circular and triangular amalgams. Following in line with Hermetic principles, it is an interactive dichotomy of scale based on opposite poles. The natural flow is from one pole to the other, but when energy is added to the system, the flow's direction can be reversed. For example, heat flows from hot to cold, air flows from high pressure to lower pressure, electricity flows from a higher to a lower potential, quantum states jump from elevated to lower levels, and a gravity funnel attracts things from a higher point to a lower point. The steady-state flow can be from circular to triangular, or triangular to circular. By inputting energy, the flow can be reversed in the opposite direction on the scale.

Sometimes it is better to dwell more in the triangular region, other times it is better to dwell more in the circular region and sometimes exchanges between both ranges are needed for desired results. The relationship and interactions between triangular and circular components can either be in harmony (producing a greater result) or in discord (producing a lesser result). When in harmony, the result is greater than the sum of the individual contributing components. When in discord, the result is less than the sum of the individual contributors. Our interactions and decisions consist of juggling daily triangular and circular influencers. When we choose to rise above the duality or traverse them simultaneously in parallel, we become non-duality and merge the antinomes.

—Λ*—

"He is an instant, she is an eternity. God is the duality and everywhere within, in between and above resulting in the transcendence throughout." – AO

—*Ω—

The interplay of dualities or opposites exists far into the cosmos when one considers that the darkest thing in the universe, a black hole, generates the brightest thing in the universe, a quasar. Perhaps the stars themselves are the Empyrean abode of God, gods, or goddesses and reserved for those souls among us that are truly worthy. The exchanges between the poles of duality can build upon themselves to reach infinity or annihilate themselves into nothingness. The gnosis of understanding the relationships of duality and properly applying the model of triangular and circular elements will promote more revelations from the mind of that which is All. Gnosis is embracing the paradoxes and situating your fulcrum of psyche and decisions at the proper location between the poles to maximize goodness. Perhaps the interplay of triangular and circular elements can be referred to as a new theory of everything – it is God's elixir of creation; a taxonomy for all occasions. With duality, confusion can surface which requires one to settle in on what is truly important above the scattering details. Sometimes being closer to the triangular is considered the "good" or better choice and other times being closer to the circular is considered the "good" or better choice. When the fulcrum between the triangular and circular is close to its proper position (this is not always in the center between the poles), harmony and equilibrium occur. By applying the Hermetic Law of Neutralization, we can maintain our fulcrum, our pendulum, closer to the pole of goodness than the pole of evil. It calls upon the will to be good, a *modus operandi* of benevolent behavior, rather than evil.[1210] Between the duality of love and hate, acceptance and fear, is love and acceptance not the better choice when applied with the appropriate cautions?

—A*—

"Gnosis is being conscious of both poles of your identity – your humanity and your divinity. Encountering the thoughts of God comes to us with more of a surrender rather than through a search." – AO

—*O—

When you start to notice the symbols or shapes of Δ and O or close approximations (i.e., Λ, Ω, A, O) during religious investigation and in your daily environment, it means that you are starting to understand this chapter and a basic pattern of the universe. Upon encountering moments of divinity and rising above the duality of Alpha and Omega, the triangle and the circle, the delineation of the beginning and end may become irrelevant, insignificant or non-existent. The hermetic vessel of an aspect of God's mind has been unveiled to your mind – your eyes have been opened to a new unfolding reality. As you start to understand the abstract relationship between triangular and circular components, it means that you are starting to awaken the Buddha within, your consciousness is rising to a higher state of existence, the fiber of your being is redefining as you become witness to a new and truer reality that is unfolding before your very eyes and mind. When one understands and comprehends the duality between circular and triangular elements, transcendence takes place which raises one above the influence of space and time. This transcendence can either be for a brief moment or a long duration, depending on its epiphanic impact. Having now been made aware of the abstract interplay between circular and triangular components, you will start to see, encounter and recognize their dynamics. Those readers of this book who are spiritual advanced enough to understand and implement its message will start to see the interplay of triangular and circular elements on a more regular basis. Do not fear them, but embrace them! For you are encountering bursts of synchronization with the universe – being blessed with the thoughts of God.

—Λ*—

"You are both Author and character. *Daemon* and *eidolon*. Spirit and body. Subject and object. Essence and appearance. Imagination and image. God and man." – fictional quote by Mary Magdalene[1211]

—*Ω—

Chapter 25
Omega – Our And God's Conclusions

"WHEN I AM WITH GOD in my own mind for the briefest of moments, I am Love." – you, the reader, AO

• • • •

ACTING AS A KABBALISTIC reference and a soteriology for all true religions (those that have a creed of love and lowering the ego as the basis of their tenets), this text was written to inspire within you the notion of balance, moderation, proper tolerance, positive exploitation and healthy affection during your existence here in this world. An even greater endeavor is to go beyond just tolerance by embracing coexistence and compassion through active pluralism. There is the duality between how so many religions share commonalities and yet there are still differences. Religion is both unified and diverse, yet interwoven through common threads. Remember, there are many conduits and spokes for connecting with divinity. Some are true, some are false, and some contain elements which are both. Focus on those paths that exemplify truth and minimize falsehoods. A healthy religious attitude is an element of the psyche whose importance to our historical continuity is indispensable and it should not be overlooked.[1212]

Reading this book has hopefully invoked an even deeper connection to something that is much greater than the actions of your daily routine, awakened that divine receiver within and brought you closer to your truer self. By trying to reconnect you to an eternal wisdom which started far back in time and continues to grow with each generational advancement in evolution of thought and awareness, it is an egalitarian energy of anamnesis which predates all known prophets, saints, messiahs, imams, sages and religious vehicles and yet exists as a seed, an ancient encrypted creature, dwelling within the very central core of our being. Our task is to tap into this prodigious providence, acknowledge it, nourish it and recognize its place within each moment of existence. Understand that we are a feature or an aspect of the universe experiencing itself. As Baal Shem Tov would have most likely said,[1213] mysticism is the recognition of divinity within every moment of our existence.

Various labels have been used interchangeably throughout these chapters to refer to something much greater than ourselves. A model of the universe has been presented in terms of triangular and circular elements interacting with each to form scales and degrees between extremes and diversity among the ether of God. Existing in the root meaning of such words as **Tao**, **Ago**, **Yoga**, **Atmon**, **Creator**, **Atone**, **Oath**, **Alone**, **Manifestor**, **Atom**, **Iota**, **Absolute**, **Chaos**, **Archon**, **Aeon**, **Sophia**, **Mohammad**, **Daimon**, **Havoc**, **Achamoth**, **Godman**, **Polar**, **Adonai**, **Reason**, **Anthropos**, **Pythagoras**, **Socrates**, **Plato**, **Aristotle**, **Tarot**, **Monad**, **Zoroaster**, **Ignorance**, **Passion**, **Zodiac**, **Mortal**, **Pharoah**, *Koran*, *Torah*, *Zohar*, **Ain** Soph and *Apokalypsis* (*Απολυψις*), that universal mind incorporates both the alpha and omega of existence. It even reveals its poles in the words "Father" and "Mother" and "hate" and "love." For simplification, the most overused labeling term of this supreme consciousness has been the word "God." Although trying to describe all that the Lord is or is not, becoming both nonviable and subjective, various figurative analogies (i.e., forms of water, electrical grid, an ocean's wave) have been used within this book in attempts to do so. In addition, various analogies (i.e., paths, tools, vehicles, tree branches) have also been used to describe the multitude of religious options and variants. The label of "love" is another word that has been overused with necessity in this book for it is the *magnum opus* for truly interacting with divinity. Love is the soul of the universe, and this soul knows no bounds – it embraces all people, all countries, and all true religions.[1214] Although the term "God" is often ambiguous at times, the word "love" is always lucid. The Almighty can be mysterious, vague and nebulous, but love is clear, distinct and straightforward. Allah is <u>sudurdarsam</u>, love is obvious. Love is found in the Tao, the Tao is found in God, and God is found in love – they are all aspects of the same force. The quintessence of the Philosopher's Stone, the Emerald Tablet and the Holy Grail is love, serenity and contentment in surrendering to the Lord, that higher and true God. Their secret is to always project and emanate love, not hatred. Comprehension of this requires that we already have a fragment of them within our core. By journeying on our path of illumination, we enlarge the stone, increase the tablet and expand the grail. Bernard of Treves finally realized this well into his eighties; you have the opportunity to understand this now.[1215]

The location of your behavioral fulcrum, your temperament and precepts, is something that you must determine and modify when necessary, to achieve the most efficient flow between yourself and society, the inner universe and the external universe. Boundaries are necessary, but they also need to be flexible. If humanity is to survive into the next millennium and enter into its next gilded era, it must select to participate only in organizations and entities that do not negatively exploit their constituents. In the coming age of Positive Empathetic Equilibrium, it is not just about applying a sense of fairness and abstract reasoning when imagining the feelings and perspectives of others; it is about deciding whether to nurture and adjust our perceptions to more closely and compassionately align. In doing so, we rejoin that group collective of the Universal Mind of humanity and feel a reciprocating relational belonging. With the globe becoming metaphorically smaller due to faster transportation and quicker communication, we are exposed to new ideas and cultural influences at an extraordinary pace. In recognizing and accepting these reductions while becoming citizens of planet Earth, we need to embrace the spectrum of cultural variety, work past the significances of our differences, put away our eschatonphobias and find the proper balance between maintaining links to our family heritage, preserving our nationalities and engaging in a world perspective.

Corporations must raise the bar of all employees and reduce the drastic incentive differential between those on the upper rungs of the corporate ladder and those on the lower rungs. Otherwise, pure monetary capitalism will continue to progress towards mimicking pyramid schemes in which much work is done by those in the lower ranks to subsidize those in the upper ranks. When egos and benefits of those on the upper rungs become too inflated, the ladder or pyramid becomes top-heavy and collapse is inevitable. A healthy organization functions as a rotating wheel, where every spoke is necessary to keep the rim properly spinning and centered about its axis. Those in warehouse positions are just as important as those in the executive offices for maintaining the balanced rotation of the rim around the axle. The balanced pull of both the worker and the manager, the officer and the enlistee, are necessary to maintain the trueness of the rim's rotation. Without the correct proportion of either's input and influence, the wheel will wobble. The amount of wobble, vibration or eccentricity is dependent on the degree of dysfunctionality within an organization's day-to-day operations. The objective is to minimize such organizational dynamics of dysfunctionality.

The statements of Buddha, Jesus (the Prince of Peace), Mohammad and others, are presented to us in the scriptural writings: "As ye think, so shall ye be."[1216] What you choose to focus on is what you will become. Remember, you are the sum of your thoughts and results of your actions. Listen to your internal voice and be aware of your discernment and volition – choose your ways wisely. It is not of primary importance if one believes in God, or the words of this book or any other spiritual text. It is not one's religion that Allah pays attention to, it is one's morality. The particular source of faith or beliefs is up to the individual to determine and whether they wish to become religious or choose no ideology, become pagan or non-pagan, select the orthodox or heterodox or opt for the denominational or non-denominational. It is, however, of primary importance that one strives to be good, genuine, sincere, merciful, truthful, honest and respectful of others as well as respectful of their universe. Consider the atheist who doesn't believe in God or anything beyond the physical death, but still treats his or her world with respect. The strangest look of surprise will be upon their face after leaving this realm as the face of God reveals itself to them. The Lord shall say, "Even though you didn't believe in me, your actions towards others pleased me. Therefore, I chose to believe in you." We are judged not by our beliefs or disbeliefs, but by our works – what we bring into the world.

—Δ*—

"My religion is very simple. My religion is kindness." – XIV Dalai Lama[1217]

—*O—

It doesn't matter to God which path you choose to use on your journey to find him or her so long as that path is based on a set of core values designed around the notion of healthy love and the advancement of our species' relationship with itself and the world around us. Allow the multiplicity of religious paths based on love to flourish and grow, even without having a single interpretation of the Supreme Consciousness of the Universe and its revealed thoughts. The evolving of a one-world religion that we mistakenly fear is actually the recognition of the truths within all the religions of love – it is pluralistically embracing the diversity of paths. All true religions should be welcomed under a protective umbrella, an unofficial leviathan of differential syncretism of which they may join or leave at any time, not a state-backed Church of dogmatic enforcement. God welcomes the multiple paths and for you to find him or her.

Don't be overly concerned with the afterlife, previous lives or your physical death; it will come on its own in the future. Allocate energy and effort on improving the here and now of your current existence. Every day we will be faced with confrontations and decisions that force us to be less than perfect – this is the dilemma of being human. Our lifetime duty, however, is to leave this world in better condition than we found it. The amount of freedom in the next realm is determined by our behavior in this realm. Never forget that we are emanations of God's love. Remember that Creation is diversity so embrace the wonder in all the variety of Allah's forms. God manifests and grows through diversity, for it is what creates balance and moderation in the universe for maintaining thriving and prosperous systems. Worship the Lord by embracing the beauty in all the diversity of her arrangements. Bestowing upon us diversity in particles, molecules, rocks, minerals, plants, creatures, and people, his/her variety is found in the multitude of skin tones, faces, cultures, ethnicities and religions. When we intertwine our differences, we are stronger and more durable as a species, or even as advanced intelligent sentient beings. Given the same overall diameter, a rope made of many strands is much stronger than a rope made of a single strand. This analogy applies to diversity.

Many of the ancient scriptures make statements about being the word of God. They are all correct. They are the words of God, but as interpreted by human beings and transcribed mostly in antiquated times and seemingly primarily by the male of the species. Parts of those texts relate to only the bygone time period in which they were written and portray certain historical events, potentially outdated laws and based on the society's level of ignorance, the related extreme punishments for violating such laws. Other sections focus on family relationships or ancient genealogy such as who beget which son or daughter.[1218] As humanity spiritually advanced, those laws and the related punishments changed to match our perception, whether correct or incorrect, of what God wanted. Modern books on anatomy, surgery, biology and astronomy would never have come about if it wasn't for the exploratory and experimental foundations established in older versions. The same holds true for spiritual and religious texts which evolve as our relationship with divinity becomes purer and as the average of our species becomes closer to enlightenment. Other parts of the various scriptures reference the past and relate to the future. The truly relevant ones relate to all of eternity. This book is also the word of God. It is the word of God as interpreted by a human, so it is fallible and receptive to errors. Words and ideas, either deliberately or inadvertently, may become subject to misinterpretation or exaggerated out of context. If so, I only hope that any phrases or interpretation taken out of context and applied beyond the author's intent is done so for benevolent purposes.

Ideas may become obsolete or out-of-date as our species advances in balance with its universe; the healthy growth of a sentient species is dependent on welcoming that which is new in balance with that which is old. Do not be afraid to redefine your relationship with Allah and perspectives on what constitutes divinity – strive for being spiritually centered and avoid dwelling on the extremes of religious fanaticism. Be cautious of absolutes, most things in the universe are probabilities, with some events being much more likely to occur than others. A willingness to seek truth, even if the truth may change our understanding of God is a sign of divine balance. Weaving the tapestry of our days and calligraphing the story of our moments, we manifest Allah into our being with the diverse threads of duality. She comes to us when we lower our ego and allow our internal being to encompass and absorb her divine attributes of love. In doing so, we blend in unity with the Supreme Consciousness, putting into action movements of healthy compassion to heal the wounds of the world. As you are refining your relationship with God, also consider redefining your relationship with the group collectives that you identify with or belong to. Should our identity as a nation or ethnicity take precedent over our identity with the global populace and the collective of humanity? Are we ready to rise above the narrow bands of parochialism?[1219] We must look beyond being just part of our neighborhoods, beyond being just part of our states, beyond the nationalism and pride we have as countrymen, and look to participating as humble citizens of the global community. Shifting views from a regional vantage point to a global one, and eventually to a galactic perspective, our identity with the planetary population as a whole needs to override our local affiliations with tribes, villages, districts and nations. The diverse coalition of humanity should be the dominating focus as we expand our communal loyalties to the global scale. Transcending from individual responsibilities, then to global responsibilities, then to universal responsibilities, will lead us in the direction of peace.

The surest sign of a strong faith in some grander consciousness is striving for a better future for ourselves and all of humanity. I have faith that this book will help to propel humanity forward via a quantum leap into a prosperous future; one of cooperative opportunities and abundance for all in a balanced relationship with our home planet's ecological environment, resources and the greater universe. There will be some who will say this book is unorthodox, foolishness, heretical and blasphemous nonsense. They have every right to do so provided it is done via peaceful means and without strife. No matter how much the teacher tries to present the lesson, some students will not be receptive to the meaning. It is an unfortunate but necessary side effect of free will. We all make choices of behavior as we become the sum of our actions. This book was written as a Gospel of Love, not as a Doctrine of Doom. It is not for those who wish to remain in their isolated and comfortable world of religious intolerance; it is for those seeking truth. God willing, may it change the world for the better.

—Λ*—

"What is proper is your praise that you will sing to God so that it might be written in this imperishable book." – *The Discourse on the Eighth and Ninth*[1220]

—*Ω—

We are all on this planet in the physical realm for relatively brief periods. How we spend our time here will determine our degree of contentment in our final days and our degree of freedom in the next realm. Did we spend our life in anger over those who trespassed against us or did we choose to move on and focus our energy on improving the world we live in? Were we willing to expose ourselves to new experiences for the continued enrichment of our being or did we remain in fear of growth and change? Are we going to spend our precious minutes relying excessively on artificial chemicals and destructive behavior to stimulate our being or are we going to learn to balance our emotions and our relationships with the world around us? Will we continue to start empty debates in the comment sections of the virtual world of social media or will we learn to express our ideas without antagonizing others and perhaps even quell the arguments? Will we have spiritualized ourselves enough at the moment of death to abandon our worn or broken body without regrets while crossing over into the eternity of divinity?

Our emotional balance is dependent on experiences, not material accumulation. The experience of being comfortable in our own solitude, the experience of being comfortable with others, the experience of being at peace with ourselves and the experience of helping others is the determination of our character. Finding the perfect balance of being in this world, but not of it, enthusiastically engaging this material realm with the connection of a Catholic and the simplicity of a Cathar – this life and the soul's journey are about service and love. We are not to renounce the material world, but on the contrary, we are to work to find our stable equilibrium within it. How we perceive, absorb and enjoy our time on this planet or on others is up to our course of thoughts and actions. It is up to each one of us to pursue our desired dreams with stable preparation and allow for any changes that occur along the way. Good and bad things will happen in life. Focus on the good while attending to the bad. We each need to accept the responsibility of our spiritual growth and that of the universal human consciousness. We need to raise our own consciousness to a higher state. We need to decide the direction of our species, the civilizations promulgating forth and the future for our offspring.

Do not become fixated on determining or proving the nature of a prophet's relationship with divinity, but instead focus on the truth of his/her message and its implementation. Be they a great teacher, healer, imam, saint or incarnation, focus on the aspects of eternal truths within their message, and not so much on their particular relationship with God. If their message portrays violence as a means of enforcing an ideology, I can assure you that aspect of their path is false. Resorting to initiating violence or negative exploitation as a means to promote any religion or any cause is a grievous sin and goes against the word of Allah/God. If their message focuses on decency and striving for balanced and healthy righteousness, then their path is true. Treat all true religious paths with humble respect and remember above all else, that God, divinity, Allah, the Supreme Consciousness, or any other suitable name is all the same essence of everything – that is love and truth. The universe came into being out of love, and into this love, all things shall return. It is just a matter of when this return occurs.

—A*—

"By love he knows me in truth, who I am and what I am. And when he knows me in truth he enters into my Being." – Krishna speaking to Arjuna[1221]

—*O—

When reading any true religious text, be aware that a percentage is the word of God. This leaves the remaining percentage under the influx of human frailty and influence of fallible human interpretations. If 10% to 20% of a book is incorrect or outdated, do we throw out the rest of it as well? I would think not. Some parts (i.e., those condoning or accepting of violence or negative exploitation) of scripture may seem counter intuitive to spiritual growth, but other phrases and stories are timeless in their value. The living words of true paths written in sacred books are eternal and infinitely above their commentators.[1222] Scripture does not provide all the answers, but it does act as a map for travelling the road of life. How we use that map on our journey is up to us.

—Δ*—

"The meek of faith and spirit shall inherit the Earth; the strong of faith and spirit shall inherit the Earth, the Universe and the domain of God." – AO

—*O—

Our being is shaped by circumstances imposed on it from the external environment, but it is also morphed by the reaction of our internal environment. We have to rise above our thoughts to recognize what they are doing. Are they stuck in a repetitive pattern that causes us and others harm? Are they leading us forward on the path of enlightenment? Being in control of our thoughts doesn't mean suppressing them, but rather being aware of them. Sometimes we need to be deep in thought and other times we need the mind to be clear. Enlightenment is knowing when each state is the most appropriate and being able to enter, exit and remain there when appropriate. If the thoughts are destructive, then we need to clear the mind to make room for those that are beneficial. The weeds must be pulled so the flowers can grow.

—Λ*—

"We look forward to the time when the Power of Love will replace the Love of Power. Then will our world know the blessings of peace." – William Ewart Gladstone[1223]

—*Ω—

We must all strive for an internal mantra of peace, compassion, wisdom and love to develop ourselves into higher beings. This is done by expanding congruently both the humanity and divinity within towards enlightenment, illumination, heaven, nirvana, jannah or whatever name you choose to call it. When the internal voice is balanced within boundaries of moderation, an external composition of happiness and productivity can be our gift to the world. We are all born into this realm to do the work of the Father and/or the Mother and to become an instrument of their divine love through the song and music of the Holy Spirit. Humbly becoming a higher being involves approaching all our decisions with an awareness of the dualities from both sides of an issue, then engaging with a baseline of love, not anger or hatred, and a willingness to educate ourselves to seek truths. If you default to love and compassion, it will be God experiencing the universe through you. If you default to hate and anger, it will be Satan experiencing the universe through you. Which one do you want to provide with the most experiences? Remember, angels are attracted to and feed upon love, demons are attracted to and feed upon hatred. Which would you rather have hovering overhead and influencing you? Once we achieve resonance as a higher being and dwell in an elevated state of existence, our experiences will be more vibrant, vivid and harmonious.

The Yahweh of yesterday is not entirely the same as the God of today. For Allah is both static and dynamic, fixed and moving, all-knowing and forever learning. As we grow and evolve as a species, so too, does God. Since Allah is all encompassing, he consists of both ancient wisdom and progressive change. She is the duality of all, interacting in a triangular and circular manner that propels the universe forward. No matter how disappointed God is with humanity's spiritual progress at times, he or she will continue to reach out to us because that is what a loving parent does. Let us forgive and look past the imperfections that religions' prophets may have had due to conforming to societal norms considered acceptable for their historical time period. How perfect are any of us? Future generations will be judging our actions, deeds and behaviors as well relative to their evolved norms and ethics of their coming time period. We should forgive the universe for its perceived mistakes, just as the universe has forgiven ours many times over.

Yahweh is sorry that he lost his temper and threw Adam and Eve out of the Garden of Eden. He now asks for our forgiveness and to help him repair, refurbish and rebuild the Garden back into the plush paradise it was. The destructive nature of our contamination, toxification and collective negative exploitation of our biosphere (the damage we are doing to Mother Earth) has a tremendous cultural inertia that can be challenging to overcome, but it can be tamed and then redirected. Gaea is not ours to destroy and she will shake us off like fleas (figuratively) if we continue our disrespectful behavior. As a species, we must strive for balance between ourselves and the growth of our collective entity. We must be willing to cut back on the unhealthy desires of excess consumption and strive for harmony with the surrounding universe. We should learn to play the roles of teacher, philosopher, artist and lover. We need to be our own role models so that we can be healthy role models for others. We need to restore our connection with divinity so that our species will thrive. We need to become our own saviors and stewards of our home world, preserving ourselves and that glorious, swirling, finite, blue, white, green, brown and tan marble floating in a backdrop of darkness from which our species originated. Our living globe is a gift from God, the gods and the goddesses and we are to protect it, not destroy it. We need to focus on providing a future of healthy and balanced altruistic actions to reduce suffering and improve the living conditions of others. We need to summon the will to preserve civilization by repairing the planet as a legacy for our children and future generations beyond the fig tree.[1224] The seeds of divinity have been planted in each and every one of us. Like the mustard seed, it needs spiritual nourishment in the form of faith, hope, love and insight to put forth sprouts and blossom forth.[1225] All of us are given the same mission in life, to somehow improve the human condition, if ever so slightly. Part of our journey, our path, is to determine the individual details and components of that mission. We travel our own highway of life that intermingles and meanders with other travelers on their way to the same common destination of eventual reintegration with that loving being of the cosmos.

We must ask ourselves, are we willing to curb our appetite for excess to preserve the future for our offspring? Are we willing to give up our extremes of material pursuits for our own happiness and that of others? Are we willing to take the steps needed to regain our balance with nature? Are we willing to pull together as a species to preserve our place in the Universe? Can we handle Globalization without destroying ourselves? If so, then we need to shift the fulcrum of our human consciousness from the isolated singularity of our own egos and expand it to a balanced focus between our individual beings, the universal principle of oneness, and a common future of balanced prosperity for all. We must strive to improve the human condition by finding the proper balance between serving our individual wants and needs, and those of others. Our vision starts with protecting that which is sacred by providing upcoming generations of children a legacy of love – agape towards the young and those not yet born. This legacy is denoted by preservation of the ecological environment, a rebuilding of our Eden, fostering of benevolent traditions, promoting inclusive prosperity and investing for the long-term future.

"We must do this" and "we must do that" if we are going to change the world for the better. But how as human beings with limited time, life spans, energy and resources can we focus our attention on accomplishing all that "what must be done?" Have there been too many "we must", "we need to" and "we should" printed within this book placing even more demands on our already overburdened shoulders? We all have limited reserves of time and energy, so choose those that you feel are the most important and focus on them. The most difficult part of any mass project is the beginning. The direction we head and choices we make are based on our most internal intentions. We can only hope that those who reach positions of leadership within militaries, governments and corporations have learned to discipline the temptation of their own nafs and not allow them to dictate their decisions.

The potential for a Golden Age of all the cultures of humanity is very high. Entrance into a Golden Age is dependent, however, on numerous factors. How will we handle the Beast and its Number? Will our monetary pursuits result in a limited number experiencing massive wealth and the reminder dwelling in poverty? Or will our monetary pursuits result in many achieving limited wealth? How many of us will finally figure out that happiness is not found in the quantity of material possessions that we own or in the power that we think we have over others? Will we choose to exercise our minds in a quest for knowledge? We have limited time in our mortal bodies while in this earthly plane. Will we choose mental stimulation that advances our relationship with the universe and others or will we choose to seek only self-destructive moments of instant gratification? Are we willing to step out of our religious comfort zone and open our eyes to the multitude of pathways to God? Are we secure enough with our own religious convictions to chance experiencing the convictions of others? Will compromise and negotiation become the dominant interaction rather than conflict or violence for settling our differences?

There is a universal dream within the Global Consciousness of Humanity. It is a dream which calls for an advanced state of human existence; a dream which calls for a better life for each individual; a dream in which all intelligent sentient beings have access to the resources and education to raise their well-being; a dream in which understanding and tolerance is more persuasive to the mind than the words and actions of the ignorant, and a dream which resonates with the Supreme Universal Consciousness. Enlightenment is the synchronization of our actions with this dream, pulling it into our secular reality. The goal is to make this dream a part of our awakened state. This is the same dream that Martin Luther King, Jr. talked about, the same transcendental message that *The Beatles* and John Lennon sang about, and the same realization that Gautama awakened into become the Buddha. The methods and means of attaining this awaken dream state have been left by the sages and prophets within the scriptures of all the great religions. Although the universal dream of peace for humanity seems to become disrupted by patterns of destructive narcissistic behavior frothing into positions of leadership, it is up to us to steer the future into a direction which will allow our children to value themselves, their world, and their potential to bring the universal dream into a reality. It is a dream coming into a reality of healthy love, tolerance (or better yet: pluralism) and a respect and wonder for that which is both similar and different.

Each of us can have a quest in life to do what we can to preserve and advance our species and our relationship with the universe. We can't all be like Mother Teresa and perhaps we shouldn't,[1226] but emitting just a fraction of her compassion would do a lot to change the world. We can, however, implement the practices of Saint Therese of Lisieux by doing the "little things" to make the world a better place – saving it with small incremental actions that build into bigger actions. What if every intelligent being could emanate just one one-thousandth of such saintly qualities in helping others? Think of how our cosmos could change for the better. What does God expect of us and what should we expect of God? That is simple. *The Lord's Prayer* pretty much sums that up for the Kingdom of God starts within you.[1227] "Thy will be done on Earth as it is in Heaven" is a mantra for the mystic and prophet within all of us, regardless of which true religious path that we follow.[1228] Allah expects actions and works from us in the service of love towards all people.

—Δ*—

"The man that moves a mountain must start by moving small stones."
– Chinese proverb[1229]

• • • •

"BE A STAR ONTO YOURSELF and become your own illuminating beacon." – AO

—*O—

Being only human, we can't change the world all at once nor should we. However, it is the small little strings of action that can result in catalytic webs of action. These little strings of action branch out in time and geography, having a grander affect than first realized. At the end of our lifetime, being able to say that our actions contributed to a better world for all is the ultimate reward and something to be strived for. The poetic visualization of improving conditions is one thing, making a genuine effort to bring it into reality is something more. Both the dreams and the efforts are needed. In striving to becoming a Bodhisattva, money will have less meaning to the Self, for the Atmon within is not of the material world. We should all thrive to become a Mahasattva through our chosen religious path and in doing so, to ask ourselves, is this our final material cycle before reaching the Eastern version of Enlightenment? Are we going to be returning again for another "go round" or is this our home stretch? Have we come to the finish line in the race of purity? Will our karma at last be wiped clean in this lifetime?

—A*—

"As long as space endures, as long as sentient beings remain, until then, may I too remain and dispel the miseries of the world." – Shantide-va[1230]

—*O—

As a collective species, our greatest ongoing battle is correcting ignorance. How do we catalyze every individual and generation of human beings to seek truth, disdain from hatred, and avoid becoming trapped within isolated perspectives? How do we assure that every member of society feels connected and maintains a balanced emotional state when interacting with others? How can we assure to head in the direction of becoming an empathetic society rather than a narcissistic one? The starting point has always been through positive educational systems and supportive family structures, but what causes some beings to thrive and others to go astray with hostility and chosen ignorance even when better opportunities are present? Why do some still choose a perspective of contempt for those of different religious, ethnic and racial backgrounds than that of their own? Is it out of unwarranted fear? Is it from a desire to feel superior to those that are different? Are they scared to embrace a larger world view than their isolated and sheltered egos? Did empathetic intelligence fail to develop within the cores of their beings? In the next thousand years, we may never completely end ignorance and poverty, but we can certainly minimize them to levels much lower than where they are now. Even so, extreme global poverty has already been cut in half during the period from 2004 to 2019.[1231] With the implementation of financial infusions with proper oversight, supply chain management, distribution and opportunities, we can end extreme poverty by 2030 – this is an achievable goal. There will be occasional outbreaks of indigence but keeping them in check can be done with proper monitoring, routine maintenance, treatment and benevolent social adjustments. No one individual religious or spiritual path can cure all of society's ills, but keeping one's mind open and receptive to the multiple of true methods for communing with that permeating Supreme Consciousness will certainly minimize its woes. Our religious psychology must embrace all true paths.

Otherwise, we are still stuck in the Middle Ages and bottled within an Era of Ignorance.

—Δ*—

"A true path, a true religion, a true way, will always have love at the core of its tenets and will never initiate violence nor be a part of its continuance." – AO

—*O—

Understanding that the universe operates through interchanges between opposite poles and degrees of extremes, the objective is to harness these dualistic tendencies for the productive improvement of our world. To do this, sometimes we need to be immersed in the dualities and other times to transcend above them. The way to become closer to the godhead is through continuing the development of our cores by choosing the proper course between the dualities of good and evil, positive and negative exploitation, and following through on actions that support a better state of mind for both ourselves and others. Our degree of synchronization with the higher mind is dependent on our willingness to lower our egos at the appropriate times and to rise above negative situations in preference over becoming entangled in them. Seek enlightenment by continually illuminating the habit of virtue from within. Love, gratitude, and forgiveness put into action; these are the principles by which a practitioner of the divine arts abides. This is the trilogy that needs to become the roots of all our cores and by which to live.

The bottom line is that if we want to survive as a species, we must be willing to expand the boundaries of our formal existence and stretch the borders of our religious preconceptions. It is time for humanity to decide where to go as we progress forth into the future. If we want our offspring and the next generations to succeed, we must be willing to curb our appetite for excess and focus on the quality of experience, not on the quantity. We have the tools of religion for raising our consciousness to a higher state, the tools of economic diversity for driving away poverty, the tools of government for social stability and the tools of the internet for expanded communication. Using these tools with benevolent application and the direction humanity goes from here is up to you; steer yourselves wisely.

Coming to terms with the multitude of religious paths walked by humanity to reach the Divine Spirit of the Universe (in its many forms and names) is a prerequisite if we are to ever interact with advanced intelligent sentient beings from other worlds. Our anthropocentric attitudes will come to a halt at the start of such interactions. No religion, race, culture or species has a monopoly for accessing God or a hegemony over others. Upon awakening to our true Self, the essential Self, while becoming aware of our connection and oneness to the whole, we will start to sense that same greater consciousness as described by the religious voices and the sacred languages of all cultures. For if we are unable to embrace with healthy tolerance and pluralism the variety of true religious paths used here on planet Earth to connect with divinity, how will we ever accept the true paths used by intelligent sentient non-Terra dwellers? If humanity as an average whole cannot accept the pluralism of multiple paths to Allah, the gods, or the goddesses, then how will we be capable of interacting with lesser, equally or more advanced non-terrestrial sentient beings that have their own mythologies, prophets and paths to the godhead? If we do not learn to tolerate and respect that there are multiple acceptable paths to God on this planet and among our own species, how will we ever deal with the potential multiple religious paths of sentient and sapient beings from other planets within the Milky Way galaxy and those beyond? If we cannot accept the variety of cultures, ethnicities and minute differences among humanity here on planet Earth, how will we ever tolerate those of sentient beings from other worlds? If we are unable to embrace diversity on our own home planet Earth, that pale blue dot swirling all of us into existence, how will we ever embrace the diversity among the star systems?

—Λ*—

"Just as there are infinite rays emanating from our Sun, so too, are there infinite paths for connecting with God." – AO

—*Ω—

The hypothetical outcome of the variables in the Drake Equation shows that there could be a vast number of civilizations capable of communication from beyond our solar system.[1232] It is just a matter of time before we encounter other spacefaring species and their true religions from other worlds based on non-terrestrial prophets. To think our planet is the only one in which God presented himself or herself to AISBs is preposterous. Some of these alien religions could be thousands of years older than Hinduism and have probably encountered their own distortions as well. Remember, we are all gentiles and heathens to religions not of our own and should embrace the diversity of paths, not admonish them. Alien sentient beings would approach us with the same timid curiosity, genuine caution and protective skepticism as we would have towards them. Whether they are "little green men" or tall like the "Coneheads",[1233] there would be initial concerns of rogue violence from resistive protesters and then the potential spreading of new diseases and plagues between both parties. We don't want to repeat decimations similar to that transmitted upon the indigenous people of the Americas or the Aboriginals of Australia by the introduction of smallpox and other diseases from Europeans travelling to the new continents. To prevent the repeat of such occurrences, introductions to other spacefaring beings should proceed with contaminative caution. This is to protect both them and us, from exposure to and transmission of any foreign hostile pathogens. There is also the concern on whether the interaction will result in the creation of allies or foes. Is it a relationship to be favored or to be feared? We have already seen recent patterns of behavior in intelligent marine animals that seem to risk approaching a scuba tanked diver for interaction or the removal of entangled hooks, fishing lines, plastic loops and netting. Perhaps alien sentient life will learn to recognize advanced righteous human beings and be less fearful of those in a space suit. Through the words of Fr. José Gabriel Funes and Monsignor Corrado Balducci, even the Vatican was courageous in expressing a receptiveness to welcoming AISBs from other planets with open arms.[1234]

—A*—

"Misperceptions produce fear and true perceptions foster love." - *Accept This Gift*[1235]

—*O—

There are those who feel expansion beyond the influence of our nearest star's gravitational pull will result in the annihilation of the human species due to continued diversification beyond recognition from evolution occurring in unique isolated planetary biospheres. Occurring over hundreds of thousands of years, is this something really to be feared? Doesn't evolutionary diversity contribute to the survival of our genes? Do our descendants millions of years from now really need to still look like us? Humanity evolving into higher states of existence and branching off into customized evolutionary tracks suitable to their environments and new religious currents should be the natural welcomed progression of nature and divinity. There are also those who fear first contact with celestial intelligent beings (i.e. smart aliens) since any advanced civilization capable of interstellar travel could wipe us out. Well guess what folks, as mentioned previously in Chapter 21 discussing the verdict of our future, we are perfectly capable of doing that on our very own without any outside help. If we are being watched by extraterrestrials for a possible invasion, then logic dictates that the invasion should have occurred long before humanity learned to take to the air in our flying machines, if conquering is truly their goal. Delaying an invasion of our planet only gives more time for us to technologically advance and harder to defeat. Despite the science fiction horror shows and movies, I would think that any species that has evolved to the point of interstellar travel would also have evolved beyond the desire to be invaders, predators and conquerors. Look how much work, energy, costs, resources, hardship and failure that go into attacking and/or occupying other nations on our own planet. How often do such invading dominations from hostile foreign forces endure before rebellious undercurrents prove more victorious? I'm sure advanced extra-terrestrial species have better things to do with their time than deal with molding and training us to be their slaves. Just like humans, I'm sure some will be hostile, but the vast majority would be benevolent, kind, helpful, receptive and open to trade and barter. Once we have passed the initial hurdles of first contact and encountering one another, mutualism can proceed and sprout forth. The worst of obvious sins is the negative exploitation of a being from a sentient spacefaring species or one that is capable of developing interplanetary exploration. Leaving the nest of our planetary home and becoming a spacefaring species is encoded into our DNA, and because of the possibility of panspermia, most likely within the molecules of non-terra AISB life forms as well. It is necessary for our survival, for if we do not open the doorways into becoming a spacefaring species, we will fade and then become extinct.

Proceeding forth with our evolution into space depends on humanity reaching a critical mass threshold of spiritual understanding, religious pluralism, love and engagement in continued learning – a runaway positive feedback loop which embraces both the enlightened and the disenfranchised. Reawakening a sense of belonging, inclusive preparation for the journey will give the discouraged and the addict a recharged vitality of spirit to overcome their obstacles, a sense of purpose, a newfound usefulness to society and to find value in their life and the lives of others. "Give people a cause worth following and the dignity of a necessary role for every one of every age and they will respond – not quickly or easily, perhaps, but if patiently gathered, they will respond."[1236] For it is the power of purpose and will that can lead the depressed, the apathetic and the chemically dependent from their pit of despair, malaise of the soul and false perceptions of self-worthlessness. Although chemical dependence is not always cured and can be a chronic disease for those who cannot escape the artificialness of its bait, it can be treatable for the determined through proper counseling channels and by substituting and replacing the addiction with a constructive passion and a healthy obsession. An addict can articulate the consequences of the behavior, but there is a failure to retrain the mind to act accordingly.[1237] The addict and mentally afflicted are merely looking for something else to take possession of them, steer them to meaning, form substance amidst the confusion of internal conflict and neurosis, and change their epitome to a whole new outlook upon life. For neurosis is an inner conflict of battling oneself and aspects of dissociated personalities fighting to merge into a stable equilibrium. Victory is obtained when the Ego finally accepts itself and no longer has to prove its worth. Do not make the mistake of thinking that lowering one's ego is the same as reducing one's self-worth and value, for they are polar opposites. This post-war peace after victory has been obtained is when the self is contented – it has found enlightenment by just being. Addiction can be overcome if we are willing to surrender to a consciousness much greater than ourselves and allow it to fill and replace the emptiness of destructive cravings. Upon dropping the external false self, that part of us that lacks permanence and impedes intimacy, we can begin again by allowing the internal true Self to come forth. To erase the surface behavior of addiction, our deeper being needs to rebuild and connect to a more eternal meaning. Providing the focus of a future purpose for the essential Self to emerge and the addicted self to die, we can then be reborn as the glorious version of who we were meant to be.[1238] When the addict starts to shift the center of gravity of their personality, only then will they start to find significance in their value to society. A purpose of service to the universe should become our call, placing us in a commonality of experiences as we all inclusively participate in the expansion into the frontiers of space and the healing of our planet of birth. It is internal circumstances that give so much more to life's meaning than external circumstances. There is plenty of internal growth and development that has occurred within your reading span of the past 25 chapters and there are lots of marvelous things that can be accomplished just within the space of the upcoming twenty five years – "a lot of things can happen in 25 years."[1239] There is nothing wrong with striving for an extraordinary tomorrow, insha'Allah.

—Λ*—

"If the moon is beautiful as it reflects the light of the sun at so great a distance, what will be the beauty of the saints who for all eternity and not at a distance, will reflect the divine image of God!" – Solanus Casey[1240]

—*Ω—

Militarizing space exploration based on individual national objectives will be a self-fulfilling doom, since inevitably, international mutual support is mandatory to address the hurdles of travelling into the vastness between planets, moons, nebulas and stars. We will fail to enter the final frontier and extend beyond if the governing national leadership among our species continues down such a path of myopic cultural isolationism. If done properly, however, our flourishing into the vastness of the heavens has the propensity to unite all nations in a federation of interstellar exploration and healthy, balanced, respectful expansion into the cosmos based on redefined economic realities. Our trek across the universe should be based on global participation, not on national supremacy.

—A*—

"If you want to go quickly, go alone. If you want to go far, go together." – African proverb[1241]

—*O—

We have already witnessed the cooperative success of the International Space Station. Continuing on this explorative path calls for the first craft to place men and women on Mars to consist of representatives of several nations – the United States of America, Canada, the Russian Federation, People's Republic of China, India, Japan, members of the European Space Agency, and others in conjunction with corporate partners. If the warring city-states of ancient Greece could look past their differences and continue to send athletic representatives to the Olympic events, I'm sure current feuding nations can provide astronautic expertise. The craft itself can be a conglomerate of technologies, scientific sections and modular components designed and built by different nations and assembled while still orbiting Earth – this would help alleviate any national security concerns. Working through the collaborative initiatives of the United Nations Office for Outer Space Affairs (UNOOSA), space exploration can become the unifying vehicle of all nations, an enterprise of common goals. The next step towards peace and healing our home planet is by making the United Nations (UN) the benevolent leviathan that it was always meant to be. What if the UN had unlimited funds in which to clean up the contaminated oceans, heal the polluted lands, encourage civil rights through incentives, redevelop slums into vibrant communities, reduce the rate of climate change, respond rapidly to natural and humanitarian disasters, educate on cultural diversity, promote true religious pluralism and teach the masses how to feed themselves through proper agrarian management? Through the mining of asteroids this is not a fantasy, for such celestial objects contain billions if not trillions of dollars' worth of minerals and metals. The mining operations of asteroids should be conducted by the UN, not by corporate or national objectives of greed. The UN can redirect the profits from the sale of those extraterrestrial commodities into funding ventures for healing our home world and improving the human condition. This is a very real and feasible path to peace among nations.

With the discoveries and perils to be encountered, we need each other if our species is going to surpass the Odyssean distances reached by the twin Voyager space probes. One day these probes will become protected historical spacemarks, drifting artifacts visited by stellar tour ships – tours that will most likely first visit the historically protected final resting place of the Mars rovers named Spirit and Opportunity. Reliance upon peoples of all nations is mandatory if we are going to successfully traverse beyond and into the vastness of the cosmos. The lessons learned in the importance of productive national cooperation for containing the COVID-19 pandemic and minimizing its damages can be well applied to how we need to interact for entering the final frontier – this can be our turning point. Be assured of this, doorways to the stars will automatically reveal themselves when enough of humanity reaches this united juncture. If all of us come together as a cooperative interacting species that accepts, tolerates and respects the multiple cultural differences and peaceful paths for connecting with divinity, interstellar doorways will be revealed much sooner – *ad astra*!

—Δ*—

"There is no discord among the inhabitants of heaven. All have one purpose, one mind, one feeling – for they are bound by the spell of love into one harmonious whole." – *The Hermetica*[1242]

• • • •

"YOU MUST ALL STAND fast in the faith and love one another. And do not be weakened by what we have gone through." – Saint Perpetua[1243]

• • • •

"LORD, THROUGH YOUR love and guidance, we are ready to heal the world and expand beyond it. Let it begin." – AO

—*O—

Faith and prayer can heal us through the combination of both the internal mind and the universal (external) mind – it is the culminating effects of both that provide miracles. When we are ready for such miracles, then we will start to receive them. Our greatest supplication to the universe should be for sufficient prosperity, good health and spiritual growth for all as we induce forward into the Era of Positive Empathetic Equilibrium, transitioning into a perpetual period of Satya. If we take the initiative, recognize and seize the current zeitgeist, then there will be no apocalypse to be feared, no divinely implemented doomsday of despair, no destructive battle of Armageddon, no Hour of Doom, no ending Ragnarok, no final savage cataclysm and no wrath of God. Such eschatological timelines have already been significantly altered due to certain predominant anomalies and intercessions occurring in the common era of human history. There is enough good fruit among humanity to continue our existence and growth. Namely, the realization of the sacredness of civil rights, the divine right of freedom of true religion, the virtues of self-determination, and that many of us are starting to recognize the interlacing benevolent connections between all the great religions. For religion was never supposed to be about beating the unbeliever into submission or defeating and slaying our enemies. True religion was supposed to be and is about generating a constructive relationship with the universe through a covenant of love. In the short term, sometimes humanity may temporarily lose confidence on its spiritual evolution, but as a species we must look at the long-term growth of ourselves over the past 25, 50, 100, 500, 1,000, 2,000 and 4,000 years. Although our species still has elements of turmoil and will encounter bumps along the way, its average good sense has grown tremendously over the recent centuries. It is by love and compassion that we will outwit Satan, casting him away and bounding him for a millennium, thus initiating the End of the Age.[1244]

The End of Times will be a benevolent change, a metamorphosis into a new direction, not the annihilation of existence. It will not be the end of the world, but on the contrary, it will be new beginnings. It will actually become the Days of Glory, bringing with them the beginning of humanity's rise and ascension beyond the gravity wells of the Earth and the Sun, both in the physical and spiritual sense with the start of a new Earth (the healing of our home planet and the genesis of humanitarian non-invasive colonies and embassies on other habitable worlds) and a new Heaven (the unlimited boundaries of space where seas are absent between the vast planetary distances).[1245] Venturing further into the frontiers of space, some will choose to journey to distances beyond seeing the direct light from our own sun and the reflected light from our own moon as the stars seem to flash and fall past them during their travels.[1246] Time will start to fluctuate from linear to non-linear, depending on our point of reference in space-time. The actuality coming out of the eschatological beginnings of all the great religions' prophecies will be much more wonderful than what was expected, **not** a reckoning of hailstones, fire, smoke and brimstone. It will **not** be the elimination, destruction and the ending of life, but on the contrary, it will be its rebirth, regeneration, rejuvenation and preservation. It will **not** be a violent cataclysm of epic proportions, but on the contrary, it will be the awakening of love within our species to a level beyond imagination. This is how the new Earth and new Heaven will unfold from the Buddhist, Christian, Islamic and other eschatological prognostications – the realigning and balancing of the physical with the spiritual. The end of the tribulations, the latter days that we are currently within, will become the beginning of our deliverance. It will be the start of the true New Age coinciding with the precession of the equinoxes transitioning from the Age of Pisces and into the Age of Aquarius, as the commandment of love, even when you don't understand why, virally spreads across the globe dissipating the skotosphere into oblivion due to its wake.[1247] This shock wave of love and tears of joy will lead the way to an extension of intercultural peace, bringing harmony into the world and cooperation among nations.[1248] Great nations deserving of praise provide their citizens with one of the most fundamental of human rights: that is freedom of religion. Having the right to search, question, define, and redefine what God is on a personal level allows each and every individual the ability to expand and grow their connection with divinity and achieve enlightenment.

Emerging from the Beginning of Sorrows, with our minds opening to a higher state of consciousness and awareness, we will be moved to sobs with each step towards heaven and enlightenment. There is a duality with these cries – some will be a cathartic release of tears of sadness and others will be tears of joy from an overwhelming sense of understanding. There will be tears of mourning for what we were as a child prior to the innocence lost to adulthood, weeping over how we have been living in denial of our true Self, and crying in shame of what we have become or still are. There will be deluges from our eyes both due to sadness for how we've been living our lives so far and from the joy upon the realization of where we will be headed. The wailing or gnashing of teeth will then become from the rapturous holy tears of overwhelming jubilation among the multitudes and of anticipatory ecstatic excitement as the future unfolds. For most, there will be tears of spiritual joy, happiness and especially love; intense feelings of love and felicity will burst us into crying and cause "butterflies" (bitterness) in our stomachs due to the excitement.[1249] To the mind, the words within this book may be as sweet as honey, yet they may make the stomach feel sour. Upon the completion of this chapter, the tears in your eyes and feeling developing in your belly region is your conduit to God being cleansed, but step back once you are ready to regain your composure – limit overdoing ecstatic stimulation.

—Λ*—

"The day your love touches me, I'll become so mad that lunatics will run away." – Rumi[1250]

—*Ω—

For some, the truth will be too threatening for those who are not ready, nor willing to listen. For others, it will be weeping of guilt over the realization of what they have become as they acknowledge negative deeds of past. Eyes will fill with tears as the truth unfolds before them. Initially overcome with emotion, there will be temporary madness of joy for the worthy, temporary madness of shame for the sinners, but most of us will encounter a bit of both. There will be tears of cleansing and tears of healing as fear, worries, and anxieties will be cleansed out of us in the form of weeping. The Atmon within shall be reborn through this cleansing of tears and voyage to the depths of our souls, forming with beauty, the pearls of Self. You may have already encountered some of those gushing tears during the reading of this book and may find many more coming forward upon its completion. After the tribulation period ends, the awakening will begin as the inertia of love spreads across the global community. During this awakening, we are remade in a transformation of our Atmon, the Self, and we will more consistently tune into and vibrate at the higher frequencies of love without being overwhelmed, fragmented or off-balance. We will become aware of our primordial unity to the light within that illuminates and reconnects to the light throughout. This newfound reality beyond the ego will at first appear frightening, agitative, and send us into religious shock, but as it becomes accepted into the Self, balance will return. During the emergence from this awakening and astonishment, focus will be restored as logic and emotion will again stabilize as proper equanimity and samatva take hold. The world shall again return to its proper equilibrium, but at a higher level of existence.

—A*—

"Lift up your head and be of good cheer; for behold, the time is at hand, and on this night shall the sign be given, and on the morrow come I into the world, to show unto the world that I will fulfill all that which I have caused to be spoken by the mouth of my holy prophets." – Writings of Moroni[1251]

* * * *

"THE SOUL OF EVERY PROPHET of God, of every divine messenger, hath thirsted for this wondrous day." – Bahá'u'lláh[1252]

—*O—

Believe or not, humanity is on the cusp of a great leap forward and entering into a paradigm shift of both a scientific and a spiritual rise – the developing momentum of this Fourth Great Awakening and perhaps the absolute and final one.[1253] We are about to undergo the next jump along the timeline of our bio-spiritual evolution as the unitive conjuncture of matter and spirit again reveals itself, a genuine Aquarius Age of Realization. In doing so, we will accelerate our quest to discover everything that God is about as our knowledge substantially increases. The great days of the Almighty are upon us as the final phases are revealed. There will be birthing pains during the interregnum of a shift in social order as new beginnings rising from endings; the alpha coming out of the omega, the triangle coming forth from the circle. It is up to us to fulfill the prophesy of improving conditions as we open the door, lift the veil, and uncover a continuous expansive existence unto which love far surpasses hatred and reason outshines shortsightedness.

Our salvation as a species is dependent upon improving the interplay between science/technology and metaphysical ideology. It will be through the proper application of geometric physical principles, the Euclidian and Pythagorean elements of the triangle and circle that establish predictability in navigation, architectural structure, surveying, electromechanical design, and the movements of the heavenly bodies. It will be through the proper application of the metaphysical principles of the triangle and circle that establishes a means of becoming closer to God. For both the physical and metaphysical interplay between the triangle and the circle are the soul of science and religion.[1254] The truest pursuit of knowledge is built upon the intermixing of science, religion and spirituality as we transcend beyond the simple reality of the physical plane and into the realm of the outer spheres. Science will take us only so far into the reaches of outer space; it has its limits. For the rest of the journey, it calls upon true religion to bring us beyond the confines of self, in order to understand and explore the Self. Both the tools of true science and the tools of true religion are needed to trek beyond the influence of Earth's and Sun's gravitational domains. It won't just be our bodies that will need to adapt and adjust for adventures beyond the Moon, it will also call for a strengthening and refining of our consciousness and the identifying constituents of our core. Although neither science nor religion will provide all the answers, the voyage requires that we become practitioners and masters of each as we edify ourselves into becoming both terrestrial and celestial citizens of the cosmos during our self-actualization.

Once we come to the realization and acceptance that there are multiple pathways to the godhead, each conduit being paved with the ethical traditions, customs, anecdotes and wisdom of the true religions, then we are properly aligned in the direction of understanding Allah's thoughts. True religion is the incorporation of the Lord's message of love into our everyday existence and guides us in repairing ourselves, our planet and our universe. It is not a feeling of being a chosen elite in the eyes of God, better or more blessed than those around you, nor does it concern itself with focusing on questionable literary interpretations of scripture. It is a beacon of healthy and moderate behavior for which we should all strive to follow throughout our lives. We are all inwardly divine, but some of us have degraded or tarnished our connection. It is time to heal our religious outlook, forgive any distortions we may have encountered, and rebuild ourselves anew as we find and redefine our place in the universe. To regain and polish your contact, become a student and practitioner of the divine arts by going back and regenerating the lineage to your religious roots, no matter how obsolete the heritage may seem – work to revitalize and improve upon the shibboleths. Readopt the appropriate family traditions from the past, linking to the spiritual wisdom of ancestors and follow and implement the mystical energy of the Divine Benevolent Principles. The primary principle is Love; the secondary principles are Forgiveness and Gratitude; the tertiary principles are Truth, Peace, Humility; the quaternary principles are Joy, Humor, Wisdom, Compassion; the quinary principles are Faith, Hope, Liberty, Justice and Freedom; and the senary principles are Patience, Kindness, Goodness, Faithfulness, Gentleness, and Self-control.[1255] Feel free to continue the sequence with additional magnanimous abstract qualifying nouns. By implementing and mastering these principles, you will come to know God and God will come to know you. These are the principles by which power and healing strength reveal themselves; these are the methods that Jesus, the Buddha and other spiritual masters were trying to teach us – that the Christos Logos is accessed from within and is then to be released throughout. This is how we open the doorway from the inside that will take us beyond the illusion of this material realm and access unity with Allah. As a movement of global empathy and compassion, a benevolent juggernaut forming within the consciousness of humanity, we must all take the step forward from the present into the future with a leap of faith as we heal our home planet, reverse the trend of climate change, preserve the kaleidoscope of life, explore both the physical and metaphysical universes and multiverses, and savor the cosmic vistas.

As you approach the completion of this book, hopefully the synaptic circuitry within your brain and body have further tapped into, strengthened and soldered their connections with the Universal and Supreme Consciousness. Should we be suspicious of "inner experiences" and "imaginative symbols" that appear as junctures between the material and the spiritual? Don't we all crave the occasional influence of the supernatural miracle to jolt our humdrum routine?[1256] The concept of divine immanence and emanations being real will terrify the unbeliever. To the believer, however, they interject a rapturous joy of ecstatic bliss. Recognizing encounters with miracles would comfort us by indicating something greater to our individual existence and the fact the God cares enough to enter into our lives.[1257]

If there be any sorcery, spells or incantations in this book, then let it be an enchantment of expanding love and divine wisdom. If I have been discovered subliminally leading your thoughts to draw certain desired conclusions, then my influence has been exposed. If the image of an Asterox as shown on the front cover is an artifice, then let it be duping you into love of God and of Self as it becomes a symbol of the future manifesting in the collective consciousness. If there be any suspect of legerdemain, then follow and research the endnote references and bibliography to remove any skepticism. If I appear to be a conjurer, then let my intentions remain noble. If I am a trickster, then let the benevolent agenda of my antics and games improve humanity. Remember always, that which is spiritual, cannot be controlled by physical laws.[1258] As you define and color the contours of your reality, it is up to you to decide if the thoughts and concepts you read and encountered within these chapters were fact or opinion, foresight or fantasy, madness or understanding, coincidence or synchronization, apophenia or randomania, a prophetic view of a vi-able future or idealistic wishful perceptions of grandeur from an overactive imagination.[1259]

—Δ*—

"The soul should always stand ajar, ready to welcome the ecstatic experience." – Emily Dickinson

—*O—

Did you succumb to the brush strokes of a painted false reality or was it the authentic unveiling and genuine revealing of a greater one, a landscape of philosophic and religious truth? What would Carl Jung, Joseph Campbell, Arthur Guirdham, Eckhart Tolle, Samael Aun Weor and Stephan Hoeller have to say about the ideas and mysteries revealed in these pages? What would Elaine Pagels, Birger Pearson, Karen King, Timothy Freke, Peter Gandy, Sean Martin, Gary Lachman, Bart Ehrman, Ismo Dunderberg, April DeConick, Miguel Conner, Paul Wallis and their contemporary colleagues have to say about an engineer whose world works on reason, yet was able to put forth much of this book based on something beyond logic and before even knowing of their names? Was it schizophrenic ramblings and nonsense or was it relevant exposure to a greater existence? Was it merely the desired delusions of an insane mind or a wealth of meaning from the influence of inspired genius? Were you led by the power of suggestion, agreement from your own conclusions, or by faith? Are you becoming brainwashed into loving thy neighbor as thyself, within reason? Were you guided into believing by subliminal hypnosis from the non-vocal internal voice in your head or is a real awakening being triggered within you? Is this all fiction of my own making or a truth beyond all others? Will you be choosing the "blue pill", the "red pill" or opt for the "gold pill?" Can you correctly decipher which sentences in this composition were figurative expressions and which were literal facts? Like the Cathars' vision as described by Margaret Long, did I expose you to insights more intense, more real, more piercing and more utterly truthful than any intuition?[1260] Were these words inspired from the likes of Seshat, Isis, Athena, Orunmila, Saraswati, Anahita, Saint Sophia, Asherah, Saint Francis de Sales, Saint Paul and a combination of all the other divine influencers of wisdom and writing? Will you be able to encapsulate the contradictions and find the correct fulcrum location between perception and paranoia? Perhaps all speculative possibilities are valid to some degree. You must decide for yourself where in the duality they lay between reality and imagination and where in the duality you will choose to dwell. You may choose that these writings were either an illusion or a truth. In choosing, you will see what you want to see, and based on your decision, will need to let go of the other choice. Whatever you accept as being real, will become your reality. We see intelligence when we want to and beauty where we want to. Succumbing to the influences of our internal archons, it is human nature to judge based on desire and to fear what is not understood. The unity of all true spiritual insight, however, rises above duality in the form of sound reason and the application of proper sapience. No matter where in the duality that you choose to dwell, always remember to <u>default to a steady state of love, gratitude and forgiveness</u>, even when feeling the pressures, fears, anxieties and demands of being human. As spiritual beings living out a human experience, the objective is to minimize these negative influences by focusing on defaulting to a steady state of love. By doing so, our thoughts become redirected in a constructive manner towards positive courses of actions and words for improving the outcome. It allows for solutions and options to surface. Most situations are best dealt with when in a state of peaceful serenity. For this is when we think in the correct direction, rather than emotionally "hot" react in the wrong direction. The Supreme Consciousness knows how tough it sometimes is to be human.

Love is risk, but hatred is riskier. Love is vulnerability, but hatred is vile. Love is logical, hatred is illogical. Love is courageous, hatred is cowardice. Make love your constant even when under duress, for with love you will see much more into reality than with hatred. In doing so, you will be more astute, perceptive, insightful, confident and intelligent when dealing with the situations that life throws at us. Love is the most efficient and most powerful binding energy of consciousness in the universe and with it comes increased acuity. <u>Maintaining an internal state of love, gratitude, and forgiveness is the best way to deal with external affairs, stop madness and to stay focused on what really matters.</u> Learning to avoid sinful overreactions to insignificant affronts upon our ego and conditioning our minds to default to a steady state of love rather than retaliation in response to provocations, kindles the proper amount of healthy patience and mitigates the demons within.[1261] It is love that disarms demons, keeps them at bay and even turns them into angels. By defaulting to love, you will radiate love and rise above the negative influences and testing temptations put forth by archons, passing their trials and examinations and graduating into the positive influential spheres of the aeons. For the archons operate within the realm of time, matter and ego, while the aeons operate beyond the realm of time, matter and ego. Life should be viewed as a gift, and with that gift our ultimate pursuit should be increasing our degree and contribution of happiness and joy. Focus on peace, harmony, good health, and contentment as the driving force behind your intentions and actions to prevent hatred, anger, hostility and ill-will from robbing you of your vitality.[1262]

—Λ*—

"Relinquish anger, then forgive, then trust in God." – AO

—*Ω—

Interlacing the power of our little minds with the Universal Consciousness and the big mind of God, is the spiritual goal of all of us as we ascend into the outer influential fields of the Supreme Consciousness. When we think with and open ourselves up to the mind of the All Mighty Being in its many forms, we are closer to vibrating as pure thought and perceptive energy, the destination of illumination and enlightenment. May these words provide the exogenous trigger to excel humanity and other advanced intelligent sentient beings into the next phases of existence. Even with all his/her might, unlimited power and glory, there are a few things that the Lord is "incapable" of: they are hatred, healing those who do not want to be healed, rescuing those who do not want to be rescued, helping those who do not want to be helped, saving those who do not want to be saved, curing the apathetic and teaching those who do not want to listen.

The universe is eternal but it is always changing. So is God. As one of the Lord's unique creations we must decide whether we are also going to grow in the wake of her divine expansion. The building of a New Jerusalem and the establishment of Zion is the renovation and repair of the Gaia-Sophia principle, the healing of Mother Earth. This planet is our species' inheritance; it is to be invested and cared for, not squandered and pillaged. The Resurrection will not be the physical reviving of flesh and bone from the grave, but rather, it is the raising from the death of ordinary consciousness into a higher state – into a life of gnosis.[1263] It will be a global anastasis, the awakening of the Logos within by following the valid tenets of one's chosen true religious path. The Rapture is not about being physically left behind, it is about spiritually being left behind due to one's own choosing.[1264] Succumbing to emotional cowardness and being too afraid to make that journey of looking into the infinite interior of their own cores to access God, some will remain behind spiritually because they are not willing to comprehend adjusting their ego to advance the Self. Constricted by the dominance of their ego-self, they will not awaken their Atmon, the universal Self, and will continue to interact with the world in a dysfunctional manner and be ruled by and stuck in their lower self. One finds their Ego, their true Self, by lowering their ego. Some will choose to maintain their narrow world perspective, a lower state of consciousness by becoming estranged to both their past and future. Our human perspective is often restricted in time, molded by regrets of prior events and the desires for improved future ones. Our core, our soul, however, is emancipated from the concept of the clock's movements – it has no restriction of chronology. In choosing not to embrace the divine presence, the mana of love, some will become their own judges and executioners by living in contradiction to their Atmon, their essential, eternal Self.[1265] Comprehension of Allah's grace and the lucidity of the message is up to the receiver – the student of Yahweh does not always understand the lesson. Peace be with you and may you live long and prosper as we manifest a greater destiny while entering the next aeon.[1266]

Were the pages of this book inspired and influenced by a holy heavenly authority and the Atmon within? I leave that up to you to conclude.

If so, then it is time for all of us to become God Seekers in our own unique way, to form our own individual Logos as we investigate our place in the ultimate mystery and formulate our own spiritual elixir and roadway for mingling with the divine. Following and taking a Gnostic or Orthodox approach to pull order from the chaos and to encounter gnosis, there is no one set of beliefs or practices that are suitable for everyone. If we do not create our own personal religious synthesis, our own mythopoeia, then we are left to partially or solely rely upon the previous systems of others – faith is our resort when we do not yet fully understand the nature of our destiny. Our mission is to rescue and free Sophia's wisdom and compassion from her material constraints, falling in love with her again as we release her back into the common spirit of the human psyche. After all, the etymology of the English word "philosophy" is from the Greek *philosophia* and the French *philosophie* – the loving of Sophia. Every philosopher is a lover of wisdom and knowledge.

One's individual conditioning and belief structure is unique, but with overlapping commonality of experiences, depending on the merger level of Self with the divine. Communing with God is a personal journey of our divine spark that varies from person to person or group to group among the many strands of theological diversity.[1267] The particular route traveled, our personal idea of what constitutes Allah and the details of how we get there are unique to each of us, our local collective identities, our communities and our cultures. However, the destination of our journey is all the same and all true paths eventually converge. Believing in the immortality of the soul is not enough; through solidarity of purpose, we must also work on its development and investment by projecting and releasing the individual consciousness of love into the global consciousness of a rational world order – for it is love which destroys sin and induces forth miracles.

—A*—

"One who knows God, becomes God." – *Mundaka Upanishad*[1268]

—*O—

The weaving of love and truth into our global cultural matrix is what will define this and future eras, for it is time for the great spirit of divinity and healing to come upon humanity – upon every man, woman, girl, boy, adult and child. The Cosmic plan is unfolding as it needs to through Sophia's desire for humanity and it is time for us to join in the nexus of its direction. It is time for those who are willing to listen to develop their own illimitable connection with the godhead.[1269] "Now is the time of revelation of John's message, the time of the return of the Troubadours, the return of the path of the heart and the wisdom that liberates."[1270] It is time to allow for and put in place a Gnostic praxis of skill and implementation of the mystical and spiritual arts from all the true religious tenets. It is time to remember our original intention, sifting through our anamnesis and for the re-enchantment and *tikkun* of our world. It is time to move beyond the panic of hoarding and hatred and into the passion of sharing and love. It is time for our disturbed world to make sense again as we wean ourselves away from the addictions of materialism and back to the balance provided by the fulfillment of spirituality. It is time to regain our natural dopamine high from the reading of good books, the achieving of genuine accomplishments, the stimulating of our mind and the participation in religious and spiritual exercises. It is time to rebuild the human psyche back to its spiritual Father and Mother, our Heavenly parents, bringing them above the horizon of consciousness and to make amends with the natural globe that we are destroying. It is time to merge The Gospel of Wealth with The Gospel of Love, to create a Gospel of The World to Come. It is time to embrace an epoch of theology and to end the quibbles of speculation over minutiae while transcending above the semantical specifics, unclear metaphors, religious conspiracy theories, polemics and redundancies of doctrinal points as we rediscover the awe of the Almighty's presence within our lives. It is time to align with a modern perception of what religion is supposed to be about, that is, communing with the Creator by walking a path of love, gratitude and forgiveness. It is time to dampen the swings of the Hermetic pendulum between misogyny and misandry and reach the understanding that we are all just people trying to make the best of the dualities between the sexes. It is time for our pilgrimage forward into a peaceful and prosperous future to be much different than the cyclical brutish wars of past that we leave behind. It is time to draw from the better aspects of a Hyperian culture by merging the best of both opposites into a higher unity of existence. It is time to renew the living spirit and embrace its many manifestations. It is time for us to move closer to those sublime and ineffable experiences in restoring our relationship with Allah and rectifying the sanity within our species.[1271] It is time to give back to nature what nature has given to us – sustenance for existence. It is time for the next root race to evolve in a season of the New Spring.[1272] It is time to come to terms with our location between the duality of forgiveness for Satan and love for God, positioning ourselves at the optimum juncture between atheism and godism.

The start of this third millennium and beginning of the 21st century can finally be the course correction needed to bring genuine religion to a perpetual zenith, a never-fading crescendo and diapason, an everlasting springtime of faith and hope, returning it back to a foundation of comfort, the search for truth, civility to others, decency in politics, integrity of character and the illumination of the Self. It is time for the grace of the Lord, without intimidation or fear, to suddenly and powerfully re-enter the lives of us ordinary people. It is time to wake up the Buddha within and arise to a better universe than the one we fell asleep to. It is time to switch on those vast portions that we have neglected to use of our inhibited brain by changing our behavior to a programming of respect for both those stronger and weaker than ourselves. It is time to increase the degree of Christ living within us as we increase how much we live in him. It is time to fix the broken rhythm of the human family, both the individual and the collective.[1273] It is time to understand that Abraxas is not tormenting and torturing us, he is teaching, training and then testing us – to purify us to a level worthy of uniting with and marrying one of his divine daughters (aka a Sophia) or a divine son. It is time to find the proper balance between the masculine and the feminine, working steadily towards this goal of life by practices of ethics and spirituality as described in the *Zohar*.[1274] It is time to bring ourselves into alignment with the connections between our past, present and future and to strive for a unitive integration between the subconscious and the conscious. It is time to veer the egregore of our Global Consciousness far from the pole of hate and towards the pole of love. It is time to change the average person's life from bitter and hardness into joy and empowerment. It is time to shift xenophobic currents into a multicultural, multi-faith and multi-compassionate global Alexandria. It is time to forgive the Demiurge, that being of the *Old Testament* who was either immature and tormenting or just limited intellectually and morally, for creating a not so perfect material world and assist in making amends for his errors introduced into this physical realm. It is time to bring our mindset beyond its current bounds of ego and into actions of love while aiding Sophia in repairing our fractured species and mending our home planet. It is time for a call of hope and guidance for the human race as we evolve beyond Plato's cave. It is time to tap into the *spiritus mundi* and lift ourselves beyond the limits of myopic perceptions. It is time to rouse the ardor of true religion as we implement activism of compassion to rescue each other from damnation. It is time to resurface the Hermetic idea that we are greater than the sum of our thoughts, yet keep our egos lowered and calmly excited. It is time to follow our intuition in fulfilling Jehovah's design for each of our lives and determine what incarnate piece we are in the grand puzzle's scheme. It is time to embrace the re-embodiment of ancient wisdoms and apply them to modern science and psychoanalysis.[1275] It is time to realize that the Lord and the Lady, although not always perfect, are now received as a god and goddess of love. It is time to recognize and acknowledge our ecological footprint while doing everything feasibly possible to minimize its destructiveness and make it a blended part of the environment, not in spite of it. It is time to forge ahead with an amalgam of mysticism and common sense.[1276] It is time to reawaken both the morals and morale of our human psyche as we venture forth among the stars. It is time to merge the best of our humanity with the best of our divinity to achieve profound accomplishments. That which must be done, let it be done quickly and within the twinkling of an eye![1277] All the scriptural trumpets are sounding, telling us the moment has arrived for us to rise to the next level of awareness in expanding our beings and ascending our consciousness to a higher state. Wake up – it is time! It is time.

• • • •

<u>NOTE OMEGA/CIRCLE</u>: Have you solved the arcana presented in the note at the end of Chapter 1, *Alpha – In The Beginning And The Growth Of God*? If not, then read this book one more time from start to finish and see beyond the Duality of dualities. *ΕΠΙΣΤΡΟΦΗ ΣΤΟ ΑΛΦΑ*

Epilogue

HAVING REACHED THIS part of the book, by now you should have an understanding that God and Love are synonymous, but not always perfect. Enlightenment is about love, always was about love and always will be about love. The words "we must" appear on at least 90 occasions in this book, the word "love" appears more than 600 times and the word "God" appears greater than 1300 times. Combining them forms the sentence "We must love God." Putting them into action can be done through acts of healthy compassion. Charity is a manifestation of compassion, for it is love which washes away sin. The armies of the Lord mentioned in *Revelation* (*Ἀποκάλυψις*) are the legitimate charities across the world continuing to do good works. In the spirit and purity of which this book was written, the author/scriber is donating a portion of financial profits obtained from the original purchase of this book (in both print and electronic format) to charitable organizations and causes.

• • • •

FULL DISCLOSURE: ALTHOUGH not the intention of this publication, the author may directly and indirectly financially profit from activities associated with its release. Being a productive member of society requires that we earn, when medically possible, an honest living to sustain our physical existence. Likewise, the author of this book needs to purchase food, pay bills and fund expenses just like every other responsible wage earning being.

— Anon Omous (AO) —

• • • •

AsteroxRising.com

Appendix 1 – Words Of Duality

THE CATEGORY OF A PARTICULAR word in the following lists (or any word for that matter) as being triangular or circular is subjective to the perspective of the one doing the categorizing. A word can even appear in both categories, depending on the approach and perspective of which it is being classified. There is nothing precluding from switching the categorical location of a particular pair of poles, since the datum is arbitrary and based on subjective reference. Being open to different reasoning and points of view, others may prefer or choose to switch the classification of a particular opposite pairing. In categorizing a word, the rationale behind a given selection may vary depending on the definitional circumstance or instance. Although the author has provided some guidance in Chapter 24 for typical categorizing methods, variations exceptions and alternates are acceptable. The mind of God, the universe, operates by locating or cycling at various degrees between the poles, the opposites, and sometimes by merging the duality into unity. The following are classification examples of some relational dichotomies and their trends, but it is not a perfect or absolute model.

Triangular	Circular	Notes
abnormal	normal	
abrupt	gradual	
absolute	relative	
absolution	confession	
abundance	poverty	
Abzu	Tiamat	Sumerian
acceptance	rejection	
active	contemplative	
actuality	fiction	
actuality	possibility	
Adam	Eve	
adjust	monitor	
Adlerian	Freudian	
adult	child	
Advaita	Dvaita	
after	before	
aggression	ambition	
aggression	cooperation	
aging	youthful	
Ahriman	Ormuzd	
Ahriman	Ohrmazd	
ajiva	jiva	
Aletheia	Nous	Valentinus' Gnostic
alike	opposite	
all	one	

Triangular	**Circular**	**Notes**
all	nothing	
alliance	betrayal	
alliance	competition	
ally	foe	
amen	omen	
America	Europe	
Amor	Roma	
ancient	modern	
and	or	
and	both	
angels	demons	and vice-versa
animus	anima	
answer	question	
ant	grasshopper	
antipathy	sympathy	
anxiety	anticipation	
anxious	bored	
any	none	
appearance	disappearance	
apple	orange	
Apollonian	Dionysian	
Aristotelian	Platonic	
Aristotle	Plato	
arrogance	humility	
As Above	So Below	Hermeticism
asceticism	hedonism	
asleep	awake	

<u>Triangular</u>	<u>Circular</u>	<u>Notes</u>
assertive	passive	
atheism	godism	
atma	paramatma	
Atman	Eidolon	
attachment	detachment	
authority	subversion	
back	front	
back	forth	
bad	good	
bat	owl	
bātin	zāhir	Batiniyya
BCE	CE	
bear	cow	*Isaiah* 11:6-9
beauty	ugliness	
beginning	end	
belief	skepticism	
below	above	
beneficial	destructive	
benefit	cost	
bhukta	bhokta	
birth	death	and vice-versa
black	white	
bleach	ammonia	
blessings	woes	
bondage	liberation	
brake	accelerator	

Triangular	**Circular**	**Notes**
bravado	confidence	
buy	sell	
buyer	seller	
calf	lion	*Isaiah* 11:6-9
calm	stormy	
calmness	enthusiasm	
Cassandra	Pollyanna	
cat	dog	
catch	throw	
cathode	anode	
Catholic	Orthodox	
cattle	horses	
cause	effect	
cause	outcome	
chaos	order	
cheating	fairness	
Christ	Sophia	
citizen	civilization	
clarity	confusion	
clean	dirty	
clergyman	psychotherapist	
coalesce	dissipate	
cognition	emotion	
cold	hot	
consequentialist	deontologist	

Triangular	Circular	Notes
conservative	liberal	
conserving	consuming	
contraction	expansion	
contractive	expansive	
converge	diverge	
convergent	divergent	
cooperation	defection	
cost	benefit	
creation	destruction	
creation	dissolution	
credit	debit	
culture	religion	
curse	blessing	
customer	vendor	
daemon	eidolon	
dark	light	
data	intuition	
dawn	dusk	
death	birth	and vice-versa
decay	growth	
defeat	triumph	
defense	offense	
dammed	blessed	
demons	angels	and vice-versa
depression	euphoria	
depression	enthusiasm	

Triangular	Circular	Notes
descent	ascent	
destruction	re-construction	
differentiation	connection	
digital	analog	
dim	amplify	
discourage	encourage	
doubt	faith	
dread	pleasure	
Earth	Cosmos	
earth	heaven	
ecstasy	agony	
ego	sacred-self	
Ekklesia	Anthropos	Valentinus' Gnostic
electron	photon	
elephant	donkey	
endarkenment	enlightenment	
Ennoia	Bythos	Valentinus' Gnostic
entrance	exit	
equal	opposite	
esoteric	exoteric	
eternal	transient	
Evangelicals	Mormons	
evil	good	
existence	non-existence	
fact	opinion	
failure	success	

Triangular	Circular	Notes
faith	doubt	
faith	gnosis	
faith	hope	
faith-Pistis	wisdom-Sophia	
far	close	
fate	free-will	
fate	freedom	
father	mother	
fear	courage	
fear	love	
finite	infinite	
first	last	
flesh	spirit	
Flintstones	Jetsons	
fractional	whole	
Frater Mysterium	Soror Mystica	
full	empty	
gain	loss	
Giddianhi	Gidgiddoni	*3 Nephi, Book Of Mormon*
giving	receiving	
goat	leopard	*Isaiah* 11:6-9
Graeco	Roman	
hand	foot	
hard	soft	
hard cover	soft cover	
harm	care	

Triangular	Circular	Notes
harmony	discord	
hate	love	
haves	have nots	
hawk	dove	
heat	cool	
Hebdomad	Ogdoad	Valentinus' Gnostic
helping	hurting	
heredity	environment	
Human	God	Nestorianistic perspective; dyophysitism
humility	hubris	
ignorance	wisdom	
ignorance	knowledge	*The Thunder: Perfect Mind*
immanent	transcendent	
impious	pious	
implementation	imagination	
independence	dependence	
individual	tribe	
individual	collective	
in-drawing	outpouring	
infallible	fallible	
inhale	exhale	
inhibit	foster	
initiate	hierophant	
inner	outer	
inside	outside	
insular	cosmopolitan	

Triangular	Circular	Notes
intake	exhaust	
intellectual	emotional	
internal	external	
intimate	impersonal	
introversion	extraversion	
introvert	extravert	
introverted	extraverted	
isolated	connected	
isvara	jivas	
Jachin	Boaz	
Jehoshaphat	Jehoram	biblical monarchs
Judah	Israel	division of nations
Kenoma	Pleroma	
Khadr	Moses	
king	queen	
lamb	lion	
lamb	wolf	*Isaiah* 11:6-9
laughing	crying	
law	order	
left	right	
life	death	
literalism	gnosticism	
Literalists	Gnostics	
logic	emotion	
Logos	Zoe	Valentinus' Gnostic
Logos	Sophia	

<u>Triangular</u>	<u>Circular</u>	<u>Notes</u>
low	high	
lower	higher	
Luna	Sol	
male	female	
malice	negligence	
Man	God	
man	woman	
many	one	
masculine	feminine	
material	spiritual	
matter	soul	
me	you	
medieval	modern	
meditation	contemplation	
microcosm	macrocosm	
misery	bliss	
misery	happiness	
Moab	Edom	biblical kingdoms
monarchy	democracy	
mundane	sacred	
naked	clothed	
Narcissist	Empathic	
nature	nurture	
nearness	remoteness	
negative	positive	
Nei Tan	Wei Tan	

Triangular	Circular	Notes
nutrients	poison	
objective	subjective	
observer	object	
odd	even	
off	on	
oneness	crowd	
oppression	liberty	
ordinary	transcendent	
Orthodox	Gnosticism	
Osiris	Isis	
ousia	hypostatis	religion and philosophy
pain	pleasure	
pain	joy	
paranoia	perception	
participant	observer	
particle	wave	
passive	active	
peasant	nobility	
perfect	flawed	
perishable	eternal	
permanence	impermanence	
permanent	fleeting	
personal	impersonal	
pessimism	optimism	
play	record	

Triangular	**Circular**	**Notes**
play	work	
position	speed	
prayer	work	
precise	approximate	
presence	absence	
present	absent	
preservation	annihilation	
proletarian	plutocrat	
psyche	consciousness	
purchase order	invoice	
pure	filthy	
pure	impure	
purity	impurity	
Quantum Mechanics	General Relativity	
qurb	bu'd	
reaction	action	
realism	abstract	
reality	ideology	
reason	passion	
reason	faith	
red	green	
regulated	unrestricted	
Rehoboam	Jeroboam	biblical monarchs
rejection	acceptance	

Triangular	Circular	Notes
religion	spirituality	
Republican	Democrat	
required	optional	
resistance	flow	electrical current and fluids
rest	motion	
restraint	indulgence	
retreat	advance	
retrieve	store	
reverse	forward	
rigid	flexible	
rose	lotus	
rumination	meditation	
sacred	profane	
same	different	
Samsara	Nirvana	
sanctity	degradation	
Satan	God	
science	religion	
secular	divine	
security	risk	
self	community	
self-control	impulsive	
self-definition	attachment	
self-preservation	self-annihilation	

Triangular	Circular	Notes
separate	joined	
Seth	Horus	Egyptian pantheon
shame	boldness	*The Thunder: Perfect Mind*
Shias	Sunnis	
Shiva	Shakti	
short term	long term	
silence	sound	
sink	rise	
sinking	rising	
soul	super-soul	
south	north	
spiritual	temporal	
start	finish	
starvation	gluttony	
static	dynamic	
static	moving	
stay	go (flee)	
stop	start	
sturdy	fragile	
subconscious	conscious	
subject	object	
subjective	objective	
success	failure	
suffer	enjoy	

Triangular	**Circular**	**Notes**
Sunni	Shiite	
sunrise	sunset	
supply	demand	
tangible	nontangible	
tea	coffee	
teacher	student	
teacher	disciple	
temporal	spiritual	
terrestrial	celestial	
The Beatles	The Rolling Stones	
today	tomorrow	
traditional	modern	
tragic	comic	
tranquility	commotion	
truth	lie	
truth	dishonesty	
union	dissolution	*The Thunder: Perfect Mind*
unique	common	
uniqueness	conformity	
unite	divide	
unity	diversity	
unity	discourse	
upload	download	
us	them	

Triangular	**Circular**	**Notes**
valued	worthless	
vice	virtue	
victim	perpetrator	
villain	hero	
visible	unseen	
voluntary	involuntary	
war	peace	*The Thunder: Perfect Mind*
warm	cool	
wealth	poverty	
wealthy	poor	
west	east	
winning	losing	
within	without	
Woman	**Go**ddess	
Yin	Yang	

Appendix 2 – Additional Prayers And Poems

PSALM 19:1-14 (KJV)

The heavens declare the glory of God; and the firmament sheweth his handywork.

Day unto day uttereth speech, and night unto night sheweth knowledge.

There is no speech nor language, where their voice is not heard.

Their line is gone out through all the earth, and their words to the end of the world. In them hath he set a tabernacle for the sun,

Which is as a bridegroom coming out of his chamber, and rejoiceth as a strong man to run a race.

His going forth is from the end of the heaven, and his circuit unto the ends of it: and there is nothing hid from the heat thereof.

The law of the LORD is perfect, converting the soul: the testimony of the LORD is sure, making wise the simple.

The statutes of the LORD are right, rejoicing the heart: the commandment of the LORD is pure, enlightening the eyes.

The fear of the LORD is clean, enduring for ever:

the judgments of the LORD are true and righteous altogether.

More to be desired are they than gold, yea, than much fine gold: sweeter also than honey and the honeycomb.

Moreover by them is thy servant warned: and in keeping of them there is great reward.

Who can understand his errors? cleanse thou me from secret faults.

Keep back thy servant also from presumptuous sins; let them not have dominion over me: then shall I be upright, and I shall be innocent from the great transgression.

Let the words of my mouth, and the meditation of my heart, be acceptable in thy sight, O LORD, my strength, and my redeemer.

• • • •

THE SPACIOUS FIRMAMENT On High

Recompilation and paraphrase of the 19th Psalm
Written by Joseph Addison,
The Spectator Magazine 1712

The spacious firmament on high,
With all the blue ethereal sky,
And spangled heavens, a shining frame,
Their great Original proclaim.
The unwearied sun, from day to day,
Does his Creator's power display;
And publishes to every land
The work of an Almighty hand.
Soon as the evening shades prevail,
The moon takes up the wondrous tale,
And nightly to the listening earth
Repeats the story of her birth:
Whilst all the stars that round her burn,
And all the planets in their turn,
Confirm the tidings as they roll,
And spread the truth from pole to pole.
What though in solemn silence all
Move round this dark terrestrial ball;
What though no real voice or sound
Amidst their radiant orbs be found;
In reason's ear they all rejoice,
And utter forth a glorious voice,
Forever singing as they shine,
"The hand that made us is divine."

Lord's Prayer

(Older modified version as kept within the Franciscan Order)[a]
All-Father-Mother
All-Father-Mother, All One
Of the All, in the All
Holy and secret are Your names
You live in activity and Light
Let Your desire be with mine
Here now and in the All
Touch me, feed me with your astonishment
To fulfil Your desire
My surrender to You, the other and the All.
Accept me, that I am not yet whole,
Not yet connected to You
Forgive my hesitant effort
To connect myself with You
As I accept my fellow-man
His being un-whole,
His being un-healed.
Lead me away from show and ignorance
And free me of what keeps me from the Light
Because in You and from You
Is the Light, the Power and the Life
Here, now and for ever
Always

a) Patrick, Dave-editor; *The Cathar View*; as cited by Jeanne D'Août pg. 169

• • • •

PATER NASTOR

(Modern modified version)
Our Father and Mother, who art in Heaven,
hallowed be Thy names.
Thy kingdom come. Thy will be done,

on earth as it is in Heaven.
Give us this day our daily bread
and forgive us our trespasses,
as we forgive those who trespass against us.
Lead us not into temptation,
but deliver us from evil.
For thine is the kingdom,
the power and the glory,
for ever and ever.

• • • •

VENI CREATOR SPIRITUS[b]

Come, Creator, Spirit, come
from your bright heavenly throne,
come take possession of our souls,
and make them all your own.

You who are called the Paraclete,
best gift of God above,
the living spring, the viral fire,
sweet christ'ning and true love.

You who are sev'nfold in your grace,
finger of God's right hand;
his promise, teaching little ones
to speak and understand.
O guide our minds with your blest light,
with love our hearts inflame;
and with your strength, which ne'er decays,
confirm our mortal frame.

Far from us drive our deadly foe;
true peace unto us bring;
and through all perils lead us safe
beneath your sacred wing.

Through you may we Father and Mother know,
through you th' eternal Son and Daughter,
and you the Spirit of them all,
thrice-blessed Three in One.

All glory to the Father and Mother be,
with their co-equal children;
the same to you, great Paraclete,
while endless ages run.

b) Modified to include the feminine; Hymn attributed to Rabanus Maurus, a 9th century archbishop living in Germany; Ghezzi, Bert; *Mystics & Miracles*; Afterword pgs. 175-177

• • • •

POSTCARD FROM POMPEII – The Integrated Self[c]

Frozen in place by fire of longing
Bright shadow blaming
All other wronging
We must deposit something
So sandy a stand
For we and thing is doubly grand
Each soul a lens of collective most flowing
Light upon light
God's knowing, growing
You are dreamed and dreamer
Cease pictures and posing
Me in the instant, not judging and closing
Thinking like nature, Jung says we'll feel better
Losing our lonely, personal fetter
Intuition is key, so here's my hunch
If the small gods eat ego, why feed them free lunch?

c) Author unknown, presented by a member of the audience during a 2005 seminar by James Hillman on Carl Jung

• • • •

TO THE MUSES IN OUR Midst^d

Deep within us lies a flame,
slumbering on another plane,
the relic of a genius lost,
a house so cold its blood is frost.
Dormant it lies, but not yet dead,
it catcalls demons, in your head,
Caught in traps of your own making,
it's not just you whom she is faking.
Empty and shallow, no fuel for the fire,
you know not what the heart truly desires.

In the doldrums of the day,
no wind to sail, the soul decays.
Lost all hope a Self unknown.
He needs a push to guide him home.
In the frigid winter air,
he can move without a care.
From outside he looks mellow,
though deep within he is yellow.
Blooming in a cold abyss
the Metamorphosis of Narcissus.

Far below he hears a sound.
but questions what his eyes have found.
Staring in eternity,
a reflection looks back fervently.
On the edge he stands beside,
a choice to be made, he cannot hide.
To his left a Book of Red,
sign your name your Soul is dead.
To his right a pool so blue,
seize your shot, a dream come true.

In good faith the Fool leaps forward,
without a plan to move toward.
Sinking fast he starts to see,
just how deep this hole will be.
Now below what was above,
he's found a world there is no love.

In the Darkest of the Nights,
He looks back up for the Light,
So far gone it is not there,
just abyss and more despair.
No one left who will listen,
he prays for her and has a vision.
Letting go and giving in,
he takes on all that's meant for him.

What's worth having won't come easy,
Wisdom is true but not for the queasy,
Mother of whores she's costly to see,
won't hold your hand till you've paid her fee.
Stand beside her just for a minute,
a light so bright, you cannot win it.

Blink for a second the passion is gone.
Back in the Tower no longer a fawn.
At one with the light not in division,
come back to earth with a new mission.
A phoenix he rises and quickly begins
to work his magick and pull from within.

Sent down beside him to guide his foresight
a muse is delivered in the midst of the night.
She'll twist and turn, push, pull, tease and twirl,
in the end she'll give him a whirl,
she will do what she can

to chisel the man.

Fortune has it it's just the beginning,
the end of an aeon return of divinity.
The planets aligned a new star was born,
choose from which world you will be torn
In the end in jest is best
after all this was just a test.

Lesson learned he'll keep silent,
abide his time and wear the violet,
make his mark and pave the way,
plant his seed and fade away,
One more sign it's just a ruse,
truth be told he's the muse.

d) By Anthony Kemarowz; 2021, published with permission

Appendix 3 – Recommended Media List

ALTHOUGH THE AUTHOR has presented the list below for recommended reading or viewing, it does not mean that he/she agrees 100% with all their content. Read them while applying your own insightful distinctions between what seems sound, reasonable and valid and what does not. Apply epiphanic common sense and spiritual logic to determine what should be allowed into your core. Some sentences and sections may be outdated or obsolete. This does not, however, negate the importance or relevance provided in the rest of the book. The date in the curly brackets { } is the approximate year the media was first read or read again by the author.

Everyone should read the *Bible*, *The Koran* and their own selection of Hindu, Taoist and Buddhist texts at least once in their live(s). The reading of them should be a prerequisite for understanding humanity.

• • • •

RECOMMENDED BOOKS

The Practical Cogitator {started 1999, finished 2010}
The Better Angels of Our Nature {2018}
Eternal Quest {1994, 2019}
The Bible – both the old and new testament {1990}
The Koran {1998, 2019}
The Gita {1999, 2019}
Various Buddhist texts
The Upanishads, translation by Juan Mascaró {2002, 2018}
Tao Te Ching {2019}
Age of Reason by Thomas Paine {1994, 2020}
The Power Of Negative Thinking {2018}
The Power Of Positive Thinking {2019}
A Wrinkle In Time {1977, 2018}
Al-Muhaddithat: The Women Scholars in Islam by Mohammad Akram Nadwi
365 Days of Wonder {2020}

• • • •

FOR THE ADVANCED THEOLOGIAN, initiate and metaphysical traveler

> *The Kybalion* {2019}
> *Nine Faces of Christ* {2019}
> *The Hermetica, The Lost Wisdom of the Pharaohs* {2019}
> *Sufism, The Transformation of the Heart* {2019}
> *The Modern Christian Mystic* {2019}
> *The Gnostics, The First Christian Heretics* {2020}
> *The Cathar View* {2020}
> *Accept This Gift* {2020}
> *The Return Of Arthur Conan Doyle* {2020}
> *Jesus And The Lost Goddess* {2020}
> *The Sophia Teachings* {2020}
> *Voices of Gnosticism* {2020}
> *Other Voices of Gnosticism* {2020}

• • • •

PERSONAL NOTABLE MOVIES

> *The Fiend Without A Face, Yellow Submarine, Heavy Metal, Stand By Me, Rain Man, The Shipping News, The Shawshank Redemption, The Music Never Stopped, Inside Out, Arrival*

• • • •

FAVORITE MEMORABLE Video Games

> *Slither-IO, Halo 2, Zaxxon, Asteroids, Space Invaders, Breakout, Atari-Combat*

RECOMMENDED WEBSITES

Most of these sites are recommended for further reading although some may have questionable ideologies and unsubstantiated conspiracies within the links on their pages. Use your God given critical thinking skills to sift through what makes sense to your soul as you proceed forward in your investigation and search.

••••

ABWOON NETWORK, THE https://abwoon.org/
    Aeon Byte Gnostic Radio https://thegodabovegod.com/
    Ananda https://www.ananda.org/
    Anthroposophical Psychology https://anthroposophicpsychology.org/
    Anthroposophical Society https://anthroposophy.org/
    Astrogeographia http://www.astrogeographia.org/index.html
    Awakening The Artist Of Your True Self http://www.rebellesociety.com/
    Awakening The World https://awakentheworld.com/
    BBC's website on religions http://www.bbc.co.uk/religion/religions/
    Beliefs https://www.beliefnet.com/
    C. G. Jung Society of the Triangle http://jungnc.org/
    Divine Spark https://www.divinespark.co/home
    Esoteric Traditions and the Occult https://thothermes.com/
    Gnostic Church http://gnosis.org/eghome.htm
    Gnostic Sanctuary https://www.gnosticsanctuary.org/index.html
    Gnostic Society, The http://www.gnosis.org/welcome.html
    Gnostic Teachings https://gnosticteachings.org/
    Golden Rosycross Community https://goldenrosycrosscommunity.org/
    Golden Sufi Center, The https://goldensufi.org/
    Hellenic Faith https://hellenicfaith.com/
    Joseph Campbell Foundation https://www.jcf.org/
    Jung Currents http://jungcurrents.com/

Learn Religions https://www.learnreligions.com/

Lonerwolf https://lonerwolf.com/

Monk Within, The https://themonkwithin.net/

Nour Foundation https://www.nourfoundation.com/

Pluralism Project, The http://pluralism.org or http://pluralism.org/religions/

Rosicrucian School https://www.lectoriumrosicrucianum.org/

Sophia Foundation https://sophiafoundation.org/

Sophia Lineage http://sophialineage.com/

Spiritual Awakening http://www.spiritualawakeningradio.com/

Tanenbaum https://tanenbaum.org/

Tasawwuf Teachings https://www.safinasociety.org/

Temple of Wisdom – Sophia https://www.ourspirit.com/

Theosophical Society, The https://www.theosophical.org/

Urantia Foundation https://www.urantia.org/

White Eagle Lodge https://www.whiteaglelodge.org/

On Transitioning from ego to Self

https://thoughtcatalog.com/ryan-holiday/2016/06/25-ways-to-kill-the-toxic-ego-that-will-ruin-your-life/

Appendix 4 – Locations Where Written

THE LAST TIME I ATTENDED any church or organized religion on a regular basis was over 35 years ago, so where did such thoughts and revelations come from? Portions of this book were drafted, developed and compiled at numerous geographical locations including but not limited to:

• • • •

REGIONS WITHIN THE United States

Atlanta, Georgia
Baltimore, Maryland
Bennington, Vermont
Chicago, Illinois
Cincinnati, Ohio
Clinton, New Jersey
Dallas, Texas
Danbury, Connecticut
Detroit, Michigan
Dover, Vermont
Durham, North Carolina
Flagstaff, Arizona
Greenwood, Maine
Hoboken, New Jersey
Houston, Texas
Iowa City, Iowa
Kanab, Utah
Las Vegas, Nevada
Los Angeles, California
Memphis, Tennessee
Miami, Florida
Minneapolis, Minnesota
Murfreesboro, Arkansas
Nashville, Tennessee

New Orleans, Louisiana
New York City, New York
Newark, New Jersey
Oklahoma City, Oklahoma
Old Lyme, Connecticut
Orlando, Florida
Philadelphia, Pennsylvania
Phoenix, Arizona
Portland, Oregon
Princeton, New Jersey
Rapid City, South Dakota
Red Lodge, Montana
Rochester, New York
Sacramento, California
San Diego, California
San Francisco, California
Sandy, Utah
Sedona, Arizona
Sioux Falls, South Dakota
St. Louis, Missouri
Trenton, New Jersey
Tulsa, Oklahoma
Washington, D.C.

• • • •

REGIONS OUTSIDE OF The United States

Aruba, Bahamas, Canada, France, Germany, Jamaica, Netherlands, Portugal, Mexico

Glossary

AS MENTIONED IN THE section titled Navigational Reading Instructions, words that typically have a straight or zig-zagged line underneath them (i.e., <u>example</u>) are listed in this glossary. The line will only appear under the first, second or third appearance of the word within this book.

Aeons – Beings or emanations from higher realms considered benevolent towards humankind. They are mentioned in Hermeticism, the Gnostics scriptures found at Nag Hammadi and elsewhere; an eon or large segment of time.

Agape – The love of God for humanity and of humanity for God; the love originating from God or Christ for humankind.

Ahimsa – Sanskrit term for minimizing or causing no harm, nor injury to others; nonviolence.

Ananda – Sanskrit term for achieving moments of joy or eternal bliss which allows one to work through crises with the least amount of emotional damage.

Apeirokalia – Greek word meaning lack of experience in things beautiful or unable to experience or perceive beauty.

Aphar – From Hebrew meaning dust, ashes or debris.

Archons – From Gnosticism, forces or entities that strive to keep humans ignorant of their divine nature and beginnings beyond the material cosmos. Perhaps they are just misunderstood rather than a threat.

Atman (or **Atmon**) – The radiant part of our self that does what is correct and hears the true wisdom of that ancient being often referred to as God. The term is mentioned in *The Upanishads* and other spiritual texts.

Bhakti – Sanskrit term for surrendering to the Lord with love, devotion, piety, belonging and engagement.

Bodhisattva – From Mahayana Buddhism, a person who is able to reach nirvana but delays doing so out of compassion in order to save others.

Bu'd – From Sufism, meaning feeling distant from God; feeling like our mind, ego and heart is still connected to Allah, but at a distance since the bar for the next epiphany has been moved to a higher level in order to continue our spiritual training.

Chinvat – The bridge or border separating this realm from the next as mentioned in the religion of Zoroastrian; (aka As-Sirāt).

Deism – A philosophical view that rejects revelation as a source of religious knowledge and that observation and reason alone are enough to account for the presence of a divine consciousness or Supreme Being.

Demiurge – a being said to have bunglingly created the material realm in an incompetent manner and mistakenly started to think that he was the true God. He represents the dysfunctional version of Yahweh within much of the *Old Testament* and is considered an unwanted or neglected offspring of Sophia.

Diakrisis – Greek word meaning to make a distinction; to decide; to give judgment.

Egregore – Greek word meaning "wakeful" and it relates to an occult concept of an entity arising from a collective; a group mind forming a common purpose.

Empyrean – The highest of heavens; the dwelling place of God and his celestial beings.

Enantiodromia – Initially from Heraclitus and further coined by Carl Jung, it designates the play of opposites in the course of events causing everything that exists to turn into its opposite; the flipping of emotional poles.

Eschatonphobia – Fear of the end of the world.

Eudaimonia – Greek word meaning internal happiness; (asa eudaemonia).

Fana – From Sufism, the passing away or annihilation of self as "to die before one dies".

Fiqh – The human imperfect interpretation and changeable understanding of the divine Islamic law (Sharī'ah) as revealed in the *Koran* and the *Sunnah*.

Gnosis – Divine knowledge of an intuitive and intrinsic understanding of many of the universe's mysteries, provided by both deism and revelation.

Gnosticism – The acceptance that there are many true ways, paths and tools for connecting to divinity, which can be a combination of personal experiences and scriptural writings; any path not considered of the Orthodox as determined by the 4th century meeting of the Council of Nicaea.

Hagiographer – The writer, author or biographer of a saint, religious founder or an ecclesiastical leader.

Haram – Forbidden based on the interpretations of Islamic perspectives, though often subjective according to the intentions and illumination level of the interpreter.

Inculcate – Teaching by repetition of importance.

Jinas – From Jainism, perfected-beings who serve as role models and revered teachers to guide the faithful on the proper path to liberation from the endless cycles of rebirth.

Karsati – Sanskrit term meaning our individual struggles endured and actions taken to maintain our existence.

Kenoma – The abyss and voids that leave us uncertain and empty within the material realms; abode of the Archons.

Koinonia – Greek word for joint participation or fellowship.

Ksama – Sanskrit term meaning extreme patience and applying a practice and state of forgiveness.

Kubera – Sanskrit for a god of wealth, but also a term emanating within Judaic folklore.

Mahasattva – From Mahayana Buddhism, a person who is an advanced Bodhisattva and very high up on the path to enlightenment.

Mammon – From the Greek word *mamōnas* (see *Matthew* 6:24 and *Luke* 16:9–13) and from Aramaic *māmōn* "riches", it means wealth regarded as an evil influence or false object of worship and devotion.

Maranatha – An Aramaic or Koine Greek phrase (see *1 Corinthians* 16:22 and *Revelation* 22:12) which is broadly applied to mean the coming or return of the Lord or the return of an official representative of the Lord.

Moksha – A Sanskrit term for various forms of liberation and enlightenment. It can mean a release from ignorance, the attainment of self-actualization or the freedom from continuous cycles of birth and death.

Monopsychism – A belief that we share the same eternal consciousness or soul and that we are all somehow connected through a common mind.

Naf – An Arabic word meaning self and referring to an unrefined state(s) of ego considered the lowest dimension of a person's inward existence; it is the destructive animal and satanic nature dwelling within all of us.

Naga (or **Nagas**) – Sanskrit term for serpent like deities that are part human and part cobra which exhibit enlightened wisdom and are beneficial to good humans.

Nirvana – In a simplistic sense, it is a Sanskrit term for heaven, but it can have a variety of meanings and specific details beyond that. It can represent the final desired destination of all of our spiritual journeys, a state of peace, joy and bliss which arises in the absence of desires, seeking and striving or a balancing of our individualism as we ecstatically merge with the godhead.

Orrery – A display, diorama or model of our Solar System that illustrates or predicts the relative positions and motions of the planets and moons relative to each other and their rotation around the Sun.

Paramatma – Sanskrit term for the absolute Atman (ama Atmon), or supreme Self. It is the "Primordial Self" or the "Self Beyond" which meshes and blends in identical union with the Supreme Consciousness of the Universe. It identifies with the Brahman in which our individuality both exists and does not.

Parthenogenesis – The biologic reproduction from an ovum without fertilization; self-pregnancy induced without the need for a male member's sperm.

Path – The metaphorical, metaphysical and mystical journey that one takes to connect with divinity based on either religion, spirituality or both.

Pleroma – The fullness of certainty and divinity that guides us within the spiritual realms; abode of the Aeons.

Prakrti – Sanskrit term for the original form of primary substance and the cosmic elementary constituent that characterizes all natures.

Purusha – Sanskrit term for the mostly masculine essence of the cosmic being which dwells within all of us.

Qurb – From Sufism, meaning gaining proximity to God; having our mind, ego and heart near to Allah; a temporary epiphany beyond the boundaries of time.

Religion – An organized theological "club", school and/or doctrine that one associates with.

Religious Path – The metaphorical, metaphysical and mystical journey that one takes to connect with divinity based on a particular organized religion or aspects from multiple religious perspectives.

Ruach – From the *Tanakh* and Hebrew for spirit, the breath of life; See *Job* 33:4 and *Psalm* 51:11.

Rubedo – From true alchemy and Carl Jung's framework of psychology, it is the initiation and manifestation into one's true Self by building upon all life experiences and welding their dualities into a complementary whole; it is the final stages of transmuting one's consciousness into a higher state of existence.

Sahu – From ancient Egyptian religion it refers to the incorruptible spiritual body or perfect soul that could dwell in the heavens. It can also refer to the personification myths of the constellation Orion.

Sama – This term has a dual meaning: from Sanskrit, it is a Hindu practice or form of mental conditioning which consists of directing the mind inward and preventing counterproductive ideas from externalizing; it is a method for dissipating unnecessary or negative exploitive thoughts and/or emotions. It is also a Japanese term for someone worthy of admiration based on the merits of their behavior; the God within.

Samādhi – Sanskrit term for unification of the mind with the thoughts of the cosmos, an ecstatic merging of the soul with God. Also referred to as samapatti, it is considered the highest state of meditative consciousness in Hinduism, Buddhism, Jainism, Sikhism and among schools of yoga.

Samatva – Sanskrit term for equanimity; balanced behavior and stable mindedness.

Satori – Sudden enlightenment as defined by the framework of Japanese Zen Buddhist tradition; seeing one's true nature through experiences of understanding.

Satya – Sanskrit term for truth, but going much deeper, it represents the greatest of all the four Yugas (eras).

Satyam – Sanskrit term for that which is for the benefit of that which is true; the ultimate truth.

Scripture – The written words and texts of any religion, whether true or false.

Shekinah – Hebrew term for the mostly feminine essence of the cosmic being who dwells within all of us.

Shibboleth – Hebrew term for a custom, principle, or belief unique to a particular religion, sect or ethnicity that seems outmoded, not important or no longer applicable.

Spirituality – One's personal relationship with divinity.

Sudurdarsam – Sanskrit term for difficult to see or understand; hidden from plain view.

Sunyata – From Buddhism, it is the void or bubble that constitutes ultimate reality by the releasing of all apparent entities, distinctions, and dualities. It is not a negation of existence but rather a reaffirmation of it through lowering or removing the boundary lines that constitute our ego-self.

Svatstika – Sanskrit term for conducive to well-being.

Tanha – Derived from Vedic Sanskrit, it is a concept from Buddhism, meaning the desires and cravings which cause suffering.

Tao (or **Dao**) – The essence of the universe that we can mesh with, but cannot describe. When we try to describe it, we lose our place with it.

Taqiyya – From Shiite Islam, the allowable practice of denying or even lying to protect one's religion, permissible when one is faced with persecution and regarded as a means of preserving the religion from annihilation.

Tauba – From Sufism, repentance and renouncing the ways of evil as one steers back towards God.

Tektōn – Ancient Greek term for an artisan/craftsman, in particular a carpenter, wood-worker, mason, builder, teacher or engineer.

Tian – Ancient Chinese term for heaven and a key concept in their mythologies, philosophies, and religions. It was considered the realm of divinity's influence and a destination that our soul should strive for.

Tzvarnoharno – A term put forth by King Solomon of Judea, it is a force of *status quo* that rises amongst people leading to the destruction of anyone trying to raise consciousness or help humanity; it is the nemesis to bodhisattvas and mahasattvas.

Wahdat al-wujud – From Sufism, meaning oneness of being or unity with the Supreme Consciousness.

Bibliography

PRINT MATERIAL

The following listing of books, pamphlets and websites is not all-inclusive and does not imply an endorsement. It merely indicates that it was read by the author and/or used as an information source. The various references cited in the endnotes may or may not appear here in the bibliography.

• • • •

ANDERSON, FRED; *The War That Made America*; VIKING; Penguin Group Publishing; 2005; ISBN 0-670-03454-1

Ankerberg, John; *The Case For Jesus The Messiah*; Harvest House Publishers; 1989; ISBN 0-89081-772-3

Ayres, Ed (edited by); *God's Last Offer: Negotiating For A Sustainable Future*; Basic Books; 1999; ISBN 978-1-56858-125-5

Aziz, Zahid; *Introduction to Islam*; Ahmadiyya Association for the Propagation of Islam; 1993; ISBN 0-913321-08-7

Barrett, T.H. (introduction by); *Zen, The Reason Of Unreason*; Chronicle Books (Labyrinth Publishing); 1993; ISBN 0-8118-0403-8

Beattie, Melody; *Codependent No More*; Hazelden; 1992; ISBN 978-0-89486-402-5

Bercholz, Samuel and Kohn, Sherab Chödzin (edited by); *An Introduction To The Buddha And His Teachings* (Originally titled as *Entering The Stream*); Marboro Books/Barnes & Noble; 1997; ISBN 0-7607-0636-0

Bloom, Paul; *Just Babies, The Origins Of Good And Evil*; Crown Publishers; 2013 ; ISBN 978-0-307-88684-2

Bolles, Richard Nelson; *What Color Is Your Parachute?*; Ten Speed Press; 2000; ISBN 1-58008-123-1

Bunsun, Matthew E.; *The Wisdom And Teachings Of The Dalai Lama*; A Plume Book/Penguin Group; 1997; ISBN 0-452-27927-5

Burgo, Joseph; *The Narcissist You Know*; Touchstone (Simon & Schuster); 2015; ISBN 978-1-47678-568-4

Campbell, Joseph; *The Hero with a Thousand Faces*; Princeton University Press; 1972; ISBN 0-691-01784-0

Capra, Fritjof; *The Tao Of Physics*; Shambhala Publications; 1975, 1999; ISBN 978-1-59030-835-6

Chinmoy, Sri; *God is...*; Aum Publications; 1997; ISBN 0-88497-059-0

Cohen, Daniel; *The New Believers*; M. Evans & Co.; 1975; ISBN 0-87131-174-7

Conner, Miguel; *Voices of Gnosticism*; Bardic Press; 2011; ISBN 978-1-960834-12-8

Conner, Miguel; *Other Voices of Gnosticism*; Bardic Press; 2016; ISBN 978-1-906834-30-2

Cooke, Ivan (edited by); *The Return Of Arthur Conan Doyle*; The White Eagle Publishing Trust; 1980; ISBN 0-85487-045-8

Curtis, Charles P. Jr. and Greenslet, Ferris (edited by); *The Practical Cogitator*; Houghton Mifflin Company; 1962; ISBN 0-395-34635-5

Daniel, Alma; Wyllie, Timothy; Ramer, Andrew; *Ask Your Angels*; Ballantine Books (a division of Random House); 1992; ISBN 0-345-36358-2

Davison, Gerald C. and Neale, John M.; *Abnormal Psychology: An Experimental Clinical Approach*; John Wiley & Sons; 1986; ISBN 0-471-88876-1

Dawkins, Richard; *Climbing Mount Improbable*; W.W. Norton and Company; 1996; ISBN 0-393-03930-7

Dawkins, Richard; *The Selfish Gene*; Oxford University Press; 1978; ISBN 0-195-2000-0-4

Dawood, N.J. (translated by); *The Koran, With Parallel Arabic Text*; Penguin Books; 1997; ISBN 0-14-044542-0

Dhammapada, Thomas (translated by); *The Sayings Of Buddha*; Bantam Books; 1994; ISBN 0-553-37376-5

Dyer, Dr. Wayne W.; *You'll See It When You Believe It*; William Morrow and Company; 1989; ISBN 0-688-08040-5

Dyer, Dr. Wayne W.; *Manifest Your Destiny*; Harper Paperbacks (a division of Harper Collins Publishing); 1997; ISBN 0-06-109494-3

Effendi, Shoghi; *Gleanings From The Writings Of Bahá'u'lláh*; Bahai Publishing Trust; 1976; ISBN 0-87743-111-6

Elahi, Bahram; *The Path of Perfection: The Spiritual Teaching of Nur Ali Elahi*; Element, Inc.; 1993; ISBN 1-85230-392-1

Epstein, Mark (M.D.); *Going To Pieces Without Falling Apart*; Broadway Books; 1998; ISBN 0-7679-0235-1

Esslemont, J.E.; *Bahá'u'lláh And The New Era*; Bahá'í Publishing Trust; 1980; ISBN 0-87743-160-4

Fadiman, James and Frager, Robert; *Essential Sufism*; Castle Books; 1997; ISBN 0-7858-0906-6

Farah, Caesar E.; *Islam, Beliefs and Observances*; Barron's Educational Series; 1994; ISBN 0-8120-1853-2

Ferrel, L. Emerson; *Becoming The Master's Key*; Voice Of The Light Ministries; 2009, 2016; ISBN 978-1-933163-06-2

Finley, Mitch (introduction by); *The Saints Speak To You Today*; Charis Books (Servant Publications); 1999; ISBN 1-56955-141-3

Flescher, Andrew; *Moral Evil* ; Georgetown University Press; 2013; ISBN 978-1-62616-010-1

Flowers, Charles; *A Science Odyssey: 100 Years Of Discovery*; William Morrow and Company; 1998; ISBN 0-688-15196-5

Freke, Timothy and Gandy, Peter; *The Hermetica: The Lost Wisdom Of The Pharaohs*; Jeremy P. Tarcher/Penguin; 1997; ISBN 978-1-58542-692-8

Freke, Timothy and Gandy, Peter; *The Gospel of the Second Coming*; Hay House; 2007; ISBN 978-1-4019-1552-0

Freke, Timothy and Gandy, Peter; *Jesus And The Lost Goddess*; Harmony Books; 2001, ISBN 0-609-60767-7

Gawande, Atul; *Being Mortal:, Medicine and What Matters in the End*; Metropolitan Books, Henry Holt and Company; 2014; ISBN 978-0-8050-9515-9

Ghezzi, Bert; *Mystics & Miracles: True Stories of Lives Touched by God*; Loyola Press; 2002; ISBN 0-8294-1772-9

Gibran, Kahlil; *The Prophet*; Alfred A. Knopf, Inc.; 1951; ISBN 978-0-39445-094-0

Gill, Debbie; *Religions Of The World*; HarperCollins Publishers; 1997; ISBN 0-00-471008-8

Gladwell, Malcolm; *Blink: The Power of Thinking Without Thinking*; Little, Brown and Company; 2005; ISBN 0-316-17232-4

Gleitman, Henry; *Psychology*; W.W. Norton & Company; 1981; ISBN 0-393-95102-2

Greene, Arthur; *A Guide To The Zohar*; Stanford University Press; 2004; ISBN 0-8047-4908-6

Greive, Bradley Trevor; *The Meaning of Life*; Andrews McMeel Publishing; 2002; ISBN 0-7407-2336-7

Hamilton, Edith; *The Greek Way*; W. W. Norton & Company; 1958; ISBN 0-393-31077-9

Hanh, Thich Nhat; *Living Buddha, Living Christ*; River Head Books (a division of Penguin Putnim); 1997; ISBN 1-57322-568-1

Harpur, James; *The Miracles Of Jesus (Bible Wisdom for Today)*; Reader's Digest Association; 1997; ISBN 0-89577-907-2

Harvey, Andrew; *A Journey In Ladakh*; Houghton Mifflin Company; 1983; ISBN 0-395-36670-4

Hill, Napoleon; *Think & Grow Rich*; Ballantine Books; 1960; ISBN 0-449-21492-3

Hoff, Benjamin; *The Tao of Pooh*; Penguin Books; 1982; ISBN 0-14-006747-7

Horn, Sandra; *Relaxation: Modern Techniques For Stress Management*; Harper Collins; 1986; ISBN 0-7225-1187-6

Jones, Landon Y.; *Great Expectations: America and the Baby Boom Generation*; Ballantine Books; 1980; ISBN 0-345-29750-4

Jung, Carl Gustav (C.G.); *Modern Man In Search Of A Soul*; A Harvest Book, Harcourt; 1933; ISBN 0-15-661206-2

Kaufman, Josh ; *How To Fight A Hydra*; Wordly Wisdom Ventures LLC; 2018; ISBN 978-0-9796695-0-7

Kita, Joe; *Wisdom Of Our Fathers*; Daybreak Books, Rodale Press Inc.; 1999; ISBN 1-57954-041-4

Kluger, Jeffrey; *The Narcissist Next Door*; River Head Books (a division of Penguin Putnim); 2014; ISBN 978-1-59448-636-4

Knight, Bob; *The Power Of Negative Thinking*; Houghton Mifflin Harcourt; 2013; ISBN 978-0-544-02771-8

LaChance, Albert J.; *The Modern Christian Mystic: Finding the Unitive Presence of God*; North Atlantic Books; 2007; ISBN 978-1-55643-669-7

Lewis, James R.; *Encyclopedia of Death and the Afterlife*; Visible Ink Press; 1995; ISBN 1-57859-107-4

Lovecraft, H.P.; *Cthulhu Mythos Tales*; World Cloud Classics, Canterbury Classics; 2017; ISBN 978-1-68412-133-5

Malkin, Dr. Craig; *Rethinking Narcissism*; HarperCollins Publishers; 2015; ISBN 978-0-062348-10-4

Martin, Sean; *Alchemy & Alchemists*; Pocket Essentials; 2015; ISBN 978-1-84344-609-5

Martin, Sean; *The Gnostics - The First Christian Heretics*; Pocket Essentials; 2006; ISBN 978-1-904048-56-5

Martin, Sean; *The Cathars: The Rise And Fall Of The Great Heresy*; Pocket Essentials; 2014; ISBN 978-1-84344-336-0

Mascaró, Juan (aka Joan Mascaró Fornés) (interpreted by); *The Upanishads*; Penguin Group; 1965; ISBN 0-14-044163-8

McCullough, David; *1776*; Simon & Schuster; 2005; ISBN 978-0-74322-671-4

McKnight, C.J. and Catto, Jeremy I. (introduction by); *Alchemy: The Art Of Knowing*; Labyrinth Publishing; 1994; ISBN 0-8118-0473-9

McKnight, C.J. and Catto, Jeremy I. (introduction by); *Mysticism: The Experience Of The Divine*; Labyrinth Publishing; 1994; ISBN 1-85538-374-8

McWilliams; Peter; *I Marry You Because...*; Wilshire Publications; 1997; ISBN 0-934081-15-8

Mitchell, Stephen (interpreted by); *Tao Te Ching*; Harper & Row; 1988; ISBN 0-06-091608-7

Moore, Thomas; *Soul Mates: Honoring the Mysteries of Love and Relationships*; Harper Collins Publishing; 1994; ISBN 0-06-016928-1

Murphy, Joseph; *The Power Of Your Subconscious Mind*; Wilder Publications; 1963, 2007; ISBN 1-60459-201-X or 978-1-60459-201-6

Needleman, Jacob (introduction by); *The Spiritual Emerson: Essential Works by Ralph Waldo Emerson*; Jeremy P. Tarcher/Penguin; 2008; ISBN 978-1-58542-642-3

Paine, Thomas; *The Age of Reason*; Random House; originally published as Part I & II in the mid-1790s, 1993; ISBN 0-517-09118-6

Palacio, R.J.; *365 Days of Wonder*; Alfred A. Knopf, Inc.; 2014; ISBN 978-0-399-55918-1

Parsons, John Denham; *Our Sun-God, Or, Christianity Before Christ*; Printed by Hazell, Watson & Viney, Ld.; 1895; ISBN N/A, https://archive.org/details/oursungodorchri00parsgoog

Patrick, Dave (edited by); *The Cathar View: The Mysteriouis Legacy Of Montségur*; Polair Publishing; 2012; ISBN 978-1-905398-28-7

Peale, Norman Vincent; *The Power Of Positive Thinking*; Simon & Schuster, Touchstone Edition; 1952, 2015; ISBN 978-0-7432-3480-1

Peale, Norman Vincent; *Life Beyond Death*; Zondervan Publishing House; 1996; ISBN 0-310-20908-0

Peck, Scott; *The Road Less Travelled*; Simon & Schuster; 1978; ISBN 0-671-24086-2

Pinker, Steven; *The Better Angels Of Our Nature: Why Violence Has Declined*; VIKING; Penguin Group Publishing; 2011; ISBN 978-0-670-02295-3

Pirsig, Robert M.; *Zen And The Art Of Motorcycle Maintenance*; Quill; 1974; ISBN 0-688-17166-4

Powell, Robert; *The Sophia Teachings*; Lindisfarne Books; 2001; ISBN 978-1-58420-048-2

Prophet, Clare Elizabeth; *Saint Germain's Prophecy For The New Millennium*; Summit University Press; 1999; ISBN 0-922729-45-X

Redfield, James; *The Celestine Prophecy: An Adventure*; Transworld Pub; 1994; ISBN 978-0-55340-902-4

Robinson, James M. (edited by); *The Nag Hammadi Library*; HarperCollins Publishers; 1990; ISBN 0-06-066935-7

Schwartz, David Joseph; *The Magic of Thinking Big*; Simon & Schuster; 1987; ISBN 0-671-64678-8

Sekida, Katsuki; *Zen Training*; Weatherhill; 1975, 1997; ISBN 0-8348-0114-0

Shoghi, Effendi; *The World Order Of Bahá'u'lláh: Selected Letters*; Bahá'í Publishing Trust; 1993; ISBN 0-87743-231-7

Shreve, Mike; *In Search Of The True Light*; Deeper Revelation Books; 2007; ISBN 978-0-942507-73-7

Sizer, Theodore R.; *Horace's Hope*; Mariner Books; 1997; ISBN 978-0395877548

Smith, Huston; *The Illustrated World's Religions: A Guide To Our Wisdom Traditions*; Harper, San Francisco; 1994; ISBN 0-06-067440-7

Smith, Peter; *A Concise Encyclopedia of the Bahá'í Faith*; Oxford: Oneworld Publications; 2000; ISBN 978-1-85168-184-6

Smith, Joseph; *The Book Of Mormon: Another Testament of Jesus Christ*; Published by The Church of Jesus Christ of Latter-day Saints; 1830, #1990, 1981edition; ISBN N/A

Star, Jonathan (translated by); *Rumi, In the Arms of the Beloved*; Jeremy P. Tarcher/Penguin; 1997; ISBN 978-1-58542-693-5

Storr, Anthony; *The Essential Jung*; Princeton University Press; 1983; ISBN 0-691-02455-3

Strauss, William and Howe, Neil; *Generations: The History of America's Future, 1584 to 2069*; Quil, William Morrow and Company; 1991; ISBN 0-688-11912-3

Swedenborg, Emanuel; *Divine Love And Wisdom*; Swedenborg Foundation; 2003; ISBN 0-87785-481-5

Swedenborg, Emanuel; *Heaven and Hell*; Swedenborg Foundation; 2000; ISBN 0-87785-476-9

Tayé, Jamgön Kongtrul Lodrö; *Myriad Worlds*; Snow Lion Publications; 1995; ISBN 1-55939-033-6

Taylor, Barbara Brown; *Learning To Walk In The Dark*; HarperCollins Publishers; 2014; ISBN 978-0-06-202435-0

Teodoro, Andrian; *The Power Of Positive Energy*; 2017; ISBN 978-1537222790

Tickle, Phyllis (foreword by); *The Four Gospels*; Jeremy P. Tarcher/Penguin; 2008; ISBN 978-1-58542-677-5

Titmuss, Christopher; *An Awakened Life: Uncommon Wisdom from Everyday Experience*; Shambhala Publications; 2000; ISBN 1-57062-564-6

Vaughan, Frances and Walsh, Roger; *Accept This Gift*; Jeremy P. Tarcher/Penguin; 1983; ISBN 978-1-58542-619-5

Vaughan-Lee, Llewellyn; *Sufism: The Transformation of the Heart*; The Golden Sufi Center; 2012; ISBN 978-0-9634574-4-8

Waley, Muhammad Isa; *Sufism: The Alchemy Of The Heart*; Chronicle Books (Labyrinth Publishing); 1993; ISBN 0-8118-0410-0

Walker, Barbara G.; *Man Made God, A Collection of Essays*; Stellar House Publishing; 2010; ISBN 978-0-9799631-4-8

Wallis, Paul; *Escaping From Eden*; Axis Mundi Books (John Hunt Publications); 2020; ISBN 978-1-78904-387-7

Walsh, Neale Donald; *Conversations with God: An Uncommon Dialogue*; G. P. Putnam's Sons (a member of Penguin Putnam); 1995; ISBN 0-399-14278-9

Weinersmith, Kelly and Zach; *Soonish*; Penguin Press; 2017; ISBN 978-0-399-56382-9

White, David Manning; *Eternal Quest*; Paragon House; 1991; ISBN 1-55778-475-2

Whitworth, Eugene E.; *Nine Faces of Christ: Quest of the True Initiate*; Great Western University Press; 1972; ISBN 0-944155-00-6

Wilczek, Frank and Devine, Betsy; *Longing For The Harmonies: Themes and Variations from Modern Physics*; W.W. Norton & Company; 1988; ISBN 0-393-02482-2

William, James; *The Varieties of Religious Experience: A Study in Human Nature*; Barnes & Nobles Classics, Sterling Publishing; 1902, 1929; ISBN 978-1-59308-072-3

Young, John V.; *Kokopelli: Casanova of the Cliff Dwellers*; Filter Press; 1990; ISBN 0-86541-026-7

Zagami; Leo Lyon; *The Invisible Master: The Puppeteers Invisible Power*; Consortium of Collective Consciousness Publishing; 1999; ISBN 978-188872-970-2

Zeilik; Michael; *Astronomy: The Evolving Universe*; John Wiley & Sons; 5th Edition, 1988; ISBN 0-471-60523-9

Zeilstra, Kim (managed by); *Bible Promises For You: New International Version*; Inspirio, The Zondervan Corporation; 2006; ISBN 978-0-31081-268-5

A.C. Bhaktivedanta Swami Prabhupada; *Bhagavad-Gita, As It Is*; Bhaktivedanata Book Trust International Inc.; 1997; ISBN 0-89213-134-9

The Three Initiates; *The Kybalion: A Study Of The Hermetic Philosophy Of Ancient Egypt And Greece*; Rough Draft Printing; 2012; ISBN 978-1-60386-478-7

XIV Dalai Lama; *The Dalai Lama's Book Of Wisdom*; Thorsons (An Imprint of HarperCollins Publisher; 1999; ISBN 0-7225-3955-X

The Lockman Foundation; *New American Standard Bible*; Thomas Nelson, Publishers; 1977; ISBN N/A

Holy Bible, Authorized King James Version; Landoll/ Ottenheimer Publishers, Thomas Nelson; 1993, 1994; ISBN 1-56987-087-X

Short Description Of Gods, Goddesses And Ritual Objects Of Buddhism and Hinduism In Nepal; Handicraft Association of Nepal (Subhash Printing Press); 1998; ISBN N/A

The Quiet Mind: Sayings Of White Eagle, White Eagle Publishing Trust, William Clowes Limited; 1990; ISBN 0-85487-009-1

Aesop's Fables; Magnum Books (Lancer Books); 1968; ISBN N/A

• • • •

WEBSITES

Please accept our apologies if some of the following links are broken or no longer valid. They are provided as an information source only and their inclusion in this bibliography should not be interpreted as an endorsement.

Alchemy	https://www.alchemywebsite.com/index.html
Alchemy	http://www.levity.com/alchemy
Antichrist	https://www.britannica.com/topic/Antichrist
Antichrist	https://www.pbs.org/wgbh/pages/frontline/shows/apocalypse/antichrist/quiz.html
Antichrist	https://encyclopedia2.thefreedictionary.com/Antechrist
Antichrist	https://en.wikipedia.org/wiki/Antichrist
Antichrist	https://cathstan.org/posts/who-or-what-is-the-antichrist-a-reflection-on-the-biblical-teaching-3
Awakening Intuition	http://www.awakening-intuition.com/
BBC Religion & Ethics	http://www.bbc.co.uk/religion/religions/
Bible	https://biblehub.com/
Bible Versions	https://www.biblica.com/resources/bible-faqs/why-are-there-so-many-versions-of-the-bible-in-english/
Buddhism	https://www.pbs.org/edens/thailand/buddhism.htm
Buddhism	http://www.buddhanet.net/
Buddhism	https://tricycle.org/magazine/noble-eightfold-path/
Cathars	http://www.cathar.info/
Cathars	https://www.newdawnmagazine.com/articles/the-cathars-and-reincarnation-the-strange-revelations-of-arthur-guirdham
Crysta Links	http://www.crystalinks.com/shinto.html
Deism	https://en.wikipedia.org/wiki/Deism
Developing A Healthy Sense Of Self	https://thoughtcatalog.com/ryan-holiday/2016/06/25-ways-to-kill-the-toxic-ego-that-will-ruin-your-life/
Druids	https://www.encyclopedia.com/philosophy-and-religion/ancient-religions/ancient-religion/druids
Druids	https://en.wikipedia.org/wiki/Druidry_(modern)
Filianism	http://www.mother-god.com/filianism.html
Filianism	http://www.daughtersofshiningharmony.com/introductory/filianism/
Filianism	https://priestessofholywisdom.wordpress.com/

	Hermeticism
Hermeticism	https://en.wikipedia.org/wiki/Hermeticism
Hermeticism	https://ascendingpassage.com/Wisdom-The-Vision-of-Hermes-Trismegistus-7.htm
Hermeticism	https://www.crystalinks.com/emerald.html
Hermeticism	https://www.youtube.com/watch?v=hbfeE7OC_uU
Hinduism	https://www.hafsite.org/
Hinduism	https://study.com/academy/lesson/the-hindu-belief-system-darma-karma-and-moksha.html
Human Design	http://humandesign.net/index.html
Human Origins And Preserving Our Beginnings	https://www.ancient-origins.net/
Institute Of Noetic Sciences	https://www.noetic.org/
Islam	http://aboutislam.net/
Islam	https://www.alislam.org/
Islam: A religion of peace or not?	https://www.thereligionofpeace.com/
Islam: A religion of peace or not?	https://www.meforum.org/1913/religion-of-peace
Islam: A religion of peace or not?	https://en.wikipedia.org/wiki/Religion_of_peace
Jainism	https://sites.fas.harvard.edu/~pluralsm/affiliates/jainism/jainedu/mahavir.htm
Karma quotes	http://www.wiseoldsayings.com/karma-quotes/
Krishna, Bhagavad-Gita	http://www.krishna.com/
Krishna, Bhagavad-Gita	https://krishna.org/
Krishna, Bhagavad-Gita	https://www.gitadaily.com/
Krishna, Bhagavad-Gita	https://asitis.com/
Krishna, Bhagavad-Gita	https://www.holy-bhagavad-gita.org/
Krishna, Bhagavad-Gita	https://www.bhagavad-gita.org/Gita/chapter-13.html

Krishna, Bhagavad-Gita	https://bhagavadgita.io/
Learn Religions	https://www.learnreligions.com/
Lectorium Rosicrucianum	https://www.rosycross.org/
Mahatma Gandhi	https://www.mkgandhi.org/main.htm
Mary Magdalene	https://www.bbc.co.uk/religion/religions/christianity/history/marymagdalene.shtml#h4
Muhammad Marriages	https://www.theguardian.com/commentisfree/belief/2012/sep/17/muhammad-aisha-truth
Nafs	https://www.livingislam.org/nafs.html
Nirvana	https://www.hinduwebsite.com/Hinduism/concepts/nirvana.asp
On Saint Paul (Saul of Tarsus)	https://jewsforjesus.org/publications/issues/issues-v03-n04/was-paul-the-founder-of-christianity/
On the word "Allah"	https://christiananswers.net/q-eden/allah.html
On Violence In Scripture	http://archive.boston.com/bostonglobe/ideas/articles/2009/03/08/dark_passages/?page=1
Orthodox Christianity	https://myocn.net/
Pahana	http://www.pahanalives.com/hopi.html
PanEuRythmy	http://www.paneurhythmy.us/index.html
Rosicrucian Fellowship	http://www.rosicrucian.com/index.html
Rosicrucian Order AMORC	https://www.rosicrucian.org/
Sikhism	https://www.sikhs.org/
Sikhism	http://www.searchsikhism.com/
Sikhism	http://pluralism.org/religions/sikhism/introduction-to-sikhism/guru-nanak/
Socrates, Plato and Aristotle	https://www.diffen.com/difference/Aristotle_vs_Plato
Sufism	http://www.dar-al-masnavi.org/rumi-shams.html
Sufism	https://medium.com/@mo.issa/13-rumi-poems-to-awaken-the-love-within-us-2fcba19ca1c6
Sufism	https://qspirit.net/rumi-same-sex-love/

Sufism	https://en.wikipedia.org/wiki/Sufism
Sufism	https://en.wikipedia.org/wiki/History_of_Sufism
Terrorism	https://ourworldindata.org/terrorism
Terrorism	https://press.princeton.edu/titles/9012.html
Terrorism	http://archive.boston.com/bostonglobe/ideas/articles/2009/03/08/dark_passages/
The Bahá'í Faith	http://www.bahai.org/
The Bahá'í Faith	https://en.wikipedia.org/wiki/Bah%C3%A1%CA%BC%C3%AD_Faith
The Bahá'í Faith	https://en.wikipedia.org/wiki/New_world_order_(Bah%C3%A1%CA%BC%C3%AD)
The Church of Latter Day Saints (LDS), (aka Mormon Church)	https://www.churchofjesuschrist.org/?lang=eng
The Church of Latter Day Saints (LDS), (aka Mormon Church)	https://www.josephsmithpapers.org/paper-summary/book-of-mormon-1830/6
The Church of Latter Day Saints (LDS), (aka Mormon Church)	https://www.history.com/topics/religion/mormons
The Pluralism Project	https://pluralism.org/ or https://pluralism.org/religions
The Quran	https://quran.com/
Unitarian Universalist	https://uucolumbusga.org/newcomers/uu-principles/
Unitarian Universalists Association	https://www.uua.org/
White Eagle Lodge	https://www.whiteagle.org/
White Eagle Lodge	https://www.encyclopedia.com/philosophy-and-religion/other-religious-beliefs-and-general-terms/miscellaneous-religion/white-eagle-lodge
Women's Rights In The Muslim World	http://s.telegraph.co.uk/graphics/projects/koran-carla-power/index.html
Yin and Yang (aka Yab and Yum)	https://www.ancient.eu/Yin_and_Yang/

Yin and Yang (aka Yab and Yum)	https://www.ancient-origins.net/history/legendary-symbol-born-chaos-philosophy-yin-and-yang-009081

• • • •

DIGITAL MEDIA

Joseph Campbell and The Power Of Myth; Interview by Bill Moyers; Mystic Fire Video

Cosmos: A Spacetime Odyssey; Narrated by Dr. Neil deGrasse Tyson; Created by Cosmos Studios, Inc. and Distributed by 20th Century Fox

The Story of Islam: A History of the World's Most Misunderstood Religion; MPI Home Video

The Story of God With Morgan Freeman; television series which premiered on the National Geographic Channel

• • • •

USPTO S/N

88424958, 88424880, 88424750, 75927367

References And Notes

<u>FRONT MATTER</u>

[1] With slight modification; *Proverbs* 31:10-11

[2] Blog/Podcast by Chris Knowles; *Secret Sun*; and https://thegodabovegod.com/10-definitions-gnosis-experts-will-lead-mind-god/

[3] Storr, Anthony; *The Essential Jung*; pg. 50

[4] With modification; Beattie, Melody; *Codependent No More*; pg. 10

[5] Wachowski, Lilly and Lana-directors; circa 1999 cinematic science-fiction movie classic titled *The Matrix*

[6] "Know thyself." is a maxim from the Oracle at Delphi, a pagan temple in Greece.

[7] Parsons, John Denham; *Our Sun-God, Or, Christianity Before Christ*; per Julian (?), pg. 125

[8] Storr, Anthony; *The Essential Jung*; pg. 20

[9] Patrick, Dave; *The Cathar View*, contributed by Ani Williams; pg. 67 and http://www.usccb.org/prayer-and-worship/liturgical-year/easter/easter-proclamation-exsultet.cfm

[10] Book One, Chapter X, *The Order of the Heavenly Spheres* in *Copernicus: On the Revolutions of the Heavenly Spheres* (1543), trans. A. M. Duncan (1976), pgs. 49-51

[11] Mascaró, Juan, translator; *The Upanishads*; First Question, pg. 68

[12] Dante – 13th and 14th century Italian philosopher and poet and Palacio, R.J.; *365 Days Of Wonder*; February 9

[13] Swedenborg, Emanuel; *Divine Love and Wisdom*; Part 2, Section 83, pg. 83

[14] Palacio, R.J.; *365 Days of Wonder*; pg. April 3

[15] Freke, Timothy & Gandy, Peter; *Jesus And The Lost Goddess*; pg. 32 and Hippolytus, Ref., 5.3 and see Mead, G. R. S.; pg. 200

[16] Smith, Joseph; *3 Nephi* 6:30, *The Book Of Mormon, Another Testament of Jesus Christ*; 1830, #1990, ©1981 edition

[17] Angela of Foligno (1248–1309), Franciscan nun known as "Mistress of Theologians" and later canonized into a saint; *Mysticism, The Experience Of The Divine*; pg. 37 and outer rear dust cover

[18] With modification; LaChance, Albert J.; *The Modern Christian Mystic*; pg. 100

[19] Green, Arthur; *A Guide To The Zohar*; pg. 6

[20] http://www.akashicrecordsofsouls.com/read-akashic-records and https://medium.com/holisticism/what-are-the-akashic-records-ede3bee05673 and

https://www.gaia.com/article/akashic-records-101-can-we-access-our-akashic-records and https://en.wikipedia.org/wiki/Valis_(novel)

[21] The encountered cloud like mist that I saw seems similar to that shown surrounding the image of Arthur Conan Doyle from beyond the grave; Cooke, Ivan-editor; *The Return Of Arthur Conan Doyle*; pgs. 67-68

[22] Robinson, James M. (General Editor); *The Nag Hammadi Library*; *The Apocryphon of John*, pg. 116

[23] The initial spelling of "Abraxas" was most likely "Abrasax" from the Greek (Αβρασαξ). The consonants were probably switched due to a confusion between the Greek letters of *sigma* and *xi*. See https://greece.greekreporter.com/2020/12/04/greek-immigrant-in-roman-era-london-used-amulet-to-ward-off-plague/ and https://blogs.bl.uk/european/2015/10/the-tale-of-m%C3%A9lusine.html and https://www.pitt.edu/~dash/melusina.html

[24] *Jesus And The Lost Goddess*; pgs. 47-48 and https://plato.stanford.edu/entries/boethius/

[25] https://www.thecenterforsophiologicalstudies.com/post/jacob-boehme-on-the-virgin-mary-as-the-incarnation-of-sophia and http://www.berdyaev.com/berdiaev/berd_lib/1930_351.html and http://www.naturasophia.com/Intuit-Imagin.html and Powell, Robert; *The Sophia Teachings, The Emergence Of The Divine Feminine In Our Time*; pgs. 58-62

[26] https://www.newworldencyclopedia.org/entry/Hieros_gamos

[27] https://www.ancient.eu/Amaterasu/ and https://www.nippon.com/en/japan-topics/g00748/amaterasu-the-japanese-sun-goddess.html?pnum=1 and https://en.wikipedia.org/wiki/Amaterasu

[28] https://en.wikipedia.org/wiki/Tara_(Buddhism) and https://www.britannica.com/topic/Tara-Buddhist-goddess and https://en.wikipedia.org/wiki/Guanyin and https://www.crystalinks.com/kwanyin.html and https://www.nationsonline.org/oneworld/Chinese_Customs/Guan_Yin.htm and https://viking-styles.com/blogs/history/top-10-viking-goddesses and https://www.youtube.com/watch?v=aFiORPps_rg&feature=youtu.be

[29] https://www.ccel.org/ccel/wace/biodict.html?term=Helena,%20companion%20of%20Simon%20Magus and *Jesus And The Lost Goddess*; pgs. 90-91

[30] http://esoteric.msu.edu/Hobgood-Oster.html and https://www.sophian.org/forum/viewtopic.php?t=670 and http://gnosis.org/genesis.html

[31] Effendi, Shoghi; *Gleanings From The Writings Of Bahá'u'lláh*; pg. 45

[32] https://ascendingpassage.com/Wisdom-The-Vision-of-Hermes-Trismegistus-7.htm

[33] *The Sophia Teachings*; pgs. 54-56 and https://en.wikipedia.org/wiki/Hildegard_of_Bingen

[34] Jung, C.G.; *Modern Man In Search Of Soul*; pg. 79

[35] *Modern Man In Search Of Soul*, pg. 101

[36]   https://www.newscientist.com/article/2120135-one-time-or-another-our-best-5-theories-of-the-fourth-dimension/

[37] With modification; *Modern Man In Search Of Soul*; pg. 171

[38] Conner, Miguel; *Aeon Byte Gnostic Radio: Daemons, Divination, and the Return of the Witch*; August 27, 2020

[39] With modification; Gawande, Atul; *Being Mortal*; review by *Financial Time*, pg. vii

[40] Parsons, John Denham; *Our Sun-God, Or, Christianity Before Christ*; pg. 17

[41] Whitworth, Eugene E.; *Nine Faces of Christ*; pgs. 1-2

[42] With modification; Pinker, Steven; *The Better Angels of Our Nature*; pg. 478

[43] https://quotesgram.com/hypatia-quotes/ and https://www.laphamsquarterly.org/roundtable/killing-hypatia and http://www.math.wichita.edu/history/Women/hypatia.html and https://www.britannica.com/biography/Hypatia

[44]   https://www.ancient.eu/article/1041/the-origin-and-history-of-the-bcece-dating-system/

[45] https://www.baltimoresun.com/news/bs-xpm-2005-06-12-0506110147-story.html   and   https://www.mohammedamin.com/Community_issues/Koran-or-Quran.html

[46] https://en.wikipedia.org/wiki/Muhammad_(name)

[47] With much modification; Jung, C.G.; *Modern Man In Search Of A Soul*; pg. 11

[48] Paraphrase of comment by Bonomo; Conner, Miguel; *Aeon Byte Gnostic Radio, Finding Hermes 2*; September 15, 2020

[49] Gopnik, Alison; Sept. 2015; https://getpocket.com/explore/item/how-an-18th-century-philosopher-helped-solve-my-midlife-crisis

[50] Knight, Bob; *The Power Of Negative Thinking*; pg. 222

• • • •

CHAPTER 1

[51]   Conner,   Miguel;   *Other   Voices   of   Gnosticism*;   pg.   200   and http://www.blakearchive.org/

[52] With modification; Smith, Houston; *The Illustrated World's Religions*; pg. 242

[53] With modification; Freke, Timothy & Gandy, Peter; *Jesus And The Lost Goddess*; pg. 59

[54] Green, Arthur; *A Guide To The Zohar*; pg. 36

[55] With modification; Cooke, Ivan-editor; *The Return Of Arthur Conan Doyle*; pg. 2

[56] White, David Manning; *Eternal Quest*; pg. xx in the preface and outside rear cover

[57] Jung, C.G.; *Modern Man In Search Of A Soul*; pg. 131

[58] The Three Initiates; *The Kybalion*; pg. 8

[59] Freke, Timothy & Gandy, Peter; *The Hermetica, The Lost Wisdom of the Pharaohs*; pg. 32

[60] Einstein is known to have quoted variations on the notion of God rolling dice.

[61] *Modern Man In Search Of A Soul*; pg. 8

[62] Paine, Thomas; *The Age of Reason*; pg. 177

[63] Vaughan-Lee, Llewellyn; *Sufism, The Transformation of the Heart*; pg. 52

[64] With slight modification; *Eternal Quest*; pg. x in the preface

[65] With modification; *Jesus And The Lost Goddess*; pg. 142

[66] LaChance, Albert J.; *The Modern Christian Mystic*; pg. 28

[67] Verbatim; Pinker, Steven; *The Better Angels Of Our Nature*, pg. 628

[68] With modification; *The Better Angels Of Our Nature*, pg. 629

[69] With modification; Weinersmith, K&Z; *Soonish*; p. 186

[70] Patrick, Dave; *The Cathar View*; contributed by Hristo Madjarov; pg. 120

[71] Wallis, Paul; *Escaping From Eden*; pg. 25

[72] Utnapishtim (asa Utanapishtim) is a character in the *Epic of Gilgamesh* whose actions closely resemble that of Noah; see https://en.wikipedia.org/wiki/Epic_of_Gilgamesh

[73] Martin, Sean; *The Gnostics, The First Christian Heretics*; pgs. 56-57

[74] *Our Sun-God, Or, Christianity Before Christ*; pgs. 38-41

[75] *Our Sun-God, Or, Christianity Before Christ*; pgs. 186-187

[76] Early 2nd or 3rd century Christian author from Carthage, Rome; *Our Sun-God, Or, Christianity Before Christ*; pg. 177

[77] *Our Sun-God, Or, Christianity Before Christ*; pg. 178 and see Chapter 4 under Zoroastrianism for more on Ohrmazd.

[78] *Our Sun-God, Or, Christianity Before Christ*; pg. 73

[79] *Our Sun-God, Or, Christianity Before Christ;* pg. 178

[80] Deoxyribonucleic acid; the organic material that forms the replicating codes of life on Earth.

[81] *Modern Man In Search Of A Soul;* pg. 103

[82] The chart of the "Spheres of Evolving Life and Consciousness" can also be found in: *The Return Of Arthur Conan Doyle;* pgs. 108-109

[83] *The Age of Reason;* pgs. 98, 101

[84] *The Age of Reason;* pg. 156

[85] *The Age of Reason;* pg. 107

[86] *The Age of Reason;* pg. 109

[87] *The Age of Reason;* pg. 133-136

[88] *The Age of Reason;* pg. 175

[89] *Isiah* 7:14

[90] *Our Sun-God, Or, Christianity Before Christ;* pgs. 146-147

[91] Wallis, Paul; *Escaping From Eden;* pg. 24

[92]   https://www.cnn.com/2020/03/09/us/komodo-dragons-parthenogenesis-scn-trnd/index.html

[93] *The Age of Reason;* pg. 143-144

[94] *The Age of Reason;* pg. 157

[95] For example, *1 Kings* 18:31

[96] Powell, Robert; *The Sophia Teachings;* pgs. 126-127

[97] *Jesus And The Lost Goddess;* pg. 113 and Plato*; Laws;* pg. 745d-e

[98] *Our Sun-God, Or, Christianity Before Christ;* pgs. 41-54, 61-62, 100-101, 151-152, 186 and *The Sophia Teachings;* pg. 118 and https://en.wikipedia.org/wiki/Ascension_of_Jesus

[99] *The Age of Reason;* pg. 147

[100] *Matthew* 1:18-25, *Luke* 1:26-38

[101] Unbeknownst previously to the author, the Bhagavad-Gita, Émile Durkheim and Carl Jung reference forms of a collective consciousness, collective subconscious, or a collective unconscious.

[102] Examples of shortened variations are "collective consciousness of humanity" or "supreme consciousness of humanity"

[103] https://en.wikipedia.org/wiki/Collective_unconscious

[104] The meaning of "triangular" and "circular" will be explained in Chapter 24

[105] Egyptian sun-god; *Poimandres*, The Barque of Isis, https://ascendingpassage.com/Wisdom-The-Vision-of-Hermes-Trismegistus-7.htm

[106] Star, Jonathan – translator; *Rumi, In the Arms of the Beloved*; pg. 152

[107] *Sukkah* 53a; (*Talmud*)

[108] Groening, Matt; creator of the humorous and often dysfunctional antics of a cartoon family called *The Simpsons* and their associates. Mentioned during presentations as a guest speaker at a PMI virtual expo; circa 2018.

[109] *Modern Man In Search Of A Soul*; pg. 168

[110] *Modern Man In Search Of A Soul*; pg. 169

[111] https://medium.com/@mo.issa/13-rumi-poems-to-awaken-the-love-within-us-2fcba19ca1c6

[112] Vaughan, Frances and Walsh, Roger; *Accept This Gift*; Mind, pg. 12

[113] With modification; *Modern Man In Search Of A Soul*; pg. 29

• • • •

CHAPTER 2

[114] "When it comes right down to it" is a cliché or expression which means focusing in on the root of what is important.

[115] http://www.mother-god.com/ and http://www.daughtersofshiningharmony.com/introductory/filianism/

[116] https://gnosticismexplained.org/barbelo/ and Scopello, Madeleine & Meyer, Marvin; *The Gospel of Philip* in *The Nag Hammadi Scriptures*; footnote 16, pg. 164

[117] *Bhagavad-Gita, As It Is*, 9.11

[118] Powell, Robert; *The Sophia Teachings*; pgs. 137-139

[119] https://ascensionglossary.com/index.php/Achamoth

[120] Freke, Timothy & Gandy, Peter; *Jesus And The Lost Goddess*; pg. 133

[121] https://thegodabovegod.com/10-definitions-gnosis-experts-will-lead-mind-god/

[122] *Jesus And The Lost Goddess*; pg. 95

[123] Martin, Sean; *The Gnostics, The First Christian Heresy*; pg. 90 and http://gnosis.org/naghamm/exe.html

[124] *The Gnostics, The First Christian Heresy*; pg. 89 and *Thunder:Perfect Mind, The Gnostic Bible*, pg. 226

[125] Troubadour Arnaut Daniel (1180–1200); Patrick, David, Editor; *The Cathar View*; contributed by Ani Williams; translation by Henry Lincoln, pg. 50

[126] *The Gnostics, The First Christian Heresy*; pg. 76 and *The Apocryphon of John*, pg. 139

[127] https://www.sophian.church/about

[128] *Exodus* 3:14

[129] 13th century Sufi mystic; from poem *When All You Had Was Him*; Rumi, *In the Arms of the Beloved*; pg. 48

[130] Existential quote by Popeye the Sailor, a fictional muscular American cartoon character created in 1919 by Elzie Crisler Segar and famous for saving his friends after eating a can of empowering spinach and http://extraordinaryconversations.com/thought-leadership/2018/1/3/i-am-what-i-am

[131] With modifications; Introduction by Juan Mascaró; *The Upanishads*; pg. 25

[132] *Metaphysics*; White, David Manning; *Eternal Quest, Volume 1, The Search For God*; pg. 9

[133] Parsons, John Denham; *Our Sun-God, Or, Christianity Before Christ*; pgs. 92

[134] *Our Sun-God, Or, Christianity Before Christ*; pgs. 91-92

[135] *Our Sun-God, Or, Christianity Before Christ*; pg. 132

[136] *Our Sun-God, Or, Christianity Before Christ*; pgs. 87-89

[137] *Romans* 8:15

[138] *1 Corinthians* 12:4-6

[139] Conner, Miguel, *Voices of Gnosticism*; pg. 187

[140] https://www.youtube.com/watch?v=DMx_JKJbvJI&feature=youtu.be

[141] Vaughan-Lee, Llewellyn; *Sufism, The Transformation of the Heart*; pg. 22

[142] *Sufism, The Transformation of the Heart*; pg. 26

[143] Dawood, N.J. – translator; *The Koran* and https://simple.m.wikipedia.org/wiki/Names_of_God_in_Islam

[144] With slight modification; The Three Initiates; *The Kybalion*; pgs. 15, 25, 33

[145] With slight modification; Mascaró, Juan; *The Upanishads*; pg. 72

[146] LaChance, Albert J.; *The Modern Christian Mystic*; pg. 104

[147] *Bhagavad-Gita, As It Is*; 1.15

[148] *The Upanishads*; pg. 72

[149] http://www.native-languages.org/mohegan-legends.htm

[150] White, David Manning; *Eternal Quest*; pg. 3

[151] https://www.youtube.com/watch?v=-XagZt80bTs&list=WL; Indigenous Native American Prophecy

[152] Storr, Anthony; *The Essential Jung*; pgs. 69-70

[153] *The Kybalion*; pgs. 27, 28, 31 and *The Hermitica*; pg. 36

[154] Wickersham, John M. – Editor; *Myths and Legends of the World*; ©2000/2001; Macmillan Library Reference

[155] *Revelation* 18:3

[156] *The Upanishads*; pg. 73

[157] Roman stoic philosopher; (4 BCE–65 CE)

[158] *Eternal Quest*; pg. 3

[159] *The Upanishads*; pg. 101

[160] *The Modern Christian Mystic*; pg. 31

[161] With modification; Peale, Vincent; *The Power Of Positive Thinking*; pg. 5

[162] *Deuteronomy* 31:6; *Joshua* 1:9; *Isiah* 41:10; *Matthew* 18:20, 28:20; *Romans* 8:38-39; *Hebrews* 13:5-8

[163] Primary religious scriptures of Zoroastrianism; Cooke, Ivan-editor; *The Return Of Arthur Conan Doyle*; pg. 18

[164] With modification; *The Modern Christian Mystic*; pg. xxvi

[165] *Jesus And The Lost Goddess*; pg. 131 and Armstrong, K.; *The Divine Names*, 7.3; pg. 149

• • • •

CHAPTER 3

[166] Some sources refer to angels and demons as the duality of the same being. When guiding, assisting or helping humanity, they are angelic. When punishing, tempting or testing humanity, they are demonic. Jinn, from Arabic mythology, are considered at the same hierarchical ranking or lower than angels and demons.

[167] *Gopala-tapani*, 1.21; *Bhagavad-Gita*; pg. 417

[168] Paine, Thomas; *The Age of Reason*; pg. 114

[169] *Jonah* 1:5-6

[170] *Jonah* 1:12-13

[171] *Jonah* 1:15

[172] Paine, Thomas; *The Age of Reason*; pgs. 137-138 and *Jonah* 1:14

[173] https://en.wikipedia.org/wiki/S%C3%B8ren_Kierkegaard and Palacio, R.J.; *365 Days of Wonder*; pg. April 7

[174] 19th century Unitarian minister and transcendentalist; *The Collected Works of Theodore Parker: Lessons From The World Of Matter And The World Of Men*; published 1872, pgs. 38-39 and *Eternal Quest*; pg. xxii

[175] https://www.newadvent.org/cathen/05740c.htm and https://en.wikipedia.org/wiki/Frederick_William_Faber and *365 Days of Wonder*; pg. May 4

[176] Mascaró, Juan; *The Upanishads*; pg. 89

[177] From a bronze plaque located in the hallway of a New Jersey elementary school.

[178] *The Modern Christian Mystic*; pg. 8

[179] *John* 15:5

[180] Storr, Anthony; *The Essential Jung*; pg. 278

[181] With modification; Vaughan-Lee, Llewellyn; *The Transformation of the Heart*; pg. 72

[182] http://www.jwmt.org/v1n3/treeoflife.html and https://en.wikipedia.org/wiki/Tree_of_life_(Kabbalah)

[183] With slight modification; Whitworth, Eugene E.; *Nine Faces of Christ*; pg. 313

[184] Freke, Timothy & Gandy, Peter; *Jesus And The Lost Goddess*; pg. 64

[185] *The Upanishads*; Part 6, pg. 65

[186] https://www.humanitiestexas.org/programs/tx-originals/list/karle-wilson-baker and https://en.wikipedia.org/wiki/Karle_Wilson_Baker and *365 Days of Wonder*; pg. April 25

[187] The fictional child protagonist in the animated series *Avatar: The Last Air Bender*, circa 2005-2008 and https://en.wikipedia.org/wiki/Aang and Palacio, R.J.; *365 Days of Wonder*; pg. February 11

[188] *John* 14:6

[189] Latin expression for "the highest good"

• • • •

CHAPTER 4

[190] A.C. Bhaktivedanta Swami Prabhupada; rear cover of *Bhagavad Gita, As It Is*

[191] *Galatians* 6:7-8

[192] https://www.hinduwebsite.com/Hinduism/concepts/nirvana.asp

[193] https://www.hinduwebsite.com/Hinduism/concepts/nirvana.asp

[194] https://en.wikipedia.org/wiki/Hermeticism

[195] The Three Initiates; *The Kybalion*; pg. 11

[196] From poem titled The Dome of the Inner Sky; *Rumi, In the Arms of the Beloved*; pg. 125

[197] *Alchemy, The Art Of Knowing*; pg. 18

[198] *Alchemy, The Art of Knowing*; pg. 20; see also Herman Boerhaave (1668–1738), Dutch physician

[199] *Genesis* 5:21-24

[200] *The Koran*; Verse 19:56-57

[201] With modification; Freke, Timothy & Gandy, Peter; *The Hermetica*; pg. xvii

[202] http://www.newworldencyclopedia.org/entry/Hermeticism

[203] http://www.newworldencyclopedia.org/entry/Hermeticism

[204] *3 Nephi* 28:4-12, 36-40, *The Book of Mormon*; and *Revelation* 14:6-16, *The New Testament* and https://www.bibleinfo.com/en/questions/three-angels-messages and https://en.wikipedia.org/wiki/Three_Angels%27_Messages

[205] http://www.jwmt.org/v3n24/chapel.html

[206] *The Hermetica*; pg. 106

[207] *Alchemy, The Art Of Knowing*; pg. 57 & rear outside of dust cover

[208] Patrick, David-editor; *The Cathar View*; contributed by Nick Lambert; pg. 89 and "The Visions of Isaiah", http://gnosis.org/library/Cathar-Vision-Isaiah.htm

[209] With modification; *Alchemy, The Art Of Knowing*; pg. 24

[210] https://siimland.com/the-7-hermetic-principles/

[211] LaChance, Albert J.; *The Modern Christian Mystic*; pg. 145

[212] https://ultraculture.org/blog/2016/04/19/hermetic-initiates-magick-study-reality/

[213] Parsons, John Denham; *Our Sun-God, Or, Christianity Before Christ*; pg. 122

[214] Martin, Sean; *The Cathers, The Rise And Fall Of The Great Heresy*; pg. 19

[215] *Our Sun-God, Or, Christianity Before Christ*; pg. 148-150 and https://en.wikipedia.org/wiki/Biblical_Magi

[216] Martin, Sean; *The Gnostics, The First Christian Heretics*; pg. 25

[217] Martin, Sean; *The Gnostics, The First Christian Heretics*; pg. 25

[218] https://en.wikipedia.org/wiki/Jain_symbols

[219] https://en.wikipedia.org/wiki/Jainism and *Hinnells, John R.; Who's Who of World Religions*; pgs. 145-146

[220]   https://en.wikipedia.org/wiki/Ahimsa_in_Jainism#cite_note-FOOT-NOTEJain192948-32

[221] Religions of the World, Collins Gem; Gill, Debbie; Harper Collins Publishing, 1997, pg. 39.

[222] *Mystics & Miracles*; pg. 45

[223] Ghezzi, Bert; *Mystics & Miracles*; pgs. 119-120

[224] Jung, C.G.; *Modern Man In Search Of Soul*; pg. 45 and Paine, Thomas; *The Age of Reason*; pg. 9

[225]http://gnostic-unrest.blogspot.com/2009/12/somatics-psychics-pneumatics.html

[226] *Zen, The Reason Of Unreason*; pg. 42

[227] Greek pre-Socratic philosopher and follower of Pythagoras.

[228] *Wax and wane* is an idiom which means to cyclically increase and decrease. Written reference to the expression first occurred in the 14th century to describe the various light intensities of the Moon's phases.

[229] With modification; Martin, Sean; *Alchemy & Alchemists*; pg. 83

[230] Ames, Roger T. and Mei, Yi Pao; https://www.britannica.com/biography/Mozi-Chinese-philosopher

[231] Tignor, Robert; Adelman, Jeremy; Brown, Peter; Elman, Benjamin; Liu, Xinru; Pittman, Holly; Shaw, Brent (2013-10-24); *Worlds Together Worlds Apart Volume One: Beginnings Through the 15th Century (Fourth ed.)*; pg. 167

[232] Ames, Roger T. and Mei, Yi Pao; https://www.britannica.com/biography/Mozi-Chinese-philosopher

[233] https://en.wikipedia.org/wiki/Mozi

[234] Ames, Roger T. and Mei, Yi Pao; https://www.britannica.com/biography/Mozi-Chinese-philosopher

[235] http://www.uh.edu/engines/epi2080.htm and R. Temple; *The Genius of China: 3000 Years of Science, Discovery and Invention.* (Intr. by Jos. Needham; New York: Simon & Schuster Inc.; © 1986.

[236] http://www.crystalinks.com/shinto.html, Doctrines – Concept of the Sacred

[237] *Mystics & Miracles*; pg. 158

[238] *1 Kings* 18

[239] *1 Kings* 18:40

[240] Patrick, Dave-editor; *The Cathar View*; writings of Maurice Magre; pg. 190

• • • •

CHAPTER 5

[241] Freke, Timothy & Gandy, Peter; *The Gospel of the Second Coming* and Parsons, John Denham; *Our Sun-God, Or, Christianity Before Christ*; pgs. 155-159

[242] Freke, Timothy & Gandy, Peter; *Jesus And The Lost Goddess;* pg. 56

[243] Conner, Miguel; *Voices of Gnosticism*; pg. 97

[244] *Voices of Gnosticism*; pgs. 72-74

[245] *Voices of Gnosticism*; pgs. 159-160

[246] *Jesus And The Lost Goddess;* pg. 130freke

[247] *The Gospel of the Second Coming*; pg. 7

[248] https://en.wikipedia.org/wiki/Ginza_Rba and https://en.wikipedia.org/wiki/Mandaeans

[249] Conner, Miguel; *Other Voices of Gnosticism*; pg. 128

[250] *Other Voices of Gnosticism*; pgs. 184-185

[251] *Other Voices of Gnosticism*; pg. 189 and *Matthew 11:11* (NIV) and *Luke7:28* (NIV) and *Gospel of Thomas*, saying (46); http://gnosis.org/naghamm/gthlamb.html

[252] *3 Nephi* 27:13, *The Book of Mormon*

[253] *Gospel of Thomas*; saying (39); http://gnosis.org/naghamm/gthlamb.html

[254] *Our Sun-God, Or, Christianity Before Christ*; pg. 211

[255] LaChance, Albert J.; *The Modern Christian Mystic*; pg. 28

[256] Whitworth, Eugene E.; *Nine Faces of Christ*; pg. 236

[257] http://www.badnewsaboutchristianity.com/df0_nativity.htm and Walker, Barbara G.; *Man Made God, A Collection of Essays*; Chapter 14, footnote 7, pg. 307

[258] *Matthew* 1:20-21, 2:13, 2:19-20 and *Luke* 1:26-38

[259] *The Koran* (3:45)

[260] Martin, Sean; *The Gnostics-The First Christian Heretics*; pg. 86

[261] https://www.britannica.com/topic/Christology/The-Arian-controversy

[262] Powell, Robert; *The Sophia Teachings*; pgs. 40-43

[263] *Jesus And The Lost Goddess;* pgs. 44-45

[264] *The Gnostics-The First Christian Heretics*; pg. 12

[265] *Aeon Byte Gnostic Radio; Hidden Meaning & Structure In The Gospel Of Thomas*; interview with John Munter; September, 2018 and https://thegodaboveg-od.com/the-textable-gospel-of-thomas/

[266]   https://www.behindthename.com/name/thomas   and https://en.wikipedia.org/wiki/Thomas_(name) and https://www.name-doctor.com/name-didymos-meaning-of-didymos-40069.html and

[267] http://gnosis.org/thomasbook/intro.html and https://en.wikipedia.org/wiki/Substitution_hypothesis

[268] Patrick, Dave-editor; *The Cathar View*; contributed by Deirdre Ryan; pgs. 84-85

[269] *Luke* 2:41-52

[270] *John* 3:16

[271] With modification; *Jesus And The Lost Goddess;* pg. 115

[272] Martin, Sean; *The Gnostics, The First Christian Heretics*; pg. 96

[273] Paine, Thomas; *The Age of Reason*; pgs. 47-48

[274] *The Gnostics, The First Christian Heretics*; pg. 92 and *The Cathar View*; contributed by Val Wineyard; pgs. 133-134 and Conner, Miguel; *Other Voices of Gnosticism*; pg. 33 and https://en.wikisource.org/wiki/1911_Encyclop%C3%A6dia_Britannica/Ophites

[275] *Our Sun-God, Or, Christianity Before Christ*; pg. 209

[276] https://catholicgnosis.wordpress.com/2014/11/10/the-platonic-triad/ and https://www.athensjournals.gr/humanities/2018-5-1-2-Burgin.pdf and *Jesus And The Lost Goddess;* pg. 66

[277] https://gnosticismexplained.org/barbelo/

[278] *The Sophia Teachings*; pgs. 87-89 and https://en.wikipedia.org/wiki/Valentin_Tomberg

[279] *Voices of Gnosticism*; pg. 86

[280] Cleary, Thomas - translator; *The Secret Of The Golden Flower*; pg. 78

[281] *Jesus And The Lost Goddess;* pgs. 78, 140, 149

[282] Storr, Anthony; *The Essential Jung*; pg. 212

[283] *The Sophia Teachings*; pg. 4

[284] *The Sophia Teachings*; pg. 40

[285] 19th century American journalist, social reformer, Unitarian minister and reflector of the zeitgeist of his era.

[286]   https://en.wikipedia.org/wiki/Binitarianism   and   http://www.ccg.org/weblibs/study-papers/p127b.html

[287] Pinker, Steven, *The Better Angels of Our Nature*; pg. 6

[288] Conner, Miguel; *Voices of Gnosticism*; pgs. 196-197

[289] *The Gnostics, The First Christian Heretics*; pg. 19

[290] Martin, Sean; *The Cathars, The Rise And Fall Of The Great Heresy*; pgs. 26 & 153

[291] *Our Sun-God, Or, Christianity Before Christ*; pgs. 27-32, 190-191 and https://www.newyorker.com/magazine/2012/08/13/i-nephi

[292] *Our Sun-God, Or, Christianity Before Christ*; pg. 191

[293] *Our Sun-God, Or, Christianity Before Christ*; pgs. 84-86

[294] *Voices of Gnosticism*; pg. 47

[295] *Voices of Gnosticism*; pg. 104

[296] Saul was his Hebrew name as a Jew growing up in Tarsus, a city in Asia Minor and a center of Gentile Culture. Paul was his name in Greek.

[297] *Religions of the World*, Collins Gem

[298] *The Cathar View*; contributed by Roger Shorter; pg. 114

[299] *The Age of Reason*; pgs. 178-179

[300] With modifications; https://en.wikipedia.org/wiki/Jehovah%27s_Witnesses

[301] https://www.history.com/topics/religion/mormons

[302] Smith, Joseph; *The Book of Mormon, Another Testament of Jesus Christ*; Introduction, 1830, #1990, ©1981 edition

[303] https://en.wikipedia.org/wiki/Joseph_Smith_and_the_criminal_justice_system and https://en.wikipedia.org/wiki/Death_of_Joseph_Smith

[304] https://en.wikipedia.org/wiki/Joseph_Smith_1844_presidential_campaign

[305] https://www.newyorker.com/magazine/2012/08/13/i-nephi

[306] https://www.history.com/this-day-in-history/the-mormon-church-officially-renounces-polygamy

[307] https://www.history.com/topics/religion/mormons and https://www.history.com/this-day-in-history/the-mormon-church-officially-renounces-polygamy

[308] https://knowhy.bookofmormoncentral.org/knowhy/what-does-the-book-of-mormon-say-about-polygamy

[309] Testimony Of The Prophet Joseph Smith; *The Book Of Mormon*

[310] Wallis, Paul; *Escaping From Eden*; pgs. 71-74

[311] https://www.newyorker.com/magazine/2012/08/13/i-nephi and https://www.ldsliving.com/What-Mark-Twain-Really-Thought-About-Mormons/s/78635

[312] This quote is also stated in Chapter 3 within this book.

[313] *Escaping From Eden*; pgs. 38-39

[314]   https://www.newadvent.org/cathen/01150a.htm   and https://en.wikipedia.org/wiki/Adoptionism

[315] https://uucolumbusga.org/newcomers/uu-principles/

[316]   http://www.adherents.com/largecom/fam_unitarian.html   and https://en.wikipedia.org/wiki/List_of_Unitarians,_Universalists,_and_Unitarian_Universalists

[317] Although discovered in 2005 during an expedition by Italian researchers to sites between the Nile valley and the Gilf Kebir Plateau, its existence was not revealed until 2016.

[318] *The Cathar View*; contributed by Nick Lambert; pg. 99

[319] Conner, Miguel; *Other Voices of Gnosticism*; pgs. 105-106

[320] *The Cathar View*; contributed by Jaap Rameijer; pgs. 255-256

[321] *The Cathar View*; contributed by Nick Lambert; pg. 98

[322] *The Cathar View*; contributed by Val Wineyard; pg. 135

[323] https://en.wikipedia.org/wiki/Gospel_of_Mary

[324]   https://www.bbc.co.uk/religion/religions/christianity/history/marymagdalene.shtml#h4 see *Mary Magdalene, the clichés*

[325]   https://www.bbc.co.uk/religion/religions/christianity/history/marymagdalene.shtml#h4; see *Mary's biggest moment*

[326] *The Cathar View*; contributed by Jaap Rameijer; pg. 256

[327]   https://en.wikipedia.org/wiki/Islam_by_country   and https://www.ncbi.nlm.nih.gov/pmc/articles/PMC3705684/

[328] http://s.telegraph.co.uk/graphics/projects/koran-carla-power/index.html

[329] *Jesus And The Lost Goddess;* pg. 207

[330] Farah, Caesar E.; *Islam: Beliefs and Observations*; pg. 96

[331] *Islam: Beliefs and Observations*; pg. 95

[332] *Islam: Beliefs and Observations*; pg. 2

[333] Martin, Sean; *Alchemy & Alchemists*; pg. 52

[334] *The Koran* ≈ (4:29)

[335] *The Koran* (2:237)

[336] *Islam: Beliefs and Observations*; pg. 54

[337] *Islam: Beliefs and Observations*; 85

[338]   https://www.imb.org/2019/05/24/difference-between-shiite-sunni-muslims/

[339] *Sufism, The Alchemy Of The Heart*; pg. 11

[340] Vaughan-Lee, Llewellyn; *Sufism, The Transformation of the Heart*; pg. xvi

[341] Star, Jonathan-translator; *Rumi, In the Arms of the Beloved*; pg. xvii

[342] *Sufism, The Transformation of the Heart*; pg. 27

[343] https://qspirit.net/rumi-same-sex-love/

[344] Seale, Patrick with the assistance of McConville, Maureen; *Asad of Syria: The Struggle for the Middle East*; Berkeley: University of California Press; 1989, c1988

[345] *The Cathar View*; writings of Walter Birks; pg. 191

[346] https://en.wikipedia.org/wiki/Alawites

[347] https://www.reuters.com/article/us-syria-crisis-deaths/death-toll-in-syria-likely-as-high-as-120000-group-idUSBRE94D0L420130514 and https://www.middleeastmonitor.com/20170420-150000-alawites-killed-in-6-year-syria-war/

[348] *The Cathar View*; writings of Walter Birks; pg. 192

[349] *The Cathar View*; writings of Walter Birks; pg. 191

[350] https://www.globalsecurity.org/military/intro/islam-alawi.htm

[351] *The Cathar View*; writings of Walter Birks; pg. 196

[352] *The Cathar View*; writings of Walter Birks; pg. 194

[353] https://www.britannica.com/topic/Druze

[354] *Islam: Beliefs and Observations*; pg. 179

[355] More on nafs; https://www.livingislam.org/nafs.html

[356] https://www.newworldencyclopedia.org/entry/Druze

[357] *Voices of Gnosticism*; pg. 125

[358] https://www.newworldencyclopedia.org/entry/Druze and Shen et al. 2004; *Reconstruction of Patrilineages and Matrilineages of Samaritans and Other Israeli Populations From Y-Chromosome and Mitochondrial DNA Sequence*; Variation Research Article - *evolutsioon.ut.ee*; retrieved October 17, 2007

[359] https://theconversation.com/solving-the-1-000-year-old-mystery-of-druze-origin-with-a-genetic-sat-nav-68550

[360] https://www.jstor.org/stable/40926501?seq=1#page_scan_tab_contents

[361] Gill, Debbie; *Religions of the World*, pg. 193

[362] https://www.sikhs.org/summary.htm

[363] "Earning one's keep" is an expression which means working for a living and earning wages so as not to be a burden upon others or on society.

[364] *NewScientist*; 24/31, December 1987 No 1592/1593; pg. 15

[365] https://en.wikipedia.org/wiki/Christian_Rosenkreuz

[366] *Rumi, In the Arms of the Beloved*; pgs. xiii & xix and https://www.whiteagle.org/childrens-stories/roses-of-kindness-and-love   and   https://www.whiteaglelodge.org/ and https://www.whiteagle.org/who-we-are/principles and Cooke, Ivan-editor; *The Return Of Arthur Conan Doyle*; pgs. 35, 36, 47

[367] https://www.britannica.com/topic/Rosicrucians

[368] *NewScientist*; 24/31, December 1987 No 1592/1593; pg. 15

[369] https://www.rosycross.org/article/what-goal-rosicrucians-lectorium-rosicrucianum

[370] https://www.rosicrucian.org/mystical-path

[371] https://www.rosicrucian.org/highest-potential

[372] *Luke* 17:21

[373] *The Koran* (16:77)

[374] Smith, Peter; *"Eschatology"*, *A concise encyclopedia of the Bahá'í Faith*; pgs. 133–134

[375] *The Koran* (7:40)

[376] Effendi, Shagdi; *The World Order Of Bahá'u'lláh, The Goal of a New World Order*; pgs. 34–35 and https://reference.bahai.org/en/t/se/WOB/wob-14.html

[377] Bunson, Matthew E.; *The Wisdom And Teachings Of The Dalai Lama*; pg. 67

[378] https://en.wikipedia.org/wiki/Bah%C3%A11%27%C3%AD_Faith_and_gender_equality

[379] *Bhagavad-Gita* 9.11

[380] https://www.astronism.com/ and https://www.astronism.org/

[381] https://astronism.wikia.org/wiki/Omnidoxy

[382] *Our Sun-God, Or, Christianity Before Christ*; pgs. 56-57 and *Genesis* 37:9

[383] *Stella Polaris*; Dec-Jan, 1991-1992 Edition; Volume 41, Number 1; pg. 31

[384] Swedenborg, Emanuel; *Divine Love And Wisdom*; pg. 7

[385] Produced by Gene Roddenberry, *Star Trek* is science fictional television show that first aired in September of 1966. It later expanded into movies, additional series and has become a cult phenomenon.

[386] http://startrekdom.blogspot.com/2007/04/gene-roddenberrys-atheism-in-his-own.html and https://humanism.org.uk/humanism/the-humanist-tradition/20th-century-humanism/gene-roddenberry/

[387] Parker, Trey-creator, producer and Stone, Matt-creator, producer; *South Park*; circa 1997 to present

[388]   https://www.nytimes.com/2004/12/19/fashion/fooey-to-the-world-fes-tivus-is-come.html and https://en.wikipedia.org/wiki/Festivus and https://fes-tivusweb.com/index.php and http://www.kwillis.com/festivus.html

[389] Animated comical science-fiction series created by Matt Groening and David X. Cohen; *Godfellas*, episode first aired March 17, 2002 and *When Aliens Attack*, episode first aired on November 7, 1999 and http://www.cc.com/shows/futurama and https://en.wikipedia.org/wiki/When_Aliens_Attack

[390] MacFarlane, Seth-creator, producer; *The Father, the Son and the Holy Fonz, Family Guy*; first aired on December 18, 2005, 18th episode, 4th season

[391] With modification; *Sufism, The Transformation of the Heart*; pg. xxvii

[392] *Nine Faces of Christ*; pg. 5

[393] *The Koran*, (47:38)

[394] *Sufism, The Transformation of the Heart*; pgs. i & iv

• • • •

CHAPTER 6

[395] Buildings, machines, clothes, furniture, infrastructure, textiles, food, toys, art, is a non-inclusive list of material items that we, as sentient beings, create through fur-ther manipulating stardust (atoms & molecules).

[396] *Unus mundus* is Latin for "one world" and refers to the notion of an underly-ing unified reality from which everything emerges and to which everything returns. It first appeared as early as the 13th century but become popularized in the 20th century by Carl Gustav Jung.

[397] *2 Kings* 23:5

[398] Cooke, Ivan-editor; *The Return Of Arthur Conan Doyle*; pg. 114

[399] Martin, Sean; *The Gnostics-The First Christian Heretics*; pg. 13

[400] Swedenborg, Emanuel; *Divine Love And Wisdom*; pg. 21 within the Introduc-tion

[401] Many of the true prophets of history encountered visions upon direct and un-filtered exposure to God's influence. The original inhabitants of the Americas consider visions as divine guidance from the Great Spirit.

[402] *The Return Of Arthur Conan Doyle*; pg. 59

[403] *The Koran* ≈(74:32)

[404] *Matthew* 7:2 NAS

[405] *The Koran* (4:111)

[406] *The Koran* (99:8)

[407] Dr. Wayne Dyer; exact source unknown

[408] *Galatians* 6:7

[409] Freke, Timothy & Gandy, Peter; *Jesus And The Lost Goddess*; pg. 23

[410] Jung, C.G.; *Modern Man In Search Of A Soul*; pg. 66

[411] Conner, Miguel; *Other Voices of Gnosticism*; pgs. 198-199 and https://www.poetryfoundation.org/poets/william-blake

[412] With modification and interpretation: Mascaró, Juan; *The Upanishads*; Introduction, pg. 27

• • • •

CHAPTER 7

[413] *Matthew* 5:48

[414] *Futurama*; animated comical science-fiction series created by Matt Groening and David X. Cohen; *The Problem with Popplers*; Season 2, Episode 18 and first aired on May 7, 2000 and http://www.cc.com/shows/futurama

[415]   https://monkeyland.co.za/unacceptable-practice-of-eating-monkey-brains_article_op_view_id_615 and

https://www.mapotic.com/worlds-scariest-foods/110151-live-monkey-brain and https://www.mirror.co.uk/news/uk-news/savages-chop-helpless-monkeys-skull-10002740

[416] *Genesis* 2:2-3

[417] *The Bhagavad Gita – As It Is*; pg. 385

[418] American football player, coach and National Football League executive; (b1913 – d1970)

[419] *Isaiah* 40:31

[420] The Three Initiates; *The Kybalion*; pgs. 1, 11

[421] Parsons, John Denham; *Our Sun-God, Or Christianity Before Christ*; pgs. 143-144 and https://www.britishmuseum.org/collection/term/BIB6467

[422] *Genesis* 1:27

[423] *Genesis* 2:7 and 2:22

[424] Original film directed by Roland Emmerich and co-wrote and produced by Dean Devlin, circa 1994.

[425] Wallis, Paul; *Escaping From Eden*; pg. 65

[426] https://interestingengineering.com/the-clovis-comet-and-the-forging-of-human-civilization-as-we-know-it   and   https://www.ncdc.noaa.gov/abrupt-climate-change/The%20Younger%20Dryas

[427] *Escaping From Eden*; pg. 80, 87

[428] Paine, Thomas; *The Age of Reason*; pgs. 84-86

[429] *Genesis* 1:29

[430] *Genesis* 2:17

[431] *Genesis* 3:22

[432] *Genesis* 3:6

[433] Jung, C.G.; *Modern Man In Search Of A Soul*; pg. 98

[434] LaChance, Albert J.; *The Modern Christian Mystic*; pg. 104

[435] Conner, Miguel; *Other Voices of Gnosticism*; pg. 8

[436] *Genesis* 3:9 (NAS)

[437] *Genesis* 3:4

[438] *The Koran*, ≈(7:20)

[439] *The Koran*, ≈(7:21)

[440] Conner, Miguel; *Voices of Gnosticism*; pg. 122

[441] *Other Voices of Gnosticism*; pg. 57

[442] Martin, Sean; *The Gnostics, The First Christian Heretics*; pg. 35

[443] Patrick, Dave-editor; *The Cathar View*; contributed by Ani Williams; pg. 66

[444] https://en.m.wikipedia.org/wiki/Glycon

[445] *The Cathar View*; contributed by Ani Williams; pgs. 66-67

[446]   https://forums.catholic.com/t/the-word-vatican/141802   and
https://www.quora.com/Does-the-name-Vatican-mean-Divining-Serpent   and
https://wedg.millenniumweekend.org/forum/forum/wedg-forums/general-prophe-cy-related/24088-does-vatican-really-mean-prophetic-serpent

[447] *John* 3:14-15

[448] *Genesis* 11:1-9

[449] *Escaping From Eden*; pgs. 83-86

[450] *Acts* 2:6-12

[451] *Matthew* 27:46-50

[452] Freke, Timothy & Gandy, Peter; *Jesus And The Lost Goddess*; pg. 122 and Walker, B.; *The Women's Encyclopedia of Myths and Secrets*; pg. 30

[453] With modification; Pinker, Steven; *The Better Angels of Our Nature*; pg. 607

[454] With modification; Mascaró, Juan, interpreter; *The Upanishads*; pg. 110

[455] *The Better Angels Of Our Nature*; pgs. 135-136

• • • •

CHAPTER 8

[456] Martin, Sean; *Alchemy & Alchemists*; pg. 47

[457] Beattie, Melody; *Codependent No More*; pg. 125

[458] Mascaró, Juan, interpreter; *The Upanishads*; Introduction, pg. 13

[459]   https://www.learnreligions.com/how-to-recognize-archangel-metatron-124277

[460] 20th century Jesuit Catholic priest, paleontologist and geologist involved in the discovery of the Peking Man.

[461] With Modification; Vaughan, Frances & Walsh, Roger; *Accept This Gift*; pg. 75

[462] Palacio, R.J.; *365 Days of Wonder*; pg. December 8

[463] LaChance, Albert J.; *The Modern Christian Mystic*; pg. 164

[464] "Upon a pedestal" is an expression that means giving someone uncritical respect or admiration without ever questioning their judgment or behavior.

[465] Storr, Anthony; *The Essential Jung*; pgs. 418-419

[466] Schwartz, David Joseph; *The Magic of Thinking Big*; pg. 154

[467] Murphy, Joseph; *The Power Of Your Subconscious Mind*; pgs. 45, 56

[468] Hill, Napoleon; *Think & Grow Rich*; pgs. 32-34

[469] With much modification; words of Adolphe Tanquerey; Ghezzi, Bert; *Mystics & Miracles*; pg. 103

[470] Peale, Vincent; *The Power Of Positive Thinking*; pg. 41

[471] *Mystics & Miracles*; pg. 16

[472] With modification; Paine, Thomas; *The Age of Reason*; pg. 28

[473] Book of Job; *Old Testament* and *The Koran* (21:83), (67:2)

[474] Fascinating how much ancient scripture can relate to the modern day: from section 61 of the *Tao Te Ching* written over 2,500 years ago by Lao-tzu from the region of China.

[475] Gibran, Kahlil; *The Prophet*; the orator speaking about freedom, pg. 51

[476] With slight modification: http://www.awakening-intuition.com/The-Ego-and-Its-Opposite.html

[477] Written by Paul the Apostle; *Galations* 2:20

[478] https://siimland.com/the-7-hermetic-principles/

[479] With modification: *The Upanishads*; pg. 126

[480] With modification: *The Upanishads*; pg. 39

[481] Vaughan-Lee, Llewellyn; *Sufism, The Transformation of the Heart*; pg. 134

[482] *The Power Of Positive Thinking*; pg. 12

[483] Knight, Bob; *The Power Of Negative Thinking*; pg. 96

[484] Alexander, Bevin; *Lost Victories: The Military Genius of Stonewall Jackson*; Henry Holt & Company; 2004

[485] *I Corinthians* 15:30-32

[486] With modification; Murphy, Joseph; *The Power Of Your Subconscious Mind*; pg. 131

[487] With modification; Pinker, Steven; *The Better Angels of Our Nature*; pgs. 540-541

[488] *The Upanishads*; pg. 140

[489] *365 Days of Wonder*; pg. June 13

[490] *365 Days of Wonder*; pg. June 8

[491] With modification; Teodoro, Andrian; *The Power of Positive Energy*; pg. 37

[492] *The Modern Christian Mystic*; pg. 101

[493] With slight modification; *John* 14:12

[494] With slight modification; Whitworth, Eugene E.; *Nine Faces Of Christ*; pg. 64

[495] Corpse meditation is also a way to desensitize those having to deal with the proper disposal of death and decay, such as First Responders to emergency situations or morticians.

[496] With modification; *The Power Of Positive Thinking*; pg. 84

[497] Dowling, Colette; *The Cinderella Complex*; pg. 22

[498] Jung, C.G.; *Modern Man In Search Of A Soul*; pg. 34

[499] *Modern Man In Search Of A Soul*; pg. 93

[500] Bloom, Paul; *Just Babies: The Origins of Good and Evil*; variation of concluding paragraph, pg. 218

[501] *The Koran* (5:13)

[502] *Luke* 6:31 and *Matthew* 7:12

[503] *Udanavarga* 5:18

[504] https://tanenbaum.org/about-us/

[505] Writings of Confucius; *Analects* 15:23

[506] *Mahabharata* 5:1517

[507] *3 Nephi* 14:12, *The Book Of Mormon*

[508] With modification; Martin, Sean; *The Gnostics, The First Christian Heresy*; pg. 122 and *1 Corinthians*

[509] *Hylics/somatics, psychics* and *pneumatics* are the various levels of existence and conscious awareness based on Valentinian Gnostic classifications; *The Gnostics, The First Christian Heretics*; pg. 50 and *1 Corinthians*

[510] Freke, Timothy & Gandy, Peter; *Jesus And The Lost Goddess*; pg. 28

[511] The Three Initiates; *The Kybalion*; pgs. 76, 77

[512] With slight modification; Whitworth, Eugene E.; *Nine Faces of Christ*; pg. 274

[513] Note in a thank-you card from a friend of the author.

[514] With modification; Gawande, Atul; *Being Mortal*, pg. 116

[515] The meaning of (Δ) and (O) will be revealed in Chapter 24

[516] Notice both the alpha and omega geometric representation within the word **Tao.**

[517] Freke, Timothy & Gandy, Peter; *The Hermetica The Lost Wisdom Of The Pharaohs*; pg. 126

[518] Host extraordinaire of *Aeon Byte Gnostic Radio; Finding Hermes 2: Alcoholism, Vedanta, Tarot & Free Will*; September, 2020

[519] *The Modern Christian Mystic*; pg. 70

[520] With modification; *The Modern Christian Mystic*; pg. 14

[521] "Hand-in-hand" is an expression meaning things that are closely correlated.

[522] *Sufism, The Transformation of the Heart*; pg. 129 and https://www.sloww.co/enlightenment-chop-wood-carry-water/

[523] *Matthew* 4:4

• • • •

CHAPTER 9

[524] The meaning of these geometric terms will be elaborated upon in Chapter 24

[525] With modification; White, David Manning; *Eternal Quest*; pgs. xx, xxi in the preface

[526] Murphy, Joseph; *The Power Of Your Subconscious Mind*; pg. 55

• • • •

CHAPTER 11

[527] With modification: *The Bhagavad-Gita: As It Is*, pg. 258

[528] With modification; Paine, Thomas; *The Age of Reason*; pg. 59

[529] *The Koran* (5:13), see also (5:41)

[530] *The Koran* (3:78)

[531] *Matthew* 10:34

[532] *Matthew* 19:16-19; *Mark* 10:17-23

[533] Freke, Timothy & Gandy, Peter; *Jesus And The Lost Goddess*; pg. 39 and *The Jesus Mysteries*, Glorious Gore, footnote, 225

[534] Patrick, Dave-editor; *The Cathar View*; contributed by Nick Lambert; pg. 96

[535] With slight modification; *The Cathar View*; pg. 96

[536] With slight modification; *The Cathar View*; pg. 123

[537] *The Cathar View*; contributed by Jeanne D'Août; pg. 166

[538] Reference to *Star Wars* and the works of Joseph Campbell

[539] Freke, Timothy & Gandy, Peter; *The Gospel of the Second Coming*; pgs. 64, 67

[540] Parsons, John Denham; *Our Sun-God, Or, Christianity Before Christ*; pgs. 188-189

[541] With modification: *The Cathar View*; contributed by Hristo Madjarov; pg. 121

[542] With slight modification; *Matthew* 5:17; *3 Nephi* 12:17; *3 Nephi* 15:6

[543] Martin, Sean: *Alchemy & Alchemists*; pg. 48

[544] *Our Sun-God, Or, Christianity Before Christ*; pg. 15

[545] The Library Genesis is a wonderful index portal for accessing greater knowledge; http://libgen.rs/

[546] https://www.britannica.com/biography/Constantine-I-Roman-emperor/Commitment-to-Christianity

[547] Conner, Miguel; *Voices of Gnosticism*; pg. 62

[548] *Our Sun-God, Or, Christianity Before Christ*; pg. 14

[549] Martin, Sean; *The Cathars, The Rise And Fall Of The Great Heresy*; pg. 28-29

[550] Martin, Sean; *The Gnostics, The First Christian Heretics*; pg. 105

[551] *The Age of Reason*; pg. 25

[552] *The Gospel of the Second Coming*; pg. 68

[553] *The Gospel of the Second Coming*; pgs. 44-46

[554] *Jesus And The Lost Goddess*; pg. 31

[555] Freke, Timothy & Gandy, Peter; *The Hermetica*; pg. xvii

[556] https://qz.com/1183992/why-europe-was-overrun-by-witch-hunts-in-early-modern-history/

[557] https://www.goodreads.com/author/quotes/5771553.Hypatia and https://www.realmofhistory.com/2016/04/14/hypatia-last-great-philosopher-alexandria/

[558] *Voices of Gnosticism*; pg. 125 and https://en.wikipedia.org/wiki/Manichaeism

[559] *The Gnostics, The First Christian Heretics*; pg. 67

[560] *The Gnostics, The First Christian Heretics*; pg. 65

[561] *The Cathars, The Rise And Fall Of The Great Heresy*; pgs. 30 & 61

[562] *Voices of Gnosticism*; pgs. 119-120

[563] *The Gnostics, The First Christian Heretics*; pg. 65

[564] *The Cathar View*; pg. 51 and https://www.vocabulary.com/dictionary/heretical

[565] https://en.wikipedia.org/wiki/James_A._Michener and https://www.biblio.com/james-a-michener/author/635 and Palacio, R.J.; *365 Days of Wonder*; pg. July 25

[566] *The Cathar View*; contributed by Jaap Rameijer; pg. 254

[567] *Jesus And The Lost Goddess*; pg. 49 and Ellerbe, H.E.; pg. 77

[568] *The Cathar View*; contributed by Jaap Rameijer; pg. 257

[569] Ghezzi, Bert; *Mystics & Miracles*; pg. 89

[570] *Jesus And The Lost Goddess*; pg. 48 and Ellerbe, H.E.; pgs. 72-73

[571] https://en.wikipedia.org/wiki/Monty_Python_and_the_Holy_Grail

[572] Sumption, Jonathan; *The Albigensian Crusade*; pgs. 15-16

[573] O'Shea, Stephen; *The Perfect Heresy: The Revolutionary Life and Death of the Medieval Cathars*; pgs. 239-246 and *The Albigensian Crusade*; pgs. 242-243 and Conner, Miguel; *Other Voices of Gnosticism*; pg. 117

[574] Freke, Timothy & Gandy, Peter; *Jesus And The Lost Goddess*; pg. 48 and *Against the Bogomils*, quoted in Lacarrière, J.; pg. 113

[575] *The Cathar View*; contributed by Hristo Madjarov; pg. 123

[576] *The Cathar View*; contributed by Val Wineyard; pg. 233

[577] *The Cathar View*; contributed by Val Wineyard; pg. 235

[578] *The Cathar View*; contributed by Dimitar Mulushev; pg. 110

[579] *Jesus And The Lost Goddess*; pg. 46

[580] *Jesus And The Lost Goddess*; pg. 46

[581] https://www.newdawnmagazine.com/articles/trickster-pack-at-the-end-of-deception-a-gnostic-view-of-disclosure

[582] Ghezzi, Bert; *Mystics & Miracles*; pg. 41

[583] Outlined in an MSNBC.com November 10, 2008 article titled "Monks brawl at Jesus' tomb"

[584] Wallis, Paul; *Escaping From Eden*; pg. 132

[585] http://archive.boston.com/bostonglobe/ideas/articles/2009/03/08/dark_passages/?page=5

[586] https://philphilips.com/35-facts-about-tuts-father-akhenaten-and-the-origins-of-the-monotheistic-sun-god-aten/

[587] *Old Testament, Deuteronomy* 7:16, 20:17-18 and *The Koran* (2:22), (4:48), (4:116), (14:35), (6:162-164)

[588] https://masadarain.wordpress.com/2016/09/16/idol-worship/

[589] *Genesis* 22

[590] *Jesus And The Lost Goddess*; pg. 52

[591] *The Koran* ≈ (4:27), (4:92), (4:93)

[592] *The Koran* (29:6) and repeated in other chapters of this book.

[593] Pinker, Steve; *The Better Angels Of Our Nature*; pg. 347

[594] *The Better Angels Of Our Nature* pg. 349; referencing Cronin, Audrey Kurth; How Terrorism Ends: Understanding the Decline and Demise of Terrorist Campaigns; Princeton University Press 2009; pgs. 93, 215

[595] Conner, Miguel; *Voices of Gnosticism*; pg. 189

[596] *Jesus And The Lost Goddess*; pg. 187

[597] There is actually no mention of promised virgins in *The Koran;* see *Matthew* 25:1and https://www.theguardian.com/books/2002/jan/12/books.guardianreview5

[598] A.C. Bhaktivedanta Swami Prabhupada ; *Bhagavad-Gita, As It Is*; pg. 55

[599] With modification; *The Better Angels of Our Nature*; pg. 557

[600] Bloom, Paul; *Just Babies-The Origins of Good and Evil*; pg. 201

[601] ≈ (4:29), see also (4:92), (4:93)

[602] *The Cathars, The Rise And Fall Of The Great Heresy*; pg. 50

[603] *Our Sun-God, Or, Christianity Before Christ*; pg. 78

[604] https://www.newyorker.com/magazine/2012/08/13/i-nephi

[605] *Matthew* 28; https://myocn.net/stone-rolled-away-entry-tomb/

[606] *The Koran* (2:256)

[607] *The Koran* (109:6)

[608] Conner, Miguel; *Other Voices of Gnosticism*; pgs. 42-43

[609] *The Cathar View*; contributed by Ani Williams; pg. 56

[610] Wallis, Paul; *Escaping From Eden*; pg. 15

[611] https://cathstan.org/posts/who-or-what-is-the-antichrist-a-reflection-on-the-biblical-teaching-3

[612] *Mark* 3:25 and *Matthew* 12:25

[613] *3 Nephi* 14:18, *The Book Of Mormon*; saying (45), *The Gospel Of Thomas*; *Luke* 6:43; *Apocalypse of Peter* (Codex VII, 3, 72, 4-6)

[614] From *Matthew* 12:25-37 and *Luke* 6:45; also indirectly from *Luke* 11:17-28

[615] *Voices of Gnosticism*; pg. 210

[616] https://biblehub.com/proverbs/23-7.htm

[617] *The Koran* (2:27)

[618] *1 Corinthians* 1:27 (KJV)

[619] Mistakenly romanticized, the Crusades not only involved atrocities against Muslims and Jews, but also against other Christians and pagans.

[620] *Mark* 3:21

[621] *John* 10:19-20

[622] *John* 10:21

[623] *Mark* 3:31-35

[624] *John* 19:25-28

[625] https://en.wikipedia.org/wiki/Mental_health_of_Jesus

[626] https://archive.org/details/lafoliedejsus01binegoog/page/n4/mode/2up

[627] https://en.wikipedia.org/wiki/Mental_health_of_Jesus and Murray, Evan D.; Cunningham, Miles G.; Price, Bruce H.; *The Role of Psychotic Disorders in Religious History Considered*; *Journal of Neuropsychiatry and Clinical Neurosciences, American Psychiatric Association*; October 2012

[628] Storr, Anthony; *Feet of Clay; Saints, Sinners, and Madmen: A Study of Gurus*

[629] *Matthew* 17:1-8, *Mark* 9:2-8, *Luke* 9:28-36 and *2 Peter* 1:16-18

[630] Ghezzi, Bert; *Mystics & Miracles*; pg. xii

[631] *The Gospel of the Second Coming*; pgs. 24-33 and Freke, Timothy & Gandy, Peter; *The Jesus Mysteries* and Murdock, D.M. (aka Acharya S); *The Christ Conspiracy*

and *Our Sun-God, Or, Christianity Before Christ*; pgs. 74-78, 150-152 and https://www.equip.org/article/the-jesus-mysteries-was-the-original-jesus-a-pagan-god/

[632] *Jesus And The Lost Goddess*; pg. 12

[633] http://www.vexen.co.uk/books/jesusmysteries.html

[634] *Our Sun-God, Or, Christianity Before Christ*; pgs. 33-35

[635] Murray, Evan D.; Cunningham, Miles G.; Price, Bruce H.; *The Role of Psychotic Disorders in Religious History Considered*; *Journal of Neuropsychiatry and Clinical Neurosciences, American Psychiatric Association*; October 2012

[636] Schweitzer, Albert; *The Psychiatric Study of Jesus: Exposition and Criticism*; 1948 and Martinez, Pablo; Sims, Andrew; *Mad or God? Jesus: The healthiest mind of all*; 2018

[637] "crammed down people's throats" is an idiom. It is an expression meaning to force something upon a recipient against their desire or will. Scripture is filled with ancient idioms, which due to their meaning becoming lost with time, are sometimes mistakenly interpreted literally in modern eras.

[638] *John* 14:6

[639] *John* 14:2

[640] *Our Sun-God, Or, Christianity Before Christ*; pg. 70

[641] *The Better Angels of Our Nature*, pg. 200

[642] With modification; *The Better Angels of Our Nature*; pg. 367

[643] *The Age of Reason*; pg. 173

[644] *The Better Angels of Our Nature*; pg. 140

[645] Lyrics within *The Rolling Stones'* song Jumpin' Jack Flash refers to a dysfunctional teaching method by the means of a "strap right across my back"; circa 1968

[646] 16th century Carmelite nun and Spanish mystic; *Mystics & Miracles*; pg. 125

• • • •

CHAPTER 12

[647] Freke, Timothy & Gandy, Peter; *The Hermetica*; pg. 106

[648] Paine, Thomas; *The Age of Reason*; pg. 46

[649] McKnight, C.J. & Catto, Jeremy I.-introduction; *Mysticism, The Experience Of The Divine*; pg. 36

[650] Conner, Miguel; *Other Voices of Gnosticism*; pg. 164

[651] Hellenistic and Judaic philosopher living in Alexandria, Egypt both before and after the life of Jesus; see Parsons, John Denham; *Our Sun-God, Or Christianity Before Christ*; pg. 198

[652] More on this in Chapter 24

[653] With modification; *Mysticism, The Experience Of The Divine*; Miguel de Molinos (1628–1696); pg. 56

[654] With modification of various interpretations; *The Bhagavad-Gita*; 18:58

[655] Swedenborg, Emanuel; *Divine Love and Wisdom*; Part 1, Section 78, pg. 80

[656] With slight modification; Palacio, R.J.; *365 Days of Wonder*; pg. June 2

[657] https://www.hki.org/helen-kellers-life-and-legacy/ and https://www.biography.com/activist/helen-keller and *365 Days of Wonder*; pg. September 20

[658] With modification; Vaughan-Lee, Llewellyn; *Sufism; The Transformation of the Heart*; pg. 89

[659] *The Koran* ≈(2:26)

[660] McKnight, C.J. & Catto, Jeremy I.-introduction; *Alchemy, The Art Of Knowing*; pg. 34

[661] Cooke, Ivan-editor; *The Return Of Arthur Conan Doyle*; pgs. 101-102

[662] With slight modification; Mascaró, Juan; *The Upanishads*; pg. 61

[663] With slight modification; LaChance, Albert J.; *The Modern Christian Mystic*; pg. 100

[664] https://www.britannica.com/biography/Henry-Ward-Beecher and https://ohiohistorycentral.org/w/Henry_W._Beecher and Palacio, R.J.; *365 Days of Wonder*; pg. July 7

[665] *Alchemy, The Art of Knowing*; pg. 19

[666] *365 Days of Wonder*; pg. January 14

[667] With modification; *The Modern Christian Mystic*; pg. 4

[668] *The Modern Christian Mystic*; pg. 84

[669] https://medium.com/nakshatra/the-nature-of-nothingness-understanding-the-vacuum-catastrophe-c04033e752f4

[670] The Three Initiates; *The Kybalion*; pg. 14

[671] *The Upanishads*; pg. 53

[672] With slight modification; Whitworth, Eugene E.; *Nine Faces of Christ*; pg. 303

[673] *The Upanishads*; pg. 62

[674] Hand-in-hand is an idiom/expression meaning things that are very closely connected or related.

[675] *The Wisdom of the Egyptians*; writings of Hermes and Plato, pg. (?)

[676] *The Wisdom of the Egyptians*; writings of Hermes and Plato, pg. (?)

[677] 19th century American philosopher, lecturer and essayist

[678] *The Bhagavad-Gita: As It Is*; pg. 260, 601

[679] With modification; *Sufism, The Transformation of the Heart*; pg. vi

[680] With modification; Murphy, Joseph; *The Power Of Your Subconscious Mind*; pg. 128

[681] Vaughan, Frances & Walsh, Roger; *Accept This Gift*; pg. 47

[682] *Bhagavad Gita – As It Is*; pg. 519

[683] With modification; *The Kybalion*; pg. 53

[684] With modification; *The Kybalion*; pg. 48

[685] Bunson, Matthew E.; *The Wisdom Teachings Of The Dalai Lama*; pg. 65

[686] *The Upanishads*; pg. 81

[687] *365 Days of Wonder*; pg. February 6

[688] Gibran, Kahlil; *The Prophet*; pg. 85

[689] Freke, Timothy & Gandy, Peter; *Jesus And The Lost Goddess*; pg. 72 and *Poimandres*, translation by Barnstone, Willis; pg. 573

[690] With modification; *Jesus And The Lost Goddess*; pg. 175 and Clement of Alexandria; *Stromata*; 4.22

[691] https://ascendingpassage.com/Wisdom-The-Vision-of-Hermes-Trismegistus-7.htm *The Wisdom of the Egyptians*; Brian Brown; 1923

[692] Paine, Thomas; *The Age of Reason*; pg. 30

[693] *The Modern Christian Mystic*; pg. 5

[694] Hawking, Stephen; *A Brief History Of Time*; 1998

[695] With modification; *The Modern Christian Mystic*; pg. 5

[696] With modification; *The Modern Christian Mystic*; pg. 6

[697] https://www.patheos.com/blogs/americanbuddhist/2016/04/the-story-of-god-a-buddhist-perspective-on-creation.html and https://aeon.co/videos/hinduism-has-not-just-one-creation-story-but-many-one-for-each-universe

[698] *The Prophet*; the orator speaking about time, pg. 68

[699] *The Modern Christian Mystic*; pg. 12

• • • •

CHAPTER 13

[700] With modification; Pinker, Steven; *The Better Angels Of Our Nature*; pg. 657

[701] With modification; *The Better Angels Of Our Nature*, pg. 693

[702] This is due to all the analytical software and algorithms used to provide a given internet protocol (IP) address with customized advertisements and viewing preferences based on past historical searches.

[703] Peale, Vincent; *The Power Of Positive Thinking*; pg. 70

[704] https://www.popsci.com/gear-amp-gadgets/article/2009-06/worlds-small-est-vga-display-literally-size-thumbnail/

[705] Articles circa 1907 from *Agricultural Advertising*, Volume 16, pg. 577

[706] From a tea bag label

[707] With slight modification; Peale, Vincent; *The Power Of Positive Thinking*; pg. 3.

[708] With slight modification; Jung, C.G; *The Modern Man In Search Of A Soul*; pg. 67

[709] Vaughan-Lee, Llewellyn; *Sufism, The Transformation of the Heart*; pg. 38

[710] With slight modification; *The Modern Man In Search Of A Soul*; pg. 220

[711] As described by Redfield, James in *The Celestine Prophecy*; ©1993

[712] With modification; *Power Of Positive Thinking*; pg. 180

[713] Ghezzi, Bert; *Mystics & Miracles*; pg. 107

[714] Emphasis on "temporarily" retreating from society

[715] With modification; Mascaró, Juan; *The Upanishads*; pg. 60

[716] 19th century Scottish philosopher; from *Sartor Resartus*; *The Power of Positive Thinking*; pg. 22

· · · ·

CHAPTER 14

[717] Patrick, Dave-editor; *The Cathar View*; contributed by Margaret Long; pg. 241

[718] With modification; Vaughan-Lee, Llewellyn; *Sufism, The Transformation of the Heart*; pg. 49

[719] With modification; Pinker, Steven; *The Better Angels of Our Nature*; pg. 520

[720] http://doctor-ramani.com/ and http://drlescarter.com/

[721] Most likely from *Galatians* 6:7

[722] Daniel, Alma; Wyllie, Timothy; Ramer, Andrew; *Ask Your Angels*; pg. 27 and *The Better Angels of Our Nature*; pg. 496

[723] https://www.catholicculture.org/culture/library/view.cfm?recnum=6341

[724] *Matthew* 5:45; *3 Nephi* 12:45

[725] Martin, Sean; *The Gnostics, The First Christian Heretics*; pg. 35

[726] Martin, Sean; *The Cathars, The Rise And Fall Of The Great Heresy*; pg. 133

[727] Wallis, Paul; *Escaping From Eden*; pg. 12

[728] *The Gnostics, The First Christian Heretics*; pg. 25

[729] https://en.wikipedia.org/wiki/Marcionism

[730] *Escaping From Eden*; pgs. 50-53

[731] *The Gnostics, The First Christian Heretics*; pg. 124

[732] Curtis, Charles. P. Jr and Greenslet, Ferris; compilers and editors; *The Practical Cogitator: The Thinker's Anthology*; Henry Adams, pg. 276

[733] The opening track of the *Rolling Stones*, a British rock band, 1968 album *Beggars Banquet* is titled *Sympathy for the Devil*. It was written by the band's members Mick Jagger and Keith Richards.

[734] "Last-ditch effort" is and idiom that means making a final attempt before it is too late; a last stand to avoid defeat

[735] *Revelation* 14:8, 18:3

[736] Cooke, Ivan-editor; *The Return Of Arthur Conan Doyle*; pg. 128

[737] With modification; *Sufism, The Transformation of the Heart*; pg. 103

[738] "Gaslighting" is a tactic of negative exploitation in which a person or entity, in order to gain more power, makes a victim question their reality. Anyone who is not enlightened is susceptible to gaslighting and it is a common technique of abusers, dictators, narcissists, and cult leaders. It is done slowly, so victims don't realize how much they've been brainwashed. The name is based on the movie *Gaslight* (circa 1944), where a man manipulates his wife to the point where she thinks she is losing her mind. The antidote for defending against it is by applying logic of facts, which counteracts the emotions behind the "gaslighting" attacks.

[739] Exact wording varies depending on interpretation and the version; *The Koran*; (24:64)

[740] *The Koran*; (29:6) and repeated in other chapters of this book

[741] Even the remains of the dead were dug up and burnt if found post mortem guilty of heresy; *The Cathars, The Rise And Fall Of The Great Heresy*; pgs. 104, 129 & 139

[742] Sources vary on whether those suffering from bubonic plague (aka The Black Death) were sealed in and left to die or were well cared for by the compassionate folks of Edinburgh, Scotland.

[743] *Book of Mosiah* 29; *Book of Alma* 46, 51, 61, 62; *Book of Helaman* 6

[744] *The Better Angels of Our Nature*; pg. 233

[745] Singer M, Evans JM: Water Wary: Understandings and Concerns about Water and Health among the Rural Poor of Louisiana. In *Environmental Anthropology: Future Trends*. Edited by: Kopnina H, Shoreman-Ouimet E. New York and Oxford: Routledge; ©2013; pgs. 172–187

[746] Storr, Anthony; *The Essential Jung*; pg. 91

[747] An exploitive campaign declaimed by US Senator Joseph McCarthy in the years 1950–1954 against alleged communists or communist sympathizers in government and other institutions. It was based on fearmongering and many of the accused were blacklisted or lost their employment based on little evidence, although most did not have any associations with the Communist Party.

[748] Bloom, Paul; *Just Babies, The Origins of Good and Evil*; pg. 133

[749] With slight modification; Jung, C.G.; *Modern Man In Search Of A Soul*; pg. 203

[750] Freke, Timothy & Gandy, Peter; *Jesus And The Lost Goddess*; pg. 49

[751] Pearle, Vincent; *The Power Of Positive Thinking*; pg. 154

[752] His Divine Grace A. C. Bhaktivedanta Swami Prabhupada; *The Bhagavad-Gita, As It Is*; 2.19, pg. 44

[753] With modification; *The Gnostics, The First Christian Heretics*; pg. 38

[754] *The Gnostics, The First Christian Heretics*; pg. 95 and *Pistis Sophia*; pg. 72

[755] *1 Peter* 3:1-7, Timothy 2:9-15, *Titus* 3:3-5

[756] Translation from *Vedānta-Sūtras* (2.1.34)

[757] *The Cathar View*; contributed by Margaret Long; pgs. 240-241

[758] Ghezzi, Bert; *Mystics & Miracles*; pg. xiii

[759] *Exodus* 20:5-17

[760] *Deuteronomy* 21:10-14 (NIV) and *Numbers* 31:18 (NIV)

[761] *The Koran* ≈(4:111)

[762] *The Koran* (2:256); even the intention of this statement has a duality among its various translations and interpretations.

[763] *Stella Polaris*; Dec-Jan, 1991-1992 Edition; Volume 41, Number 1; pg. 5

[764] *The Gnostics, The First Christian Heretics*; pg. 104

[765] With modification; *Modern Man In Search Of Soul*; pg. 54

[766] https://www.amnestyusa.org/a-clear-scientific-consensus-that-the-death-penalty-does-not-deter/ and https://deathpenaltyinfo.org/policy-issues/deterrence

[767] https://deathpenaltyinfo.org/policy-issues/innocence/executed-but-possibly-innocent and http://www.ncadp.org/pages/innocence

[768] https://deathpenaltyinfo.org/news/studies-death-penalty-adversely-affects-families-of-victims-and-defendants

[769] https://vittana.org/15-biggest-capital-punishment-pros-and-cons

[770] An interpretation of "turning the other cheek", a teaching of Jesus, is also to move on and go in a different direction when life gives you hurdles, walls and obstructions. One can continue to pound against an immovable barrier or one can find an alternate means around it.

[771] Murphy, Joseph; *The Power Of Your Subconscious Mind*; pg. 123

[772] With modification; *The Better Angels of Our Nature*; pg. 590

[773] Source not confirmed; https://www.quora.com/How-should-one-overcome-fear-according-to-Bhagavad-Gita

[774] Ancient Greek stoic philosopher and former slave living just after the time of Christ; *The Return Of Arthur Conan Doyle*; pg. 131

• • • •

CHAPTER 15

[775] McDermott, Robert A.; *Rudolf Steiner and Anthroposophy*, in Faivre and Needleman, *Modern Esoteric Spirituality*, pgs. 299–301; 288ff

[776] LaChance, Albert J; *The Modern Christian Mystic*; pg. 100

[777] *The Modern Christian Mystic*; pg. 150, 39

[778] Martin, Sean; *The Gnostics, The First Christian Heretics*; pg. 92

[779] Beattie, Melody; *Co-dependency No More*; pg. 60

[780] With slight modification; *Co-dependency No More*; Earnie Larson; pg. 32

[781] With slight modification; Vaugh, Frances and Walsh, Roger; *Accept This Gift*; pg. 6

[782] Palacio, R.J.; *365 Days of Wonder*; pg. November 4

[783] https://www.theguardian.com/artanddesign/2005/jan/12/art

[784] With modification; *The Modern Christian Mystic*; pg. 159

[785] With slight modification; Dr. Wayne W. Dyer

[786] Dorothy James, Phyllis; author and novelist.

[787]   YouTube video; The Impact of Early Emotional Neglect; https://www.youtube.com/watch?v=aymvX-OrlS0

[788] https://thoughtcatalog.com/ryan-holiday/2016/06/25-ways-to-kill-the-toxic-ego-that-will-ruin-your-life/

[789] *Codependent No More*; pgs. 134-140 and Elisabeth Kübler-Rose; *On Death and Dying*

[790] *Codependent No More*; pg. 114.

[791] With modification; Murphy, Joseph; *The Power Of Your Subconscious Mind*; pg. 101

[792] With modification; *Codependent No More*; pg. 227

[793] With modification; Hill, Napoleon; *Think & Grow Rich*; pg. 21

[794] *365 Days of Wonder*; pgs. April 30 to May 1
and https://www.thequotablecoach.com/play-the-tiles-you-get/

[795] Earliest known similar publication appears in a January 1957 issue of *Reader's Digest* magazine and the expression later became popularized in 1980 within lyrics by John Lennon, a former member of a British based musical band called *The Beatles*

[796] https://www.bl.uk/people/e-m-forster and https://en.wikipedia.org/wiki/E._M._Forster and *365 Days of Wonder*; pg. July 31

[797] With modification; https://alyjuma.com/euthymia/

[798] François VI, Duc de La Rochefoucauld, Prince de Marcilla; French 17th century author of *Memoirs* and *Maxims*.

[799] Waley, Muhammad Isa; *Sufism, The Alchemy Of The Heart*; pg. 27

[800] *The Bhagavad-Gita;* (2.48) and https://www.hinduwebsite.com/HINDUISM/concepts/buddhiyoga.asp

[801] With modification; Pinker, Steven; *The Better Angels of Our Nature*; pg. 637

[802] https://philosophyterms.com/telos/

[803] Malkin, Dr. Craig; *Rethinking Narcissism*; pg. 206

[804] Murphy, Joseph; *The Power Of Your Subconscious Mind*; pg. 73

[805] Marcus Aurelius; 2nd century Roman philosopher and sage.

[806] *365 Days of Wonder*; pg. January 30

[807] https://thebiography.us/en/claraso-serrat-noel and https://es.wikipedia.org/wiki/Noel_Clarasó and *365 Days of Wonder*; pg. December 30

[808] With modification; Murphy, Joseph; *The Power of Your Subconscious Mind*; pg. 109

[809] Child poet, peacemaker, spiritual savant and divine prodigy.

[810] *365 Days of Wonder*; pg. January 7

[811] Peale, Vincent; *The Power of Positive Thinking*; pg. 169

[812] Written in German on the stationary of the Tokyo's Imperial Hotel in 1922, the note fetched $1.6 million at an auction held almost 95 years later.

[813] *Accept This Gift*; pg. 75

[814] A saying of the author's father.

[815] From poem titled *The Dome of the Inner Sky*; *Rumi, In the Arms of the Beloved*; pg. 124

[816] *365 Days of Wonder*; pg. February 19

[817] *365 Days of Wonder*; pg. April 11

[818] With modification; *365 Days of Wonder*; pg. May 11

[819] *365 Days of Wonder*; pg. June 11

[820] https://www.pbs.org/wgbh/aia/part4/4p1539.html and https://www.biography.com/activist/frederick-douglass and *365 Days of Wonder*; pg. September 10

[821] Knight, Bob; *The Power Of Negative Thinking*; pg. 18

[822] With modification; Hill, Napoleon; *Think & Grow Rich*; pg. 8

[823] With modification; Knight, Bob; *The Power Of Negative Thinking*; pgs. 116, 124

[824] With slight modification; C. G. Jung; *Modern Man In Search Of Soul*; pg. 4

[825] Dunning, David and Kruger, Justin; 1999 Cornell Paper and https://www.psychologytoday.com/us/basics/dunning-kruger-effect

[826] Patrick, Dave-editor; *The Cathar View*; contributed by Anna Hayward, pg. 202

[827] http://www.bbc.co.uk/history/historic_figures/johnson_samuel.shtml and https://www.samueljohnson.com/briefbio.html and *365 Days of Wonder*; pg. July 4

[828] https://www.radio.com/news/gallery/bill-gates-quotes-about-success

[829] Gawande, Atul; *Being Mortal*; pg. 262

[830] *The Power of Your Subconscious Mind*; pg. 48

[831] Whitworth, Eugene E.; *Nine Faces of Christ*; pg. 363

[832] *The Power Of Negative Thinking*; pg. 92

[833] *The Power Of Negative Thinking*; pg. 88

[834] *Being Mortal*; pg. 232

[835] From the 1973 movie titled *Magnum Force* in which a San Francisco police inspector named Harry Callahan (played by the actor Clint Eastwood) investigates a series of killings by vigilante police officers and https://www.youtube.com/

watch?v=uki4lrLzRaU   and   https://www.imdb.com/title/tt0070355/characters/
nm0000142

[836] With slight modification; *Accept This Gift*; pg. 46

[837] With modification; *The Bhagavad-Gita, As It Is*; pg. 586

[838] https://www.jcf.org/ and *365 Days of Wonder*; pg. April 18

[839] With modification, *The Dalai Lama's Book Of Wisdom*, pgs. 77-79

[840] *Isaiah* 40:28-31

[841] https://americanliterature.com/author/henry-van-dyke and *365 Days of Wonder*; pg. April 17

[842] Cooke, Ivan; *The Return Of Arthur Conan Doyle*; pgs. 188-190

[843] Yung, C.G.; *Modern Man In Search Of A Soul*; pg. 71

[844] https://austinkleon.com/ and *365 Days of Wonder*; pg. April 29

[845] *Proverbs* 23:7; credit for variations thereof can also be given to Bruce Lee, a famous martial arts expert, and Dr. Wayne Dyer, a motivational spiritual speaker/counselor.

[846] Poem titled *From Black Soot*; *Rumi, In the Arm of the Beloved*; pg. 31and http://sunlightgroup.blogspot.com/2006/08/from-black-soot.html

[847] Dyer, Wayne; *You'll See It When You Believe It: The Way To Your Personal Transformation*

[848] With slight modification; Mascaró, Juan-interpreter; *The Upanishads*; pg. 103

[849] *365 Days of Wonder*; pg. March 10 and Bunson, Matthew E.; *The Wisdom Teachings Of The Dalai Lama*; pg. 41

[850] *The Cathar View*; contributed by Margaret Long; pg. 245

[851] Conner, Miguel; *Other Voices of Gnosticism*; pg. 209

[852] *The Power of Your Subconscious Mind*; pg. 88

[853] *Think & Grow Rich*; pg. 2

[854] *The Power Of Negative Thinking*; pg. 119

[855] *The Power Of Your Subconscious Mind*; pg. 87

[856] Ghezzi, Bert; *Mystics & Miracles*; pg. 46

[857] Stephen, Mitchell-interpreter; *Tao Te Ching*; pg. 44

[858] German poet, playwright, historian & philosopher [1759 – 1805]; *Modern Man In Search Of A Soul*; pg. 66

[859] With modifications; mid-18th to mid-19th century American essayist; *The Treasure Chest*, see *Codependent No More* and http://www.repplier.net/Agnes_Repplier.html

[860] Puppeteer, PBS Advocate, Presbyterian Minister, Saint; In testimony before the United State's Congress, Fred Rogers (aka Mr. Rogers) quoting "L'essentiel est invisible pour les yeux.", a line from the children's book *The Little Prince* by Antoine de Saint-Exupery, ©1943

[861] *365 Days of Wonder*; pg. July 18

[862] Freke, Timothy and Gandy, Peter; *The Hermitica*; pg. 23

[863] *Modern Man In Search Of A Soul*; pg. 66

[864] German Dominican theologian writer, philosopher and mystic (1260–1328 ?); *Mysticism, The Experience Of The Divine*; pg. 46

[865] With slight modification; *The Bhagavad-Gita, As It Is*; pg. 356

[866] Storr, Anthony; *The Essential Jung*; introduction, pgs. 18-19

[867] Internet public social media commenter from Italy; 2019

[868] Skakus is a realistic fictional(?) character considered a reincarnate of Socrates; *Nine Faces of Christ*; pg. 284

• • • •

CHAPTER 16

[869] Ghezzi, Bert; *Mystics & Miracles*; pg. 49

[870] *Luke* 6:27-29; *Matthew* 5:38-42

[871] *Matthew* 18:21-22.

[872] Beattie, Melody; *Codependent No More*; pg. 213

[873] Bunson, Matthew E.; from *Thinking Globally: A Universal Talk*; *The Widsom Teachings Of The Dalai Lama*; pg. 73

[874] "Being a doormat" is an expression which means allowing people to walk all over you; succumbing to negative exploitation.

[875] Paine, Thomas; *The Age of Reason*; pg. 175

[876] *The Koran* (2:264)

[877] LaChance, Albert J.; *The Modern Christian Mystic*; pg 171

[878] *The Koran* (6:160)

[879] *The Age of Reason*; pg. 175

[880] *The Koran* (3:126)

[881] "Under your skin" is an expression that means to irritate without relief and alludes to burrowing or stinging insects that work their way into flesh. It also has the polar opposite meaning of to declare being limitlessly in love with someone.

[882] *Proverbs* 24:17-18, *Saying* 28

[883] Vaughan, Frances & Walsh, Roger; *Accept This Gift*; pg. 63

[884] *Matthew* 7:2; *The Bible* (NIV)

[885] *Stella Polaris*; Dec-Jan, 1991-1992 Edition; Volume 41, Number 1; pg. 16

[886] *Omnidoxy*; https://www.astronism.com/cometanic-quotes?pgid=ju2s7ed9-a37b8e07-16e8-4b96-9434-7a7ea19a6128

[887] With modification; Pinker, Steven; *The Better Angels of Our Nature*; pg. 537

[888] Original author unknown

[889] Here again is how confusing language can be. The phrase "at one's disposal" means available for one to use whenever or however one wishes. The word "disposal" standing alone means to throw out or get rid of.

[890] The Akashic records are thought recordings of human data considered by theosophists to exist in the etheric plane.

[891] *The Koran* (6:147), (33:143)

[892] *Luke* 10:25

[893] *Luke* 10:30-35

[894] *Luke* 10:36-37

• • • •

CHAPTER 17

[895]Jenkins, Philip; Edwin Erle Sparks Professor of Humanities Emeritus at Pennsylvania State University and http://archive.boston.com/bostonglobe/ideas/articles/2009/03/08/dark_passages/?page=2

[896] Stanley, Kubrick (producer); considered a cult-classis, *Clockwork Orange* is a dystopian film portraying horrific juvenile gang violence; circa 1971 and https://en.wikipedia.org/wiki/A_Clockwork_Orange_(film)   and https://www.imdb.com/title/tt0066921/

[897] Jenkins, Philip; http://archive.boston.com/bostonglobe/ideas/articles/2009/03/08/dark_passages/

[898] *Psalms 137, Verse* 9

[899] Freke, Timothy & Gandy, Peter; *Jesus And The Lost Goddess*; pg. 27

[900] Paine, Thomas; *The Age of Reason*; pg. 18

[901] *The Age of Reason*; pgs. 89-90 and *Numbers* 31

[902] Parsons, John Denham; *Our Sun-God, Or Christianity Before Christ*; pgs. 101-104 and *Numbers* 21:7-9,

[903] *1 Kings* 12:28-29 (KJV)

[904] *2 Kings* 10 (KJV)

[905] *2 Kings* 15:14-16 (NIV)

[906] *2 Kings* 2:23

[907] Bloom, Paul; *Just Babies: The Origins of Good and Evil*; pg. 202

[908] *1 Samuel* 5:9; *Genesis*; 38:9-10

[909] https://truthfaithandreason.com/a-case-for-the-old-testament-old-testament-apologetics-every-christian-should-know/

[910] *Numbers* 25:1-15

[911] https://en.wikipedia.org/wiki/Phineas_Priesthood

[912] *The Age of Reason*; pg. 98

[913] *Job* 38:31-32 and *The Age of Reason*; pg. 113

[914] *Timothy* 2:11-14, *The Koran* (4:34) and https://ffrf.org/component/k2/item/23729-why-women-need-freedom-from-religion

[915] *The Koran* (2:229)

[916] http://s.telegraph.co.uk/graphics/projects/koran-carla-power/index.html

[917] https://en.wikipedia.org/wiki/Muhammad%27s_wives#Aisha_bint_Abu_Bakr

[918] https://en.wikipedia.org/wiki/Fatima_al-Fihri

[919] http://s.telegraph.co.uk/graphics/projects/koran-carla-power/index.html

[920] http://s.telegraph.co.uk/graphics/projects/koran-carla-power/index.html

[921] Islamic scholar, http://s.telegraph.co.uk/graphics/projects/koran-carla-power/index.html

[922] *Deuteronomy* 22:24

[923] *The Koran*, ≈ (5:38)

[924] *The Koran*, ≈ (8:39)

[925] https://quran.com/8/

[926] CNN internet article on the Medina bombing; by Haroon Moghul; July 5, 2016; https://www.cnn.com/2016/07/04/opinions/medina-attack-opinion-haroon-moghul/index.html

[927] *John* 7:53-8:11.

[928] *Isaiah* 2:4, *Micah* 4:3

[929] *Bhagavad-Gita, As It Is*; pgs. xv-xvii

[930] *Matthew* 18:3

[931] LaChance, Albert J.; *The Modern Christian Mystic*; pg. 116

[932] *The Gita*; 13.27-28

[933] *The Atlantic Monthly,* April 2001; Brooks, David; *The Organization Kid*, pg. 43

[934] *Deuteronomy* 21:18-21

[935] *Proverbs* 13:24

[936] With modification; Pinker, Steven; *The Better Angels of Our Nature*; pg.432

[937] With modification; *The Better Angels of Our Nature*; pg. 632

[938] *Deuteronomy 22:22, Leviticus 20:10* (NIV)

[939] Jenkins, Philip; http://archive.boston.com/bostonglobe/ideas/articles/2009/03/08/dark_passages/?page=5

• • • •

CHAPTER 18

[940] Cooke, Ivan-editor; *The Return Of Arthur Conan Doyle*; pg. 43

[941] Freke, Timothy & Gandy, Peter; *Jesus And The Lost Goddess*; pg. 71

[942] With modification; Pinker, Steven; *The Better Angels of Our Nature*; pg. 47

[943] *The Return Of Arthur Conan Doyle*; pg. 143

[944] 19th century priest in Turin, Italy from which the order of Salesians was established, see https://www.salesians.org/; Ghezzi, Bert; *Mystics & Miracles*; pg. 143

[945] With slight modification; *The Return Of Arthur Conan Doyle*; Preface, pg. vii

[946] Mitchell, Stephen-interpreter; *Tao Te Ching*; pg. 16

[947] With modification; from poem titled *You Hold This* by Paul Weiss of Bar Harbor, Maine and cited by LaChance, Albert J. in *The Modern Christian Mystic*; pg. 134

[948] *The Modern Christian Mystic*; pg. 103

[949] Paneurhythmy is a term developed by Peter Deunov (1864–1944) to denote the proper flowing with the pulse and rhythm of the universe, often expressively celebrated in a cicular dance.

[950] With modification; Freke, Timothy & Gandy, Peter; *The Hermetica*; pg. 100

[951] *The Return Of Arthur Conan Doyle*; pg. 105

[952] Palacio, R.J.; *365 Days of Wonder*; pg. January 9

[953] *Jesus And The Lost Goddess*; pg. 76 and Plato; *Cratylus*; pg. 400c

[954] Gawande, Atul; *Being Mortal*; pgs. 140, 147, 210

[955] *Jesus And The Lost Goddess*; pgs. 76-77

[956] *The Return Of Arthur Conan Doyle*; pg. 141

[957] *Jesus And The Lost Goddess*; pg. 114 and Guthrie, K.S. pg. 145

[958] Ghezzi, Bert; *Mystics & Miracles*; pg. 113 and *Ephesians* 5:14-16

[959] https://ascendingpassage.com/Wisdom-The-Vision-of-Hermes-Trismegistus-7.htm

[960] Birks, Walter and Gilbert, R.A.; *The Treasure of Montsegur* and Patrick, David-editor; *The Cathar View*; contributed by Ani Williams; pg. 67

[961] Sean, Martin; *The Gnostics, The First Christian Heretics*; pg. 85 and *The Gnostic Bible*; pg. 260

[962] Circa 1983/1984 song lyric by author, age 17

[963] A more detailed sorting into 12 stages of life: https://www.institute4learning.com/resources/articles/the-12-stages-of-life/

[964] *The Return Of Arthur Conan Doyle*; pg. 110

[965] Powell, Robert; *The Sophia Teachings*; pg. 118

[966] *The Return Of Arthur Conan Doyle*; pg. 112

[967] *The Return Of Arthur Conan Doyle*; pg. 113

[968] Consider this sentence a metaphor.

[969] *The Koran* ≈(75:15)

[970] *The Koran* (24:64)

[971] *The Koran* (16:119)

[972] *Luke* 23:32-43, *Mark* 15:27, *Matthew* 27:38-44

[973] With slight modification; Whitworth, Eugene E.; *Nine Faces of Christ*; pg. 177

[974] With modification; Mascaró, Juan-interpreter; *The Upanishads*; pg. 62

[975] Conner, Miguel; *Voices of Gnosticism*; pg. 24

[976] *365 Days of Wonder*; pg. July 11

[977] *365 Days of Wonder*; pg. October 5

• • • •

CHAPTER 19

[978] Jung, C.G.; *Modern Man In Search Of A Soul*; pg. 173

[979] Ghezzi, Bert; *Mystics & Miracles*; pg. 138

[980] *Modern Man In Search Of A Soul*; pg. 176

[981] With modification; Freke, Timothy & Gandy, Peter; *Jesus And The Lost Goddess*; pg. 10

[982] https://aeon.co/ideas/why-religion-is-not-going-away-and-science-will-not-destroy-it and https://agnostic.com/discussion/453337/why-religion-is-not-going-away-and-science-will-not-destroy-it?page=1&order=replies

[983] The saying "The Right Tool For The Right Job" became popularized by advertising for True Temper tools around 1907; see *Agricultural Advertising*, Volume 16, pg. 547. The statement is akin to the saying "Don't crack a nut with a sledgehammer".

[984] Dr. John Jackson quoted from an article on the Shroud Of Turin; https://www.cnn.com/travel/article/shroud-of-turin-mystery-italy/index.html

[985] A slight variation from that previously quoted in Chapter 1, *Alpha - In The Beginning And The Growth Of God*

[986] *Jesus And The Lost Goddess*; pg. 193

[987] https://en.wikipedia.org/wiki/Richard_Dawkins

[988] http://www.rebellesociety.com/2018/05/04/anaiyasophia-archons/ and Wallis, Paul; *Escaping From Eden*; pgs. 20-21

[989] https://thegodabovegod.com/10-definitions-gnosis-experts-will-lead-mind-god/

[990] Paine, Thomas; *The Age of Reason*; pg. 180

[991] Cooke, Ivan-editor; *The Return Of Arthur Conan Doyle*; pg. 70

[992] https://www.scientificamerican.com/article/are-virtual-particles-rea/ and https://profmattstrassler.com/articles-and-posts/particle-physics-basics/virtual-particles-what-are-they/ and http://math.ucr.edu/home/baez/physics/Quantum/virtual_particles.html

[993] https://www.nytimes.com/1977/06/05/archives/13th-floor-anyone-13th-floor-anyone.html

[994] With modification; *Modern Man in Search of a Soul*, preface by Cary F. Baynes

[995] (aka Ibn Daisan), 2nd and 3rd century philosopher, scholar and poet and Freke, Timothy & Gandy, Peter; *Jesus And The Lost Goddess*; pg. 166 and Mead, G. R. S.; pg. 403 and https://en.wikipedia.org/wiki/Bardaisan

[996] Palacio, R.J.; *365 Days of Wonder*; pg. March 19

[997] Primates and some other animals have been trained to present abstract displays of colors, but is the animal actually projecting a part of themselves, a reflection of their soul, into the displays as a true artist would? A paint brush attached to a robotic arm can create similar works with very basic random number algorithms.

[998] *The Age of Reason*; pg. 180

[999] With modification; Gawanda, Atul; *Being Mortal*; pg. 6

[1000] https://mythology.net/demons/belphegor/

[1001] Martin, Sean; *Alchemy & Alchemists*; pg. 15

[1002] https://science.nasa.gov/astrophysics/focus-areas/what-is-dark-energy

[1003] This notion is denoted by the canvas acrylic painting titled *Creation Redefined*, still unfinished as of circa 2020

[1004] With modification; *The Better Angels of Our Nature*; pg. 612

[1005] *The Selfish Gene* is a book published in 1976 by Richard Dawkins and the intent of its contents is often misinterpreted and misapplied.

• • • •

CHAPTER 20

[1006] *There really are 50 Eskimo words for 'snow'*; Robson, Davis; *Health & Science, The Washington Post*; January 14, 2013

[1007] Beattie, Melody; *Codependent No More*; pg. 210

[1008] With slight modification; Jung, C.G.; *Modern Man In Search Of A Soul*; pg. 216

[1009] Lachance, Albert J.; *The Modern Christian Mystic*; pg. 90

[1010] *The Modern Christian Mystic*; pg. 77

[1011] *The Modern Christian Mystic*; pg. 80

[1012] Hill, Napoleon; *Think And Grow Rich*; pg. 156

[1013] With slight modification; pg. 8

[1014] 19th century and early 20th century Russian philosopher, author and activist

[1015] With modification; *Modern Man In Search Of Soul*; pg. 22

[1016] Gibran, Kahlil; *The Prophet*; pg. 80

[1017] https://www.wbur.org/hereandnow/2016/05/20/oneida-silverware and http://www.nyhistory.com/central/oneida.htm

[1018] https://www.businessinsider.com/comparing-genetic-similarity-between-humans-and-other-things-2016-5

[1019] With modification; Murphy, Joseph; *The Power Of Your Subconscious Mind*; pg. 94

[1020] https://www.psychologytoday.com/us/blog/hide-and-seek/201801/the-pros-and-cons-polygamy

[1021] Vallely, Paul; *Independent; The Big Question: What's the history of polygamy, and how serious a problem is it in Africa?* Wednesday, 6 January and https://www.independent.co.uk/news/world/africa/the-big-question-whats-the-history-of-polygamy-and-how-serious-a-problem-is-it-in-africa-1858858.html

[1022] Vallely, Paul; *Independent*; *The Big Question: What's the history of polygamy, and how serious a problem is it in Africa?* Wednesday, 6 January 2010 and https://www.independent.co.uk/news/world/africa/the-big-question-whats-the-history-of-polygamy-and-how-serious-a-problem-is-it-in-africa-1858858.html

[1023]   https://www.psychologytoday.com/us/blog/hide-and-seek/201801/the-pros-and-cons-polygamy

and https://fragilestatesindex.org/

[1024] *1 Kings* 11:1-3 (NIV)

[1025] *Deuteronomy* 21:15 (NIV)

[1026] Powell, Robert; *The Sophia Teachings*; pgs. 6-22

[1027] *Independent*; Vallely, Paul; *The Big Question: What's the history of polygamy, and how serious a problem is it in Africa?* Wednesday, 6 January 2010 and https://www.independent.co.uk/news/world/africa/the-big-question-whats-the-history-of-polygamy-and-how-serious-a-problem-is-it-in-africa-1858858.html

[1028] *Independent*; Vallely, Paul; *The Big Question: What's the history of polygamy, and how serious a problem is it in Africa?* Wednesday, 6 January 2010 and https://www.independent.co.uk/news/world/africa/the-big-question-whats-the-history-of-polygamy-and-how-serious-a-problem-is-it-in-africa-1858858.html

[1029] Paine, Thomas; *The Age of Reason*; pg. 116

[1030] *Leviticus* 20:13, *Romans* 1:25-32, *The Koran* (7:81), *1 Corinthians* 6:9

[1031] *1 Corinthians* 13:7, *The Koran* (30:21), (28:56), https://www.answering-islam.org/Quran/Themes/love.htm

[1032] Freke, Timothy & Gandy, Peter; *The Gospel of the Second Coming*; pgs. 36, 50

[1033] https://www.bbc.com/news/magazine-34290981 and http://sitn.hms.harvard.edu/flash/2016/gender-lines-science-transgender-identity/ and https://www.ncbi.nlm.nih.gov/pmc/articles/PMC5841333/

[1034] Freke, Timothy & Gandy, Peter; *The Hermetica*; pg. 61

[1035] *The Sophia Teachings*; pg. 112

[1036] With modification; *The Modern Christian Mystic*; pg. 69

[1037] With modification; *The Modern Christian Mystic*; pg. 68

[1038] Mitchell, Stephen-interpreter; *Tao Te Ching*; Chapter 6, pg. 89

[1039] Martin, Sean; *The Gnostics, The First Christian Heretics*; pg. 112

[1040] Ghezzi, Bert; *Mystics & Miracles*; pgs. 90-91

[1041] Patrick, Dave-editor; *The Cathar View*; contributed by Maurice Magre; pgs. 188-189

[1042]   https://www.sciencealert.com/remote-town-in-the-dominican-republic-some-girls-turn-into-boys and http://www.newser.com/story/213135/in-this-town-girls-become-boys-at-puberty.html   and   https://www.bbc.com/news/maga-zine-34290981

[1043] Gardner, Howard; first proposed in *Frames of Mind: The Theory of Multiple Intelligence*; ©1983 and

https://www.verywellmind.com/gardners-theory-of-multiple-intelligences-2795161 and https://www.verywellmind.com/howard-gardner-biography-2795511

[1044] Emphasis on "monogamous": With either heterosexual or homosexual rela-tionships, engaging in non-exclusive interaction with multiple physical partners con-tributes to the spread of diseases, the potential for viral & bacterial mutations morphing into more harmful forms and the emotional wounding of a person's inner core and psy-che.

[1045] *The Modern Christian Mystic*; pg. 88

[1046] https://lonerwolf.com/twin-flame/

• • • •

CHAPTER 21

[1047] Mitchel, Stephen-interpreter; *Tao Te Ching*; pg. 39

[1048] https://quoteinvestigator.com/2013/01/22/borrow-earth/

[1049] https://www.gandhiheritageportal.org/ , there have been other summarized and condensed variations of this quote still credited to Gandhi.

[1050] Lachance, Albert J; *The Modern Christian Mystic*; pg. 13

[1051] *Genesis* 1:26, 28-30

[1052] From the song *Breathe* on the classic Pink Floyd album *The Dark Side of the Moon*; circa 1973

[1053] With modification; based on insightful speech by Carl Sagan presented at Cornell University, October 13, 1994

[1054] With modification; *Sufism, The Transformation of the Heart*; pg. 73

[1055] Curtis, Charles. P. Jr and Greenslet, Ferris; compilers and editors; *The Practi-cal Cogitator: The Thinker's Anthology*; Henry George, *The Master Motive*; pg. 636

[1056] On the strength of diversity appearing in a February 14, 2018 CNN article

[1057] The Frrrozen Haute Chocolate ice cream sundae costing $25,000 (£12,000), became part of the menu of the Serendipity 3 restaurant in New York City on in 2007; https://www.guinnessworldrecords.com/world-records/most-expensive-dessert

[1058] For those without peanut allergies, make it a peanut butter and jelly sandwich

[1059] Patrick, Dave-editor; *The Cathar View*; contributed by L. Shannon Anderson; pg. 150

[1060] https://amturing.acm.org/award_winners/kay_3972189.cfm and https://www.thefamouspeople.com/profiles/alan-curtis-kay-637.php

[1061] Palacio, R.J.; *365 Days of Wonder*; pg. January 12

[1062] *365 Days of Wonder*; pg. March 17

[1063] https://www.janastanfield.com/ and *365 Days of Wonder*; pg. August 13

[1064] *Revelation 8-11* and *The Koran* (39:68)

[1065] *Revelation 7:3*

[1066] https://www.cnn.com/2020/04/08/europe/pope-francis-coronavirus-nature-response-intl/index.html

• • • •

CHAPTER 22

[1067] Farah, Caesar E.; *Islam: Beliefs and Observations*; pg. 26 cite W.R. Smith; *Religion of the Semites*; pg. 2

[1068] Ghezzi, Bert; *Mystics & Miracles*; pg. 116

[1069] *The Koran* (22:75)

[1070] Effendi, Shoghi-translator; *Gleanings From The Writings Of Bahá'u'lláh*; pg. 78

[1071] *Mark* 6:2-4

[1072] *Matthew* 13:57 (NLT), *Mark* 6:4 (BSB), *John* 4:44 (NAS)

[1073] *The Gospel Of Thomas*; saying (31); http://gnosis.org/naghamm/gthlamb.html

[1074] https://en.wikipedia.org/wiki/Baltasar_Graci%C3%A1n and Palacio, R.J.; *365 Days of Wonder*; pg. August16

[1075] *Matthew* 5:17

[1076] "In the nick of time" is an expression which also means without a moment to spare. https://www.phrases.org.uk/meanings/in-the-nick-of-time.html;

Whitworth, Eugene E.; *Nine Faces Of Christ*; p. 27

[1077] *Thessalonians* 5:2

[1078] With modification; *Nine Faces Of Christ*; pg. 276

[1079] https://en.wikipedia.org/wiki/List_of_messiah_claimants and https://en.wikipedia.org/wiki/List_of_people_claimed_to_be_Jesus and https://en.wikipedia.org/wiki/List_of_Buddha_claimants

[1080] *Matthew* 2:16

[1081] *Matthew* 24:36

[1082] *Mark* 13:32-33, *Matthew* 24:36-44

[1083] Attributed to William Blake, 18th to 19th century poet and artist; Conner, Miguel; *Other Voices of Gnosticism*; pg. 194 and https://en.wikipedia.org/wiki/William_Blake

[1084] Jung, C.G.; *Modern Man In Search Of A Soul*; pg. 236

[1085] Jung, C.G.; *Modern Man In Search Of A Soul*; pg. 236

[1086] Freke, Timothy & Gandy, Peter; *The Hermetica*; pg. 112

[1087] White, David Manning; *Eternal Quest*; pg. xix in preface

[1088] Patrick, Dave-editor; *The Cathar View*; contributed by Alphedia; pg. 225

[1089] Cooke, Ivan-editor; *The Return Of Arthur Conan Doyle*; pg. 145

[1090] https://www.alislam.org/articles/demystifying-the-second-coming/

[1091] *Luke* 11:49

[1092] *3 Nephi* 7:20

[1093] Freke, Timothy & Gandy, Peter; *Jesus And The Lost Goddess*; pg. 191

[1094] https://en.wikipedia.org/wiki/Horton_Hears_a_Who!

[1095] Martin, Sean; *The Gnostics, The First Christian Heretics*; pg. 70

[1096] *Jesus And The Lost Goddess*; pg. 152 and Plato, *The Republic*; 7.517a

[1097] *Acts* 5:39

[1098] *The Koran* (3:22)

[1099] *3 Nephi* 10:12, *Book Of Mormon*

[1100] *Gleanings from the Writings of Baha'u'llah*, pgs. 57-58

[1101] From the *Asclepius*, a section within the contents of *Corpus Hermeticum*

[1102] *Jesus And The Lost Goddess*; pg. 66

[1103] Martin, Sean; *The Gnostics, The First Christian Heretics*; pgs. 70,71 and *The Discourse on the Eighth and Ninth, The Nag Hammadi Library In English*; pg. 322

[1104] *The Gnostics, The First Christian Heretics*; pg. 87 and *The Gospel of Mary, The Nag Hammadi Library In English*; pg. 525

[1105] *Gleanings From The Writings Of Bahá'u'lláh*; pg. 277

[1106] With modification; *The Nine Faces Of Christ*; pg. 76

[1107] With slight modification; *Modern Man In Search Of Soul*; pg. 51

[1108] *Matthew* 22:14 and *Nine Faces of Christ*; pg. 196

[1109] *Mystics & Miracles*; pg. 86

[1110] *Genesis* 9:20-27

[1111] *Mystics & Miracles*; pg. 124

[1112] LaChance, Albert J.; *The Modern Christian Mystic*; outside rear cover

[1113] *The Modern Christian Mystic*; pg. 152

[1114] Sheikh Mohammad Akram Nadwi, Islamic, 20th and 21st century Islamic Scholar and http://s.telegraph.co.uk/graphics/projects/koran-carla-power/index.html

[1115] *The Cathar View*; contributed by Jeanne D'Août; pg. 170

[1116] 365 *Days of Wonder*; pg. March 12

[1117] With modification; *The Cathar View*; contributed by Alphedia; pg. 225

[1118] *Nine Faces of Christ*; pg. 196

[1119] Taylor, Barbara Brown; *Learning To Walk In The Dark*; pg. 10

[1120] National Oceanic and Atmospheric Administration - global atlas of light pollution, circa 2016

[1121] *Jesus And The Lost Goddess*; pg. 65

[1122] *The Cathar View*; contributed by Jeanne D'Août; pg. 165

[1123] With modification; Mascaró, Juan-interpretor; *The Upanishads*; pg. 83

[1124] With modification; Weinersmith, Kelly & Zach; *Soonish*; pg. 293

[1125] *John* 13:34

[1126] *Gleanings From The Writings Of Bahá'u'lláh*; pgs. 316, 317

[1127] *The Upanishads*; Part 1, Chapter 2, pg. 77

[1128] *Brihad-Aranyaka Upanishad*; *The Upanishads*; pg. 127

[1129] *The Nine Faces of Christ*; pgs. 61, 195

[1130] Cooke, Grace; *The Shining Presence*; pg. 36 and Hayward, Colum with *The Cathar View*; pg. 185

[1131] With modification; *Nine Faces of Christ*; pg. 143

[1132] *The Cathar View*; contributed by Hristo Madjarov; pg. 120

[1133] *The Koran* (10:3)

[1134] *Luke* 9:56

[1135] *365 Days of Wonder*; pg. January 25

• • • •

CHAPTER 23

[1136] Pinker, Steven; *The Better Angels Of Our Nature*; pgs. 75-76

[1137] *The Koran* (2:275-276)

[1138] *The Better Angels Of Our Nature*; pg. 609

[1139] The notion of being productive, whenever feasible, and not deliberately becoming a burden to society is implied in the *Bhagavad-Gita: As It Is*; *Karma-yoga* (3.7-3.9), pg. 94

[1140] *Titus* 1:11 (KJV)

[1141] *Genesis* 4:9

[1142] Murphy, Joseph; *The Power Of Your Subconscious Mind*; pg. 74

[1143] *Gospel of Thomas*, saying (110); http://gnosis.org/naghamm/gthlamb.html

[1144] *Matthew* 19:24; *Mark* 10:25, *Luke* 18:25

[1145] Wallis, Paul; *Escaping Eden*; pg. 142

[1146] *Escaping Eden*; pgs. 142-143

[1147] With modification; Mascaró, Juan-interpreter; *The Upanishads*; pg. 57

[1148] *Revelation* 13:18

[1149] *1 Kings* 10:14

[1150] *Revelation* 13:16-17, 14:9-11 (NKJV)

[1151] Paine, Thomas; *The Age of Reason*; pg. 16

[1152] As defined by Stephan A. Hoeller, a modern Gnostic; *The Gnostics, The First Christian Heretics*; pg. 39

[1153] *The Power Of Your Subconscious Mind*; pg. 69

[1154] Mythological markers from antiquity for the Strait of Gibraltar

[1155] https://en.wikipedia.org/wiki/Dollar_sign

[1156] Martin, Sean; *Alchemy & Alchemists*; pg. 18

[1157] *The Age of Reason*; pg. 21

[1158] Philip K. Dick supposedly also underwent similar transmission through time. Perhaps there was a temporary swap or merger of consciousness between he and the writer of the *Book of Revelation*.

[1159] Circa 1843

[1160] Circa 1964

[1161] Circa 1973

[1162] Circa 1976

[1163] Circa 1977

[1164] *The Koran* (59:9)

[1165] Communism and socialism are not the same thing. One is a form of government, the other is a form of policy. The public K-12 education systems and social security are examples of benevolent socialist programs operating within the capitalistic society of the United States.

[1166] "The Capitalist Tool" is the motto of the iconic Forbes investment magazine

[1167] Curtis, Charles. P. Jr and Greenslet, Ferris; compilers and editors; *The Practical Cogitator: The Thinker's Anthology*; *Political Love*, Henry Demarest Loyd; pg. 635

[1168] *The Koran* ≈(9:34)

[1169] *3 Nephi* 27:31, *The Book of Mormon*

[1170] *The Age of Reason*; pg. 25-26

[1171] Weinersmith, Kelly and Zack; *Soonish*; pg. 221

[1172] *The Koran* ≈(7:128)

[1173] *Revelation* 14:9-12

[1174] Hill, Napoleon; *Think & Grow Rich*, pg. vi

[1175] *The Koran* ≈(16:96)

[1176] An English proverb implying or meaning that you can't have the best of both dualities.

[1177] Patrick, Dave-editor; *The Cathar View*; contributed by L. Shannon Anderson; pg. 161

[1178] With slight modification; MacFarlane, Seth-producer; fictional science fiction character and commander of *The Orville* on socio-economics, Season 2, Episode 5; circa 2018-2019

• • • •

CHAPTER 24

[1179] http://www.languedocmysteries.info/dualism.htm

[1180] Martin, Sean; *The Cathars, The Rise And Fall OF The Great Heresy*; pg. 16

[1181] Galilei, Galileo; *The Assayer*; circa1623

[1182] With slight modification; The Three Initiates; *The Kybalion*; pg. 18

[1183] Jung, C.G.; *Modern Man In Search Of A Soul*; pg. 86

[1184] *Matthew* 18:3 (NIV)

[1185] *Modern Man In Search Of A Soul*; pg. 163

[1186] *Modern Man In Search Of A Soul*; pg. 163

[1187] *Genesis* 11:1-9

[1188] Vaughan-Lee, Llewellyn; *Sufism, The Transformation of the Heart*; pg. 80

[1189] Storr, Anthony; *The Essential Jung*; pg. 275

[1190] *Modern Man In Search Of A Soul*; pg. 189

[1191] *Modern Man In Search Of A Soul*; pg. 120

[1192] https://www.ancient-origins.net/history/legendary-symbol-born-chaos-philosophy-yin-and-yang-009081

[1193] https://www.ancient.eu/Yin_and_Yang/

[1194] *Sufism, The Transformation of the Heart*; pg. 37

[1195] *Matthew* 10:34 and *Revelation* 1:16, 2:12

[1196] *Hebrews* 4:12

[1197] *Sri Guru Granth Sahib*; (a section within the *11th Sikh Guru*); pg. 534

[1198] *Sri Guru Granth Sahib*; (a section within the *11th Sikh Guru*); pg. 1087

[1199] *The Kybalion*; pgs. 72-73

[1200] See the Pauling epistles and/or the Acts of the Apostles

[1201] Swedenborg, Emanuel; *Divine Love and Wisdom*; pgs. 31-32

[1202] Freke, Timothy & Gandy, Peter; *Jesus And The Lost Goddess*; from Simon Magus, pg. 64

[1203] *The Kybalion*; pg. 84

[1204] Paine, Thomas; *Age of Reason*; pgs. 181-182. It should be noted that Paine's comment only relates to the Newtonian world, for the Einsteinian world was not conceived of yet.

[1205] With modification; *Sufism, The Transformation of the Heart*; pg. 67

[1206] *Sufism, The Transformation of the Heart*; pg. 133

[1207] Palacio, R.J.; *365 Days of Wonder*; pg. September 1

[1208] https://www.roerich.org/roerich-pact.php

[1209] "black & white" is an expression denoting that things are not always clearly only one way or another; there can be meshing or overlap and boundaries are not always definite.

[1210] *The Kybalion*; pgs. 76, 77

[1211] Freke, Timothy & Gandy, Peter; *The Gospel of the Second Coming*; pg. 87

• • • •

CHAPTER 25

[1212] Jung, C.G.; *Modern Man In Search Of A Soul*; pg. 67

[1213] 18th century mystical rabbi and regarded as the founder of Hasidic Judaism

[1214] Star, Jonathan-translator; *Rumi, In the Arms of the Beloved*; pg. xvii

[1215] An Italian alchemist who may have been fictional, allegedly to have lived from 1406–1490

[1216] Variation of *Proverbs* 23:7

[1217] Palacio, R.J.; *365 Days of Wonder*; pg. November 11

[1218] Typical examples of this can be found in the Old Testament books and the *Bhagavad-Gita*

[1219] White, David Manning; *Eternal Quest*; pg. xxiii in the preface

[1220] Sean, Martin; *The Gnostics, The First Christian Heretics*; pg. 71 and Robinson-general editor, *The Discourse on the Eighth and Ninth, The Nag Hammadi Library*; pg. 325

[1221] *Bhagavad-Gita*; 18.55 and Mascaró, Juan; *The Upanishads*; Introduction, pg. 29

[1222] With modifications: *The Upanishads*, Introduction, pg. 36

[1223] Quote by William Ewart Gladstone (British Prime Minister) from the 19th century and also re-worded by the guitar virtuoso named Jimi Hendrix in the 20th century; see Patrick, Dave-editor; *The Cathar View*; pgs. 283-284 and https://www.brainyquote.com/quotes/jimi_hendrix_195397 and http://kscequinox.com/2014/04/the-power-of-love-will-probably-never-overcome-the-love-of-power/

[1224] *Matthew* 24:32-35, *Mark* 13:28-31, *Luke* 21:29-33

[1225] With modification; Jung, C.G.; *Modern Man In Search Of A Soul*; pg. 226

[1226] Critics revealed some questionable comments, motives and practices in protest of Mother Teresa's recognition to sainthood by the Catholic Church in 2016; https://www.nytimes.com/2016/08/27/world/asia/mother-teresa-critic.html and https://www.cnn.com/2016/08/31/asia/mother-teresa-controversies/index.html and https://www.nbcnews.com/news/world/mother-teresa-s-canonization-controversy-clouds-nun-s-work-n641181

[1227] *Matthew* 6:9-13

[1228] *Matthew* 6:10

[1229] *365 Days of Wonder*; pg. March 24

[1230] 8th century Indian Buddhist monk; *The Dalai Lama's Book Of Wisdom*; pg. 115

[1231] According to an OXFAM statement, those living on less than $1.25 per day (the World Bank's definition of extreme poverty) has been dramatically reduced from 36% to 18%

[1232] https://www.seti.org/drake-equation-index

[1233] "The Coneheads" is a comedy sketch from Saturday Night Live (SNL) circa 1977 and portrays beings not native to Earth adapting to and trying to fit in to human culture.

[1234] Wallis, Paul; *Escaping From Eden*; pgs. 112-115, and https://www.catholic-newsagency.com/news/believing_in_aliens_not_opposed_to_christianity_vati-cans_top_astronomer_says and https://www.youtube.com/watch?v=SdQn-77QIJA and https://www.catholicnewsagency.com/news/belief_in_aliens_not_necessari-ly_against_the_faith_vatican_official_says and https://www.iarga.it/en/2018/11/13/ufos-and-churchmen/

[1235] Vaughan, Frances and Walsh, Roger; *Accept This Gift*; pg. 18

[1236] Sizer, Theodore R.; *Horace's Hope*; pg. 138

[1237] Gladwell, Malcolm; *Blink*; pg. 60

[1238] LaChance, Albert J.; *The Modern Christian Mystic*; pg. 38

[1239] *3 Nephi* 5:8, *Book of Mormon* and quote of fictional character of Captain Jean Luc Picard during final episode titled *All Good Things...*(circa 1994) of the science fiction series of *Star Trek: The Next Generation*

[1240] Ghezzi, Bert; *Mystics & Miracles*; pg. 26; Solanus was a humble, yet exalted 19th and 20th century priest who worked at the frontlines with people

[1241] *365 Days of Wonder*; pg. August 21

[1242] Freke & Gandy, Timothy & Peter; *The Hermetica*; pgs. 129-130

[1243] An early Christian martyred for her faith in 203; *Mystics & Miracles*; pg. 59

[1244] *Revelation* 20 and https://www.pbs.org/wgbh/pages/frontline/shows/apoc-alypse/readings/white.html

[1245] *Book of Isaiah* (KJV) 65:17, 66:22; *2 Peter* (KJV) 3:13; *Revelation* 21:1

[1246] *Matthew* 24:29

[1247] "Skotosphere" is a term first coined by Albert J. LaChance and relates to a collective fog or shadowy cloud of insanity or evil that can form in a region or around a planet. The notion of skotosphere is also indirectly presented in the fictional children's novel *A Wrinkle In Time* circa 1962.

[1248] With modification; Whitworth, Eugene E.; *Nine Faces of Christ*; pg. 380; For those reading this in the early part of the 21st century, you are witness to and part of the birth of the New Age. For those reading in the millenniums to follow, you will already understand why.

[1249] *Revelation* 10:10 (KJV) and an intimation of extraordinary proportions

[1250] From poem titled *O Beloved, Be Like That To Me*; *Rumi-In the Arms of the Beloved*; pg. 27

[1251] *3 Nephi* 1:13, *Book Of Mormon*

[1252] Effendi, Shoghi; *Gleanings From The Writings of Baháʼuʼlláh*; pg. 11

[1253] "on the cusp" is an idiom meaning the point at which something is about to change; and, Fogel, William Robert; *The Phases of the Four Great Awakenings* and https://www.press.uchicago.edu/Misc/Chicago/256626.html

[1254] With modification; Paine, Thomas; *The Age of Reason*; pgs. 35-38

[1255] Senary list from partial of *Galatians* 5:22

[1256] Ghezzi, Bert; *Mystics & Miracles*; pg. xi

[1257] *Mystics & Miracles*; pg. xi

[1258] *Nine Faces of Christ*; pg. 111

[1259] Refer back to the end of Chapter 6 for what imagination actually entails.

[1260] *The Cathar View*; contributed by Margaret Long; pg. 249

[1261] With modification; Pinker, Steven; *The Better Angels of Our Nature*; pg. 585

[1262] With modification; Murphy, Joseph; *The Power Of Your Subconscious Mind*; pg. 119

[1263] *The Gnostics, The First Christian Heretics*; pg. 83

[1264] There is no explicit mention of the "Rapture" in *Revelation*. It was a conjecture and a "pious opinion" put forth by a 19th century theologian named John Nelson Darby. The "dead" referred to in *1 Corinthians* 15:52 relates to those who are "dead in spirit", for they will have a spiritual awakening.

[1265] With modification; *The Modern Christian Mystic*; pg. 57

[1266] "Live long and prosper" is commonly held as a salutation created by the actor Leonard Nimoy in his portraying of the science fictional *Star Trek* character of Spock. Based on a Hebrew blessing, it also has roots in an ancient Egyptian phrase and in the *Old Testament, Numbers* 6:22-27

[1267] *The Gnostics, The First Christian Heretics*; pg. 41

[1268] *The Upanishads*; Introduction; pg. 14

[1269] Cooke, Ivan-editor; *The Return Of Arthur Conan Doyle*; pg. 130

[1270] *The Cathar View*; contributed by Ani Williams; pg. 68

[1271] https://thegodabovegod.com/10-definitions-gnosis-experts-will-lead-mind-god/

[1272] *The Cathar View*; contributed by Hristo Madjarov; pgs. 124-125

[1273] *The Return Of Arthur Conan Doyle*; pg. 175

[1274] Conner, Miguel; *The Other Voices of Gnosticism*; pgs. 57-58

[1275] Freke & Gandy, Timothy & Peter; *Jesus And The Lost Goddess*; pg. 50

[1276] *The Cathar View*; contributed by Margaret Long; pg. 252

[1277] *John* 13:27, *Nine Faces of Christ*; pg. 318, *The Koran* (16:67)

About the Author

Anon Omous is a layperson observer of human nature with a limited understanding of the patterns of both functional and dysfunctional behaviors. As a mechanical tektōn by profession, he constantly seeks religious and spiritual knowledge to better combine the poles of logic and emotion while being immersed in the daily routine of life. Preferring to put the religious mysteries into everyday practice rather than dwell and obsess on the alleged divine relationships of human characters, although occasionally drifting, he seeks to maintain a spiritual core. Relying on an inner intuition and unique sensitivity, he constantly seeks information on how to form a better perspective on what defines reality and what makes us better people. Realizing that we all must occasionally put on masks to be actors within environments of ignorance and to choose our battles wisely, he hopes to improve world conditions by awakening the savoir in all of us.

Read more at https://www.asteroxrising.com/.

Made in the USA
Middletown, DE
10 February 2023

24443336R00446